"This textbook effectively explains complex evidential concepts and rules in a way that can be easily understood and places the law in context with practical examples. It is also a useful revision tool as it provides students with a range of practice questions."

Holly Greenwood, *Lecturer, Cardiff University*

"This book is excellent. It is a clear, comprehensive and well-researched introduction to the principles, practice and procedures of the law of evidence, highlighting with concision the historical context and academic debates arising in this interesting area. Certainly of considerable benefit to students, academics and practitioners alike."

Alexander McColl, *Barrister*

"Comprehensive yet accessible, this text expertly and critically discusses all key topics of evidence law and more. It is a superb example of co-collaboration. Student needs are fully accounted for through key learning points, examples, and practice questions alongside excellent analysis."

Lucy Welsh, *Reader in Criminal Justice, University of Sussex*

Evidence: Law and Context

Evidence: Law and Context explains the key concepts of evidence law in England and Wales clearly and concisely, set against the backdrop of the broader political and theoretical contexts. The book focuses on the essential topics commonly found on Evidence courses, covering both criminal evidence and civil evidence. Taking a contextual approach, the authors show how wider policy debates and societal trends have impacted upon the recent evolution of the law, helping to explain how and why the law has developed.

The sixth edition has been revised to include: the impacts of the COVID-19 pandemic, the introduction of the Solicitors Qualifying Examination (SQE), and updates on previous statistics on the increase in the use of 'show pleas,' false confessions, and miscarriages of justice, alongside a comparative perspective on how the American criminal practice has evolved along a parallel line. Learning points summarise the major principles and rules covered and practical examples are used throughout the text to give better understanding as to how the technical rules are applied in practice. Self-test questions are included in the book, helping students to test their understanding and prepare for assessment.

Well written, clear, and with a logical structure throughout, it contains all the information necessary for any undergraduate evidence law module.

Claire McGourlay is Professor of Legal Education and the Director of External Relations in the School of Social Sciences at the University of Manchester.

Mark Thomas is a practising barrister, specialising in criminal law.

Suzanne Gower is a lecturer in criminal evidence and miscarriages of justice at the University of Manchester, UK.

Joyce Claudia Choo is an International Legal Studies LLM candidate at New York University School of Law, US, and a Transitional Justice Scholar with the Centre for Human Rights and Global Justice (CHRGJ).

Evidence: Law and Context

Sixth Edition

Claire McGourlay, Mark Thomas, and Suzanne Gower

With contributions from Joyce Claudia Choo

Routledge
Taylor & Francis Group
LONDON AND NEW YORK

Designed cover image: Aliaksandr Zadoryn / Getty Images ®

Sixth edition published 2024
by Routledge
4 Park Square, Milton Park, Abingdon, Oxon, OX14 4RN

and by Routledge
605 Third Avenue, New York, NY 10158

Routledge is an imprint of the Taylor & Francis Group, an informa business

First edition published by Law Matters Publishing 1995

Fifth edition published by Routledge 2018

British Library Cataloguing-in-Publication Data
A catalogue record for this book is available from the British Library

ISBN: 978-1-032-54278-2 (hbk)
ISBN: 978-1-032-54277-5 (pbk)
ISBN: 978-1-003-41609-8 (ebk)

DOI: 10.4324/9781003416098

Typeset in Joanna
by Deanta Global Publishing Services, Chennai, India

Contents

About the Authors

Claire McGourlay is Professor of Legal Education and the Director of External Relations in the School of Social Sciences at the University of Manchester. She is also a National and Principal Fellow of the Higher Education Academy. She teaches criminal evidence, miscarriages of justice and runs the Manchester Innocence Project. Claire completed her doctoral studies at the University of Sheffield, where she previously taught.

Mark Thomas is a practising barrister, specialising in criminal law. Mark has taught law for several years at both undergraduate and postgraduate levels, with a focus on criminal law, evidence and procedure. Mark is the author of a number of academic textbooks concerned with the criminal law and sits on the Management Committee for The Advocate's Gateway.

Suzanne Gower is a lecturer in criminal evidence and miscarriages of justice at the University of Manchester. She is an experienced criminal defence solicitor (non-practising) and has higher rights of audience for criminal advocacy. She was previously the Managing Director of APPEAL, the charity law practice dedicated to challenging miscarriages of justice. Suzanne is carrying out doctoral research in the area of wrongful allegations of historic sexual abuse.

Joyce Claudia Choo is an International Legal Studies LLM candidate at New York University School of Law, and a Transitional Justice Scholar with the Centre for Human Rights and Global Justice (CHRGJ). She has a first class LLB from the University of Manchester and obtained the highest marks in her cohort for Criminal Evidence and Counterterrorism and Human Rights. Joyce is a graduate editor for the N.Y.U Journal of International Law & Politics and serves as a judicial Intern for the Hon. Gerald Lebovitz of the New York State Supreme Court.

Preface

We would like to dedicate this book to the late Mark George KC, Garden Court North Chambers. Mark was one of the most generous, wonderful people you could have the good fortune to meet and he helped and inspired generations of students and colleagues.

This is the sixth edition of our textbook, and we are delighted to welcome Suzanne Gower and Joyce Claudia Choo. Suzanne was in criminal practice for 15 years and brings her practical experience to this edition and Joyce is a recent graduate of the University of Manchester, who has given us a student perspective. On a more personal note, since the previous edition Mark has now qualified as a barrister, and Claire has been made an associate member of Garden Court North Chambers, congratulations Claire and Mark. Unfortunately, Jonathan Doak has now stepped back from wiring with us, but we want to thank Jonathan for his invaluable contribution of the past 5 editions.

Since the last edition the world has changed, COVID 19 impacted on every part of life, the criminal justice system is in crisis, we might be heading for a new era of political change and the shake-up of legal education following the SRA's introduction of the Solicitors' Qualifying Examination (SQE) has now happened. The law of evidence, or at least the study of the law of evidence, did not change that dramatically between editions 5 and 6 but the future remains uncertain. A new project was launched in parliament earlier this year by the All-Party Parliamentary Group on Miscarriages of Justice ('APPGMJ'), that being the Future of Justice project. It is being run by experienced appellate lawyer, Glyn Maddocks KC (Hon.), and the campaigning journalist and academic, Jon Robins. The Future of Justice Project has now been registered as a charity under the governance of Maddocks and Robins who have been joined as trustees of the charity by Barry Sheerman MP, the Chair of the APPGMJ and Sue James, the Chief Executive Officer of the Legal Action Group ('LAG'). The project will take over the role of providing the secretariat to the APPGMJ as they look to build upon the impressive work done by the Westminster Commission on Miscarriages of Justice, whose investigation and 2021 Report into the workings of the Criminal Cases Review Commission has formed the basis for the wide ranging review of the laws concerning criminal appeals currently being undertaken by the Law Commission. This could present a once in a generation opportunity for reform in this complex and often over-looked area of law. The Future of Justice Project will begin their work in late 2023 by launching inquiries into five different areas of the criminal justice system which they have identified as needing reform: Science & the Courts; Media; Legal Policy; the Legal Profession; and Criminal Appeal. At the same time the Law Commission is also looking at reforms in this area.

We hope that this edition continues to reflect the balancing exercise that we, as authors wish to conduct with the subject that is evidence. The law of evidence does not always lend itself to the integration of a contextual perspective, but we have tried, where possible, to discuss how wider policy debates and societal trends have impacted upon the recent evolution of the law.

This edition aims to include all major developments in the law of evidence, both in terms of legislation and case law, since our previous edition in 2018. Mainly, this edition updates our previous statistics on the increase in the use of 'show pleas', false confessions, and miscarriages of justice, alongside a comparative perspective on how the American criminal practice has evolved along a parallel line. Specifically, we would like to thank Justin Brookes for kindly allowing us to utilise the new case-studies and data in his contemporary book, 'You Might Go To Prison, Even if You're Innocent', which allows us to update our illustrations on the dangers associated with police interrogation techniques and its effect on false confessions. This edition also updates academic commentary towards Article 3 and Article 6 of the ECtHR case-law, and new critique on the CJPOA, including (as mentioned above), Mark George KC's previous comments on how these acts are utilised in practice. New evidentiary findings within DNA and Forensic evidence were revised, specifically focusing on contemporary sociological research into the current role of racial injustice within the criminal justice system, with a particular focus on new research into the prejudicial effects of admitting rap music into the trial process. New perspectives on the genuine probative value of admitting prior allegations of sexual history evidence were revisited, and comparatives were drawn between the way other jurisdictions treat this crucial area were updated. Lastly, relational assessments were drawn between how expert evidence is treated in other jurisdictions, namely Australia, New Zealand, U.S. and Hong Kong were updated, and new academic commentary on the subjects were put forward.

As authors, we recognise the importance of the Criminal and Civil Procedure Rules and their continued significance in practice. As such, we continue to pay particular attention to the relevant procedural rules explaining how the 'theory' of evidence interacts with the 'practice' of evidence. The Criminal Procedure Rules underwent significant change in 2015 with a complete overhaul of the structure and numbering of the Rules and the official recognition of the Rules being abbreviated to 'Crim PR'. These changes continue to be reflected in the text.

We hope that this latest edition will result in a textbook which both students and lecturers find accessible and stimulating. From the inception of this book (first published in 2005), we have aimed to provide a text that takes a contextual approach to the law of evidence in an effort to rouse the interest of students and allow them truly to appreciate evidence law outside of the theoretical legal vacuum. We have continued in our style of avoiding the taking of a broad doctrinal sweep of the law of evidence to allow us to focus more attention and detail on those topics that tend to feature commonly on Evidence courses. This is the reason why we invited Joyce to be part of our team, to put what we preach into practice, to work on partnership and co- creation with students.

As with every edition, we have sought to improve on the pedagogical features of the book, updating the use of tables, flow-charts and other diagrams where we have felt these would be of assistance to students. Many of these diagrams are used by the authors in teaching their own students and we feel it useful to share these diagrams with our readers.

We wish to express our sincere gratitude to the team at Routledge for commissioning this latest edition and their continued support of this text in the present financial market. Our thanks also go to our academic peers and students who have provided very useful feedback on the previous editions. As with previous editions, we remain indebted to the late Ken Lidstone, who supplied us with a wealth of material which laid the foundations of this book and to the late Mark George KC for his ongoing support and comments on the last 2 editions.

As authors, we accept full responsibility for any errors or omissions in the text. We have endeavoured to state the law as it stood at November 7th 2023.

Professor Claire McGourlay, University of Manchester
Mark Thomas, Nottingham Trent University
Suzanne Gower, University of Manchester
Joyce Claudia Choo, University of Manchester Alumni

List of figures and tables

Figures

Tables

Table of statutes

D

E

P

R

S

T

W

Y

Table of statutory instruments

E

M

P

Y

Table of international instruments

Table of codes of practice, guidance and practice directions

Table of Cases

C

D

E

F

G

H

I

J

K

L

M

N

O

P

Q

R

S

T

U

V

W

X

Chapter 1

Introduction

Basic Concepts

Chapter contents

DOI: 10.4324/9781003416098-1

1.1 Introduction

All material that is produced at court is subject to regulation by the laws of evidence. Decisions on the application of these rules are taken by the trial judge and will often be concerned with whether or not the evidence should be admitted. The law of evidence is said to be an 'adjectival' rather than a 'substantive' form of law. So, while the substantive law concerns matters such as the elements of a criminal offence or a tort or the circumstances leading to discharge of a contract, the adjectival law relates to practice and procedure. The law of evidence concerns the use of material to prove the existence or non-existence of any elements of the substantive law; see Figure 1.1.

It should be underlined, however, that the adjectival law is not an entirely separate entity from the substantive law. Often, there will be some degree of overlap between the two. For example, in a murder case, the jury will often have to decide whether the defendant intended to kill or to cause serious bodily harm. The trial judge will direct them that there has to be a 'virtual certainty of death' and that the defendant(s) had to have an 'appreciation that such was the case.'[1] These aspects of the trial relate to the elements of the offence, and fall within the remit of the substantive criminal law. However, a number of evidential rules will regulate how the case is prosecuted in court. They will dictate where the burden and standard of proof lies, what material may be used by the parties, the form of questioning that can be adopted by the advocates, and the manner in which the jury should assess the evidence. It is therefore unsurprising that, in practice, knowledge of the operation of evidential rules is essential to a full understanding of the legal process as a whole. No matter how well versed a lawyer may be in substantive law, they will be unable to provide advice to a client, or to prosecute a case, without a firm grasp of the law of evidence.

As a starting point for studying the law of evidence, it is worth bearing in mind the Latin maxim *ei incumbit probatio qui dicit, non qui negat* ('the burden of proof lies on he who seeks to affirm something, not on he who denies it'). In practice, this means that it is for the prosecution to prove the case against the accused, or, in the civil courts, for the claimant to prove the case against the defendant. We shall consider this principle in some depth in Chapter 3, but for present purposes it is worth noting that even in cases in which the facts may appear relatively straightforward, in practice, evidential rules can complicate the task of proving guilt.

Example 1.1

James, a young adult with severe learning difficulties, is found dead. The autopsy shows that a blow to the head killed him, probably from his head coming into contact with a wall or similar hard, flat surface. James was seen alive the day before he was found dead. Only his parents had contact with James during this period.

At first glance, this might appear to be an open-and-shut case against the parents. However, this is by no means the case. For example, his parents may maintain their right to refuse to answer questions and refuse to offer any explanation for James' death. Without evidence that one or the other, or both, committed the act that killed the deceased, neither can be charged with murder or manslaughter. It is not sufficient simply to charge both and let the jury decide who was responsible. If both parties were charged, each could refuse to give evidence, which would not then be tested through

1 *R v Woollin* [1999] AC 82; *R v Matthews and Alleyne* [2004] QB 69.

cross-examination. Since the Criminal Justice and Public Order Act 1994 came into force, the jury may draw proper inferences from the failure to answer policy questions or to give evidence, but these provisions do not replace the requirement for evidence that the defendant intentionally, recklessly, or negligently did an act, or failed to do an act, which caused the death of James. Therefore, if there were a prosecution in this case, the lack of evidence would almost certaily result in an acquittal.

If, however, subsequent forensic evidence uncovered some years later tended to implicate the mother and her boyfriend in James' death, they could then face a retrial.[2] In these circumstances, the prosecution may well find it easier to discharge the burden of proof and convince the jury beyond reasonable doubt that the defendants were responsible for the killing of James.

1.2 Facts

To begin with, we must distinguish facts in issue (also known as 'principal facts') from collateral facts (also known as 'subordinate facts').

1.2.1 Facts in issue

At the centre of the criminal trial are the facts in issue. In a nutshell, these are the facts that are being contested by the parties. A fact in issue is one where the party bearing the responsibility of proving the fact (known as the burden of proof) must do so to the appropriate standard (known as the standard of proof). In the majority of cases, the burden of proving a fact in issue rests with the prosecution (and claimant in a civil case); in some cases, however, the burden falls on the defendant.

In some cases, an accused may plead not guilty and simply deny any knowledge of the offence. In this case, all the elements of the offence effectively become facts in issue, since they are contested by both parties. Here the prosecution must prove all elements of the offence. In the case of theft, contrary to section 1 of the Theft Act 1968, the prosecution must prove that the defendant dishonestly appropriated property belonging to another with the intention of permanently depriving the other of that property. This reflects Lord Goddard CJ's observation in *Sims* that when a defendant pleads not guilty, 'everything is in issue and the prosecution has to prove the whole of its case, including the identity of the accused, the nature of the act and the existence of any necessary knowledge or intent.'[3]

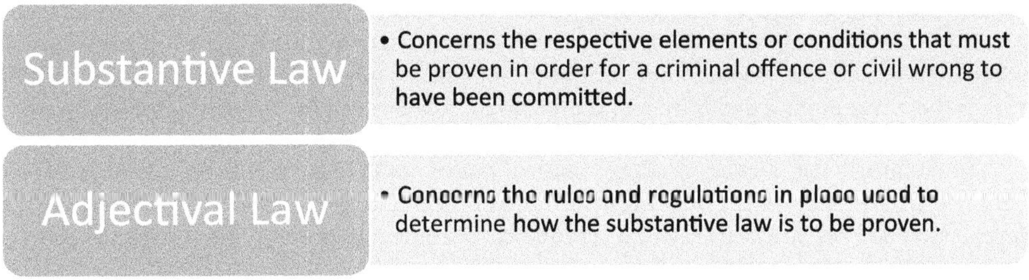

Figure 1.1 Understanding the law of evidence

2 Previously, the rule against double jeopardy stipulated that an acquitted defendant could not thereafter be tried again for the same offence. However, Pt 10 of the Criminal Justice Act (CJA) 2003 provides for the retrial of a person who has been acquitted of a qualifying offence where there is new and compelling evidence that the person was guilty of that offence.

3 *R v Sims* [1946] KB 531, at 539 (Lord Goddard CJ).

Most often, however, the defence will make out that one element of the offence has not been proven. We can observe this in Example 1.2 with the offence of theft.

> **Example 1.2**
>
> Emma is charged with theft after lifting a silver bracelet in the changing room at her local gym. She pleads 'not guilty' on the ground that she lacked dishonest intent. Defence counsel admits that she appropriated property belonging to someone else, but argues that Emma was not dishonest as she genuinely believed she was the true owner of the bracelet.

In these circumstances, the act of taking the bracelet will not, therefore, constitute a fact in issue, since the defence will not attempt to rebut the prosecution's evidence on this point. Instead, the defence will concentrate their efforts on countering the one fact in issue, which is the prosecution's contention that the accused acted dishonestly.

In many rape cases, the fact that intercourse took place is admitted, and the trial will thus revolve around the issue of consent. Since the defendant is admitting that the intercourse took place, the only fact in issue here is whether the complainant consented (or the defendant held a reasonable belief that she was consenting). Similarly, in a civil trial, facts in issue are the matters contested between the parties. As opposed to a criminal trial where the facts in issue arise upon the entering of a not guilty plea by the accused, in a civil trial, facts in issue arise much earlier with the issuing, filing, and serving of a statement of case.[4] Where, in a criminal or civil case, a defence is raised to the allegations made, this also will give rise to a fact in issue (namely whether or not the defendant may rely on such a defence). As discussed in Chapter 3, the burden of proving a defence varies according to the type of defence and whether it is a criminal or civil trial.

Importantly, if a fact in issue is proven (to the requisite standard), the law treats that fact as having happened; if the burden has not been discharged to the necessary standard, then the fact is taken as having not happened. It is important to now consider a number of different ways by which a fact in issue is taken as being proven. For this, we will consider formal admissions.

1.2.1.1 Facts in issue and formal admissions

Formal admissions (more commonly referred to in practice as 'agreed facts') are any facts which are formally admitted to by either party to the proceedings. Where a fact has been formally admitted, it ceases to be a fact in issue (i.e. it is treated as having been proved in law). Formal admissions ensure that evidence does not need to be called where the fact is not contested; this means that time, money, and resources can be saved. Any fact can be formally admitted between the parties.

In a criminal case, section 10 of the Criminal Justice Act 1967 prescribes the relevant rules for admitted facts. Section 10 provides that a formal admission can be made orally, but in practice the prosecution and defence will create an agreed facts document that will be put before the jury (as

4 A statement of case which initiates a claim is known as a Claim Form (more specifically, an N1 Form) and must have contained within it or served with it a Particulars of Claim, unless the claimant seeks to serve the Particulars at a later date (no later than 14 days after service of the Claim Form): Civil Procedure Rules 1998, r 7.4(1).

part of their bundle of papers).[5] Section 10 covers 'any fact of which oral evidence may be given in any criminal proceedings'; this means that the opinion of an expert, or inadmissible evidence such as hearsay, cannot be admitted under section 10.

> **Example 1.3**
>
> James is charged with assaulting David, occasioning him actual bodily harm, contrary to section 47 of the Offences Against the Person Act 1861. James accepts that he assaulted David and that the assault caused actual bodily harm (a small cut to the back of the head, requiring three stitches). James claims that he acted in self-defence.

In this example, the prosecution and defence will be able to create an agreed facts document which details the assault and injury caused to David. By admitting the injury caused to David, the jury would not have to hear from the medical practitioner who examined David on the relevant day. The jury would thus be able to focus their minds on the issue of self-defence.

Facts can also be admitted in civil cases. Rule 14.1(1) of the Civil Procedure Rules (CPR) 1998 provides that any party 'may admit the truth of the whole or any part of another party's case.' By r 14.1(2), such admission must be given in writing.

1.2.2 Collateral facts

Those facts that are not directly relevant to the facts in issue are known as 'collateral facts.' Collateral facts are usually only relevant to the court insofar as they go to the credit of the witness, or to the credibility of primary evidence – such as the admissibility of a confession. Thus, counsel may carry out cross-examination purely designed to undermine the credibility of the witness in the eyes of the jury and persuade them to give less weight to the evidence of the particular witness or a particular piece of evidence. As we shall see in Chapter 6, the law now limits such questioning in relation to collateral facts through the 'finality rule,' which usually obliges the cross-examiner to accept the answer given, and denies the advocate the opportunity to introduce rebutting evidence.

Although attacks on the credibility of opposing witnesses may be seen as a necessary, and even a desirable, process for undermining deceitful or mistaken witnesses, it is clear that the

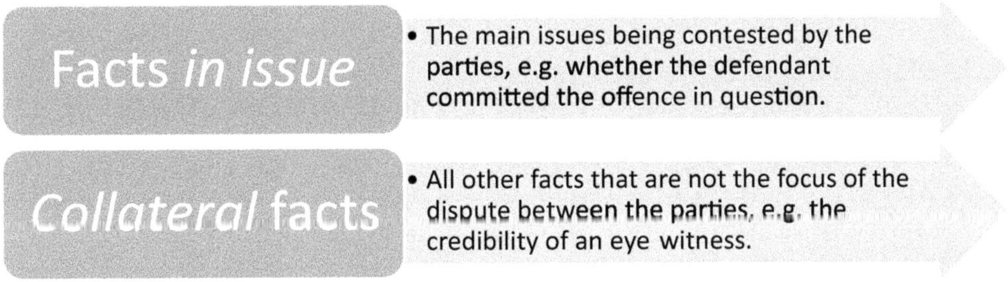

Figure 1.2 Understanding different facts

5 Indeed, r 24.6(2) (magistrates' court trial) and r 25.13(2) (Crown Court trial) of the Criminal Procedure Rules 2020 provide that where a party introduces in evidence a fact admitted by another party, or parties jointly admit a fact, then unless the court otherwise directs, 'a written record must be made of the admission.'

nature of many such attacks continues to be a problem, particularly for victims and vulnerable witnesses. It is often suggested that witnesses are mistaken or, even worse, liars, and many who have given evidence at a criminal trial will say that it felt as if they were on trial and they would think twice before volunteering to give evidence in future. Section 100 of the Criminal Justice Act 2003 restricts the admissibility of the bad character of a non-defendant with the intention of preventing some of the abuses of cross-examination of witnesses. Until relatively recently, the accused was permitted to cross-examine their alleged victim in person. Children and adult victims of rape and other offences were particularly intimidated by this practice. One of the most notorious instances occurred in 1996, when defendant Ralston Edwards subjected the victim of rape to a six-day cross-examination that he carried out while wearing the same clothes he was alleged to have worn while raping her. The Youth Justice and Criminal Evidence Act 1999 changed the law to prevent cross-examination by the defendant in person of children or victims of sexual offences, and judges have discretion to prevent such cross-examination in other appropriate cases. In addition, the Act seeks to control the use of evidence of the sexual behaviour of the complainant in a case of rape and other sexual offences.[6] In the past, it was not unusual for the previous sexual behaviour of the complainant to be used by the defence to suggest that the complainant was of loose moral character and probably consented to the intercourse that took place. This was a factor in the extremely low conviction rate for rape, particularly the form known as acquaintance rape, where the defendant and complainant were known to each other and might well have been intimate in the past. Recent years have seen judges exert much closer control over how collateral facts are used by advocates, although the widely reported treatment of the deceased's stepfather in the Milly Dowler murder trial suggests that the problem is far from having been laid to rest.[7]

These matters will be discussed in depth in Chapter 5.

1.3 Admissibility, relevance, and weight

Before we consider the different forms of evidence, we must first consider whether any such evidence would be admissible in court. The general rule in the law of evidence is that if the evidence is potentially relevant to a fact in issue, then, subject to any exclusionary rules, the evidence is also admissible. Vice versa, should the evidence prove to be irrelevant, or not sufficiently relevant, then it should be treated as inadmissible. Even where evidence is admissible, the weight to be placed on that evidence by the arbiter of fact remains to be seen. In this section, we discuss the issues of relevance, weight, and contesting admissibility (see Figure 1.3 for an overview of these concepts).

1.3.1 The concept of relevance

Before a party can adduce any evidence at trial, it must first be shown that the evidence in question is relevant. The legal definition of relevance was laid down by Lord Simon in *DPP v Kilbourne*.[8] Evidence is considered to be relevant if 'it is logically probative or disprobative of some matter which requires proof.'[9] This definition is not a decisive indicator as to what evidence should be excluded and what should be included; it does not amount to a legal test for relevance.

---

6 Youth Justice and Criminal Evidence Act 1999, s 41; Ch 6.

7 See further 'Milly Dowler family's court ordeal "appalling" says victims czar Louise Casey,' *Daily Telegraph* (24 June 2011) http://www .telegraph.co.uk/news/uknews/crime/8595906/Milly-Dowler-familys-court-ordeal-appalling-says-victims-czar-Louise -Casey.html (last accessed 2 February 2023).

8 [1973] AC 729.

9 Ibid., 756.

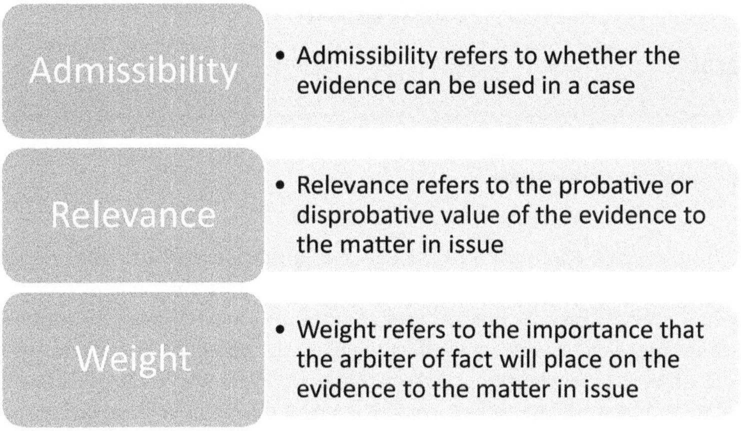

Figure 1.3 Admissibility, relevance, and weight

The House of Lords took relevance to what may be described as its logical extreme in *R v Blastland*.[10] The accused was charged with the murder of a young boy. He claimed that the murderer was another man, M, who had been in the vicinity while the accused was with the boy. M was investigated by the police, and had made a number of statements in which he admitted the crime, but he later withdrew them. These were inadmissible at Blastland's trial because they were hearsay. However, the defence wished to call a number of witnesses who would say that M had told them of the boy's death at a time when the only way in which he could have known of it was if he himself had killed him. The House of Lords upheld the trial judge's decision to exclude the evidence of these witnesses on the ground that it was not relevant. The issue at the trial was whether Blastland had committed the crime, and what was relevant to that issue was not the fact of M's knowledge but how he came by it. Since he might have come by it in a number of different ways, there was no rational basis on which the jury could be invited to draw an inference as to how M came by that knowledge or that M, rather than the accused, was the killer.

There are thus various degrees of relevance: at one end of the spectrum, a fact may be only of peripheral significance, while at the other, the entire case may hang on its existence or non-existence. Relevance is therefore a matter of degree, determined by common sense and experience.[11]

In practice, most facts will lie somewhere between these two extremes. Yet it remains the case that the question of relevance often boils down to subjective interpretation and, as such, has been subject to considerable criticism from various quarters. Feminist commentators, in particular, have attacked the way in which the concept of relevance has been applied in rape and sexual assault cases. Jennifer Temkin, for example, highlighted that 'relevance is in the mind of the beholder and all too often it can be swayed by stereotypical assumptions, myths, and prejudice.'[12] As we shall see in Chapter 6, this often resulted in complainants in rape cases being cross-examined in detail about their previous sexual history and lifestyle choices; trial judges frequently deemed such matters relevant to the issue of consent. Delayed complaints are often a suggestion that any allegation has been fabricated or exaggerated; in these cases, an appropriate direction to the arbiter of fact will be necessary to avoid this evidence being purely pejorative against the complainant.[13]

---

10 [1986] AC 41.

11 *R v Randall* [2003] UKHL 69, [2004] 1 WLR 56, at [20] (Lord Steyn).

12 Temkin, J., *Rape and the Legal Process*, 2nd edn (Oxford University Press, 2002), at 199.

13 See the likes of *R v Miller* [2010] EWCA Crim 1578 and *R v Smith* [2012] EWCA Crim 404.

Figure 1.4 The spectrum of relevance

Another controversial application of the concept of relevance relates to evidence of previous convictions or bad character. As with sexual history evidence, a simple application of whether a previous conviction would be 'more or less probative' to the accused having committed the offence in question would prove to be entirely ineffective given the potential overwhelming effect of this type of evidence. Likewise, evidence of the apparent good character of a prosecution witness must be questioned as to its value and relevance; if the good character is designed to merely bolster the credibility of the prosecution witness, it should not be treated as relevant.[14] Traditionally, the common law deemed that a high degree of probative value was required in order to outweigh the prejudicial effect of admitting such evidence. The rules relating to the use of such evidence have long since become complex and have been overhauled on various occasions. The most recent body of rules, contained in the Criminal Justice Act 2003, will be examined in Chapter 11.

1.3.2 The weight of evidence

It should be underlined, however, that the *degree* of relevance does not usually affect the *admissibility* of the evidence, although the less relevant the evidence is, the less weight the factfinder will generally be prepared to place upon it.

> **Example 1.4**
>
> Carol has positively identified Ibrahim as the person she saw running away from the scene of a bank robbery. Her evidence would probably have very little weight attached to it if she had caught only a fleeting glimpse of the offender on a dark night as he ran from the scene. The evidence would still be relevant (and admissible), but would probably carry little weight. If, on the other hand, Carol was in the bank and saw Ibrahim's face for a period of time at close hand, the evidence would probably be seen as being highly relevant, and doubtless the jury would give much greater weight to it.

The weight of the evidence will also be affected by the way in which it is given, the character of the witness, and whether or not that witness is discredited in cross-examination. Thus, a witness may give what appears to be highly relevant evidence, which is then discredited in cross-examination. For example, if the eyewitness in the scenario above claims to recognise the defendant as a person with whom she went to school, and the defence show this witness to have held a long-standing grudge against the defendant, the weight of her evidence may be diminished in the eyes of the jury since she may no longer be considered a reliable witness.

An example of witnesses who may have been improperly motivated to testify can be found in the infamous trial of one of Britain's most notorious serial killers, Rosemary West, which took

14 *R v Mader* [2018] EWCA Crim 2454.

place in the autumn of 1995.[15] West had been placed on trial alongside her husband for the torture and murder of ten young women in the 1970s. It came to light that a number of witnesses had been paid by newspapers, or had entered into lucrative contracts with newspapers, to publish their stories if West was convicted.[16] Their evidence, although highly relevant, was still admissible, but may have carried relatively little weight in the eyes of the jury since the witnesses may have been motivated to embellish their testimony to ensure a guilty verdict. Indeed, the West case is not the only example in which money has played a factor in discrediting witnesses. In 1979, the former Liberal Party leader, Jeremy Thorpe, was acquitted of various offences, in part because a central prosecution witness had been promised more money for his story if Thorpe was convicted.[17] Similarly, in the Damilola Taylor murder trial, a 15-year-old witness known as Bromley had been promised a reward of £50,000 in return for evidence leading to the conviction of those responsible for the killing.[18] The discussion of the reward with the interviewing police officer, which suggested more interest in the reward than in giving honest evidence, was a factor in the judge's decision to instruct the jury that her evidence was not credible. However, legislation to prohibit such payments to witnesses has not been forthcoming to date.

The Editors' Code of Practice,[19] a code governing the press, provides that '[n]o payment or offer of payment to a witness – or any person who may reasonably be expected to be called as a witness – should be made in any case once proceedings are active.'[20] It goes on to say that '[w]here proceedings are not yet active but are likely and foreseeable, editors must not make or offer payment to any person who may reasonably be expected to be called as a witness.'

Weight is also important regarding how certain types of evidence are treated in civil cases. As we shall see in Chapter 12, section 4(1) of the Civil Evidence Act 1995 provides that, in estimating the weight to be given to hearsay evidence in civil proceedings, the court shall have regard to any circumstances from which any inference can reasonably be drawn as to the reliability or otherwise of the evidence. When making this assessment, the court must take into account the list of factors set out in subsection (2).[21]

1.3.3 Contesting the admissibility of evidence

Where the admissibility of evidence is contested, a number of options are open to the court. Such issues are often resolved as part of the Plea and Trial Preparation Hearing (PTPH) (formerly the Plea and Case Management Hearing), which generally takes place within 28 days of the magistrates' court sending the defendant for trial in the Crown Court. Where there is a guilty plea, the purpose of the hearing is to formally record this and put in place arrangements for sentencing. Where the accused pleads not guilty, the prosecution and defence must outline the facts in issue, the witnesses they propose to call, any special requirements that are required by such witnesses, and the evidence they propose to rely on, and they should also raise any matters pertaining to the admissibility of evidence.

However, not all admissibility decisions are taken in advance of the trial. As the Court of Appeal held in *Murray*,[22] it may be appropriate to hear submissions as to admissibility at the beginning of the trial before opening speeches are made to the jury. Here it was held that making the

15 See generally Masters, B., *'She Must Have Known': The Trial of Rosemary West* (Corgi Publications, 1997).

16 'Newspapers paid West witnesses,' *The Independent* (13 November 1995) http://www.independent.co.uk/news/newspapers-paid-west-witnesses-1581685.html (last accessed 2 February 2023).

17 Waugh, A., *The Last Word: An Eye-witness Account of the Thorpe Trial* (Michael Joseph, 1980).

18 'Damilola witness: give me the £50,000,' *The Guardian* (7 February 2002) https://www.theguardian.com/uk/2002/feb/07/ukcrime1 (last accessed 24 July 2017).

19 Independent Press Standards Organisation, *Editors' Code of Practice* (2021), at para 15(i).

20 Ibid., para 15(ii).

21 See Ch 12.

22 *R v Murray* (1950) 34 Cr App R 203.

objection before the opening to the jury was justified on the basis that prosecuting counsel would be unable otherwise to explain the case for the Crown in opening.

Alternatively, a *voir dire*, or trial within a trial, may be held. In trials on indictment, the judge will ask the jury to leave the courtroom in order to hear arguments from the prosecution and defence about whether or not a particular piece of evidence should be admitted in evidence. One of the more common scenarios is where the prosecution proposes to rely on a confession made by the accused, which the defence argues is inadmissible because it was obtained in breach of section 76 of the Police and Criminal Evidence Act 1984, or in some other way that renders it liable to exclusion under section 78 of that Act. In practice, counsel for the defence will have informed the prosecution that they intend to object to the admissibility of a particular piece of evidence. At the point at which the prosecution would have adduced the evidence in question, counsel will intimate to the judge that a point of law has arisen that falls to be determined in the absence of the jury. Counsel are often very astute as to the way in which they raise a point of law in front of the jury. Particularly, jurors may question why they are being excluded from the courtroom and will no doubt ponder what exactly is being hidden from them. In any event, the jury will then be asked to retire and the issue of admissibility will be determined by the judge. Witnesses may be called by both parties in what is essentially a mini trial arising from a contested issue in the case.

It will often be necessary for the defendant to give evidence, particularly if they allege some malpractice or illegality in the obtaining of the evidence. If the judge decides that the evidence is not admissible, the jury are recalled and the trial continues, but the jury hear nothing of the excluded evidence.[23] If the evidence is deemed admissible, the jury are recalled and the evidence is presented in the normal way.

In magistrates' courts, where the magistrates are adjudicators of both law and fact, and in the civil courts, where juries rarely operate, there are obvious difficulties that arise when adjudicators are called on to decide both the elements of legal and factual decision-making. In these settings, it will generally be for the opposing party to raise an objection where it is felt that the evidence should not be taken into account. The rules regarding the holding of a *voir dire* in the magistrates' court are varied. For example, where the court is determining the admissibility of a confession under section 76, it has been held that the magistrates are under a legal obligation to hold a *voir dire*.[24] On the other hand, where an application is made to exclude the evidence under section 78, a magistrates' court has the discretion whether to deal with the admissibility of evidence by way of *voir dire* or not.[25]

1.4 The role of discretion

Even where evidence is deemed to be relevant, it does not necessarily mean that it will be included in the trial. It should be already apparent from the discussion above that various types of evidence are excluded both by rules contained within statutes and by the common law. Failure to properly apply an exclusionary rule may well constitute grounds for a successful appeal. The other main means by which evidence is excluded is through the role of judicial discretion. This involves the judge weighing a number of factors against each other in order to make a determination as to whether the evidence ought to be admitted, usually on the grounds that it would be unfair or prejudicial to do so. Unlike exclusionary rules, it is extremely rare for the appellate courts to interfere with the exercise of judicial discretion at first instance, providing the judge takes into account all relevant matters in doing so, and disregards those that are deemed to be irrelevant.[26]

23 *Mitchell v R* [1998] AC 695.

24 *Liverpool Juvenile Court, ex parte R* [1988] QB 1.

25 *Vel v Owen* [1987] Crim LR 496.

26 *R v Scarrott* [1978] QB 1016.

The exercise of discretion has a long history at common law; judges wielded considerable discretion in the latter part of the eighteenth century.[27] In an era where defence counsel was relatively unknown, the exercise of judicial discretion over prosecution evidence was widely perceived as a protective bulwark for the accused against the potential abuse of state power, and was subject to very few controls.[28] However, as the trial became increasingly 'lawyerised' in the nineteenth century, power tended to move away from the trial judge towards counsel, causing judges to take a step back from proceedings, and the discretion became increasingly limited by the evolution of evidential rules.[29]

In the contemporary context, the scope of judicial discretion remains limited and only applies to evidence tendered by the prosecution.[30] It is no longer the case that judges may exclude evidence solely on the basis that it may be unfair to the accused to include it. Instead, the focus of the court is very much on the *quality* of the evidence, namely whether it is relevant and reliable, with fairness to the accused being very much of secondary importance. These narrow parameters, which now govern the use of common law discretion in criminal trials, were laid down by the House of Lords in *Sang*.[31] The case is discussed in some detail in Chapter 9, but for present purposes it is sufficient to note that the effect of the decision is that common law discretion may only be used in circumstances where the prejudicial effect of the evidence outweighs its probative value. Unfortunately, the courts have been reluctant to provide any real guidance as to when, precisely, such circumstances might arise. The task of determining what constitutes prejudicial effect, probative value, and the balancing exercise that needs to be carried out between them is thus both flexible and open-ended and rests solely with the trial judge.

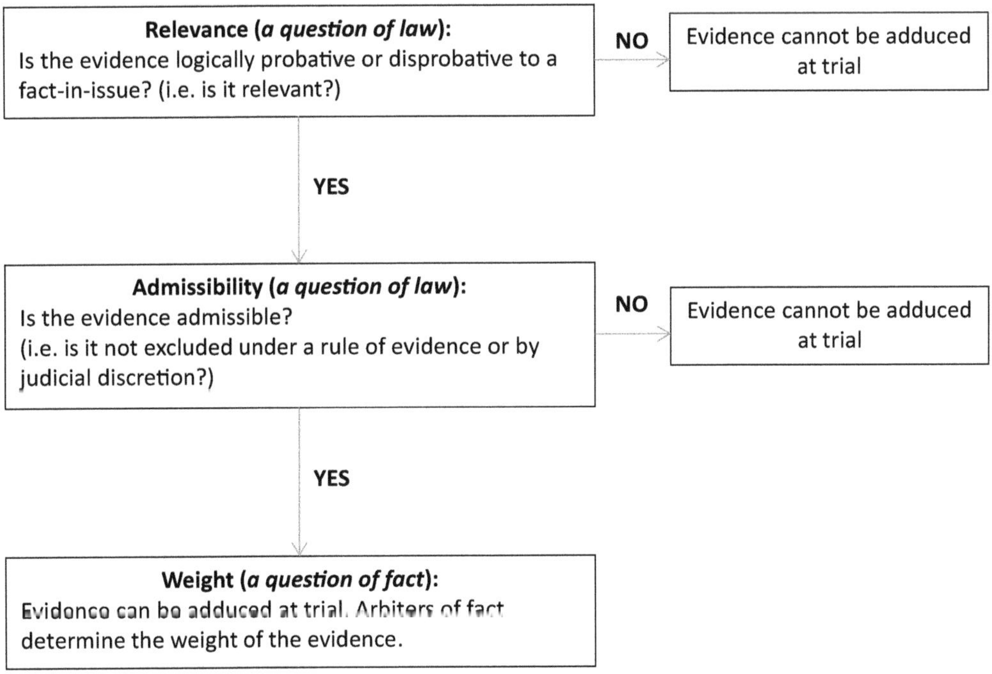

Figure 1.5 Introducing evidence

27 See Baker, J.H., *An Introduction to English Legal History*, 4th edn (Oxford University Press, 2000).

28 See further Beattie, J.M., *Crime and the Courts in England, 1660–1800* (Princeton University Press, 1986), pp. 406–36.

29 Langbein, J. H., *The Origins of Adversary Criminal Trial* (Oxford University Press, 2003). See also Ch 2.

30 *R v Randall* (n. 11).

31 [1980] AC 402. See further Ch 9.

The introduction of the Police and Criminal Evidence Act (PACE) 1984 has largely superseded the common law discretion in practice, though the latter continues to exist.[32] Section 78 provides:

> (1) In any proceedings, the court may refuse to allow evidence on which the prosecution proposes to rely to be given if it appears to the court that, having regard to all the circumstances, including the circumstances in which the evidence was obtained, the admission of the evidence would have such an adverse effect on the fairness of the proceedings that the court ought not to admit it.

The standard of unfairness is thus essentially the same as under the common law, though the provision is also broader than the common law discretion for a number of reasons. First, it can take into account the manner in which the evidence was obtained when determining its effect on the fairness of the trial. Thus, unlike the common law discretion, it may cover instances of entrapment by agents provocateurs.[33] Second, it applies not only to confessions and evidence obtained after the commission of the offence, but also to *any* form of evidence on which the prosecution proposes to rely, notwithstanding other statutory provisions that may, *prima facie*, appear to allow their admission. However, both the statutory and the common law discretions are concerned with the effect that the evidence has on the fairness of the trial; there is no alteration to the general rule that obtaining evidence illegally or improperly will not per se afford a defence to a criminal charge.

In addition to these generic forms of exclusionary discretion, statute provides for the exercise of both inclusionary and exclusionary discretion for specific forms of evidence. As we shall see in Chapter 12, reforms to the hearsay rules and rules concerning bad character introduced under the Criminal Justice Act 2003 provide for the operation of judicial discretion, though such discretion is controlled by factors set out in the legislation.

It should be noted that the discretion to exclude evidence was long considered to be confined to criminal cases, with no equivalent power existing in the civil courts. However, the position was changed by the Civil Procedure Rules 1998. Rule 32.1 provides:

> (1) The court may control the evidence by giving directions as to –
> (a) the issues on which it requires evidence;
> (b) the nature of the evidence which it requires to decide those issues; and
> (c) the way in which the evidence is to be placed before the court.
> (2) The court may use its power under this rule to exclude evidence that would otherwise be admissible.

The provision is clearly fairly sweeping, and is considered in greater detail in Chapter 9.

There remains considerable debate concerning whether discretion plays a positive or negative role within the criminal process, and whether (depending on one's stance) that role ought to be expanded or contracted. Some practitioners find the prospect of a more widespread use of discretion to be somewhat vexing, since it tends to add to the unpredictability of decision-making and thereby makes cases more difficult to plan.[34] Moreover, if decision-making is rendered unpredictable, then there would seem to follow a greater risk of inconsistent outcomes, thereby undermining the value of law and resulting in an uneven application of justice.[35]

---

32 PACE, s 82(3). See further Ch 9.

33 *R v Christou* (1992) 95 Cr App R 264. See further Ch 9.

34 Schneider, C., 'Discretion and Rules: A Lawyer's View,' in K. Hawkins (ed.), *Uses of Discretion* (Oxford University Press, 1991), p. 47.

35 Tapper, C., 'The Law of Evidence and the Rule of Law' (2009) 68 *Cambridge Law Journal* 67.

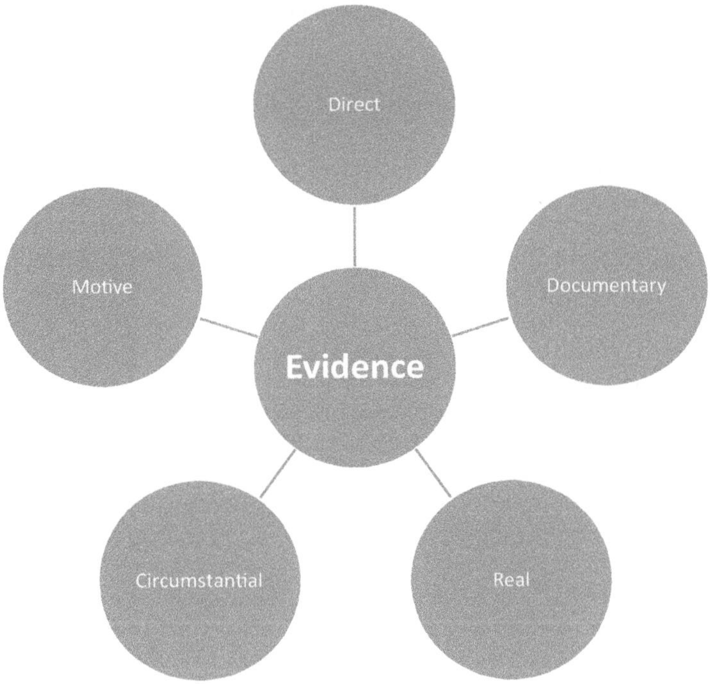

Figure 1.6 Forms of evidence

Those holding a more favourable attitude towards the use of discretion assert that such claims are misconceived, since discretion is never unfettered and is always exercised in accordance with established legal principles. Moreover, as Roberts and Zuckerman claim, previous attempts by the law of evidence to produce overly restrictive and binding directives for the judiciary rarely work in practice: '[c]reative judicial interpretation deployed to outflank procedural rules is part of the unofficial history of common law.'[36] In a more positive sense, Jones argues that judicial discretion 'can fill gaps, correct errors and resolve conflicts allowing the law to develop in line with social standards without the need for constant legislative reform.'[37]

1.5 Forms of evidence

Evidence may be received by the court in a variety of different ways, which may be broadly categorised under the following headings.

1.5.1 Direct evidence

Most commonly, evidence will take the form of direct oral testimony. This means that the witness will be called on to testify under oath in open court, and everything they say will be tendered as evidence of the truth of the facts asserted. Witnesses can only give evidence of matters that they have themselves perceived with one of their five senses – usually a witness will speak of what

36 Roberts, P. and Zuckerman, A., *Criminal Evidence* (Oxford University Press, 2010), p. 30.

37 Jones, I., 'Still Just Rhetoric? Judicial Discretion and Due Process' (2011) 32(3) *Liverpool Law Review* 251, 255.

they saw or heard. Such testimony is always admissible, providing it is relevant and the witness is competent to testify.[38]

Direct evidence need not only be adduced by a live witness in the witness box; it may also be adduced by reliance on the witness statement of that person where their statement is agreed under section 9 of the Criminal Justice Act 1967. In that case, there would be no need to call the witness to give live evidence, as it has not been challenged by the opposing party. A similar procedure applies in civil proceedings where the general rule is that a witness statement will stand in place of the evidence-in-chief[39] and the witness will not be called to give live evidence unless the calling party requests to 'amplify' their evidence.[40] In either case, they will then be tendered for cross-examination by the defendant.

In both civil and criminal proceedings, witnesses may not proffer their own opinions or speculate on matters in which they have no expert knowledge, and special rules will determine whether they may relate any hearsay evidence to the court. Hearsay evidence is any statement other than one made by the witness in the course of giving their evidence in the proceedings in question, which is tendered as evidence of the truth of the facts asserted. Such evidence is inadmissible unless subject to a common law or statutory exception. Thus, a witness may testify to the court: 'I saw D strike V.' This is direct testimony, since the witness is speaking as an eyewitness. However, should that witness be unable to testify, a friend or family member could not be called to say that 'W told me that he had seen D striking V.' That would be hearsay, since it would be tendered to prove that the defendant struck the victim. There are numerous exceptions to the rule against hearsay, though for present purposes it is worth noting that such evidence is much more readily admissible in the civil rather than the criminal courts. The rules are considered in detail in Chapter 12.

1.5.2 Documentary evidence

Not all evidence, however, needs to be received in oral form. Documentary evidence will also be admissible, and comprises not only written or typed papers but also maps, plans, graphs, drawings, photographs, tapes (audio and visual), films, negatives and disks, CDs or DVDs, and digital recordings. In short, 'documentary evidence' is used to refer to every means of communicating information other than the direct spoken word. The purpose in producing a document varies according to the document and the particular case. Maps may be produced simply to provide the court with a visual picture of the scene of an accident or a crime. For example, in the Rosemary West trial, detailed plans of the house in which a number of bodies were found were produced to provide a visual picture of the location of the various bodies. The formal evidence of the finding of the bodies came from the police and forensic pathologists.

The situation becomes more complex when we consider the circumstances in which documentary evidence may replace the direct oral evidence of witnesses. Typically, most witnesses in criminal cases will have given a written statement to the police or to a solicitor. However, since these statements have been made out of court and have not been made under oath, the law of evidence places tight constraints on the extent to which they can be used at court. As we shall discuss below, these written statements may be used by the witness to refresh their memory before or while giving evidence if the statement was made fairly soon after the events described.[41] Furthermore, statements in a document, whether made by a witness to the crime or a business

---

38 See Ch 4.

39 CPR 1998, r 32.5(2).

40 Civil Procedure Rules 1998, r 32.5(3).

41 See Ch 6.

document made for the purposes of the business, are admissible in evidence subject to certain conditions and judicial discretion.[42]

1.5.3 Real evidence

In addition to documentary evidence, the court may also receive 'real evidence.' This term is usually taken to mean some material object, known as an exhibit, that is produced to the court for inspection so that the court may draw its own inference from observation of the particular object. Although real evidence will frequently feature in the cases of either the prosecution or defence, it is usually of little intrinsic value without some accompanying testimony. Thus, a knife may be produced in a murder case as a form of real evidence. However, unless other evidence is available to show that it was the murder weapon and that it is linked to the accused (e.g. it was found in their car and has the victim's blood on it), it proves nothing. Real evidence may also be an original document, a visit to the scene of the alleged crime(s) by the judge and jury, a tape-recording, photograph, or video image of the defendant. Real evidence will usually constitute an exception to the hearsay rule. For example, in *R v Robson, Mitchell and Richards*,[43] the defendants were convicted of armed robbery. The prosecution linked the second defendant with the crime by means of a computer printout of telephone calls made by the second defendant to the phone of the first defendant. It was held that the printout was not hearsay but real evidence since the printout was produced by a computer that operated automatically and independently without human intervention.[44]

1.5.4 Circumstantial evidence

Circumstantial evidence is evidence of relevant facts from which the existence, or non-existence, of the facts in issue may be inferred. Such evidence may include any of the above forms of evidence except, of course, direct testimony relating to the facts in issue. It is with direct oral testimony that circumstantial evidence is contrasted. Popular fiction and televised legal dramas often portray circumstantial evidence in rather derogatory terms; phrases such as 'the case against the accused is merely circumstantial' are relatively commonplace. However, in practice, circumstantial evidence is relied upon by the parties just as much as they rely on direct oral testimony. This is, perhaps, unsurprising, since it is in the nature of most crimes, and the 'luck' of civil wrongs, that they are not committed in the presence of eyewitnesses, and thus circumstantial evidence may be the only available evidence. However, as the Court of Appeal acknowledged in *R v Pinnock*,[45] contrary to popular perception, circumstantial evidence may be highly cogent:

> [I]t is our experience that appeals against conviction are all too often launched on the basis that where the Crown has little or no direct evidence upon which it can rely, but invites the court to draw inferences from circumstantial evidence, that this is in itself a good indicator of the weakness of the prosecution case. In our combined experience this is simply not the case. Circumstantial evidence can provide and often does provide a very strong case against an accused person. Provided the inferences the Crown invite the jury to draw from the circumstances are safe and proper inferences, then defence counsel will have a difficult job in persuading this court that a conviction secured upon them is unsafe.[46]

42 See Ch 12.
43 [1991] Crim LR 362.
44 See Ch 12.
45 [2006] EWCA Crim 3119.
46 Ibid., at [68].

This view is shared by Cross and Tapper who, citing Pollock CB in *R v Exall* (1866) F & F 922, liken such evidence to a multi-stranded rope:

> One strand of the cord might be insufficient to sustain the weight, but three stranded together might be of sufficient strength. Thus ... there may be a combination of circumstances, not one of which would raise a reasonable conviction or more than mere suspicion: but the three taken together may create a conclusion of guilt with as much certainty as human affairs can require.[47]

Example 1.5

Sahira is charged with the murder of Julia by stabbing her in an alleyway behind a club they both frequented. On the night of Julia's death, Sahira and Julia had an argument in the club, which resulted in Julia being thrown out at around 9.30 pm. Around 30 minutes later, Sahira was seen leaving the club in an agitated state through the back door, which led into the alleyway where Julia's body was later found. At about 10.15 pm, a woman fitting Sahira's description was seen running away from the alleyway a few minutes after witnesses heard loud voices followed by a scream. Sahira's jacket was stained with lime wash, which was identical to that used on a wall in the alley where Julia was found, and a button from Sahira's jacket was found at the scene of the murder. The murder weapon, a carving knife, was of the same brand as those contained in a knife block in Sahira's kitchen. One knife is missing from the block.

In the above example, while no witnesses may have seen Sahira stab Julia, there is plenty of circumstantial evidence to suggest she was involved. When we tie the various strands of it together, there appears to be a very strong case against the accused. The Rosemary West trial, noted above, provides a very infamous and poignant example of a real case in which circumstantial evidence was used as the primary basis for multiple murder convictions.[48]

1.5.5 Evidence of motive

Those familiar with substantive criminal law will be aware of the distinction between motive and mental element. The fact that the defendant holds a grudge against a victim, or stood to benefit from the death of a particular person, contributes nothing to the question of whether the defendant intended to kill the victim when they struck them.[49] However, it may still be regarded as a useful piece of evidence, insofar as it makes it more probable that the defendant was responsible for a particular act.[50] By itself, evidence of motive is not sufficient to convict the defendant, but when considered alongside the other pieces of evidence, it will strengthen the prosecution case. Equally, the absence of a motive may serve to weaken the prosecution case. The Privy Council dealt with evidence of motive demonstrated through a feud between neighbouring families. The Privy Council noted that evidence of motive does not become irrelevant simply because others had

---

47 Tapper, C., *Cross & Tapper on Evidence*, 12th edn (Oxford University Press, 2010), p. 30.

48 For a case discussing the use of circumstantial evidence, see *R v Kelly* [2015] EWCA Crim 817.

49 *R v Moloney* [1985] AC 905; *R v Mohan* [1976] QB 1.

50 See e.g. *R v Ball* [1911] AC 47.

the same motive. The Privy Council concluded that despite motive being shared between members of a family, the accused's motive still demonstrates why he may have committed the offence.[51]

1.6 Human rights and the law of evidence

Although the United Kingdom ratified the European Convention on Human Rights (ECHR) in 1951, like most international treaties, it carried only persuasive authority before domestic courts and was not legally binding. The rights of individuals throughout the criminal process were protected at common law on a largely piecemeal basis, and the notion of a particular 'human right' to do or to be free from something amounted to no more than the absence of legal restraint upon a particular course of action. In short, there were no legal limits set on the power of the state to behave as it saw fit. For example, in the case of *Malone v Metropolitan Police Commissioner No. 2*,[52] the High Court found that telephone tapping by the police was not unlawful, as it did not violate any particular law and the concept of a 'right to privacy' could not be enforced at common law.

As with all other areas of English law, the enactment of the Human Rights Act 1998 radically altered how evidential rules were treated by the courts. The Act gives effect to the European Convention on Human Rights in domestic law and renders it directly applicable in national courts. While a detailed discussion of the legislation is outside the remit of this text, three key points should be borne in mind:

- Section 2 of the Human Rights Act provides that all courts must take into account the jurisprudence of the European Court of Human Rights and other Strasbourg organs in all cases that come before them.
- Under section 3 of the Human Rights Act, all legislation must be interpreted and given effect as far as possible in a way that is compatible with Convention rights. Where it is not possible to do so, section 4 stipulates that a court may quash or disapply subordinate legislation or, if it is a higher court, it may make a declaration of incompatibility in relation to primary legislation.
- Section 6 of the Act makes it unlawful for a public authority to act in a way that is incompatible with Convention rights and gives cause of action for individuals to bring cases before UK courts or tribunals where it is alleged that a public authority has acted thus. However, a public authority will not have acted unlawfully under the Act if, as the result of a provision of primary legislation (such as another Act of Parliament), it could not have acted differently. Crucially, as far as the law of evidence is concerned, public authorities include the police, the Crown Prosecution Service (CPS), and the courts.

The Convention itself seeks to protect a wide range of rights, but some of these are more pertinent than others to the study of the law of evidence. Foremost among these is the right to a fair trial, contained in Article 6. As the European Court of Human Rights (ECtHR) explained in *Delcourt v Belgium*,[53] the right to a fair hearing holds such a prominent place in a democratic society 'that a restrictive interpretation of Article 6(1) would not correspond to the aim and purpose of that provision.'

The Article itself is lengthy and comprises a number of separate constituent elements which have been developed over time by the court's jurisprudence:

---

51 *Myers v R* [2015] UKPC 40 at [45].

52 [1979] 2 All ER 620.

53 (1970) 1 EHRR 355.

1. In the determination of his civil rights and obligations or of any criminal charge against him, everyone is entitled to a fair and public hearing within a reasonable time by an independent and impartial tribunal established by law. Judgment shall be pronounced publicly by the press and public may be excluded from all or part of the trial in the interest of morals, public order, or national security in a democratic society, where the interests of juveniles or the protection of the private life of the parties so require, or to the extent strictly necessary in the opinion of the court in special circumstances where publicity would prejudice the interests of justice.
2. Everyone charged with a criminal offence shall be presumed innocent until proved guilty according to law.
3. Everyone charged with a criminal offence has the following minimum rights:
   (a) to be informed promptly, in a language which he understands and in detail, of the nature and cause of the accusation against him;
   (b) to have adequate time and the facilities for the preparation of his defence;
   (c) to defend himself in person or through legal assistance of his own choosing or, if he has not sufficient means to pay for legal assistance, to be given it free when the interests of justice so require;
   (d) to examine or have examined witnesses against him and to obtain the attendance and examination of witnesses on his behalf under the same conditions as witnesses against him;
   (e) to have the free assistance of an interpreter if he cannot understand or speak the language used in court.

While most observers welcome Article 6 as providing important protections to persons accused of a crime by the state, the provisions are not without controversy. Often, they may entail balancing the rights of the accused with victims, witnesses, or indeed, society as a whole. For example, in Chapter 3 we shall explore the issue of reverse burdens of proof (i.e. where the defence must effectively disprove one or more of the elements of the case against them); these stand in *prima facie* opposition to Article 6(2). In Chapter 6, we shall reflect on the case of *R v A*,[54] where the House of Lords decided that the defence ought to be able to cross-examine a rape complainant about her previous sexual history with the accused, despite legislation stipulating otherwise. This was essentially because the accused's right to a fair trial was violated by the fact that he was unable to elicit evidence that the court deemed relevant to his defence. In Chapter 12, we shall consider the tension around the ability of the defence to challenge hearsay evidence; the Strasbourg Court has found that provisions contained in the Criminal Justice Act 2003 contravene Article 6(3)(d) since they did not provide the defence with an adequate opportunity to challenge the hearsay evidence adduced by the prosecution.[55]

A number of other provisions of the Convention are also relevant to the study of the law of evidence. These include Article 5, which contains the right to liberty and security of person, and Article 8, which provides for the right to privacy. Both provisions are relevant to the gathering of evidence against the accused and the treatment of the accused in police custody. These provisions will be discussed further in Chapters 8 and 9.

1.7 The changing nature of evidence law

Over the past 20 years, both the civil and the criminal realms of evidence law have undergone significant changes. Writing in the *Modern Law Review* in 1993, Cyril Glasser argued that the civil process was undergoing a 'slow erosion' of the basic practices of adversarial justice and of the

54 [2002] 1 AC 45.
55 *Al-Khawaja and Tahery v UK* (2009) 49 EHRR 1.

orality principle in particular. This was occurring, he argued, in response to changing attitudes in modern litigation, because of increased pressure on public funds.[56] His article proved to be imminently prophetic; in 1996, the Woolf Report contended that many civil litigation problems in England and Wales derive to a large extent from the unrestrained adversarial culture of the system.[57] The Report proposed adopting certain inquisitorial-style features such as greater case management for judges and a more cooperative pre-trial regime of discovery. Emphasis was also placed on the desirability of the early settlement of disputes and financial penalties for parties who unreasonably refused to attempt negotiation or to consider alternative dispute resolution. It was acknowledged by Lord Woolf that such a move would require a 'radical change of culture for all concerned.'[58] Such a change did indeed occur in subsequent years following the introduction of the Civil Procedure Rules in 1998.

At the same time as the civil justice system was being overhauled, a number of well-publicised miscarriages of justice, such as the Birmingham Six, Judith Ward, and the Guildford Four, attracted a crisis of confidence in the criminal justice system. In response to these concerns, the Government established the Royal Commission on Criminal Justice,[59] which recommended a number of key changes to evidential and procedural rules relating to disclosure and other safeguards for the defence. Yet, as the decade progressed, specific components of the criminal justice system continued to be placed under scrutiny. These included: the treatment of victims and witnesses in court;[60] problems arising from adjournments and delays;[61] and the role of the Crown Prosecution Service.[62]

Sir Robin Auld's *Review of the Criminal Courts of England and Wales*[63] contained a number of radical proposals designed to streamline criminal procedure and radically overhaul the law of evidence. The Review recommended the adoption of a number of inquisitorial-style features into the English system. For example, it was conceded that adversarial combat in the pre-trial phase was inappropriate and a more cooperative regime of disclosure was recommended. Other features were somewhat reminiscent of practices in continental jurisdictions and were aimed at tempering the very partisan nature of the adversarial justice system. These included the recommendation to codify the criminal law and law of evidence, a greater managerial role for trial judges, and further pre-trial cooperation between the parties. Sir Robin's observation that the adversarial system should 'move away from technical rules of inadmissibility to trusting judicial and lay fact finders to give relevant evidence the weight it deserves'[64] also reflects the approach followed in most inquisitorial trials. Therefore, judges would play a much more proactive role in the trial and have a much broader discretion in relation to the admissibility of evidence.

It is also worth noting that Lord Justice Auld acknowledged some of the drawbacks of oral evidence, including the effects of stress and delay upon witnesses. He appears to have used this observation as a springboard for a number of his recommendations, which included the relaxation of the rules on admissibility of previous witness statements, the relaxation of the hearsay rule, and the extension of the use of televised evidence. He seemed to accept that indirect testimony can, in certain circumstances, be as reliable and cogent as direct oral evidence.

---

56 Glasser, C., 'Civil Procedures and the Lawyers: The Adversary System and the Decline of the Orality Principle' (1993) 56(3) *Modern Law Review* 307, 317.

57 Woolf, Lord H., *Access to Justice: Final Report* (HMSO, 1996).

58 Ibid., p. 7.

59 Royal Commission on Criminal Justice, *Report*, Cmnd 2263 (HMSO, 1993).

60 Home Office, *Speaking Up for Justice* (HMSO, 1998).

61 Audit Commission, *The Route to Justice* (HMSO, 2002).

62 Glidewell, I., *Review of the Crown Prosecution Service*, Cmnd 3960 (HMSO, 1998).

63 Auld, Sir R., *Review of the Criminal Courts of England and Wales*, Cmnd 9376 (HMSO, 2002).

64 Ibid., at [2.17].

Over recent years, while there has been limited reform to criminal procedure and law of evidence in England and Wales, attention should be given to issues that persist relating to the role of the defendant and their participation in the criminal process. Legislative reforms which have impacted them include those to the right to silence and pre-trial disclosure, specifically through the introduction of the Criminal Procedure Rules, and as highlighted by Owusu-Bempah, the increasingly narrow interpretation and application of the privilege against self-incrimination. It is recommended that anyone studying evidence should give critical consideration to the wider implications of the recent trend requiring increased defendant participation in the criminal process, and in particular consider whether the principles governing the right to silence, and pre-trial disclosure can still stand against these developments. Consequently, readers should be very mindful to study the law of evidence with regard to these wider developments and the implications they have on the traditional doctrinal exploration of the law.

The Criminal Justice Act 2003 and the original Criminal Procedure Rules in 2005 gave legislative effect to most of these reforms, signifying a shift away from a rigid regime of exclusionary evidential rules towards a broader freedom of proof. In many ways, this development mirrored what had happened to the rules of evidence in the civil courts in the previous decade.

While the full impact of these reforms will be discussed in subsequent chapters, it is worth noting at this juncture that the hearsay rule has undergone substantial erosion, as have rules relating to the automatic exclusion of bad character evidence. Furthermore, the Criminal Procedure Rules in 2010 consolidated the earlier set of rules produced in 2005 and laid down a new 'overriding objective' that courts and everyone involved in a criminal case must pursue: to deal with the case justly.[65] The priority afforded to a particular principle or value in this way is something that is very much alien to the common law tradition but has been preserved in the latest version of the rules, the Criminal Procedure Rules (Crim PR) 2020. The years following the introduction of the 2005 Rules have provided some interesting insights as to how the courts apply such principles in practice. We shall see this in our discussion in the forthcoming chapters. Technology is also changing the ways in which evidence is given. Already evidence can be given via satellite link, so that witnesses overseas are able to give evidence without appearing in person.[66] Similarly, the Crime (International Co-operation) Act 2003 allows evidence requested by foreign countries to be taken by telephone. Technology has also brought benefits to lawyers, judges, and jurors: instead of poring over mountains of documents, it is now possible in many cases for evidence to be viewed on a screen. This may be of particular value in fraud cases, where juries may be asked to consider a range of complex financial documents.

Perhaps the most important advances for technology have been the benefits reaped for vulnerable witnesses in criminal proceedings. As we shall see in Chapter 5, the Youth Justice and Criminal Evidence Act 1999 provides that children and other vulnerable witnesses can give their evidence-in-chief by means of a pre-recorded video, and also may be cross-examined and re-examined on video so that they need never be present in court. Doubtless, the rules of evidence will continue to be amended and modified for the new age. It is not improbable that in the future we will be able to give evidence via a mobile phone with a video picture being transmitted.

Some commentators have argued that tinkering with evidential and procedural rules and introducing new technology are unlikely to tackle many of the system's current problems in an effective manner.[67] As we shall see in the next chapter, while some have gone so far as to argue that the common law adversarial process should be substituted with a more continental style of

---

65 Criminal Procedure Rules 2005, r 1.1 (which remains in the Crim PR 2020).

66 CJA 2003, Pt VIII.

67 See e.g. Ellison, L., *The Adversarial Process and the Vulnerable Witness* (Oxford University Press, 2001); Doak, J., *Victims' Rights, Human Rights and Criminal Justice: Reconceiving the Role of Third Parties* (Hart Publishing, 2008).

process, others have proceeded to defend staunchly the retention of the adversarial system with what has been described as 'self-righteous adoration.'[68] The Auld *Review of the Criminal Courts* was happy to recommend the grafting of certain elements of inquisitorial procedure on to the adversarial framework. However, not all commentators are agreed that such an approach can work effectively: Edwards comments that cherry-picking and transplanting individual components of inquisitorial systems risks diffusing 'the worst tendencies of combativeness in the Anglo-American system, while retaining some of the salutary features of the continental inquisitorial system.'[69]

The transplantation of certain aspects of the law of evidence from elsewhere is already, however, something of a *de facto* reality in the global village of the twenty-first century. Increasingly, policymakers are seemingly more ready to acknowledge the shortcomings of the existing rules and structures and look to other jurisdictions for new ideas that might work more effectively or more efficiently. Pizzi has observed that among the judiciary, legislature, and legal profession there is 'less attachment to failed doctrinal structures of the past and a willingness to look for what will work.'[70]

The restriction of the right to trial by jury, the dismantling of a number of exclusionary rules of evidence and corresponding drift towards free proof, and the expansion of opportunities for witnesses to give evidence by alternative means are all recent developments that sit uneasily alongside traditional perceptions of the common law adversarial trial.

The willingness to move away from traditional components and try new things is not exclusively seen in common law countries. States that have traditionally had inquisitorial models have also been willing to experiment with adversarial ideas. There has been a 'circulation of legal ideas between legal systems.'[71] Examples include Italy's attempt to adopt an adversarial style of proceedings[72] and the adoption of jury systems in Spain and Russia.[73]

New international criminal trial systems, such as the International Criminal Court and the various ad hoc bodies, such as the International Criminal Tribunals for Rwanda and the former Yugoslavia, have been instrumental in developing something approaching an international consensus on best trial practice.[74] Indeed, the emphasis placed on the rights of victims and witnesses within these institutions probably acted as a catalyst for the improved protections now available to vulnerable witnesses and the erosion of exclusionary rules of evidence. We should also not underestimate the impact of the European Court of Human Rights. Over the past decade, there has been an increased willingness of the court to venture into areas concerning the law of evidence, around which it has traditionally steered a wide berth. Indeed, Jackson has observed a discernible shift from the way in which we have tended in the past to categorise systems of evidence according to the adversarial or inquisitorial spectrum and argues that the court is in the process of developing a new model of proof that might more accurately be characterised as 'participatory.'[75] While it may be some time before the full impact of this shift upon the parameters of the adversarial system can be fully ascertained, it seems certain that international harmonisation and the expan-

68 Van Kessel, G., 'Adversary Excesses in the American Criminal Trial' (1992) 67 *Notre Dame Law Review* 403, 409.

69 Edwards, H., 'Comments on Mirjan Damaska's "Of Evidentiary Transplants"' (1997) 45 *American Journal of Comparative Law* 853, 855; see also Corker, D., 'The Worst of Both Worlds' (2002) 152 *New Law Journal* 1741.

70 Pizzi, W., *Trials Without Truth* (New York University Press, 1999), p. 231.

71 Langer, M., 'From Legal Transplants to Legal Translations: The Globalization of Plea Bargaining and the Americanization Thesis in Criminal Procedure' (2004) 45 *Harvard International Law Journal* 1, 5.

72 See Pizzi, W. and Montagna, M., 'The Battle to Establish an Adversarial Trial System in Italy' (2003–04) 25 *Michigan Journal of International Law* 429; and Panzavolta, M., 'Reforms and Counter-Reforms in the Italian Struggle for an Accusatorial Criminal Law System' (2004–05) 30 *North Carolina Journal of International Law* 577.

73 See Thaman, S., 'Europe's New Jury Systems: The Cases of Spain and Russia' (1999) 62 *Law and Contemporary Problems* 233.

74 Jackson, J.D. and Summers, S.J., *The Internationalisation of Criminal Evidence: Beyond the Common Law and Civil Law Traditions* (Cambridge University Press, 2012).

75 Jackson, J., 'The Effect of Human Rights on Criminal Evidentiary Processes: Towards Convergence, Divergence or Realignment?' (2005) 68 *Modern Law Review* 737.

sion of human rights norms will continue to inform the operation of the rules of evidence for the foreseeable future.

Within the European perspective, recent developments include the introduction of 'mutual recognition' within member states, which applies to the criminal minimum standards of procedural rights for suspects and accused persons set out in Article 6 of the ECHR. However, there have also been ever-increasing obstacles to fairness that must be addressed. Recently, there has been academic focus towards how criminal unfairness can be located outside the eye of a public trial, as well as how a 'liberal conception' of the dignity of individuals can be kept within an increasingly punitive and managerial criminal justice system. Strasbourg decisions such as *Salduz v Turkey*[76] explore the interaction between how international human rights jurisprudence should intersect with the jurisprudence of the domestic courts. Aside from those developments, there has also been a recent focus on institutions and the various patterns of criminal responsibility, duties, and rights between the multitude of players within the court system.

1.8 Key learning points

- The 'facts in issue' are those matters that are being contested by the parties.
- 'Collateral matters' are extraneous to the facts in issue and will usually be admissible only if they are relevant to the credibility of a witness.
- Questions of admissibility are decided within a *voir dire*, otherwise known as a 'trial within a trial.'
- All evidence adduced at the trial must be relevant; the determination of relevancy is a matter for the trial judge.
- Evidence can be categorised into a number of types or forms, including direct evidence, documentary evidence, real evidence, and circumstantial evidence.
- Globalisation and the Human Rights Act 1998 have brought about major changes to the pace and direction of reform relating to the law of evidence.

1.9 Suggested further reading

Galligan, D.J., *Discretionary Powers: A Legal Study of Official Discretion* (Clarendon Press, 1986).

Jackson, J., 'The Effect of Human Rights on Criminal Evidentiary Processes: Towards Convergence, Divergence or Realignment?' (2005) 68 MLR 737.

Jackson, J.D. and Summers, S.J., *The Internationalisation of Criminal Evidence: Beyond the Common Law and Civil Law Traditions* (Cambridge University Press, 2012).

Jones, I., 'Still Just Rhetoric? Judicial Discretion and Due Process' (2011) 32(3) Liverpool Law Review 251.

Roberts, P. and Hunter, J., 'Introduction – The Human Rights Revolution in Criminal Evidence and Produce' in P. Roberts and J. Hunter (eds), *Criminal Evidence and Human Rights – Reimagining Common Law Procedural Traditions* (Hart Publishing, 2012).

Sharpe, S., *Judicial Discretion and Criminal Investigation* (Sweet & Maxwell, 1998).

Tapper, C., 'The Law of Evidence and the Rule of Law' (2009) 68 Cambridge Law Journal 67.

---

76 App No. 36391/02, [2008] ECHR 1542, (2009) 49 EHRR 19, 26 BHRC 223, IHRL 3268 (ECHR 2008).

Chapter 2

The Adversarial Trial

Chapter contents

DOI: 10.4324/9781003416098-2

Criminal trial systems differ vastly around the world. From indigenous 'sentencing circles' used in North America to the Islamic courts of the Middle East and parts of Africa and Asia, societies have long striven for the best way to do justice. In the Western world, two major 'families' of trial system prevail. These are known as the adversarial and inquisitorial methods and differ substantially in terms of both their procedures and underlying rationales. This chapter contains an overview of the adversarial nature of the English criminal trial. It begins by outlining the course of the trial, and highlights how it is structurally geared to maximise the power of the parties (i.e. the prosecution and defence in criminal cases and the claimant and defendant in civil cases). It then proceeds to highlight some of the most prominent structures and processes that are corollaries of the adversarial label. Next, we consider a number of pertinent questions relating to the rationale for the adversarial mode of trial: why, for example, does the 'fight' theory continue to prevail in law while inquiries are typically favoured in many other disciplines? Does (or should) the adversarial model enhance prospects for truth-finding? Finally, we consider the operation of one of the main alternative models, the inquisitorial paradigm, which is followed in most continental legal systems. How does such a system work in practice, and is it better placed to do 'justice' than its adversarial counterpart?

2.1 The course of the adversarial trial

The English trial, like its North American counterpart and 'descendants' throughout the common law world, is often described as adversarial in nature. As Landman comments, the adversarial system began to fully develop throughout the 18th and 19th centuries. However, many of its components had been developing in parts over the centuries, including the rise of the jury and the idea of party participation.[1] Before the emergence of the adversarial trial was the period most often referred to as the 'altercation' trial. This process was described by Langbein[2] as being the phase where the 'accused speaks' because the defendant was effectively forced to speak to defend himself from the charge against him.

The adversarial label connotes the fact that the trial is organised as a two-way contest between the parties, in which the parties are charged with producing evidence to substantiate their own case, and to puncture the arguments of their opponent. The emergence of the adversarial system also impacted defendant participation as we will explore further below. One example is how it affects the concept of the burden of proof, as in the early adversarial trial, the court could dismiss a case if the prosecution had presented its case and offered defensive evidence. Accordingly, the recognition of the prosecution's burden, combined with the use of defence counsel to test if the burden had been met, materially reduced the amount of speaking the accused had to do to defend himself effectively.[3] As the Australian Law Reform Commission has recognised, the idea of adversarialism is popularly associated with bipartisan competitiveness and hostility:

1 Landsman, S., *The Adversary System: A Description and Defense* (American Enterprise Institute for Public Policy Research, 1984), 8–10.

2 Langbein, J.H., *The Origins of the Adversary Criminal Trial* (Oxford University Press, 2003).

3 Ibid., 177 and 261.

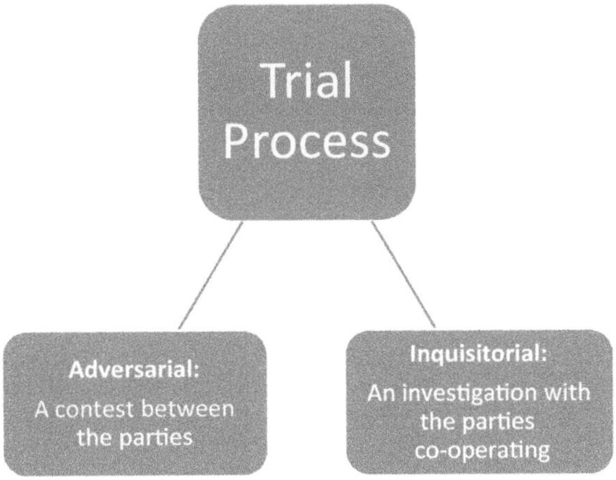

Figure 2.1 Comparing adversarial and inquisitorial approaches

> The term 'adversarial' connotes a competitive battle between foes or contestants and is popularly associated with partisan and unfair litigation tactics. Battle and sporting imagery are commonly used in reference to our legal system. These different meanings associated with an adversarial system have confused the debate concerning legal system reform.[4]

2.1.1 Phases of the adversarial trial

The adversarial trial can be divided into a number of broad phases. The description of these phases below reflects what occurs in both criminal and civil cases (although, for the purposes of simplicity, the terminology applied here relates to criminal cases only).[5] For example, the English system retained a number of traditionally adversarial characteristics, yet has shifted away from adversarialism due to an increased focus on accurate fact-finding, moving away from its continental European counter-parts.[6] The first task of the prosecution is to adduce sufficient evidence to persuade the judge that there is a case to answer. Assuming that there is, the prosecutor has an unfettered right to open the case (known as an opening speech) in either the magistrates' court or Crown Court.[7] In very simple summary trials, they may choose not to do so. Typically, prosecutors shall introduce themselves and defence counsel to the trier of fact. They will then proceed to explain the charge put to the defendant, give an overview of the facts of the case at hand with brief reference to the relevant law (if necessary

4 Australian Law Reform Commission, *Review of the Adversarial System of Litigation: Rethinking the Federal Civil Litigation System*, Issues Paper No. 20 (Australian Government Publishing Service, 1997), [2.29]. For a consideration of how the English system operates alongside its European continental counterparts and American counterparts, see W.T. Pizzi, 'Soccer, Football, and Trial Systems' (1995) *Columbia Journal of European Law* 369.

5 Thus, the term 'claimant' can here be substituted for 'prosecution' in order to reflect practice in civil procedure.

6 Niljboer, J.F., 'Common Law Tradition in Evidence Scholarship Observed from a Continental Perspective' 41 *American Journal of Comparative Law* 299, 308 (1993).

7 The right to make an opening speech in the Crown Court is vested in the common law. The right to make an opening in a summary trial is found in the Criminal Procedure Rules 2020, r 24.3(3)(a), which provides that the prosecutor may summarise the prosecution case, identifying the relevant law and facts.

or complex), and will normally inform the magistrates or jury of the burden and standard of proof (see Chapter 3).

From 4 April 2016, Rule 24.3 of the Criminal Procedure Rules (trial in magistrates' courts) and Rule 25.9 (trial in the Crown Court) were amended by Rules 9 and 10(a) of the Amendment Rules to provide for the identification of issues by the defence at the beginning of the trial.

The Rule in the Crown Court provides:

> where there is a jury, to help the jurors to understand the case and resolve any issue in it the court may—
>
> (i) invite the defendant concisely to identify what is in issue, if necessary in terms approved by the court,
>
> (ii) if the defendant declines to do so, direct that the jurors be given a copy of any defence statement served under rule 15.4 (Defence disclosure), edited if necessary to exclude any reference to inappropriate matters or to matters evidence of which would not be admissible.[8]

It was not intended that the defence would use this to make a traditional opening speech, but merely help the jury to focus on the issues in the case. It is increasingly the practice that either the prosecution will state what the defence issues are, or defence counsel will make such a short statement of issues for the jury.

Next, the prosecution will call its witnesses, who will be led through their evidence by counsel (examination-in-chief). As part of the examination-in-chief, the questioner will seek to paint a picture of the witness as someone who is confident of their facts and will aim for clear and spontaneous answers to the questions that are posed.[9] Cross-examination will follow the witness's evidence-in-chief. The cross-examiner will carefully pick through the testimony that the witness has given in evidence-in-chief, since it is assumed that a party who fails to dispute a fact in cross-examination has accepted the facts relayed by the witness under examination-in-chief.[10] In contrast to the party calling the witness, the cross-examiner may use leading questions in an apparent attempt to persuade the witness that they are either lying or are mistaken. In order to discredit the testimony, the cross-examiner may also attack the character of the witness.[11]

Following cross-examination, the counsel for the prosecution will have an opportunity to re-examine the witness. Importantly, unless the court grants leave, questions in re-examination are confined to matters arising out of cross-examination.[12] Further, as is the rule in examination-in-chief, no leading questions may be asked of the witness in re-examination.[13] Re-examination will be used to emphasise the evidence given and to restore the credibility of the witness if damaged in cross-examination. Once sufficient evidence has been presented to persuade a trial judge that there is a case to answer, the prosecution or claimant's case is closed and it is not permissible for this party to introduce any further evidence except evidence in rebuttal, fresh evidence not previously available to the court, or evidence that was inadvertently omitted from the Crown's case.[14] The prosecution case may, however, be strengthened by cross-examination of the defendant and/

---

8 The Criminal Procedure Rules 2020, https://www.gov.uk/guidance/rules-and-practice-directions-2020#trial (accessed 13 June 2023).

9 McEwan, J., *Evidence and the Adversarial Process* (Hart Publishing, 1998), p. 100.

10 *R v Wood Green Crown Court, ex p Taylor* [1995] Crim LR 879.

11 This is subject to a number of restraints that are discussed in Ch 11.

12 *Queen Caroline's Case* (1820) 2 B&B 284.

13 *Ireland v Taylor* [1949] 1 KB 300.

14 *R v Rice* [1963] 1 QB 857.

or any witnesses for the defence. Equally, cross-examination of the complainant and any prosecution witnesses, together with evidence from the defendant and/or defence witnesses, may weaken the prosecution case. Here, Beattie has previously argued that securing the defendant as an informational resource is a central preoccupation of the adversarial trial. Facing the defendant with the evidence in court for the first time was thought to help the judge and jury ascertain the truth of the matter, allowing no room for the privilege against self-incrimination and the right to silence.[15]

At the end of the prosecution case, the defence may submit that there is 'no case to answer,' known colloquially as a 'half-time submission,' if there appears to be insufficient evidence to persuade a reasonable jury of the defendant's guilt. This submission is made in the absence of the jury. In such an event, the principles laid down in *R v Galbraith* will be followed:[16]

- The submission should succeed if the judge comes to the conclusion that the prosecution evidence, taken at its highest, is such that a jury, properly directed, could not properly convict on it. Here, the judge should direct the jury to acquit.
- The submission should fail if the strength or weakness of the prosecution case depends on the view to be taken of the reliability of a witness or whether there is a case to answer.

If the judge agrees, the prosecution will have failed to discharge the evidential burden and the judge will withdraw the case from the jury and direct an acquittal.[17] Where the submission is unsuccessful, no reference or comment should be given to the jury.[18] In most cases, the prosecution will succeed in discharging the evidential burden, which means that the defence will also present their case. However, this is not to say that the prosecution has successfully discharged the burden of proof; the jury must be persuaded of the defendant's guilt beyond reasonable doubt.[19]

If the prosecution succeeds in producing sufficient evidence to persuade the judge that there is a case to answer, the case proceeds to the next phase, with the defence presenting its evidence. In the magistrates' court, defence counsel has no right to make an opening speech.[20] In the Crown Court, section 2 of the Criminal Evidence Act 1898 provides that there is no right to make an opening speech when the only defence witness as to fact is the defendant. Therefore, the defence may only make an opening speech where there are two witnesses to be called (the defendant and any other witness).

One of the key decisions to be taken at this juncture is whether the accused will testify in person. As Owusu-Bempah recognises,[21] even though the central purpose of the criminal trial was to hear the defendant speak, he spoke unsworn until the Criminal Evidence Act 1898. Counsel for the defence will be aware that section 35 of the Criminal Justice and Public Order Act 1994 provides that inferences may be drawn from the failure of the accused to give evidence or if they, without good cause, refuse to answer questions.[22] The section provides for a procedure under which the court must at the end of the prosecution case satisfy itself (in the case of proceedings on indictment) that the accused is aware that the stage has been reached at which evidence can be given for the defence and that they can, if they wish, give evidence. The accused will also be told of the effect of their failure to give evidence or without good cause to answer questions (that a

15 Beattie, J.M., 'Scales of Justice: Defense Counsel and the English Criminal Trial in the 18th and 19th Century' (1991) 9 *Law and History Review*, 221, 223.

16 (1981) 73 Cr App R 124.

17 *Practice Direction (Submission of No Case)* [1962] 1 WLR 227.

18 *R v Smith and Doe* (1986) 85 Cr App R 197.

19 See Ch 3.

20 Crim PR 2020, r.24.3(3)(f) gives the defence the right to 'introduce evidence.' There is no provision within the Crim PR that allows the defence to make an opening speech.

21 Owusu-Bempah, A., *Defendant Participation in the Criminal Process* (Routledge, 2016).

22 See Ch 7.

proper inference may be drawn). This puts the defendant under some degree of coercion to give evidence, but the strength of the prosecution case will also exert a certain pressure. This aligns with the idea first proposed by Blake and Ashworth,[23] in that 'the defence advocate represents more than the client – he or she is simultaneously responsible for maintaining fundamentally guarantees central to the Criminal Justice System.' If the prosecution has presented a strong case that calls for an answer, the failure of the accused to answer it suggests to the jury that they have no answer. The jury may then accept the evidence presented by the prosecution and conclude that the accused is guilty as charged. If the defendant does give evidence, they may succeed in casting sufficient doubt on the prosecution's case to justify an acquittal.

However, it should be underlined that it is also possible that defence evidence may actually serve to strengthen the prosecution case. Where a defendant, or indeed any witness, gives evidence, it is evidence for all purposes, and may be evidence not only for them but also against their co-accused.

For example, a defence witness may admit under cross-examination that she lied to help the defendant, or the defendant herself may make damaging admissions under cross-examination. In cases where more than one defendant is being prosecuted, it is not uncommon for each accused to run a so-called 'cut-throat' defence, where each alleges that the other(s) played a more important role in the offence.

Example 2.1

John and Mary are jointly charged with murder. Mary testifies in her examination-in-chief that John had regularly beaten her and placed her under duress to stab the victim. Thus, the prosecution case against John will have received a substantial - although indirect - boost through what Mary has said as part of her examination-in-chief.

At this point in the trial the defence may have an evidential burden to adduce sufficient evidence of a defence they are relying on. In Example 2.1, Mary sought to plead duress. Depending on the circumstances, there are a range of other defences she might have sought to rely on: diminished responsibility or loss of self-control might be the most obvious. If the defence do not adduce sufficient evidence of a particular defence to make it a live issue in the case, and there is no other evidence of that defence, the trial judge will not allow that defence to be put to the jury, and the prosecution are not required to adduce evidence rebutting that defence. It thus follows that if the defence are relying on a particular defence, the accused or defence witnesses will usually have to give evidence of that defence. Just as a defence witness may sometimes assist the prosecution case, sometimes a prosecution witness may inadvertently assist the defence.

Example 2.2

Anna is on trial for inflicting grievous bodily harm (GBH) to Cara. Marvin, a witness for the prosecution, gives evidence that he saw Cara punch the accused, who then hit her around the head with a hockey stick. This would tend to suggest that self-defence might apply - even though it was first raised as an issue by a prosecution witness.

23 Ashworth, A., 'Four Threats to the Presumption of Innocence' (2006) 10 *International Journal of Evidence and Proof*, 241.

Defence witnesses may also give evidence of the existence of a defence, but few juries will accept any defence if the accused does not testify in person about it and is not subjected to cross-examination. If there is sufficient evidence to make the particular defence an issue – and this will be for the trial judge to determine – the prosecution will usually be required to disprove that defence. As we shall see in Chapter 3, exceptions to this rule exist for diminished responsibility and insanity, where the defence will bear the burden of proving the existence of the defence.

Like prosecuting counsel, defence counsel will lead the witness through their evidence and will re-examine defence witnesses after cross-examination. Sometimes the defence will bear the legal or persuasive burden of proving certain defences, for example insanity or diminished responsibility, or they may need to show that a defendant has an excuse or justification for their action. Reversing the legal or persuasive burden means that the defence must persuade the jury (on the balance of probabilities) that the defendant was insane or suffering from diminished responsibility, or has the excuse or justification pleaded.[24] However, there has been some concern that within the English system, the defendant's current role cannot be labelled as strictly adversarial,[25] and instead, the increasing preoccupation with efficiency in fact-finding has influenced the criminal procedure, such that greater emphasis is now placed on the defendant's participation, as the case of Haywood demonstrated.[26]

After the conclusion of all of the evidence and closing speeches,[27] the jury will be asked to consider their verdict. Before they begin this task, however, the trial judge must sum up the case.

The judge must direct the jury on the relevant substantive law, remind them of the evidence that has been given, and explain a number of evidential matters. A typical direction will begin with an explanation as to which side bears the burden of proof and against what standard those elements will need to be proved. The judge will normally take the jury through the prosecution evidence and, importantly, point out any defence that that evidence discloses, even if the defence have not relied on that particular defence. For example, on a charge of murder, the defendant may plead self-defence, but the evidence may also point towards a loss of self-control. In these circumstances, the jury will be directed to consider self-defence first, but, if that fails, they should proceed to consider loss of self-control in the alternative. This is because self-defence is a 'full' defence, meaning that if a defendant is found not guilty, they will walk free; whereas loss of self-control is a 'partial' defence, and a defendant may still be found guilty of voluntary manslaughter. The particular nature of the evidential directions that are given will depend on the features of each individual case. Thus, where the case depends wholly or substantially on identification evidence, a direction on the special need for caution will be required.[28] If there are a number of defendants, but only one of them has confessed, the jury must be directed that the confession is evidence only against that particular defendant.[29]

24 See Ch 3.

25 Langer, M., 'The Long Shadow of the Adversarial and Inquisitorial Categories,' in Dubber and Hoernle (eds), *Oxford Handbook of Criminal Law* (Oxford University Press, 2014); Field, S., 'Fair Trials and Procedural Tradition in Europe' (2009), 29 *Oxford Journal of Legal Studies* 365; McEwan, J., Marshall, S., and Tadros, V., *The Process* (Hart Publishing, 2004).

26 David Dixon, 'Integrity, Interrogation and Criminal Injustice', in Hunter, J., Roberts, P., Young, S.N.M., and Dixon, D. (eds), *The Integrity of the Criminal Process: From Theory into Practice* (Hart Publishing, 2016), p. 117.

27 Rule 24.3(3)(h) of the Criminal Procedure Rules 2020 provides that, in the magistrates' court, a prosecutor may make final representations in support of the prosecution case, where (i) the defendant is represented by a legal representative, or (ii) whether represented or not, the defendant has introduced evidence other than their own. Similarly, for the defence, r 24.3(3)(i) provides that after the close of the prosecution's closing speech, the defendant may make final representations in support of the defence case. In the Crown Court, the prosecution is generally entitled to make a closing speech except in situations where the defendant is not defended by counsel and calls no witnesses to the facts except herself, or calls no evidence. Section 2 of the Criminal Procedure Act 1865 provides that the defence always has a right, in the Crown Court, to make a closing speech at the conclusion of the evidence.

28 See *R v Turnbull* [1977] QB 224, discussed in Ch 10.

29 See Ch 8.

The judge may also comment on the plausibility and credibility of witnesses, and on the weight that might be attached to particular evidence.[30] The judge may express a fairly strong opinion on such matters, but the jury will be told that, ultimately, they are the arbitrators of fact, and may reject any such opinions if they see fit to do so. By the same token, however, the judge should be careful not to give an express indication of his or her belief or disbelief in a particular piece of evidence. It would be quite wrong, for example, for a judge to comment that 'it is obvious to everyone in this court that the accused is lying,' although it would be acceptable for them to comment thus: 'You may think that the defendant's explanation is not worthy of belief, but that, ladies and gentlemen of the jury, is a matter for you.' Importantly, a judge is entitled to direct a jury to acquit a defendant, possibly due to a successful submission of no case to answer or a knowledge that any conviction would be unsafe. However, a judge may never direct a jury to convict a defendant, as was expressly stipulated by the House of Lords in *R v Wang*.[31]

Despite the Court of Appeal having stipulated that trial judges should confine themselves to stating matters 'impartially, clearly and logically,'[32] some commentators argue that the summing-up often unduly influences the jury and could be dispensed with altogether. In the United States, judges are prohibited from giving any indication of how they evaluate the evidence. Apart from interfering with the paradigmatic judicial role as a passive arbiter, any comment on the weight of the evidence also risks usurping the function of the jury by putting pressure on them to arrive at a particular verdict.[33] In one of the most notorious miscarriages of justice of the last century, Lord Bingham made a stinging criticism of the summing-up of one of his predecessors in title, Lord Goddard, in the case of Derek Bentley, which was heavily biased in favour of a conviction.[34] Indeed, there are numerous cases in which a conviction has been quashed on appeal because of improper comment by the trial judge, but these cases do represent a very small minority.[35] In the great majority of cases, judges tend to be extremely circumspect, and, in any case, it is difficult to ascertain the full extent of their influence over the jury in the absence of any definitive research. Since the law does not permit such research, we may never know the true impact of the summing-up upon the deliberations of the jury.[36]

At the end of the trial, the jury will deliver its verdict, which – unlike many inquisitorial systems – need not be accompanied by reasons. A not guilty verdict will result in an acquittal, while a guilty verdict will mean that the case proceeds to sentencing. Once the jury have given their verdict, they will often be thanked by the judge for their service and will be sent home. Unlike the United States,[37] the jury have no say, influence, or comment on any sentence that is to be given with the return of a guilty verdict. Their job as factfinders has ended.

It should be underlined, however, that although it is commonly supposed that a verdict of not guilty equates with innocence, this is not necessarily the case. It simply means that the prosecution has failed to satisfy the jury of the defendant's guilt beyond reasonable doubt. The failure to satisfy the jury is often due to a lack of evidence, or to an inability to adduce relevant evidence

---

30 See, e.g. the judge's comments on the evidence of the witness 'Bromley' in the *Damilola Taylor* case ('Damilola judge rejects witness as a liar,' *The Daily Telegraph* (28 February 2002), http://www.telegraph.co.uk/news/uknews/1386257/Damilola-judge-rejects-witness-as-a-liar.html (last accessed 4 July 2017)).

31 [2005] 1 WLR 661.

32 *R v Berrada* (1989) 91 Cr App R 131.

33 See generally Wolchover, D., 'Should Judges Sum Up on the Facts?' [1989] Crim LR 781.

34 'Judge is accused of basic errors; The Derek Bentley case,' *The Times* (31 July 1998), p. 6.

35 See e.g. *R v Berrada* (n. 32), in which the trial judge described the defendant's allegations that the police had fabricated evidence as 'really monstrous and wicked.'

36 Section 8 of the Contempt of Court Act 1981 prohibits interviewing jurors in connection with their deliberations.

37 On occasion, juries in the United States may be asked to make factual findings on particular issues relevant to sentencing, such as any aggravating or mitigating factors. Indeed, in *Blakely v Washington*, 542 US 296 (2004), the Supreme Court stated that juries ought to exercise this role in all capital cases, since having judges alone determine such factors would violate the citizen's right to a jury trial.

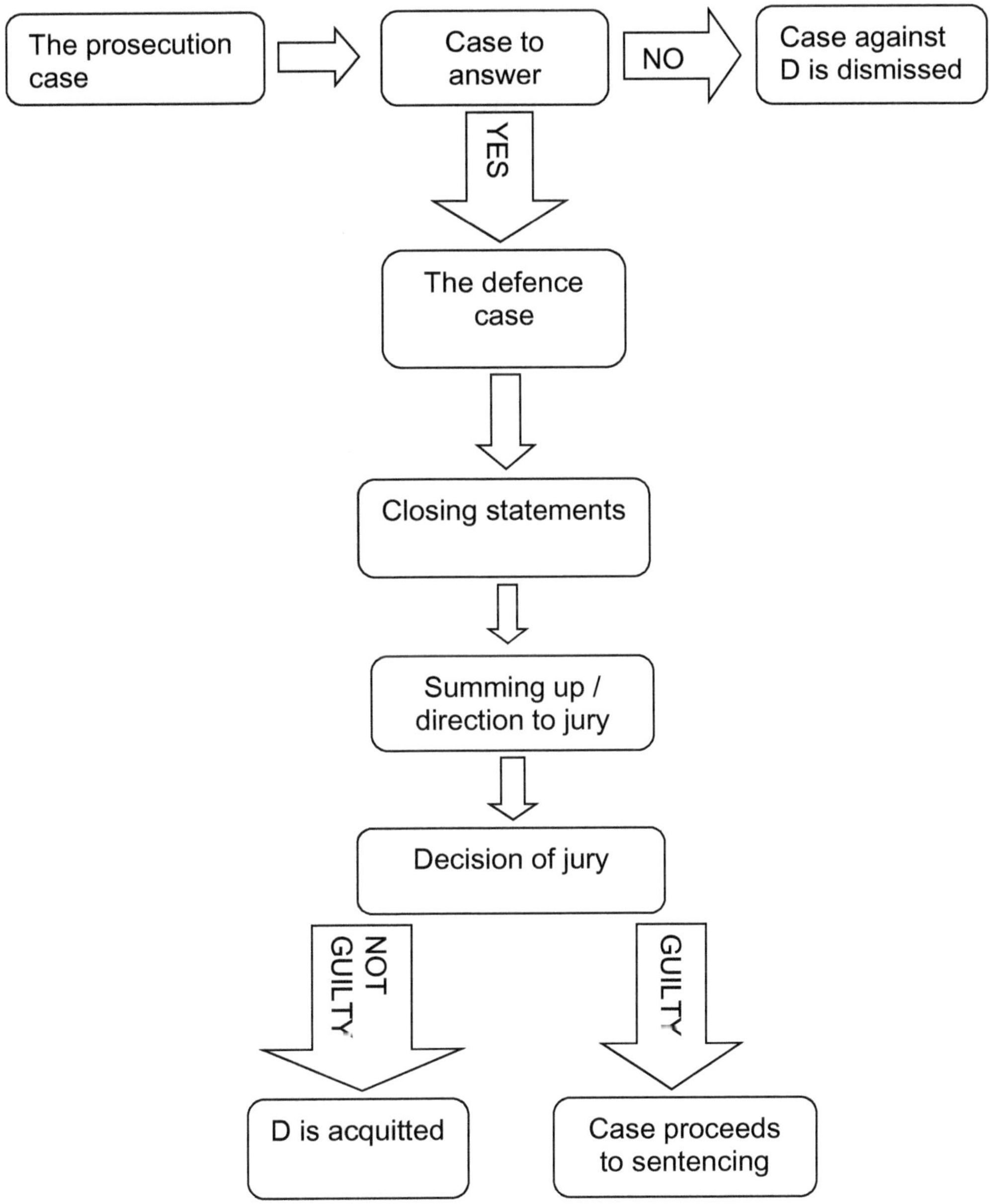

Figure 2.2 Phases of the adversarial criminal jury trial

because it is excluded or inadmissible. Alternatively, the evidence (including any confession by the accused) may be excluded because of some improprieties in how it was obtained.[38]

In law, the term 'not guilty' carries a specific legal meaning and essentially means that the prosecution has failed to discharge the burden of proof. In contrast, media communication

38 See further Ch 9.

frequently represents both acquittals at first instance and successful appeals as authoritative statements of innocence and full acceptance of the defence cases, thereby both reinforcing and responding to the general public expectation that a verdict of not guilty equates to a declaration of innocence. In a similar vein, one may also note the fact that where an appellate court quashes a conviction, it does not necessarily mean that the convicted person was in fact innocent. A higher court will occasionally declare that the convicted person is innocent of the crime, but more often the conviction is quashed because it is seen as unsafe.[39] This may be because of a fault in the trial, such as the judge's failure to give an appropriate direction to the jury.

2.2 What makes the trial system adversarial?

While the English trial has historically been regarded as adversarial in nature, most observers agree that it is wrong to think of any one model of justice as a perfect prototype. Care should thus be taken to avoid the overuse of the adversarial label in relation to 'a single technique or a collection of techniques.'[40] Overall, however, it can be said that the interaction and mutual dependability of certain themes and features of the trial process allow it to be defined as adversarial in character. Four such features are often regarded as pre-eminent and are thus worth considering in some further detail. These are the principles of orality, party control, zealous advocacy, and judicial non-intervention.

2.2.1 The principle of orality

Lord Devlin once remarked that 'the centrepiece of the adversary system is the oral trial.'[41] The principle of orality states that evidence should normally be received through the live oral testimony of witnesses in court, speaking of their own direct knowledge. As noted in the previous chapter, although the use of documentary and real evidence does play a role in criminal proceedings, the adversarial trial is primarily geared to receiving evidence in oral form before an open court. The view that oral evidence is an intrinsically superior form of evidence is widely accepted within the courts and the legal profession. Its perceived advantages were outlined by the High Court of Australia in *Butera v DPP*:[42]

> A witness who gives evidence orally demonstrates, for good or ill, more about his or her credibility than a witness whose evidence is given in documentary form. Oral evidence is public; written evidence may not be. Oral evidence gives to the trial the atmosphere which, though intangible, is often critical to the jury's consideration of the witnesses. By generally restricting the jury to consideration of testimonial evidence in its oral form, it is thought that the jury's discussion of the case in the jury's room will be more open and the exchange of views among jurors will more easily occur than if the evidence were given in writing or if the jurors were each armed with a written transcript of the evidence.[43]

Adversarial theory holds that by placing a witness in the austere surroundings of the courtroom and subjecting them to the processes of examination and cross-examination, the truth will be elicited. The emphasis placed upon live oral testimony is also backed up by a number of common

39 Criminal Appeal Act 1968, s 2.

40 Landsman, S., op. cit., n. 1, at 2.

41 Devlin, P., *The Judge* (Oxford University Press, 1979), at 54.

42 (1987) 167 CLR 180.

43 Ibid., 189, as cited by Dennis, I., *The Law of Evidence*, 3rd edn (Sweet & Maxwell, 2007), at 491.

law rules designed to enhance the principle of orality in ensuring that the witness tells the truth, as Dennis explains:

> There is firstly the general rule that a witness may give testimony only about matters of which the witness has personal knowledge. Secondly, testimony must be given on oath or affirmation ... Thirdly, a requirement for oral testimony enables the factfinder to observe the demeanour of the witness when giving evidence, and to take this into account in deciding the weight to be attached to the testimony. Fourthly, witnesses who give oral testimony can be cross-examined in person at the time, thereby enabling the cross-examiner to maximise the impact and efficiency of the questioning. Fifthly, collateral evidence of the witness's credibility can sometimes be adduced in the form of evidence of the witness's bias, previous convictions, discreditable conduct ... and reputation for veracity.[44]

Yet, in spite of these purported advantages, the alleged superiority attached to oral evidence is something that is to be found uniquely in the Anglo-American common law tradition. As we shall see below, it is not widely adhered to in many continental jurisdictions, where a distinct preference is often placed on documentary sources. Indeed, one French legal treatise speaks of 'the primacy of written proof and the mistrust which is *prima facie* inspired by oral testimony,' which is seen as highly subjective.[45] The heavy emphasis attached to oral evidence is a product of our legal culture rather than being rooted in any empirical justification that oral evidence constitutes a more reliable basis for fact-finding. Spencer and Flin are particularly sceptical about the supremacy routinely afforded to oral evidence for two main reasons:

> First, it is nearly always given a long time after the event in question. Secondly, when giving evidence live at trial a witness is normally suffering from stress. If there are two scientific facts about the psychology of the human memory which are clear beyond any doubt, one is that memory for an event fades gradually with time, and the other is that stress beyond a certain level can impair the power of recall.[46]

In addition to stress, psychologists have noted that human powers of perception, memory, and recall will often taint the way in which evidence is perceived by the court. Human memories are susceptible to changes over time and become conflated with other real or imaginary events.[47]

Events are interpreted and reinterpreted over time, and the time gap between the events in question, giving a statement to the police, and then testifying at trial will often run into many months or even years. In such circumstances, the brain actively represses memories about stressful past events.[48] In the context of the criminal trial, witnesses who are asked to testify about a past traumatic event may give muddled and confused testimony as a result of the brain's selective processing of information. Other witnesses will be limited in their ability to articulate clearly what they recall, perhaps because of age, disability, or illness.[49]

---

44 Ibid.

45 Cited by McEwan, J., 'Documentary Hearsay Evidence: Refuge for the Vulnerable Witness?' [1989] Crim LR 629, 631.

46 Spencer, J. and Flin, R., *The Evidence of Children* (Butterworths, 1993), at 268.

47 For an overview of the psychological literature, see Loftus, E., Wolchover, D., and Page, D., 'General Review of the Psychology of Witness Testimony,' in A. Heaton-Armstrong, E. Shepherd, G. Gudjonsson, and D. Wolchover (eds), *Witness Testimony: Psychological, Investigative and Evidential Perspectives* (Oxford University Press, 2006).

48 See further Ernsdorff, G.M. and Loftus, E.F., 'Let Sleeping Memories Lie? Words of Caution about Tolling the Statute of Limitations in Cases of Memory Repression' (1993) 84 *The Journal of Criminal Law & Criminology* 129.

49 Most commonly (although not exclusively), this affects child witnesses, the elderly, and witnesses with learning disabilities. For a general overview, see Murphy, G. and Clare, I., 'The Effect of Learning Disabilities on Witness Testimony,' in A.

It may well be the case that the vast majority of witnesses who testify in court give a bona fide account according to their memory. But this does not mean that their testimonies constitute a reliable source of information. Some witnesses may be honestly mistaken about certain key facts, whereas in other cases social attitudes and prejudices can influence the way in which the witness perceives an event, albeit at a subconscious level.[50] Other witnesses may actively choose to be dishonest in order to assist the prosecution or defence with their efforts to secure a conviction or acquittal. By contrast, other witnesses may be adversely affected by a sense of 'extreme eagerness' to assist the police with their inquiries.[51] Taking all of these factors into account, it is perhaps questionable whether the principle of orality really merits the esteemed position it has traditionally enjoyed within the English adversarial system. Recently, there has been a growing movement to substitute the oral public trial with a process of negotiated justice. As Langer[52] comments, this development can now be increasingly demonstrated across both common law and civil traditions. Although, it should be noted that it would be problematic to permit any waiver of the trial based on the accused's consent, since an accused should not be able to consent to fundamentally unfair processes, as Weigend[53] highlighted.

Furthermore, there has been a shift in the adversarial narrative, specifically in relation to the situation of suspects who are questioned prior to their detention. Here, the European Court of Human Rights (ECtHR), in *Zaichunko v Russia*, considered the undesirable price of questioning suspects outside the formal police interview context. It noted that,

> in examining whether a procedure has extinguished the very essence of the privilege against self-incrimination, the Court must examine the nature and degree of the compulsion, the existence of any relevant safeguards in the procedures and the use to which any material so obtained is put.

As Judge Spielman noted in his partly dissenting opinion,

> Nothing should have prevented the police officers from apprising the applicant immediately ... of his right to legal assistance and asking him to accompany them to the police station where the interview could have been conducted in conditions complying with the requirements of Article 6(3)(c).[54] The Supreme Court ruling in Ambrose v. Harris gives further guidance on this issue.[55]

2.2.2 Party control

Parties in the adversarial trial hold a near-complete autonomy to gather, select, and present evidence before the tribunal of fact. The commencement, conduct, and termination of proceedings rest largely in their hands. The parties will decide which facts are in issue and which are not. They

Heaton-Armstrong et al., op. cit., n. 47; and Davis, G. and Westcott, H., 'Investigative Interviewing with Children: Progress and Pitfalls,' in A. Heaton-Armstrong et al., op. cit., n. 47.

50 See Greer, D.S., 'Anything but the Truth? The Reliability of Testimony in Criminal Trials' (1971) 11 *British Journal of Criminology* 147.

51 Gudjonsson, G., 'The Psychological Vulnerabilities of Witnesses and the Risk of False Accusations and False Confessions,' in A. Heaton-Armstrong et al., op. cit., n. 47, at 66.

52 Langer, M., 'From Legal Transplants to Legal Translations: The Globalization of Plea Bargaining and the Americanization Thesis in Criminal Process' (2004) 45 *Harvard International Law Journal*.

53 See the arguments in Weigend, T., 'The Delay of Inquisitorial Ideal: Plea Bargaining Invades German Criminal Procedure,' in J. Jackson, M. Langer, and P. Tillers, p. 118.

54 *Aleksandr Zaichenko v Russia* No. 39660/02, 18 February 2010.

55 UKSC 43 [2011] 1 WLR 2435.

will determine how to go about generating proofs, and which witnesses will be called to aid them in that task. They will generally have a free hand in examining and cross-examining witnesses, including the accused and the complainant. The state, personified by the trial judge, will generally adopt a *laissez-faire* attitude to much of the conduct of the parties. The only legal controls on the parties are the rules of evidence, and the extent to which the trial judge enforces them or uses their discretion to protect the individual witness.[56] Non-legal limitations are also set out in the General Council of the Bar's Code of Conduct. These include a general duty to the court over and above that in relation to counsel's client and a duty not to knowingly or recklessly mislead the court.[57]

A fundamental premise of the party control system means that witnesses will rarely be permitted to convey their own version of events to the court. The questioning is advocate-led (although the trial judge and jurors may also pose questions). However, from a practical perspective, it is vital that counsel does not give the witness too much leeway in their responses lest the witness should inadvertently say something that might damage the questioner's case. This is particularly important for cross-examination where the witness needs to be tightly controlled in order to ensure the testimony does not damage the cross-examiner's overall case.[58]

In seeking to take control of the witness, counsel will try to elicit only those facts that they feel should be included and will do everything to avoid the witness speaking about anything that counsel feels should be omitted from the testimony. The goal, essentially, is to manipulate witness testimony in such a way that victory is made more likely. Testimony is closely regulated through carefully crafted questions and answers, in order to keep a tight rein on the witness. This process was critiqued by Jerome Frank, an American judge and legal philosopher, in the following terms:

> The witness often detects what the lawyer hopes to prove at the trial. If the witness desires to have the lawyer's client win the case, he will often, unconsciously, mould [sic] his story accordingly. Telling and re-telling it to the lawyer, he will honestly believe that his story, as he narrates it in court, is true, although it importantly deviates from what he originally believed.[59]

It has been said that the adversarial system 'turns witnesses into weapons to be used against the other side.'[60] The party calling them will seek to control carefully what witnesses say in an effort to make sure that their testimony fits in with the narrative that counsel puts forward. Their testimony must be shaped to bring out its maximum adversarial effect,[61] and witnesses are thereby confined to answering questions within the parameters set down by the questioner.

Advocates are trained to use a number of specific devices to exert maximum control over a witness. These include the projection of confidence and control, role-playing, intimidation, the use of suggestion, and the carefully devised linguistic techniques designed to limit the witness's scope for free narrative. In addition, advocates are encouraged to construct a 'case theory,'[62] or a version of events that they believe took place. The advocate should then explain this to the court in the form of a story. In his manual on cross-examination, Marcus Stone explains:

56 See further Ch 6.

57 The Bar Standards Board, Handbook, Part II – Code of Conduct (General Council of the Bar), [rC3.1].

58 Danet, B. and Bogoch, B., 'Fixed Fight or Free for All? An Empirical Study of Combativeness in the Adversary System of Justice' (1980) 36 *British Journal of Law & Society* 41.

59 Frank, J., *Courts on Trial* (Princeton University Press, 1974), at 86.

60 Pizzi, W., *Trials Without Truth* (New York University Press, 1999), at 197.

61 Ibid.

62 Stone, M., *Cross-Examination in Criminal Trials*, 2nd edn (Butterworths, 1995), at 82.

> Almost every criminal trial is essentially a conflict between two stories about a human event, not a legal debate ... All the advocate's arts, including techniques and devices of cross-examination, should converge to tell a party's story, in such a way as to persuade the court that it is true.[63]

The tribunal of fact will therefore ultimately receive the evidence in a manipulated and reconstructed form. Facts are decontextualised, recategorised, and their significance is augmented or diminished according to how it might impact on the prospects of victory. The way in which the jury perceive this evidence may be intensified or diminished as counsel attempts to highlight or downplay respective aspects. Doreen McBarnet provides an insightful description as to how this impacts upon the work of counsel:

> To process a case through to conviction as quickly as possible, the prosecution requires sufficient factual information to incriminate the accused but no extras which might introduce ambiguities that surround real-life incidents. He wants the issues kept clear cut – there is an offence; there is a victim who is blameless and an offender who is guilty; there are no reasonable doubts. He thus needs a victim-witness who gives clear, precise evidence on the relevant facts as he defines them, who is personally credible and who is the blamelessly white side of the black and white adversarial dispute. He wants no grey areas introduced in relation to the facts, credibility or culpability for the defence to pounce on in cross-examination.
>
> Grey areas are, of course, exactly what the defence lawyer does want raised and especially from the central witness, the victim. Techniques in dealing with the victim are thus developed by the prosecutor and defence to respectively play down and play up the extra information that the victim might or might not provide, and both can involve treating the victim in a way which he or she experiences as degrading.[64]

Since the adversarial trial is limited to two versions of events, there is always going to be only one winner and one loser. The factfinder must then determine the outcome of the trial by fully awarding complete gain or loss through a guilty or not guilty verdict in respect of each individual charge.[65] Both parties must be sent away either victorious or defeated. The exception to this is if the jury is 'hung' and cannot reach a verdict. In these circumstances, the prosecution must decide whether to pursue a retrial or drop the charges. In theory, there is often scope for the jury to convict the accused of a lesser charge,[66] thus in effect allowing the factfinder to partly transcend the terms of the dispute as framed by the parties. However, it remains the case that the trier of fact bases any such decision on the material presented by the parties themselves. Although in theory

---

63 Ibid., at 120.

64 McBarnet, D., 'Victim in the Witness Box: Confronting Victimology's Stereotype' (1983) 7 *Contemporary Crises* 293, at 296.

65 It is, however, open to the jury to acquit the accused of some charges while convicting on others.

66 By virtue of s 6(3) of the Criminal Law Act 1967, where a person is tried on indictment for any offence except treason or murder and the jury find them not guilty of the offence specifically charged in the indictment, the jury may find them guilty of an alternative offence if the allegations in the indictment expressly or by implication amount to, or include, an allegation of the alternative offence, provided that the alternative offence falls within the jurisdiction of the court of trial. Section 6(2) of the Act deals with alternative verdicts to a count of murder. For example, if the defendant is charged with robbery, it may be possible to convict them of theft if the element of force is not proved. On occasions, the prosecution may also charge the accused with two or more offences in the alternative. In these circumstances, if the defendant is convicted of the more serious offence, the jury should be discharged from giving a verdict on the lesser charge.

jurors may question witnesses themselves,[67] they are almost entirely dependent upon the advocates as their source of information.

There is therefore a clear difference between the historical truth and the constructed truth,[68] and the concealment of the historical truth may better serve the advocate's end than its discovery. The exclusion of free-flowing witness narrative from the process highlights a certain irony in the adversarial trial process. Witnesses are put under oath 'to tell the truth, the whole truth, and nothing but the truth,' yet the manipulation of their testimony means that few witnesses are able to tell the truth in their own words.

The attenuated role afforded to witnesses also sits in stark contrast to the rapid ascendancy of victims' rights discourse. While the criminal justice system has traditionally been conceptualised as a mechanism for the state to resolve its grievances against suspects, defendants, and offenders, it is now broadly accepted that justice cannot be administered effectively without due recognition of the rights and interests of victims and witnesses. Psychologists have known for some time that one of the primary means to attain closure and overcome trauma and anxiety is through account-making. Indeed, contemporary psychotherapy and counselling practice – the so-called talking therapies – are founded on the premise that externalising traumatic experiences through verbalisation constitutes an effective coping mechanism for many people facing upheavals from major life-changing events, including violent crime.[69] Thus it is sometimes asserted that, for victims of crime and serious human rights violations, storytelling – while usually a painful process – can be valuable and empowering in the longer term by helping to restore a sense of esteem and self-worth.

Thus, if it is accepted that healing victims ought to be a function of the criminal justice system, then the parameters of the criminal trial and the law of evidence ought to be adapted to better facilitate therapeutic outcomes.[70] The inability of victims to tell their story to the court in their own words may well serve to exacerbate suffering – or at the very least it could be argued that the criminal justice system is 'missing a trick' in terms of how it might assist in the emotional restoration of victims. However, whether or not the criminal trial is the appropriate forum for this to take place, or whether the law is the appropriate tool to achieve this, are questions that are not easily resolved, considering the myriad of other functions that the criminal justice system is expected to perform.[71]

2.2.3 Zealous advocacy

Advocates are more interested in pursuing victory over their opponent than objectively uncovering information. Jerome Frank is one of many commentators who have drawn comparisons between the adversarial trial and a fight or some other form of physical showdown:

---

67 As Doran notes, jurors rarely ask questions since adversarial trials are not conducive to this practice: Doran, S., 'The Jury,' in M. McConville and G. Wilson (eds), *The Oxford Handbook of the Criminal Justice Process* (Oxford University Press, 2002), at 395.

68 See comment by Haines J in *R v Lalonde* (1971) 15 CRNA 1, 4: 'A trial is not a faithful reconstruction of the events as if recorded on some giant television screen. It is an historical recall of that part of events to which witnesses may be found and presented in an intensely adversary system where the object is the quantum of proof. Truth may only be incidental.'

69 See Smyth, J. and Pennebaker, J., 'Sharing One's Story: Translating Emotional Experiences into Words as a Coping Tool,' in C.R. Snyder (ed.), *Coping: The Psychology of What Works* (Oxford University Press, 1999).

70 Sveaass, N. and Lavik, N., 'Psychological Aspects of Human Rights Violations: The Importance of Justice and Reconciliation' (2000) 69 *Nordic Journal of International Law* 35.

71 The argument that the legal system can and should be used as a therapeutic tool is commonly advanced by proponents of the therapeutic jurisprudence movement. See e.g. Wexler, D.B. and Winick, B.J., *Law in a Therapeutic Key* (Carolina Academic Press, 1996).

> In short, the lawyer aims at victory, at winning in the fight, not at aiding the court to discover the facts. He does not want the trial court to reach a sound educated guess, if it is likely to be contrary to his client's interests. Our present trial method is thus the equivalent of throwing pepper in the eyes of a surgeon when he is performing an operation.[72]

The reward of a personal victory over one's opponent acts as a powerful incentive for energetic and zealous advocacy. This explains why proceedings are so highly confrontational and why the adversarial system leaves little room for human concern as advocates discharge their duties.[73] This is particularly true in trials for rape and sexual offences, in which many complainants feel as though they have been put on trial, as opposed to the accused. Frequently, they will have details of their private lives played out before an open court, which can be particularly embarrassing and humiliating in cases. This issue is examined further in Chapter 6, although for present purposes it can be noted that complainants in non-rape trials have reported similar experiences.[74]

2.2.4 Judicial non-intervention

The criminal trial involves questions of both law and fact. In trials on indictment, the general rule is that questions of law are to be decided by the trial judge, while questions of fact are to be decided by the jury. Thus, matters such as the competence of witnesses, the admissibility of evidence, and matters relating to the substantive law are matters of law for the judge, whereas those such as the credibility of a witness, the weight to be attached to the evidence, and the existence or non-existence of the facts in issue are questions of fact, and will be determined by the jury. In the case of trials in the magistrates' courts, the lay justices or stipendiary magistrates will determine questions of both law and fact, and will typically rely heavily on the legally qualified clerk in deciding questions of law.[75]

However, the theoretical distinction that is frequently made between the judge and jury is not always reflected in practice. Jackson has pointed out that:

> the traditional view that judges have responsibility merely for the law and juries for the facts is a misleading one, and it is more apt to characterise the factual function as one in which responsibility is shared between the judge and the jury.[76]

There are occasions on which the judge must investigate the preliminary facts in order to decide, for instance, whether evidence is admissible, or to determine whether there is sufficient evidence on a particular issue to go before a jury and to evaluate the evidence in order to comment on it when summing up the evidence for the jury.

---

72 Frank, op. cit., n. 59, at 84.

73 Barrett, E.F., 'The Adversary System and the Ethics of Advocacy' (1962) 37 *Notre Dame Law Review* 479, 481.

74 Brereton, D., 'How Different Are Rape Trials? A Comparison of the Cross-Examination of Complainants in Rape and Assault Trials' (1997) 37 *British Journal of Criminology* 242.

75 The Diplock courts of Northern Ireland, which (until 2007) heard trials related to alleged terrorist offences, were presided over by a single judge who was the sole arbiter of both law and facts. A proposal to introduce a similar system for complex fraud cases in England and Wales was contained in the Fraud (Trials Without a Jury) Bill 2007, but the proposed legislation was blocked by the House of Lords. Section 43 of the Criminal Justice Act 2003 made it possible for a judge to hear a complex fraud case without a jury; however, this provision was never brought into force. Further, as a result of the Protection of Freedoms Act 2012, the right to a juryless fraud trial has been repealed. See Wilson, W., '"Collaring" the Crime and the Criminal? "Jury Psychology" and Some Criminological Perspectives on Fraud and the Criminal Law' (2006) *Journal of Criminal Law* 70 for a discussion of the use of juryless trials.

76 Jackson, J., 'The Adversary Trial and Trial by Judge Alone,' in M. McConville and G. Wilson (eds), *The Oxford Handbook of the Criminal Justice Process* (Oxford University Press, 2002).

Furthermore, there are a number of grey areas in which questions of fact may be treated as questions of law, or in which questions of law are essentially treated as questions of fact. For example, while the construction of a statute is a matter of law, the construction of ordinary words used in the statute may be a question of fact. The phrase 'insulting behaviour' in section 5 of the Public Order Act 1936 was thought to be a matter of law, but in *Brutus v Cozens*,[77] the House of Lords held that where a word in a statute is used in its ordinary sense, it is a question of fact for the jury or magistrates to determine whether the proved conduct amounted to insulting behaviour. Similarly, in *R v Feeley*,[78] the word 'dishonestly' as used in the Theft Act 1968 was held to be an ordinary word in common use and therefore a question of fact for the jury.[79] Of particular relevance to the law of evidence is the decision of the Court of Appeal in *R v Fulling*,[80] in which the word 'oppression' in section 76(2)(a) of the Police and Criminal Evidence Act 1984 (which governs the admissibility of confessions) was given its ordinary dictionary meaning despite a partial definition in section 76(8).

In practice, however, *Brutus v Cozens* is often ignored, and there is little consistency in approach as to whose function it is to determine the meaning of words. Even the House of Lords disregarded the decision in *MPC v Caldwell*,[81] in which the word 'recklessly,' as used in the Criminal Damage Act 1971, was said to be used in its ordinary sense and yet was given a legal definition that differed from that given in the case of *R v Cunningham*.[82] There are countless other examples of ordinary words being legally defined simply because, without such definition, juries (and judges) are likely to produce different interpretations.

One of the key roles often attributed to the trial judge is that of umpire of the contest between the prosecution and defence. Traditionally, the adversarial paradigm has granted criminal advocates a considerable freedom in how they present their cases at court, and the manner in which they question witnesses. This freedom is not, however, unfettered. The conduct of the advocates and the way in which evidence is elicited from witnesses are subject to the oversight of the trial judge. However, judicial intervention is not regarded as a feature of the adversarial system, since control of the trial and evidence rests with the parties. While the judge has a role in ensuring that proceedings are conducted in accordance with the rules of evidence and procedure, they will generally refrain from intervening when witnesses are being questioned by counsel. Lord Denning famously summed up the role of the judge in the adversarial trial in *Jones v National Coal Board* in the following terms:

> The judge's part in all this is to hearken to the evidence, only himself asking questions of witnesses when it is necessary to clear up any point that has been overlooked or left obscure; to see that the advocates behave themselves seemly and keep to the rules laid down by law; to exclude irrelevancies and discourage repetition; to make sure by wise intervention that he follows the points the advocates are making and can assess their worth and at the end to make up his mind where the truth lies.[83]

---

77 [1973] AC 854. The 1936 legislation has now been replaced by the Public Order Act 1986.

78 [1973] QB 530.

79 A further example can be found in *DPP v Stonehouse* [1978] AC 854, in which it was held that the question of whether an act is 'more than merely preparatory to the commission of an offence' for the purposes of s 1 of the Criminal Attempts Act 1981 is one of fact.

80 [1987] QB 426. See discussion in Ch 8, pp. 210–29.

81 [1982] AC 341.

82 [1957] QB 396. In *R v G* [2004] 1 AC 1034, the House of Lords reconsidered its decision in *Caldwell* and departed from it, holding that it was just to do so (recklessness is now subjective, as in *Cunningham*, as opposed to objective, as in *Caldwell*).

83 *Jones v National Coal Board* [1957] 2 QB 55, at 64.

The adversarial model of justice dictates that the decision-maker, whether judge or jury, must rely on the parties exclusively for all of the material facts.[84] The jury is regarded in adversarial theory as the arbitrator of facts, and opposing sides should be able to rely on a broad freedom of proof to present their cases to the court with minimal interference from the bench. In a widely cited comment, Judge Frankel argued in the following terms that an overly active bench would serve to thwart the strategies of both parties to a case:

> The judge views the case from the peak of Olympian ignorance. His intrusions will in too many cases result from partial or skewed insights. He may expose the secrets one side chooses to keep never becoming aware of the other's. He runs a good chance of pursuing inspirations that better informed counsel have considered, explored, and abandoned after further study. He risks at a minimum the supplying of more confusion than guidance by his sporadic intrusions ... Without an investigative file, the American Trial Judge is a blind and blundering intruder, acting in spasms as sudden flashes of seeming light may lead or mislead him at odd times.[85]

Essentially, therefore, excessive judicial intervention in the trial risks usurping the functionality of the adversarial process. Indeed, an overly interventionist judge thus runs the risk of not only appearing to be partial to one side, but also of having a conviction overturned on appeal.[86] This danger was recognised by the Court of Appeal in *Sharp*:[87]

> The judge may be in danger of seeming to enter the arena in the sense that he may appear partial to one side or the other. This may arise from the hostile tone of questioning or implied criticism of counsel who is conducting the examination or cross-examination, or if the judge is impressed by a witness, perhaps suggesting excuses or explanations for a witness's conduct which is open to attack by counsel from the opposite party.[88]

While the role of the trial judge as an impartial and neutral umpire is often regarded as fundamental to the adversarial process, questions remain as to the degree to which practice reflects theory.[89]

For example, judges occasionally exercise common law powers to question witnesses themselves,[90] and may even call witnesses of their own motion.[91] They are also under a duty to intervene in order to prevent over-zealous or protracted cross-examination of an offensive or oppressive nature.[92]

However, in contemporary criminal practice, the primary role of the judge lies in overseeing the enforcement of evidential and procedural rules. By contrast, the parties in the trial hold a near-complete autonomy to gather, select, and present evidence before the tribunal of fact. The commencement, conduct, and termination of proceedings rest largely in their decisions. They dictate which facts are in issue and which are not, which proofs to generate, and which witnesses will be called to assist them in the pursuit of victory. The high level of party control is not really

---

84 Damaska, M., *The Faces of Justice and State Authority* (Yale University Press, 1986), at 36.

85 Frankel, M.E., 'The Search for Truth: An Umpireal View' (1975) 123 *University of Pennsylvania Law Review* 1031, 1042. This comment does, however, overlook the fact that, in civil cases and in the magistrates' courts, the umpire, as the trier of both law and fact, is effectively brought down from the heights of 'Olympian ignorance' into the trial arena.

86 See e.g. the Court of Appeal decision in *R v Gunning* [1980] Crim LR 592.

87 [1993] 3 All ER 225.

88 Ibid., at 231.

89 McEwan, op. cit., n. 9, at 13.

90 *R v Hopper* [1915] 2 KB 431; *R v Cain* (1936) 25 Cr App R 204.

91 *R v Wallwork* (1958) 42 Cr App R 153.

92 *Mechanical and General Inventions Co Ltd and Lehwess v Austin and Austin Motor Co Ltd* [1935] AC 346; *Wong Kam-ming v R* [1980] AC 247.

surprising, given that the opportunity to present one's arguments and then confront those of the opposing party lies at the heart of the adversarial process.[93]

As explained above, the only legal controls on the parties are the rules of evidence, and the extent to which the trial judge enforces them or exercises discretion to place limits on the parameters of the questioning process. In recent years, however, concerns over the manner in which witnesses are treated in court have been instrumental in focusing the attention of academics and policymakers on the need for more effective rules to govern the questioning of witnesses. These rules are mostly located within the Youth Justice and Criminal Evidence Act 1999 and the Criminal Justice Act 2003.

As they are the umpires of the contest, it might be asked why judges do not take an active role in ensuring that witnesses are not manipulated in the ways described above. Judicial intervention is not regarded as a feature of the adversarial system, since control of the trial and evidence rests with the parties. As seen above, while the judge has a role in ensuring that proceedings are conducted in accordance with the rules of evidence and procedure, they will generally refrain from intervening when witnesses are being questioned by counsel.[94]

2.3 The rationale for the adversarial trial

Commentators have long been intrigued by the question of what the overriding purpose, or function, of the adversarial trial ought to be. For some, the adversarial trial provides the best way in which to determine the truth of what witnesses are saying. Live oral evidence, given to the court under oath and tested by the parties, has traditionally been regarded as the best means of reaching the truth. Although Jerome Frank disliked the fight theory that underpinned the adversarial model of justice, he nonetheless defended its ability to seek out the truth. In his eyes, parties that have a clear focus on victory will produce the best information for the tribunal of fact to make a determination:

> Many lawyers maintain that the best way for the court to discover the facts in a suit is to have each side strive as hard as it can, in a keenly partisan spirit, to bring to the court's attention the evidence favourable to that side. Macauley said that we obtain the fairest decision 'when two men argue, as unfairly as possible, on opposite sides' for then 'it is certain that no important consideration will altogether escape notice.'[95]

An alternative justification for the adversarial process is that although adversarial structures do not always lend themselves to accurate truth-finding, it is nonetheless the dispute resolution model that is best placed to ensure that outcomes are as fair as possible to the parties to the case. Landsman, for example, is quite happy to defend the adversarial system on the basis that truth is not its primary goal:

> [A] preoccupation with material truth may be not only futile but dangerous to society as well. If the objective of the judicial process were the disclosure of facts, then any technique that increases the prospect of gathering facts would be permissible.[96]

93 Stone, M., *Cross-Examination in Criminal Trials*, 2nd edn (Butterworths, 1995), at 114.
94 Unless the witness is vulnerable; see Ch 5.
95 Frank, op. cit., n. 59, at 80–81.
96 Landsman, op. cit., n. 1, at 37.

Landsman proceeds to list examples, such as the use of psychoactive drugs and/or torture as a means to produce truth. Thus, by necessity, a *truth at all costs* approach to criminal trials is unworkable given that exclusionary evidential rules, coupled with certain due process protections, are designed to maintain the integrity of the criminal justice process. Instead, Landsman defends the adversarial trial on the basis that truth plays second fiddle to the overriding need for justice. Procedural requirements such as party control, an impartial decision-maker, and commitment to winning the contest mean that the process should be broadly equal. Fundamental rights are safeguarded through evidential rules, which go some way towards offsetting the broader range of resources at the disposal of the prosecution, as well as maintaining integrity and public confidence in the criminal justice system.

In a similar vein, Thibaut and Walker argue for a form of 'distributive justice,' whereby the outcomes of proceedings will naturally reflect the inputs of the parties.[97] In their eyes, the truth-finding aspect of the adversarial system is subservient to the overriding goal of justice or fairness. Therefore, maximum control must rest with the parties. In their view, this is a more satisfactory basis for resolving legal disputes than scientific enquiry, since 'the information attained would be of little or no significance and the cost of attaining it would be a significant diminution in the perceived fairness of the outcome.'[98] At one level, Thibaut and Walker's theory provides a useful conflict resolution analysis of the adversarial trial. However, it is arguably overly clinical, and also overlooks the fact that truth is often synonymous with justice. A decision is more likely to be regarded as 'just' or 'fair' if it reflects the truth of what actually happened, as opposed to the party input, although it does not guarantee that the truth has been elicited.

A more persuasive argument is put forward by Goodpaster. He contends that truth and justice are 'intimately connected' and should therefore be considered to be twin objectives of the adversarial system. Fair procedures are more conducive to accurate fact-finding, whereas unfair procedures may lead to erroneous fact-finding.[99] Such a view also underpinned Jeremy Bentham's famous image of '[i]njustice, and her handmaid [f]alsehood.'[100] It is important, however, to bear in mind that the concept of fairness should not only focus on the extent to which the rights of the accused are protected. A truly fair process would seek to minimise both the trauma of victims and the risk of prejudice to the accused, and would also, arguably, meet society's demands for the criminal justice system to be both fair and perceived as such. Furthermore, a truly fair outcome is not only dependent upon fair processes, but also requires that the relevant processes are geared to uncovering the truth. This raises significant questions as to whether the adversarial trial can be genuinely described as fair for the accused, the victim, or indeed society as a whole. Jackson and Summers[101] argue that the assumption that a 'non-legally qualified accused' will be able to present his case in accordance with the procedural rules seems 'downright absurd.' This argument becomes more pronounced when considering cases in which the accused is expected to cross-examine the witness and object to procedurally improper activities undertaken by the prosecution. The US Supreme Court has noted that within the context of the adversarial trial, they consider that it is 'virtually impossible' to ensure the fairness of the proceedings without granting the accused the assistance of defence counsel.

---

97 Thibaut, J. and Walker, L., 'A Theory of Procedure' (1978) 66 *California Law Review* 541.

98 Ibid., at 556.

99 Goodpaster, G., 'On the Theory of the American Adversary Criminal Trial' (1987) 78 *Journal of Criminal Law and Criminology* 118; for a consideration of the same system, see Grande, E., 'Dance of Criminal Justice: Thoughts on Systems Differences, and the Search for the Truth,' and Lempert, R., 'Anglo-American and Continental Systems: Manuscripts and Mammals of the Law,' both in Jackson et al. (eds).

100 Bentham, J., *Rationale of Judicial Evidence*, Vol. 1 (Hunt and Clarke, 1827; Garland, 1978).

101 Jackson, J. and Summers, S., *Obstacles to Fairness in Criminal Proceedings: Individual Rights and Institutional Forms* (Hart Publishing, 2018).

In practice, the underlying structures and processes of the adversarial model may impede the ability of the trial to uncover the truth. In specific relation to the rules of evidence, the most obvious evidential constraint in the common law system is that the court itself cannot undertake a search for relevant evidence; it must rely almost entirely upon the prosecution and defence to supply it with relevant information.[102] As Landsman argues, proactively seeking further information outside what the parties were presenting would heighten the risk of perceived partisanship:

> Adversary theory suggests that if he [the judge] diverges from passivity by attempting to develop the evidence at trial, or to arrange the compromise of the case, he runs a serious risk of undermining his ability to evaluate neutrally the adversaries' presentations.[103]

Therefore, evidence that may be perceived as being neutral, yet may still be relevant, is often overlooked. McEwan gives the example of the evidence of a key witness whom neither side wishes to call, since both sides fear what that witness may do to their case.[104] Evidential rules make no provision for the admissibility of such a witness's testimony, and thus truth-finding is arguably made more difficult.

It should be noted that Dworkin has previously argued that the Criminal Procedure Rules were being used as a scapegoat to divert legal attention away from the social causes relating to the increased crime rates. He has argued against 'defendant-centered subjectivity' noting that it is easiest to erode the rights of unpopular groups.[105] The expectation of cooperation is incompatible with principles of adversarial, sits uneasily with the presumption of innocence, and assists the prosecution in discharging the burden of proof.

Furthermore, for the fight theory to work effectively, the prosecution and defence must be relatively equal in terms of resources. The difficulty here is that the potential for the defence to embark on their own evidence-gathering process is significantly hindered in terms of resources. The defence will be highly dependent on the Crown Prosecution Service (CPS) to comply with disclosure obligations in order to sift through the evidence gathered by the police.[106] However, there is a risk that such evidence will already have been selectively filtered by the police or CPS, even on a subconscious level, as cases are constructed against suspects.[107] For example, it can be assumed that certain aspects of evidence that sat uneasily alongside the initial case theory of the police or the CPS may have been set to one side; certain lines of enquiry may not have been probed; certain witnesses may not have been interviewed; and certain questions may not have been asked. It is thus the case that the truth of past events is routinely deconstructed by criminal investigations, with a new 'truth' being reconstructed within the trial as the parties attempt to persuade the factfinder that their presentation of events represents a historically correct narrative. In this sense, it is arguable that the adversarial model of proof constitutes a poor vehicle for delivering justice that is ultimately based on the truth.[108]

---

102 In theory, judges can widen the scope of the fact-finding process. For example, they may call witnesses of their own motion (*R v Wallwork* (1958) 42 Cr App R 153). However, this power should be used sparingly (*R v Roberts* (1984) 80 Cr App R 89).

103 Landsman, op. cit., n. 1, at 491.

104 McEwan, op. cit., n. 9, at 4.

105 Dworkin, *The Times* (London, 4 December 1972).

106 The Criminal Procedure and Investigations Act 1996 requires disclosure by the prosecution of previously undisclosed material. This is to be followed by the defence disclosing to the prosecution certain information about the defence case. On receipt of that evidence, the prosecution will be required to disclose any material relevant to the defence case as disclosed. See also Part 5 of the CJA 2003, which amends this procedure to increase the nature of the disclosure obligations on the defence.

107 See further McConville, M., Sanders, A., and Leng, R., *The Case for the Prosecution* (Routledge, 1991). The authors argue that the police, although normatively neutral, will seek to build a strong case for the prosecution in the investigation of the crime and in the collection of evidence.

108 See further Doak, J., *Victims' Rights, Human Rights and Criminal Justice* (Hart Publishing, 2008), Ch 4.

2.4 An alternative: the inquisitorial approach

Criminal proceedings in inquisitorial countries can be divided into three broad phases: (1) the investigative phase, (2) the examining phase, and (3) the trial.[109] Each stage is formally documented, and is strictly governed by the principle of legality. The investigative phase begins once a crime has been reported. It will be brought to the attention of the prosecutor (*procureur*), who will request a formal judicial investigation. Mirfield notes that these provisions intended that 'the suspect is recruited as an active part of the investigation process.'[110] In France, this request goes to a separate panel of three judges who are responsible for the charging process, known as the *Chambre d'Instruction*. If the panel agrees that an investigation is warranted, it will appoint an examining magistrate (*juge d'instruction*), who will begin an investigation into all of the circumstances surrounding the offence. In other jurisdictions, including Germany and Austria, the prosecutor herself controls the pre-trial investigation, and is viewed as a neutral representative of the state rather than an opponent of the suspect.

In addition to collecting information relating to the particular facts of the incident in question, the investigation also conducts an extensive inquiry into the suspect's *personalité*, which includes the gathering of information on their upbringing, family life, education, job history, behaviour, financial situation, and psychological make-up. Once this evidence has been collected, the examining magistrate will begin the examination phase. During this stage of the procedure, they will interview all pertinent witnesses, and interviews are usually recorded in a verbatim transcript. Normally, the questioning of the lead suspect will form a central part of the examination phase. Although defendants cannot be compelled to answer questions, there is a strong expectation that they will do so and lawyers will normally instruct their clients to give truthful answers to all questions asked. The examination phase can be lengthy: a wide range of witnesses are typically called, including the family, friends, co-workers, and neighbours of the accused, to gather a more rounded picture of the suspect's *personalité*.[111]

The investigations and examinations conducted in the pre-trial phase will be recorded in the dossier, or case file. The dossier will usually consist of several hundred separate documents, including witness statements, expert reports, and photographs. The defence normally has an absolute right to inspect the full dossier prior to trial, and may make submissions to the investigating magistrate on any additional investigations or tests that ought to be instigated. It is therefore vital that the dossier is both objective and complete. This is guaranteed, in theory at least, by the supervisory role exercised by the prosecutor over the police and also by the investigating magistrate, who has an overall duty to ensure that the investigation is carried out fairly and impartially. When the investigation has been completed, the examining magistrate will then determine whether there is reasonable cause for trial. In some jurisdictions, including France and Belgium, this decision is taken by an indicting chamber of three judges. If it is decided that the case should proceed, the court then assumes control over the case, replacing the prosecutor and the investigating magistrate for the commencement of the trial proper.

As a consequence of the way in which evidence is assembled in the pre-trial phase, the conduct of the trial proper bears little resemblance to its common law counterpart. Daly has described

---

109 Merryman, J.H., *The Civil Law Tradition* (Stanford University Press, 1985), at 129.

110 Mirfield, R., 'Two Side Effects of Section 34 to Section 37 of the Criminal Justice and Public Order Act 1994' (1995) Crim LR 613, 616.

111 See Daly, M., 'Legal Ethics: Some Thoughts on the Differences in Criminal Trials in Civil and Common Law Legal Systems' (1999) 2 *Journal of the Institute for the Study of Legal Ethics* 65, 67–68. Daly notes that the investigation of *personalité* is derived from the French legal maxim, *On juge l'homme, pas les faits* ('One judges the man, not the facts'). In many civil law jurisdictions, both the prosecution and defence are prohibited from interviewing witnesses, although at this stage the defence will normally be able to exercise a right of allocution to protect their client's interests, calling certain matters to the attention of the court and advising the client on how he or she should respond to judicial questioning.

the trial as 'anticlimactic,' since the fact-finding has already been largely completed through the pre-trial investigation.[112] Thus, proceedings are generally conducted with less formality than in adversarial jurisdictions.[113] The evidence has already been taken and the record made: the function of the trial is to present this evidence to the trier of fact and allow the prosecutor and defence to argue their respective cases on the basis of the evidence contained in the dossier.[114] Proceedings are therefore structured in the form of an inquiry rather than a contest, which, depending on the jurisdiction, will often be presided over by a single professional judge or a mixed panel comprising laypersons and other professional judges.

The tone and atmosphere of the inquisitorial trial are seemingly very different indeed from its adversarial counterpart. Generally, it is much more businesslike in tone. Consider the following observations of Renée Lettow Lerner, an American law professor who observed the murder trial of one Thierry Gaitaud at the French Cour d'Assises in 1999:

> Introduction of each witness was minimal ... [The judge] asked each witness 'What do you have to tell us?' There was no direct or cross-examination as we know of it. The witness started off testifying in narrative form, usually for several minutes without interruption ... When the witness finished his or her story or the testimony got murky, Corneloup [the judge] began asking questions, directing the witness's attention to key points. He often read the former statements of a witness from the dossier in framing his questions. When he was done, he turned to the assesseurs and jurors to see if they had any questions, then to the prosecutor, then to defence counsel. Bilger [the prosecutor] and defence counsel usually asked between one and three questions each.[115]

Lerner's description of the trial highlights the lack of any clear-cut division between the prosecution case and the defence case. Indeed, some inquisitorial jurisdictions, including Germany, Austria, Norway, and Sweden, permit victims to assist the prosecutor as a 'subsidiary prosecutor'. Rather than being viewed as the property of the prosecution or defence, witnesses are instead regarded as the property of the court, and it would be unusual for their characters to come under attack in a way that is so commonplace within the adversarial system.

In most jurisdictions, the defendant is questioned before other witnesses, first by the presiding judge, and then by the prosecutor and defence counsel. In some jurisdictions, questioning may be conducted indirectly through the trial judge. Other witnesses, including the *juge d'instruction*, are then usually questioned in a similar way, with most of their testimony being elicited through the relatively informal questioning by the presiding judge. Further evidence is presented in documentary form.

In contrast to the adversarial trial, in which evidence is contemporaneously presented and tested by the parties, the examination of witnesses and the assessment of their credibility will have already been completed by the *juge d'instruction* as part of the pre-trial phase. The primary function of the inquisitorial trial is thus to assess the weight of individual pieces of evidence.

This impacts how advocates carry out their business. Witnesses are not usually extensively questioned about background information relating to their credibility as any real combat will

---

112 Ibid., at 66.

113 Van Kessel notes that the presiding judge sits closer to the parties and to the public than in adversarial jurisdictions, and lawyers will generally address the judge with a greater degree of familiarity: Van Kessel, G., 'Adversary Excesses in the American Criminal Trial' (1992) 67 *Notre Dame Law Review* 403, 413.

114 Merryman, op. cit., n. 109, at 130.

115 Lerner, R.L., 'The Intersection of Two Systems: An American on Trial for an American Murder in the French *Cour d'Assises*' (2001) 19 *University of Illinois Law Review* 791, at 804.

have already taken place in the investigation and examination phases.[116] There is no conceptual equivalent of cross-examination, although the accused may rely on the 'principle of contradiction,' which effectively amounts to a right to challenge evidence adduced against them. Therefore, only the principle of adversarial testing, which provides the defence with the opportunity to challenge crucial incriminating evidence before it is evaluated before the court, seems capable of doing justice to fair standards. As the Al-Khawaja[117] case demonstrates, the ECtHR accepted that the existence of other corroborative evidence rests upon witness statements in respect of which there is an absence of supporting or undermining evidence; fairness demands an opportunity to examine these witnesses. The manner in which the defence may exercise the principle of contradiction varies considerably between jurisdictions. Defence lawyers have very limited rights to question the witness directly in France or Belgium;[118] other jurisdictions, such as Spain and the Netherlands, permit the parties to play a subsidiary role in posing questions after the examining magistrate has conducted questioning. Other civil law countries, including Italy and Denmark, provide for a more extensive questioning regime, which bears some resemblance to adversarial cross-examination, although the judge retains very close control over the questions posed and generally ensures that witnesses are treated with respect.

Most commentators agree that questioning is much less aggressive in form, regardless of whether it is carried out by the parties or by the trial judge. Van Kessel, for example, notes that, by and large, questioning tends to be 'informal and more natural,'[119] and Langbein has commented that the tone was 'crisp and business-like, but not hostile.'[120] Similarly, the eminent comparative scholar Mirjan Damaska states that:

> Anglo-American observers of the court scene are regularly struck by the rarity and the subdued nature of the challenges to the witnesses' credibility. If such a challenge occurs, it mainly focuses on the witness's reliability with respect to the facts to which he has been disposed and seldom escalates into a general attack on his character or reputation for untruthfulness.[121]

As a result, witnesses in inquisitorial trials may be more relaxed and often more forthcoming with information than their adversarial counterparts.[122] As Wohler comments, however, a change of system, from adversarial to a mixed system, must be compatible with the principle of fairness and expediency. An example of a mixed model system would be the international criminal tribunals, which attempt to create a criminal procedure that meets the minimum fairness standards across a broad spectrum of legal traditions.[123] Moreover, as Pizzi and Perron observed, the fact that the majority of the questions are posed by the judge can help to lessen the emotional impact of relaying detailed events about a distressing event: 'It is often easier for victims to answer questions concerning painful, distasteful, or embarrassing events when these questions come from professional judges who are expected to be both impartial and fair.'[124]

---

116 Daly, op. cit., n. 111, at 66.
117 [2012] 54 EHRR 23.
118 Spencer, J., 'Evidence,' in M. Delmas-Marty and J. Spencer (eds), *European Criminal Procedures* (Cambridge University Press, 2002), at 629. Spencer points out, however, that it is very rare for the parties to make such a request.
119 Van Kessel, op. cit., n. 113, at 464.
120 Langbein, J.H., *Comparative Criminal Procedure: Germany* (West Publishing, 1977), at 74.
121 Damaska, M., *Evidence Law Adrift* (Yale University Press, 1997), at 80.
122 Lerner, op. cit., n. 115, at 808.
123 Wohlers, W., 'The Role of Counsel in Criminal Proceedings'.
124 Pizzi, W. and Perron, W., 'Crime Victims in German Courtrooms: A Comparative Perspective on American Problems' (1996) 32 *Stanford Journal of International Law* 37, at 46.

After all of the evidence has been received, parties will present their closing arguments before the trier of fact retires to consider the verdict, which, unlike the common law model, must be issued with reasons. The trier of fact will often take the form of a mixed panel involving both professional judges and lay assessors (usually volunteers). For example, the French Cour d'Assises, which tries serious offences carrying a minimum sentence of 10 years' imprisonment, sits with a jury comprising nine lay assessors and three professional judges (including the presiding judge). A majority of eight is needed to convict.[125] Similarly, Spain and Russia both reformed their criminal justice systems and have reintroduced the use of lay jurors after they were abolished in the late nineteenth century.[126] In Spain, the jury is composed of nine jurors and one presiding judge, whereas Russia and Belgium both have common law-style juries comprising 12 laymen. By contrast, Dutch criminal courts are composed entirely of professional judges.

The historical lack of lay involvement in the inquisitorial tradition underlines the degree of faith that is placed in the machinery of the state to investigate, prosecute, and adjudicate objectively alleged criminal behaviour. This can be contrasted with a basic underlying scepticism that seems to exist in adversarial jurisdictions about trusting the state to produce the truth while simultaneously protecting the interests of the accused. Thus, the jury has historically been perceived as an institutional bulwark against the abuse of power by the state. The differing approaches to lay participation also go some way towards explaining the very different regimes of evidential rules. It is broadly accepted that a complex and exclusionary system of evidential rules is primarily needed in adversarial proceedings to safeguard the risk of laypersons attaching undue weight to potentially prejudicial evidence such as previous convictions or hearsay evidence. For their part, inquisitorial systems are characterised by a lack of prescriptive rules, meaning that these types of evidence are usually freely admitted.[127] It is something of an irony that the right to trial by jury is often portrayed in adversarial jurisdictions as a fundamental civil liberty, and yet the criminal justice system is not quite prepared to fully trust jurors to properly weigh up the probative value of certain forms of evidence – such as bad character – against its prejudicial effect. There is no solid reason for the belief that judges are better able to deal with prejudicial evidence than juries, and paternalism towards juries would seem to be a problem contrived exclusively by the common law.

2.4.1 The rationale for the inquisitorial model

Truth-finding is widely regarded as the overriding goal of the inquisitorial paradigm. Whereas adversarial theory dictates that the truth is more likely to be elicited through a 'sharp clash of proofs,'[128] the inquisitorial attitude dictates that the search for truth is best effected through what Damaska has termed a 'a self-propelled judicial inquiry ... only slightly affected by party initiative.'[129]

The emphasis placed upon truth-finding is reflected in the general principles contained in the criminal codes of many inquisitorial jurisdictions. For example, the German Code of Criminal Procedure explicitly provides that the inherent objective of the German criminal justice system is to 'investigate thoroughly all the facts to arrive at the objective truth.' Section 244(ii) of the Code also provides for the principle of material truth, and states that 'in order to search out the truth,

125 On appeal, the court sits with a jury of 12 laypersons and three judges, with a majority of ten needed to uphold a conviction from the first instance.

126 See further Thaman, S., 'Europe's New Jury Systems: The Cases of Spain and Russia' (1999) 62 *Law and Contemporary Problems* 233.

127 Although there is an absence of formal rules relating to the admissibility of evidence, two key principles are usually applied. First, the principle of free evaluation of evidence means that the factfinder should have access to all of the relevant evidence before coming to a decision. In many jurisdictions, this principle is considered alongside the principle of proportionality, which emphasises the need to balance the due process rights of individuals against the state's interest in fighting crime.

128 Landsman, S., *Readings on Adversarial Justice: The American Approach to Adjudication* (West Publishing, 1988), at 2.

129 Damaska, op. cit., n. 121, at 107.

the court shall on its own motion extend the taking of evidence to all facts and means of proof that are important for the decision.' The close judicial supervision of the preliminary fact-finding process means that the inquisitorial model arguably does a better job than its adversarial counterpart in ensuring that all relevant information is factored into key decision-making.

In contrast to the low priority seemingly afforded to truth-finding by adversarial processes, many specific structures of the inquisitorial process are designed to maximise its potential. The model 'erects few evidentiary barriers that restrict the information the judge can consider in determining guilt.'[130] The lack of exclusionary evidential rules means that the trier of fact is thereby entrusted with the ability to exercise due objective diligence when assessing the evidence, by attaching variable weight to different forms of evidence. For example, it might be assumed that whereas forensic DNA evidence placing the accused at the scene of the crime would be highly probative, hearsay evidence would attract comparatively little weight (although such evidence would not usually be excluded altogether). Instead, the court will usually take steps to test the reliability of second-hand or third-hand statements, by asking other witnesses and checking documents, and through considering the circumstances in which the original statements were made.[131] All evidence will therefore be weighed up, taking into account its differing weight and credibility. Such evidence (particularly relating to the character of the accused) is often seen as being crucial in enabling the trier of fact to form an *intime conviction* concerning the guilt or innocence of the accused.[132] It would therefore make little sense to place burdens on parties who played subsidiary roles to the trial judge.

In contrast to the tightly regulated rules of evidence of the adversarial process, the lack of any rigid regime of evidential rules in inquisitorial systems means that a wide array of information is to be presented to the trier of fact. Since the collection of evidence is supervised by the investigating judge rather than the parties, this should avoid the selective filtering of information that occurs in the adversarial process. Arguably, relevant evidence is thereby much less likely to be excluded, and the lack of any evidential filtering of relevant information should mean that, in general, justice is more likely to be delivered to both victims and defendants.

However, there are also arguably certain aspects of criminal procedure for which the adversarial model is better adapted. Some proponents of adversarial procedure contend that the inquisitorial model is fundamentally unfair to the accused.[133] For instance, the emphasis placed on judge-led questioning in many continental systems raises the question as to whether defendants are offered sufficient opportunity to challenge evidence against them. It can be noted, for instance, that the vast majority of challenges brought before the Strasbourg Court under Article 6(3)(d) (the right of the accused 'to examine or have examined witnesses against him') have been brought against systems operating an inquisitorial style of procedure. Arguably, adversarial cross-examination provides the best means for exercising this right to challenge through providing the defence with an opportunity to put their case directly to the opposing witness.[134] The ability of the defence to do this varies considerably across inquisitorial jurisdictions, but recent years have

130 Pizzi, W. and Marafiorti, L., 'The New Italian Code of Criminal Procedure: The Difficulties of Building an Adversarial Trial System on a Civil Law Foundation' (1992) 17 *Yale Journal of International Law* 1, 7.

131 Lerner, op. cit., n. 115, at 810.

132 The concept of *intime conviction* reflects the standard of proof in criminal cases. Although it has no direct English equivalent, Lerner has suggested that it amounts to the factfinder deciding whether they are 'deeply and thoroughly convinced': Lerner, op. cit., n. 115, at 796. The standard of proof thereby takes a very different form from the adversarial standard, which reflects the judge-led nature of proceedings.

133 See, e.g., Landsman, S., 'The Decline of the Adversary System' (1980) 29 *Buffalo Law Review* 487; Ammodio, E. and Selvaggi, E., 'An Accusatorial System in a Civil Law Country: The 1988 Italian Code of Criminal Procedure' (1999) 62 *Templeton Law Review* 1213.

134 Friedman, R., 'Confrontation Rights of Criminal Defendants,' in J.F. Nijboer and J.M. Reijntjes (eds), *Proceedings of the First World Conference on New Trends in Criminal Investigation and Evidence* (Open University of the Netherlands, 1997).

witnessed a discernible shift towards affording greater opportunities for the defence to directly challenge prosecution evidence in many continental systems.[135] Swart, for instance, has observed the impact of the increasing effect of the European Convention in the Dutch courts, which have been 'forced to change their course' by giving the defence more opportunities to question witnesses from the prosecution.[136]

A further charge frequently levied at inquisitorial systems is that the state-led nature of the evidence-gathering process is not subject to adequate checks and balances. The level of trust placed in the state to conduct the 'inquiry' means that the accused cannot be guaranteed a fair trial given that the judge is a representative of the state and has a strong political interest in increasing conviction rates and being seen to be tough on crime. The risks of injustice are thereby perceived by some to be higher in inquisitorial settings. For example, Landsman has commented: 'Generally, the inquisitorial process will not serve as a check on government power. Inquisitorial judges ... are bureaucrats who identify with the governments and whose advancement in judicial hierarchy depends on accommodation rather than confrontation.'[137]

Placing such a heavy emphasis upon the role of the state appears to sit uneasily alongside the exponential growth of both restorative justice and alternative dispute resolution initiatives in recent years. Whereas these programmes tend to focus on empowering the parties and devolving the dispute resolution process into the hands of those primarily affected by it, the inquisitorial model's adherence to the principle of legality and rejection of plea negotiation suggests that the systems of continental Europe are less well equipped than the adversarial systems to accommodate such developments.

2.5 Caveat: the adversarial-inquisitorial spectrum

Notwithstanding the above discussion, it is worth underlining that there is no such thing as a prototype adversarial or inquisitorial model. Such labels are simply used to describe the general character and structure of proceedings. Adversarial and inquisitorial systems differ widely in respect of how the trial is organised. Jackson and Doran explain the dangers of these labels in the following terms:

> Anglo-American systems cannot adequately be characterised as 'adversarial' or contest-based ... continental systems do not conform purely to 'inquisitorial' or inquest-based methods of procedure. Nevertheless, it has to be assumed that, beyond the level of description, these terms are useful ways of idealising the essential attributes of Anglo-American and European legal procedures.[138]

There is an inherent danger in drawing assumptions that a particular rule of procedure that has been identified in one particular jurisdiction will apply in all jurisdictions, and is thus perceived as a *sine qua non* of the inquisitorial paradigm. It is thus important to bear in mind that such models do not represent an empirical reality for any one individual jurisdiction, but rather assist in the interpretation of structures and values that are commonly found in the majority of trial systems of a particular type. No single legal system constitutes an absolute apotheosis of either model. Such

135 See further Van Kessel, G., 'European Trends towards Adversary Styles in Procedure and Evidence,' in M. Feeley and S. Miyazawa (eds), *The Japanese Adversary System in Context* (Macmillan, 2002).

136 Swart, A., 'The Netherlands,' in C. Van Den Wyngaert (ed.), *Criminal Procedure Systems in the European Community* (Butterworths, 1993), p. 298.

137 Landsman, op. cit., n. 1, at 50.

138 Jackson, J. and Doran, S., *Judge Without Jury: Diplock Trials and the Adversary System* (Clarendon Press, 1995), at 299.

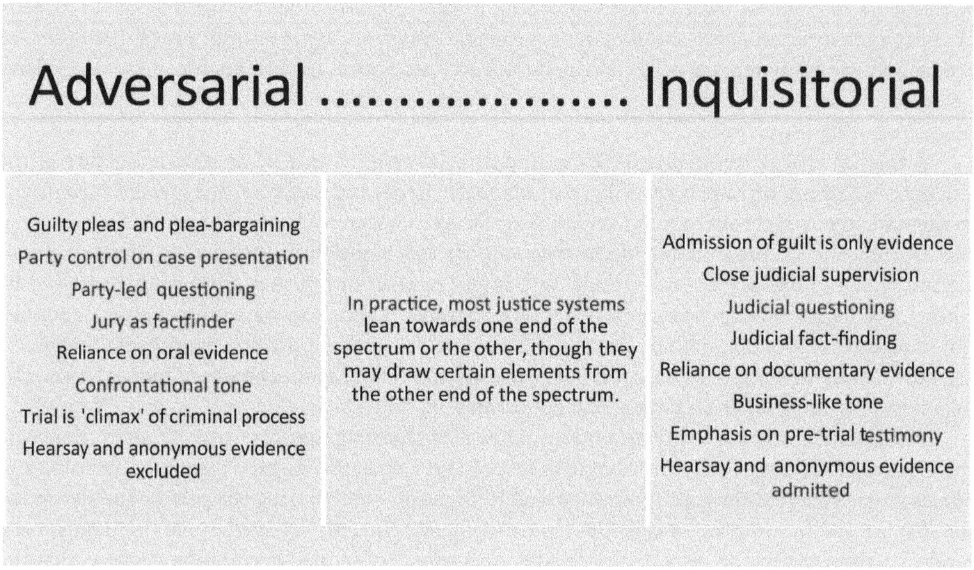

Figure 2.3 The adversarial–inquisitorial spectrum

designations are typically used in a relatively loose way, to describe very general features of different legal models.[139] As Figure 2.3 indicates, the labels 'adversarial' and 'inquisitorial' are perhaps best thought of as descriptors that can be placed at either end of a spectrum, with most systems conforming to a greater or lesser extent with the classic perceptions of either model. The models help us to understand the nature of various criminal justice systems around the world, but do not provide a definitive explanation of what one will find in an 'inquisitorial/adversarial' system of criminal justice. The empirical reality is much more complex than the adversarial/inquisitorial model will have us believe, but the models do help us *begin* to understand the many different features that exist in different systems.

As regards the English trial model, it would be a fundamental misconception to think of the English model as *purely* adversarial, since it does possess some inquisitorial features, such as the recent drift towards a freer regime of proof. As we shall see in subsequent chapters, the reforms contained in the Criminal Justice Act 2003 significantly relaxed the exclusionary regimes relating to hearsay and bad character evidence. Similarly, recent years have also seen shifts in the way in which some continental legal systems treat hearsay and anonymous evidence following rulings from the European Court of Human Rights.[140] In the case of *Stafford v U.K.*,[141] the ECtHR held that despite the defendant not having properly heard the proceedings, there was no violation of Article 6. Therefore, the right to follow proceedings in the adversarial system is now a personal one, exercisable by the defendant himself.

---

139 For a brief account of why the English system developed differently from that on the Continent, see Levy, L.W., *The Palladium of Justice* (Ivan R. Dee, 1999), at 51–53. Note, however, that Damaska warns of the dangers of such a neat distinction. He warns that the adversarial/non-adversarial classification is of only limited use beyond Western justice systems. He prefers to analyse comparative processes from a political perspective, advocating that it is key political and socio-economic factors, such as democratic values and the nature of government, which shape individual justice processes: Damaska, op. cit., n. 84.

140 See further Doak, J. and Huxley-Binns, R., 'Anonymous Witnesses in England and Wales, Charting a Course from Strasbourg' (2009) 73 *Journal of Criminal Law* 508.

141 ECHR, 28 May 2002.

2.6 Key learning points

- The adversarial trial follows a closely regulated format. The prosecution and defence will present their cases in turn, before the jury retires to consider its verdict.
- Key features of the adversarial criminal trial include the principles of orality, party control, zealous advocacy, and judicial non-intervention.
- The extent to which the adversarial trial does or should pursue truth-finding as its ultimate goal is open to debate.
- The main alternative to the adversarial trial, the inquisitorial method, is used in most of continental Europe.
- The inquisitorial model is characterised by a very relaxed regime of evidential rules and tends to prioritise truth-finding as its primary goal.

2.7 Practice questions

1. Why have the adversarial and inquisitorial systems evolved so differently?
2. Where on the adversarial–inquisitorial spectrum do you think the English criminal trial lies?
3. To what extent do the rules of evidence hinge on the historical use of juries in the adversarial system?
4. Should the criminal trial prioritise truth-finding over and above other goals?
5. Is it true that the inquisitorial system does a better job at fact-finding than the adversarial system?

2.8 Suggested further reading

Australian Law Reform Commission, *Review of the Adversarial System of Litigation: Rethinking the Federal Civil Litigation System*, Issues Paper No. 20 (Australian Government Publishing Service, 1997).

Damaska, M., *Evidence Law Adrift* (Yale University Press, 1997).

Jackson, J.D. and Summers, S.J., *The Internationalisation of Criminal Evidence* (Cambridge University Press, 2012).

King, M., 'Security, Scale, Form, and Function: The Search for Truth and the Exclusion of Evidence in Adversarial and Inquisitorial Justice Systems' (2002) 12 International Legal Perspectives 185.

Landsman, S., *The Adversary System: A Description and Defense* (The American Enterprise Institute, 1984).

McKillop, B., 'Anatomy of a French Murder Case' (1997) 45 American Journal of Comparative Law 527.

Merryman, J.H., *The Civil Law Tradition* (Stanford University Press, 1985).

Pakes, F., *Comparative Criminal Justice*, 2nd edn (Willan Publishing, 2012).

Pizzi, W., *Trials without Truth* (New York University Press, 1999).

Chapter 3

The Burden and Standard of Proof

Chapter contents

DOI: 10.4324/9781003416098-3

Whether we are concerned with a civil or a criminal trial, it is important to establish at the outset which party bears the burden of proving a particular issue. Furthermore, it is equally important to understand the standard to which the burden of proving a certain issue requires to be discharged. It is these two issues that will be explored in this chapter. Understanding the allocation of these burdens during the onset of the trial will help to determine which party should begin calling evidence and, in that vein, if there is a case to answer (Figure 3.1).[1]

3.1 The legal and evidential burden: criminal trials

A central feature of most common law jurisdictions is that the prosecution has the burden of proving the guilt of the accused person beyond reasonable doubt. In *Woolmington v DPP*,[2] the House of Lords held that it was for the prosecution to prove all of the elements of the crime, including the mental element (i.e. the *mens rea*). In *Woolmington*, the accused was charged with murdering his estranged wife. He admitted shooting her, but claimed that he had shot her by accident. The trial judge directed the jury that, once it was established that the victim had died as a result of the accused's act, the defence bore the burden of proving that it was an accident rather than an intentional killing. The House of Lords held this to be a misdirection. In the words of Viscount Sankey:

> While the prosecution must prove the guilt of the prisoner, there is no … burden laid on the prisoner to prove his innocence and it is sufficient for him to raise a doubt as to his guilt. Throughout the web of English criminal law one golden thread is always to be

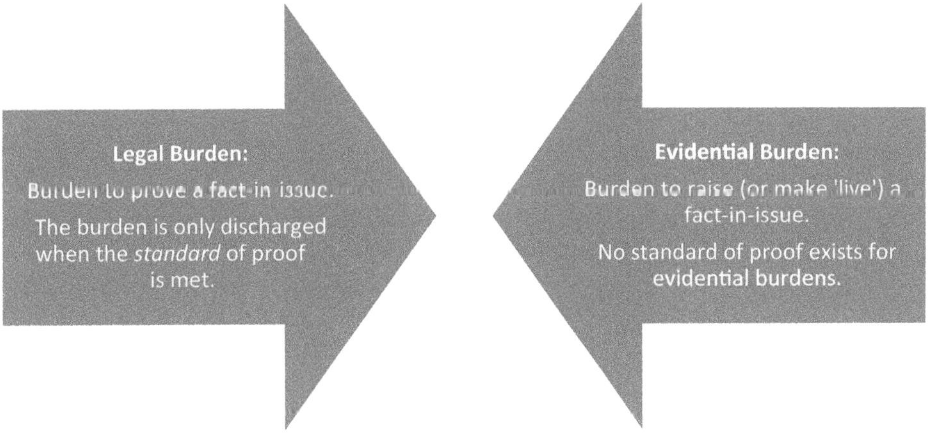

Figure 3.1 Legal and evidential burdens

---

1 For a theoretical discussion of the issues discussed along Keynesian lines, see Nance, D., *The Burdens of Proof: Discriminatory Power, Weight of Evidence, and Tenacity of Belief* (Cambridge University Press, 2016).

2 [1935] AC 462.

> seen, that it is the duty of the prosecution to prove the prisoner's guilt subject to the defence of insanity and subject also to any statutory exception ... No matter what the charge or where the trial, the principle that the prosecution must prove the guilt of the prisoner is part of the common law of England (and Wales) and no attempt to whittle it down can be entertained.[3]

It was this decision in 1935 that first clearly established the so-called golden thread of English criminal law: the principle that it is for the prosecution to prove the defendant's guilt. As the House of Lords proceeded to state, this rule was subject only to the common law exception of insanity and any statutory exception created by Parliament (see Section 3.2).

Thus, the expression 'burden of proof' properly describes the legal (also known as persuasive[4] or probative[5]) burden, that being the obligation on the prosecution to prove all of the facts necessary to establish the defendant's guilt. However, the term is also (incorrectly) used to describe the evidential burden – the obligation upon either the prosecution or the defence to produce sufficient evidence to establish the facts. It is perhaps more accurate to describe this duty as the 'burden of adducing evidence.' The importance of distinguishing between the two forms of burden cannot be overestimated.[6]

So far as the prosecution is concerned, the legal and evidential burdens are two sides of the same coin – without adducing sufficient evidence of the facts of the offence, they would not be able to discharge their legal burden. If the prosecution adduces sufficient evidence to establish a *prima facie* case, the defence may then respond by calling its own witnesses. Nevertheless, it should be noted that the defence do not have to *disprove* the prosecution case (although they may seek to do so). It is sufficient for counsel to raise a reasonable doubt in the minds of the factfinder. The defence may take the chance that the prosecution case will not satisfy the jury beyond reasonable doubt and decide not to call any evidence. However, it will be apparent that such a strategy is *replete with risk*, so, in the majority of cases, the defence will challenge the evidence of the prosecution by calling its own witnesses as well as the accused in person. On occasion, the evidence on which the defence proposes to rely to discharge the evidential burden may emanate from the prosecution's case. Such a scenario could, for example, arise where a prosecution witness has given evidence of the victim attacking the defendant and the defendant then retaliating. This would generally be considered good grounds on which to put the issue of self-defence to the court. The prosecution will then bear the legal burden of disproving the defence beyond reasonable doubt.[7]

Self-defence is just one example of a defence that will impose an evidential burden on the accused. Others include non-insane automatism,[8] intoxication,[9] duress,[10] diminished responsibility,[11] and loss of self-control.[12] Professor Glanville Williams[13] remarked that the imposition of an evidential burden on the defence is twofold in its purpose; firstly, to save the prosecution

3 Ibid., at 481.
4 Williams, G., *Criminal Law: The General Part*, 2nd edn (1961) [289].
5 *DPP v Morgan* [1976] A.C. 182 HL.
6 See Lord Hope's comments in *R v DPP, ex p Kebilene* [2000] 2 AC 326. For a discussion of the rationale for the presumption of innocence, see Stumer, A., *The Presumption of Innocence* (Hart Publishing, 2010), especially Chs 1 and 5.
7 *R v Lobell* [1957] 1 QB 547.
8 *Bratty v Attorney-General for Northern Ireland* [1963] AC 386.
9 *R v Foote* [1964] Crim LR 405.
10 *R v Gill* (1963) 47 Cr App R 166.
11 Homicide Act 1957, s 2(2).
12 *Mancini v DPP* [1942] AC 1.
13 Williams, G., op. cit., n. 4.

the trouble of meeting a defence that wasn't raised and secondly, to force the defence to the witness box to give evidence if he wishes to deny a state of mind. In practical terms, this will usually mean that the defendant must give evidence himself or call witnesses to substantiate any defence raised. A failure to do so will result in the prosecution's case being uncontested. Indeed, if the prosecution has presented strong arguments and there is no good reason why the accused should not give evidence, the jury will probably draw a common-sense inference that the defence has no answer, or no good answer, to the prosecution's case. Thus, a practical consequence of such an evidential burden is likely to be that the defendant is compelled to go into the witness box and give evidence of the defence, since the jury may be likely to convict in the absence of such testimony.[14]

It should be noted that there are circumstances in which the accused may raise a particular defence that is potentially inconsistent with another that they choose to run concurrently.

Example 3.1

Assume that Kim is charged with the murder of her boyfriend, Rodney. She claims Rodney verbally abused her for a period of hours before physically attacking her. She then admits having stabbed him with a kitchen knife. The best defence for Kim may be self-defence, which, if it succeeds, will result in an acquittal. Alternatively, she may be able to argue loss of self-control. In either case, she will bear an evidential burden and the prosecution will bear a legal burden to disprove the defences. However, a key difference is that loss of self-control essentially amounts to a guilty plea to manslaughter, and would also potentially undermine her argument of self-defence. If, however, there is sufficient evidence of loss of self-control, the judge is under a duty to put that defence to the jury alongside any other defence – even where defence counsel has not raised it.[15] Since the defence must disclose their defence(s) to the prosecution before trial,[16] the prosecution will be aware of the possibility of potentially contradictory defences being put to the jury, and may use this information to highlight potential inconsistencies in an effort to show that neither defence will apply.

As explained below, there is one common law provision (insanity), as well as many statutory provisions, that place the legal burden of proving a defence on the accused. In such cases, the accused stands to be convicted if the defence fails to convince the jury on the balance of probabilities. Previously, when faced with a statutory provision that placed a reverse legal burden on the accused, the courts had to accept that this was the will of Parliament and apply the law, no matter how unfair it may have seemed. However, since the Human Rights Act 1998 took effect in October 2000, courts may now declare any reverse burden to be incompatible with the European Convention on Human Rights, or, relying on section 3, interpret the statutory provision so as to avoid any incompatibility. As we shall see below, this provision has been relied on in the appellate courts to 'read down' legislation that imposes a reverse legal burden of proof on the defendant.

14 As noted in Ch 7, under s 35 of the Criminal Justice and Public Order Act 1994, the trial judge may direct the jury that they may draw 'such inferences as appear proper' from the failure of the accused to give evidence. An accused who adopts this approach clearly runs the risk that the jury will in fact convict them. This is often referred to as a 'tactical burden' on the accused. See further Roberts, P. and Zuckerman, A., *Criminal Evidence* (Oxford University Press, 2010), p. 230. See also *R v Zafar* [2008] QB 810, [2008] EWCA Crim 184; *Grayson v UK* (2009) 48 EHRR 30.

15 See Doran, S., 'Alternative Defences: The "Invisible Burden" on the Trial Judge' [1991] Crim LR 878; and *R v Watson* [1992] Crim LR 434.

16 Disclosure obligations for both parties are contained in the Criminal Procedure and Investigations Act 1996 (as amended by the Criminal Justice Act 2003).

Thus, the word 'prove' is interpreted as requiring the defendant to adduce sufficient evidence to make it an issue that the prosecution must disprove (i.e. an evidential burden) rather than imposing a requirement on the defendant to prove the issue on the balance of probabilities (i.e. a legal burden). Following the readiness of the courts to adopt this strategy, Parliament seems to be increasingly accepting the fact that reverse legal burdens are not always necessary. For example, section 118 of the Terrorism Act 2000 expressly converts a number of reverse burdens contained in various provisions of the Act to evidential burdens.

3.2 Criminal trials: tarnishing the thread – exceptions to *Woolmington*

Despite their Lordships' proclamation in *Woolmington v DPP*[17] that no whittling down of the principle should be entertained, there has been a significant tarnishing of the golden thread in the years since this decision. For the most part, this has been brought about by an increasing number of express statutory provisions reversing the burden of proof or creating presumptions against the defence. While the House of Lords accepted that Parliament had the power to reverse the burden of proof, their Lordships cannot have anticipated that departures from the golden thread would be so commonplace in the early years of the twenty-first century. Where Parliament intends that the accused will bear the full legal burden, this will normally be stipulated clearly in the relevant legislation. Problems tend to arise on those occasions on which the intended construction of the statute is less clear, thereby charging the courts with the task of ascertaining the legislature's intentions. Certainly, it would have been open to the courts to uphold the fundamental nature of the principle in *Woolmington* by refusing to accept any displacement of it without a clearly expressed statutory provision. However, in *R v Hunt*,[18] the House of Lords accepted that the fundamental principle can also be displaced by implication, as well as by an express statutory provision.

Before examining the reversal of the burden of proof by statute in detail, we first turn to those circumstances in which the common law places the burden on the defence.

3.2.1 Criminal trials: common law exceptions

During the eighteenth and nineteenth centuries, it was generally accepted that, in trials on indictment, it was for the prosecution to prove guilt beyond reasonable doubt. However, in practice, juries were often offered vastly different judicial directions on this point. For example, Chitty's *Practical Treatise on Criminal Law*, first published in 1816,[19] stated that the direction ought to be that the jury should convict if guilt were proved (or clearly proved) to their (complete) satisfaction, or if they believed the prosecution witnesses.[20] Despite this straightforward indication that the burden of proof fell on the prosecution, there was a growing body of opinion that such a burden did not include a duty to disprove defences raised by the accused at trial. Both jurists and judges appeared open to the suggestion that the burden of proving defences was on the accused. A body of case law developed in which the legal burden of disproving defences fell on the accused in relation to defences such as duress or self-defence. In cases of murder, it was accepted that once the prosecution had proved that the accused had killed the victim, the burden was then on the accused to establish that the case was not one of murder by proving that the killing was an accident or was in self-defence (or was manslaughter due to a loss of self-control or lack of an intent to kill). It

17 [1935] AC 462.

18 [1987] AC 352. See also *DPP v Wright* [2009] EWHC 105, a case involving the Hunting Act 2004, s 1.

19 Chitty, J., *A Practical Treatise on Criminal Law*, Vol. 1 (Valpy, 1816).

20 For a discussion on cases which have multiple components of a defence, see *R v Moore* [1992] Crim LR 882.

followed that, throughout the greater part of the nineteenth century, the rule that the prosecution bore the burden of proof referred only to the prosecution's duty to prove that the act alleged to be criminal had been committed by the accused – which in modern times is described as the *actus reus*. The law on proving the mental element (*mens rea*) required in major crimes such as murder had yet to be clarified. In murder cases, the law presumed malice aforethought[21] from the fact of killing, but it is clear that the prosecution was not required to prove an intention to kill; rather, it was for the accused to prove a lack of such an intention.[22]

Over time, the common law gradually modified its position, and by the time *Woolmington* came before the House of Lords, insanity was the only defence that the accused was required to prove at common law. This had been clear law since *Arnold's Case*,[23] and was confirmed by the decision in *M'Naghten's Case*,[24] which remains the leading authority on insanity in English criminal law. Today, the defence of insanity remains the sole common law exception to the principle that the prosecution shoulder the legal burden of proof. As with the other circumstances in which the burden is reversed, the defence must prove insanity on the balance of probabilities, as opposed to 'beyond reasonable doubt' (see Section 3.6).

3.2.2 Criminal trials: express statutory reversal

With the exception of the defence of insanity, which was expressly excluded from the scope of the rule by Lord Sankey L.C., the golden thread established in *Woolmington* thus remains intact at common law and the burden is on the prosecution to prove guilt. However, Lord Sankey L.C. also recognised that constitutionally, the courts must accept the will of Parliament, and also excluded "any statutory exception"[25] from the general rule, as where the legislature clearly places the burden of proof on the defence, the courts cannot override the sovereignty of Parliament by disapplying a statute. There is generally less concern about the placing of burdens on the defendant when the offence is triable only as a summary offence.[26] It follows that Parliament is more ready to reverse the burden of proof in such cases.[27] Such offences are often regulatory offences, and generally the courts have had little difficulty in determining the reverse legal burden to be justifiable in these circumstances.[28]

Parliamentary draftsmen use a number of different mechanisms to reverse the burden of proof. In most cases, the legislation will stipulate quite clearly that the defence must prove certain circumstances to be in existence in order to make use of an available defence.[29] Another common device is to include a presumption of fact or law that the court must accept as proved unless the defence rebut that presumption. Take, for example, how the burden of proof is framed in relation to driving with excess alcohol. The proportion of alcohol in a person's body will depend on a number of factors: most importantly, when they last consumed alcohol. If a driver has recently

21 Until the enactment of the Criminal Justice Act 1967, s 8.

22 Cross and Tapper note that at this juncture of loss of control defence, since the passing of the Human Rights Act 1998, this defence has been made into an explicit evidential burden on the defendant. See Coroners and Justice Act 2009, S54(6). This provision is perhaps unusually detailed. Compare the sparer formula in Sexual Offences Act 2003, S75(2).

23 (1724) 16 St Tr 694, 764.

24 (1840) 10 Cl & Fin 200.

25 *Woolmington* [1935] A.C. 462

26 That is, where the offence is considered to be minor and punishable by a fine and no more than 6 months' imprisonment for a single offence or 12 months for two or more either-way offences.

27 See Prevention of Crime Act 1953, s 1; Criminal Justice Act 1988, ss 139 and 141; Criminal Justice and Public Order Act 1994, s 69; Health and Safety at Work Act 1974, s 40; and Insolvency Act 1986, s 206(1).

28 *L v DPP* [2002] Crim LR 320; *R v Alleyne* [2004] QB 69.

29 For example, the Criminal Justice Act 1988, s 139(4) provides a defence for an accused charged with possession of a bladed weapon in a public place if they can establish some 'lawful authority or reasonable excuse' for being in possession of the offensive article.

consumed alcohol, the amount in the bloodstream will be rising steadily as the body absorbs it. On occasions, this can work in the driver's favour since a breath sample or blood sample may not show excess amounts before all of the alcohol has been absorbed. There will also come a point at which the body ceases to absorb the alcohol and starts to destroy it. Some drivers, when they fail a breath test and are later required to provide a specimen of blood or urine at the police station, seek to take advantage of this process by delaying the taking of a sample until a time when they believe their body has destroyed enough alcohol to return a legal sample. Alternatively, the driver may claim that the sample (which shows an illegal amount of alcohol) taken an hour or more after they had ceased to drive did not reflect the lower, legal amount that it was when they were driving. In order to counteract these possibilities (and suggestions of post-offence consumption of alcohol), the statute provides for back-calculation to establish the blood alcohol level at the time of the offence. Section 15(2) of the Road Traffic Offenders Act 1988, as amended by the Road Traffic Act 1991, provides:

> Evidence of the proportion of alcohol or any drug in a specimen of breath, blood, or urine provided by the accused shall, in all cases ... be taken into account and ... it shall be assumed that the proportion of alcohol in the accused's breath, blood or urine at the time of the alleged offence was not less than the specimen.

This section goes further than simply placing the legal burden of proof on the defendant. It is, in effect, an irrebuttable presumption that the proportion of alcohol in the defendant's blood at the time of the offence was not less than that shown in the specimen. The presumption will not apply if the accused proves that they consumed alcohol before the specimen was provided, but after they ceased to drive, attempted to drive, or were in charge of the vehicle.[30] However, there is no opportunity to rebut the presumption by proving that the proportion of alcohol in the blood was less than that shown by the analysis.

The absence of such an opportunity to prove that the blood alcohol level at the time of the offence was in fact less than shown by the specimen was subject to challenge under the Human Rights Act 1998 in *Parker v DPP*.[31] The defendant failed a roadside breath test and, roughly one hour later, provided a specimen of blood that exceeded the prescribed proportion of alcohol. He was convicted of driving with excess alcohol, and appealed, arguing that the presumption contained in section 15(2) was incompatible with Article 6(2) of the European Convention on Human Rights. Dismissing the appeal, Waller LJ rejected the contention that the only way in which the provision could be valid would be if words were read into the section to the effect that the assumption would not be made 'unless proved to the contrary.' In the view of the court, since it was the alcohol consumption prior to driving at which the offence was aimed, it did not tarnish the presumption of innocence to assume that the quantity of alcohol in the sample taken at the police station was the quantity that the motorist had in his blood at the material time. Even if that were taking it too far, having regard to the importance of what is at stake – pedestrians' and other motorists' lives – the presumption was a reasonable one and, in the view of the court, this did not amount to an infringement of Convention rights.

Section 15(3) of the Road Traffic Offenders Act 1988 prevents the presumption in subsection (2) from operating if the accused proves that they consumed alcohol before they gave the specimen and after they had ceased to drive, attempted to drive, or were in charge of a motor vehicle. This was the subject of the appeal in *R v Drummond*.[32] D had driven into a scooter, killing the pas-

30 Road Traffic Offenders Act 1988, s 15(3).
31 [2001] RTR 240.
32 [2002] RTR 21.

senger and seriously injuring the driver. D admitted that he had been aware that his car had struck something on the road, but that, seeing nothing else around, he had driven on. In his defence, D stated that he was in a state of shock when he arrived home and saw the extent of the damage to his car. He claimed his wife had given him two measures of gin to calm him down, which explained why he provided two positive samples of breath shortly after his arrest. He was convicted of causing death by careless driving, and appealed, arguing that the stipulation in section 15(2) that he should prove that he had consumed the alcohol after the alleged incident constituted a violation of the presumption of innocence under the Human Rights Act 1998. In the view of the Court of Appeal, the statutory reversal of the presumption of innocence was wholly justifiable, and was no greater than necessary to minimise the social evil of drink-driving.

Similar facts were present in *Sheldrake v DPP*.[33] Here, the defendant was found to be over the alcohol limit in his car in a public place, but later claimed that he had been trying to get a lift from a friend. Section 5(2) of the Road Traffic Act 1988 affords a potential defence if it can be proved that, at the time of the alleged offence, the circumstances were such that there was no likelihood of the motorist driving the vehicle while they remained above the prescribed limit. It was held that this placed the legal or persuasive burden of proof on the defendant. In this case, having failed to persuade the court on the balance of probabilities that there was no likelihood of him driving while over the limit, the defendant was convicted.

The Divisional Court allowed the appellant's appeal by a majority of 2:1. Clarke LJ stated two clear points. First, the prosecution had failed to show that it was necessary to impose a legal burden on the accused; second, the prosecution had been unsuccessful in showing that there was no likelihood of the defendant driving while over the limit. To do so would be disproportionate. Thus, the court held that section 5(2) of the 1988 Act should be read down under the Human Rights Act 1998 so as to impose an evidential burden only.

However, a different view was taken by the House of Lords. Assuming that the section infringed the presumption of innocence and that it was directed to a legitimate object – the prevention of death, injury, and damage caused by unfit drivers – Lord Bingham asked whether the provision met the test of acceptability identified in the Strasbourg jurisprudence.[34] Accepting that it plainly did, he went on to state that he did 'not regard the burden placed on the defendant as beyond reasonable limits or in any way arbitrary.' He also concluded that it was not 'objectionable to criminalise a defendant's conduct in the circumstances without requiring a prosecutor to prove a criminal intent.' This was on the basis that:

> the defendant has a full opportunity to show that there was no likelihood of his driving, a matter so closely conditioned by his own knowledge and state of mind at the material time as to make it more appropriate for him to prove on the balance of probabilities that he would not have been likely to drive than for the prosecutor to prove, beyond reasonable doubt, that he would.[35]

In their Lordships' opinion, the imposition of a legal burden did not go beyond what was necessary and it was not unfair to the defendant, given the legitimate object of the legislation of protecting society from the very real dangers of driving with excess alcohol. *Sheldrake* is a good example of a case where neither the form of drafting, nor seriousness of the offence charged, nor the maximum penalty, is to determine the justifiability of allocating a persuasive burden to the

33 [2005] 1 AC 264; see also *DPP v Wright (Anthony)* [2009] 3 All ER 726, at 234. In *Wright*, the court read down a provision relating to an offence of unlawful hunting.

34 See discussion below.

35 *Sheldrake*, op. cit., n. 33, at [41].

accused. From Lord Bingham's comments in *Sheldrake*,[36] and his subsequent disapproval in *Attorney General's Reference (No. 4 of 2002)*,[37] it suggests that it is for the judge to determine where, if so, a persuasive burden lies, apart from the considerations discussed above. Unfortunately, not all statutes are clearly expressed, and it may be unclear in some cases who should shoulder the burden. Some statutes contain provisions in which the burden of proof is clearly placed on either the prosecution or defence, while others are silent on the matter. For example, *Polychronakis v Richards and Jerrom Ltd*[38] highlighted an apparent ambiguity in section 80(1) of the Environmental Protection Act 1990. The legislation contained two subsections that clearly imposed the legal burden of proving a specified defence on the accused. However, a third subsection provided for a defence of reasonable excuse, without specifying whether the prosecution should prove the absence, or the defence the presence, of that excuse. The magistrates' court imposed the burden upon the accused. On appeal, the Divisional Court held that it had been wrong to do so, and stated that, in such circumstances, the court must interpret the statute or section and endeavour to determine whether Parliament intended to place the legal burden of proof on the prosecution or the defence.[39] In this particular instance, it was held that, once the defendant had laid the proper evidential basis for the contention of a reasonable excuse, it was for the prosecution to satisfy the court to the criminal standard of proof that the excuse was not a reasonable one. How the persuasive, evidential, tactical, and ultimate burdens interact with one another was illustrated in the civil case of *Ratford v Northavon District Council*,[40] where in proceedings of non-payment, the district council authority bore both the evidential and persuasive burdens of showing the rate had been made. In this case, the adduced evidence showed that they had not taken possession of the relevant premises, therefore raising the evidential burden upon that issue satisfied, where Cross and Tapper comment that this was when the burden shifted in a tactical sense.

In criminal cases, it is also tactically common for issues to arise where evidence is equivocal between the two defendants who are co-accused, and both allege that the crime was committed by the other, a so-called 'cut-throat defence,' where then both must normally be acquitted, even in instances where it is *prima facie* clear the crime must have been committed by one or the other of them. See, for instance, *R v Banfield and Banfield* [2013][41] for a judicial consideration of this tactical issue.

3.2.3 Criminal trials: implied statutory exceptions

It might be expected that, for a statutory displacement of the fundamental presumption of innocence to arise, there would be an express provision within the legislation stipulating that the prosecution must prove all aspects of the offence. However, this has rarely been the case, meaning that it is frequently left to the courts to ascertain Parliament's intentions.

When considering the intersection between the presumption of innocence and the burden of proof, it is important to frame this relationship in the context of a criminal trial, and to ask if there are alternative ways of understanding the presumption of innocence that might offer a different view of understanding fairness in the criminal process. Farmer articulates that *Woolmington* led towards the developing distinction between probative and evidential burdens of proof when the

---

36 Ibid., n. 33, at [41].

37 [2003] EWCA Crim 762, [2003] 3 WLR 1153.

38 [1998] Env LR 346.

39 However, as we shall see below, parliamentary intention is no longer sufficient in itself to justify a reverse legal burden. Under the Strasbourg jurisprudence, any such reverse burden must be justifiable and proportionate to the particular mischief that the statute seeks to counter.

40 [1981] QB 357.

41 *R v Banfield and Banfield* [2013] EWCA Crim 1394.

House of Lords held that in murder offences, malice cannot be presumed, and the burden of proof always rests on the prosecution. This 'hardening distinction' can essentially be categorically understood as the distinction between fact and law, offences and defences, and evidence and procedure. Understanding the distinction that arose from the golden thread in *Woolmington* in this manner might be useful when considering the wider implications of this distinction as the criminal law moves towards an 'inculpatory model.' Propounding support for this inculpatory model of criminal evidence and proceedings, Glanville Williams even referred to the *Woolmington* principle as 'hearsay.' Farmer frames this 'inculpatory model' as being linked to the idea of subjective responsibility within the presumption of innocence and argues that this would mean that the presumption acts as the nexus between criminal procedural fairness and individual responsibility when thinking of the substantive criminal law.

Therefore, it could be valuable to contextualize the entire discussion surrounding the burden of proof within the context of the institutional advancements previously addressed. It's crucial to recognize that the evolution of the law of evidence has been a gradual process, originating in the nineteenth century with the eventual establishment of presumptions. This evolution progressed incrementally, shaping the overarching concept of a probative burden, and leading to the delineation of various standards of proof, especially in situations where courts relied on circumstantial evidence. Therefore, looking at the burden of proof holistically within its historical significance, and the evolution of its rules and values that made up the foundations of the modern presumption of innocence. Therefore, a firm understanding of the burden of proof within criminal proceedings requires a holistic comprehension of the elements that underpin the modern-day legal principles. It should even be said that the focus on innocence acting as a normative core of the right to a fair trial produces a narrative of fairness within criminal trials which 'share an almost instinctive orientation that rests on the belief that the most serious threat to justice is that innocence will be targeted.'

3.2.3.1 Criminal trials: summary offences

As Parliament grew in strength during the eighteenth and nineteenth centuries, it began to create a new range of statutory offences. Many of these were comparatively minor in nature and were triable as summary offences in magistrates' courts. In the middle of the nineteenth century, Parliament sought to bring the trial of summary offences into line with the trial of indictable offences by passing the Summary Jurisdiction Act 1848. This Act required that where the defendant relied in their defence upon any exemption, proviso, excuse, or qualification, then it was for them to prove that they came within any such exception. After the statute took effect, the common law and statute law proceeded on a parallel course, with both modes of trial placing the burden on the defendant to prove any defence relied upon in the nature of an excuse (such as accident or self-defence) in relation to indictable offences, or that the defendant fell within any exception, exemption, etc. in relation to summary offences. The 1848 legislation has been re-enacted over the years, and the equivalent provision is today contained within section 101 of the Magistrates' Courts Act 1980. As the title of the legislation suggests, the provision applies only to magistrates' courts, meaning that it covers only summary offences or 'either way' offences that are tried summarily. However, it should be noted that as of 2022, there is still little comparative authority on the construction of this section.[42] Section 101 states:

> Where the defendant to an information or complaint relies for his defence on an exception, exemption, proviso, excuse or qualification whether or not it accompanies the description of the offence or matter of complaint in the enactment creating the offence or on which the

---

42 Cross and Tapper (2018) comment that a claim of right was held to fall outside S101's New Zealand equivalent in *R v Gorrie* [2008] 3 NZLR 620.

complaint is founded, the burden of proving the exception, exemption, proviso, excuse or qualification shall be on him and this notwithstanding that the information or complaint contains an allegation negativing the exception, etc.

There are numerous examples of statutes expressly worded so as to render a certain act an offence unless done by someone licensed or qualified to do the act, or if done without lawful authority or excuse. For example:

- driving a motor vehicle without being the holder of a licence to drive;[43]
- selling intoxicating liquor without a licence;[44]
- possessing a firearm without a licence;[45]
- possessing certain drugs without a doctor's certificate;[46]
- delivering a child while not being a qualified midwife;[47]
- practising medicine when unqualified;
- obstructing the highway without lawful authority or excuse;[48]
- possessing forged currency without lawful authority or excuse;[49]

and many more besides. These are all offences that fall within the scope of section 101, thereby placing the burden of proof on the accused.

In *Gatland v Metropolitan Police Commissioner*[50] and *Nimmo v Alexander Cowan Ltd*,[51] it was held that the defendant in cases to which section 101 applies bears the legal burden of proving that they come within the exception, proviso, excuse, or qualification upon which they rely, and not simply the evidential burden to the same effect. Thus, it is not sufficient to produce some evidence of a defence and leave it to the prosecution to rebut it, as may be done with specific defences such as self-defence, duress, or an alibi. Instead, defence counsel must prove that the relevant exception applies, but need only do so on the balance of probabilities. It was argued in *Nimmo* that such a reversal of the burden appears logical since the defendant would be in a better position to discharge it. In *Nimmo*, Lord Pearson considered that, while exceptions, exemptions, and provisos would be easily recognisable with words such as 'except,' 'provided always,' in the Factories Act 1961, the words 'excuses or qualifications' indicate that the courts should read the law on substance rather than form.[52] From the outset, this consideration blatantly contradicts Viscount Sankey's golden thread; it will be recalled that, in *Woolmington*, the House of Lords referred specifically to the fact that the fundamental principle would apply 'no matter what the charge or where the trial.' However, since Parliament is supreme, the fundamental principle must give way to any statutory reversal. Lord Sankey's Principle was once again considered regarding section 54(5) of the Coroners and Justice Act 2009, in the case of *R v Dawes (Carlos)*,[53] on the defence of loss of control and where the burden of adducing sufficient evidence to raise an issue with respect to the defence was considered.

---

43 Road Traffic Act 1988, s 87.
44 Licensing Act 2003, s 136.
45 Firearms Act 1968, s 1.
46 Misuse of Drugs Act 1971.
47 Midwives Act 1902; repealed and replaced by the Midwives Act 1951.
48 Highways Act 1980, s 137.
49 Forgery and Counterfeiting Act 1981, s 16.
50 [1968] 2 QB 279.
51 [1968] AC 107.
52 See Zuckerman's analysis on Nimmo in Zuckerman (1976) 92 LQR 402.
53 *R v Dawes (Carlos)* [2013] EWCA 322, [2014] 1 WLR 947.

When this type of case comes to court, the magistrates must first analyse the statute in question in order to determine whether section 101 applies. Naturally, the defence will frequently deny that it does and claim that the prosecution bears the entire legal burden. Section 101 distinguishes between 'the description of the offence' and 'any exception.' Any matter that is part of the description of the offence must be proved by the prosecution; it is only with regard to exceptions, provisos, excuses, or qualifications that the onus of proof is on the defendant.

While there is no doubt that such provisions significantly whittle down the presumption of innocence, it is unlikely that they will be found to be in breach of Article 6(2) of the European Convention on Human Rights (ECHR). In *Salabiaku v France*,[54] the European Court of Human Rights accepted that all of the Convention States make use of reverse burdens and presumptions. Such burdens were not contrary to the Convention per se, provided that they were confined within 'reasonable limits,' and framed in such a way as to take into account the importance of what is at stake, while maintaining the rights of the defendant. Given that a summary conviction is punishable by way of a fine or a sentence of imprisonment not exceeding six months, or 12 months for multiple either-way offences, the offence is not usually seen as so serious as to prevent the burden being reversed. On the one hand, many such reversals are regulatory offences passed for the protection of society, which tends to justify the imposition of a reverse burden.[55] On the other hand, some commentators view such offences as stretching beyond the traditional remit of the criminal law, and have called for them to be decriminalised. As Padfield suggests, the time has come for 'a category of administrative regulations which would carry little stigma and no possibility of imprisonment. Only for such "non-crimes" should strict liability or reverse burdens be acceptable.'[56] Drawing the point back to the idea that the presumption of innocence can be construed in either a 'narrow' or 'wide' fashion (in Section 3.3), this brings interesting implications for thinking about how this applies to reverse burdens. Owusu-Bempah contends that reverse burdens of proof cannot be reconciled with the 'narrow' interpretation of the presumption of innocence, arguing that the imposition of a legal burden of proof on the defence creates a participatory requirement, where the defence is required to actively participate in the trial proceedings to actively discharge the burden, by way of raising arguments and adducing the appropriate evidence. Therefore, placing this form of participatory requirement on the defendant contradicts both the narrow and wide view of the presumption of innocence and throws fairness concerns within fact-finding eventual procedures into sharp regard.

3.2.3.2 Criminal trials: indictable offences

Although section 101 of the Magistrates' Courts Act 1980 applies only to summary proceedings, in *R v Edwards*, the Court of Appeal enunciated an almost identical principle that applies to trials on indictment.[57] In the view of the Court of Appeal, the forerunner to section 101 was simply a codification of an older common law rule. This was deduced from the fact that the origins of the provision are to be found in section 14 of the Summary Jurisdiction Act 1848, which stated: 'It shall not be necessary for the prosecutor or complainant in that behalf to prove a negative, but the defendant may prove the affirmative thereof in his defence, if he would have advantage of the same.' In passing this legislation, Parliament was doing no more than putting into statutory form an old common law rule, which, as we have seen, was applied by the trial court and the Court of Appeal in *Woolmington* (although later overruled by the House of Lords). Since the majority of offences were statutory in nature, the Court of Appeal saw no reason why the rule in what is now

54 (1991) 13 EHRR 379.

55 See e.g. the discussion of Road Traffic Offenders Act 1988, ss 15(2)–(3), above.

56 Padfield, N., 'The Burden of Proof Unresolved' (2005) 64 *Cambridge Law Journal* 17.

57 [1975] QB 27.

section 101 of the Magistrates' Court Act 1980 should not be applied by the common law so that indictable and summary offences would be treated alike. After all, there appeared to be no sound rationale as to why an 'either-way' offence should be tried according to different rules depending on whether it was tried summarily or on indictment.

In *Edwards* itself, the defendant was convicted of selling alcohol without a justice's licence under section 160 of the Licensing Act 1964.[58] The prosecution called no evidence that the appellant did not hold a justice's licence, leaving him to show, if he could, that he did possess one. The conviction was upheld by the Divisional Court and by the Court of Appeal. In the words of Lawton LJ:

> In our judgment this line of authority establishes that over the centuries the common law, as a result of experience and the need to ensure that justice is done both to the community and to defendants, has evolved an exception to the fundamental rule of our criminal law that the prosecution must prove every element of the offence charged. This exception, like so much else in the common law, was hammered out on the anvil of pleading. It is limited to offences arising under enactments which prohibit the doing of an act save in specified circumstances or by persons of specified classes or specified qualifications or with the licence or permission of specified authorities. Whenever the prosecution seeks to rely on this exception, the court must construe the enactment under which the charge is laid. If the true construction is that the enactment prohibits the doing of acts, subject to provisos, exemptions and the like, then the prosecution can rely upon the exception.[59]

Clearly, the Court of Appeal had taken into account the fact that it would have been just as easy for the defendant to produce evidence of the possession of a licence (if he had one) as for the prosecution to prove that he did not.[60] Such records are kept by clerks to the justices, and are readily available to anyone on request. However, the decision in *Edwards* is not limited to cases in which the defendant has peculiar knowledge, or one party can more easily prove the particular defence. Instead, it is based on the particular linguistic structure adopted within a piece of legislation. Where words or a phrase within a statute prohibit certain acts subject to provisos, exemptions, and the like, the defendant bears the legal burden of proving that proviso, exemption, etc. It follows from this that the Court of Appeal confined the decision of the House of Lords in *Woolmington* to common law offences, such as murder, and statutory offences that are not framed to prohibit the doing of acts subject to some form of exception. Those statutory offences that are framed to prohibit the doing of acts subject to a proviso or exemption are placed outside the fundamental principle expressed in that case.

The decision in *R v Edwards* received qualified approval by the House of Lords in *R v Hunt*.[61] The House of Lords, in *Hunt*, stated that Lawton LJ's statement was better regarded as merely a guide to a statute's construction rather than as an exception to the rule that the prosecution bear the burden of proof. Their Lordships laid down a subjective approach, stating that the question of whether the defendant bears a legal burden of proof should not always be determined by the wording of the particular statute. The words 'any statutory exception' in *Woolmington* were not confined to statutory exceptions in which the burden of proof was expressly placed on the defendant. A statute can do so expressly or impliedly on its true construction. Therefore, when the statute was not clear, it

58 Now a summary offence, but when *Edwards* was heard, it was triable on indictment.
59 *Edwards*, op. cit. n. 43, at 39–40.
60 See also Bayley J's comments in *R v Turner*, which Lawton LJ addressed in *Edwards*.
61 [1987] AC 352.

was a matter of construction, and a number of considerations then applied. Among the factors to be taken into account were:

- whether Parliament intended to place a heavy burden on the defendant;
- the nature of the mischief the legislation sought to resolve; and
- whether that mischief was serious in its nature.

Most importantly, their Lordships in *Hunt* declared that any ambiguities within the legislation should be resolved in favour of the accused.

The defendant in *Hunt* was charged with possession of a controlled drug, morphine, contrary to section 5(2) of the Misuse of Drugs Act 1971. A search of his house revealed a fold of paper containing morphine, which was mixed with caffeine and atropine (which were not controlled drugs). The prosecution called no evidence as to the proportion of morphine in the mixture. The defence submitted that there was no case to answer because Schedule 1 to the Misuse of Drugs Regulations 1973[62]provided that a preparation containing not more than 0.2 per cent morphine, which was not readily recoverable, did not fall within section 5. Since the prosecution had failed to prove that the amount of morphine in the mixture exceeded this volume, the defence argued that they had not proved that the mixture constituted a controlled drug for the purposes of the Act. The trial judge rejected this submission, and the accused was convicted.

On appeal, the court upheld this ruling on the ground that the defendant bore the burden of proving that the mixture fell within the exception provided by Schedule 1 to the 1973 Regulations. The House of Lords, however, overturned this decision, holding that the prosecution bore the burden of proving that the mixture did not come within the exception. Properly analysed, the offence consisted not of being in possession of morphine itself, but of being in possession of morphine other than a preparation specified in Schedule 1. The percentage of morphine was part of the description of the offence, not an exception to it. It followed that the prosecution had to prove that the levels of morphine within the mixture were above 0.2 per cent.

It is arguable that the courts, applying the common law, significantly failed to protect their own fundamental principle of the presumption of innocence by allowing its displacement by implication, rather than insisting on an express provision as the House of Lords did in *Hunt*. If the courts had seized the opportunity to insist on express provisions to reverse the burden, such a declaration would have had the effect of placing the responsibility of undermining such a fundamental right of its citizens squarely on the shoulders of Parliament. In turn, Parliament would then be under a duty to give reasons for imposing a reverse burden of proof on defendants in particular statutes. Instead, the courts conspired – wittingly or unwittingly – in the undermining of fundamental rights by using the smokescreen of an unspoken intention of Parliament to justify a reversal. This led to a loss of respect in the legislature for the presumption of innocence and meant that a potential buffer between the practical power of the State and the comparative weakness of the individual was considerably diminished.[63]

However, in contemporary practice, it is suggested that the decisions in *Edwards* and *Hunt* are now primarily of historical interest for three main reasons.[64] First, as Lord Griffiths himself stated in *Hunt*:

62 SI 1973/797, as amended by the Misuse of Drugs (Amendment) Regulations 1983 (SI 1983/788).

63 For a more detailed discussion on how the reasoning of the House of Lords in *Hunt* was scathingly critiqued by academic commentators, see *Davies v Health and Safety Executive* [2002] EWCA Crim 2949, [2003] ICR 586 [1].

64 For a discussion on how *Hunt*'s dictum has been applied, see *DPP v Wright* on the application of Schedule 1 of the Hunting Act 1999, and see *R v Clarke (Roy)* [2008] EWCA Crim 893 on the application of *Hunt* towards the Immigration and Asylum Act 1999, S84(2).

> the principle is limited ... I have little doubt that the occasions on which the statute will be construed as imposing a burden of proof on a defendant which do not fall within this formulation are likely to be exceedingly rare.[65]

Second, in the years since *Hunt*, the implied statutory reversals of indictable offences have become extremely rare, if not extinct. Almost all implied statutory reversals now concern comparatively minor offences, triable only in magistrates' courts. Even the offence of which *Edwards* was convicted today lies within the exclusive jurisdiction of the magistrates' court.

Third, the Human Rights Act 1998 (discussed in greater depth below) has significantly altered the way in which such reversals should be handled by the courts.[66] If there is a serious indictable offence that prohibits the doing of an act in specified circumstances – this covers, for example, persons of a specified class, those without specified qualifications, persons without a licence or permission from specified authorities – the court would be obliged to take into account an array of new factors, including the concept of proportionality under Article 6(2) of the Convention, and the post-Human Rights Act case law. Such factors are likely to operate in favour of the accused, and courts may be prepared to read down any implied reverse burden so that the defence will bear only an evidential burden.

3.3 The impact of the Human Rights Act 1998

The idea that the presumption of innocence can be thought of as either 'narrow' or 'wide,' as termed by Ashworth, is helpfully explained by Ho: the 'narrow' view of the presumption of innocence would be taking the view that the presumption should be confined to being a common law principle, but the 'wider' view of the presumption would view the presumption as a wider human rights principle which permeates through the entire criminal justice system. It should be noted, however, that while Ashworth's work supports the idea of wider integrity and human rights in evidence and procedure, he has been highly critical of attaching this wider integrity towards 'public attitude' in avoiding the criminal justice process adopting principles based on shifting public attitudes that may be contrary to fundamental human rights.[67]

More widely, incorporating an analysis of wider human rights is crucial for a holistic analysis of evidence and procedure, as Young[68] highlights using the case of *R v Sang*,[69] where prior to the rise of domestic human rights law as expounded above,[70] where it was held to effectively uphold the rule of law, wider accounts of integrity must be incorporated into the criminal procedure.

3.3.1 Article 6(2) of the European Convention on Human Rights

Article 6(2) of the ECHR mirrors the golden thread of *Woolmington* in providing that everyone charged with a criminal offence shall be presumed innocent until proved guilty according to law.

---

65 *Hunt*, op. cit. n. 46, at 375.

66 For an in-depth discussion on the application of the Human Rights Act 1998 on statutory reversed burdens specifically, see Tadros and Tierney (2004) 67 MLR 405; and Dennis [2005] LR 901. Cross and Tapper have also commented that similar statutory conundrums have arisen in various jurisdictions, although their relevance towards modern English law was marginalised in *Sheldrake* [2004] UKHL 42 [2005], 1 AC 264, [33] and [58].

67 Ashworth, A., 'Exploring the Integrity Principle in Evidence and Procedure,' in P. Mirfield and R. Smith (eds), *Essays for Colin Tapper* (Oxford University Press, 2003), 107, 108; Roberts, P. and Zuckerman, A., op. cit., n. 14, at 189, referring to 'the integrity of the administration of criminal justice.'

68 Young, S.N.M., 'A Public Law Conception of Integrity in the Criminal Process,' in J. Hunter, P. Roberts, S.N.M. Young, and D. Dixon (eds), *The Integrity of Criminal Process: From Theory into Practice* (Hart Publishing, 2016), pp. 36–52.

69 *R v Sang* [1980] AC 402.

70 See earlier development of an integrity-based public policy ground for exclusion in Australia: *R v Ireland* (1970) 126 CLR 321 (HC).

Importantly, the imposition of an evidential burden on the defence does not automatically render it incompatible with Article 6(2), as demonstrated in *R v Bianco*,[71] where the evidential burden to raise evidence of duress was 'not incompatible with Article 6.' Although there have been relatively few cases in which the Strasbourg organs have considered the principle, it did arise in *X v United Kingdom*.[72] Here, the Commission upheld the reverse burden formerly contained in section 30(2) of the Sexual Offences Act 1956.[73] Under this provision, any man who lived habitually with a prostitute, or who exercised control or influence over her movements in a way that showed that he was aiding and abetting or compelling her prostitution, would be presumed to be knowingly living on the earnings of prostitution unless he proved the contrary. The Commission held that, provided that the presumption was rebuttable and reasonable, it would not violate Article 6(2). It proceeded to emphasise, however, that where such a provision was widely or unreasonably worded, it could have the same effect as a presumption of guilt and would contravene the Convention.

The leading Strasbourg case is that of *Salabiaku v France*,[74] which concerned a provision of the French Criminal Code that placed the burden of proof squarely on the defendant to prove that he was not guilty of smuggling where he was found to be in possession of prohibited goods. In rejecting the complaint, the Court stated that:

> Presumptions of fact or law operate in every legal system. Clearly the Convention does not prohibit such presumptions in principle. It does, however, require the Contracting State to remain within certain limits in this respect as regards criminal law ... Article 6(2) does not, therefore, regard presumptions of law or fact with indifference. It requires States to confine them within the reasonable limits which take into account the importance of what is at stake and maintains the rights of the defence.[75]

The guidance in *Salabiaku* was applied in *H v United Kingdom*,[76] in which the Commission rejected the applicant's contention that the burden on the accused to prove insanity on the balance of probabilities in criminal proceedings was contrary to the presumption of innocence and therefore in violation of Article 6. Similarly, in *Bates v United Kingdom*,[77] the Court dismissed the applicant's argument that section 5(5) of the Dangerous Dogs Act 1991 contravened the Convention standards.[78] This provision creates a presumption that the dog is one to which the Act applies unless the contrary is shown by the defence.[79] Additionally, in *R v Foye*,[80] the Court of Appeal (Criminal Division) upheld the imposition of a persuasive burden in cases concerning the special partial defence of diminished responsibility, where placing a reverse burden on the defendant can be justified under Article 6 when it can be distinguished as involving the defendant proving entitlement to a statutory defence rather than a requirement for the defendant to discharge a persuasive burden in relation to an element of the criminal offence charged.

---

71 [2001] EWCA Crim 2516, [15].

72 App. No. 5124/71 (23 March 1972).

73 Now the Sexual Offences Act 2003, s 52.

74 (1991) 13 EHRR 379.

75 Ibid., at [28].

76 App. No. 15023/89 (4 April 1990).

77 App. No. 26280/95 (16 January 1996).

78 For a discussion on the vestigial nature of the burden put on the defence, see the Court of Appeal's judgment in *R v S* (trade mark defence) [2002] EWCA Crim 2558, [2003] 1 Cr App Rep 35, 220.

79 See also *R v Drummond* [2002] EWCA Crim 527, [2002], 2 Cr App Rep 25, [35], where the Court of Appeal decided whether evidential burdens could be discharged by producing very specific pieces of evidence, and the implications this has for wider persuasive and evidential burdens.

80 *R v Foye (Lee)* [2013] EWCA Crim 475, (2013), 177 JP 449.

In an important series of decisions, the European Court of Human Rights has now held that the protections guaranteed under Article 6(2) extend to the protection of individuals charged with or even suspected of a crime. Within wider academic literature, some scholars have argued that these protections should not only be confined to the trial process itself, but also the pre-trial and post-arrest procedures, as well as the treatment of defendants during the post-sentencing phase. Therefore, it is widely believed that the presumption of innocence has thus become central to a firm understanding of how state power should be limited in the pursuit of criminal justice.

3.3.2 The Prevention of Terrorism (Temporary Provisions) Act 1989 (now repealed)

Even before the Human Rights Act 1998 took effect, the Convention standards had begun to infiltrate decision-making processes in the domestic courts. In *R v DPP, ex p Kebilene and Others,*[81] three Algerians were prosecuted for offences under sections 16A and 16B of the Prevention of Terrorism (Temporary Provisions) Act 1989.[82] These provisions created the offences of 'possession of articles for the purposes of terrorism' and of 'collecting or recording information for such a purpose.' In both cases, the burden of proof was placed clearly and unequivocally on the defendant. Section 16A stipulated that the accused would have to prove that the possession of the articles was not for the purposes of terrorism, or else that he was not in possession of those articles; similarly, in relation to the offence under section 16B, the defendant had to prove that he had a reasonable excuse for collecting or recording the information.

At the close of the prosecution case, the defence obtained a ruling that the sections were incompatible with Article 6(2) of the European Convention on Human Rights. The Director of Public Prosecutions (DPP), whose consent was required before a prosecution could be undertaken, appeared before the trial judge to argue that the judge's ruling was wrong. The trial judge maintained his position and the case was appealed to the Divisional Court, which agreed with the trial judge. At the time, the Human Rights Act 1998 was not yet in force, its implementation having been delayed until October 2000. Despite this, the Divisional Court decided that the sections undermined the presumption of innocence protected by Article 6(2) in a 'blatant and obvious way.' It proceeded to point out that the prosecution would be a waste of time and money since the defendants would, if convicted, appeal. In addition, if the appeal were to go ahead at a time when the Human Rights Act 1998 was in force, it would almost certainly be allowed. The Divisional Court therefore held that the DPP had acted unlawfully, and granted a declaration to this effect.

The DPP appealed to the House of Lords, which held that the courts had no power to review a decision of the DPP. That was sufficient to dispose of the appeal, and, unfortunately, the majority expressed no concluded views on the compatibility of the sections with Article 6(2). Lord Hobhouse, however, noted that the provisions were arguable, but emphasised that presumptions and reverse burdens were not uncommon within European States, nor were they necessarily incompatible with the Convention. Lord Hope, meanwhile, adopted the suggestion of counsel for the Director of Public Prosecutions that three questions should be considered in determining whether a reverse burden strikes a balance between the rights of the individual and those of the State.[83]

1. What does the prosecution have to prove in order to transfer the onus to the defence?
2. What is the burden of the accused? Does it relate to something that is likely to be difficult for him to prove, or does it relate to something that is likely to be within his knowledge or to which he readily has access?
3. What is the nature of the threat faced by society that the provision is designed to combat?

81 [2000] 2 AC 326.

82 Repealed by the Terrorism Act 2000.

83 As will be seen, these questions have been applied in later cases.

However, despite posing these questions, Lord Hope stated that no definitive view could be expressed as to the question of compatibility in the instant case since the trial itself had not yet been concluded. Nonetheless, in suggesting that the matter was open to argument, he appeared to disagree with the Divisional Court's view that they were incompatible.[84]

3.3.3 The Terrorism Act 2000

In 2000, Parliament decided to repeal the Prevention of Terrorism (Temporary Provisions) Act 1989, which required annual renewal by Parliament, and to replace it with a permanent statute. Parliament responded to the comments in *Kebilene*[85] by re-enacting sections 16A and 16B of the 1989 Act as sections 57 and 58 of the Terrorism Act 2000, but added section 118, which converts these reverse legal burdens into evidential burdens. Section 58 makes it an offence, punishable to the same extent as section 57, to collect or make a record of information likely to be useful to a person committing or preparing an act of terrorism, or to possess a document or record containing information of that kind. Section 58(3) also provides that it is a defence for a person charged with an offence under this section to prove that they had a reasonable excuse for their action or possession. Sections 12(4), 39(5)(a), 54, 77, and 103 also contain provisions making it a defence for the accused to prove certain facts or for presumptions to be made. For example, the court may assume that the accused possessed the article or object in question, unless they prove that they did not know of its presence on the premises or that they had no control over it.

At first sight, it appeared that the Government was ignoring the opinion of the House of Lords in *Kebilene*. However, section 118 contains provisions that make it clear that the defendant charged with offences under the relevant sections bears only an evidential burden. This means that the matter must be taken as proved against the accused unless the accused adduces *sufficient* evidence to raise an issue on the matter in court. Thereafter, if the evidential burden is discharged, the prosecution face the burden of satisfying the legal burden beyond reasonable doubt.[86] In addition, the use of the phrase 'a live issue'[87] within the statute means that it is not enough merely to allege a potentially relevant fact; the accused must raise sufficient evidence to make it an issue that can be put to the court or jury. In jury trials, this will be a matter for the judge to determine. If they are satisfied that the matter is an issue, the jury will be directed to consider whether, in the light of that evidence, the prosecution have disproved that evidence beyond reasonable doubt. If, however, the judge decides there is insufficient evidence to raise the issue, they will direct the jury to consider the matter proved in accordance with the provisions of the particular statutory provision.

In years to come, we shall almost certainly see new challenges brought in respect of this legislation. Consider, for example, section 57 of the Act, which provides:

> 1 A person commits an offence if he possesses an article in circumstances which give rise to a reasonable suspicion that his possession is for a purpose connected with the commission, preparation or instigation of an act of terrorism.
>
> 2 It is a defence for a person charged with an offence under this section to prove that his possession of the article was not for a purpose connected with the commission, preparation or instigation of an act of terrorism.
>
> 3 In proceedings for an offence under this section, if it is proved that an article –
> (a) was on any premises at the same time as the accused, or

---

84 The case then proceeded to trial, but was abandoned after a witness, said to be an agent working for MI5, refused to give evidence because he feared for his life. Unfortunately, the compatibility of the sections therefore remained untested.

85 [2000] 2 AC 326.

86 See the rule as to evidential burdens stated in *R v Gill* (1963) 47 Cr App R 166, 172, set out above.

87 Or, as in sub-ss 118(2) and (4), simply 'an issue.'

(b) was on premises of which the accused was the occupier or which he habitually used otherwise than as a member of the public, the court may assume that the accused possessed the article, unless he proves that he did not know of its presence on the premises or that he had no control over it.

Here, the legal or persuasive burden on the prosecution has been softened by the fact that there need only be 'reasonable suspicion' that the article is possessed for the purposes of terrorism. Reasonable suspicion is normally sufficient to ground an arrest, but is not proof that an offence has been committed. The need to prove possession arises only if the accused adduces evidence that the article, although in their possession, was not possessed for the purposes of terrorism. Only then need the prosecution prove beyond reasonable doubt that it was possessed for that purpose. Similarly, where the article is on the premises occupied or habitually used by the accused, possession is assumed unless the accused adduces evidence that they did not know of its presence, or, if they did, that they had no control over it. Only if such evidence is adduced is the prosecution required to prove that the accused knew or had control over it. It follows that if the accused decides not to give evidence, they might be convicted by virtue of presumptions against them and on reasonable suspicion falling short of proof.

This is one of the reasons why the Divisional Court in *Kebilene*[88] believed that the predecessor of section 57 was in breach of the European Convention on Human Rights. Ironically, long before the Human Rights Act 1998 was conceived, the Criminal Law Revision Committee recommended that whenever a statute places a burden on the accused, it should be treated as an evidential rather than persuasive burden.[89] Section 118 of the Terrorism Act 2000 accomplishes this in respect of most of the provisions within that Act, and that is to be welcomed. However, it should not be assumed that a serious offence cannot be the subject of a reverse legal burden. Not all reverse legal burdens in the Terrorism Act 2000 are covered by section 118. Parliament expressly intended that, for some offences, the legal burden of proof should fall squarely on the defendant. Traditionally, that would have meant that the courts were bound by such an intention.[90] However, in *Attorney General's Reference (No. 4 of 2002); Sheldrake v DPP (Conjoined Appeals)*,[91] the House of Lords held that section 11(2) of the Terrorism Act 2000 did not impose a reverse burden of proof on the defence and did not infringe the presumption of innocence so as to breach Article 6(2) of the Convention:

> The task of the court is never to decide whether a reverse burden should be imposed on a defendant, but always to assess whether a burden enacted by Parliament unjustifiably infringes the presumption of innocence. It may nonetheless be questioned whether ... 'the assumption should be that Parliament would not have made an exception without good reason'. Such an approach may lead the court to give too much weight to the enactment under review and too little to the presumption of innocence and the obligation imposed on it by section 3 [of the Human Rights Act 1998].[92]

This statement underlines the impact of the Human Rights Act 1998 in altering the orthodox role of the courts in statutory interpretation: the express intention of Parliament to impose a reverse burden is no longer conclusive – it must be shown that a reverse onus is both necessary and proportionate in relation to the particular statute.

---

88 [2000] 2 AC 326.

89 Criminal Law Revision Committee, *Eleventh Report: Evidence (General)*, Cmnd 4991 (HMSO, 1972).

90 *Attorney-General's Reference* (No. 4 of 2002) [2003] 3 WLR 1153.

91 [2005] 1 AC 264.

92 Ibid., at [31] (Lord Bingham).

3.3.4 Misuse of Drugs Act 1971/Homicide Act 1957

In *R v Lambert, Ali and Jordan*,[93] the first appellant, Lambert, had been convicted of possession of a Class A drug with intent to supply, contrary to section 5 of the Misuse of Drugs Act 1971. The section makes it clear that it is for the accused to prove, *inter alia*, that they neither knew nor suspected the existence of some fact alleged by the prosecution if they are to be acquitted of the offence charged. Ali and Jordan had both been convicted of murder, but had pleaded the defence of diminished responsibility under section 2 of the Homicide Act 1957. Like the common law exception of insanity, the defence of diminished responsibility must be proved by the accused. All three appellants complained that the respective statutory provisions under which they had been convicted were in breach of Article 6 of the European Convention on Human Rights, but their arguments were rejected by the Court of Appeal.

So far as the defence of diminished responsibility was concerned, the court had no difficulty in finding no breach of Article 6. The fact that the prosecution had no power to compel a defendant to testify meant that it would be exceedingly difficult for the prosecution to prove a negative. Similarly, the court also took account of the fact that the prosecution was required to prove all of the ingredients of the offence. Section 2 of the Homicide Act 1957 was of benefit to defendants who were in a position to take advantage of it. In the view of the court, it did not matter whether it was treated as creating a defence to a charge of murder or an exception – section 2 did not contravene Article 6.

Lambert, who was found in possession of a controlled drug, argued that he did not know that the bag he carried contained such drugs. However, section 28(3) of the Misuse of Drugs Act 1971 provides that the accused:

> shall not be acquitted of the offence charged by reason only of proving that he neither knew nor suspected nor had reason to suspect that the substance or product in question was the particular controlled drug alleged; but shall be acquitted … if he proves that he neither believed nor suspected nor had reason to suspect that the substance or product in question was a controlled drug.

In relation to section 28, the court emphasised the fact that for the defendant to be guilty of possession of drugs, the prosecution must prove an identifiable *actus reus* and *mens rea*. However, it was not necessary to prove that the defendant knew that the box contained drugs, only that he knew it contained something that proved to be drugs. This was a deliberate policy of Parliament, and the substance of the offence was reflected in the language of the statute. Sections 5(4) and 28 did not impose additional ingredients that had to be proved to complete the offence, but rather provided a way of avoiding liability for what would otherwise be an offence. Noting that it was commonplace for a defendant to seek to avoid guilt by saying that they thought they had pornography or gold and not drugs in a box or package, the court stated that such defence was difficult for the prosecution to rebut. In essence, the formulation of this statutory provision was designed to make the defendant responsible for making sure they did not take into their possession containers that, in fact, contained drugs.

In addition, the court held that there was a clear social objective in discouraging trading in drugs, and that the level of sentence would reflect the extent to which the defendant was responsible for the drugs in his possession. In the opinion of the court, there was an objective justification for the choice in the case of drugs, and the justification was not disproportionate. This particular

93 [2001] 1 All ER 1014.

part of the decision, in respect of the defendant Lambert and section 28 of the Misuse of Drugs Act 1971, was the subject of an appeal to the House of Lords.[94]

By a majority of 4:1, with Lord Hutton dissenting, the appeal was dismissed on the somewhat technical ground that the Human Rights Act 1998 could not be applied retrospectively. However, in respect of section 28 itself, their Lordships accepted that the prosecution had to prove only that the accused had a bag with something in it in his custody and control, and that the something in it was a controlled drug. It was not necessary for the prosecution to prove that the accused had known that the contents constituted a controlled drug, let alone a particular controlled drug.[95] The accused might then seek to establish one of the defences in section 5(4) or section 28. Lord Steyn, giving judgment for the majority, stated: 'It follows that a legislative interference with the presumption of innocence requires justification and must not be greater than necessary. The principle of proportionality must be observed.'[96]

While accepting that there was an objective basis for the justification, his Lordship went on to stress that any such justification must be proportionate. The burden was on the state to show that the legislative means were not greater than necessary. Where there is an objective justification for some inroad into unsettling the presumption of innocence, the legislature had to choose whether it was more appropriate to impose a legal burden or an evidential burden on the accused. A transfer of a legal burden amounted to a far more drastic interference with the presumption of innocence than the creation of an evidential burden. A reverse legal burden involved the risk that the jury might convict where the accused had not discharged the legal burden resting on them. However, it left the jury unsure on the point. Such a risk was not present if the nature of the burden was evidential only.

In respect of section 28, his Lordship observed that the prosecution must establish that the prohibited drugs were in the possession of the defendant and that he knew that the package contained something. The accused must then prove, on a balance of probabilities, that he did not know that the package contained controlled drugs. If the jury were in doubt on this issue, they must convict. This might occur where the accused adduced sufficient evidence to raise a doubt about his guilt, but the jury were not convinced on a balance of probabilities that his account was true. Indeed, it obliged the court to convict if the version of the accused was as likely to be true as not.

This particular aspect of the decision has far-reaching consequences, insofar as a guilty verdict may be returned in respect of an offence punishable by life imprisonment even though the jury might consider that it is reasonably possible that the accused has been duped. Moreover, there may be real difficulties in determining the real facts upon which the sentencer must act in such cases. In any event, the burden of showing that only a reverse legal burden can overcome the difficulties of the prosecution in drugs cases is a heavy one. Lord Steyn pointed out that some of the difficulties faced by the prosecution are already dealt with by the practicalities of procedure and the rules of evidence. Thus, the relevant facts are peculiarly within the knowledge of the possessor of the container. This presumptively suggests, in the absence of evidence to the contrary, that the person in possession of the container knew what was in it. This would be a complete answer to a submission of 'no case to answer,' and it would also be a factor that the trial judge would put before the jury. After all, it is common sense that possession of a package containing drugs demands a full and adequate explanation.

Lord Steyn concluded that he was satisfied that the transfer of the legal burden in section 28 did not satisfy the criterion of proportionality and that, in the current legal system, section 28 was a disproportionate reaction to difficulties faced by the prosecution in drug cases. It was therefore

---

94 *R v Lambert* [2002] AC 545.

95 See *R v McNamara* (1988) 87 Cr App R 246.

96 Ibid., at [34].

sufficient to impose an evidential burden on the accused. It followed that section 28 should be 'read down' in a way that is compatible with Convention rights by reading the words 'prove' and 'proves' as meaning giving sufficient evidence. Reading these words in such a way had the effect of imposing an evidential-only burden on the accused.

3.3.5 The Insolvency Act 1986

The decision in *Lambert*[97] was applied in *R v Carass*.[98] The defendant was charged with concealing debts in anticipation of a winding-up, contrary to section 206(1)(a) of the Insolvency Act 1986. Section 206(4) provides that it is a defence for the accused to prove that they had no intent to defraud. On an interlocutory appeal against a finding by the trial judge that section 206(4) of the 1986 Act imposed a legal burden of proof on the accused, the Court of Appeal held that the word 'prove' in section 206(4) must be read as 'adduce sufficient evidence,' thereby imposing an evidential rather than a persuasive burden. Waller LJ, giving the judgment of the court, stated that if a reverse legal burden were to be imposed on an accused, it had to be justified and demonstrated why a legal or persuasive burden (rather than an evidential burden) was necessary. Their Lordships did not believe that a legal burden was justifiable or necessary. Common sense dictated that if concealment of the debt were proved, the evidential burden itself would be quite difficult for the defendant to satisfy. Even if the accused were to satisfy it, it would be less than satisfactory if he could still be convicted if the jury were not sure that he had intended to defraud. Nothing their Lordships had seen demonstrated a justification for that being a possible result under section 206 because of some 'threat faced by society.'[99] It was therefore held that the judge was wrong insofar as he felt obliged to direct the jury that section 206(4) imposed a legal burden on the defendant. The burden was evidential only and it was appropriate to read the word 'prove' in section 206(4) as 'adduce sufficient evidence.' On this point, however, it should be noted that the House of Lords, in *Attorney General's Reference (No. 4 of 2002); Sheldrake v DPP (Conjoined Appeals)*,[100] concluded that *Carass* had been wrongly decided.

3.3.6 Discussion

The above decisions clearly indicate that, at least in relation to the most serious offences, statutory reversals of the burden of proof will frequently be read down by the courts as imposing only an evidential burden on the accused under the Human Rights Act 1998. It will be recalled that section 118 of the Terrorism Act 2000 makes almost all reversals of the burden of proof within that Act evidential burdens. This statute, together with the decision of the House of Lords in *Lambert*, suggests that Parliament and the courts have been coming around to the idea that placing the legal burden of proof on the accused can rarely be justified under the European Convention on Human Rights. There are few more serious offences than those contained in the Terrorism Act 2000, and few offences that are so serious a threat to society as the abuse of drugs; if these offences do not justify the imposition of a legal burden of proof on the accused, it seems difficult to envisage offences that might. There may, however, be a difference of approach in relation to offences that, although serious in their effect on society and in terms of the punishment imposed on conviction, are essentially regulatory and are not seen as truly criminal.[101]

97 [2001] 1 All ER 1014.
98 [2002] Crim LR 316.
99 *R v DPP, ex p Kebilene* [2000] 2 AC 326.
100 [2005] 1 AC 264.
101 See *R v S (Trademark Defence)* [2003] 1 Cr App R 602 and *Davies v HSE* (2002), *The Times* (27 December 2002).

This was a point that was probed further by the House of Lords in *R v Johnstone*.[102] Here, their Lordships recognised that the law still lacked some measure of clarity and sought to outline a fresh set of principles for determining when a reverse burden would be justifiable under the Human Rights Act 1998. Johnstone was convicted of an offence under section 92(1)(b) of the Trade Marks Act 1994 by illegally copying CDs by Bon Jovi and others. He had sought to rely, *inter alia*, on a defence provided in section 92(5), which stipulates that:

> It is a defence for a person charged with an offence under this section to show that he believed on reasonable grounds that the use of the sign in the manner in which it was used, or was to be used, was not an infringement of the registered trademark.

The defendant's appeal was allowed on other grounds, although the Court of Appeal had read section 92(5) as imposing no more than an evidential burden on the defendant. It was on this point (which was not, in the end, determinative of the appeal) that the House of Lords disagreed. Lord Nicholls, giving judgment with which the majority agreed, came to the conclusion that section 92(5) imposed a legal burden on the accused. The court took a variety of factors into account in reaching this decision:

> A sound starting point is to remember that if an accused is required to prove a fact on the balance of probabilities to avoid conviction, this permits a conviction in spite of the fact-finding tribunal having a reasonable doubt as to the guilt of the accused ... This consequence of a reverse burden of proof should colour one's approach when evaluating the reasons why it is said that, in the absence of a persuasive burden on the accused, the public interest will be prejudiced to an extent which justifies placing a persuasive burden on the accused. The more serious the punishment which may flow from conviction, the more compelling must be the reasons. The extent and nature of the factual matters required to be proved by the accused, and their importance relative to the matters required to be proved by the prosecution, have to be taken into account. So also does the extent to which the burden on the accused relates to facts which, if they exist, are readily provable by him as matters within his own knowledge or to which he has ready access. In evaluating these factors the court's role is one of review. Parliament, not the court, is charged with the primary responsibility for deciding, as a matter of policy, what should be the constituent elements of a criminal offence.[103]

In the instant case, Lord Nicholls found a number of compelling reasons why the burden should be legal rather than evidential in nature, including the urgent international pressure to restrain fraudulent trading in counterfeit goods, the framing of offences against section 92 as offences of 'near absolute liability,' and the dependence of the section 92(5) defence on facts within the defendant's own knowledge. There were, in particular, clear policy reasons for imposing the burden on the accused, including that fewer investigations and prosecutions into counterfeit goods would occur where the burden of proving dishonesty fell upon the prosecution.[104]

It was recognised in *Attorney General's Reference (No. 1 of 2004)*[105] that there appeared to be a significant difference in emphasis between the approach of Lord Steyn in *Lambert*[106] and that of Lord

102 [2003] 1 WLR 1736. *Johnstone* was considered by the Supreme Court in *R v M & Others* [2017] UKSC 58.

103 Ibid., at [50].

104 See *Beezadhur v Independent Commission Against Corruption* [2014] UKPC 27.

105 [2004] 1 WLR 2111.

106 [2001] 1 All ER 1014.

Nicholls in *Johnstone*.[107] Evidently, the former had a much more robust approach to the question of compatibility; one that, if followed, would mean that a great number of legal burdens should in future be read down so as to constitute an evidential burden only. In expressing a clear preference for the approach of Lord Nicholls, the Lord Chief Justice noted that his angle was considerably more flexible and reflective of the intention behind the Human Rights Act 1998, which aimed to strike a balance between the role of Parliament and that of the courts. It was also more up to date and, unlike Lord Steyn's speech, was endorsed by all of the other members of the House. Thus, the decision in *Carass* was impliedly overruled.

The Court of Appeal proceeded to note that, where courts were confronted with a reverse burden, three pertinent questions should be addressed:

1. whether the particular provision placed an evidential or a legal burden on the defendant;
2. if it did impose a legal burden, whether the legal burden could be justified; and
3. if it could not be justified, whether it could be read down so that it was an evidential burden.

In determining whether the imposition of the burden was justifiable, the court stated that ten general factors could be borne in mind (although it recognised that these might not be appropriate in all situations).

(a) Courts should strongly discourage the citation of authority to them other than *Johnstone's case* and this guidance. *Johnstone* is at present the latest word on the subject.
(b) The common law and the language of Article 6(2) had the same effect. Both permitted legal reverse burdens of proof or presumptions in appropriate circumstances.
(c) Reverse legal burdens were probably justified if the overall burden of proof was on the prosecution – that is, the prosecution had to prove the essential ingredients of the offence. There were, however, situations in which significant reasons present themselves as to why it is fair and reasonable to deny the accused the general protection normally guaranteed by the presumption of innocence.
(d) Where the exception went no further than was reasonably necessary to achieve the objective of the reverse burden – and was proportionate – it was sufficient if the exception was reasonably necessary in all of the circumstances. The assumption should be that Parliament would not have made an exception without good reason. While the judge must make their own decision as to whether there was a contravention of Article 6, the task of a judge was to review Parliament's approach, as Lord Nicholls indicated in *Johnstone*.
(e) If only an evidential burden were placed on the defendant, there would be no risk of contravention of Article 6(2).
(f) When ascertaining whether an exception was justified, the courts must construe the provision to ascertain what would be the realistic effects of the reverse burden. In doing so, the courts should be more concerned with substance than form. If the proper interpretation were that the statutory provision created an offence plus an exception, that would in itself be a strong indication that there was no contravention of Article 6(2).
(g) The easier it was for the accused to discharge the burden, the more likely it was that the reverse burden was justified. That would be the case where the facts were within the defendant's own knowledge. How difficult it would be for the prosecution to establish the facts was also indicative of whether a reverse legal burden was justified.
(h) The ultimate question was: would the exception prevent a fair trial? If it would, it must either be read down, if that were possible, or declared incompatible.
(i) Caution must be exercised when considering the seriousness of the offence and the power of punishment. The need for a reverse burden was not necessarily reflected by the gravity of the offence – although, from a defendant's point of view, the more serious the

107 [2003] 1 WLR 1736.

offence, the more important it was that there was no interference with the presumption of innocence.

(j) If guidance was needed as to the approach of the European Court of Human Rights, that was provided by *Salabiaku v France*: 'Article 6(2) does not regard presumptions of fact or of law with indifference. It requires states to confine them within reasonable limits which takes into account the importance of what is at stake and maintains the rights of the defence.'[108]

As the law stood in the light of the decisions in *Johnstone* and *Attorney General's Reference (No. 1 of 2004)*, it was considerably easier to persuade the court that Parliament knew what it was doing in enacting a reversal of the burden of proof and that imposing a reverse legal burden was necessary, reasonable, and proportionate in the particular circumstances. In the case of *Euro Wines (C & C) Ltd v CMRS for HM Revenue & Customs* [2018],[109] Lord Bingham rehearsed the reasoning of Lord Nicholls in *R v Johnstone* to reverse the burden in excise duty cases under S154(2) of the Custom and Excise Management Act 1979. However, the decision of the House of Lords in *Attorney General's Reference (No. 4 of 2002); Sheldrake v DPP (Conjoined Appeals)*[110] has further modified the position. Lord Bingham of Cornhill made it clear that both *Lambert* and *Johnstone* were decisions of the House of Lords, binding on all lower courts for what they decided:

> Nothing said in R v Johnstone suggests an intention to depart from or modify the earlier decision, which should not be treated as superseded or implicitly overruled. Differences of emphasis ... were explicable by the difference in the subject matter of the two cases. Section 5 of the Misuse of Drugs Act 1971 and section 92 of the Trade Marks Act 1994 were directed to serious social and economic problems. But the justifiability and fairness of the respective exoneration provisions had to be judged in the particular context of each case.[111]

In light of this decision, the guidelines laid down in *Attorney General's Reference (No. 1 of 2004)* were modified. *Lambert* or *Johnstone* can now be cited according to the particular context in which the provision under consideration operates. *Johnstone* is the latest word on economic offences that, although serious, may not be considered 'truly criminal'; *Lambert* is the latest word on 'truly criminal offences,' and the court agreed with Lord Bingham's comments in *Attorney General's Reference (No. 1 of 2004)* that *Carass* had been wrongly decided. The assumption contained in guideline (d) above, that Parliament would not have made an exception without good reason, was also erroneous, since it might lead a court to give too much weight to the enactment under review and too little to the presumption of innocence and the obligation imposed on it by section 3 of the Human Rights Act 1998.

The combined effect of the Terrorism Act 2000 and the decisions in *Lambert* and *Carass* appeared to be moving towards an endorsement of the recommendation of the Criminal Law Revision Committee's Eleventh Report,[112] which suggested that whenever a statute placed a burden of proof on the accused, it should be treated as evidential rather than legal in nature. However, *Johnstone* and *Attorney General's Reference (No. 1 of 2004)* clearly put a brake on the movement towards the replacement of legal burdens with evidential-only burdens and the restoration of the fundamental nature of the presumption of innocence. The latest decision of the House of Lords, in *Attorney General's Reference (No. 4 of 2002); Sheldrake v DPP*, suggests not so much a brake on the movement as an acceptance that

---

108 Ibid., at [52].

109 *Euro Wines (C & C) Ltd v CMRS for HM Revenue & Customs* [2018] EWCA Civ 46, [2018], IWLR 3248.

110 [2005] 1 AC 264.

111 Ibid., at [30].

112 Criminal Law Revision Committee, op. cit., n. 89.

there can be different approaches in relation to what may be termed 'real crime' and what may be termed 'regulatory offences,' which are not truly criminal.

It can thus be confidently forecast that many statutes, including the Official Secrets Act 1989 and the Terrorism Act 2000, which concern serious criminal offences and place a reverse burden on the defence, will be the subject of a challenge in the future. The essential question for the courts will be whether the provisions are necessary, justifiable, and proportionate, but despite two House of Lords decisions (*Lambert* and *Sheldrake*), and numerous recent Court of Appeal decisions, there remains no definitive test that can be applied by the lower courts to determine whether a particular provision is Convention-compliant. The courts have rejected the formulation of any generic rule or test, preferring instead to treat each case on its own merits.[113] The closest the courts have come to offering any general guidance is the Court of Appeal's formulation of a list of factors to take into account. However, even these have had to be modified in light of the House of Lords' decision in *Attorney General's Reference (No. 4 of 2002); Sheldrake v DPP*, and there is no guarantee that those aspects of the guidance that remain good law will remain so indefinitely.

However, on the basis of recent trends, the likelihood is that in future years we shall see many more statutes being read down and interpreted in such a way as to impose an evidential burden only. Indeed, this is precisely what happened to certain provisions of the Official Secrets Act 1989 in *R v Keogh*.[114] The defendant, civil servant David Keogh, was charged with allegedly leaking a document containing what was purported to be a discussion between then Prime Minister, Tony Blair, and US President, George W. Bush, concerning policy in Iraq to his co-defendant, Leo O'Connor, a political researcher for Parliament. The trial judge ruled that sections 2(3) and 3(4) of the 1989 Act created strict liability offences that imposed a reverse legal burden on the defendant and that they were justifiable. On appeal, Keogh contended that the burden to be shouldered under these provisions was arduous and unjustifiable.

Allowing the appeal, the Court of Appeal mooted whether the reverse burden contained within the challenged sections was necessary for the effective operation of the 1989 Act. They concluded that, procedurally, the trial would be 'completely unbalanced' if – according to the reverse burden – the prosecution were to wait until the defendant gave evidence as to his *mens rea* before advancing with their case. It was established that the trial would better (and more effectively) proceed if the burden of proving the defendant's *mens rea* were to lie with the prosecution from the outset. Therefore, the reverse burdens contained within sections 2(3) and 3(4) of the Official Secrets Act 1989 were, by their natural meanings, 'disproportionate and unjustifiable' and should be read down to form evidential burdens only.[115]

While some statutory reversals of the burden of proof can be justified as being confined within reasonable limits given the importance of what is at stake, it is clear, nonetheless, that placing an evidential burden on the accused achieves the same purpose, while better maintaining the rights of the defence. Placing an evidential burden on the accused requires them to raise issue(s) that the prosecution must then rebut. This process still assists the prosecution by clarifying the issue(s) with which they must deal and, given the disclosure provisions that now apply to the defence, the prosecution can be made aware of those issues before trial, thus enabling them to deal with them efficiently. This, it could be contended, is fair to the accused since, as an individual, they are arguably best placed to know what those issues are, and how to access relevant evidence to prove them. However, by the same token, it should be borne in mind that placing a legal burden of proof on the defence may lead to an unfair trial and result in the conviction of a

113 See *Lambert*, n. 94, at [34]; *Sheldrake*, n. 26, at [21].

114 [2007] 1 WLR 1500. See also Glover, R., 'Pause for Thought' (2007) 157 New Law Journal 1344.

115 Ibid., at [33].

defendant in circumstances in which the jury continues to harbour some degree of doubt as to the accused's guilt.

In *R v Brook*,[116] the appellant alleged, somewhat unusually, that being asked questions in cross-examination by the prosecution was tantamount to a reversal of the burden of proof. The defendant was charged with and convicted of seven counts of rape, three of attempted rape, and six of indecent assault. During cross-examination, counsel for the prosecution applied to the judge to be allowed to ask the defendant whether he could think of any reasons why the complainants should lie. The judge gave permission and the question was put to the defendant. Following his conviction and sentence of 11 years' imprisonment, the defendant appealed. The grounds for appeal were, *inter alia*, that it was unfair and tantamount to a shifting of the legal burden of proof for the prosecution to have been permitted to ask that question.

Giving the judgment of the court, Rose LJ stated that the question under scrutiny was one that had been widely, if not invariably, put in such cases for at least 40 years without any recorded expression of disapproval from the courts. Indeed, in this jurisdiction, there was no authority on the point. Having considered authorities from other jurisdictions, it was held that the question put at trial was not unfair and did not shift the burden of proof. It was an admissible question because it was relevant. For example, if something were known to the defendant that provided a reason for the complainant to lie, that would tend to undermine the complainant's credibility – and if a defendant unexpectedly gave a positive answer, that might be relevant to their own credibility.

In the case of *R v BD*,[117] the Court of Appeal was faced with another atypical challenge in a case involving an alleged sexual assault. At first instance, the defendant was convicted on five specimen counts of indecent assault on a female who, at the time, was between 13 and 14 years old. During the trial, the defendant sought to cross-examine the complainant over an earlier complaint of indecent assault that she made against another man, X, who was subsequently acquitted. The defendant also sought to call X as a witness in a bid to prove that the complainant's allegation against him was, like her complaint against X, based on collusion and fabrication. Applying the finality rule,[118] the judge allowed the defence counsel to ask each witness about their previous complaints and whether they had concocted them.[119] However, the court refused to allow the defence to call X, since it was apparent that the purpose of calling him had more to do with discrediting the complainant, rather than adducing evidence surrounding the matters in issue.

It was held, dismissing the appeal, that if X were called and his evidence submitted, the situation would be tantamount to the reversal of the burden of proof onto the complainants. Essentially, the defence had been attempting to equate the previous acquittal of X with an automatic presumption of innocence in favour of the defendant in the immediate case. In addition, to cross-examine X if he were called would have effectively resulted in a retrial of his guilt for an offence that took place nearly nine years earlier.

3.4 Restoring the fundamental nature of the 'golden thread'?

The advent of the Human Rights Act 1998 and the incorporation of the European Convention on Human Rights into domestic law have provided means by which the fundamental nature of the right to be presumed innocent can be restored. However, as the cases considered above

---

116 *The Times* (3 March 2003).

117 [2007] EWCA Crim 4.

118 See Ch 6.

119 If they had admitted making up their previous accusations, further questioning would have been permissible.

make clear, the provisions of Article 6 are not absolute and can be displaced for good reason.[120] Nevertheless, as Mark George KC has commented, it remains unlikely that a provision that allows a jury to convict a defendant while still harbouring doubts about their guilt would survive a challenge in the appellate courts.[121]

It must be borne in mind that the European Convention on Human Rights was a document prepared by European nations with diverse legal cultures, political histories, and criminal processes. It was drafted by governments for governments, and as such the original framers of the Convention tended to agree on the lowest common denominator: the majority of rights within it are qualified and can be displaced in the public interest when it is necessary and reasonable to do so. It follows that the Convention can provide only limited protection by requiring States to show that displacement of the fundamental right is necessary, justified, and proportionate. It is, for example, unlikely that reverse burdens and presumptions in a majority of summary offences will be found to be in breach of Article 6, as some of the decisions already made under the Human Rights Act 1998 make clear.[122]

As the law currently stands, it is only the reverse burdens and presumptions that apply to serious indictable offences that are likely to contravene Article 6[123] and, as the guidance in *Attorney General's Reference* (No. 1 of 2004) makes clear, the seriousness of the offence and the punishment to be imposed are not the sole criteria. Courts are required to look to the realistic effect of imposing a reverse burden.[124] For example, Pearson, in assessing how reverse burdens operate, comments that the defence bears the explicit statutory reverse burden to provide that they did not go onto the playing area without a lawful excuse. Where the offence is regulatory in nature and intended to protect the public, reverse legal burdens are unlikely to be seen as incompatible with Article 6(2) if the effect of reading them down to evidential burdens is to make the investigation and prosecution of such offences more difficult. In the years to come, it may be that serious offences such as terrorism and dealing in prohibited drugs will be seen as truly criminal and thus more deserving of the protection provided by the presumption of innocence.

The incorporation of the Convention provisions into domestic law has obliged the courts to consider whether provisions that *prima facie* contravene Article 6 can be justified. In future, Parliament will itself have to justify any new statutory provision that is incompatible with Article 6, and the courts must decide whether existing reverse burdens that place a legal burden of proof on the defence can also be justified. The early promise of the Terrorism Act 2000 and the decisions in *Lambert*[125] and *Carass*[126] – that few such provisions in relation to the more serious offences can or will be justified – is now less likely to be realised. Instead, the more pragmatic approaches of the Court of Appeal in *Johnstone* and *Attorney General's Reference* (No. 1 of 2004), and the House of Lords in *Sheldrake*, will hold sway. This approach is likely to lead to an acceptance of reverse burdens in relation to a majority of regulatory offences in which reverse burdens are prevalent despite the seriousness of the offence and punishment. There are few truly criminal offences containing reverse burdens and it is in relation to such offences that one might expect the courts to read

120 See the case of *R v Webster* [2010] EWCA Crim 2819, in which the Court of Appeal allowed an appeal against conviction under the Prevention of Corruption Act 1916, s 2, which created a reversal of the legal burden of proof.

121 See *Garden Court North, Criminal Law Update*, Issue 28 (25 January 2011) http://www.gcnchambers.co.uk/gcn/areas_of_specialisation/areas/criminal_defence/criminal_law_updates/criminal_law_update_25_1_11 (last accessed 15 December 2014).

122 See e.g. *L v DPP* [2003] QB 137; *Parker v DPP* [2001] RTR 240; *Sheldrake*, op. cit., n. 26.

123 See e.g. the decisions in *Lambert*, op. cit., n. 94 and *Kebilene*, op. cit., n. 61.

124 See Pearson, G., 'A Beautiful Law for the Beautiful Game? Revisiting the Football Offences Act 1991' (2021) 85(5) *The Journal of Criminal Law* 362–74 for a discussion on how the defence offered under s4 Football Offences Act 1991 may not now operate as a lawful reverse burden.

125 [2001] 1 All ER 1014.

126 [2002] Crim LR 316.

down legal burdens. Therefore, it is likely that future researchers asking how many indictable or either-way offences contain reverse burdens will find no significant reduction from the 40 per cent found by researchers prior to the Human Rights Act 1998 and no great advance for the cause of the rights of the defence.[127]

Interestingly, the Criminal Law Revision Committee, which contended that reverse burdens should be evidential only, also advocated the effective abolition of the right to silence along the lines of what are now sections 34 to 38 of the Criminal Justice and Public Order Act 1994.[128]

One consequence of placing an evidential burden on the accused is that the accused must adduce evidence of the particular defence or risk being found guilty. The right to remain silent, to decline to give evidence, and to require the prosecution to prove one's guilt is no longer available to the accused where the offence-creating statute includes a reverse burden that requires the accused to adduce sufficient evidence. The accused is not required to prove their innocence, but is required to adduce sufficient evidence of a particular defence that will create a reasonable doubt – unless the prosecution disprove the defence beyond reasonable doubt. In adducing the required evidence, the defendant, in theory, does not have to give evidence herself, but in practice she must almost always go into the witness box as most of the evidence she wishes to adduce will be within her own exclusive knowledge. If the accused does decide to appear in the dock, she will then be exposed to cross-examination, which is likely to assist the prosecution in proving her guilt.

As was indicated by Waller LJ in *Carass*,[129] the evidential burden can be difficult for the defence to satisfy where, as in a case under section 206(1)(a) of the Insolvency Act 1986, the prosecution prove a concealment of the debt. At first sight, it may appear to be unimportant whether the burden on the accused is legal or evidential, since in both instances the accused will be placed under pressure to give evidence and be exposed to cross-examination. There is, however, one very significant difference. As was made clear by Lord Steyn in *Lambert*,[130] placing a legal burden on the accused can result in conviction where the jury have a reasonable doubt that the defence has not made out its case sufficiently, while placing an evidential burden does not carry that risk – it is a much lower threshold for the defence to overcome. The other key difference is that imposing a legal burden may be incompatible with Article 6 of the European Convention on Human Rights, while imposing an evidential burden will not.

Some will argue that the imposition of the evidential burden is only the lesser of two evils, since it will still require the accused to give evidence and, in that sense, may be seen as another attack on the accused's right to silence alongside that imposed by section 35 of the Criminal Justice and Public Order Act 1994.[131] Others will argue that, like section 35, the imposition of an evidential burden does little to change the position of the accused, particularly where they are confronted with overwhelming evidence. In practice, the pressure of the prosecution case is in itself usually enough to require most defendants to give evidence or risk conviction by not doing so. Whichever position is preferred, the fact remains that the golden thread of English criminal law is qualified by the imposition of a reverse burden of proof, and it might be legitimately argued that 'a qualified fundamental principle' is something of a contradiction in terms.

Contemporarily, after the Covid-19 pandemic, the question of statutory burdens of proof was considered in the Health Protection Regulations Act 2020.[132] The new act included extensive powers of detention for 'the purposes of screening, assessment, and the imposition of any restrictions or requirements under Regulation 5' where a registered health professional has 'reasonable

127 Ashworth, A. and Blake, M., 'Presumption of Innocence in English Criminal Law' [1996] Crim LR 306.

128 Criminal Law Revision Committee, op. cit., n. 89, at [140]. See further Ch 7.

129 [2002] Crim LR 316.

130 [2001] 1 All ER 1014.

131 See Ch 7.

132 Health Protection Regulation Act 2020.

grounds to believe that the person is or may be infected or contaminated with Coronavirus,' carrying the 'risk that s[he] may infect or contaminate others.' Interestingly, the regulation specifies that those who fail to comply with the above restrictions 'without reasonable excuse' will have committed an offence under section 15 of the Act. Applicably, this statutorily reverses the burden towards the defence to provide a reasonable and lawful excuse for breaching lockdown regulations while being symptomatic.

3.5 The burden of proof in civil cases

In civil trials, the general rule is that the Latin maxim *ei incumbit probation qui dicit* (he who asserts must prove) applies. So, normally, the overall burden of proof will lie with the claimant. A defence which simply denies an element of the claimant's case does not raise any new facts and thus does not impose any burden of proof on the defendant. Thus, for example, in a tort action for negligence, the claimant bears the legal burden of proving all of the elements of negligence: namely, the existence of a duty of care, breach of that duty, and the consequential loss. However, if the defendant wishes to introduce new facts to support a defence (such as contributory negligence, for example), the burden of establishing such facts will switch to the party seeking to prove them.

The case of *The Glendarroch*[133] provides a useful illustration. The plaintiff (the pre-1998 term for 'claimant') was seeking damages from the shipowners for breach of contract for the non-delivery of goods. Under the bill of lading, the defendants were exempt from liability for loss or damage to goods caused by perils of the sea, unless the defendants had been negligent. When determining with whom the burden for establishing such negligence would lie, it was held that the legal duty was on the plaintiffs to establish a contract for the delivery of goods. However, if the defendants sought to rely on the exemption clause (i.e. that they were not liable if damage was caused as a result of perils of the sea), the burden of proving the clause applied then fell on them. If that burden were subsequently satisfied, the onus would revert back to the plaintiff to establish that the defendant had indeed been negligent.

This reasoning was followed by the somewhat similar case of *Munro, Brice & Co. v War Risks Association*.[134] The case was brought against the defendant insurers by the shipowner plaintiff following the loss of his ship, as in *The Glendarroch*, through the perils of the sea. The insurance company sought to rely on an exemption clause, which provided that it would not be liable in the event of capture, seizure, or in consequence of hostility. Bailhache J held that it was only for the plaintiff to prove to the court that the ship had been lost; it was then for the defendant to show that one of the excepted causes applied.

In *Rhesa Shipping Co. SA v Edmunds*,[135] the plaintiffs were owners of an old ship, which was known to have been in bad condition. In 1978, the ship sank while sailing in the Mediterranean. The weather was good and there was evidence that water had entered through a hole in the side. The shipowners brought actions against the underwriters, arguing that the ship's loss was caused by collision with a submarine. The underwriters had rejected this claim, and contended that the hole had been caused by the ship's poor condition. At first instance, the court found for the owners on the grounds that the defendants had little evidence to support their claim (although some doubt was also cast on the owners' version of events). The case proceeded to the House of Lords, where the underwriters' appeal was allowed. It was held that, in a case such as this in which there was real doubt as to the cause of loss in question, the overall burden of proof remained with the

133 [1894] P 226.
134 [1918] 2 KB 78.
135 [1985] 1 WLR 948.

plaintiff. The reason for the ship's sinking was unclear, and the owners had thus failed to show the loss was occasioned by a peril insured against.

Burdens of proof in the civil sector were once again considered in *R v MK*, where the issue of where the burden of proof is to be attributed was considered, in relation to the increasing amount of English legislation which implements Directives of the European Union.[136]

3.6 The standard of proof

3.6.1 Criminal trials

The 'standard of proof' refers to the level or degree of proof that must be established. There are only two standards: the criminal standard of proof, which is 'proof beyond reasonable doubt'; and the civil standard, which is proof 'on the balance of probabilities.'

3.6.1.1 Criminal trials: proof beyond reasonable doubt

Where the prosecution bear the legal or persuasive burden, they must establish a defendant's guilt beyond reasonable doubt. This has also been expressed as 'a,' 'any,' or 'all' reasonable doubt. This standard applies in all criminal trials, whether before magistrates or on indictment before a jury. If there is a reasonable doubt created by the evidence adduced either by the prosecution or by the defence, the prosecution have not made out their case and the defendant must be acquitted.[137] Many judicial attempts have been made to define what is, or is not, reasonable doubt. For the most part, these efforts have generally shed little light on the term. One of the better definitions, however, was that given by Lord Denning in *Miller v Minister of Pensions*:[138]

> It need not reach certainty, but it must carry a high degree of probability. Proof beyond reasonable doubt does not mean proof beyond a shadow of a doubt. The law would fail to protect the community if it admitted of fanciful possibilities to deflect the course of justice. If the evidence is so strong against a man as to leave only a remote possibility in his favour which can be dismissed with the sentence, 'of course it is possible but not in the least probable', the case is proved beyond reasonable doubt but nothing short of that will suffice.[139]

Even this relatively clear definition has been subject to criticism, and there has been no shortage of attempts in the intervening period to define reasonable doubt in terms that a jury might better understand. Thus, in *Walters v The Queen*,[140] the Privy Council approved the definition as 'that quality of doubt which when you are dealing with matters of importance in your own affairs, you allow to influence you one way or another.'[141] However, this was disapproved of in *R v Gray*[142] because it pitched the standard too low. The reference to 'important affairs,' however, was deemed acceptable, since decisions regarding such important matters invoke a more reflective thought process, and thus one in which a higher standard is likely to be applied. In *R v Ching*,[143] the analogy between

136 See *R v MK* [2018] EWCA Crim 667, [2018] 2 Cr App R 14 (Directive 2011/36/EU), and the Modern Slavery Act, Section 45.

137 *Woolmington v DPP* [1935] AC 462. See also *Re D* [2009] 1 AC 11; *R v Majid* [2009] EWCA Crim 2563; *R v Layton* [2009] SCC 36 (a case dealt with by the Supreme Court of Canada). For a discussion on the issues surrounding the question of whether a trial system that utilises only two verdicts (guilty or not guilty) serves the interests of justice, see Laudan, L., 'Need Verdicts Come in Pairs?' (2010) 14 *International Journal of Evidence and Proof* 1.

138 [1947] 2 All ER 372.

139 Ibid., at 373.

140 [1969] 2 AC 26.

141 Ibid., at 28.

142 (1973) 58 Cr App R 177.

143 (1976) 63 Cr App R 7.

buying a house and taking out a mortgage was approved: the jury would have to be as sure as they would be in taking out a residential mortgage before they had proof beyond reasonable doubt. All such definitions, however, merely highlight the fact that the jury are making an important decision and do little to indicate what degree of doubt justifies an acquittal. Their decision is also highly subjective and relative to individual jurors' experiences. The Court of Appeal in *Ching* advised that judges would be well advised not to attempt any gloss on what is meant by 'sure' or 'reasonable doubt'; in *R v Adey*,[144] the Court of Appeal cautioned against any attempt at a more elaborate definition of 'being sure' or 'beyond reasonable doubt.'[145]

In *R v Kritz*,[146] Lord Goddard CJ expressed the view that, as opposed to beyond reasonable doubt, it was better to tell the jury that before they convict they must be 'satisfied so that they are sure' of the guilt of the accused (*obiter*). This form of direction on the standard of proof has frequently been used by judges since then and continues to be used.[147] The reason for Lord Goddard's *dicta* was clearly that some judges had found difficulty in explaining what was meant by 'reasonable doubt.' The most prominent authority on use of the 'sure' direction is that of *R v Majid*,[148] where the Court of Appeal supported Lord Goddard's *dicta* and held that counsel and the judge must avoid use of 'beyond reasonable doubt' and should instead refer only to the standard of 'sure.' By contrast, the editors of *Archbold* have also given opinions on the matter. In particular, it has been submitted by the editors of *Archbold* that it is better to give the 'reasonable doubt' direction and cite approval by many Court of Appeal authorities.[149] In *R v Bentley (Deceased)*,[150] the Court of Appeal said, as to the standard of proof, that a jury should be instructed that if, on reviewing all the evidence, they are unsure or left in any reasonable doubt as to the accused's guilt, that doubt must be resolved in the accused's favour.

The need to use the correct wording of the standard of proof in open court was evident in *JS (A Child) v DPP*.[151] In this case, the magistrates referred to the word 'viable' in reaching their decision to convict a minor of tampering with a motor vehicle contrary to section 25 of the Road Traffic Act 1988. The appellant appealed by way of case stated to the High Court on the basis that the magistrates had applied the incorrect standard of proof. The High Court allowed the appeal and concluded that, although the magistrates may have used the correct standard of proof, they created an impression in open court that they may not do so. On that basis, the conviction was unsafe.

The most recent edition of the *Crown Court Compendium* suggests an example direction using 'sure' rather than 'beyond reasonable doubt':[152]

> The prosecution will only succeed in proving that D is guilty if you [the jury] have been made sure of D's 'guilt'. If, after considering all … the evidence, you are sure that D is guilty, your verdict must be 'Guilty'. If you are not sure that D is guilty, your verdict must be 'Not Guilty.'[153]

---

144 Unreported (97/5306/W2) (1998).

145 See also *R v Stephens* (2002), *The Times* (27 June 2002), in which the Court of Appeal echoed the Judicial Studies Board's specimen direction, in stating that it was unhelpful to differentiate between being 'sure' and being 'certain.'

146 (1949) 33 Cr App R 169 at 177.

147 Expressly approved by the Privy Council in *Walters v R* [1969] 2 AC 26 at 30.

148 [2009] EWCA Crim 2563.

149 *Archbold: Criminal Pleading, Practice and Evidence*, 65th edn (Sweet & Maxwell, 2017), p. 512.

150 [2001] 1 Cr App R 21.

151 [2017] EWHC 1162 (Admin).

152 For further discussion, see Crim LR 2022, 11, 893–907

153 Judicial College, *The Crown Court Compendium* (London: Judicial College, 2022), Pt 1, 5, Legal Summary, Directions, Example 1. https://www.judiciary.uk/guidance-and-resources/crown-court-compendium/ (last accessed 21 February 2023).

3.6.1.2 Criminal trials: proof on the balance of probabilities

On those relatively rare occasions on which the defence bears the legal burden on an issue at trial (e.g. where insanity or diminished responsibility is pleaded, or where an express or implied statutory exception applies), the relevant standard is the balance of probabilities. In *Miller v Minister of Pensions*,[154] Lord Denning summarised the nature of this standard effectively when stating: 'If the evidence is such that the tribunal may say "we think it is more probable than not" the burden is discharged, but if the probabilities are equal it is not.'[155]

The Judicial College has suggested that in circumstances where the defendant carries a burden of proof that the following example direction should be given:

> When you are considering {specify} this is for D to prove. D has to show that it is more likely than not that {specify}. D does not have to make you sure of it.[156]

Something to note on the criminal standard of proof directions is that *Ukpabi v CPA*[157] ruled in 2008 that within the Magistrate's summing up, it is important that the correct standard of proof be applied. Here, the conviction was overturned on the basis that there was a misdirection given that gave the impression that a lower standard of proof was applied. In general, the case laid down that the standard of proof must keep in mind the broader context that 'we tend to believe the officers and therefore find the defendant guilty.' Recently, this judgment on the standards of criminal proof was revisited in the case of *R v Broughton*[158] in 2020, where the court commented that 'Taken at its highest, the evidence adduced by the prosecution was incapable of proving caution to the criminal standard of proof.' Therefore, it has recently been confirmed by the courts that the criminal standard of evidential proof has not been watered down and, instead, remains firmly rooted in established criminal jurisprudence

3.6.2 Civil trials

The civil standard of proof is on the balance of probabilities, which basically amounts to the question of whether something is more possible than not.[159] It is lower than the criminal standard. Although not generally controversial, there was some ambiguity until recently whether a higher standard of proof might apply in certain types of case that involved serious and potentially criminal allegations. For example, in *Re a Solicitor*,[160] the Divisional Court held that it was correct to apply the criminal standard of proof given the nature of the allegations of professional misconduct, which involved the commission of a criminal offence. Similar approaches have been advocated in respect of cases involving domestic violence and child abuse, given the nature of the allegations that are often advanced against the parties. For example, in *Re G (A Minor)*,[161] Sheldon J proposed that:

---

154 [1947] 2 All ER 372.

155 Ibid., at 374.

156 Judicial College, *The Crown Court Compendium* (London: Judicial College, 2022), Pt 1, 5, Legal Summary, Directions, Example 2. https://www.judiciary.uk/guidance-and-resources/crown-court-compendium/ (last accessed 21 February 2023).

157 *Upkabi v CPA* [2008] EWHC (Admin) 952.

158 *R v Broughton* [2020], EWCA Crim 1093.

159 See Lord Hoffmann's comment in *In Re B (Children)* [2008] UKHL 35, 13: 'The time has come to say, once and for all, that there is only one civil standard of proof and that is proof that the fact in issue more probably occurred than not.'

160 [1992] QB 69.

161 [1987] 1 WLR 1461. See also *Bater v Bater* [1951] P 35.

> a higher degree of probability is required to satisfy the court that the father has been guilty of some sexual misconduct with his daughter than would be needed to justify the conclusion that the child has been a victim of some such behaviour of whatever nature and whoever may have been its perpetrator.[162]

However, the House of Lords has put such uncertainties to rest with the decisions in *Re H and Others (Minors) (Sexual Abuse: Standard of Proof)*[163] and *Re B (Children)*.[164] This line of reasoning in SB was also confirmed in the case of *GB v Stoke City Football Club Ltd*.[165] It is thus now clear that the observation by Denning LJ in *Hornal v Neuberger Products Ltd*[166] to the effect that 'the more serious the allegation, the higher the degree of probability that is required' is blatantly incorrect.[167]

The imposition of a higher standard of proof in criminal cases may explain why a defendant in a criminal case who is found not guilty can nevertheless be found liable for damages in a civil claim. In civil cases, the standard of proof is based on the balance of probabilities. Thus, while a jury in a criminal trial can return a not guilty verdict, a civil court can find the same person liable under the law of tort on identical evidence. To some extent, this differentiation may be explicable by the absence of the jury in civil cases (with the exception of libel). When someone is sued in a claim that suggests dishonesty or serious criminality, it might be argued that the applicability of the civil standard of proof is in real terms little different from the criminal standard, and the consequences of finding against the defendant in certain circumstances are arguably so serious as to justify the imposition of a heightened standard of proof. The real difference for the preservation of the legal justification may be that it is the trial judge who acts as the tribunal of fact in the vast majority of civil cases, and is (perhaps incorrectly) assumed to be less likely to be prejudiced by irrelevant issues and/or prejudicial evidence than the lay jury. Contemporarily, in the case of *Constandas v Lysandrou*,[168] the court confirmed that upon demonstration that an issue is found to be too evenly balanced to determine the imposition of proof on the matter, then the issue must be determined by evidence of the persuasive burden. This seems to follow the decision of the then

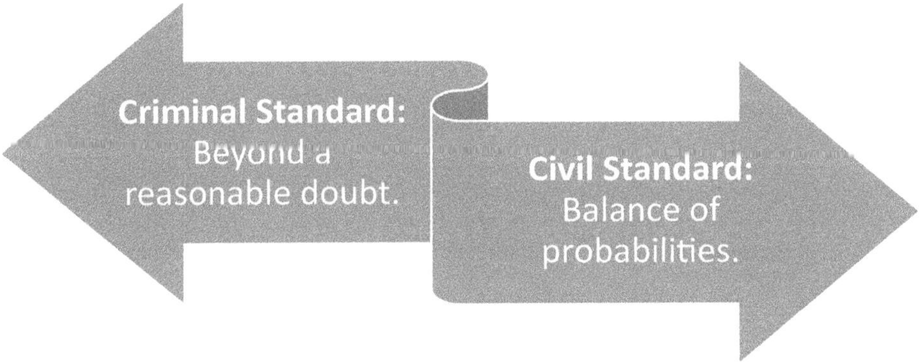

Figure 3.2 Standard of proof

162 Ibid., at 1466.
163 [1996] AC 563.
164 [2009] 1 AC 11.
165 See *GB v Stoke City Football Club Ltd* [2015] EWHE 2663 (QB).
166 [1957] 1 QB 247.
167 Ibid., at 258.
168 *Constandas v Lysandrou* [2018] EWCA Civ 613.

House of Lords in *Rhesa Shipping Co SA v Edmunds*. [169] This issue was revisited regarding the entry into force of the Anti-Social Behaviour, Crime and Policing Act 2014, Section 22 ASBO, which concerns the standard of proof within the exercise of judgment, as indicated by *DPP v Bulmer*.

In conclusion, there is now seemingly a growing consensus in academic literature on the importance of public confidence within the law on evidence and procedure. For example, Paul Roberts and Adrian Zuckerman argue that the entire moral edifice and legitimacy of the system of law as a whole must be based on the public confidence of the general public, and built on a foundation of respect for the system.[170] Professor Ian Dennis, with the agreement of Duff,[171] takes this reasoning even further, contending that the 'aims of the law of Evidence are ultimately referable to an overall objective of promoting legitimacy of decision in adjudication.'[172]

3.7 Key learning points

- The golden thread of English criminal law encapsulates the general principle that the burden of proof falls on the prosecution.
- Burdens may be either legal or evidential in nature.
- There is one established common law exception to the principle (insanity), as well as numerous express and implied statutory exceptions.
- Provided that reverse burdens are confined within 'reasonable limits,' and are framed in such a way as to take into account the importance of what is at stake, they will not violate Article 6(2) ECHR.
- There is no universal 'test' that can be applied to determine whether a reverse burden is justifiable.

3.8 Practice questions

(1) The Terrorism (Further Measures) Bill 2017 [fictional] contains the following provisions:

Clause 1

1 It shall be an offence for any person to assist another in any way whatsoever whether by act or omission in the commission, preparation or instigation of an act of terrorism.

2 Where the prosecution has proved assistance in the commission, preparation or instigation of an act of terrorism by an act or omission it is a defence for the accused to prove that he either did not know or had no reason to suspect that the assistance given was in the commission, preparation or instigation of an act of terrorism.

This offence is punishable on indictment by a maximum of ten years' imprisonment. Clause 25(1) of the Bill further provides that where, in accordance with a provision mentioned in clause 25(2), it is a defence for a person charged with an offence to prove a particular matter, if the person adduces sufficient evidence to raise an issue with respect to the matter, the court or jury

169 *Rhesa Shipping Co SA v Edmunds* [1985] 1 WLR 948, 955–956 (Lord Brandon); see also in Ireland, *Quinn v Mid Western Health Board* [2005] 4 IR 1, [59].

170 Roberts, P. and Zuckerman, A., op. cit., n. 14, at 111.

171 Duff, P., 'Admissibility of Evidence Obtained in Physical Evidence in the Scottish Criminal Trial: The Search for Principle' (2004) 8 *Edinburgh Law Review* 152, 171–76.

172 Dennis, I., *The Law of Evidence* 4th edn (Sweet & Maxwell, 2010), 49.

shall assume that the defence is satisfied unless the prosecution proves beyond reasonable doubt that it is not. Clause 25(2) lists a number of clauses but not clause 1.

Consider whether the above provision, if enacted in the above terms, would be compatible with Article 6(2) of the European Convention on Human Rights, and, if not, how it may be amended so as to be compatible.

(2) No matter what the charge or where the trial, the principle that the prosecution must prove the guilt of the prisoner is part of the common law of England and no attempt to whittle it down can be entertained.

Woolmington v Director of Public Prosecutions (1935) AC 462, 481 (Viscount Sankey LC)

To what extent has the principle been safeguarded in the years following *Woolmington v DPP?*

(3) The presumption of innocence, one of the central tenets of a fair trial as enshrined in Article 6 of the European Convention on Human Rights, is epitomised by the requirement that the prosecution prove the guilt of the accused beyond all reasonable doubt. In practice, however, the principle has been whittled down by parliamentary intervention and judicial interpretation. It is hoped that reliance on the Human Rights Act 1998 will serve to restore the principle to its fundamental status.

Discuss the issues raised in the above statement.

3.9 Suggested further reading

Allen, J., 'Rethinking the relationship between reverse burdens and the presumption of innocence'. The International Journal of Evidence & Proof (2021) 25(2), 115–134.

Allen, R.J., 'Burdens of Proof' (2014) 13(3/4) Law, Probability & Risk 195.

Ashworth, A., 'Four Threats to the Presumption of Innocence' (2006) 10 E & P 241.

Dennis, I., 'Reverse Onuses and the Presumption of Innocence: In Search of Principle' (2005) Crim LR 901.

Dingwall, G., 'Statutory Exceptions, Burdens of Proof and the Human Rights Act 1998' (2002) 65 MLR 450.

Hamer, D., 'The Presumption of Innocence and Reverse Burdens: A Balancing Act' (2007) 66 CLJ 142.

Hamer, D., 'Presumptions, Standards and Burdens: Managing the Cost of Error' (2014) 13 LP & R 221.

Hjalmarsson, J., 'The Standard of Proof in Civil Cases: An Insurance Fraud Perspective' (2013) 17 E & P 47.

Lippke, R.L., 'Justifying the Proof Structure of Criminal Trials' (2013) 17 E & P 323.

Padfield, N., 'The Burden of Proof Unresolved' (2005) 64 CLJ 17.

Pearson, G., 'A Beautiful Law for the Beautiful Game? Revisiting the Football Offences Act 1991'. The Journal of Criminal Law (2021) 85(6), 362–374.

Roberts, C., 'Reversing the burden of proof before human rights bodies'. The International Journal of Human Rights (2021) 25(10), 1682–1703.

Roberts, P., 'The Presumption of Innocence Brought Home? Kebilene Deconstructed' (2002) 118 LQR 41.

Sumter, A., *The Presumption of Innocence* (Oxford University Press, 2010).

Tadros, V. and Tierney, S., 'The Presumption of Innocence and the Human Rights Act' (2004) 67 MLR 402.

Whitman, J.Q., *The Origins of Reasonable Doubt* (Yale University Press, 2008).

Chapter 4

Witnesses I

Competency, Compellability, and Oath Taking

Chapter contents

DOI: 10.4324/9781003416098-4

Historically, the common law placed a number of restrictions on who could be called to give evidence in both civil and criminal cases. In addition, rules also developed as to when a witness could be legally obliged to testify, under threat of punishment in the event that they failed to do so. This chapter examines the rules relating to competence and compellability of witnesses. The term 'competency' is concerned with who *may* lawfully testify as a witness, whereas the term 'compellability' is concerned with who may be lawfully *obliged* to testify. Both are matters of law to be resolved by the trial judge prior to the witness giving evidence.

We start our discussion with the law relating to the swearing of an oath or solemn affirmation. We start here and base our discussions relating to competence on oath taking given the historical background and link between the two. We then proceed to discuss compellability separately.

4.1 The oath and solemn affirmation

At one time, the principle of orality required that all witnesses testify under oath on the Bible. The courts appeared to regard it as a form of acknowledgement by the witness of a belief that, if they did not keep to it, the consequence would be to suffer 'some kind of divine punishment, although it need not be as bad as hell-fire.'[1] In practice, this rule served to exclude all non-Christians and atheists, who were considered incompetent to testify.

4.1.1 Administering the oath

Prior to a witness entering the court room, or the witness box, they will be asked whether they wish to swear an oath or make a solemn affirmation. If they indicate that they wish to take the oath, they will then be asked upon which holy book they wish to take the oath.

The modern law in respect of both civil and criminal cases is to be found in the Oaths Act 1978. Section 1(1) provides for the manner of the administration of the oath to Christians and

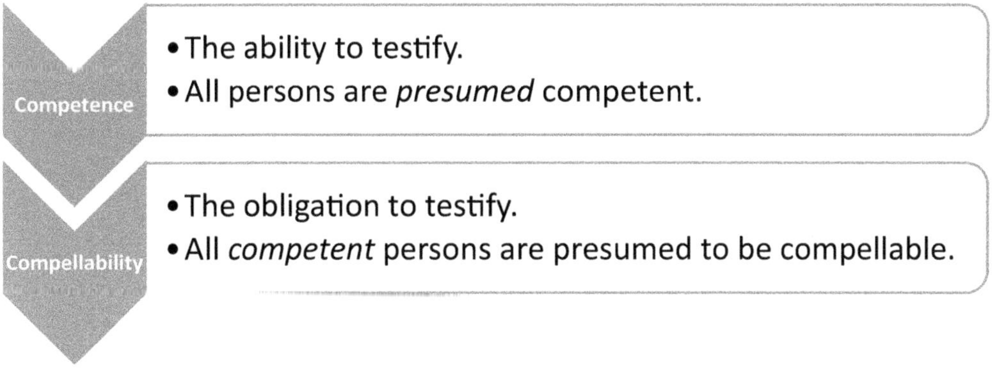

Figure 4.1 Competence and compellability

1 Spencer, J. and Flin, R., *The Evidence of Children* (Blackstone, 1993), p. 51, citing Brett MR in *Attorney General v Bradlaugh* (1885) 14 QBD 667.

those of the Jewish faith. In the case of witnesses of a different religion (i.e. not covered by s 1(1)), the Act provides that the oath shall be administered in any lawful manner.[2] There are, nevertheless, numerous exceptions to the general rule in civil cases, one prominent example being where the case is brought on the small claims track.[3]

4.1.2 Swearing an affirmation

In an increasingly secular society, it is now common for a witness to object to taking a religious oath and to opt to make a solemn affirmation.[4] Section 5(4) states that an affirmation is of the same force and effect as an oath and thus it is improper to question a witness as to why they did not swear an oath,[5] unless there is a real risk that the jury will attach less weight to their evidence.[6] Section 5(2) also provides that a person may make an affirmation where the court finds itself unequipped to administer an oath in the manner appropriate to a person's particular religious belief. Such cases may include where the court does not have a copy of the appropriate book to swear on.

4.1.3 Practicalities of oath taking

The issue as to whether an oath is lawful or not does not depend on the intricacies of the particular religion, but on whether the oath appears to the court to be binding on the conscience of the witness and, if so, whether the witness in question considers the oath to be binding on their conscience.[7]

To avoid the possibility that a non-religious witness might claim that their evidence given on oath is invalid, section 4(2) of the Oaths Act 1978 provides that the fact that a person had at the time of taking the oath no religious belief 'shall not for any purpose affect the validity of the oath.' If a witness wilfully makes a material statement on oath or affirmation that they know is false or does not believe to be true, they will have committed the offence of perjury.[8] Regardless of whether the witness takes the oath or gives a solemn affirmation, they are recognising and acknowledging to open court the importance that is placed on them giving a truthful account in a criminal trial.

There have been a number of proposals to abolish the religious oath altogether, though to date nothing has come of these, and it would seem that the oath in its present form is likely to continue unaltered in the short term at least; Rule 25.11(3)(b) of the Criminal Procedure Rules 2020 provides that, prior to the giving of evidence, a witness must be sworn or give a solemn affirmation, unless legislation otherwise provides.

4.2 Child witnesses (competence and oath taking)

There are, however, certain categories of witnesses who may give evidence unsworn. Traditionally, children who were deemed capable of distinguishing between good and evil were expected to

2 Oaths Act 1978, s 1(3).
3 Rule 27.8(4) of the Civil Procedure Rules 1998 provides that 'the court need not take evidence on oath.'
4 Oaths Act 1978, s 5(1).
5 See *R v Majid* [2009] EWCA Crim 2563.
6 *R v Mehrban* [2002] 1 Cr App R 561.
7 *R v Kemble* [1990] 1 WLR 1111.
8 Perjury Act 1911, s 1(1).

take the oath and give evidence orally from the witness box in open court.[9] However, in time, this rule came to be considered unsatisfactory and led to enactment of section 38 of the Children and Young Persons Act 1933 (now repealed), which permitted a child of tender years (under the age of 14) to give evidence unsworn, provided that the child understood the duty to speak the truth, and was of sufficient intelligence to justify the reception of their evidence. Following *R v Hayes*,[10] the key question for the trial judge became:

> whether the child has a sufficient appreciation of the solemnity of the occasion and the added responsibility to tell the truth which is involved in taking an oath, over and above the duty to tell the truth which is an ordinary duty of normal social contact.[11]

The test in *Hayes* remains good law for child witnesses in civil cases. Anyone under the age of 18 who does not meet this threshold may still give evidence unsworn in civil cases if they understand the 'duty to speak the truth' and have 'sufficient understanding' to justify the reception of the evidence.[12]

Yet for much of the twentieth century, the testimony of children continued to be treated with considerable suspicion. In *R v Wallwork*,[13] Lord Goddard CJ stated that it was 'ridiculous to suppose that a jury could attach any value to the evidence of a five-year-old child' – a view that was endorsed by the Court of Appeal as recently as 1987.[14] However, the 1990s witnessed a considerable shift in thinking, with both policymakers and the judiciary increasingly expressing unease about the longstanding assumption that children were inherently less reliable as witnesses than adults.[15] Following the publication of *Speaking Up for Justice* in June 1998,[16] the rules concerning competency were finally overhauled by the Youth Justice and Criminal Evidence Act (YJCEA) 1999. The Act provides that no witness under the age of 14 is to be sworn, and that witnesses over 14 are eligible to be sworn only if they understand the solemnity of a criminal trial and that taking an oath places a particular responsibility on them to tell the truth.[17] Such witnesses may, however, give evidence unsworn[18] provided that they can understand questions and give answers that can be understood.[19] This could conceivably exclude a very young child or an adult with severe learning or communicative disabilities. If doubts are raised as to the competence of a witness, it is for the party calling the witness to prove that they are able to communicate intelligibly on the balance of probabilities.[20] In practice, any objection as to the competency of a witness ought to be taken

9 *R v Brasier* (1779) 1 Leach 199.
10 (1977) 64 Cr App R 194.
11 Ibid., at 196.
12 Children Act 1989, s 96(2).
13 [1958] 42 Cr App R 153.
14 See comments of Ognall J in *R v Wright and Ormerod* (1990) 90 Cr App R 91, 94: 'That was nearly 30 years ago. So far as this Court is aware, the validity of, and good sense behind, that proposition has remained untrammelled in the practice of the criminal courts.'
15 See further Spencer and Flin, op. cit., n. 1, pp. 46–74.
16 Home Office, *Speaking Up for Justice: Report of the Interdepartmental Working Group on the Treatment of Vulnerable or Intimidated Witnesses in the Criminal Justice System* (Home Office, 1998). See Ch 5.
17 Youth Justice and Criminal Evidence Act 1999, s 55(2)(a).
18 Ibid., s 56. In *R v Day* [1997] 1 Cr App R 181, it was held that where a child, aged under 14 when the video was made but over 14 when the video is presented as evidence, is cross-examined in court or via a TV link, the child should be sworn. This remained the position under the 1999 Act. It follows that fewer children may now appear in court, but if the situation in *Day* is repeated and the child witness is then over 14 years of age when the video is tendered in evidence, then, consistent with s 55(2), they can only give sworn evidence. It is the practice when video-taping an interview with a child close to 14, who might well be over that age when appearing in court, for the child to affirm that fact at the beginning of the interview.
19 Youth Justice and Criminal Evidence Act 1999, s 53(3).
20 Ibid., s 54(2).

prior to the moment the witness is sworn or gives evidence.[21] Further to this, section 54(4) of the YJCEA 1999 provides that any proceedings held for the determination of competency shall take place in the absence of the jury (if there is one). In evaluating competency, the court will often consult a child psychologist and may also watch any video-taped interview with the child or ask questions of the child.[22]

4.2.1 Applying the competency test to child witnesses

In *R v MacPherson*,[23] the appellant was charged with having committed indecent assault upon S, a 4-year-old girl. The trial judge, having watched the video-recorded interview, rejected the defence's contention that the witness was incompetent, and allowed her evidence. The appellant was convicted, and appealed on the grounds that the judge erred in determining S's competence on the basis of her video testimony alone, that he had no or insufficient regard to the requirement that he assess the child's ability to understand and answer questions within the forensic forum as a witness as required by section 53 of the Act, and that, in reaching his decision, he had no or insufficient regard to the girl's ability to participate meaningfully in cross-examination. These arguments were, however, dismissed by the Court of Appeal. It was held that the judge had properly assessed the child's ability to 'understand questions put to her as a witness and give answers to them which could be understood.' In particular, the court noted that the words 'put to him as a witness' within section 53(3)(a) meant the equivalent of 'being asked of him in court,' so that a child who could only communicate in baby-language with his mother would not ordinarily be competent, but a young child like the girl in the instant case, who could speak and understand basic English with strangers, would be competent. Moreover, the Act laid down no requirement that the child should be aware of their status as a witness: questions of credibility and reliability were matters for the jury and were not relevant to the issue of competence.

The importance of applying the correct test for competence was demonstrated in *R v F*, where the Court of Appeal overturned a conviction on the grounds that it was unsafe as the judge had applied the wrong test of competence.[24] In that case, the judge had considered the court's difficulties in communicating with the witness, who had learning difficulties and was profoundly deaf, rather than considering the appellant's ability to understand questions put to him and give answers that could be understood.

As Professor Spencer has observed, the rules introduced by the 1999 Act governing the competency of child witnesses are of symbolic, as well as practical, importance:

> [The rules] mark the final transition from a system where the courts refused to hear all sorts of persons for fear they might not tell the truth, to one where the courts listen to everybody, and try to decide whether they are truthful or not on the basis of what they have said.[25]

---

21 See *R v Yacoob* (1981) 72 Cr App R 313, where it was held that the appropriate time for determining the competency of a witness was at the beginning of a trial. However, there is no strict rule to this effect.

22 *DPP v M* [1997] 3 Cr App R 70.

23 [2006] 1 Cr App R 459.

24 *R v F* [2013] 1 WLR 2143.

25 Spencer, J., 'The Youth Justice and Criminal Evidence Act 1999: The Evidence Provisions,' *Archbold News*, January 2000, at 5–8.

Such an approach was followed by the Court of Appeal in the leading case of *R v Barker*.[26] The case concerned the anal rape of a toddler, X, who was the sister of the recently deceased Baby P.[27]

Following the death of her brother, X was taken into foster care and made a number of allegations concerning sexual abuse by Barker. She was interviewed on video shortly afterwards, and was available for cross-examination at trial, by which time she was 4 years old. Despite objections from the defence, the judge determined that she fulfilled the statutory criteria and was competent to give evidence. Dismissing the appeal, it was held that the provisions of the YJCEA 1999 were clear and unequivocal and no further interpretation was required. In each case in which a party sought to introduce the testimony of a young child, the trial judge was called on to make a judgment as to whether the witness fulfilled the statutory criteria. Although the age of the child would inevitably help to inform the decision regarding competence, the decision was not to be based on age alone since the age of the witness did not necessarily reflect their ability to give truthful and accurate evidence. The court further noted that the witness need not understand every single question or give a readily understood answer to every question. Moreover, in the case of *R v IA & Others*, the Court of Appeal reaffirmed the trial judge's words that competence is 'witness, trial and issue specific.'[28] Combined with the range of special measures that have been made available to assist such witnesses,[29] the above decisions send a positive signal that children testifying in English courtrooms can now expect to be respected and protected in a much more comprehensive fashion than has traditionally been the case.

4.3 Witnesses with cognitive and learning disabilities

Witnesses who suffer from cognitive or mental disabilities that impact upon their ability to communicate have traditionally presented problems for the courts. At common law, 'persons of unsound mind' who were not capable of understanding the nature of the oath and of giving rational evidence were not competent witnesses. Historically, the applicable test was whether the witness understood the nature of the oath and the divine sanction. Thus, in *R v Hill*,[30] the witness was an inmate of a lunatic asylum who suffered from the delusion that he was possessed by spirits who talked to him. Medical evidence was given that the witness was capable of giving an account of any transaction that he witnessed. The Court of Appeal held that the judge had correctly ruled that the witness was competent. In any such case, it was for the trial judge to examine the witness and determine, on the basis of the responses to his questions, whether the witness understands the nature of the oath.

Surprisingly, the requirement of belief in some form of divine sanction if one failed to tell the truth continued to underpin the test of competency for adults with learning disabilities until the decision of the Court of Appeal in *R v Bellamy*.[31] The case concerned the testimony of a rape complainant, aged 33, but with a mental age of ten. At trial, the judge heard evidence from the complainant's social worker and questioned the complainant both about her belief in God and about her understanding of the importance of telling the truth. He decided that she was a competent witness, but lacked a sufficient belief in the existence of God to take a binding oath. The Court of Appeal held that her appreciation of the theological intricacies of the oath should have been

26 [2010] EWCA Crim 4; [2011] Crim LR 233.

27 The infamous case of 'Baby P' was widely reported in the media in autumn 2008. Peter Connelly was a 17-month-old boy who died after he sustained more than 50 injuries over an eight-month period while in the care of his mother and her boyfriend. See further *The Guardian* (12 November 2008).

28 *R v IA, TA & FA* [2013] EWCA Crim 1308, [70].

29 See Ch 5.

30 (1851) 2 Den 254.

31 (1985) 82 Cr App R 222.

discarded as irrelevant. The answers the complainant had given to initial questioning indicated that she satisfied the *Hayes* test. Although *Hayes* had only been regarded as an authority in respect of child witnesses, the Court of Appeal held that the same test should be applied for adult witnesses under the modern law. Thus, applying *Hayes*, the trial judge would have to ascertain whether the witness had a sufficient appreciation of the solemnity of the occasion and the added responsibility to tell the truth that is involved in taking an oath.

Under the YJCEA 1999, witnesses in criminal cases who suffer from cognitive impairment or a learning disability are subject to the same test for competency as children.[32] Thus, under section 53 of the Act, all witnesses are presumed to be competent unless it is shown that they are unable to understand the questions and give answers that can be understood. In practice, this presumption will rarely be called into question, but where the issue is raised, it is for the parties to satisfy the court on the balance of probabilities that the witness is competent to give evidence. For such evidence to be given under oath, the witness must also have a sufficient appreciation of the solemnity of the occasion and of the particular responsibility to tell the truth that is involved in taking an oath.[33] It can be noted that, in civil cases, all adult testimony must be received under oath; so witnesses who fail the *Hayes* test will be unable to provide evidence.

In *R v Sed*,[34] the trial judge admitted the video statement of an 81-year-old woman suffering from Alzheimer's disease. Although the woman's answers on the video were somewhat confused, she stated that a man had had sexual intercourse with her without her consent. Expert medical evidence indicated that, at the time of her interview, she was not fit to give evidence in court owing to her dementia. Applying the test of competence set out in section 53 of the 1999 Act, the judge ruled that the witness was competent, and admitted the video statement.

The accused was convicted, and his appeal was dismissed. The question for the Court of Appeal centred on which test of competence ought to be applied for the purposes of a documentary statement admissible under section 23 of the Criminal Justice Act 1988 (repealed). Even though the trial had taken place before section 53 of the 1999 Act came into force, Auld LJ said that its formulation of a new notion of competence was a reasonable, although not obligatory, approach for the judge to adopt when considering whether to admit the hearsay evidence. Ultimately, it was concerned with assessing the extent and impact of any mental or psychiatric illness at the time the statement was made.[35]

The competency of a 13-year-old girl with a severe mental handicap was challenged in *DPP v R*.[36] In her evidence-in-chief (which was pre-recorded following a special measures direction),[37] the girl had stated that she had been subjected to a sexual assault. When she was cross-examined in court, she was unable to recall any details of the incident. The defence contended that she should be deemed incompetent, but the Divisional Court drew a distinction between her inability to recall details and an inability to give intelligible testimony. In the instant case, she was considered to be able to understand questions put to her and give intelligible answers, thereby satisfying the test in section 53 of the 1999 Act.

Although recent years have seen a gradual relaxation of the once-stringent requirements on competency, the facts of *DPP v R* appear to support the view that the adversarial environment is not conducive to facilitating the testimony of young and vulnerable people. Special measures

32 The test in *Hayes* continues to govern civil cases.

33 YJCEA 1999, s 55(2).

34 [2004] 1 WLR 3218.

35 To this end, s 123(3) of the Criminal Justice Act 2003 now makes it clear that consideration of s 53 of the 1999 Act is now obligatory when considering the admissibility of a hearsay statement contained in any document. Hearsay evidence is considered in detail in Ch 12.

36 [2007] EWHC Crim 1842.

37 See Ch 5.

Table 4.1 The competency of witnesses in criminal cases

Category of witness (W)	Legislative provision	Competent?
Child witnesses aged under 14	YJCEA, s 53(3)	Only competent to give unsworn evidence and only if W can understand questions and give answers that can be understood.
Child witnesses aged 14 and over	YJCEA, s 55(2)(a)	Competent to give sworn evidence only if W understands the solemnity of a criminal trial and that taking an oath places a particular responsibility on them to tell the truth.
Witnesses with cognitive impairment or learning difficulties	YJCEA, s 53(3); s 55(2)	Presumed competent to give evidence unless it is shown that they are unable to understand the questions and to give answers that can be understood. For sworn evidence, W must also have a sufficient appreciation of the solemnity of the occasion and of the particular responsibility to tell the truth that is involved in taking an oath.
Accused/co-accused	YJCEA, s 53(4)	Incompetent for prosecution.
Spouse of the accused	YJCEA, s 53(1)	Competent for either party unless jointly charged with the accused.

directions (considered in the next chapters) have undoubtedly helped greater numbers of such people to give evidence, but problems clearly remain when they are required to give live evidence in court. The difficulties faced by such witnesses will be considered in detail in Chapter 5. Table 4.1 shows the categories of competency of witnesses.

4.4 The compellability of witnesses

At every stage in criminal proceedings, all persons are (whatever their age) presumed competent to give evidence. Unlike the criminal system, where the general rule has been put on a statutory footing,[38] there is no such footing in civil proceedings. However, in both systems, it is well established that all competent witnesses are compellable. In other words, all witnesses are under a legal obligation to give evidence if called upon do so and may be subject to a legal penalty for failure to carry out that duty. A competent witness can be compelled to give evidence by the threat of being held in contempt (punishable by imprisonment) for failing to do so.[39] It should however be noted that there has been an increase in concern for the interests of complainants and other witnesses in the criminal justice process, as Hall[40] and Doak[41] identified.

As regards operation of the rule in practice, in a criminal case both the prosecution and defence are responsible for the attendance of their witnesses, and therefore they require a summons

38 YJCEA 1999, s 53(1).

39 See e.g. *R v Renshaw* [1989] Crim LR 811; *R v Holt and Bird* (1996), *The Times*, 31 October.

40 Hall, M., 'The Relationship between the Victim and Prosecutor: Defending Victim Rights?' [2010] Crim LR 31.

41 Doak, J., *Victims' Rights, Human Rights and Criminal Justice* (Hart Publishing, 2008).

in order to get the witness to court. In the Crown Court, a witness can be compelled to attend trial,[42] and a compellable witness who ignores a summons is in contempt of court and can face imprisonment for up to three months.[43] In the magistrates' court, the attendance of witnesses can be secured by a witness summons or a warrant.[44] Should a witness fail to attend court on a summons, the court may issue a warrant for their arrest.[45] Refusal to be sworn or give evidence may result in a punishment of up to one month's imprisonment and/or a maximum fine of £2,500.[46]

In civil cases, Part 34 of the Civil Procedure Rules 1998 provides that the attendance of a witness can be secured by the issuing of a witness summons. Under Rules 34.2–34.7, a witness can be compelled to give oral evidence or produce a document.[47] Failure to obey a summons from the High Court is contempt of court with a maximum sentence of two years' imprisonment and/ or a fine,[48] whereas failure to obey a summons from the County Court may result in a fine up to £1,000.[49]

Although it is usually the case that competence will automatically give rise to compellability, there are three major exceptions to this rule that apply in criminal cases. First, the spouse of an accused is now a competent witness by virtue of section 53(1) of the YJCEA 1999. However, as we shall see below, they are only compellable for the prosecution against the accused, or a co-accused in very limited circumstances.[50] Second, the accused was made a competent witness in their own defence by the Criminal Evidence Act 1898, but is not a competent witness for the prosecution in any proceedings so long as they remain charged with an offence in the proceedings. An accused person is not compellable, but, as noted below, if they choose to give evidence, there is no privilege against self-incrimination in respect of the offences with which they are charged.[51] As noted in the case of Saunders,[52] the privilege against self-incrimination has value in its ability to prevent wrongful conviction, to secure the acquittal of innocent suspects by preventing false confessions or the disclosure of unreliable information. In the same vein, the broader application of privilege towards non-testimonial and material evidence has been explored by Choo,[53] where, for example, in the demand for the handling of a specific pre-existing document, or the provision of a bodily sample, there is no wider danger of the suspect falsely confessing. Corresponding with Choo's research, the case of Tully confirmed that under material evidence, the contents of a document or sample will 'speak for itself.'[54] Lastly, diplomats, foreign heads of state, and the sovereign are competent, but are not usually compellable witnesses.[55] Correspondingly, Siedmann and Stein[56] also offer an alternative way to link the presumption of innocence to witness compellability, where they claim that allowing suspects to remain silent and not incriminate themselves discourages guilty defendants from giving false accounts.

42 Criminal Procedure (Attendance of Witnesses) Act (CPA) 1965, s 2.
43 Ibid., s 3(2). See further *R v Yusuf* [2003] All ER (D) 91; *R v Renshaw* [1989] Crim LR 811.
44 Magistrates' Courts Act 1980, s 97.
45 Ibid., s 97(3).
46 Ibid., s 97(5).
47 Rule 17.3 of the Criminal Procedure Rules 2020 provides that before a magistrates' court may issue a warrant under section 97(3) of the 1980 Act, the witness must first be paid or offered a reasonable amount for costs and expenses.
48 Contempt of Court Act 1981, s 14(1).
49 County Courts Act 1984, s 55(1).
50 Unless the spouse is jointly tried with the defendant, in which case they will not be competent for the prosecution.
51 Criminal Evidence Act 1898, s 1(2).
52 *Saunders v U.K.* (1997) 23 EHRR, 313, [68].
53 Choo, A.L-T., *The Privilege Against Self-Incrimination and Criminal Justice* (Hart Publishing, 2013), 5.
54 *AT & T Istel Ltd v Tully* [1993] AC 45 [HL] 57.
55 See further Diplomatic Privileges Act 1964, Consular Relations Act 1968, and State Immunity Act 1978.
56 Siedmann, D.J. and Stein, A., 'The Right to Silence Helps the Innocent: A Game-Theoretic Analysis of the Fifth Amendment Privilege' (2001) 114 *Harvard Law Review* 430.

4.4.1 Exceptions to the rule

4.4.1.1 The spouse or civil partner of the accused

The common law rules relating to the competence and compellability of the accused's spouse were complex and confused. The wife or husband of a person charged in the proceedings was generally considered to be incompetent, except in respect of a small number of serious offences. The House of Lords' decision in *Hoskyn v Metropolitan Police Commissioner*[57] changed this view, and thereafter the common law rule was that the wife or husband of a defendant could not give evidence for the prosecution no matter how serious the charge.

The issue was considered by the Criminal Law Revision Committee in 1972. The Committee accepted that a wife ought not to be compelled to testify against her husband on the grounds that such a move could disrupt marital harmony by placing one partner in the invidious position of having to incriminate the other.[58] It concluded, however, that public policy dictated that wives should be compellable to testify for certain offences against the person of the wife or children (aged under 16) of the same household as the accused; otherwise, these offences might go undetected – or, if detected, unpunished – given that there are rarely any other witnesses to domestic crimes of this nature. It was further felt that, in relation to crimes against children of the household, the wife might be guilty of some complicity and for that reason reluctant to testify without the compulsion of law. However, the Committee emphasised that the seriousness of the offence was not in itself sufficient to justify compelling a spouse to testify against the other spouse.[59]

No action was taken in terms of reforming the law until some 12 years later. As the Police and Criminal Evidence Bill was going through Parliament, a number of high-profile cases of child sex abuse persuaded the Government to extend compellability to include sexual offences against, or assaults upon, any child under 16. Section 80 of the Police and Criminal Evidence Act (PACE) 1984, as amended by the YJCEA 1999, forms the basis of the current legal framework.

Section 80(2A) makes a spouse or civil partner compellable for the prosecution or a co-defendant (unless jointly charged) if, and only if, the offence constitutes a 'specified offence.' Under section 80(3), an offence is defined as a specified offence for the purposes of section 80(2A) if:

> (a) it involves an assault on, or injury or threat of injury to, the wife or husband or a person who was at the material time under the age of 16;
> (b) it is a sexual offence alleged to have been committed in respect of a person who was at the material time under that age; or
> (c) it consists of attempting or conspiring to commit, or of aiding, abetting, counselling, procuring or inciting the commission of, an offence falling within paragraph (a) or (b) above.

A spouse or civil partner is now competent in all cases (unless also charged in the proceedings) and can give evidence in any case but can only be compelled to do so in the limited circumstances provided for in section 80(3)(a), (b), and (c) (a specified offence).[60] This provision does, however, create anomalies. For example, a wife cannot be compelled to give evidence against her husband charged with the rape and murder of a girl aged 16 years and 1 month but can be compelled to give evidence against her husband if he is charged with committing a sexual assault

---

57 [1979] AC 474.

58 *Criminal Law Revision Committee, Eleventh Report, Evidence (General)*, Cmnd 4991 (HMSO, 1972).

59 Ibid., at [143]–[157].

60 Civil Partnership Act 2004, s 84(1) provides that: 'Any enactment or rule of law relating to the giving of evidence by a spouse applies in relation to a civil partner as it applies to the spouse.' Marriage (Same Sex Couples) Act 2013, s 11(1) provides that: 'In the law of England and Wales, marriage has the same effect in relation to same sex couples as it has in relation to opposite sex couples.'

on a 15-year-old girl by pinching her bottom. This position is consistent with the Criminal Law Revision Committee's refusal to be swayed simply by the seriousness of the offence. A high-profile example of this aberration can be found in the infamous case of the serial killer Fred West. He and his wife were jointly charged with more than ten murders of young girls. If the wife had not been charged with West, she would have been compellable for the prosecution on charges of rape and murder of girls aged under 16, but not in respect of the same charges where the victims were 16 or over.

West's case highlights a further peculiarity: where multiple victims are involved, a spouse may be compellable in respect of one offence, but not the other.

Example 4.1

Suppose Keith and Jane are married with two children, Hilda (16) and Tammy (15). Keith is charged with the rape of both of his daughters. In practice, however, were such a case to come to court, the accused would almost certainly be tried for the two different counts of rape at the same trial. Since rape is a specified offence for the purposes of section 80(3)(b), Jane will be compellable by the prosecution in respect of the alleged offence committed against Tammy, but not in relation to the alleged rape of Hilda. In respect of this latter offence, Jane will be entitled to refuse to give evidence. This is likely to create problems for the prosecution and court, who must determine what evidence is relevant to which offence, and what evidence the wife can be compelled to give and what evidence she can refuse to give. Evidence may very well be intermingled, so although technically the jury should consider Jane's evidence only in respect of Tammy, it may be difficult for them to draw a clear line of division to separate the evidence in respect of the two different offences.

When the Government took the opportunity to revise section 80 as part of the reforms introduced by the YJCEA 1999, it would have been logical to provide that, where the accused is charged with a specified offence in respect of which their spouse is compellable, and with other offences in respect of which they are not compellable, they should be compellable in respect of all offences charged. However, no such reform was ever undertaken.

As the law stands, the spouse has been given a *de facto* privilege against being compelled to give evidence against the other spouse unless the offence falls within section 80(3). They can waive the privilege and give evidence in those cases to which section 80(3) does not apply. However, any such decision must be made in full knowledge of their right not to give such evidence. Thus, where a spouse who is not compellable chooses to give evidence, the trial judge must ensure that the decision to give evidence is made in the knowledge that they are not compelled to do so.[61] Given the fact that one of the core functions of the criminal justice system ought to be protection of the public at large, it seems highly questionable, particularly in serious cases, that a spouse should effectively hold a form of veto on a conviction.

It is also doubtful whether the scope of section 80(3)(a) includes a sexual offence against the spouse. Could it be the case, for example, that the wife of the accused could be compellable to give evidence against her husband accused of raping her? This question was not considered by the Criminal Law Revision Committee in 1972, nor by the framers of the PACE 1984, because at that time there was no offence of marital rape. When the husband's immunity at common law for

61 *R v Pitt* [1983] QB 25.

marital rape was abolished by the decision of the House of Lords in *R v R*,[62] the question was thus raised as to whether, in such cases, the wife may be compellable by the prosecution.

Given that rape usually involves an assault or the threat of an assault, the question would seem to be answerable in the affirmative. However, the Law Commission has drawn attention to the presumably intended contrast between section 80(3)(a), which refers to assault, and section 80(3)(b), which refers to 'sexual' offences[63] committed against persons under 16.[64] If rape is considered to be a sexual offence, it follows that a woman is not compellable on a charge against her partner of raping her. This view is supported by the redefinition of 'rape' in section 1 of the Sexual Offences Act 2003, which, while including lack of consent, speaks of 'intentional penetration.' It is likely that the courts will interpret rape as including an assault for the purposes of section 80(3)(a), given that any touching without consent constitutes an assault. Such an interpretation is supported by section 2 of the 2003 Act, which creates the offence of assault by penetration by parts of the body or by any object other than the penis. Since the offences are almost identically worded, it would seem that rape of a spouse would now fall within the ambit of section 80(3)(a) of the 1984 Act. This issue may have been answered by the important case of *R v BA*,[65] where the Court of Appeal embraced the opportunity to define exactly what is meant by an assault in section 80(3)(a). The court concluded that:

> the word 'it' in subsection (3)(a) plainly refers back to the word 'offence' in the opening words of subsection (3). Although this demonstrates that the focus is upon the nature of the offence … the word 'involved' can be given a broad construction within that constraint. Thus the offence itself does not have to have as one of its ingredients 'an assault on or injury or threat of injury' to the spouse or person under the age of 16. It is sufficient if the offence encompasses the real possibility of an assault or injury or threat of injury.[66]

In light of this ruling, it now seems that three types of offences will suffice for the purposes of the test contained in section 80(3)(a):

1. The legal offence of assault (under section 39 of the Criminal Justice Act 1988).
2. An offence which has as one of its ingredients an assault (e.g. actual bodily harm (ABH)).
3. An offence which encompasses the 'real possibility' of an assault.

Therefore, given that rape involves an assault (through unwanted touching), it would appear that rape of the spouse falls within the list of specified offences in section 80(3)(a). However, the court proceeded to state that the anomalies arising in section 80(3) were ultimately a matter for Parliament; it remains to be seen whether such issues will be addressed in due course.

When section 80(3) was first formulated, it was hoped that the provision might assist in the prosecution of domestic violence cases, which, like child abuse, have a notoriously high attrition rate. It is often the case that a wife withdraws her complaint before a file is passed to the Crown Prosecution Service (CPS), and in these circumstances the CPS will tend not to bring charges (or will later drop charges) on the grounds that there is little prospect of a conviction.[67] In such cases, it would be open to the prosecution to use section 80(3) and threaten the wife with a charge of

62 [1992] 1 AC 599.
63 Defined in the YJCEA 1999, 80(7).
64 Law Commission, *Rape Within Marriage*, Report No. 205 (HMSO, 1990).
65 *R v BA* [2012] 1 WLR 3378.
66 Ibid., The President of the Queen's Bench Division, at [18].
67 See further Her Majesty's Chief Inspector of Constabulary and Her Majesty's Chief Inspector of the Crown Prosecution Service, *Violence at Home* (HMSO, 2004).

contempt if she refuses to testify. This course of action would, however, be extremely undesirable in that it could result in the absurd situation in which the victim is punished and the alleged perpetrator would go unpunished. There is also some evidence from other jurisdictions that a policy of pursuing prosecutions regardless of the witness's reluctance to testify can serve to discourage victims from reporting domestic violence.[68] If the victim is in fear because of threats of intimidation, she may be eligible for such measures, which may assist her to give evidence.[69] There is also the possibility that her statement of evidence may be admissible in documentary form under sections 114(1)(d) or 116(2)(e) of the Criminal Justice Act 2003.[70] While such provisions may alleviate to some extent the victim's fear of testifying, they will not ultimately affect the privilege provided by section 80(3), or the refusal to testify based on the emotional tie between victim and offender.

Even where a reluctant spouse does testify, they may refuse to give the expected testimony. In these circumstances, they can be treated as a hostile witness, and previous statements made to the police that are inconsistent with what the witness says in the witness box can be put to the witness and, if accepted as correct, be put in evidence.[71] However, the weight given to such evidence is much reduced by the process, and the jury may not give much credence to a witness who has said one thing to the police and something else in court.

It will be apparent from the above discussion that section 80(3) is something of a minefield of potential difficulties, a number of which confronted the Court of Appeal in the case of *R v L*.[72]

The accused was on trial for a number of rapes and indecent assaults on his daughter. It was alleged that the indecent assaults had taken place over a number of years from the age of 10, and that she had been raped since the age of 16. The prosecution sought to introduce a towel into evidence that had been found near a sofa in the complainant's flat with traces of the accused's semen on it. The defendant claimed that he had used the towel following sex with his wife on the sofa on a previous occasion, but when questioned by police the defendant's wife stated that she did not think that they had ever had sex in her daughter's flat, and if they did it would have taken place only in the bedroom. However, at trial his wife declined to testify. She was not a compellable witness since this evidence related to a rape when the complainant was aged 19. Nevertheless, the prosecution successfully argued that the statement be introduced under section 114(1)(d) of the Criminal Justice Act 2003, which provides that certain out-of-court hearsay statements may be admitted in the 'interests of justice.'[73]

The accused was convicted and appealed, contending that his wife's statement should not have been admitted for two reasons: first, because, in admitting the statement, the trial judge had effectively circumvented the non-compellability provisions in PACE; second, because his wife ought to have been advised before she was questioned that she could not be compelled to give evidence against her husband. Both of these arguments were rejected by the Court of Appeal. On the first point, it stated the legislation reflected that 'the interests of convicting a husband of child abuse take precedence over the demands of marital duty and harmony,'[74] and, as such, in the instant case the interests of justice were best served by the admission of the defendant's wife's evidence. The second ground of appeal was also rejected on the basis that there was no legislative requirement for the police to have informed the spouse that she would not be compellable. It was, however, stated *obiter* that 'there may be circumstances where the police would be well advised to make it

---

68 See generally Buzawa, E. and Buzawa, C., *Domestic Violence: The Criminal Justice Response*, 3rd edn (Sage, 2003).

69 See Ch 5.

70 See Ch 12.

71 Criminal Procedure Act 1865, s 3. See further Ch 6.

72 [2009] 1 WLR 626.

73 See further Chapter 12.

74 *R v. L* [2015] EWCA Crim 741, at 634.

plain that a wife need not make a statement that implicated her husband.'[75] Indeed, the policy requirements underpinning the current legal approach were considered valid by the Strasbourg Court, which held in *Van Der Heijden v Netherlands* that although compelling a spouse to testify interfered with her right to respect for family life under Article 8(1) of the European Convention on Human Rights (ECHR), such interference was held to be necessary under Article 8(2).[76]

It should be noted that it is only the wife, husband, or civil partner who has the right to refuse to give evidence in those cases not covered by section 80(3). Cohabitees, no matter how long they have lived together, are competent and compellable in all cases, as are all children, parents, siblings, and other close relatives. This is somewhat anomalous given the increasing tendency to place live-in partners on the same legal footing as spouses,[77] and the fact that the blood relationship can be as strong as, if not stronger than, the marital bond. Compelling a partner, son, or daughter to give evidence against the other partner or parent, or compelling the partner or parent to give evidence against their children, is likely to have as great an impact on the family and relationship as compelling the legal spouse. Seemingly, the law is not concerned with what compelling a spouse to give evidence does to the family, only with what it might do to the marriage. In *R v Pearce*,[78] the Court of Appeal confirmed that cohabitees and children were not within section 80(3). In that case, it was argued on behalf of the appellant that compelling partners and children of the marriage to give evidence constituted a breach of Article 8(1) of the ECHR. However, the Court of Appeal rejected the argument, holding that such compulsion was necessary in a democratic society to prevent crime.

The institution of marriage has, of course, undergone radical transformation in the decades since section 80 came into force. With around 40 per cent of marriages now ending in divorce, and with two-thirds of people believing that there is little difference between marriage and cohabitation,[79] it might be asked whether a more modern approach should be enacted that would place on the spouse the same social responsibility to give evidence as non-spouses. This would involve repealing section 80 and putting spouses under the same moral and legal obligation as any other witness who can choose not to testify, but on pain of punishment. A priest has no legal privilege and cannot lawfully refuse to disclose matters confided to him, even under the seal of the confessional.[80] Journalists have gone to prison rather than testify as to the source of information obtained.[81] It is increasingly difficult to justify a more privileged position for the spouse.

Alternatively, it may be argued that the emphasis should be on preserving family relationships, so that the privilege should be extended to include partners, children, and close relatives. However, given the increase in abuse within families, the exceptions contained in section 80(3) must remain if the family members are to be protected from criminal abuse. A number of Australian states, including Victoria, New South Wales, and South Australia, have adopted a discretionary approach in various forms, whereby the spouse is compellable in all cases, but the trial judge has a discretion to exempt the spouse from giving evidence where the public interest in obtaining the spouse's evidence is outweighed by private interests, such as the likely damage to the marital relationship or the harshness of compelling the spouse to testify. Factors to be considered

75 Ibid., at 626.

76 (2013) EHRR 13.

77 See e.g. Civil Partnership Act 2004.

78 [2002] 1 Cr App R 551.

79 National Centre for Social Research, *British Social Attitudes Survey* 2008 (NCSR, 2008).

80 *Butler v Moore* (1802) 2 Sch & Les 249; *R v Gilham* (1828) 1 Mood CC 186.

81 For example, in 2005 the prominent *New York Times* journalist Judith Miller was sentenced to 18 months' imprisonment for refusing to reveal the identity of a confidential source of information for an article about a CIA informer. Journalists are better protected in England and Wales, with s 10 of the Contempt of Court Act 1981 stipulating that they cannot be required to disclose a source (or held in contempt for refusing to reveal it) unless a court is satisfied that such disclosure is necessary 'in the interests of justice or national security or for the prevention of disorder or crime.'

in exercising that discretion include the nature of the offence charged, the likely significance of the spouse's evidence in the case, the state of the relationship between the spouses, and the likely effect upon it of compelling the spouse to testify. Under such a discretionary system, a wife is unlikely to be compelled to testify against her husband who is charged with a minor offence, but is likely to be compelled when she has evidence of some significance and the offence is a serious one.

It is worth noting that the failure of the spouse of the accused to give evidence shall not be made the subject of any comment by the prosecution.[82] The judge may comment on the failure of the spouse to testify, but there is little that can be said about the wife whose loyalty to her husband causes her to decline to give evidence against him. Although a spouse is not compellable as a witness, they, on their own accord, may still give evidence by waiving the privilege. Moreover, the trial judge should ensure the decision to give evidence is made in knowledge that the spouse is under no legal obligation to do so. This is not a strict rule or course of action that must be followed, but if the judge decides to offer such a warning, they must do so in the absence of the jury.[83]

4.4.1.2 Former spouses, future spouses, and polygamous 'spouses'

Under section 80(5) of the PACE 1984, former spouses are competent and compellable to give evidence as if that person and the accused had never been married. Only those who have had the divorce decree made absolute are compellable.[84] The position regarding future spouses was considered in *R (Crown Prosecution Service) v Registrar-General of Births, Deaths and Marriages*,[85] in which the accused, charged with murder and held on remand, sought permission to marry his long-term partner. Since she was a witness for the prosecution, and would by virtue of section 80 of the 1984 Act cease to be a compellable witness at his trial, the CPS attempted to persuade the Registrar-General and the director of the prison not to allow the marriage to take place until after the trial. When both declined to do so, their decision was challenged by way of judicial review. The Court of Appeal held that there was no power to prevent, on the grounds of public policy, the marriage between a prisoner on remand and his long-term partner, despite the fact that the marriage would make her a non-compellable witness at his forthcoming trial for murder. It was accepted that the duty of the Registrar-General under section 31 of the Marriage Act 1949 was absolute. There were, however, circumstances in which that absolute duty would be subject to implied limitations on public policy grounds. Authorities were cited to show that no person should profit from their own serious crime, and that statutes should be interpreted to prevent a grave crime being committed or the course of justice perverted. Despite the consequences that followed from the provisions of section 80 of the 1984 Act, entering into a lawful marriage did not amount to perverting the course of justice.

The application of section 80 to a polygamous marriage was considered by the Court of Appeal in *R v Khan*.[86] Khan, who was already married under English law, underwent a Muslim marriage taking a second 'wife.' The marriage was not recognised in England, and it was thus held that his second 'wife' was competent and compellable for the prosecution on the charges against Khan. Although this case was decided before section 80 came into force, the decision would be the same under section 80, either because the woman is not married to a person charged in the proceedings and must therefore be treated as any other witness, or because section 80(5) operates to treat her as not married.

---

82 PACE 1984, s 80A.
83 *R v Pitt* [1983] QB 25.
84 *R v Cruttenden* [1991] Crim LR 537.
85 [2003] 1 QB 1222.
86 (1987) 84 Cr App R 44.

4.4.1.3 The accused

Prior to 1898, accused persons were incompetent to give evidence in their own defence. Instead, a defendant could make an unsworn statement from the dock, which could be taken into account by the trier of fact, but was not technically regarded as evidence.[87] Section 1 of the Criminal Evidence Act 1898 provided that accused persons were competent to give evidence in their own defence. However, it remained the case that they could not be compelled to do so, thus the phrasing 'upon his own application' in section 1(1) of the 1898 Act.

Thus, where the accused decides to give evidence, they will be treated as any other witness and be exposed to cross-examination. They can be questioned in relation to any matter as to the offence charged,[88] although no questions may be asked in relation to previous bad character or previous convictions, except in the circumstances provided for in the Criminal Justice Act 2003.[89] By virtue of section 1(4) of the 1898 Act, any defendant who exercises their right to give evidence must do so from the witness box, unless otherwise ordered.[90]

Table 4.2 describes a broad overview of the category of witnesses in a trial, the legislative provisions that govern them, and whether they can be compelled.

Table 4.2 The compellability of witnesses in criminal cases

Category of witness		Legislative provision	Compellable?
	for himself	s 1(1) CEA 1898	No, due to the privilege against self-incrimination.
Accused/ co-accused	for a co-accused	NA	No, due to the privilege against self-incrimination.
	for the prosecution	NA	No, as not competent for the prosecution (s 53(4) YJCEA 1999).
	for the defence	s 80(2) PACE 1984	Yes, unless they too are a co-accused (s 80(4) PACE 1984).
Spouse/civil partner of the accused	for a co-accused	s 80(2A) PACE 1984	No, unless the offence is a 'specified' one.
For the prosecution	s 80(2A) PACE 1984	No, unless the offence is a 'specified' one.	
Former spouse/ civil partner of the accused		s 80(5)/(5A) PACE 1984	Yes. These witnesses are treated as though they were never married to the accused (decree absolute required).

87 The right to make an unsworn statement from the dock as an alternative to testifying was abolished by the Criminal Justice Act 1982, s 72.

88 Section 1(2) of the Criminal Evidence Act 1898 makes it clear that the accused has no privilege against self-incrimination in respect of the offence charged.

89 See further Ch 11.

90 *R v Symonds* (1924) 18 Cr App R 100. Such cases normally concern defendants who have difficulty walking or those who are too violent to be controlled in the witness box.

The accused is also a competent witness for a co-accused,[91] but is not compellable.[92] However, a defendant is not competent to testify for the prosecution so long as they are a 'person charged' in the proceedings, who is named in the indictment, whether alone or with others.[93] The justification for this is that when the defendant is obliged to actively participate (i.e. is compelled) the purpose of this is to secure him as a source of evidence, therefore using the defendant within the fact-finding process, as opposed to respecting the rights of the defendant, per Jackson and Summers.[94] Section 53(5) of the YJCEA 1999 provides that 'a person charged in criminal proceedings does not include a person who is not, or is no longer, liable to be convicted of any offence in the proceedings (whether as a result of pleading guilty or for any other reason).' Therefore, there are four ways in which an accused can be removed from the indictment, thus making them a competent and compellable witness for the prosecution. These arise where:

- D is acquitted, with the prosecution offering no evidence;
- D pleads guilty and is subsequently removed from the indictment;[95]
- the Attorney-General enters a *nolle prosequi*;[96]or
- D is removed from the indictment and is tried separately.

In each of these circumstances, the defendant is then a competent and compellable witness for the prosecution against a co-accused.

However, relatively recently, both the English courts and the European Court of Human Rights (ECtHR) have taken a 'silence is an indicator of guilt' approach in their assessment of the Criminal Justice and Public Order Act (CJPOA) 1994 and wider principles of self-incrimination. For the most part, they have adopted an expansive interpretation of the provisions based on the belief that drawing inferences from silence is a matter of 'common sense' for the courts.[97]

Compare this with the French system, where the defendant is expected to contribute towards the truth-finding process; he does have the right to remain silent, but psychologically, this becomes almost impossible to maintain, as identified by Hodgson.[98]

Jackson and Summers have advanced an argument of the ECtHR recognising the right to adversarial procedure. In fact, the reference towards an 'adversarial procedure' began to appear in the European Court judgments as early as the late 1980s, often linked to the equality of arms principle.[99] This was illustrated in *O'Donnell v U.K.*, where Judge Wotjtczeh expressed that 'A restriction on the right to silence affects the way in which the presumption of innocence operates in practice and entails a de facto reallocation of the burden of proof.'[100] This judgment should be read in line with Buche et al., who also found that there was a difference in opinion among criminal justice practitioners as the burden of proof shifts accordingly.

---

91 Youth Justice and Criminal Evidence Act 1999, s 53(1).

92 Criminal Evidence Act 1898, s 1(1).

93 Youth Justice and Criminal Evidence Act 1999, s 53(4). See, *R v Marsh-Smith* [2015] EWCA Crim 1883.

94 Jackson, J. and Summers, S., *The Internationalization of Criminal Evidence: Beyond the Common Law and Civil Law Traditions* (Cambridge University Press, 2012) 245.

95 If those who were their co-accused plead not guilty, they go to trial. See further *R v McEwan* [2011] EWCA Crim 1026.

96 A *nolle prosequi* is essentially a writ that stays the prosecution against the person named on it. Thus, if the accused is the subject of such a writ, they cannot be prosecuted in respect of the offence(s) with which they are charged and are removed from the indictment. The trial will then proceed against anyone else named in the indictment.

97 *Murray v DPP* [1994] 1 WLR 1 (HL); *R v Webber* [2004] UKHL 1, [2004] 1 WLR 404, [33].

98 Hodgson, J., *French Criminal Justice* (Hart Publishing, 2005).

99 Jackson, J. and Summers, S., op. cit., n. 94.

100 *O'Donnell v U.K.* [2015] ECHR, 16667/0, concurring opinion of Judge Wojtyczek [3].

Cases such as *Jalloh* and *O'Halloran*[101] have also contributed to an increasingly difficult system where it can be suggested that there is now an inherent danger and unfairness in the criminal process.[102] At the very least, the CJPOA 1994 reduces the force of the presumption of innocence by implying the guilt of the defendant from their silence. As Auld LJ commented previously:

> the whole basis of Section 34, in its qualification of the otherwise general right of an accused to remain silent and to require the prosecution to prove its case, is an assumption that an innocent defendant ... would give an early explanation to demonstrate his innocence.[103]

Attempts have been made to rationalise the privilege against self-incrimination by aligning it with defendants and suspects facing a 'cruel trilemma' of having to choose between being penalised for non-cooperation, providing the authorities with incriminating evidence, or lying and risking prosecution for perjury, as argued by Redmayne[104] as one of the strongest defences for maintaining the privilege.

However, not all commentators agree with viewing the right to silence this way. For example, Bentham[105] labelled these arguments as those proposed by 'old women,' and supporting this, Dolinko[106] explains that conviction, punishment, and condemnation are often the desired end result of the criminal system, and therefore should not be labelled cruel. Yet, students should consider the argument that compelling individuals to inflict harm on themselves aggravates the cruelty of simply inflicting it on them without their participation. This is because, especially within the context of the right to silence, the cruelty does not necessarily lie in the consequence of the trial itself, but within the circumstances in which the truth was obtained. Correspondingly, self-incrimination may be considered cruel when viewed from the perspective that it forces people to make these exceptionally difficult choices.[107] Dolinko even goes as far as to say that it would be 'contrary to the basic human instinct of self-preservation' to make these choices.

4.5 Key learning points

- Competency is concerned with who may lawfully testify as a witness.
- Compellability is concerned with who may be lawfully *obliged* to testify. Refusal to do so may lead to a charge of contempt of court.
- Witnesses will usually be required to take a religious oath or to make a solemn affirmation before giving evidence.
- Those who are incompetent to give sworn evidence may provide unsworn evidence in criminal courts. Only children may do so in civil courts.
- Even those giving unsworn evidence must be capable of providing intelligible testimony.
- The general rule is that all competent witnesses are compellable.
- Exceptions to the rule apply with respect to child witnesses, witnesses with physical and mental disabilities, the spouse of the accused, and the accused.

---

101 *Brown v Scott* [2003] 1 AC 681, (PC) 705, *O'Halloran and Francis v U.K.* (2008) 46 EHRR 21 [17].

102 See, for example, *Saunders v U.K.* (1997) 23 EHHR 313; *R v S(F)* 2008 EWCA Crim 2177, [2009] 1 WLR 1489; *Beghal v DPP* (2018) UKSC 49, [2015] 2 WLR 344. See also Choo, A.L-T., op. cit., n. 53, 50, 115.

103 Langbein, J.H., *The Origins of the Adversarial Criminal Trial* (Oxford University Press, 2003), see Ch 4.2.

104 Redmayne, M., 'Rethinking the Privilege Against Self-Incrimination' (2007) 27 *Oxford Journal of Legal Studies*, 209, 221.

105 Lewis, A., 'Bentham's View of the Right to Silence' (1990) 43, *Current Legal Problems* 135, 148.

106 Dolinko, D., 'Is There a Rationale for the Privilege Against Self-Incrimination?' (1986) 33 *UCLA Law Review* 1063, 1103.

107 Theophilopoulous, C., 'The Privilege Against Self-Incrimination and the Distinction Between Testimonial and Non-testimonial Evidence' (2010) 127 *South African Law Journal* 107, 118.

4.6 Practice questions

1. Sanjay, aged 8, has witnessed a burglary at his parents' home. The prosecution wants to call him to give evidence concerning the identity of the accused. Will the prosecution be able to call him to give evidence?
2. The prosecution wishes to call David's estranged wife, Clara, to testify against him on sexual abuse charges against his 12-year-old niece. Clara is reluctant to testify; can she be compelled to give evidence?
3. Pauline, aged 18, has an IQ of 70 and a reading age of 8. She is stopped on her way out of a local clothes shop by a security guard who accuses her of placing a T-shirt in her bag without paying for it. Is Pauline competent to testify in her own defence?
4. Why do you think special exemptions exist to limit the compellability of diplomats and foreign heads of state? Are these exceptions justifiable?
5. 'The rules concerning the compellability of spouses in English law are outdated and in pressing need of reform.' Do you agree with this statement?

4.7 Suggested further reading

Brabin, J., 'A Criminal Defendant's Spouse as a Prosecution Witness' (2011) Crim LR 613.
Creighton, P., 'Spouse Competence and Compellability' (1990) Crim LR 34.
Law Commission, *Rape within Marriage*, Report No. 205 (HMSO, 1990).
Munday, R., 'Sham Marriages and Spousal Compellability' (2001) 64(1) Journal of Criminal Law 98.

Chapter 5

Witnesses II

Vulnerable Witnesses

Chapter contents

DOI: 10.4324/9781003416098-5

For the vast majority of witnesses, the courtroom will be an unfamiliar and austere environment, dominated by lawyers and court officials. It is perhaps unsurprising that research has uncovered that many witnesses may find the process of giving evidence alienating and stressful.[1] The formality of the procedure, the forbidding atmosphere, and the presence of wigs and gowns are likely to contribute to this general sense of unease, which results in many witnesses feeling like outsiders to a highly ritualised and professionalised process.[2]

5.1 The experiences of vulnerable witnesses

While feelings of stress, anxiety, or consternation are commonplace among many witnesses with diverse characteristics testifying in very different types of cases, it is well established that such emotions are likely to be exacerbated among certain classes of witness. There is a considerable body of research charting the plight of child witnesses, complainants in sexual cases, witnesses suffering from learning disabilities, and witnesses in fear of intimidation. Not only may their sense of despondency cause them undue distress before, during, and after giving testimony, but, from the point of view of the legal system, it may also negatively impact their ability to recall past events accurately.[3] Measures that may be taken in order to enhance the experience for witnesses include witness pre-trial familiarisation with the courtroom layout, etiquette, and procedure, characterised by the court as 'sensible preparation for the experience of giving evidence,' which assists the witness to give his or her best at the forthcoming trial.[4]

5.1.1 Child witnesses

Many child witnesses find the prospect of testifying extremely daunting and confusing. Research has shown consistently that children experience considerable anxiety in the lead-up to a court appearance, as well as experiencing so-called secondary victimisation while giving evidence.[5,6]

In particular, stress levels are exacerbated by the unfamiliar language used in court by barristers. Davies and Noon's study of child witnesses in England found that 25 per cent of all questions were inappropriate to the witness's age.[7] Brennan and Brennan's survey of child witnesses in Australia identified 13 different linguistic devices that were used regularly to confuse child

---

1 See Angle, H., Malam, S., and Carey, C., *Witness Satisfaction: Findings from the Witness Satisfaction Survey 2002* (HMSO, 2003). The researchers reported that 21 per cent of all witnesses surveyed felt intimidated either by the process of giving evidence or by the courtroom environment. See also Shapland, J., Willmore, J., and Duff, P., *Victims in the Criminal Justice System* (Gower, 1985); Whitehead, E., *Witness Satisfaction: Findings from the Witness Satisfaction Survey 2000* (HMSO, 2001).

2 See generally Rock, P., *The Social World of the English Crown Court* (Clarendon, 1993).

3 For an overview of the literature on this point, see Ellison, L., *The Adversarial Process and the Vulnerable Witness* (Oxford University Press, 2001), pp. 19–23.

4 Home Office, 'Rebalancing the Criminal Justice System in Favour of the Law-Abiding Majority' (HMSO, 2006); Home Office, *Justice for All*, CM 5563 (The Stationery Office, 2002); Jackson, J.D., 'Justice for All: Putting Victims at the Heart of Criminal Justice' (2003) 30 *Journal of Law and Society* 309.

5 See e.g. Goodman, G., Taub, E.P., Jones, D., England, P., Port, L., Rudy, L., and Rado, L., *Testifying in Criminal Court: Emotional Effects on Child Sexual Assault Victims* (University of Chicago Press, 1992).

6 Ibid., p. 121. Hayes, D., and Bunting, L. 'Just Be Brave': The Experiences of Young Witnesses in Criminal Proceedings in Northern Ireland' (2013) 22(6) *Child Abuse Review* 419; Plotnikoff, J. and Woolfson, R. *Measuring Up? Evaluating Implementation of Government Commitments to Young Witnesses in Criminal Proceedings* (NSPCC/The Nuffield Foundation, 2009).

7 Davies, G. and Noon, D., *An Evaluation of the Live Link for Child Witnesses* (HMSO, 1991). Only 36 per cent of barristers made extensive efforts to adapt their language so as to make it suitable for the child.

witnesses. The use of complex sentence structures and advanced vocabulary served to exacerbate the unfamiliar situation in which children found themselves, and the researchers found that questions were frequently highly stylised (e.g. 'I put it to you ... '; 'I suggest to you ... ') or employed complex grammatical structures involving negatives (e.g. 'Now you did have a bruise, did you not, near one of your breasts?'; 'Now this happened on a Friday, did it not?'). In the words of the researchers:

> Cross-examination is that part of court proceedings where the interests and rights of the child are most likely to be ignored and sacrificed ... The techniques used are all created with words, since they are the only currency of the court ... Under conditions of cross-examination the child is placed in an adversarial and stressful situation which tests the resilience of even the most confident of adults ... The right of the lawyer to directly oppose the evidence given by the child witness, the implicit hostility which surrounds cross-examination, alien language forms, and the sheer volume of questions asked, all conspire to confuse the child. It is a quick and easy step to destroy the credibility of the child witness.[8]

In 2004, a survey of 50 child witnesses carried out on behalf of the National Society for the Prevention of Cruelty to Children (NSPCC) by Plotnikoff and Woolfson found that over half the children interviewed said that they did not understand some words or found some questions confusing.[9] Just five of the child witnesses interviewed described defence lawyers as 'polite,' but 19 said the lawyers were not polite. Defence counsel were described as 'aggressive,' 'sarcastic,' 'cross,' 'shouting,' 'rude,' 'harassing,' 'disrespectful,' 'arrogant,' 'overpowering,' 'badgering,' 'scary,' and 'pushy.' Other studies have arrived at similar findings. Cordon et al., for example, describe how advocates will frequently try to lure child witnesses into a false sense of security, by asking non-substantive questions about the child's background and interests, before subtly moving on to elicit substantive information that contradicts the child's original testimony.[10] They also present evidence that suggests that cross-examiners typically capitalise on children's tendencies to be suggestible and to fantasise. The goal in many cross-examinations, they argue, is to 'keep the child off balance to increase the chance of inconsistencies.'[11] To that end, the NSPCC produced a report, which was endorsed by the Judicial Studies Board (now the Judicial College) in July 2009, stating the sort of procedures that ought to be followed when dealing with a young witness. Such procedures include, and are not limited to:

1. Use simple, common words and phrases;
2. Repeat names and places often;
3. Avoid negatives;
4. Avoid 'Do you remember ...?' questions.[12]

---

8 Ibid., p. 91.

9 Plotnikoff, J. and Woolfson, R., *In Their Own Words: The Experiences of 50 Young Witnesses in Criminal Proceedings* (NSPCC, 2004).

10 Cordon, I., Goodman, G., and Anderson, S., 'Children in Court,' in P.J. Van Koppen and S.D. Penrod (eds), *Adversarial versus Inquisitorial Justice* (Kluwer, 2003). See also Andrews, S.J., Lamb, M.E., and Lyon, T.D. 'Question Types, Responsiveness, and Self-Contradictions When Prosecutors and Defence Attorneys Question Alleged Victims of Child Sexual Abuse' (2015) 29(2) *Applied Cognitive Psychology* 253.

11 Cordon, I., Goodman, G., and Anderson, S., ibid., pp. 175–77.

12 http://www.nspcc.org.uk/Inform/research/findings/measuring_up_guidance_wdf66581.pdf (last accessed 3 December 2014).

More recent studies suggest that, while there has been some improvement in the overall treatment of young witnesses, there remains a 'significant gap between the visions of policy and the reality of many children's experiences.'[13] In a major survey of 182 young witnesses from England, Wales, and Northern Ireland published in 2009,[14] Plotnikoff and Woolfson found that almost a third of those interviewed (30 per cent) had not been offered an opportunity to visit a courtroom or a live link facility before giving evidence. Moreover, cross-examination evidently remains problematic; almost half of the children interviewed described defence counsel as 'aggressive,' 'rude,' or 'cross,' and the same number stated that they did not understand all of the questions. Perhaps of even greater concern was the fact that a majority of witnesses (58 per cent) said the other side's lawyer tried to make them say something they did not mean or tried to put words in their mouth. On a more positive note, half of those interviewed stated that they had gained something good or positive from the experience of testifying.

5.1.2 Complainants in rape and other sexual offences

Trials for sexual offences differ from other criminal hearings in a number of respects. Often, the fact that intercourse actually took place is not a contested issue. Most rape cases usually turn on the issue of consent, which can give rise to a number of evidential difficulties, particularly where the complainant and the accused have previously engaged in a consensual sexual relationship. Since the complainant and the accused will usually be the only witnesses to the incident in question, rape trials frequently turn on a battle of credibility between the accused and the alleged victim. Historically, one of the main methods used by defence counsel was to attack the character of the rape complainant and suggest that she is sexually disreputable, alluding to loose moral values and a decadent lifestyle. By their very nature, sexual offences are notoriously invasive, and many victims will struggle with emotional and psychological consequences of victimisation for years to come.[15] Sex crimes carry a notoriously high attrition rate,[16] and it is thus particularly unfortunate that those who find the courage to testify about their ordeal in open court could be subjected to character assassination.

It is only in relatively recent times that the plight of rape and sexual assault complainants at court has been uncovered. In 1978, Holmstrom and Burgess were among the first to conduct research into the issue, and concluded that 'overwhelmingly, both adult and young [rape] victims found court an extremely stressful experience.'[17] Since then, a substantial body of literature has rapidly grown to support this view. The most stressful aspect of the court appearance is cross-examination, which is often particularly humiliating for complainants. It is not uncommon for them to be questioned in relation to intimate details of their private lives, as well as being asked to recount to a public courtroom intricate details of an invasive and traumatising attack. As Grohovsky describes, the victim's body becomes something of a crime scene in itself 'from which evidence must be collected and analysed.'[18]

---

13 Plotnikoff, J. and Woolfson, R., *Measuring Up? Evaluating Implementation of Government Commitments to Young Witnesses in Criminal Proceedings* (Nuffield Foundation/NSPCC, 2009), p. 153.

14 Ibid.

15 See e.g. Santiago, J., McCall-Perez, F., Gorcey, M., and Beigel, A., 'Long-Term Psychological Effects of Rape in 35 Rape Victims' (1985) 142 *American Journal of Psychiatry* 1338.

16 See Kelly, L., Lovett, J., and Regan, L., *A Gap or Chasm? Attrition in Reported Rape Cases*, Home Office Research Study No. 293 (HMSO, 2005).

17 Holstrom, L. and Burgess, A.W., 'Rape Trauma Syndrome' (1974) 131 *American Journal of Psychiatry* 981, 986.

18 Grohovsky, J., 'Giving Voice to Victims: Why the Criminal Justice System in England and Wales Should Allow Victims to Speak Up for Themselves' (2000) 64 *Journal of Criminal Law* 416, at 417.

The most distressing types of question are likely to be those that relate to the complainant's lifestyle and sexual history. In a survey of 116 rape complainants, Lees records complainants being asked details about their underwear, make-up, social lifestyle, menstrual cycle, and drug habits:[19]

> Questions addressed to the women in the trials I monitored included whether she had had previous sex with men other than the defendant, whether she was a single mother, whether the man she was living with was the father of her children; the colour of her present and past boyfriends ... who looked after her children while she was at work; whether she was in the habit of going to nightclubs on her own late at night; whether she smoked cannabis and drank alcohol ... what underwear she had on; whether she wore false eyelashes and red lipstick; whether the defendant had 'used her previously.'[20]

The vast majority of complainants interviewed by Lees (83 per cent) said that they felt as though they were on trial, rather than the defendant. Similarly, a 1996 survey of rape complainants by Victim Support found that 12 per cent of women said their experience in court was actually worse than the rape itself.[21] Furthermore, 41 per cent of women felt anger or that they had been revictimised in court.[22]

In *R v Uddin and Ali*,[23] Fulford LJ acknowledged the trouble that persons involved in sexual offences face. Specifically, his Lordship commented that:

> The victims of offences of this kind are frequently damaged young people. They are nearly always wholly unused to giving evidence in court. They can be difficult, emotional, contradictory, aggressive and on some occasions wholly uncommunicative. Whether in any trial their evidence is so vitiated that it is unsafe to leave the case to the jury will be a matter of careful judicial assessment. However, the courts now have a far greater understanding than hitherto as to the difficulties that exist for vulnerable witnesses and the need for care in assessing whether inconsistent or varying accounts given on different occasions necessarily mean that the underlying allegation is untruthful or unreliable. These are often matters for juries rather than judges to assess because it will be vital for the fact finder to assess the reasons for the changes or the contradictions in the witness's evidence and whether they fatally undermine the prosecution's case as regards the counts on the indictment.[24]

As noted below, while steps have been taken in recent years to limit the potential for attacks on the complainant, there are concerns that these are inadequate and are unlikely to address the fundamental difficulties faced by rape complainants.

5.1.3 Witnesses with learning disabilities

Since the adversarial system relies heavily on oral testimony, there is a presumption that all witnesses are able to communicate effectively. As we have discovered in relation to young children, this will not necessarily be the case. Witnesses with learning disabilities are also likely to find the task of understanding questions and articulating their answers extremely difficult under adversarial conditions. In a study carried out in the mid-1990s, Sanders et al. identified three key areas

19 Lees, S., *Carnal Knowledge: Rape on Trial* (Hamish Hamilton, 1996), pp. 139–49.
20 Ibid., p. 134.
21 Victim Support, *Women, Rape and the Criminal Justice System* (Victim Support, 1996).
22 Ibid.
23 [2014] EWCA Crim 2269.
24 Ibid., at [54].

that are likely to make learning-disabled witnesses at risk of heightened vulnerability in court.[25] First, such witnesses are often impaired in terms of their memory: their ability to absorb, memorise, and then recall events is often lessened. Second, such witnesses often encounter difficulties in communicating: many possess a restricted vocabulary and have, therefore, a limited means of articulating themselves. Finally, these witnesses often respond to aggressive questioning by attempting to pacify the questioners by offering the responses that they think they are looking for.

The researchers concluded that witnesses with learning difficulties suffer from enhanced levels of stress and many such witnesses were reported as feeling bullied or pressurised when testifying, which, in turn, impacted negatively upon their testimony. In addition, and in a similar fashion to the treatment of child witnesses, counsel frequently used convoluted language as a device to confuse witnesses or to make them contradict themselves.[26] In spite of their powers to do so, judges rarely intervened to prevent inappropriate questioning and failed to adapt their own language to make allowances for the witness.[27] Other studies have arrived at similar findings. Both Kebbell et al. and O'Kelly et al. have reported that lawyers did little to adjust their questioning style and that there were no significant differences in the readiness of the judiciary to intervene to clarify questioning among witnesses with learning difficulties and those without.[28]

5.1.4 Witnesses in fear of intimidation

A further group of witnesses who may be particularly vulnerable are those at risk of intimidation or reprisals as a result of giving evidence. Witness intimidation is a particular problem, especially where the alleged offenders are part of the community in which the witness lives, or where the community is hostile to the police. One intimidation incident, reported in the national press, concerned the trial of four men for causing grievous bodily harm to a witness to a murder. One prospective witness was sitting in a crowded pub when he was suddenly set upon by four masked men. His punishment for testifying was the loss of his hand, which was hacked off with a butcher's knife.[29] The Home Office publication *Working with Intimidated Witnesses*[30] envisages that the problem of witness intimidation is on the increase: the number of cases for perverting the course of justice (which includes witness intimidation) rose by over 30 per cent between 2000 and 2005. Working from the 1998 British Crime Survey, Tarling et al. concluded that intimidation occurs in almost 10 per cent of reported crime and in 20 per cent of unreported crime.[31] Intimidation of victims may take various forms, from verbal taunts or threats, to physical jousting or serious physical violence. It may range from a relatively low-key, one-off incident to a chain of events amounting to ongoing harassment and persistent threatening behaviour.[32]

---

25 Sanders, A., Creation, J., Bird, S., and Weber, L., *Victims with Learning Disabilities: Negotiating the Criminal Justice System*, Home Office Research Findings No. 44 (HMSO, 1996).

26 Ibid., p. 76.

27 Ibid.

28 O'Kelly, C., Kebbell, M., Hatton, C., and Johnson, S., 'Judicial Intervention in Court Cases Involving Witnesses with and without Learning Disabilities' (2003) 8 *Legal and Criminological Psychology* 229; Kebbell, M., Hatton, C., and Johnson, S., 'Witnesses with Intellectual Disabilities in Court: What Questions Are Asked and What Influence Do They Have?' (2004) 9 *Legal and Criminological Psychology* 23. See also Green, G., 'Vulnerability of Witnesses with Learning Disabilities: Preparing to Give Evidence Against a Perpetrator of Sexual Abuse' (2001) 29(3) *British Journal of Learning Disabilities* 103.

29 'Murder Witness's Hands Cut Off in Pub,' *The Times* (5 April 1997), p. 3.

30 Home Office, *Working with Intimidated Witnesses* (HMSO, 2006).

31 Tarling, R., Dowds, L., and Budd, T., *Victim and Witness Intimidation: Key Findings from the British Crime Survey* (HMSO, 2000).

32 Tarling et al. (ibid.) found that almost over two-thirds of incidents featured verbal abuse, 16 per cent physical assaults, and 9 per cent damage to property. However, the reasons underlying intimidation are unclear. In only a small minority of cases (8 per cent) did the victim believe that the reason behind the intimidation was to prevent them from giving evidence. In nearly 50 per cent of cases, victims thought it was simply that the offender wanted to 'annoy' or 'upset' them. For a further quarter, the intimidation was viewed as part of an ongoing series of offences against them, for example in cases of domestic violence.

Recent studies suggest that certain groups of people, or witnesses who testify in particular types of cases, are at heightened risk of intimidation. Levels of intimidation appear to be greater among poorer socio-economic groups,[33] victims of crime (particularly victims of violence),[34] racial and sexual minorities,[35] and women – particularly in cases involving domestic violence[36] or those involving sexual offences.[37] Where a case concerns organised crime or terrorist activity, it is quite possible that the associates of the accused may seek to coerce witnesses from giving evidence through duress or physical violence.

Even if witness intimidation occurs only in a relatively small proportion of cases, there is nonetheless a risk that the *fear* of intimidation may act to prevent many victims from reporting crime or giving evidence in court. Although intimidation is more often seen as a pre-trial problem, Hamlyn et al. noted that those who were intimidated were more likely to suffer secondary victimisation at court,[38] and victims were more likely to suffer than other witnesses.[39] Despite national initiatives to ensure separate waiting facilities for victims and defendants, meetings in the court precinct still seem to be commonplace.[40] One troubling finding from recent observational research conducted by Fielding was that many of the court-based professionals seemed unsure how to react and viewed it as someone else's problem.[41]

5.1.5 Other witnesses

The problems experienced by these various classes of 'vulnerable' witness are particularly well documented, but they should not detract from the fact that most lay witnesses will find the prospect of giving evidence somewhat daunting and stressful.[42] In his study of proceedings at Wood Green Crown Court, Rock found that 'as a matter of course, and in most ordinary trials, gravely wounding allegations would be put to witnesses.'[43] Witnesses, he reported, were frequently bullied, harassed, and felt as though they were on trial in 'the most charged of all secular rituals.'[44] Often, witnesses were not permitted to give their evidence at a greater rate than the desired pace of the transcriber, and on occasions were told to slow down their evidence. Rock also observed that 'nothing was allowed to remain tacit, elided, discreet or *sotto voce*,'[45] with witnesses being asked to 'speak up' if they failed to make themselves audible to the entire court.[46] Evidently, if witnesses are relaying to the court intimate details of their private lives, including past indiscretions, or even something as mundane as their addresses and occupations, they may be reluctant or embarrassed to make certain facts public knowledge. Rock noted that this can cause particular awkwardness in witnesses when they are required to flout the taboos of language, with the court hearing details of 'all the violent doings and language of the bedroom, street and public house,

---

33 Tarling et al., op. cit., n. 31.

34 Elliott, R., *Vulnerable and Intimidated Witnesses: A Review of the Literature* (HMSO, 1998). See also Angle et al., op. cit., n. 1.

35 Elliott, ibid.

36 Ibid.; Tarling et al., op. cit., n. 31.

37 Lees, op. cit., n. 19, p. 108.

38 Hamlyn, B., Phelps, A., Turtle, J., and Sattar, G., *Are Special Measures Working? Evidence from Surveys of Vulnerable and Intimidated Witnesses*, Home Office Research Study No. 283 (HMSO, 2004), p. xi.

39 Ibid., p. 19.

40 Ibid.

41 Fielding, N., *Courting Violence* (Oxford University Press, 2006), p. 215.

42 Of course, proceedings will be inevitably less stressful for those who regularly appear in court as part of their professional duties. Police officers, customs officials, and expert witnesses are much less likely to be unnerved by the process of giving evidence.

43 Rock, P., *The Social World of an English Crown Court* (Clarendon Press, 1993), at 88.

44 Ibid., at 267.

45 Ibid.

46 Ibid.

witnesses having to cite the heedless and profane speech of angry relationships.'[47] For most judges and legal professions, distress is a perfectly natural aspect of criminal trials.

Similar findings were uncovered by Fielding, who examined the conduct of trials involving violent offences.[48] Many witnesses experienced feelings of stress and alienation, but, like Rock, Fielding found that these emotions were perceived by lawyers and judges as unfortunate but essential aspects of the court hearing.[49] On occasions, judges would attempt to mitigate the experience by 'pacing' proceedings, offering tissues or water, or sympathetic words,[50] but Fielding describes how the 'fear factor' seemed to enhance credibility, with advocates engaging in a range of well-established techniques, including 'rapid fire questioning,' with witnesses being visibly upset by public interrogation about very intimate or private matters.

As research into the experience of witnesses continues to be disseminated on a regular basis, it is becoming increasingly apparent that it is the underlying adversarial paradigm itself that renders the experience of testifying so distressful for so many witnesses. We shall return to this issue later in this chapter.

5.2 Protecting vulnerable witnesses in criminal cases

The past two decades have witnessed considerable efforts to address some of the problems highlighted above, with successive governments introducing a range of measures to help reduce secondary victimisation in the courtroom. The first statutory measures were contained in the Criminal Justice Act 1988, which made provision for children, with the leave of the court, to give all of their evidence by live television link in cases involving offences of a sexual or violent nature.[51] In practice, this would mean that, subject to the discretion of the court, the child could avoid having to give evidence in the austerity of the courtroom and would not have to face the prospect of being confronted by the accused.

Shortly after the enactment of the legislation, the Government established an advisory group in 1989, chaired by Judge Thomas Pigot QC, to consider its full implications.[52] The terms of reference of the advisory group were to examine the 'growing body of support for a change in the law, so that video-recordings of interviews with victims could be readily used as evidence in trials for child abuse.' However, the Home Secretary also made clear that the Government could not contemplate the effacement of the defendant's right to cross-examination, thus effectively rejecting the possibility of pre-recorded cross-examination before the group had even commenced its inquiry. The group based its work around two 'rudimentary principles':

- that child witnesses' involvement in criminal proceedings should be concluded as rapidly as possible without compromising the interests of justice; and
- that children should give evidence in surroundings and circumstances that do not intimidate or overawe them, and the number of people present should be kept to a minimum.

---

47 Ibid., p. 50.

48 Fielding, op. cit., n. 41.

49 Ibid., pp. 38, 45–46.

50 Ibid., pp. 45–50.

51 CJA 1988, s 32. This provision was subsequently extended by the subsequent CJA 1991 to include children under the age of 17, where a sexual offence was concerned.

52 Pigot, Judge T., *Report of the Advisory Group on Video Evidence* (HMSO, 1989).

The Pigot Committee recognised that the television link was only a partial solution and recommended that:

- no child under the age of 14 (17 in sexual offences) should have to give evidence in open court when the offence involved is one of violence or of a sexual nature, or cruelty or neglect;
- children's evidence-in-chief should be replaced by a video-taped interview;
- cross-examination of the child should take place at an out-of-court preliminary hearing when the judge and counsel would be present, the videoed evidence and cross-examination being shown to the jury at the appropriate point in the trial when the child would have given evidence.

Had they been implemented, these proposals would have meant that child witnesses need never appear in court. Instead, all questioning would be pre-recorded outside the court in an informal atmosphere shortly after the charges had been brought against the accused. This radical proposal, however, met with stiff opposition, and the Criminal Justice Act 1991 that followed stopped well short of implementing the recommendations of the Pigot Committee. Instead, the Act made provision for the child's evidence-in-chief to be recorded in advance of the trial,[53] but made no equivalent provision for cross-examination or re-examination. Thus, section 54 of the Act required, as a condition of the admissibility of the video evidence, that the child be available for cross-examination – undoubtedly the most gruelling aspect of the questioning process.[54] Nonetheless, the reform was given a broad welcome. For the first time, the Government had accepted that courts had duties to safeguard the interests of certain witnesses, and acknowledged their status as victims, as opposed to mere servants of the criminal justice system. However, the legislation still fell well short of offering a fully comprehensive set of procedural protections for vulnerable witnesses, and was severely limited in a number of respects.

First, the legislation applied only to a limited class of persons for a limited range of specified offences in criminal cases only. The reforms failed to deal with other vulnerable witnesses, such as adult complainants in sexual cases, or the physically disabled and mentally ill. Second, even when child witnesses were deemed eligible to make use of such measures, the range of measures open to them remained very limited. Only the child's evidence-in-chief was to be pre-recorded, and the key recommendation of the Pigot Committee, that children should not be forced into giving any evidence in court against their will, was ignored. Third, the nature of legislation created an overly complex and piecemeal framework of rules on children's evidence, contained in three separate statutes: the Children and Young Persons Act 1933; the Criminal Justice Act 1988; and the Criminal Justice Act 1991. The Government failed to seize the opportunity to consolidate the law in the 1991 Act, and its scope thus remained uncertain and confusing.

The provisions of the 1988 and 1991 Acts were overly complex, poorly drafted, and also gave rise to numerous legal lacunae. For example, whereas the live link and the use of video-recorded evidence were limited to trial on indictment and in youth courts, no provision was made for children who had to testify in magistrates' courts. Another major omission was the lack of any comprehensive guidance or criteria, other than the rather ambiguous 'interests of justice' test.[55] Similarly, no mechanisms were in place for ascertaining the child witness's expectations or desires; there was no guidance as to whether the views of the child should be taken into account, or indeed how such views were to be ascertained. Such omissions and complexities resulted in

---

53 Note, however, that only children aged under 15 (physical abuse) or under 17 (sexual abuse) could take advantage of the provision.

54 Such cross-examination could, however, be carried out via the television link under the 1988 Act, provided that the relevant criteria were met.

55 CJA 1988, s 32A(3)(c).

an uncertain regime in which judicial discretion had a key role to play. In the absence of comprehensive guidelines, the prevailing climate of uncertainty and inconsistent practice was bound to be perpetuated.

5.2.1 The Youth Justice and Criminal Evidence Act 1999

Following the election of the Labour Government in May 1997, the new Home Secretary, Jack Straw, announced the setting up of a Home Office interdepartmental working group to examine and make recommendations on the treatment of vulnerable and intimidated witnesses within the criminal justice system. Its terms of reference included the identification of measures at all stages of the criminal justice process that would improve the treatment of vulnerable witnesses, and further measures that might encourage witnesses to give evidence in court. Members of the group were drawn from a range of government departments, and included representatives of Victim Support and the Association of Chief Police Officers. Special conferences were held to facilitate discussion with the judiciary and legal profession, and in drawing up its recommendations the group drew heavily on the findings of a number of academic studies. The group published its report, *Speaking Up for Justice*, in June 1998.[56]

The Report made a total of 78 recommendations, 26 of which required legislation. It highlighted the need for training for all those involved in the criminal justice system to assist them in responding to the needs of vulnerable witnesses, including children. A plethora of recommendations dealt with a variety of victims' issues, including measures to combat witness intimidation and a wide range of measures to protect vulnerable and intimidated witnesses at the trial itself. The group identified two categories of witness who should receive assistance at the discretion of the court. First, the Report concluded that those witnesses whose vulnerability related to the effects of age, disability, or illness (Category A witnesses) would automatically be entitled to some form of special protection. However, in the case of witnesses who may be vulnerable or intimidated for reasons relating to their particular situation or the circumstances of the case (Category B witnesses), it was recommended that the trial judge retain discretion in determining whether or not the granting of such measures would be appropriate. In contrast to the half-hearted attempt to implement the Pigot Report in 1991, most of the *Speaking Up for Justice* recommendations were implemented in Part II of the Youth Justice and Criminal Evidence Act (YJCEA) 1999.

Like the previous regime contained in the Criminal Justice Acts 1988 and 1991, the current provisions are something of a statutory minefield. Applications for special measures directions will usually be made before the trial begins during the plea and trial preparation hearing.[57] In determining whether or not to issue a special measures direction, the court has to concern itself with three issues:

- the eligibility of the witness;
- the availability of the range of special measures; and
- the desirability of making a special measures direction in the circumstances of the case.

56 Home Office, *Speaking Up for Justice: Report of the Interdepartmental Working Group on the Treatment of Vulnerable or Intimidated Witnesses in the Criminal Justice System* (HMSO, 1998).

57 See *R v Michael Boxer* [2015] EWCA Crim 1684, where the questions for cross-examination of the witness were agreed in advance with the assistance of an intermediary. See also *R v RL* [2015] EWCA Crim 1215; *R v FA* [2015] EWCA Crim 209. See further Cooper, P., Backen, P., and Marchant, R., 'Getting to Grips with Ground Rules Hearings: A Checklist for Judges, Advocates and Intermediaries to Promote the Fair Treatment of Vulnerable People in Court' [2015] *Criminal Law Review* 417.

In keeping with the recommendations of the working group, the eligibility of a witness for a special measures direction will depend upon the characteristics of an individual witness, rather than hinge on whether or not the witness falls within a list of closed categories. It is worth underlining that the legislation underwent significant amendment in June 2011 following the implementation of a raft of reforms contained in Part III, Chapter 3 of the Coroners and Justice Act 2009.

5.2.1.1 Eligibility: child witnesses

Under section 16(1)(a) of the YJCEA 1999, a child witness is eligible for special measures if they are under 18 years old at the time of the hearing.[58] However, once it has been established that a child is eligible, the court must then consider which special measure(s) should be made available. The apparent simplicity of section 16 gave way to an extremely complex framework of presumptions and rules, contained in sections 21 and 22, and which were formulated around a three-tiered hierarchy for child witnesses. At the top of this hierarchy were children testifying in sexual offences, followed by children testifying in offences involving physical assault, neglect, kidnapping, false imprisonment, or abduction under the Child Abduction Act 1984, and then, at the foot of the chain, child witnesses who fall outside these categories and who are therefore assumed not to be 'in need of special protection.'[59]

The imposition of this hierarchical straitjacket was widely criticised on the grounds that it ran contrary to the central ethos of *Speaking Up for Justice*,[60] namely that witnesses should be dealt with on the basis of their individual need rather than whether or not they fell within a particular closed category.[61] Section 100 of the Coroners and Justice Act 2009 abolished the special category of child witnesses who are 'in need of special protection,' which effectively means that all child witnesses are now on the same statutory footing, irrespective of the offence before the court. Section 21 of the 1999 Act – as revised – now stipulates a new, straightforward primary rule in respect of all child witnesses: their evidence-in-chief must be pre-recorded under section 27, and, in addition, cross-examination should take place through the live link provision under section 24.[62] This is subject to section 16(4), which provides that the court must take into account the views of the witnesses. If the witness wishes to give live evidence, the rule does not apply to the extent that the court is satisfied that not complying with the rule would not diminish the quality of the witness's evidence.[63]

In addition, the rule does not apply if for any reason the court is satisfied that compliance with it would not be likely to maximise the quality of the witness's evidence so far as practicable.[64] In either event, the court determines that this would be an appropriate course of action by taking into account the range of factors set out in section 21(4C). These factors are:

- the witness's age and maturity;
- the witness's ability to understand the consequences of giving evidence in court rather than via a video recorded statement;

58 The age limit was raised from 17 to 18 by the Coroners and Justice Act 2009, s 98. Reference to 'under 18' is exclusive of the age 18.

59 See the pre-amendment text of YJCEA 1999, s 21(1)(b).

60 See e.g. Doak, J., 'Shielding Vulnerable Witnesses from Adversarial Showdown: A Bridge Too Far?' (2000) 16 *Journal of Civil Liberties* 216; Ellison, op. cit., n. 3; Birch, D., 'A Better Deal for Vulnerable Witnesses?' [2000] Crim LR 223; McEwan, J., 'In Defence of Vulnerable Witnesses: The Youth Justice and Criminal Evidence Act 1999' (2000) 4 *International Journal of Evidence and Proof* 1.

61 Home Office, op. cit., n. 56, at [10.8].

62 YJCEA 1999, s 21(3).

63 Ibid., s 21(4)(ba).

64 Ibid., s 21(4)(c).

- any relationship between the witness and the accused;
- the witness's social, cultural, and ethnic background; and
- the nature and circumstances of the offence being tried, as well as any other factors the court considers relevant.

While the 2009 reforms are to be broadly welcomed insofar as they should ensure that all who are legally classed as minors should be guaranteed special measures protection, certain aspects of the special measures regime remain somewhat arbitrary. The so-called primary rule – while much simplified – continues to operate around two age limits. Thus, where a witness has turned 18 before they begin to give evidence, and they are not eligible for special measures for any other reason, section 21(8) stipulates that the direction should cease to have effect. However, if the witness turns 18 after they have begun to give evidence, the special measures direction will continue to apply.[65] Although these provisions were designed to reduce confusion for the witness and the court by providing a clear set of rules, it does seem questionable whether it is right to place such a high degree of emphasis on a particular date. If, for example, a child who is 17½ years old is witness to a heinous crime, the need for special measures may be just as necessary six months later, when the child turns 18.

If such a scenario were to arise in practice, other provisions contained in the Act may assist. For instance, a child who is eligible under section 16(1)(a) may also be eligible under section 17 if they are in fear or distress; if the witness is a victim of a sexual offence, section 17(4) creates a presumption that the witness is eligible for special measures. Furthermore, if the child witness is eligible under both sections, then section 21(8) will carry most effect, since it solely applies to child witnesses only eligible under section 16(1)(a). Child witnesses in need of special protection who get the benefit of special measures under sections 27 and 28 will get the benefit of these special measures after they turn 17, so long as they were under that age when the cross-examination was recorded. It follows that section 21(8) will apply only to a witness to a non-sexual offence who obtains the special measures simply on the basis of age and for no other reason. Such witnesses may well be able to cope without them.

5.2.1.2 Eligibility: adult witnesses

If the court considers that the quality of the evidence given by a witness is likely to be diminished by reason of any circumstances falling within sections 16(2) or 17(2), adult witnesses may also be eligible for special measures direction under sections 16 or 17.

5.2.1.2.1 Adults with mental impairments

Section 16(2) of the 1999 Act implements the recommendations of the working group that, like children, those suffering from mental or physical disability should automatically be entitled to

---

65 This subsection is made subject to s 21(9), which provides that where the witness is eligible only because they are under the age of 18 and the special measures direction provides for the examination-in-chief and cross-examination to be conducted by video-recording under ss 27 and 28, then the direction may still apply if the witness is over 18 by the time the trial proper commences, provided that they were under 18 when the video- recording was made. Section 22 of the Act purports to deal with the rather unusual situation in which a person under 17 is a witness to or victim of a crime, and who was under that age when a video-recording of their evidence-in-chief was made, but over 18 when the court had to determine whether any special measures should apply. They will then be deemed a 'qualifying witness' as defined by s 22(1). If they were a witness to or victim of a sexual offence, or an offence of assault or kidnapping, then they will count as a qualifying witness in need of special protection. Section 21(2)–(7) applies to such witnesses, so that they too are to be treated as child witnesses under s 21. They must, therefore, be allowed to give their evidence-in-chief by means of a video-recording and, if victims of or witnesses to sexual offences, be cross-examined on video as well. Other special measures that might improve the quality of their evidence can also be made available, as they can to child witnesses within s 21.

special measures. Such witnesses are basically those affected by mental disorder or impairment of intelligence and social functioning, and those affected by a physical disability or disorder. The court should consult witnesses prior to trial in relation to their wishes,[66] and the opinions of expert witnesses or carers may also be taken into account. Ultimately, the appropriateness of any special measure will effectively depend on the nature of the disability.

5.2.1.2.2 Adults in fear

Section 17 provides that a witness is eligible for special measures if the quality of their evidence 'is likely to be diminished by reason of fear or distress.' Yet, apart from the various exceptions outlined below, the fact that a witness produces evidence that they suffer from fear or distress about the prospect of testifying does not give rise to automatic eligibility. Section 17(2) requires the court to consider a range of factors in arriving at its determination. These are:

(a) the nature and alleged circumstances of the offence to which the proceedings relate;
(b) the age of the witness;
(c) such of the following matters as appear to the court to be relevant, namely –
  (i) the social and cultural background and ethnic origins of the witness,
  (ii) the domestic and employment circumstances of the witness, and
  (iii) any religious beliefs or political opinions of the witness;
(d) any behaviour towards the witness on the part of –
  (i) the accused,
  (ii) members of the family or associates of the accused, or
  (iii) any other person who is likely to be an accused or a witness in the proceedings.

In addition, section 17(3) provides that the court must also consider any views expressed by the witness.

5.2.1.2.3 Complainants in sexual offences, modern slavery, and domestic abuse

Under section 17(4), the court must presume that a complainant in respect of an offence listed in section 17(4A) is an 'eligible witness,' unless the witness expresses the wish not to be treated as one. The offences in section 17(4A)[67] are:

(a) a sexual offence;
(b) an offence under section 1 or 2 of the Modern Slavery Act 2015;
(c) any other offence where it is alleged that the behaviour of the accused amounted to domestic abuse within the meaning of the Domestic Abuse Act 2021 (see section 1 of that Act).

This provision is particularly welcome, in that police can guarantee complainants in sex and domestic abuse cases that, if they have to go to court, they should normally be eligible at least for one or more of the special measures.[68]

5.2.1.2.4 Adults involved in violent offences

Following reforms in the 2009 Act, complainants in sexual offences cases are not the only category of witnesses to benefit from a presumption of eligibility. Section 17(5) of the Youth Justice

---

66 YJCEA 1999, s 16(4).

67 Section 17(4A) was introduced by the Domestic Abuse Act 2021, section 62, from 19 May 2022.

68 It is important to note that complainants in domestic abuse cases can benefit from all special measures except video-recorded examination-in-chief and video-recorded cross-examination under ss 27 and 28 of the YJCEA 1999.

Table 5.1 Eligibility for special measures

Category of witness	Legislative provision	Eligibility
Child	YJCEA 1999, s 16(1)(a).	Eligible in all cases so long as under the age of 18 at time of hearing.
Adult: mental or physical disability	YJCEA 1999, s 16(2).	Eligible in all cases where their evidence is likely to be diminished as a result of their condition.
Adult: fear or distress	YJCEA 1999, s 17(2).	Eligible in all cases where their evidence is likely to be diminished by reason of fear or distress.
Adult: complainants in sexual offence cases, modern slavery cases, or domestic abuse cases	YJCEA 1999, s 17(4).	Eligible in all cases unless the witness expresses a wish not to be treated as one.
Adult: violent offences	YJCEA 1999, s 17(5).	Eligible in violent cases where a firearm or knife was used. No need to prove that their evidence would be diminished.

and Criminal Evidence Act 1999 creates a similar benefit for witnesses in any offence listed in Schedule 1A of the YJCEA 1999. These are cases involving violent offences – including homicides and offences against the person – in which firearms or knives were used. In effect, this means that the court does not need to be satisfied that the quality of the witness's evidence will be diminished for the purposes of establishing eligibility under section 17, but the court will still have to determine whether any of the available special measures will in fact improve the quality of the witness's evidence and consider whether any such measure or measures might inhibit the evidence being effectively tested as per section 19. It is hoped that extending the reach of the Act to victims involving knife and gun crime will help to secure more convictions given the apparent prevalence of such offences among gangs in London and many of the inner cities.

5.2.2 Types of special measures

Once the court determines that the adult witness is eligible for special measures direction, the decision must be made as to which measure(s) would be likely to optimise the quality of that witness's evidence under section 19. In doing so, it should have regard to all of the circumstances of the case, including, in particular, any views expressed by the witness and whether the measure or measures might tend to inhibit such evidence being effectively tested by a party to the proceedings.[69] A variety of measures are provided for in sections 23–29 of the Act, which Keane and McKeown argue are 'sensible modifications' to the orthodox trial process.[70] These are:

- screening the witness from the accused;
- giving evidence by live link;
- giving evidence in private;
- removing wigs and gowns;

69 Ibid., s 19(2)–(3).

70 Keane, A. and McKeown, P., *The Modern Law of Evidence*, 11th edn (Oxford University Press, 2016), at 149.

- video-recording the evidence-in-chief;
- video-recording the cross-examination or re-examination;
- examining the witness through an intermediary;
- providing aids to communication.

5.2.2.1 Screens (YJCEA 1999, s 23)

Section 23(1) provides that a witness, while giving evidence or being sworn in court, may be prevented, by means of a screen, from seeing the accused.[71] The provision reflects a pre-existing practice at common law, which was sanctioned by the Court of Appeal in *R v X, Y and Z*.[72] Although not formally provided for by statute, the use of screens became increasingly common for child witnesses during the 1980s and early 1990s. However, some teething troubles began to surface. Spencer and Flin pointed out that there was a considerable degree of uncertainty about when the trial judge should give leave to order their use. It therefore seemed to rest largely on chance whether or not the use of screens would be permitted.[73] There were also unanswered administrative questions over whose job it was to supply the screens. The placing of the measure on a statutory footing resolved these questions, and the measure is one of the least contentious, insofar as the witness is still seated in the actual courtroom. The witness will then sit behind a screen (in most cases, a curtain) while giving evidence. Screens are also easy to use and require few resources. Furthermore, since both the defendant and the victim will remain in the actual courtroom, the disruptive effect on proceedings will be minimal. However, under section 23(2) the witness must be able to see and be seen by: (a) the judge or justices and the jury (if there is one); (b) counsel for both sides; and (c) an interpreter. While the increasingly widespread use of screens is rightly seen as a welcome development, there are questions as to their effectiveness in relation to witnesses who are seriously fearful about giving testimony owing to the possibility of reprisals from gangs or serious criminal networks. In the case of *R v Tahery*, the court remarked that the witness's fears could not be overcome by the use of screens, which resulted in him refusing to give evidence.[74]

5.2.2.2 Live link (YJCEA 1999, s 24)

Originally provided for by section 32 of the Criminal Justice Act 1988, section 24 of the 1999 Act provides for witnesses to give evidence by live link. In most cases in which the live link is used, the jury will have sight of a large television monitor enabling them to see and hear the witness, and there will usually be at least one other monitor positioned so that the defendant, advocates, and judge can see and hear the witness's evidence. The witness will typically be seated in another room in the court precinct, facing another workstation, but sees and hears only the person speaking (i.e. counsel or the judge). They may also be accompanied by another person in the video link room.[75]

Importantly, the witness is spared the ordeal of seeing the accused. Where a witness gives evidence-in-chief by live link, there is a presumption that they will continue to give evidence in the same way throughout the proceedings.[76]

---

71 See *KL and LAK v DPP* (2002) 166 JP 369, where the court confirmed that while the witness is prevented from seeing the accused, there is no requirement that the accused should be prevented from seeing the witness.

72 (1989) 91 Cr App R 36.

73 Spencer, J. and Flin, R., *The Evidence of Children* (Blackstone, 1993), p. 101.

74 *R v Ali Reza Tahery* [2013] EWCA Crim 1053, at [13]–[14].

75 YJCEA 1999, s 24(1A) (inserted by Coroners and Justice Act 2009, s 102).

76 YJCEA 1999, s 24(3)–(4).

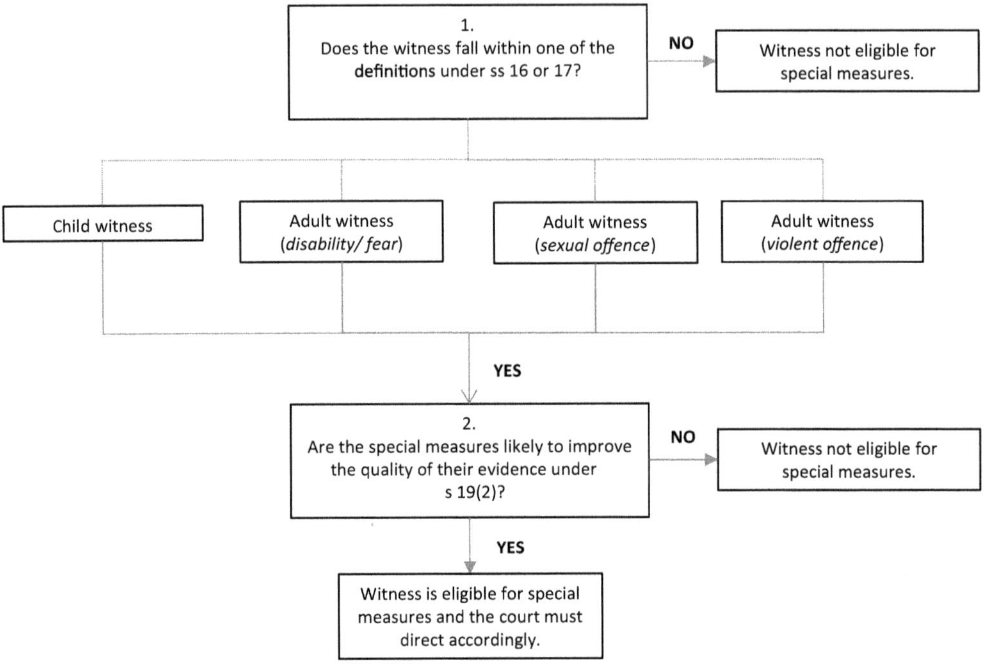

Figure 5.1 The test for special measures

Shortly after its initial roll-out under the previous statutory regimes, evaluations of the live link were carried out in England and Wales by Davies and Noon,[77] and in Scotland by Murray.[78] In both studies, findings indicate that the facility carries a range of benefits for child witnesses. Davies and Noon found that the mechanism had reduced levels of stress suffered by child witnesses, who had, as a consequence, been more forthcoming in their evidence, and Murray noted that they were more likely to say that they were fairly treated. The Australian Law Reform Commission's evaluation of the live link in the Australian Capital Territory revealed that children who knew they could use the facility when they wanted to do so were less anxious than those who were unable to use it, despite expressing a desire to do so.[79] These findings also indicated that emotional outbreaks from the child would be less likely to occur when giving evidence over the link. The professionals and parents of children in that study all said that a live link reduced stress on children as they gave evidence, and some believed that the use of the live link permitted some cases to be prosecuted that might not have proceeded without it.[80]

One particularly welcome finding is that there seems to be a solid base of support for the use of the link among practitioners. Davies and Noon found that 42 per cent of judges reported a 'very favourable' impression of the link, while a third reported a 'favourable' impression with only some reservations. Just 16 per cent believed the use of a screen to be a superior mechanism.[81] Overall, it would seem that the advent of the live link has been something that has been broadly

77 Davies, G. and Noon, E., op. cit., n. 7.

78 Murray, K., *Live Television Link: An Evaluation of Its Use by Child Witnesses* (Scottish Office Central Research Unit, 1995).

79 Australian Law Reform Commission, *Children's Evidence: Closed Circuit Television*, Report No. 63 (Canberra: Australian Law Reform Commission, 1992), p. 3.

80 Ibid., p. 4.

81 Davies and Noon, op. cit., n. 7, pp. 103–15.

accepted by most stakeholders in the criminal justice system. It undoubtedly enables children to give clearer and better-quality evidence, while significantly reducing the level of stress they feel in doing so. If the emotional impact of the evidence is diminished in this process, it would seem to be a price worth paying if it enables children to feel more comfortable about coming to court.

5.2.2.3 Evidence given in private (YJCEA 1999, s 25)

Section 25 of the 1999 Act empowers the judge to order the courtroom to be cleared of people who do not need to be present while a witness gives evidence. The direction will apply to individuals or groups of people, rather than areas of the court, and will mostly affect those in the public gallery. The court must allow at least one member of the press to remain if one has been nominated by the press, although it was held in *Richards* that a judge may go further if they feel that clearing the court is 'strictly necessary' to ensure justice is done.[82] The measure will only be available in a case involving a sexual offence,[83] or when the court is persuaded that someone has tried to intimidate, or is likely to try to intimidate, the witness.[84] These are relatively narrow grounds, which mean that many child witnesses and those with learning difficulties will not be able to benefit from such a direction. However, by section 25(2), persons not eligible for exclusion include: (a) the accused; (b) counsel for both parties; and (c) any interpreter or other person appointed. Naturally, the judge is also exempt from exclusion.

5.2.2.4 Removal of wigs and gowns (YJCEA 1999, s 26)

Section 26 of the 1999 Act stipulates that a special measures direction may provide for the wearing of wigs or gowns to be dispensed with during the giving of the witness's evidence. As with the power to clear the public gallery, such a procedure has always remained within the power of the court at common law. The potential benefits of this measure are obvious, in that witnesses may feel less daunted by the formality of the proceedings. It would particularly aid young witnesses, who may feel overawed by the austere atmosphere of the trial setting. For example, in *R v Barker*,[85] counsel removed their wigs and gowns and also used their first names with a 4-year-old witness. Unlike some of the other special measures, this has not proved to be particularly contentious and has proven to be quite commonplace in cases of children and adults with mental impairments. However, the research conducted by Sanders et al. into the experiences of witnesses with learning disabilities found that the power was used in a haphazard fashion. Witnesses who gave evidence while counsel wore their full regalia described the proceedings as scarier.[86]

It may also be suggested that some witnesses may feel that they prefer the judge and counsel to wear their wigs and gowns so that the trial is a formal rather than a casual procedure and gives them a sense that the process is being taken seriously. Ellison has also suggested that some witnesses may expect wigs to be worn from their knowledge of the legal system and may thus be thrown by their absence.[87] Obviously if a child indicates that they do not want this sort of special treatment, no such application should be made, and they should be able to give evidence in the normal setting.

82 *R v Richards* (1999) 163 JP 246, at [4.8].
83 YJCEA, s 25(4)(a).
84 Ibid., s 25(4)(b).
85 *R v Barker* [2010] EWCA Crim 4.
86 Sanders et al., op. cit., n. 25, pp. 64–65.
87 Ellison, op. cit., n. 3, p. 34.

5.2.2.5 Video-recorded evidence-in-chief (YJCEA 1999, s 27)

As a matter of course, video-recorded interviews are conducted by the police in accordance with government guidelines, *Achieving Best Evidence in Criminal Proceedings* (formerly governed by the *Memorandum of Good Practice*).[88] Although the document purports to take account of evidential rules, video-recorded interviews often contain inadmissible statements, and occasionally interviewers will allow their prejudices to show and render the video interview inadmissible because it assumed the defendant's guilt. Section 27 of the YJCEA 1999 created a new exception to the hearsay rule in providing for the admissibility of a video-recorded interview with an eligible witness to be substituted for that witness's examination-in-chief.[89]

As pre-recorded evidence is somewhat more contentious than some of the other measures provided for in the legislation, certain specific protections are in place for the accused. Foremost among these is the stipulation that such a direction may not be given if the court considers that it would be against the interests of justice to do so.[90] Furthermore, the court must balance any prejudice to the accused with the desirability of showing the whole of the recorded interview;[91] and the court may direct that the recording should not be admitted if it appears that the witness will not be available for cross-examination, or that rules of disclosure have not been followed.[92]

A witness giving evidence in this way must be called by the party tendering the evidence and may not give evidence-in-chief through means other than the recording without the permission of the court.[93]

Such protections reflect the fact that, although research has shown that pre-recorded interviews considerably reduce stress levels among users, the attitudes of practitioners are mixed. A Home Office Study, carried out by Davies et al., found that 93 per cent of judges and 41 per cent of barristers were in favour of the principle of video-taped interviews.[94] Just over one-third of barristers (37 per cent) and just over one-half of judges (53 per cent) in England and Wales considered that the admissibility of the video would serve the interests of justice or the interests of the child, while 20 per cent of judges and 50 per cent of barristers thought that it might make it more difficult to detect false allegations. The judiciary were particularly concerned about the possibility of poor interview techniques,[95] with only a handful of defence barristers agreeing that the interviewers had followed the rules of evidence.

While Pigot unanimously endorsed the value of video-taped evidence, the Report also stressed the importance of making clear to the court the nature of the original allegations, as well as the demeanour and behaviour of the child. It was also emphasised that since such interviews were both evidential and investigatory in their nature, they would need to be guided by some form of code in order to ensure that they would not be used at trial. The Home Office and the courts have been active in formulating a number of controls in relation to the manner of questioning used in the pre-recorded interviews and on how the video-recording ought to be used in evidence. Foremost among these controls was the publication of the *Memorandum of Good Practice*, which was issued jointly by the

88 Ministry of Justice, *Achieving Best Evidence in Criminal Proceedings* (HMSO, 2011).

89 As with evidence given by live link (see above), the CJA 2003 adopted the recommendation of Lord Justice Auld in his *Review of the Criminal Courts* by extending the use of video-recorded evidence beyond the rather narrow confines of the 1999 Act. Section 137 of the 2003 Act gives a judge the power to issue a direction that a video-recording of the evidence-in-chief of a witness should be admitted in trials of offences triable on indictment and prescribed offences triable either way, if it enables the witness to give better evidence and it is in the interest of justice to do so.

90 YJCEA 1999, s 27(2).

91 Ibid., s 27(3).

92 Ibid., s 27(4).

93 Ibid., s 27(5)(a).

94 Davies, G., Wilson, C., Mitchell, R., and Milsom, J., *Videotaping Children's Evidence: An Evaluation* (HMSO, 1995), p. 11.

95 Ibid., p. 12; 41 per cent of judges anticipated that this may constitute a major disadvantage.

Home Office and the Department of Health in 1992.[96] The aim of the *Memorandum* was to assist interviewers from the child protection units who would normally be responsible for producing these tapes. Although it was not intended to operate as a legally binding code, it does summarise various evidential rules, in order to discourage the use of leading or hypothetical questions.[97]

The *Memorandum* was revised and updated over the best part of two decades before it was finally replaced in 2011 by the guidance laid down in *Achieving Best Evidence in Criminal Proceedings* (The 'ABE' Guidance).[98] This document outlines best practice in conducting pre-trial interviews with vulnerable witnesses. Although it is purely advisory and is not enforceable before the courts, any significant departure from the guidance may have to be justified to the court.[99] In addition to offering technical advice, the document outlines the steps to be taken in preparation for recorded interviews and outlines basic questioning techniques. Interviewers are encouraged to follow a four-phase structure to the interview, which should begin with a 'free-narrative' phase, during which the interviewer poses a series of open-ended, general questions. From there, the interview should increasingly move on to the use of more specific questions, but without any pressure being applied to the child. Furthermore, interviewers should avoid the use of suggestion and leading questions as far as possible, and the child should not be placed under pressure to recollect. Benchmarks regarding safeguarding duties and other standards required of those who support young witnesses are also laid out in light of recommendations from a study by Plotnikoff and Woolfson.[100]

One of the more controversial issues with video-recorded evidence-in-chief is that many issues that would be inadmissible, such as evidence gained from leading questions and issues of hearsay, are also recorded. Although part of the role of the ABE Guidance is to minimise the risk of such a situation arising, there are inevitably cases where this sort of evidence permeates the recording. Usually, this occurs as a result of the interviewer's failure to follow the Guidance. In deciding whether to exclude such evidence, it was held in *R v K* that the appropriate test was whether a reasonable jury, properly directed, could be sure that the witness has given a credible and accurate account notwithstanding any breaches that occurred.[101]

5.2.2.6 Video-recorded cross-examination and re-examination (YJCEA 1999, s 28)

One of the most radical measures is contained in section 28 of the Youth Justice and Criminal Evidence Act 1999, which provides for the cross-examination and re-examination of the witness in advance of the trial. The video-recorded cross-examination may, but need not, take place in the physical presence of the judge or magistrates and the defence and legal representatives. However, a judge or magistrate will have to be able to control the proceedings. It is intended that the judge or magistrate in charge of this procedure will normally be the trial judge. All of the people mentioned in this paragraph will have to be able to see and hear the witness being cross-examined and communicate with anyone who is in the room with the witness, such as an intermediary acting under section 29 (see below).

---

96 Home Office, *Memorandum of Good Practice on Video-Recorded Interview with Child Witnesses for Criminal Proceedings* (HMSO, 1992). Such guidelines were recommended by the Pigot Report at: *Report of the Advisory Group on Video Evidence* (HMSO, 1989), at [4.8].

97 See further *Re E (a minor) (Child Abuse: Evidence)* [1987] 1 FLR 269, in which the High Court disapproved of the use of a number of videos that had been based on questioning techniques used in the therapy of children who were suspected of having been abused.

98 Home Office, *Achieving Best Evidence in Criminal Proceedings: Guidance on Interviewing Victims and Witnesses and Guidance on Using Special Measures* (Ministry of Justice, 2011).

99 Ibid., at [1.1]. See *Re E (A Child)* [2016] EWCA Civ 473, in which a number of significant defects in the ABE interview were identified by the Court of Appeal. See also *R v Krezolek* [2015] Crim LR 628.

100 Plotnikoff, J. and Woolfson, R., op. cit., n. 13.

101 [2006] 2 Cr App R 10 at [26], affirming *R v Hanton* [2005] EWCA Crim 2009. See also *G v DPP* [1997] 2 Cr App R 78.

The provision was aimed at preventing the sort of disparaging cross-examination directed at the 15-year-old witness known as 'Bromley' in the Damilola Taylor murder trial. That case showed the need for proper testing of the evidence of a witness by cross-examination, but can also be seen as an example of the abuse of cross-examination, the 15-year-old having been exposed to 15 hours of cross-examination by four experienced Oxbridge graduates. The defence claimed that she was an ill-prepared witness who, by sensitive but probing techniques of skilled criminal advocacy, was shown to be inconsistent and unreliable. Had the section 28 procedure been available to her, she would still have been subject to proper cross-examination and testing of her evidence, but under more controlled conditions.

Receipt of the entire testimony of a child outside the formal courtroom environment in advance of the trial clearly holds the potential to significantly reduce fear and apprehension and to allow the child to achieve some sense of closure within a relatively short time frame after the offence. However – citing concerns among the profession about its practical operation – the Government declined to implement this provision when most of the other special measures came into force in July 2002. In December 2004, it was announced that its implementation would be postponed indefinitely, pending a wider inquiry into children's evidence. In a subsequent Consultation Paper,[102] the Government proposed to retain section 28, but in an amended form that would cover only 'a small group of the most vulnerable witnesses,' which would include 'very young children, those with a terminal or degenerative illness and those suffering from some form of mental incapacity.'[103] As Hoyano argues, the review group seemed to overlook two crucial facts: first, that most vulnerable witnesses actually *desire* pre-recorded examination; and, second, that such schemes have operated with relative success in other jurisdictions.[104]

Nevertheless, the debate about the problems facing child witnesses did not abate, and the Ministry of Justice eventually launched fresh consultations on the matter, with a pilot programme eventually being introduced at three Crown Court Centres at the end of 2013.[105] On 10 September 2014, one Jason John Wilson became the first person to be convicted in a trial using pre-recorded cross-examination.[106] The results of the pilots, which came to an end on 31 October 2014, were assessed and its use has proven positive among witnesses who benefited from it. A Report published by the Ministry of Justice in evaluating the use of section 28 found that:

- more guilty pleas were entered in trials where section 28 was in use (48 per cent of all section 28 cases compared with 9 per cent in all section 27-only cases);
- there were fewer cracked trials in section 28 cases than there were in section 27-only cases (8 per cent compared with 27 per cent);
- there was little difference between conviction rates for trials using section 28 and trials using only section 27 (46 per cent and 54 per cent, respectively).[107]

Following the success of the pilot scheme, in 2016 Mike Penning, then Justice Minister, announced a national rollout of section 28 and the Government announced in November 2020 that the process of implementation was completed, and the special measure was now available at all 62 Crown

102 Office for Criminal Justice Reform, *Convicting Rapists and Protecting Victims: Justice for Victims of Rape – Response to Consultation* (HMSO, 2007).

103 Ibid., at [3.5].

104 Hoyano, L., 'The Child Witness Review: Much Ado about Too Little' [2007] Crim LR 849.

105 The Youth Justice and Criminal Evidence Act 1999 (Commencement No. 13) Order 2013 (SI 2013/ 3236). The three Crown Court Centres were Kingston-upon-Thames, Leeds, and Liverpool.

106 Wilson was convicted of eight counts of sexual assault on a child. See further http://blog.cps.gov.uk/2014/09/dpp-welcomes-convictions-under-pilot-scheme-of-pre-recorded-cross-examination-of-victims-.html (last accessed 11 December 2014).

107 Baverstock, J., *Process Evaluation of Pre-recorded Cross-examination Pilot (Section 28)* (Ministry of Justice, 2016) at 65–66.

Court centres across England and Wales.[108] From 1 February 2023, the protection afforded by section 28 extends to all witnesses eligible under section 16 and all complainants eligible under section 17(4).[109]

In light of the findings of the pilot scheme, changes were required to be made to the pre-trial process in cases involving eligible witnesses.[110] For a start, police need to identify them at a very early stage in order to ensure that the interview conforms with the ABE Guidance, and that appropriate arrangements are made to fix a date for the pre-recorded cross-examination. A number of issues remain, including how to deal with new evidence that comes to light after the cross-examination has occurred, and how far recordings should be edited if the questions or answers are deemed inappropriate to be placed before the jury.[111]

Clear concerns remain, particularly for defence practitioners whose ability to prepare a full defence case at an early stage in proceedings is obviously dependent upon their having received full disclosure of the prosecution evidence in a timely manner in advance of the s 28 hearing. Further concerns from a defence perspective relate to the enhanced level of case management which such cases receive through the Ground Rules Hearings (GRH), whereby the judge will be given the opportunity to review their proposed cross-examination questions and remove any unsuitable questions, thus interfering in the adversarial nature of the trial process.

A recent study by Fairclough has revealed that some serious concerns remain about the expanded use of section 28.[112] Concerns which were raised by practitioners who participated in her empirical study and had experience of conducting s 28 hearings included a possible lessening of the impact of the complainant's evidence on the jury as well as a knock-on effect on conviction rates. Other practitioners had raised concerns over a negative impact on the fairness of the trial due to problems with late and ineffective disclosure and the short preparation times which defence lawyers are given before conducting cross-examination, reducing the quality of the defence offered to the charges. Fairclough remains supportive of the measure in certain cases, in particular those with young complainants, but suggests that serious concerns exist over its expansion into cases where it is not needed and may not in fact enhance the quality of the evidence given:

> it is perceived of as a 'sticking plaster' for the huge delays experienced in the criminal justice system and has perhaps for some even become statistics-driven rather than targeted at those with true need.[113]

5.2.2.7 Examination of a witness through an intermediary (YJCEA 1999, s 29)

The most innovative measure contained in the 1999 legislation is to be found in section 29, which provides that an intermediary may not only communicate questions and answers to and from a witness, but may also explain the questions and answers to enable them to be understood. Only child witnesses and those who are eligible under section 16 of the Act can apply to be examined

---

108 https://www.gov.uk/government/news/new-courtroom-protections-for-vulnerable-victims-available-nationwide (last accessed 10 July 2023).

109 Prior to 1 February 2023, it was the case that the protection in section 28 did not apply to complainants of domestic abuse cases.

110 See 'A United Approach,' *Counsel* (February 2017) https://www.counselmagazine.co.uk/articles/united-approach (last accessed 20 July 2017).

111 See further Stevenson, M. and Valley, H., 'Pre-recorded Cross-Examination' (2014) 178(21) *Criminal Law & Justice Weekly* 312.

112 Fairclough, S., 'Section 28 Pre-trial Cross-Examination: Barristers' Experiences and Perceptions of Its Wider Use in Practice,' 2023(5) *Archbold Review* 5 https://uk.westlaw.com/Document/ICD95E920147F11EE84AEBF8582EB94E8/View/FullText.html.

113 Ibid., p. 9.

through an intermediary.[114] The judge, jury, and legal representatives must be able to see and hear the proceedings, and to communicate with the intermediary.[115] The procedure cannot be used in relation to a recorded interview with a witness, unless the court issues a further special measures direction.[116]

The idea of an intermediary was first proposed by the Pigot Committee in 1989. It was the only proposal of the Committee that was not unanimous. The rationale for the introduction of the mechanism would appear to have been that it would reduce the stress levels for child witnesses, and as such would enhance the quality of their evidence. While the use of screens, television links, and pre-recorded evidence-in-chief have now been in place for some years with relatively few opponents, the use of intermediaries is particularly contentious as it is viewed as being so alien to the nature of the adversarial process. A major perceived risk is that the traditional role of counsel would be significantly undermined, since questions would be put to the child by the intermediary, who would be free to use very different voice tones and interrogative techniques than those that defence counsel might believe to be in the interests of their client. As Hoyano points out, there is obviously the potential for a particular meaning or emphasis to be lost, which in turn could lead to disputes between the questioner and the intermediary on which the trial judge would have to adjudicate.[117]

Indeed, in the high-profile trial of Mark Bridger for the murder of schoolgirl April Jones, a number of concerns were expressed to the effect that the intermediary acted inappropriately by going 'as far as to reformulate the substance of questions which invariably contributed to a distorted and ultimately less effective line of questioning.'[118]

It is easy to imagine situations in which it might be necessary to call upon the services of an intermediary at an early stage in an investigation or proceedings involving a witness who has a particular problem in communicating. Where intermediaries are used at an early stage of the investigation or proceedings, and subsequently an application is made for a video-recording of an interview in which they were involved to be admitted as evidence, that direction can be given despite the judge, magistrate, or legal representative not having been present. However, the intermediary who was involved must still gain the court's approval retrospectively before the recording can be admitted. Intermediaries will have to declare that they will perform their functions faithfully, and will have the same obligation as foreign-language interpreters not to make a wilfully false or misleading statement to the witness or the court. If they do make such statements, they will commit an offence under the Perjury Act 1911.

As shown above, the use of the intermediary procedure is particularly alien to the adversarial process, which explains why it was not rolled out nationally for some eight years after the legislation received its royal assent. However, following a relatively positive evaluation of pilot schemes,[119] the Government finally gave the go-ahead for nationwide implementation of section 29 in September 2007. In time, this facility should serve to spare young child witnesses from some of the techniques commonly used to confuse and bewilder witnesses through complex sentence structures and the conniving manipulation of language.[120]

---

114 Witnesses who are vulnerable only by reason of fear or distress may not benefit (YJCEA 1999, s 18(2)).

115 Ibid., s 29(3).

116 Ibid., s 29(6).

117 Hoyano, L., 'Variations on a Theme by Pigot: Special Measures Directions for Child Witnesses' [2000] Crim LR 250, 272.

118 See RightsNI blog post at http://rightsni.org/2014/03/registered-intermediaries-in-northern-ireland/ (last accessed 12 December 2014).

119 See Plotnikoff, J. and Woolfson, R., 'Making Best Use of the Intermediary Special Measure at Trial' [2008] Crim LR 91.

120 See discussion above. For an example of its use with the profoundly disabled, see *R v Watts* [2010] EWCA Crim 1824, where a complainant in a sexual assault trial communicated via the movement of her eyes, with a manager at her care home acting as an interpreter when she gave evidence.

5.2.2.8 Aids to communication (YJCEA 1999, s 30)

The eighth special measure, contained in section 30 of the Act, stipulates that witnesses eligible for special measures by virtue of section 16 may be provided with such aids as the court considers appropriate. Such aids may be used to enable questions or answers to be communicated to, or by, the witness and are designed to counteract any disability or disorder that impedes effective communication. Such devices might include sign boards, communications aids for the disabled, and other aids that may allow deaf or dumb witnesses to communicate more effectively. It is not intended to include devices for disguising speech, sometimes used to preserve anonymity. Suffice to say, it is one of the least contentious measures contained within the Act.

5.2.2.9 Special measures and the accused

Since one of the most commonly cited reasons for introducing the legislation was to enable children to give the best evidence in court, it was something of an anomaly that child defendants (or indeed vulnerable accused persons of any age) were not permitted to rely on special measures. In his review of the treatment of people with mental health problems and learning disabilities in the criminal justice system, Lord Bradley condemned the fact that special measures were not extended to vulnerable defendants 'although it appears equally important in terms of exercising justice that similar support is given.'[121] Indeed, from the outset, there were fears that this stipulation could constitute a potential breach of the principle of equality of arms under the European Convention on Human Rights. This concept states that when the prosecution and defence are in court, there must be a level playing field between them. In *Delcourt v Belgium*,[122] it was held that the accused should not be placed in a position in which he is at a substantial disadvantage in presenting his case compared with that of the prosecution. This was evidently a particular concern of one former barrister, who told the House of Commons that:

> In one trial ... 58 people were in court when my client, aged 15, who was charged, with a school friend, with murdering an old lady, should have gone into the witness box to give evidence to try to save herself from a life sentence. The voyeurism in the public gallery was palpable and unavoidable, because people wanted to see the horror of young children who were said to have done horrible things. Compare her situation with that of the prosecution witnesses, also children of about 15, who had witnessed pretty small events of no great importance to them. They came to court, went straight to a room with their parents, chatted to a nice usher and watched their video on TV. They were then questioned in a quiet room by people grinning at them from the TV, just like being interviewed on a Saturday morning breakfast show. One lad had his lunch pail with him in the room. How does that amount to equality of arms between a child defendant and the prosecution?[123]

Table 5.2 describes the various sections for special measures under the Youth Justice and Criminal Evidence Act 1999, for the categories of child witnesses, vulnerable adults, and intimidated witnesses.

In the joined cases of *T v United Kingdom; V v United Kingdom*,[124] the European Court of Human Rights found a breach of Article 6 in relation to the well-publicised trial of two 10-year-olds convicted for the murder of toddler James Bulger. The Court went on to stress the need for special

---

121 Bradley, K., *The Bradley Report: Lord Bradley's Review of People with Mental Health Problems or Learning Disabilities in the Criminal Justice System* (Department of Health, 2009), at 61.

122 (1970) 1 EHRR 355.

123 Hansard, HC Deb, col. 159 (24 October 2002).

124 (1999) 30 EHRR 121.

Table 5.2 Eligibility for special measures under the Youth Justice and Criminal Evidence Act 1999

	s 16 Witnesses (children)	s 16 Witnesses (vulnerable adults)	s 17 Witnesses (intimidated/fear of distress)
Section 23 screening witness from accused	Eligible	Eligible	Eligible
Section 24 evidence by live link	Eligible	Eligible	Eligible
Section 25 evidence given in private	Only eligible in a sexual offence case or a case involving witness intimidation	Only eligible in a sexual offence case or a case involving witness intimidation	Only eligible in a sexual offence case or a case involving witness intimidation
Section 26 removal of wigs and gowns	Eligible	Eligible	Eligible
Section 27 video-recorded evidence-in-chief	Eligible	Eligible	Eligible
Section 28 video-recorded cross-examination/ re-examination	Eligible	Eligible	Eligible
Section 29 examination through an intermediary	Eligible	Eligible	Not eligible
Section 30 aids to communication	Eligible	Eligible	Not eligible

provisions to be made available for child defendants in order that they could fully participate in the proceedings against them.

In light of this judgment, the Attorney General issued guidance to the Crown Courts dealing with young defendants tried on indictment that encouraged them to consider using their common law powers to alter procedures in cases involving juveniles.[125] It was suggested, for example, that young defendants be allowed to sit with family or friends, and that counsel remove their wigs and gowns. However, the exclusion of the defendant from the regime of special measures continued with no sign of any statutory amendment coming to the aid of vulnerable accused persons.

This was a concern with which Baroness Hale seemed to identify in *R v Camberwell Green Youth Court*,[126] in commenting that the problems facing child defendants were 'very real.' However, she proceeded to note that, were the regime to be applied to the accused, a number of awkward questions would have to be addressed concerning the conduct of any video-recorded examination-in-chief or the nature of binding evidential presumption.[127] Therefore, the House of Lords concluded

125 *Practice Direction (Crown Court: Trial of Children and Young Persons)* [2000] 1 WLR 659.

126 [2005] 1 WLR 393.

127 Ibid., at [57].

that the fact such measures were not available to child defendants did not interfere with their fair trial rights under the European Convention:

> The defendant is excluded from the statutory scheme because it is clearly inappropriate to apply the whole scheme to him. There are obvious difficulties about admitting a video-recorded interview as his evidence in chief ... but the court has wide and flexible inherent powers to ensure that the accused receives a fair trial and this includes a fair opportunity of giving the best evidence he can.[128]

The dictum of Baroness Hale was considered by the Court of Appeal in *R v Ukpabio*.[129] Again, the court underlined that there was no power within the 1999 Act under which provision could be made for a fearful or vulnerable defendant to give evidence via a video link. However, Latham LJ proceeded to state that, in line with Convention requirements, 'there might be exceptional circumstances where it was appropriate for a defendant to be absent from the courtroom, but to ensure that he was able to participate in proceedings by video link where the relevant technological equipment was available.'[130] In other words, use of a video link to alleviate fear or counteract vulnerability was not permissible under the 1999 Act, but it was permissible (and arguably mandatory) for the court to make such an order, using its inherent common law powers, that would enable a defendant to participate effectively in the trial. In the case of *R v Adeojo*, the Court of Appeal held that the erection of screens in the public gallery is not capable of causing unfair prejudice to the defendant since the trial judge had clearly instructed the jury to not allow such special measures to 'colour their examination of the evidence.'[131]

In recognition of the fact that the law as it stood sat awkwardly alongside the Convention requirements of equality of arms and effective participation, section 47 of the Police and Justice Act 2006 inserted section 33A into the 1999 legislation, which largely reflects the Court of Appeal's decision in *Ukpabio*. The amendment to the 1999 Act introduces provisions whereby defendants under the age of 18 or those with mental disorders, whose ability to participate effectively as a witness is compromised by reason of mental disorder, impaired intellectual ability or social functioning, may be able to give evidence by video link. This provision is subject to two stipulations: first, the mechanism must actually be capable of improving the ability of the witness to participate (i.e. there is a causal link between the two) and, second, the court must be satisfied that it is in the interests of justice for the youth to give evidence through a live link. The use of section 33A came before the courts in the case of *R v Hamberger (Martin)*,[132] which concerned the giving of evidence by a defendant with an acute heart condition. The trial judge, in refusing an argument from the defendant that he was unfit to stand trial, granted the use of live link under section 33A in order to ensure the defendant was present within the trial. The defendant was convicted and appealed on the basis that he was unable to participate in proceedings and the trial judge was incorrect to consider live link as an appropriate alternative for the defendant. The Court of Appeal agreed that the trial judge erred in law in finding that section 33A applied to this particular defendant, noting that the trial judge failed to explain the basis on which the defendant was suffering from a mental disorder and failed to satisfy the necessary causal link. It should be stressed, however, that the new provisions are entirely self-contained within section 33A, and do not alter the fact that the accused is not classed as an 'eligible' witness for the purposes of sections 16 or 17.

---

128 Ibid., at 409.

129 [2008] 1 Cr App R 6.

130 Ibid., at [17].

131 *R v Adeojo & Anor* [2013] EWCA Crim 41 at [84].

132 [2017] EWCA Crim 273.

A similar provision exists in sections 33BA and 33BB,[133] which provide for the use of an intermediary when certain vulnerable accused persons give evidence in court where that is necessary to ensure the accused receives a fair trial, though the eligibility test is more stringent than for non-defendant witnesses.[134] As of July 2017, these provisions have not yet entered into force. However, the appellate courts have continuously recognised the use of their inherent law power to direct that a defendant be assisted by an intermediary.[135] In *R (OP) v The Secretary of State for Justice and Cheltenham Magistrates' Court*,[136] the Court of Appeal laid out what it believed to be the circumstances when an intermediary is necessary. Rafferty LJ commented that:

> [T]here are likely to be two roles during a trial for which an intermediary is fitted. The first is founded in general support, reassurance and calm interpretation of unfolding events. The second requires skilled support and interpretation with the potential for intervention and on occasion suggestion to the Bench associated with the giving of the defendant's evidence.
>
> The most pressing need for the help of an intermediary self-evidently bites at the point of maximum strain, that is when an accused should he do so elects to give an account of himself by entering the witness box and submitting to cross-examination.[137]

In determining whether an intermediary was required throughout the duration of the trial in order to ensure that the defendant had a fair trial, Rafferty LJ concluded that:

> We are not persuaded that it is essential a [registered intermediary] be available to all defendants for the duration of their trials. In many instances the provision of help centred upon the cast of mind and life experience we have described are likely to prove sufficient. The pinch point is at the giving of evidence when in our view it is unarguable that an individual in jeopardy should be put in the best position to do himself justice.

R (OP) was approved by the Court of Appeal in *R v Yahya Rashid*,[138] where Lord Thomas CJ concluded that it would be a:

> rare case where the threshold of disability is crossed such that an intermediary is required when the defendant gives his evidence ... cases in which an order will be made for an intermediary to be present for *the whole trial* will be very rare.[139]

As a last point, in *R v Cox*,[140] the Court of Appeal stated that special measures for vulnerable defendants are still very much at the discretion of the trial judge. The appeal was dismissed on the grounds that the Court felt that the trial process had already been significantly adapted to meet the defendant's needs, notwithstanding the fact that no intermediary was appointed. The remainder of the special measures contained in Part II of the legislation continue to be limited to non-defendant witnesses.

---

133 As inserted by the Coroners and Justice Act 2009, s 104.

134 See further Hoyano, L., 'Coroners and Justice Act 2009: Special Measures Directions Take Two: Entrenching Unequal Access to Justice?' [2010] 5 Crim LR 345.

135 *R (C) v Sevenoaks Youth Court* [2010] 1 All ER 735.

136 [2014] EWHC 1944 (Admin).

137 Ibid., at [34] and [36], respectively.

138 [2017] EWCA Crim 2.

139 Ibid., at [84]. Emphasis added.

140 [2012] 2 Cr App R 6.

5.2.3 The judicial role in protecting vulnerable witnesses

It was noted in Chapter 2 that, while trial judges are under a duty to intervene in order to prevent over-zealous or protracted cross-examination of an offensive or oppressive nature,[141] the umpire-like role conventionally exercised by the trial judge means that it is not always possible to discharge such a duty lest they should appear partisan to one side or the other. However, as measures designed to ease the plight of vulnerable witnesses have become more commonplace, so too has the judiciary had to undertake a much more proactive role in facilitating their evidence during the trial. In 2007, Crown Prosecutors were given a new power to conduct pre-trial interviews with potential prosecution witnesses (PTWI), including the complainant themselves.[142] In the past, the advent of PWTI was variously characterised in official publications and media reports as 'fairly radical.'[143] Indeed, the notion of the 'vulnerable witness' continues to resonate with subsequent developments in English criminal justice including the recently and widely published Crown Prosecution Service (CPS) reports.[144] The same can be said for the international perspective; prosecutors in Australia, Canada, and New Zealand interview key witnesses as part of their routine trial preparations.[145]

A relatively new procedure, known as a Ground Rules Hearing, was introduced to enable the judge and the advocates to ascertain the nature of any adaptations to trial procedure or questioning that might be required to facilitate the evidence of vulnerable witnesses, and is mandatory in all cases involving intermediaries.[146] Issues considered may include the need to avoid repetitive questioning, controlling comment, and accusations of lying; time limits on cross-examination; the type of vocabulary used in questioning; and the practicalities surrounding any intervention by the intermediary.[147] The Court of Appeal confirmed in *R v JP*[148] that such hearings are mandatory in all cases involving intermediaries and the requirement is also enshrined in the latest iterations of the Criminal Procedure Rules 2020 and the Criminal Practice Directions 2023.[149]

These procedural changes have also been reflected in a marked shift in judicial attitudes as regards their duty to protect vulnerable witnesses at trial. The Court of Appeal heard four significant cases being reported between 2010 and 2012: *R v Barker*[150] (involving the anal rape of a 2-year-old); *R v E*[151] (the rape of the accused's 6-year-old stepdaughter); *R v W and M*[152] (a sexual assault on an 8-year-old); and *R v Wills*[153] (grooming and sexual assaults on a number of children ranging from 8 to 13 years old).

---

141 *Mechanical and General Inventions Co Ltd and Lehwess v Austin and Austin Motor Co Ltd* [1935] AC 346; *Wong Kam-ming v R* [1980] AC 247. See Ch 2.

142 Roberts, P. and Saunders, C., 'Introducing Pre-trial Witness Interviews – A Flexible New Fixture in the Crown Prosecutor's Toolkit' [2008] *Criminal Law Review* 831.

143 Crown Prosecution Service, 'Pre-trial Witnesses Interviews by Prosecutors,' A Consultation Paper (London, CPS).

144 Crown Prosecution Service, 'Speaking to Witnesses at Court – Draft CPS Guidance for Consultation' (London, CPS, January 2015)

145 Public Prosecutors Service of Canada, Deskbook, (2014), [2.23], [3.17], [3.3.8], [4.1], [4.2]; *R v Regan* [2002] ISCR 297, 2002 SCC 12, see also Vasillev, S.V., 'From Liberal Extremity to Safe Mainstream? The Comparative Controversies of Witness Preparation in the United States' (2011), 9 International Commentary on Evidence, Article 5; Office of the Attorney General Pre-trial Witness Preparation by Prosecutors Report (London, 2004), Part 3 ('The Foreign Experience').

146 *Criminal Practice Directions I: General Matters*, section 3E (7 October 2013); Crim PR 3.9(3). See *R v Michael Boxer* [2015] EWCA Crim 1684, where the questions for cross-examination of the witness were agreed in advance with the assistance of an intermediary. See also *R v RL* [2015] EWCA Crim 1215; *R v FA* [2015] EWCA Crim 209.

147 Cooper, P., Backen, P., and Marchant, R., op. cit., n. 57.

148 [2014] EWCA Crim 2064.

149 Crim PR 2020 3.9(7) and Crim PD 2023, para 6.1.

150 [2011] Crim LR 233.

151 [2012] Crim LR 563.

152 [2010] EWCA Crim 1926.

153 [2012] 1 Cr App R 2.

The cases are analysed in some detail in an excellent article by Emily Henderson in the *Criminal Law Review*.[154] While limited space precludes a detailed analysis of the cases here, for present purposes it is worth noting that the line of case law elicits three key rules that cross-examiners ought to bear in mind. First, age-appropriate language must always be used. As the court remarked in *Barker*, 'the task of the advocate is to formulate short, simple questions which put the essential elements of the defendant's case to the witness.'[155] Second, cross-examiners must restrict the use of suggestion as the Court of Appeal noted in *W and M*:

> There is undoubtedly a danger of a child witness wishing simply to please. There is undoubtedly a danger of a child witness seeing that to assent to what is put may bring the questioning process to a speedier conclusion than to disagree ... It is generally recognised that particularly with child witnesses short and untagged questions are best at eliciting the evidence. By untagged we mean questions [which] do not contain a statement of the answer which is sought.[156]

Finally, in each of the four cases, the Court of Appeal was keen to stress that cross-examiners should adopt a cautious approach when challenging or seeking to undermine the testimony of a vulnerable witness. In *E*, it was stated that 'direct challenges,' such as accusations of lying, are unhelpful and risk confusion.[157] As the court explained in *Wills*, such necessary limitations to protect witnesses may carry profound implications for the traditional approach to cross-examination:

> [F]or vulnerable witnesses, the traditional style of cross-examination where comment is made on inconsistencies during cross-examination must be replaced.[158]

The Court of Appeal has again underlined the need for judicial muscularity in instances where cross-examination appears to be excessive. In *R v Steven Pipe*,[159] the trial judge stopped defence counsel's cross-examination before he had a chance to question the witness about the inconsistencies between her evidence at trial and evidence at the time of her medical appointment. The trial judge ceased counsel's questions due to the clear distress on the part of the witness, to such an extent that she could not continue. The defendant was convicted and appealed to the Court of Appeal, which in turn dismissed the appeal on the basis that the defendant did not lose his right to a fair trial as a result of the judge's actions. In fact, Coulson LJ concluded that:

> [T]he judge noted that on analysis the cessation of cross-examination would not affect the appellant's ability to rely on the alleged inconsistencies, and would instead deprive the complainant of the opportunity of explaining any such inconsistencies. He reached the conclusion that that, therefore, could not possibly prejudice the appellant. Again, we agree with him.[160]

Further, in *R v Sandor Jonas*,[161] the trial judge had restricted the questioning of a complainant in a sexual offences case as to her credibility. In that case, counsel for the defence had cross-examined the complainant for nearly a week with the majority of questions spent on the complainant's

154 Henderson, E., 'All the Proper Protections – the Court of Appeal Rewrites the Rules for the Cross-Examination of Vulnerable Witnesses' [2014] Crim LR 93.
155 *Barker*, op. cit. n. 85 at [42].
156 *W and M*, at [30].
157 *E*, op. cit. n. 99 at [28].
158 *Wills*, op. cit. n. 153 at [39].
159 [2014] EWCA Crim 2570.
160 Ibid., at [28].
161 [2015] EWCA Crim 562.

account of her life in her home country. The trial judge subsequently limited a second counsel from questioning the witness. In dismissing the appeal, Hallett LJ concluded that:

> [W]e reject the criticism that the judge intervened when she should not have done and that she in any way prevented the appellant from receiving a fair trial. On the contrary, in our view her timely and sensible interventions ensured that the whole process was fair to everyone. She protected the witness from unnecessary and oppressive questioning, but not at the expense of a fair trial for the defendants.

The restrictions placed on cross-examination were justified, and the judge's response to the suggestion that the retirement of the jury should be delayed to allow time to gather fresh evidence was understandable. In any event, her reluctance to delay the trial did not prevent her from allowing the defence sufficient time to gather the evidence and put it before the jury in a form acceptable to all.[162]

It is to be noted that, following *Sandor Jonas*, the Criminal Procedure Rule Committee amended the Criminal Procedure Rules to include a new provision in Rule 3.9(7)(b)(v) which requires the court to set ground rules concerning the allocation of questions between witnesses in cases where there is more than one defendant.

The extent to which the lower courts will respond to the Court of Appeal's prompts remains to be seen, although following *Sandor Jonas* and *Pipe*[163] it is to be hoped and expected that, in time at least, more of the judiciary will adopt a robust approach in intervening to prevent overly aggressive or inappropriate cross-examination.

It should be added that the judicial role is not confined to protecting vulnerable witnesses; the judge is also responsible for ensuring that the accused receives a fair trial. To this end, the judicial role also extends to ensuring that the jury is not prejudiced against the defendant by the very fact that special measures have been ordered. Section 32 of the Youth Justice and Criminal Evidence Act 1999 provides:

> Where on a trial on indictment evidence has been given in accordance with a special measures direction, the judge must give the jury such warning (if any) as the judge considers necessary to ensure that the fact that the direction was given in relation to the witness does not prejudice the accused.

In most cases, such warnings occur during the judge's summing-up of the case; however, in *R v Brown*, Buxton LJ ruled that a warning 'is much more likely to impress itself on the jury if it is given at the time that the witnesses give evidence than if it is repeated at a later date in the summing-up.'[164]

5.2.4 A new era for vulnerable witnesses?

Research findings into the operation of special measures have been broadly positive. Hamlyn et al. have found that vast proportions of witnesses who used special measures found them helpful,[165]

---

162 Ibid., at [37] and [38].

163 See also *R v Stephen Hamilton* [2014] EWCA Crim 1555, where the Court of Appeal noted that the trial judge had an obligation to ensure that the witness was not 'taken advantage of' by defence counsel; *R v Lubemba; JP* [2014] EWCA Crim 2064, where Hallett LJ noted (at [45]) that 'Advocates must adapt to the witness, not the other way round. They cannot insist upon any supposed right "to put one's case."'

164 *R v Brown* [2004] EWCA Crim 1620 at [21].

165 Hamlyn, B., Phelps, A., Turtle, J., and Sattar, G., *Are Special Measures Working? Evidence from Surveys of Vulnerable and Intimidated Witnesses*, Home Office Research Study No. 283 (HMSO, 2004).

and that they were significantly more confident that the criminal justice system was effective in delivering justice and meeting the needs of victims.[166] Moreover, one-third of interviewees said they would not have been willing and able to give evidence without them, and this figure rose to 44 per cent when the same question was posed to victims of sexual offences. Similar positive findings have been reported by Burton et al.[167] These researchers reported that while, overall, special measures were having a positive impact, the mechanisms used to identify vulnerable witnesses and assess their individual needs had to be improved.

It would thus appear that, on the basis of research conducted to date, special measures mark a positive step forward for vulnerable witnesses. Many witnesses will no longer have to give live oral evidence and undergo detailed questioning about their private lives in open court. In this sense, the legislation can be said to strike a better balance between the interests of the various parties involved in the criminal action. It is also indicative that certain key principles of the adversarial trial, such as orality, confrontation, and live cross-examination, may no longer be viewed as principles so sacrosanct that they ought to operate in a way that causes undue distress to victims and witnesses.

While the Youth Justice and Criminal Evidence Act 1999 has reaped considerable benefits for vulnerable witnesses, the legislation is by no means perfectly formulated. In addition to some of the concerns outlined above, it has also been argued that the legislation does not go far enough in addressing secondary victimisation. The Act will only come to the aid of witnesses who are legally eligible for assistance under the statute. The vast majority of witnesses, including victims of crime, will continue to give live, oral evidence. Even for those witnesses who do fall under the ambit of the legislation, the excesses of the adversarial trial are only partially reduced, rather than removed. Even if witnesses give evidence via a television link, for example, they will still be subjected to the same techniques and devices commonly used to disorientate or intimidate witnesses during cross-examination. It would appear that the root of the problem lies in the 'fight theory' that underpins the criminal trial. At the end of the day, it is the prospect of a heated courtroom duel that will drive counsel to pursue victory at all costs, notwithstanding the impact upon victims and witnesses.

As long as policymakers continue to view orality and cross-examination as requisite features of our mode of trial, witnesses in court are unlikely to be relieved of secondary victimisation. As Louise Ellison has argued, effective solutions to the problems facing vulnerable witnesses can be found only by looking *beyond* the adversarial system, since there is an inherent 'basic conflict between the needs and interests of vulnerable witnesses and the resultant evidentiary safeguards of the adversarial trial process.'[168] In this, the inquisitorial jurisdictions may hold valuable lessons for policymakers, since there is a relatively wide consensus that witnesses are spared much of the trauma associated with testifying.[169] However, in the short term at least, a radical overhaul of the adversarial system remains unlikely, given that many practitioners would seem to be concerned with the loss of the effect of evidence upon the jury, and view televised testimony as being 'artificial, remote and less compelling.'[170]

Other concerns with special measures stem from the idea that the accused has a 'right of confrontation' – that is, a right to be physically present to view the opposing witnesses when

---

166 One-third of all witnesses using special measures said they would not have been willing to give evidence without this help; this figure stood at 44 per cent when the witnesses were victims of sexual offences.

167 Burton, M., Evans, R., and Sanders, A., *Are Special Measures for Vulnerable and Intimidated Witnesses Working? Evidence from the Criminal Justice Agencies*, Home Office Online Report 01/06 (HMSO, 2006).

168 Ellison, op. cit., n. 3, at 7.

169 For an overview of the treatment of vulnerable witnesses in the inquisitorial systems of Europe, see Doak, op. cit., n. 60, pp. 265–84.

170 Ellison, op. cit., n. 3, at 60.

they are giving evidence against them. While this is a constitutional right in the United States,[171] such a right does not have any grounding either in English common law, or under the European Convention on Human Rights. Instead, both parties to the trial are said to have the right to put forward and effectively challenge the evidence adduced by the opposition. While the common law has traditionally recognised the right of the accused to be present during their trial,[172] there is no authority to suggest that this right should entail physical confrontation.[173]

Similarly, the right of confrontation does not appear to form part of the fair trial requirements of the European Convention. While Article 6(3)(d) gives the accused the right 'to examine or have examined witnesses against him and to obtain the attendance and examination of witnesses on his behalf under the same conditions as witnesses against him,' the wording of the Convention itself gives little guidance as to whether physical confrontation is an element of Article 6(3)(d). While the case law would appear to place an emphasis on the need for witnesses at least to attend the trial proper and be available to have their evidence challenged, it does not bear out the argument that confrontation is an essential ingredient to meaningful cross-examination. It is clear from the Convention case law that special measures to shield vulnerable witnesses from the accused will not contravene the Convention, provided that they are strictly necessary.[174]

Indeed, the compatibility of special measures with the Convention was considered by the House of Lords in the case of *R (D) v Camberwell Green Youth Court*.[175] Here, the applicants challenged the requirement for the court, under section 21(5) of the Youth Justice and Criminal Evidence Act 1999, to give a special measures direction in favour of video-recording their evidence-in-chief where child witnesses were 'in need of special assistance' (i.e. they were victims of sexual abuse). It was alleged that this requirement deprived the court of any power to consider whether the restriction on the rights of the defence was necessary or in the interests of justice. The House of Lords rejected the appeal, holding that just because some of the evidence was produced by contemporaneous television transmission, the fair trial rights of the accused were not compromised since he could see and hear the evidence, and had every opportunity to challenge and question the witnesses against him at the trial itself. Counsel for the appellants suggested that the case law should be read in the light of the adversarial tradition, whereby the core principle was that all evidence was received orally in front of the accused, but this argument was dismissed by the court, which stated that Parliament had determined that there were sound policy grounds to depart from the 'norm' of oral testimony in the accused's presence.[176]

5.3 Other protections for witnesses in fear

Outside the regime of special measures, it is worth highlighting some further mechanisms that may be of particular value for those witnesses who fear intimidation by a third party. Although the Criminal Justice and Public Order Act 1994 sought to deal with the problem by creating a new offence of witness intimidation, in practice, this has done little to reduce the amount or the effect of the practice.

---

171 In the United States, the Sixth Amendment states that 'the accused shall enjoy the right ... to be confronted with the witness against him.' This right has been described by the Supreme Court as 'one of the fundamental guarantees of life and liberty ... long deemed so essential for the due protection of life and liberty that it is guarded against legislative and judicial action by provisions in the constitution of the United States' (*Kirby v United States* 174 US 47, 55 (1899)).

172 *R v Lee Kun* [1916] 1 KB 337.

173 See further Doak, op. cit., n. 60, p. 216.

174 See *Kostovski v Netherlands* (1989) 12 EHRR 434; *Doorson v Netherlands* (1996) 22 EHRR 330; *Van Mechelen v Netherlands* (1997) 25 EHRR 647.

175 [2005] 1 WLR 393.

176 Ibid. [52]–[53].

Witness protection programmes, which are widely used in the United States, are becoming increasingly common in this country. The Metropolitan Police and Greater Manchester Police have had such a programme for some years. In extremis, what is known as 'first-tier protection' can involve moving the witness and their family from the area and changing identities. More often, a lesser degree of protection is required, which might involve supplying the witness with a panic button, a device that alerts the police to the need for assistance in the event of a threat.

In terms of testifying at the trial itself, two further arrangements are worth noting: the concealment of the identity of a particular witness; and the use of a written hearsay statement in place of oral testimony.

5.3.1 The protection of identity

The concept of concealing the identity of a witness sits uneasily alongside the principle of open justice. It is a corollary of the principle of orality and lies alongside it at the heart of the adversarial trial. As Lord Steyn noted in *Re S*:[177]

> A criminal trial is a public event. The principle of open justice puts, as has often been said, the judge and all who participate in the trial under intense scrutiny. The glare of contemporaneous publicity ensures that trials are properly conducted. It is a valuable check on the criminal process. Moreover, the public interest may be as much involved in the circumstances of a remarkable acquittal as in a surprising conviction. Informed public debate is necessary about all such matters. Full contemporaneous reporting of criminal trials in progress promotes public confidence in the administration of justice. It promotes the values of the rule of law.[178]

However, as public awareness of witness intimidation has increased, both the courts and Parliament have recognised specific circumstances that will justify a departure from the principle of open justice. The most obvious means of doing this is through the issue of an anonymity order. This will withhold the witness's name, address, and personal details from all parties in the trial, as well as the general public. Such a step, however, has never been undertaken lightly by the courts. It has always been accepted by the common law that accused persons have a fundamental right to know the identity of their accusers, including witnesses for the prosecution. This right can be denied only in rare and exceptional circumstances, and whether such circumstances exist is a matter for the trial judge to determine in the exercise of their discretion. These circumstances are considered in further depth below.

However, it is worth noting that there are some practical steps, short of outright anonymity, that are considerably less contentious and are thus more common within criminal trials. For example, the witness can be protected from undue publicity where to publicise their name and other details might endanger their safety, or where it is necessary to the fair and proper administration of justice. Thus, such witnesses may be permitted to write down their name and other details rather than identify themselves in open court. In such a scenario, the identity of the witness will only be withheld from the public record, but their identity will be known to the parties to the trial.[179]

The particular problems facing complainants in sex cases, and child witnesses, are also recognised in statute. It is a criminal offence under the Sexual Offences (Amendment) Act 1992 for

177 [2005] 1 AC 593.

178 Ibid., at [30].

179 *R v Socialist Worker, ex p Attorney General* [1975] 1 All ER 142.

any organisation to publish the victim's name, photograph, or other details that may be used to identify an individual throughout their lifetime.[180] Child witnesses, including victims and defendants, are subject to similar protections.[181] Section 44 of the Youth Justice and Criminal Evidence Act 1999 automatically prohibits the reporting of any matter that might lead the public to identify a person under the age of 18 as a potential defendant, victim, or witness as soon as a criminal investigation has begun.[182] Furthermore, legislators have now acknowledged that other adult witnesses may also desire some measure of privacy when testifying. Section 46 of the 1999 Act gives the court power to restrict reporting about certain adult witnesses (other than the accused) in criminal proceedings. Such a witness will be eligible for protection if the quality of their evidence or their cooperation with the preparation of the case is likely to be diminished by reason of fear or distress in connection with identification by the public as a witness.[183] Victims of blackmail are also permitted to give evidence incognito, a practice confirmed by the House of Lords in *Attorney General v Leveller Magazine*.[184] Section 11 of the Contempt of Court Act 1981 permits the court to prohibit the publication of the name of a witness or other matters in connection with proceedings. This will be justified only where publication would frustrate or render impracticable the administration of justice.[185]

5.3.1.1 Witness anonymity

It should be underlined that the above restrictions only cover reporting of the witness's personal details; they do not exempt them from having to give their name and address in open court. For that reason, these measures may be insufficient to ease the concerns of those witnesses who fear intimidation from defendants, or their family and friends. In particular, if individuals have roots in a particular locality and are well known in an area, they may only be willing to give evidence at trial if their identity is concealed.

Anonymity orders are (rightly) extremely rare in criminal trials and will only ever be a measure of last resort. In *R v DJX*,[186] Lord Lane CJ emphasised the overriding duty of the trial judge to see that justice is done by ensuring that the system operates fairly to all those concerned. This includes fairness to both the parties and their witnesses. If a court is satisfied that there is a real risk to the administration of justice, because witnesses for the prosecution have reasonable grounds for fearing for their safety if their identities are disclosed, then the court has the power to take reasonable steps to protect the witnesses. However, in considering what steps to take, the court must bear in mind any possible prejudice to the rights of the defence and the interests of justice. Ultimately, justice requires that the court balance any prejudice to the accused with the interests of justice generally.

---

180 Although originally limited to offences of rape, the prohibition was extended to other sexual offences by the Criminal Justice and Public Order Act 1994, Sch 9, para. 52. The Act now applies to the vast majority of offences under the Sexual Offences Acts of 1956 and 2003 and includes participatory and inchoate offences.

181 See further *R (Gazette Media Company Ltd) v Teesside Crown Court* [2006] Crim LR 157 and discussion in Gillespie, A. and Bettinson, V., 'Preventing Secondary Victimisation through Anonymity' (2007) 70 *Modern Law Review* 114.

182 This provision replaces s 39 of the Children and Young Persons Act 1933, which granted a court the power to prohibit the reporting of the name, address, school, or other particulars identifying children and young persons under the age of 17 who are involved in proceedings.

183 Quality of evidence relates to its quality in terms of completeness, coherence, and accuracy (s 46(12)(b)). The court may make a reporting restriction direction in respect of such a person if the making of such an order is likely to improve the quality of the evidence of the witness or their cooperation in the preparation (s 3), having regard to a number of factors contained in s 46(4). The court must also consider whether the making of a reporting direction would be in the interests of justice and consider the public interest in avoiding the imposition of a substantial and unreasonable restriction on the reporting of proceedings (s 46(8)).

184 [1979] AC 440.

185 *R v Malvern JJ, ex p Evans; R v Evesham JJ, ex p McDonagh* [1988] QB 540.

186 (1988) 91 Cr App R 36.

These principles were applied in *R v Watford Magistrates' Court, ex p Lenman*.[187] Here, a number of prosecution witnesses gave evidence in a case that involved a number of youths who had rampaged through the town, violently attacking a number of people, one of whom was seriously wounded by stabbing. By order of the court, the identities of the witnesses were withheld because of fears for their safety. In their statements to the police, the witnesses had been permitted to use pseudonyms; the prosecution applied for them to be allowed to give evidence from behind screens, using voice-distortion equipment to disguise their voices. The magistrates granted the application, subject to the defence solicitors being able to see the witnesses. The defendant's application for a judicial review was dismissed.

This decision was followed in *R v Taylor (Gary)*.[188] Here, the prosecution sought leave to allow Miss A, whose evidence was central to the case, to testify from behind a screen. Although counsel and the jury could still see her, it was also requested that she be allowed to remain anonymous. The defendants, who were charged with disposing of the body of a murdered man by dismembering, could not see her directly, but only through a TV monitor. The trial judge granted the application. The question raised on appeal was whether he was correct in doing so. In holding that he was, the Court of Appeal confirmed that the decision to grant witnesses protection by these means was pre-eminently one for the discretion of the trial judge. The court further recognised that the possible grounds for anonymity might include the witness's fear for their family or other persons. The court offered the following guidelines to which a trial judge should have regard in exercising their discretion:

1. There must be real grounds for fear of the consequences if evidence were given. In practical terms, it might be sufficient to draw a parallel with section 23(3)(b) of the Criminal Justice Act 1988,[189] which is concerned with the admissibility of statements where the witness does not give oral evidence through fear, but in principle it might not be necessary for the witness to be concerned for herself alone; the concern could be for other persons or for her family.
2. The evidence must be sufficiently relevant and important to make it unfair for the Crown proceed without it.
3. The Crown must satisfy the court that the credibility of the witness has been fully investigated and disclosed.
4. The court must be satisfied that there is no undue prejudice to the accused, although some prejudice is inevitable, even if it is only the qualification placed on the right of the accused to confront a witness. There might also be factors pointing the other way, for example, where the defendant could see the witness on a TV screen.
5. The court could balance the need for protection of the witness, including the extent of that protection, against the unfairness or the appearance of unfairness.
6. There is no reason in principle why the same considerations should not apply to defence witnesses.

In *R v Lord Saville of Newdigate and Others, ex p A and Others*,[190] the Divisional Court allowed an application for judicial review of a decision by a tribunal appointed under the Tribunal of Inquiry (Evidence) Act 1921 to inquire into the events of Bloody Sunday on 30 January 1972, which led to the killing of 13 civilians in Londonderry, Northern Ireland, by paratroopers. The tribunal had originally decided that the soldiers involved should not be permitted to remain anonymous, despite them having argued that their lives may have been endangered by dissident Republicans. The Divisional Court's decision was based largely on the fact that the tribunal was significantly different from

187 [1993] Crim LR 388.

188 *The Times* (17 August 1994).

189 See now CJA 2003, s 117.

190 [1999] 4 All ER 860.

ordinary adversarial proceedings. Since proceedings were generally inquisitorial in nature, its ability to discover the truth should not be impeded by granting anonymity. On those grounds, the court stated that the additional degree of openness gained by disclosure of names was so compelling for the public interest as to warrant subjecting the soldiers to a significant danger to their lives. For that reason, in a later application to the tribunal, soldiers required to give evidence were permitted to do so by means of a video link rather than by travelling to Londonderry and giving evidence in person.

However, the House of Lords' decision in *R v Davis; R v Ellis*[191] was to have profound implications in the development of the law. These two murder cases were both widely reported in the media at the time of the events in question. In *R v Davis*, two men were shot dead at a New Year's Eve party. Their deaths resulted from a surge of violence by an individual who discharged a loaded gun and killed one of his intended victims, along with an innocent bystander. A single bullet killed both men. *Ellis* concerned the shooting of a man believed to be a member of a Birmingham gang known as the Johnson Crew. The appellants were members of the rival Burger Bar Crew.

A number of witnesses at both trials had their anonymity protected by voice modulation and screens. The appellants contended that, since their conviction was based solely or substantially on the evidence of anonymous witnesses, the practice was incompatible with Article 6 of the Convention. The Court of Appeal had originally held that the use of anonymity in trials was an acceptable practice when witnesses were in a state of 'justifiable and genuine fear' and whose testimony could be tested in the adversarial process.[192] Provided that appropriate safeguards were in place, the trial would not be considered to be unfair. However, this decision was reversed by the House of Lords.

Although the reasons given by their Lordships varied, all were agreed that the use of anonymity orders in the instant cases was in breach of Article 6 of the European Convention. For Lord Bingham, a fundamental principle of the common law was that a defendant in a criminal trial should be confronted by his accusers so that he might cross-examine them and challenge their evidence. Previous decisions – including that of the Court of Appeal in the instant case – had failed to give sufficient weight to this key consideration.[193] Although his Lordship acknowledged that criminal courts did have common law powers to grant anonymity, these appeared to be restricted to the most exceptional of circumstances, which did not encompass the facts of the instant case. Lord Bingham's line of reasoning was largely endorsed by Lords Rodger, Brown, and Mance. Lord Carswell, however, seemed to embrace a wider and more flexible interpretation of the inherent common law power, and – while not dissenting – admitted that the case had caused him a great deal of difficulty. On these facts, he eventually came to the conclusion that the measures granted went beyond what was permissible and he was not 'sufficiently sure' that the trial was fair.[194]

In the immediate aftermath of the decision, the CPS warned that almost 600 cases could be affected by the ruling, and a £6 million trial at the Old Bailey was halted.[195] The case triggered considerable debate in the popular press, with cries of how 'barmy Law Lords' had 'unleashed anarchy,'[196] or how the decision had caused 'chaos in the legal system.'[197] The Government rushed through emergency legislation in the form of the Criminal Evidence (Witness Anonymity) Act

---

191 [2008] 1 AC 1128.

192 Ibid., at 3148.

193 [2006] 1 WLR 3130.

194 [2008] 1 AC 1128, at [61].

195 See 'Murder Trial Halted by Ban on Anonymity of Witnesses,' *Evening Standard* (24 June 2008); 'Court Ruling Hits Police Witnesses,' *The Independent* (8 July 2008).

196 'Anarchy is Unleashed,' *The Sun* (25 June 2008).

197 Opinion, *Daily Mirror* (25 June 2008).

2008, and subsequently proposed a longer-term solution under the auspices of the Coroners and Justice Act 2009.

The common law rules on anonymity have thus been replaced by a new statutory regime. Under section 86 of the 2009 Act, the court may adopt a number of measures to safeguard the anonymity of a witness. Applications can be made by either the prosecution or the defence, and while the court must be informed of the witness's identity, the other party need not be so informed. Section 88 prescribes three relatively stringent conditions (A, B, and C) that must be in place before such an order can be made. It is for the party seeking the anonymity order to convince the court that all of the relevant conditions have been satisfied.

Condition A is that the measures must be 'necessary' for one of two reasons: either to protect the safety of the witness or another person, or to prevent serious damage to property.[198] The accompanying Explanatory Notes make clear that there is no requirement for any actual threat to the witness or any other person.[199] The second condition is the prevention of 'real harm to the public interest.' This is likely to cover the public interest in national security, as well as the ability of police or other criminal justice agencies to conduct undercover investigations. It has, however, been questioned whether Condition A is too broad; 'serious damage to property,' in particular, would seem to be a questionable threshold for the imposition of such drastic measures.[200] There are also concerns that the Condition as it stands is overly vague, since it remains unclear as to what might constitute 'real harm to the public interest.'[201] Condition B is that the effect of the order would be consistent with the defendant receiving a fair trial. This should, in theory at least, ensure that any such order should be fully compliant with Article 6 of the European Convention, although courts will be left to decide this on a case-by-case basis. Condition C is that the witness's testimony is of such importance that, in the interests of justice, the witness ought to testify and either that the witness would not testify if the proposed order were not made, or alternatively that there would be real harm to the public interest if the witness were to testify without the proposed order being made.

Even where all three conditions are met, that is not the end of the matter. The court must then look to section 89, which details other considerations that must be taken into account, along with any other matters the court considers relevant. These considerations are:

(a) the general right of a defendant in criminal proceedings to know the identity of a witness in the proceedings;
(b) the extent to which the credibility of the witness concerned would be a relevant factor when the weight of his or her evidence comes to be assessed;
(c) whether evidence given by the witness might be the sole or decisive evidence implicating the defendant;
(d) whether the witness's evidence could be properly tested (whether on grounds of credibility or otherwise) without his or her identity being disclosed;
(e) whether there is any reason to believe that the witness –
    (i) has a tendency to be dishonest, or
    (ii) has any motive to be dishonest in the circumstances of the case, having regard (in particular) to any previous convictions of the witness and to any relationship between the witness and the defendant or any associates of the defendant;

---

198 Section 88(6) specifies that, in determining for the purposes of Condition A whether the order is necessary to protect the safety of the witness, another person, or to prevent damage to property, the court must have regard to the witness's reasonable fear of death or injury either to himself or herself or to another person or reasonable fear that there would be serious damage to property.

199 Explanatory Notes to the Coroners and Justice Act 2009, para. 469.

200 See further Doak, J. and Huxley-Binns, R., 'Anonymous Witnesses in England and Wales: Charting a Course from Strasbourg?' (2009) 73 *Journal of Criminal Law* 508.

201 See JUSTICE, *Criminal Evidence (Witness Anonymity) Bill, Briefing for House of Commons* (JUSTICE, 2008), at 10.

(f) whether it would be reasonably practicable to protect the witness by any means other than by making a witness anonymity order specifying the measures that are under consideration by the court.

These conditions are virtually identical to those contained in the original legislation that was rushed through Parliament following the decision in *Davis* (i.e. Criminal Evidence (Witness Anonymity) Act 2008), and the conditions were found to be compliant with Article 6 by the Court of Appeal in *R v Mayers*.[202] However, far from reconciling English law with the Convention standard, it has been suggested that the 2009 Act actually erodes the accused's Article 6 rights still further.[203]

While the 'sole/decisive' question is laid down as a 'relevant consideration' for the court under section 79(2)(c), courts are not bound to refuse to issue an order in these circumstances. As such, the scheme clearly envisages the possibility of an accused being convicted solely or decisively on the basis of anonymous witness testimony, which would seem to fall short of a key requirement laid down by the Strasbourg Court in respect of Article 6 of the European Convention.[204] As we shall see in Chapter 12, such problems are particularly acute where the prosecution proposes to rely on anonymous hearsay evidence.[205]

5.3.1.2 Admission of a written statement

Witnesses who are fearful of intimidation or reprisals may also avoid coming to court altogether in certain circumstances. Section 116(2)(e) of the Criminal Justice Act 2003 creates an exception to the hearsay rule, whereby a written statement of a frightened witness may be read out in court in place of oral evidence. The difficulty with this mechanism is that the defence will be unable to cross-examine the witness, so counsel may attempt to persuade the jury that little weight should be attached to it. Counsel will also be free to attack the credibility of the witness, and may actively suggest that they disbelieve its contents. For those reasons, the courts will generally prefer that the witness attends court and relies on one or more of the special measures contained in the Youth Justice and Criminal Evidence Act 1999. Section 116 is considered in greater depth in Chapter 12.

5.4 Vulnerable witnesses in civil cases

In contrast to the comparatively rapid development of protections within the criminal justice system, there has been comparatively little interest in the protections available to vulnerable witnesses in civil cases. A number of reasons may be cited for this. Perhaps, since the vast majority of issues are settled through negotiation before the court is required to decide liability or quantum, the need for witnesses to attend court very rarely arises. Even if it should, hearsay evidence is readily admissible in civil proceedings, thus avoiding the need for many witnesses to appear, particularly if they are 'vulnerable' or are otherwise indisposed. It might also be assumed that civil proceedings tend to be less adversarial in nature, with judges assuming a more managerial role. No jury is usually present, and procedures may thus take on a slightly less formal tone than their criminal counterparts. This could mean that judges would be more willing to intervene where cross-examination is perceived to be oppressive or vexatious. In contrast to the criminal courts, where any intervention carries a perceived risk of partisanship and a successful appeal in the event of a conviction,[206] judges may feel that there is less risk in taking a more proactive stance in

202 [2009] 2 All ER 145. See also *R v Powar* [2009] 2 Cr App R 8.

203 See Doak and Huxley-Binns, op. cit., n. 200.

204 *Kostovski v Netherlands* (1989) 12 EHRR 434, at [76]. See further Doak and Huxley-Binns, op. cit., n. 200.

205 See Ch 12.

206 See e.g. *R v Gunning* [1980] Crim LR 592; *R v Sharp* [1993] 3 All ER 225.

regulating advocacy. Indeed, in certain types of civil case, particularly family proceedings, judges often question children themselves.

For these reasons, it may seem that the problems facing vulnerable witnesses in civil cases are considerably less acute than in criminal cases. Yet civil justice, like criminal justice, depends upon witnesses being willing to give evidence, and being able to testify clearly and as effectively as possible. There would seem to be no sound basis for deeming that certain witnesses ought to be protected under a comprehensive statutory regime in criminal cases, but should be left in a much less certain position when testifying before the civil courts.

Civil proceedings in England and Wales are governed by the Civil Procedure Rules (CPR).[207] While there is a general rule that all hearings will be held in public,[208] courts do have the power to order that hearings be held in private in a broad range of circumstances.[209] Presumably, the court would thus be empowered to make such a direction to hear the evidence of a vulnerable witness in private where appropriate. Similarly, it is also possible for a witness to avoid giving oral evidence at all through the admission of a hearsay statement under the Civil Evidence Act 1995,[210] and the courts may also impose reporting restrictions or order that witnesses give evidence anonymously.[211]

Most witnesses will find themselves subject to Rule 32.2, which states that oral evidence should ordinarily be given by witnesses at trial. However, Rule 32.3 of the Civil Procedure Rules stipulates that '[t]he court may allow a witness to give evidence through a video link or by other means,' and Annex 3 of Practice Direction 32 gives further guidance on how the video link facility may be used. It seems likely that the rule was inserted primarily to cover the situation in which a witness was out of the jurisdiction,[212] and was unlikely to have been formulated with the protection of vulnerable witnesses as one of its primary goals. However, courts are given a very broad discretion under the Rules as to how evidence is received, and the Judicial Studies Board clearly envisaged that it may be utilised to facilitate vulnerable witnesses where appropriate:

> A judge in a civil court is given a wide discretion by the CPR as to how evidence is given in the proceedings, and may allow a witness to give evidence through a video link or by any other means. It follows that the video tape of a Memorandum interview conducted in the context of a criminal investigation may be used in a civil case ... This power is particularly important where children are concerned in terms of achieving the overriding objective set by Rule 1: that of enabling the court to deal with cases justly, including ensuring that the parties are on an equal footing.[213]

---

207 The Rules apply in all county courts, the High Court, and the Civil Division of the Court of Appeal, although family proceedings are excluded. The Family Division of the High Court is, however, bound by the Rules.

208 Rule 39.2(1).

209 Rule 39.2(3) stipulates that a hearing, or any part of it, may be in private if – (a) publicity would defeat the object of the hearing; (b) it involves matters relating to national security; (c) it involves confidential information (including information relating to personal financial matters) and publicity would damage that confidentiality; (d) a private hearing is necessary to protect the interests of any child or patient; (e) it is a hearing of an application made without notice and it would be unjust to any respondent for there to be a public hearing; (f) it involves uncontentious matters arising in the administration of trusts or in the administration of a deceased person's estate; or (g) the court considers this to be necessary, in the interests of justice.

210 Under Rule 33.4, where one party has served notice that a hearsay statement is to be relied upon and that the party does not intend to call the maker of the statement to give oral evidence, then the court may permit another party to call the maker of the statement for the purpose of cross-examining them. Under the Civil Evidence Act 1995, evidence cannot be excluded on the basis that it is hearsay.

211 In addition, Rule 39.4 states that a court may order that the identity of any party or witness must not be disclosed if it considers it necessary in order to protect the interests of that party or witness.

212 See e.g. *Garcin and Others v Amerindo Investments* [1991] 1 WLR 1140.

213 Judicial Studies Board, *Equal Treatment Bench Book* (JSB, 2004), para. 4.22.182 [2002] 4 All ER 370.

The scope of this rule was examined in two relatively high-profile cases: *Rowland v Bock*[214] and *Polanski v Condé Nast Publications Ltd.*[215]

Rowland v Bock concerned the introduction of business tycoon Tiny Rowland to Dieter Bock by Christian Norgren to facilitate the purchase of a significant share of LONRHO plc. Norgren refused to come to England to attend trial as a witness since he feared he would be arrested under an extradition order that had been issued concerning insider dealing in the United States. This was found to be sufficient reason to make an order that he should give his evidence by video link. The High Court held that there were no predefined limits as to the scope of Rule 32. No defined limit or set of circumstances should be placed upon the discretionary exercise to permit video link evidence. While the court should take into account considerations of costs, time, inconvenience, etc., there was no requirement to show a 'pressing need,' such as that a witness was too ill to attend, although the court should make 'due allowances' for any technological consequences on the demeanour and delivery of the evidence by video link.

The case of *Polanski v Condé Nast Publications Ltd* concerned a libel action brought by film director Roman Polanski following the publication of an article in the July 2002 edition of *Vanity Fair* magazine. The claimant sought to give evidence through a live video link because he feared being extradited to the United States if he entered the United Kingdom after he jumped bail in relation to a sex charge in 1977. At first instance, Eady J permitted the claimant to rely on Rule 32.3 and gave permission for evidence to be given through a video link from France. However, the Court of Appeal found that he had erred and allowed an appeal by the defendant.[216] Although the use of a video link might be appropriate in some circumstances, it was noted that Polanski had admitted that he was guilty of a serious crime; his libel claim was directly linked to the crime for which he had pleaded guilty; and Polanski had a choice of where to sue and could have alternatively brought his claim in the United States or France. It is clear that, to some extent, the Court of Appeal's decision was based in part on public policy considerations. As Parker LJ noted: 'The court should not be seen to assist a claimant who is a fugitive from justice to evade sentence for a crime of which he has been convicted.'[217]

The decision was, however, reversed on appeal to the House of Lords.[218] The majority of their Lordships held that the use of video-conferencing would be likely to contribute to the efficient, fair, and economic disposal of the litigation, as required by Practice Direction 32 of the 1998 Rules, and the respondent would not be disadvantaged to any significant extent. Approving *Rowland v Bock*, it was underlined that giving evidence by video link was entirely satisfactory if there was a sufficient reason for departing from the normal rule that witnesses gave evidence in person before the court. In these particular circumstances, if the appellant were not able to give evidence by video link, he would be gravely handicapped in the conduct of the proceedings, but it would not alter his status as a fugitive. Despite the appellant's fugitive status, he was entitled to invoke the assistance of the court and its procedures in protection of his civil rights. It would be inconsistent if a fugitive was entitled to bring his proceedings in the United Kingdom but could not take advantage of a procedural facility flowing from a modern technological development that had become readily available to all litigants. The judge at first instance had thus been correct to exercise his discretion as he had done; the fact the claimant was a fugitive from justice could amount to 'sufficient reason' for the purposes of making a video-conferencing order under Rule 32.3.[219]

214 [2002] 4 All ER 370.

215 [2004] 1 WLR 387 (CA); [2005] 1 WLR 637 (HL).

216 [2004] 1 WLR 387.

217 Ibid., at 402.

218 Lord Slynn and Lord Carswell dissented on the issue of public policy.

219 It was also stated, *obiter*, that, had a video-conferencing order been refused, the court would not have been bound to make an order excluding the claimant's statements from evidence if he did not present himself in court for cross-examination.

It was also noted by their Lordships that giving evidence via video link is always preferable to the reading of a statement pursuant to a Civil Evidence Act notice. Evidence through a video link had become a readily acceptable alternative to giving evidence in person, provided that there is a sufficient reason for departing from the normal rule that witnesses give evidence in person before the court and that fair trial rights under Article 6 of the European Convention were not endangered. Although the issue as to whether the rule would cover vulnerable witnesses was not dealt with specifically, the fact that the House of Lords recognised in *Polanski* that the use of video-conferencing was a 'satisfactory means' for vulnerable witnesses to give evidence in criminal proceedings surely implies that it ought to be so in civil proceedings too.

The Employment Appeal Tribunal (EAT) has set guidance for the civil courts when dealing with cases involving vulnerable witnesses. In *Rackham v NHS Professionals Limited*,[220] a case concerning a witness with Asperger's syndrome, the EAT stated that in future cases:

> First, we would emphasise that each case is the case of an individual ... A decision as to what it is reasonable to have to do which is then made by a Tribunal must be tailored not to some general idea of what a person with that disability, or it may be disabilities generally, needs but what the individual before the Tribunal requires.
>
> Second, we think that a considerable value should be placed upon the integrity and autonomy of the individual ... If a person entitled to make a decision affecting the conduct of their case makes that decision, it is not in general for any court to second-guess their decision and to make it in a manner which patronises that person ...
>
> Third, we think that emphasis might wish to be given in the Tribunal sphere to that which is covered in the Equal Treatment Bench Book in criminal cases, in particular where it describes ground rules hearings ...
>
> Finally, we think that there is a considerable value in taking these steps quickly. In almost any case speed is important, but it particularly may be so in the case of those who suffer from disabilities and in whose best interests as well as the interests of other parties it is sensible to resolve disputes as early as possible.[221]

5.5 Key learning points

- Research has shown that vulnerable witnesses have found the experience of testifying in adversarial proceedings to be extremely stressful.
- All child witnesses will be entitled to at least one special measure in criminal proceedings.
- All complainants in sexual cases will be presumed to be entitled to at least one special measure in criminal proceedings.
- Other witnesses may be entitled to special measures in criminal proceedings depending on the court's assessment of their needs.
- Victims of sexual offences and child witnesses will ordinarily have their identities withheld from the public and the press.
- Witnesses may only testify anonymously in exceptional circumstances.

Such an exclusionary order should not be made automatically in respect of the non-attendance of a party or other witness for cross-examination. Such an order should be made only if, exceptionally, justice so required. The overriding objective of the 1998 Rules was to enable the court to deal with cases justly. The principle underlying the Civil Evidence Act 1995 was that in general, the preferable course was to admit hearsay evidence and let the court attach to the evidence whatever weight might be appropriate, rather than to exclude it altogether.

220 [2015] UKEAT 0110_15_1612.

221 Ibid., at [58]–[61] (Langstaff J). See also *Kimathi and Others v Foreign and Commonwealth Office* [2015] EWHC 3684 (QB).

- The civil courts are able to exercise their powers under the Civil Procedure Rules to put in place various protections for vulnerable witnesses.

5.6 Practice questions

1 Consider what measures, if any, the court may put in place to assist the following witnesses:
   (a) Alec, who was subject to a series of sexual assaults when he was 8 years old and living in a local care home. He is now 16, and has just reported the incident to the police. He is likely to be 17 by the time the case comes to trial.
   (b) Sally, who was recently physically assaulted by a leader at her youth club. She is 12 years old.
   (c) Yvonne, who was raped by her stepfather at the age of 14. She is now 26 years old.
   (d) Danny, who was the victim of a hit-and-run incident. He is 84 years old, and is very frail.
   (e) Paul, 15, who witnessed his girlfriend, aged 17, suffer a violent sexual assault.
   (f) Mandy, 32, who witnessed a local gang commit a robbery at a filling station. She is fearful that she may be subject to retaliation if she gives evidence for the prosecution.

2 'The courts should only resort to anonymity orders for fearful witnesses in the most exceptional of cases. If a lesser measure would suffice, then that measure should be implemented.' Does this quotation reflect the rules relating to witness anonymity in English law?

3 'While the government may well have had honourable intentions in introducing a wide range of special measures for vulnerable witnesses, ultimately such measures are unlikely to change the experience of testifying for many. Not only is the legislative framework which created the special measures unduly complex, but also the entire culture of the adversarial form of trial means that special measures can never provide an effective means of protecting vulnerable witnesses.' Evaluate the issues raised in this quotation.

4 Should special measures apply equally to all vulnerable witnesses, irrespective of whether they testify as part of criminal or civil proceedings?

5.7 Suggested further reading

Cooper, P. and Wurtzel, D., 'A Day Late and a Dollar Short: In Search of an Intermediary Scheme for Vulnerable Defendants in England and Wales' (2013) Crim LR 4.

Cooper, P., Backen, P. and Marchant, R., 'Getting to Grips with Ground Rules Hearings – A Checklist for Judges, Advocates and Intermediaries' (2015) Crim LR 417.

Cooper, P. and Hunting, L., *Access to Justice for Vulnerable People* (Wildy, Simmonds & Hill Publishing, 2018).

Doak, J., 'One Size Fits All? The Case for Special Measures for Vulnerable Witnesses in Civil Proceedings' (2007) 58(4) NILQ 459.

Doak, J. and Huxley-Binns, R., 'Anonymous Witnesses in England and Wales: Charting a Course from Strasbourg?' (2009) 73(6) JCL 508.

Ellison, L., *The Adversarial Process and the Vulnerable Witness* (Oxford University Press, 2001).

Ellison, L. and Munro, V., 'Taking Trauma Seriously: Critical Reflections on the Criminal Justice Process' (2017) 21(3) E & P 183.

Fairclough, S., '"It Doesn't Happen . . . and I've Never Thought It Was Necessary For It To Happen": Barriers to Vulnerable Defendants Giving Evidence by Live Link in Crown Court Trials' (2017) 21(3) E & P 209.

Gillespie, A. and Bettinson, V., 'Preventing Secondary Victimisation Through Anonymity' (2007) 70 MLR 114.

Henderson, E., 'All the Proper Protections – The Court of Appeal Rewrites the Rules for the Cross-examination of Vulnerable Witnesses' (2014) Crim LR 93.

Keane, A., 'Towards a Principled Approach to the Cross-Examination of Vulnerable Witnesses' (2012) Crim LR 407.
Marcello, D., 'Testimony through a Live Link in the Perspective of the Right to Confront Witnesses' (2014) Crim LR 189.
McEwan, J., 'Vulnerable Defendants and the Fairness of Trials' (2013) Crim LR 100.
Plotnikoff, J. and Woolfson, R., *Measuring Up? Evaluating Implementation of Government Commitments to Young Witnesses in Criminal Proceedings* (NSPCC, 2009) http://www.nspcc.org.uk/Inform/research/Findings/measuring_up_report_wdf66579.pdf (last accessed 12 December 2014).
Wurtzel, D., 'The Youngest Witness in a Murder Trial: Making it Possible for Very Young Children to Give Evidence' (2014) Crim LR 893.

Chapter 6

Witnesses III

Examination and Cross-Examination

Chapter contents

DOI: 10.4324/9781003416098-6

As noted in Chapter 2, the adversarial trial model has granted the parties considerable freedom in how they present their cases at court, and the manner in which they question witnesses. While the judge has a role in ensuring that proceedings are conducted in accordance with the rules of evidence and procedure, they will generally refrain from intervening when witnesses are being questioned by counsel. By contrast, the advocates of each party hold near-complete autonomy to gather, select, and present evidence before the tribunal of fact. The commencement, conduct, and termination of proceedings rest largely in their hands. They will decide which facts are in issue and which are not, which proofs to generate, and which witnesses will be called to aid them in the pursuit of victory. The high level of party control is not surprising, given that the opportunity to present one's arguments and then undermine those of the opposing party lies at the heart of the adversarial process.[1]

The only legal controls on the parties are the rules of evidence and the extent to which the trial judge enforces them or exercises discretion to place limits on the parameters of the questioning process. In the previous chapter, we saw that some progress had been made through a recent line of cases in the Court of Appeal whereby trial judges were encouraged to intervene more readily to protect vulnerable witnesses. Notwithstanding this development, concerns remain surrounding the extent to which advocates are able to use their position not only to attack opposing witnesses, but also to create their own narrative to frame past events in a certain light that best supports their case theory. This chapter explores how witnesses are questioned at trial, and the extent to which the type of questions posed to witnesses is subject to either judicial or statutory regulation. We also examine in some depth the rules surrounding the cross-examination of rape complainants, which have been the source of considerable consternation for both commentators and victims' organisations for the best part of three decades.

6.1 Examination-in-chief

All witnesses called to testify in a criminal trial will be questioned first by the party calling them. This process is known as the examination-in-chief, and usually the questioner will

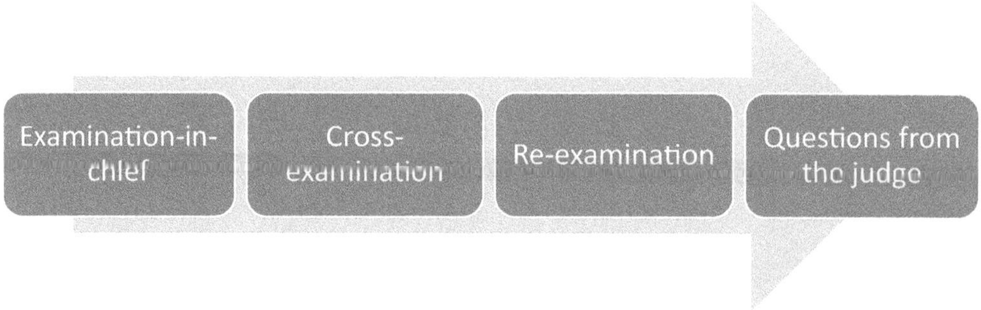

Figure 6.1 Process of witness evidence

1 Stone, M., *Cross-Examination in Criminal Trials*, 2nd edn (Butterworths, 1995), p. 114.

aim to portray the witness in a favourable light, since the testimony they give should bolster the overall strength of that party's case. Counsel will try to elicit only those facts that they feel should be included, and will do everything to avoid the witness speaking about anything that the questioner feels should be omitted from the testimony. Arguably, the principal goal is to manipulate witness testimony in such a way that victory is made more likely. The responses of witnesses are closely controlled through a series of carefully crafted questions and answers. Stone offers the following advice to counsel on how to conduct a successful examination-in-chief:

> It should be noted that controlled questioning does dictate the subject of enquiry and how it progresses, it does not involve leading. It does not suggest any answers, although the evidence is controlled by selection and editing. The witness is taken through his evidence by tightly framed questions, in small steps, and in an orderly and deliberate way, to ensure that all material facts are covered, and to avoid inadmissible, irrelevant, harmful or prejudicial evidence.[2]

Witnesses are thus confined to answering questions within the parameters set down by the questioner. In this way, testimony is shaped to bring out its maximum adversarial effect,[3] and witnesses and victims are thereby denied the opportunity to tell their story to the court using their own words.

6.1.1 Leading questions

Prior to coming to court, witnesses will usually have made a statement to the police (if a prosecution witness), or to the defence solicitor (if a defence witness). At trial, counsel will take the witness through that statement. In examination-in-chief, leading questions, which suggest the answer required or which suggest the existence of disputed facts to which the witness has not yet testified, are only allowed where the evidence being elicited is purely formal and undisputed by either party.[4]

Evidence elicited from any leading questions that are asked is still admissible but the weight to be attached to it may be reduced.[5] Table 6.1 provides some helpful examples of leading questions and their non-leading counterparts.

Table 6.1 Examples of leading and non-leading questions

Leading question	Non-leading question
X was wearing a long-sleeved shirt and trousers, that's right, isn't it?	What was X wearing?
The shirt was blue, wasn't it?	What colour shirt was he wearing?
X hit you in the face, didn't he?	Where did X hit you?
It's right that he hit you with his fist?	How did he hit you?

2 Ibid., at 94.
3 Ibid.
4 Leading questions are, however, permitted on those rare occasions when a witness is declared to be hostile. See below.
5 *Moor v Moor* [1954] 1 WLR 927.

Example 6.1

John has witnessed a fatal shooting and is called to give evidence by the prosecution. It is permissible for counsel to set the scene by asking the witness questions such as 'Your name is ...?,' 'And you work at ...?,' to which the answers are 'Yes,' but not a question such as, 'You saw the accused running from the house, just after you heard a shot?'

The dangers of such questions are obvious; John may have seen someone run from the house; he may be sure it was the accused, or merely think that it probably was. However, a simple 'yes' will serve to obscure any degree of doubt. The law of evidence thus requires that such questions be put in a form that allows the witness to say what they saw without suggesting the answer required.

Having placed John outside the house, counsel should then ask whether he heard anything. If John responds by saying that he heard a noise like a gunshot, counsel can then elicit more information by asking 'What happened next?'; the answer may be 'I saw a man running from the house.' The next question might be 'Can you identify this man?' and so on. Questions should then follow about how he was so sure it was the accused and the circumstances of the identification. Obviously, this type of question takes considerably longer than one particular leading question, but is regarded as better evidence. If this rule is contravened, evidence elicited in consequence is still admissible, although the court will generally attach less weight to it.[6]

Therefore, from the above example, you will now be aware that avoiding the trap of a leading question is a difficult task. In fact, it is worthy to note that even a question such as 'Did X do anything to you?' suggests that they did something. Owing to such difficulty, it has been noted that neither opposing counsel nor the trial judge will expect strict adherence to this rule, which has led Best in his classic work *The Principles of the Law of Evidence* (1922) to state that '"leading" is a relative, not an absolute term.'[7]

6.1.2 Refreshing memory

6.1.2.1 Out of court

All witnesses may refresh their memories from statements or other documents made reasonably close to the events about which they are to give evidence. Both prosecution and defence witnesses are entitled to a copy of their statements and to refresh their memory from them at any time up to the point at which they go into the witness box. The leading case in this area is *R v Richardson*,[8] in which the defendant was charged with two counts of burglary. Shortly before giving evidence, all five prosecution witnesses refreshed their memories from statements made to the police approximately one year beforehand. The Court of Appeal held that there was nothing improper in this:

> There can be no absolute rule that witnesses may not before trial see the statements they made at some period reasonably close to the event which is the subject of the trial. Indeed

6 Ibid.

7 W.M. Best, *The Principles of the Law of Evidence*, 12th edn (Sweet & Maxwell, 1922), at 562.

8 [1971] 2 QB 484.

> one can imagine many cases, particularly those of a complex nature, when such a rule would militate very greatly against the interests of justice.[9]

The court in *Richardson* quoted with approval the comments of the Supreme Court of Hong Kong in *Lau Pak Ngam v R*,[10] in which it was stated that if a witness is deprived of the opportunity to refresh their memory, their testimony becomes more a test of memory than truthfulness. In the view of the court, to deprive witnesses of such an opportunity would create genuine difficulties for the honest witnesses while doing little to hamper dishonest witnesses. Such a rule would also make life impossible for those police officers who daily deal with many cases and are then expected to give evidence at subsequent trials on a regular basis. In *Lau Pak Ngam* itself, a police officer met with the main prosecution witnesses the day before the trial and read aloud statements that had been taken from them shortly after the incidents occurred. All of the witnesses concerned were present at the time, so that each heard what the others intended to say. Although the Court of Appeal in *Richardson* expressed the view that it would be wrong to hand witnesses their statements in circumstances that enabled or encouraged them to compare testimonies, in the case at hand, such circumstances did not arise.

In *R v Westwell*,[11] the Court of Appeal said it was desirable, although not essential, that the defence be informed when Crown witnesses had seen their statements so that the defence might, when appropriate, draw attention to this in cross-examination. The court clearly felt that the fact that a witness has been able to refresh their memory is a matter that may then allow the jury to draw an inference that the witness who gives evidence without first refreshing their memory may be a better witness. This observation comes close to endorsing the view that testimony is more a test of memory rather than historical accuracy. The reality is that the witness who refreshes their memory is likely to be more truthful than one who does not. Since the memory may fade or be distorted by the passage of time, there is a clear benefit to the justice system as a whole in enabling witnesses to refer to previous statements before giving evidence.

6.1.2.2 In court

The rules are more stringent where witnesses wish to refresh their memory once they have begun to give evidence. The principle of orality, coupled with the desire of advocates to catch witnesses 'on the hoof,' has meant that access to previous statements for the purposes of refreshing memory has been greatly restricted.

6.1.2.3 Context: the common law position

At common law, a witness was only allowed to refresh their memory while giving evidence by reference to any written statement made or verified by that witness, while the facts were still fresh in their mind. For the most part, such statements tended to be contained in police documents or notebooks, but it was not uncommon for witnesses to refer to diaries, order/receipt books, or any other record that was relevant. Even a note scribbled on a scrap of paper or the back of a cigarette packet might have sufficed. No matter where the information was recorded, provided that the note was made or verified by the witness in question, the common law permitted it to be used as a basis for refreshing memory.[12] In criminal cases, such an approach was often scorned by the

9 Ibid., at 490 (Sachs LJ).

10 [1966] Crim LR 443.

11 [1976] 2 All ER 812.

12 It was quite common for one police officer to make a note of what was being said, and for the other to read it aloud and verify it as accurate. This was accepted as good practice by the Court of Appeal in *R v Bass* [1953] 1 QB 680, in which officers referred to the same notebook in order to refresh their memories.

defence, as prosecution counsel would generally take the witness through their original statement as part of the examination-in-chief. It thus made little sense to preclude witnesses from seeing these statements where they could serve to remind them of facts that they might otherwise have forgotten in the passage of time.

The common law also required that the statement in question must have been made or verified by the witness while the facts were still fresh in their mind. While the Court of Appeal in *Richardson* emphasised that this requirement should provide for some elasticity and should not confine witnesses to an overly short period of time, the distinction between statements that were considered to be sufficiently contemporaneous and those that were not continued to vex the courts in subsequent years. The approach of the courts was inconsistent and unpredictable, which is reflected in the fact that there was no obvious basis for imposing a contemporaneity requirement on those witnesses who refreshed their memories while giving evidence, but not on those who refreshed their memories before coming to court.[13]

In *R v Da Silva*,[14] the Court of Appeal held that the trial judge had properly exercised his discretion to allow the witness, who had started to give evidence, to refresh his memory from a statement made one month after the events to which it related. This was in spite of the fact that the statement did not concern contemporaneous events, and neither was it made while the facts were fresh in the mind of the witness. Recognising that it would have been open to the witness to have read the statement before coming into court, the court said it was equally proper to allow the witness to refresh his memory from that statement in court, subject to four conditions, as follows:

1. The witness must indicate that he or she cannot recall the details of events because of the lapse of time since they took place.
2. The witness must have made a statement much closer to the time of the events so that the contents of their statement represent their recollection at the time they made it.
3. The witness has not read the statement before coming into the witness box.
4. The witness wishes to have an opportunity to read the statement before he or she continues to give evidence.

An even broader approach was adopted in *R v South Ribble Stipendiary Magistrate, ex p Cochrane*.[15] Here, the witness had made three statements to the police. The first of these statements was made some two weeks after the events to which they referred. At committal proceedings, some 18 months later, the magistrate permitted the witness to refresh his memory from these statements, even though the witness had already spent 10 to 15 minutes reading them before he went into the witness box.

The Queen's Bench Divisional Court dismissed a judicial review application to quash the decision to commit the defendant for trial in spite of the fact that the third condition laid down in *Da Silva* had not been satisfied:

> It seems to me that a judge has a real discretion as to whether to permit a witness to refresh his memory from a non-contemporaneous document. By a real discretion, I mean a strong discretion, a choice of alternatives of free binding criteria. I do not mean the so-called weak discretion which is not a true judicial discretion at all, but simply a binding rule of law to be followed by the judge.[16]

---

13 See comments of McNeill J in *Owen v Edwards* (1983) 77 Cr App R 191, 195.
14 (1990) 90 Cr App R 233.
15 (1996) 2 Cr App R 544.
16 Ibid. at 551 (Henry LJ).

As Dennis notes, it would seem that this decision means that 'there appears to be nothing to stop a judge allowing a witness to refer repeatedly to a non-contemporaneous document in the course of testifying,' and the appeal courts should be prepared 'to give the judge a generous margin of appreciation in applying the discretion.'[17]

Moreover, the document used to refresh the memory was not evidence of the truth of its contents; the oral testimony was the evidence to be considered by the trier of fact, not the note or record to which the witness made reference. Thus, if a witness were to use a diary or other record to recall dates or entries, the other party could require the production of that diary or record and could cross-examine on it without making it evidence in the case. If the cross-examiner were to seek to probe other aspects of the document not referred to by the witness, the other party could then insist on treating the document as evidence in the case. In such an event, the document would then become an exhibit, and the jury would have a right to inspect it. However, in these circumstances, the evidential value of the exhibit was limited to showing that the witness's testimony as given in the witness box was consistent with those earlier entries. However, this rule, like those other aspects of the common law discussed above, has been subject to significant change in the Criminal Justice Act 2003.

6.1.2.4 Reform: the Criminal Justice Act 2003

The common law rules on the use of documents to refresh the memory while giving oral evidence have now been replaced by section 139 of the Criminal Justice Act 2003. Subsection (1) creates a presumption that a person giving evidence[18] in criminal proceedings may refresh their memory from a document subject to two conditions:

1. that he indicates that the document represents his recollection at the time he made it;
2. that his recollection was likely to be significantly better at the time the document was made (or verified).

These requirements reflect the common law position as finally arrived at in *ex parte Cochrane*, and it is to be hoped that the courts will construe 'at an earlier time' both more broadly and more consistently than the manner in which the contemporaneity requirement was previously handled at common law.

One of the reasons why the courts have traditionally regarded witness statements, in particular, with some measure of suspicion is that the police may, advertently or inadvertently, bias the statement towards a particular version of events. Indeed, this was the apparent fear in the case of *Cummings v CPS*,[19] where a police officer was permitted to refresh her memory as to certain details from a form that had been completed when the defendant failed to provide a breath specimen after having been stopped by the witness. The officer had not personally signed the form – which was signed by her sergeant – but had been present at the scene throughout the incident. The trial judge noted that the signature of the officer, or lack thereof, was merely an evidential consideration and what mattered was that the officer verified that the details in the form were correct.

One method of counteracting these fears is to make audio- or video-recordings of witness statements. Although this option is resource-intensive and logistically difficult, section 139(2) recognises the possibility that the transcripts of sound recordings might be used in some instances as memory-refreshing aids. While the section only refers to the use of such an aid in court while

---

17 Dennis, I., *The Law of Evidence*, 5th edn (Sweet & Maxwell, 2013), p. 581.

18 A 'person giving evidence' includes the accused: *R v Britton* [1987] 1 WLR 539.

19 Unreported, 15 December 2016.

giving oral evidence, the fact that the witness might have had the opportunity to refresh their memory before giving evidence will not affect the presumption created by section 139.

Section 120(3) of the 2003 Act is also relevant to documents used in this way. This provision preserves the common law rule that the document used to refresh the memory is not evidence unless the cross-examination probed other issues within the document beyond the specific entries to which the witness referred. As noted above, in these types of cases, the refreshing document was only evidence of the consistency of the witness's testimony. By contrast, the 2003 statutory provision stipulates that it is admissible as evidence of the truth of the matter stated, and thus constitutes an exception to the hearsay rule.[20] However, it only applies to statements made by the witness on a previous occasion and does not extend to those documents verified by them. Thus, if a witness uses a diary or other record to recall dates or entries, the other party can require the production of that diary or record and cross-examine on it without making it evidence in the case. However, if the cross-examiner goes further and introduces other dates or entries not referred to by the witness, the other party can insist on treating the document as evidence of the truth of the matters stated if the witness could have given oral evidence of those matters. As under the common law, the document thus becomes an exhibit in the case, and the jury have a right to inspect it.[21] Table 6.2 describes the procedure for refreshing and recollecting the memory of a witness.

6.1.3 Previous consistent statements

At common law, the 'rule against narrative' originally determined that witnesses should not seek to bolster their evidence by reference to the fact that they had previously said the same thing out of court on an earlier occasion. Thus, in *R v Roberts*,[22] the accused, charged with murder, claimed that the gun had gone off accidentally. He was not allowed to call evidence that two days after the shooting he had told his father that it was an accident. Such statements were excluded because they were hearsay – that is, they were made to a third party out of court. As such, they could not be used to prove the truth of the facts asserted therein.

This rule is largely maintained under section 120 of the Criminal Justice Act 2003 but is subject to a number of exceptions, which allow certain statements to be admissible as evidence of their contents.

6.1.3.1 Rebutting allegations of fabrication

Section 120(2) stipulates that previous statements are admissible in order to rebut a charge that a witness had fabricated evidence. For example, in *R v Benjamin*,[23] a police officer was allowed to produce his notebook in evidence in order to rebut a charge of fabrication. The fact that the notes were in chronological order demonstrated that they were not fabricated as alleged. Likewise, in R

Table 6.2 Procedure for refreshing the memory of the witness

Ask opposition whether you can lead.
If not, ask the witness if they made or verified a statement on the matter.
Ask when they made or verified the statement.
Ask whether the statement records his recollection at that earlier time.
Ask whether his recollection is likely to have been significantly better.
Apply to the judge!

20 See further Ch 12.

21 An application for a witness to refresh their memory will normally be made by the party calling them, but the judge, in the interests of justice, may suggest that the witness refresh their memory: *R v Tyagi Times* (21 July 1986).

22 [1942] 1 All ER 187.

23 (1913) 8 Cr App R 146.

v Oyesiku,[24] counsel for the prosecution alleged that the defendant's wife was inventing evidence. Under re-examination by the defence, counsel adduced evidence of a previous statement the witness had given to her husband's solicitor shortly after his arrest. The Court of Appeal held that the trial judge had been correct to admit the evidence, since it rebutted the allegation that she had concocted evidence in court. At common law, however, such statements could not be used as evidence of the truth of the contents of a previous statement. This position has now been altered under section 120(2) of the 2003 Act, which provides that where a previous statement is admitted to rebut a suggestion that a witness has fabricated their testimony, that statement is admissible as evidence of 'any matter stated of which oral evidence by the witness would be admissible.' Thus, in *R v MH*,[25] the accused alleged that his 3-year-old son had been coached by his mother to concoct false evidence so that he would be unable to access his children. The boy's previous complaints to his mother about his father's behaviour were admissible both to support the credibility of the witness's evidence and as evidence of the truth of their contents regarding the appellant's previous conduct. However, further complaints made by the boy to his mother following the breakdown of the marriage were deemed inadmissible for this purpose given the acrimonious nature of the relationship that then existed between the child's parents.

6.1.3.2 Refreshing memory from a document

As noted above, section 120(3) allows documents to be admitted as evidence of the truth of their contents, subject to certain conditions.

6.1.3.3 Previous statements identifying a person, object, or place

Subsections 120(4)–(7) deal with the not uncommon situation in which the witness has, in the past, made a statement to another person identifying a person, place, or thing, but cannot remember the detail when called to give evidence (such as a car registration number). Under the previous law, the witness would have been unable to rely on any document containing the relevant information if they had not verified it; the person to whom any oral statement had been made could not give evidence in person unless it fell within an established exception to the hearsay rule. Section 120(4) of the 2003 Act now stipulates that any such statement will be admissible as evidence of the facts contained within it, provided that the witness states that they made the statement and believes it to be true, and one of the conditions laid out in subsections (5)–(7) is met:

5. The first condition is that the statement identifies or describes a person, object, or place.
6. The second condition is that the statement was made by a witness when the matters stated were fresh in his memory but he does not remember them, and cannot reasonably be expected to remember them, well enough to give oral evidence of them in the proceedings.
7. The third condition is that –

    (a) the witness claims to be a person against whom an offence has been committed;
    (b) the offence is one to which the proceedings relate;
    (c) the statement consists of a complaint made by the witness (whether to a person in authority or not) about conduct which would, if proved, constitute the offence or part of the offence;
    (d) [repealed]
    (e) the complaint was not made as a result of a threat or a promise; and
    (f) before the statement is adduced the witness gives oral evidence in connection with its subject matter.

24 (1971) 56 Cr App R 240.
25 [2012] EWCA Crim 2725.

Section 120(4) therefore permits the person to whom the statement was made to give evidence, or for the document containing the relevant information to be admitted, provided that the above conditions are satisfied. Thus, where a witness has picked out a suspect in an identity parade, but cannot remember the 'number' of that person in the line-up, a police officer present may give evidence to this effect.[26]

Example 6.2

Suppose Kim witnesses a bank robbery and gives the registration number of the getaway car to Mike, a traffic warden. Mike makes a note of the number but fails to ask Kim to verify it. Kim cannot remember the registration number when called to give evidence, but she tells counsel that she made the statement and to the best of her belief, it was true. Although Kim will be unable to refresh her memory since the conditions under section 139 are not met, Mike can now testify that Kim gave him the registration number, and he can relate that number to the court directly.[27]

Section 120(4) makes it clear that a complaint is now admissible as evidence of the truth of the matters stated. Section 120(8) removes a former common law restriction that the complaint must be voluntary and should not have been made as a result of leading questions, while section 120(7)(e) requires that the complaint was not made as a result of a threat or promise. Thus, if a mother sees her daughter in a distressed and dishevelled state and says, 'He raped you, didn't he?,' a positive reply would be admissible. Questions such as 'Why are you crying?' or, as in *Osbourne*,[28] 'Why are you going home?' will not affect the admissibility of the complaint. However, if a father threatened his daughter with violence unless she told him what had happened, the subsequent complaint would not be admissible.

At common law, it was the case that the complaint should be made at the first opportunity that reasonably offered itself after the alleged offence. This rule was originally preserved – and extended to all other offences – by section 120(7)(d) of the 2003 Act.[29] However, following a government consultation, this requirement was abolished pursuant to section 112 of the Coroners and Justice Act 2009.[30]

In *R v S*,[31] questions arose as to whether evidence of complaint ought to be admitted where there were inconsistencies between the complainant's evidence and that of the person to whom she complained. The prosecution case was that the defendant started sexually abusing the complainant, S, when she was 9 or 10 years old. The abuse took the form of indecent touching, which continued until she left home at the age of 19. In her evidence-in-chief, S stated that from the age of 10 or 11 she was also subjected to more serious sexual abuse, which included sexual intercourse. The prosecution applied to adduce evidence of her complaint to a former school friend, C, in whom she had confided when she was 13 or 14 years old. C's evidence was that S had told her about the defendant touching her. However, at trial, S testified that she had told C not only about

26 *R v Osborne and Virtue* [1973] QB 678.

27 See the discussion of s 117(5) Criminal Justice Act 2003 in Ch 12 for an alternative, if more cumbersome, means of introducing the registration number.

28 [1905] 1 KB 551.

29 See e.g. *R v Valentine* [1996] 2 Cr App R 213.

30 See further Office for Criminal Justice Reform, *Convicting Rapists and Protecting Victims: Justice for Victims of Rape – Response to Consultation* (HMSO, 2007).

31 [2004] 3 All ER 689.

the indecent assaults, but also about the more serious penetrative assaults. The defendant objected to C's evidence of the sexual conduct of which S complained, but the trial judge permitted the evidence to be given.

The Court of Appeal rejected the appellant's contention that the complaint to her friend was wrongly admitted given the inconsistency between the details of her earlier complainants and her evidence. In the view of the court, the decision in each case as to whether such evidence was sufficiently consistent for it to be admissible must depend on the facts. It would not, therefore, usually be necessary for the complainant to have described the full extent of the unlawful sexual conduct alleged by the complainant in the witness box, provided that it was capable of supporting the credibility of the complainant's evidence given at trial. It was for the jury to assess the significance of any differences between the two accounts. In the instant case, although the court found that the testimony was properly admitted, the conviction itself was rendered unsafe because the judge's direction to the jury regarding the evidence was insufficient, in that he failed to draw attention to the inconsistencies between the evidence of C and that of S. The appeal was therefore allowed.

It should be emphasised, however, that evidence of a complaint may only be introduced where the complainant gives evidence in person. Thus, in *R v Wallwork*,[32] the accused was charged with incest with his daughter, aged five. The child was called to give evidence, but said nothing. Her grandmother then gave evidence that the child had complained to her about the accused's conduct. The Court of Appeal held that this evidence had been wrongly admitted because there was no evidence from the child with which it could be consistent. Section 120 does not change this common law rule. Section 120(1) stipulates that the provision applies only where the witness is called to give evidence in criminal proceedings, and section 120(4)(b) makes it clear that the previous statement is admissible only if the witness indicates that to the best of their belief they made the statement, and that to the best of their belief it contains the truth.

All of the case law discussed above – while prior to the 2003 Act – remains likely to be followed in determining the scope of section 120(7) of the 2003 Act. Furthermore, the principles apply not only to rape complainants, but also complainants in relation to many other offences. This is despite noises made by the Court of Appeal in *R v O*[33] to the effect that the provisions within the new legislation were free-standing, and courts were not bound by preceding case law. Nonetheless, in that particular case the court still seemed to echo the general tenor of the common law in the run-up to the introduction of the Act, and placed a considerable degree of emphasis on the need to consider the context of each particular complaint and the circumstances in which it was made.

6.1.3.4 Previous statements by the accused in response to accusations

Statements made by the accused to the police or other investigatory authority are commonly adduced by the prosecution whether they contain admissions or denials. Where such a statement contains an admission, it will generally constitute a confession, and will be admissible as an exception to the hearsay rule. Where such previous statements are adduced as confession evidence, they will be regarded as evidence of the facts stated and not merely as evidence of consistency. The rules relating to the admissibility of confessions are considered in detail in Chapter 8.

6.1.3.5 Statements forming part of the *res gestae*

A previous consistent statement was admissible at common law if it was part of the *res gestae* – that is, part of the transaction, story, or event to which it related. This exception to the rule against

32 (1958) 42 Cr App R 153.
33 (2006) 2 Cr App R 27.

hearsay is preserved by section 118 of the 2003 Act. Thus, in *R v Fowkes*,[34] the accused, also known as 'Butcher,' was charged with murder. A witness gave evidence that he was in a room with a police officer and his father, when the latter was killed by a shot fired through the window. Immediately beforehand, a face had appeared at the window, and the witness was permitted to testify that he had shouted, 'There's Butcher!' (the name by which the accused was known). The scope of the *res gestae* doctrine is examined in detail in Chapter 12.

6.1.4 Unfavourable and hostile witnesses

Sometimes witnesses will fail to give the evidence expected by the party that calls them. For a variety of reasons, sometimes the testimony given under oath at trial conflicts with, or substantially differs from, a previous statement. In these circumstances, the witness cannot be cross-examined as to the inconsistency between what they are saying, or not saying, in the witness box and what they said in an earlier statement. However, it is important to draw a distinction between a witness who is merely *unfavourable* to the party calling them, and one whose answers are positively *hostile* to the questioner.

A witness is considered to be unfavourable when they are simply confused about the facts or cannot remember the details. Such witnesses will not be motivated by malice or dishonesty, but their testimony is likely to undermine the examining party's case to some extent. When this happens, counsel cannot cross-examine the witness, or attack their credibility.[35] In modern times, this problem may be resolved by allowing the witness to refresh their memory from the statement made nearer to the event to which they testify.[36] If that is not possible or does not resolve the problem, other witnesses can be called to give the evidence that the unfavourable witness was expected to give, or to rebut any aspects of the testimony.[37]

Occasionally, a witness will be deemed to be hostile, and will not give the evidence expected out of malice or dishonesty. Possibly, they may be fearful of giving evidence, as in the recent case of *R v Adeojo*,[38] or may have formed their own view as to the overall merits of the case. An application for leave to treat any witness as hostile must be made by the examining party and can be made at any point in questioning, even as late as re-examination.[39] This will generally be done in the presence of the jury,[40] with a *voir dire* being saved for the most exceptional of cases.[41] Where the court grants leave to treat the witness as hostile, the party calling them may then ask leading questions,[42] and put any previous inconsistent statements to the witness.[43] In most cases, a warning should be given to the jury to approach the evidence of such a witness with caution, although the nature and extent of that warning will depend on the particular facts of the case.[44] The wording of the warning in *Mahil*[45] was contested on appeal on the grounds that the judge had said that a witness may be treated as hostile if they failed to adhere to the statement they have made, and it appears that they may be doing that deliberately. Counsel for the appellant argued that this description underplayed the notion of a hostile witness, which, in his view, was one 'who lied or

---

34 *The Times* (8 March 1856).
35 *Ewer v Ambrose* (1825) 3 B & C 746.
36 *R v South Ribble Stipendiary Magistrate, ex p Cochrane* (see text accompanying n. 15 above). See also *R v Maw* [1994] Crim LR 841.
37 *Ewer v Ambrose* (1825) 3 B & C 746.
38 [2013] EWCA Crim 41.
39 *R v Powell* [1985] Crim LR 592.
40 *R v Darby* [1989] Crim LR 817.
41 *R v Olumegbon* [2004] EWCA Crim 2337.
42 *R v Thompson* (1976) 64 Cr App R 96.
43 Criminal Procedure Act 1865, s 3. See discussion below.
44 *R v Greene* [2009] EWCA Crim 2282.
45 [2013] EWCA Crim 673.

wished to conceal the truth out of animus to the prosecution.'[46] The court rejected this argument, holding that the use of the word 'deliberately' by the judge was a 'sufficient encapsulation of the essential quality of a hostile witness, which is one not desirous of telling the truth to the court at the instance of the party calling him.'[47] As such, the judge's words were entirely adequate to convey to the jury the flavour of what is meant by a hostile witness and could not be criticised.

6.2 Principles of cross-examination

At an earlier period, all questioning in criminal trials was initiated by the judge, which usually led to a 'freewheeling discussion' between the witnesses, the defendant, and the judge.[48] The practice of witnesses being cross-examined by defence counsel appears to have emerged in the 1730s, with the purpose being to 'supplement rather than supplant questioning by the court.'[49] The practice became more commonplace during the late eighteenth century,[50] although during the nineteenth century the nature of cross-examination underwent a sea change. As the number of lawyers increased and litigation grew, the function of the judge as an active inquirer was gradually usurped.[51]

Lawyers began to assume ownership of the trial, which underlined the need for closer control of a system that was increasingly characterised by partisan advocacy.

By the first half of the nineteenth century, Landsman notes that 'flamboyant courtroom advocacy was the main avenue to success.'[52] He also observes that cross-examination took on an increasingly aggressive tone, with fierce attacks being launched on the motives and character of the witnesses:

> Accompanying the increase in counsel's participation in litigation, and especially the intensification of cross-examination, came an amplified acerbity by the advocates. Where once it was the judges who made caustic remarks, it was now the cross-examining lawyers who were sarcastic interrogators.[53]

The primacy of cross-examination as an indispensable feature of the adversarial process was established in the early nineteenth century.[54] In subsequent years, the fervent and aggressive nature of the process became deeply rooted in trial advocacy. Practitioners came to view it as having superseded the oath as an indispensable method of uncovering the truth by rooting out unreliable witnesses.[55] Indeed, since the limitations placed on defence counsel at that time forbade counsel from addressing the jury directly,[56] cross-examination was viewed as the most effective means of undermining the prosecution case.[57] Langbein cites one anonymous commentator who wrote that it was 'the most perfect and effectual system for unravelling of falsehood ever devised

46 Ibid., at [77].
47 Ibid., at [78].
48 Landsman, S., 'A Brief Survey of the Development of the Adversary System' (1983) 44 *Ohio State Law Journal* 713, 727.
49 Langbein, J.H., *The Origins of the Adversary Criminal Trial* (Oxford University Press, 2003), at 291.
50 Ibid.
51 Ibid.
52 Landsman, op. cit., n. 48, at 733.
53 Landsman, S., 'The Rise of the Contentious Spirit: Adversary Procedure in Eighteenth Century England' (1990) 75 *Cornell Law Review* at 497, 536.
54 Langbein, op. cit., n. 49, p. 246.
55 Ibid.
56 The prohibition on defence counsel addressing the jury was lifted by the Prisoner's Counsel Act 1836.
57 Ibid., p. 296.

by the ingenuity of mortals,'[58] and Bentham labelled it as a 'grand security ... against erroneous or mendacious testimony.'[59]

Towards the end of the nineteenth century, the courts came to recognise cross-examination as a fundamental right of the defence counsel. Any sworn witness was expected to undergo cross-examination as a matter of course. In conducting cross-examination, it was accepted that advocates themselves had a very broad leeway in determining their style and lines of questioning.[60] The role of defence counsel became much more proactive, and eloquent advocacy and zealous questioning were highly desirable skills.[61] The role of the prosecutor also changed. Professional advocates came to prosecute cases much more frequently, and assumed a more adversarial stance in the presentation of their cases to match the increased zeal of defence counsel.[62] As the trial moved increasingly towards the form of a duel between two parties, it became clear that this newfound fervour in the criminal courtrooms had to be 'tempered' by responsibility.[63] The conduct of advocates had to be regulated more closely, and this was primarily effected through the formulation of new rules of evidence and fresh understandings about the role of these rules within the overall context of the criminal trial. The indispensable nature of cross-examination to the criminal trial is still accepted today.[64] In its modern context, the purpose of cross-examination is said to be twofold: (1) to weaken the case for the other side, and (2) to establish facts that are favourable to the case for the cross-examiner.[65]

However, it might be added that, in modern times, the first of these objectives is achieved not by discrediting the *evidence* by demonstrating that it does not fit with other evidence before the jury, but by seeking to discredit the *witness* so that the jury will not believe, or give little credence to, their testimony. Parties have a right to cross-examine all witnesses on any relevant issue, or on any matter concerning a witness's credibility. In contrast to examination-in-chief, leading questions may be put to witnesses.[66] Strictly speaking, the cross-examiner should not 'suggest' matters to witnesses, but in practice there are few advocates who do not, at least occasionally, adopt the phrase 'I put it to you that ... ' or 'Isn't it the case that ...?' Witnesses can easily be upset by suggestions that they are mistaken or, even worse, lying. Of course, counsel will often stop short of calling the witness a liar, but phrases such as 'I suggest that what you have described never happened' have but one interpretation.

The centrality of cross-examination to the adversarial trial is underlined by the consequences of failing to cross-examine a witness. In such an event, counsel may be deemed to have accepted the witness's version of events if the testimony has gone unchallenged.[67] If a party has been prevented from cross-examining a witness, that witness's testimony may be regarded as inadmissible, or may be afforded little weight. For example, in *R v Doolin*,[68] in which the witness died before cross-examination, the testimony was still deemed to be admissible since the judge had given an appropriate warning to the jury. By contrast, in *R v Lawless*,[69] it was stated that where the testimony formed a central plank of the prosecution case, a judicial warning was not sufficient to prevent

58 Ibid.

59 Bentham, J., *The Rationale of Judicial Evidence Specially Applied to English Trials* (Hunt & Clark, 1827), as cited by Langbein, op. cit., n. 49, at 246.

60 Landsman, op. cit., n. 48, p. 539.

61 Ibid., p. 594.

62 Langbein, J., 'The Historical Origins of the Privilege against Self-Incrimination at Common Law' (1994) 92 *Michigan Law Review* 1047, 1069.

63 Cairns, D., *Advocacy and the Making of the Adversarial Trial 1800–1865* (Clarendon, 1998), p. 165.

64 *Hobbs v Tinling* [1929] 2 KB 1; *R v Paraskeva* (1982) 76 Cr App R 162.

65 Du Cann, R., *The Art of the Advocate* (Penguin, 1999), p. 114.

66 *Parker v Noon* (1836) 7 C&P 408.

67 *R v Wood Green Court, ex p Taylor* [1995] Crim LR 879.

68 (1832) 1 Jebb CC 123.

69 (1993) 98 Cr App R 342.

any prejudice to the accused. The Court of Appeal held that the entire testimony should have been excluded.

The question of admissibility will thus depend upon the nature of the evidence in question and its importance to the case as a whole. On occasions, the courts have been confronted with cases in which only a partial cross-examination has taken place. For example, in *R v Stretton*,[70] the victim of an alleged rape and indecent assault was epileptic, and fell ill while testifying. When it became clear that she was unable to continue, the trial judge directed the jury that if they felt the defence had been deprived of the opportunity properly to test her evidence, they should acquit the defendant. However, the defendant was convicted, and his appeal was dismissed on the ground that the trial judge had properly exercised his discretion to allow the trial to continue in such circumstances. The court placed considerable emphasis on the fact that cross-examination had proceeded for some time before the witness became ill, and the trial judge gave a clear warning to the jury and urged them to consider carefully the impact of the complainant's failure to complete her testimony. Similarly, in *R v Wyatt*,[71] a seven-year-old child, the alleged victim of an indecent assault, gave her evidence-in-chief via a TV link and was cross-examined for some 20 minutes before becoming too distressed to continue. Although there was no lengthy warning to the jury as there had been in *Stretton*, the Court of Appeal was satisfied that the jury had been fairly directed on the girl's evidence and upheld the conviction. If little or no cross-examination takes place, an adjournment of the trial to enable the witness to recover might assist, or a new trial might be possible. However, in cases like those above, the witness is unlikely to be helped by an adjournment, and even less likely to be able to withstand the ordeal of another trial; the choice for the trial judge is then between continuing with the trial (with an appropriate direction to the jury) or directing an outright acquittal.

6.2.1 The nature of cross-examination

Traditionally, many commentators and indeed the legal profession have maintained that the purpose of cross-examination is to investigate the truth of the witness's evidence. It was Wigmore who famously remarked that cross-examination was 'beyond any doubt the greatest legal engine ever invented for the discovery of truth.'[72] Similarly, Buckner argued that the primary purpose of cross-examination should be 'to catch truth, ever an elusive fugitive.'[73] However, such arguments have been increasingly questioned in recent years. The Australian Law Reform Commission has stated that 'so far as obtaining accurate testimony is concerned, [cross-examination] is arguably the poorest of the techniques employed at present in the common law courts,'[74] and John Langbein has described it as a 'flawed theory of truth-seeking.'[75] Cross-examination does not necessarily aim to elicit the truth, but to challenge or correct what has just been heard. Counsel will only desire that the witness testifies about those events that will lend credence to the particular case theory being advanced.

Advocacy tends to be naturally aggressive and confrontational, with cross-examiners deploying a vast range of tactics to unsettle witnesses. This in itself means that the witness will be 'in the worst possible frame of mind to be examined – he will be agitated, confused and bewildered.'[76] As

---

70 (1988) 86 Cr App R 7.

71 [1990] Crim LR 343.

72 Wigmore, J.H., *A Treatise on the Anglo-American System of Evidence in Trials at Common Law*, 3rd edn (Brown & Co, 1940), at [1367].

73 Buckner, E.R., 'Comments on the Uses and Abuses of Cross-Examination,' in F.L. Wellman (ed.), *The Art of Cross-Examination* (Simon & Schuster, 1936), p. 216.

74 Australian Law Reform Commission, *The Manner of Giving Evidence*, Research Paper No. 8 (Australian Government Publishing Service, 1982), at [10.5].

75 Langbein, op. cit., n. 49, at 247.

76 Harris, R., *Hints on Advocacy* (Little Brown, 1892), cited by Fielding, N., *Courting Violence* (Oxford University Press, 2006), at 219.

shown in Chapter 5, witnesses are often required to answer insulting and invasive questions about aspects of their lives that they would much rather were kept private. Moreover, by implication, the jury is invited to draw assumptions about the confused and distraught state of the witness, which opens the doorway to potentially inaccurate fact-finding since there is no evidence to suggest that the witness's demeanour is a reliable indicator to determine the veracity of the evidence.[77]

Recollections of past events, along with associated evidence, are routinely manipulated, decontextualised, and recategorised by the parties at trial, before any attempt is made to reorganise them so that they correspond with abstract legal principles. In particular, advocates will often resort to the use of suggestion by putting scenarios to witnesses and then asking them to comment. This maximises the likelihood that the witness will only relay those facts to the court that counsel desires. Some witnesses are more susceptible to suggestion than others. Research has indicated that suggestion is a particularly effective technique for the advocate to establish control in cases involving children[78] or those with learning disabilities,[79] particularly where such a witness views the questioner as an authority figure.[80] In this way, the testimony of individual witnesses is filtered and recast in a different light. There is no doubt that cross-examination, when properly conducted, can lead to better evidence by disclosing deliberate lies or unintended errors and misconceptions. However, the reality is that, far from acting as an effective tool for the recovery of the truth, cross-examination is all too often used to hide or obfuscate it.

6.2.2 The finality rule

While counsel retains a broad leeway in the forms of questions that are put to witnesses, cross-examination is not designed to be a 'fishing expedition.'[81] One of the most important restrictions upon counsel is the operation of the finality rule. The rule is a natural corollary of the concept of relevance,[82] and states that questions that are not directly relevant to the issue(s) in the proceedings must be regarded as final. For example, in *R v Burke*,[83] the cross-examiner alleged the witness, who was testifying through an interpreter in Irish, had been heard talking to two other people in the court precinct in English. The witness denied that this ever happened. It will be recalled from Chapter 1 that matters concerning the credit of a witness or the credibility of evidence given are generally regarded as collateral matters because they do not bear directly on the issue(s) before the court. Thus, in the instant case, the court refused to allow counsel to adduce any evidence in rebuttal, since this was deemed to be a collateral matter. While neither counsel nor the jury is required to believe the answer to a collateral question,[84] counsel is prevented from calling further evidence to demonstrate that the answer is not true.

In *Attorney General v Hitchcock*,[85] the witness had been asked whether he had said in an out-of-court statement that he had been offered money to give evidence by excise officers. He denied having said this, and it was held that counsel could not call evidence to prove that he had because it was a collateral matter. A less-than-helpful test of what constitutes a collateral matter was proposed by Pollock CB:

77 See Ch 2.
78 See Hedderman, C., *Children's Evidence: The Need for Corroboration*, Research and Planning Unit Paper No. 41 (HMSO, 1987), p 28; Spencer, J.R. and Flin, R., *The Evidence of Children*, 2nd edn (Blackstone, 1993).
79 Sanders, A., Creation, J., Bird, S., and Weber, L., *Victims with Learning Disabilities: Negotiating the Criminal Justice System*, Home Office Research Findings No. 44 (HMSO, 1996), pp. 75–76.
80 Milne, R. and Bull, R., *Investigating Interviewing: Psychology and Practice* (Wiley, 1999).
81 McEwan, J., *Evidence and the Adversarial Process*, 2nd edn (Hart, 1998), at 103.
82 See Ch 1.
83 (1858) 8 Cox CC 44.
84 *Hobbs v Tinling* [1929] 2 KB 1.
85 (1847) 1 Ex 91.

> If the answer of a witness is a matter which you would be allowed on your own part to prove in evidence – if it has such a connection with the issues that you would be allowed to give it in evidence – then it is a matter on which you may contradict [the witness].[86]

This test is, of course, something of a tautology, and is tantamount to saying that a matter is 'in issue' if it is 'in issue.' More accurately, it might be said that a fact constitutes a 'matter in issue' if it must be established by either party in order to discharge the burden of proof. Only in these circumstances will counsel be able to adduce rebutting evidence to disprove the answer of the witness. If the answer relates to collateral issues, and is thereby not relevant to any material issue in dispute, the finality rule applies and no rebutting evidence is admissible.

It was noted in Chapter 1 that the distinction between facts in issue and collateral issues can be a difficult one to draw at times, and this is particularly true in sexual cases. In *R v Funderburk*,[87] the defendant alleged that the complainant, who described in graphic detail losing her virginity to him, was lying as she was already sexually experienced. He wished to adduce evidence that the girl had told him, and others, on a number of occasions that she was sexually experienced. If such evidence was relevant to the credibility of the witness alone, it could not be adduced, although if it was relevant to the facts in issue, then it could be heard. The trial judge refused permission, although his refusal was overturned by the Court of Appeal. As that court saw it, these facts were intimately connected with the facts in issue. Similarly, in the subsequent case of *R v Nagrecha*,[88] the complainant had alleged that she had been indecently assaulted by her employer. The trial judge had ruled that the defence could not adduce evidence of similar allegations made by the complainant against other men, although the complainant denied ever having made such a complaint before. The Court of Appeal allowed the appeal and stated that such questioning should have been allowed since it went to the issue of whether an assault had actually occurred at all, and not merely to the witness's credibility.

The ultimate decision as to whether or not a matter is regarded as collateral rests with the trial judge, and will not lightly be subject to interference by the Court of Appeal.[89] As we noted in respect of the concept of relevance generally in Chapter 1, this will ultimately depend upon the trial judge's own perception of what is or is not logically probative of the facts in issue. In this sense, the judge's beliefs, experiences, social mores, prejudices, and values will all come into play, which underlines the fact that the concept of relevance and the operation of the finality rule are both fundamentally elusive and open to subjective interpretation.

In addition to some measure of uncertainty surrounding the scope of the rule, it should also be underlined that there are five established exceptions that may apply. These concern evidence of previous convictions, evidence of bias or prejudice, evidence of physical or mental disability affecting reliability evidence of a reputation for untruthfulness, and previous inconsistent statements. Each of these categories is now considered in turn.

6.2.2.1 Previous convictions

Section 6 of the Criminal Procedure Act 1865 – which applied to criminal and civil proceedings alike – provided that a

---

86 Ibid., at 99.

87 [1990] 2 All ER 482.

88 [1997] 2 Cr App R 401.

89 *R v Somers* [1999] Crim LR 744.

> witness may be questioned as to whether he has been convicted of an [offence] and upon being so questioned, if he either denies or does not admit the fact, or refuses to answer, it shall be lawful for the cross-examining party to prove such conviction.

In practice, this meant that a witness, other than the defendant, could be asked about their previous convictions in accordance with the above provision on the basis that previous convictions were always relevant to the credibility of the witness.

However, this provision has since been superseded; previous convictions in criminal cases will now fall within the definition of 'bad character' in section 98 of the Criminal Justice Act 2003. Thus, to cross-examine a non-defendant witness, the requirements of section 100 must be met.[90]

In the case of the accused, the evidence must be admitted under one of the eight gateways set out in section 101.[91] Where such evidence is admitted, it will fall outside the scope of the finality rule, even if counsel has introduced the evidence solely to attack the credibility of the witness. In civil cases, the general rule is that such evidence is admissible subject to the relevance threshold and the broad discretion of the court to control/exclude evidence.[92]

The Rehabilitation of Offenders Act 1974 does not apply to criminal trials, but in practice it is exceedingly rare for advocates to challenge the credibility of a witness through adducing evidence of spent convictions. *The Criminal Practice Directions, Part 35*[93] recommends that judges and advocates avoid making reference to spent convictions insofar as it is possible. In the case of non-defendant witnesses, section 100(3) of the 2003 Act additionally requires that the trial judge has regard to a number of factors, including the relevant time frame. Similarly, section 108 lays down a general principle that convictions obtained while the defendant was a juvenile are not normally relevant (nor would they be relevant for a non-defendant witness). In the vast majority of cases, convictions obtained by any witness as a child, or spent convictions under the Rehabilitation Act 1974, are likely to be seen as being so marginal as to be excluded, as appropriate, under either section 100 or section 101. Similarly, in civil proceedings, cross-examination about any spent convictions is prohibited,[94] unless the judge is satisfied that it is not possible for justice to be done except by admitting such evidence.[95]

6.2.2.2 Bias or partiality

A witness may be questioned about matters that suggest bias or partiality and, if denied, the necessary facts may be proved in rebuttal. Such bias or partiality, although collateral in the sense that it goes to credibility, can also impact upon the material issues in the sense that it may tend to suggest that evidence was manufactured, or that there is no case to answer. In *R v Mendy*,[96] the husband of the accused, who was to be called as a witness for her, was waiting to give evidence outside the courtroom. He was seen talking to a man who had been in court taking notes. The implication was that, knowing what evidence had been given, he could tailor his testimony to assist his wife's defence. Under cross-examination, he denied this, and the prosecution were allowed to bring evidence to rebut his denial. The Court of Appeal held that the rule of finality was not absolute and should not prevent the jury hearing evidence that suggested an attempt to pervert the course of justice, with Lane LJ commenting that '[i]t has always been permissible to call evidence to

---

90 See Ch 11.

91 See Ch 11.

92 *O'Brien v Chief Constable of South Wales Police* (2005). See further discussion in Ch 11.

93 [2013] EWCA Crim 1631.

94 Rehabilitation of Offenders Act 1974, s 4(1).

95 Ibid., s 7(3).

96 (1976) 64 Cr App R 4.

contradict a witness's denial of bias or partiality towards one of the parties.'[97] Similarly, in *R v Phillips*,[98] the defendant was charged with incest and the defence wanted to pursue a line of questioning that suggested that his two daughters, the alleged victims, had admitted to others that the allegations against their father were untrue. The children denied having made these statements, and the judge refused leave to allow the defence to bring evidence in rebuttal. However, here the Court of Appeal held that the judge was wrong to do so: the questions and the evidence went to the heart of the issue in the case and were not collateral.

More recent cases involving police evidence have given a new twist to this line of authority. In *R v Busby*,[99] it was alleged that police officers had threatened a defence witness in order to prevent him from giving evidence. This allegation was denied by the officers. The court, however, found that this was not a collateral matter, but went to the material issues, since, if true, it would show an attempt to influence the outcome of the trial. Referring to *Mendy* and *Phillips*, the Court of Appeal held that the evidence in rebuttal of the denial was clearly admissible. At the time it was reported, there was some suggestion that this case was something of a novel departure from precedent, but it is now broadly accepted that it is in line with the earlier cases, being concerned simply with a different way of seeking to pervert the course of justice.

However, the decision in *R v Edwards*[100] sits less comfortably with earlier authorities. Here, defence counsel alleged a confession had been fabricated, and wished to cross-examine the police officers about evidence they had given in previous cases that was, allegedly, tainted. The juries in these earlier cases had returned verdicts of not guilty, which tended to imply that the police officers had fabricated parts of their evidence. The Court of Appeal found that, since it could be demonstrated that the jury had disbelieved the evidence of the officers in a previous trial, the jury in the present case was entitled to be made aware of this fact. The officers could therefore be asked about their evidence in these earlier trials. Somewhat surprisingly, the court then proceeded to state that, in the event of the officers giving answers that were unfavourable to the defence, the finality rule would apply and the defence would not be able to call evidence in rebuttal. This appears to contradict the court's intention that the jury should be aware of facts that suggest that the officer is not the truthful witness they purport to be. There may be evidence to suggest that the police officer is dishonest, but we must rely on the honesty of the officer to ensure that the jury become aware of that evidence. Of course, a police officer will rarely deny facts that are in the public domain, or answer falsely and expose herself to a charge of perjury. Nonetheless, it seems strange that, on the rare occasion in which this might happen, the defence will be unable to expose the truth unless counsel is able to bring it within one of the other exceptions to the finality rule.

The *Edwards* case concerned the activities of the West Midland Serious Crime Squad in the 1980s. During the late 1980s, it became apparent that some officers had either manufactured confessions or used threats of violence to obtain them. The police and prosecution feared that the opening up of the role of the police officers in other trials would lead to an overall loss of credibility and unjust acquittals. Where an officer's background is open to an attack on their credibility, the prosecutor's natural reaction is, where possible, not to call that officer as a witness. In these circumstances, the proper course would be to call the witness and ask at the outset of the examination-in-chief whether they had been suspended or subject to other disciplinary action; otherwise the court would assume they are a serving officer.

---

97 Ibid., at 6.
98 (1936) 26 Cr App R 17.
99 (1982) 75 Cr App R 79.
100 [1991] 1 WLR 207.

Furthermore, the officer should be required to give evidence in accordance with their statement and not merely tendered for cross-examination, which is the practice when more than one officer is to give the same evidence. In *R v Haringey Justices, ex p DPP*,[101] Stuart-Smith LJ held that a witness's credibility should be determined in relation to the content of his evidence and not in relation to his credit generally. This was the correct position unless counsel argued that the evidence might be untrue because the witness had previously been found guilty of perjury, perverting the course of justice, or for some other verifiable reason. Some purely collateral act of dishonesty, whether proved or merely suspected, did not mean that a witness's evidence on a wholly unrelated matter was not credible. On the surface, such a view may appear perfectly rational, but in practice prosecution and defence counsel will seek to expose a witness's bad character and any previous convictions with a view to suggesting to the jury that they are not worthy of belief. Convictions for dishonesty are used to suggest that a person who is dishonest in one respect is probably dishonest in another respect. Other convictions will be used to suggest that the witness is of poor moral character and for that reason less worthy of belief.

In *R v Edwards (Maxine)*,[102] the Stoke Newington Drugs Squad (whose members had been the subject of an inquiry into the planting of evidence and perjury known as Operation Jackpot), arrested Edwards on suspicion of possessing crack cocaine with intent to supply. The police alleged that, when they searched her, they discovered eight foil wraps, later found to contain crack cocaine, and £175 cash. The police claimed that she had subsequently admitted that the wraps contained cocaine while in the car on the way to the police station, but had refused to sign a note of this admission. At trial, the accused denied having made any such admission, and alleged that the police had found the foil wraps in a parked car that she was standing beside. Nevertheless, she was convicted and her initial application for leave to appeal was refused.

Following the inquiry into the Drug Squad's activities and the acquittal of a number of persons arrested and charged by the Squad, the Home Secretary referred the case back to the Court of Appeal. Allowing the appeal, the court held that the appellant was one of a number of persons convicted on very similar evidence from officers of the Stoke Newington Drug Squad, and who had complained that the evidence was fabricated. Despite the fact that no charges or disciplinary proceedings had been brought against the officers who had arrested the appellant, the conviction was still regarded as unsafe:

> Once the suspicion of perjury starts to infect the evidence and permeate cases in which the witnesses have been involved, and which are closely similar, the evidence on which such convictions are based becomes as questionable as it was in the cases in which the appeals have already been allowed. It is impossible to be confident that had the jury which convicted this appellant known the facts and circumstances in the other cases in which [the witness] had been involved, that they would have been bound to convict this appellant.[103]

The above test was applied in *R v Whelan*,[104] in which the accused had been convicted of possessing cannabis. The arresting officers in the case were arrested and suspended from duty after an investigation into their conduct in other cases of alleged possession of drugs. This had led the prosecution to offer no evidence in other cases in which the arrested officers were involved. On appeal, the prosecution conceded that they had known at the time of trial that the officers were under

---

101 [1996] QB 351.
102 [1996] 2 Cr App R 345.
103 Ibid., at 350 (Beldam LJ).
104 [1997] Crim LR 353.

investigation. However, it was contended that they had not actively relied upon it. The Court of Appeal allowed the appeal and held that the prosecution was right to make the concession.

As a final point in relation to the bias exception, it should be added that, following the enactment of the Criminal Justice Act 2003, its scope in criminal proceedings is likely to be considerably narrower than it has previously been. This is because the type of evidence traditionally encapsulated under this head, particularly regarding allegations of corruption within the police, is likely to fall within the ambit of section 98 of the Act. As such, this evidence will only be admissible if the requirements of section 100 (in the case of non-defendants) or section 101 (in the case of defendants) are satisfied. The bias exception at common law is therefore only likely to come into play where the conduct in question falls short of the commission of a criminal offence or 'other reprehensible behaviour.'

6.2.2.3 Evidence of physical or mental disability affecting reliability

Almost all witnesses who give identification evidence will be cross-examined about their eyesight and whether they wear glasses. Hollywood films and televised trial dramas are replete with examples of the trial lawyer testing the eyesight of a witness in court and dramatically showing that they are unable to see how many fingers are being held up. The effect is to destroy the credibility of the witness totally. While such theatrics are seldom seen in practice, the effect of proving that the witness, who claims to have positively identified the accused from a distance of 20 metres, has defective vision and cannot see clearly beyond 5 metres, is the same. Such an example was given in the leading case on this area of law, *Toohey v The Metropolitan Police Commissioner.*[105] Here, the accused was convicted of assault with intent to rob. The defence was that the alleged victim had been drinking and, while the accused and his friends were trying to help him by taking him home, he became hysterical and accused them of attempting to rob him. The trial judge allowed evidence from a doctor that the victim had been drinking and appeared agitated when examined, but refused to allow the witness to state his opinion that the drink exacerbated the hysteria and that the victim was more prone to hysteria than the average person. The House of Lords allowed the appeal and held that the doctor should have been allowed to give his opinion on these matters.[106] Such evidence was admissible to show that the witness was unreliable, irrespective of whether it affected his credibility:

> Medical evidence is admissible to show that the witness suffers from some disease or defect or abnormality of mind that affects the reliability of his evidence. Such evidence is not confined to a general opinion of the unreliability of the witness but may give all matters necessary to show, not only the foundation of and the reasons for the diagnosis, but also the extent to which the credibility of the witness is affected.[107]

The opposing party may call expert evidence in rebuttal, but such evidence should be confined to the issues raised by the medical evidence and should not usurp the role of the jury in determining whether the particular witness is credible:

> Human evidence ... is subject to many cross-currents such as partiality, prejudice, self-interest and above all, imagination and accuracy. These are matters with which the jury, helped by cross-examination and common sense, must do their best. But when a witness through physical (in which I include mental) disease or abnormality is not capable of giving a

---

105 [1965] AC 595.

106 For further information, see Ch 13.

107 Op. cit., no. 104, at 609 (Pearce LJ).

> true or reliable account to the jury, it must surely be allowable for medical science to reveal this vital hidden fact to them.[108]

The point is further illustrated by the decision of May J in *R v Mackenney*,[109] in which a psychologist was refused permission to testify that the witness was a psychopath who was likely to be lying. A distinction was drawn between the witness who suffers from a mental disability that makes him or her incapable of giving evidence and the witness who is capable of giving reliable evidence but may not be doing so. The jury may need help with the former, but it is for them, assisted by cross-examination and common sense, to determine whether a witness who is *capable* of giving reliable evidence is, in fact, doing so.

6.2.2.4 Evidence of a reputation for untruthfulness

It has long been the case that a witness may give evidence that another witness, called by the opposing party, has a reputation for untruthfulness and should not be believed on their oath. This rule was restated in *R v Richardson* in the following terms:[110]

> 1 A witness may be asked whether he has knowledge of the impugned witness's general reputation for veracity and whether (from such knowledge) he would believe the witness's sworn testimony.
>
> 2 The witness called to impeach the credibility of another witness may also express his individual opinion (based upon his personal knowledge) as to whether the latter is to be believed on his oath, and is not confined to giving an opinion based merely on general reputation.
>
> 3 But whether his opinion as to the impugned witness's credibility be based simply upon the latter's general reputation for veracity or upon his personal knowledge, the witness cannot be permitted to indicate during his examination-in-chief the particular facts, circumstances or incidents that formed the basis of his opinion, although he may be cross-examined as to them.[111]

Although such evidence is likely to constitute hearsay, section 118(1) of the Criminal Justice Act 2003 preserves this common law exception to the rule.[112] While the law of evidence should rightfully formulate rules to protect the integrity of the criminal trial, the danger with evidence concerning poor reputations is that such disparaging charges may be entirely unearned and nothing more than the product of malicious gossip. As we shall see in Chapter 13, the general rule in relation to opinion evidence is that witnesses give evidence of facts, and only experts are permitted to express opinions to the courts. If the witness is not allowed to give evidence of particular facts on which their opinion is based, how are the jury to determine what weight to attach to such an opinion? If a witness is called for this purpose, it is open to the other side to call witnesses as to that witness's reputation, and so on, thus unnecessarily prolonging a trial.[113] However, this exception is relied upon very infrequently in practice in either the criminal or civil courts.[114]

---

108 Ibid., at 608. *Toohey* has recently been applied by the Privy Council in *Milton v The Queen* [2015] UKPC 42.

109 (1981) 72 Cr App R 78.

110 [1969] 1 QB 299.

111 Ibid., at 304–305 (Edmund-Davies LJ).

112 See Ch 12.

113 See e.g. *R v Bogie* [1992] Crim LR 302.

114 In criminal cases, any evidence that is adduced to this end may also have to meet the test laid down in s 100 of the 2003 Act if the alleged degree of 'untruthfulness' should cross the threshold of 'misconduct' under s 98.

6.2.2.5 Previous inconsistent statements

On occasions, the cross-examiner will aim to discredit a witness by revealing to the jury that they made a previous oral or written statement that is inconsistent with their testimony. If the witness denies having made such a statement, the finality rule will not apply and section 4 of the Criminal Procedure Act 1865 (which applied to criminal and civil proceedings alike) allows counsel to adduce that statement in rebuttal. The provision refers to statements that 'are relative to the subject matter of the indictment or proceedings,' and whether the statement is or is not 'relative' (i.e. relevant) is a matter for the trial judge. Under section 5 of the 1865 Act, where counsel intends to use the contents of a written statement to contradict the witness, the document must be shown to the witness, and their attention must be drawn to the contradictory aspects. The witness should be requested to read those parts and then asked whether they still wish to stand by what was said in court. If the witness accepts the contents of the statement, the document then becomes part of the evidence, replacing any earlier testimony. If the witness sticks to the oral testimony given in court, the cross-examiner may wish to use the document to contradict what the witness said. If so, counsel must prove the document and put it in evidence. The court and jury may then inspect the whole document, although the trial judge may direct that the jury see only those parts referred to in cross-examination.[115]

When a previous inconsistent statement was adduced into evidence in these circumstances, it was not evidence of the truth of its contents, but went only to the consistency and credit of the witness. The judge had to make this clear to the jury. However, following a recommendation by the Law Commission,[116] that rule has now been changed by section 119(1) of the Criminal Justice Act 2003. Under this provision, any previous inconsistent statement is now regarded as evidence of any matter stated therein, of which oral evidence by that person would be admissible. Section 119(2) makes a similar provision when a previous inconsistent statement is admitted to attack the credibility of a witness who does not give oral evidence, but whose statement is admitted under one of the exceptions to the hearsay rule created or preserved by the 2003 Act.[117] This also reflects the position relating to the use of such statements in civil proceedings.[118]

6.2.3 Character attacks on non-defendant witnesses

Since the enactment of the Criminal Justice Act 2003, evidence adduced under any of the exceptions to the finality rule that tends to attack the credibility of the witness will also have to pass the test laid down in section 100 of the legislation. In recognition of increased concern about the plight of victims and other vulnerable witnesses in court, section 100 was introduced with the aim of preventing counsel from making unfounded or irrelevant allegations of misconduct against non-defendant witnesses in criminal proceedings. This topic is dealt with in detail in Chapter 11.[119]

6.2.4 The cross-examination of rape complainants

Despite the enactment of section 100, it is in the inherent nature of all contested criminal cases that witnesses of all descriptions and backgrounds will often find their accounts of events and

115 *R v Beattie* (1989) 89 Cr App R 302.
116 Law Commission, *Hearsay and Related Topics*, Report No. 245 (HMSO, 1997), [10.92].
117 See Ch 12.
118 Civil Evidence Act 1995, s. 6.
119 See Ch 11.

their characters called into question. This section examines the experiences of victims of rape and sexual assault under cross-examination.

It should be noted that at the time of writing, the Law Commission is in the process of consulting on proposed reforms to the law, practice, and guidance in relation to sexual offences. The policy proposals that result from this consultation are likely to be published in 2024 and will be aimed at introducing strategies to counter the effect of 'rape myths' on prosecutions for sexual offences and to introduce greater judicial oversight into the process of obtaining and using evidence containing the sensitive personal information of complainants.[120]

In Chapter 2, it was noted how advocates will routinely attempt to exploit the weaknesses in the complainant's evidence, by embarking upon character assassination. During the 1980s and 1990s, research revealed astounding levels of distress caused to complainants by the manner in which questioning was conducted in court.[121] In a small minority of these cases, the complainants' distress was hugely exacerbated where defendants opted to conduct their own defence.[122] While self-representation in cases involving violence against children or child sex abuse was prohibited by the Criminal Justice Act 1988,[123] two high-profile cases in the 1990s highlighted the potentially gruelling nature of cross-examinations conducted by the accused in person.[124] In *R v Edwards (Ralston)*,[125] the defendant came to court wearing the same clothes it was alleged he had worn while committing the alleged rape, and proceeded to subject the complainant to a lengthy and deeply intrusive cross-examination about aspects of her private life and their relationship together. In *Brown (Milton)*,[126] the defendant had been convicted of raping two women at knifepoint, and had dispensed with the services of counsel and solicitors at an early stage of the trial. Like Edwards, he subjected the complainants to a lengthy and vicious cross-examination, prompting the trial judge to express alarm that the law permitted such cross-examination to occur in the first place:

> It is a highly regrettable and extremely sad aspect of this case that despite my repeated efforts during the first two days of your trial you insisted on dispensing with the services of highly competent leading and junior counsel and solicitors, the third set you had been allocated at public expense, thereafter subjecting your victims to merciless cross-examination clearly designed to intimidate and humiliate them. In the course of your questioning you made outrageous and repulsive suggestions to both witnesses ... Although I took what steps I could to minimise that ordeal by repeated efforts to prevent repetitious and irrelevant questioning, nevertheless the whole experience must for those women have been horrifying and it is highly regrettable in my view, and a matter of understandable public concern, that the law as it stands permits a situation where an unrepresented defendant in a sexual assault case has a virtually unfettered right to personally question his victim in such needlessly extended and agonising detail for the obvious purpose of intimidation and humiliation.[127]

---

120 https://s3-eu-west-2.amazonaws.com/lawcom-prod-storage-11jsxou24uy7q/uploads/2023/05/ESOS-CP-latest-version-1-1.pdf (last accessed 26 September 2023).

121 See Ch 5.

122 As a general rule, any person charged in criminal proceedings is entitled to conduct their own defence under s 2 of the Criminal Procedure Act 1865.

123 Section 34A, inserted by Criminal Justice Act 1991, s 55(7).

124 Where a defendant is unrepresented, the court has an inherent common law power to prevent the process from being abused by the defendant, but in *R v Morley* [1988] QB 601, the Court of Appeal held that this power is to be exercised exceedingly sparingly. In consequence, where a defendant was unrepresented, trial judges tended to allow more latitude in cross-examination to avoid providing grounds for a successful appeal on the basis that the defendant was not permitted to defend herself effectively.

125 *The Times* (23 August 1996).

126 [1998] 2 Cr App R 364.

127 Ibid., at 368–9.

In refusing leave to appeal, the Court of Appeal approved the decision of the trial judge and offered further guidance to judges in cases involving unrepresented defendants:

> The trial judge is, however, obliged to have regard not only to the need to ensure a fair trial for the defendant but also to the reasonable interests of the other parties to the court process, in particular witnesses, and among witnesses particularly those who are obliged to relive by describing in the witness box an ordeal to which they say they have been subject. It is the clear duty of the trial judge to do everything he can, consistently with giving the defendant a fair trial, to minimise the trauma suffered by other participants. Furthermore, a trial is not fair if a defendant, by choosing to represent himself, gains the advantage he would not have had if represented of abusing the rules in relation to relevance and repetition which apply when witnesses are questioned.[128]

Prompted by the publicity afforded to these cases, and recommendations contained within *Speaking Up for Justice*, the Youth Justice and Criminal Evidence Act 1999 restricted the right of the accused to self-representation. Unrepresented defendants are now not permitted to cross-examine child witnesses at all, nor can they cross-examine adult witnesses in certain types of cases. Furthermore, a broad discretion has been created to prohibit cross-examination by unrepresented defendants in other circumstances as the judge sees fit. Under section 34 of the Act, no person charged with a sexual offence may cross-examine a witness who is the complainant in that offence.[129] This section also replaces and extends the scope of section 34A of the Criminal Justice Act 1988, which had originally prohibited self-representation in cases concerning child violence or child sex abuse. Section 35 replaces and extends this provision to cover a much broader range of offences against children.[130]

The discretion contained in section 35 of the Act permits courts to issue directions prohibiting unrepresented defendants from cross-examining complainants in circumstances other than those covered in section 34. Such a direction may be given following the application by the prosecution or of the court's own motion, provided that the court is satisfied that the test contained in section 36(2) is satisfied. This stipulates that the court may prohibit the accused from cross-examining any witness where it appears that the quality of evidence given by the witness on cross-examination is: (a) likely to be diminished if the cross-examination is conducted by the accused in person, and would be likely to be improved if a direction were given under this section; and (b) that it would not be contrary to the interests of justice to give such a direction. Section 36(3) sets out a list of criteria for the court to take into account in determining this last question.[131] Sections 37–40 of the Act deal with practical matters relating to these directions, and include the power of the court to appoint a representative for an accused in these circumstances where she declines to do so herself.[132]

The provisions of the Act contain a number of safeguards for the accused, including the duty imposed on the trial judge under section 39 to give such a warning as they consider necessary to prevent prejudicial inferences being drawn against the accused by the jury in such circumstances. Despite these safeguards, there have nonetheless been suggestions that this provision

---

128 Ibid., at 371 (Bingham CJ).

129 Or in relation to any other offence with which that person is charged in the proceedings.

130 These are extended to include kidnapping, false imprisonment, and abduction.

131 In arriving at its determination, the court should have regard, *inter alia*, to a range of factors set out in s 36(3)(a)–(d), those being: (a) whether the witness has expressed any opinion as to whether or not they are content to be cross-examined by the accused in person; (b) the nature of the questions likely to be asked; (c) any behaviour on the part of the accused at any stage of the proceedings, both generally and in relation to the witness; and (d) any relationship between the witness and the accused.

132 YJCEA 1999, s 38.

may contravene Article 6 of the European Convention.[133] However, the case law, most notably the decision of the European Court of Human Rights in *Croissant v Germany*, does not seem to support such a view.[134]

Here, the Court held that restricting the choice of counsel for the accused did not affect his ability to challenge the evidence against him.

Of course, even where defendants are represented, the questions put to the complainant by counsel may seem just as distressing. While judges must remain impartial, the common law does permit them to exercise a discretion to take over the cross-examination of a particular witness. In *R v Cameron*,[135] a 14-year-old rape complainant broke down after 15 minutes of cross-examination, and refused to answer any more questions put to her by defence counsel. In the absence of the witness, the judge discussed the matter with counsel, and asked the defence to provide him with the material and questions that the advocate had intended to put to the witness. The judge then told counsel that he would question the witness himself, but would not use questions that were nothing more than mere comments, or those that would serve no purpose other than to inflame the witness. In the interests of fairness, the judge then told prosecuting counsel that she would have to forego re-examination. Although the Court of Appeal found that the judge was not wrong in principle to take over the questioning, the particular solution adopted here would not ordinarily be appropriate to the situation of an adult witness who, without good excuse, refused to answer questions put in cross-examination. The same principle operates in respect of civil cases.[136]

6.2.4.1 Previous sexual history evidence

Research has consistently underlined that the most difficult aspect of cross-examination for complainants in rape and sexual assault cases was the elicitation of previous sexual history evidence. On a regular basis, defence counsel would seek to elicit information concerning the previous sexual experiences of the complainant with the accused, as well as with other men. It might be assumed that since questions concerning previous sexual history were not directed to proving a fact in issue, these should be regarded as being collateral, and therefore subject to the finality rule. This, however, is not the case. The common law has traditionally accepted that, in crimes of rape, attempted rape, and assault with intent to commit rape, acts of intercourse between the victim and the accused were relevant to the issue and could thus be the subject of cross-examination and rebuttal of any denials.[137] The common law also permitted the complainant to be cross-examined about acts of intercourse with men other than the accused, but, because this was a collateral matter, her denial of such acts could not be contradicted by calling evidence of such acts of intercourse.[138] However, the fact that the finality rule applied in this situation did not prevent counsel from asking the questions that, regardless of the answer, were designed to cast doubt on the complainant's moral character and her credibility by suggesting that she was a 'loose' woman.

In *R v Bashir and Manzur*,[139] it was held that evidence that the complainant in a case of rape was a prostitute was admissible to contradict a denial, because it went to the issue of consent. Similarly, in *R v Krausz*,[140] the accused, charged with rape, alleged that he met the complainant in a pub for

133 *The Daily Telegraph* (21 May 1998), as cited by Ellison, L., 'Cross-Examination of Rape Complainants' [1998] Crim LR 606, 611. Ellison also notes that the proposal was condemned by the Criminal Bar Association and Bar Council.

134 (1993) 16 EHRR 135. There would seem to be no absolute right for an accused to access a lawyer of their own choosing. See also *Philis v Greece* (1991) 13 EHRR 741.

135 *The Times* (3 May 2001).

136 *L v H and R* [2007] 2 FLR 162.

137 *R v Riley* (1887) 18 QBD 481.

138 *R v Holmes* (1871) LR 1 CCR 334.

139 [1969] 1 WLR 1303.

140 (1973) 57 Cr App Rep 466.

the first time and she had agreed to sleep with him. After intercourse she demanded money, and complained of rape after he refused to pay. The Court of Appeal held that the judge was wrong to refuse to allow the defence to call evidence of previous similar conduct by the complainant to rebut her denial.

Yet even in the early 1970s, it was questionable whether the fact that a woman was promiscuous was of any relevance to the question of whether she consented to intercourse on a particular occasion. The Report of the Heilbron Commission in 1975 recognised that the common law rules proved to be unsatisfactory in a number of ways.[141] The advisory group expressed concern that, in many cases, the complainant's actions and character became the overriding issue at the trial rather than the culpability of the defendant's actions. The common law also failed to reflect society's changing views about sexual morality, and the group concluded that restrictions on cross-examination were needed in order to prevent questioning that 'does not advance the cause of justice but in effect puts the woman on trial.'[142] In conclusion, the Report recommended that no evidence of the previous sexual history of the complainant with persons other than the accused should be admitted unless: (a) the judge is satisfied that the evidence relates to behaviour on the part of the complainant that was strikingly similar to her alleged behaviour on the occasion of, or in relation to, events immediately preceding the alleged offence; and (b) the degree of relevance of that evidence to issues arising in the trial is such that it would be unfair to the accused to exclude it.

Section 2 of the Sexual Offences (Amendment) Act 1976 placed restrictions on the cross-examination of a complainant in cases of rape and other sexual offences, but not in the way in which the Heilbron Report recommended. The new statutory test under section 2(2) of the 1976 Act was whether 'it would be unfair to that defendant to refuse to allow the evidence to be adduced or the question to be asked.'

The principal problems with section 2 of the 1976 Act were twofold. First, the emphasis on fairness to the accused to the exclusion of any detriment to the complainant and the failure to require a high degree of relevance to an issue in the trial before the evidence could be admitted allowed evidence of past sexual history to be adduced or question(s) to be asked about such history. Ultimately, the decision whether or not to grant leave to allow the defence to cross-examine the witness about previous sexual history was a matter for the trial judge. The Court of Appeal made clear in *R v Viola*[143] that this was not a matter of judicial discretion. The judge had to determine, first, whether the evidence was relevant to the issue of consent, and then whether or not it would be unfair to the accused to disallow such questioning. The second problem was the failure of the provision to control cross-examination about previous sexual history between the accused and the complainant, since the section applied only to 'persons other than the defendant.' Given that a majority of alleged rapes involve an acquaintance, and many of these involve previous acts of intercourse between the parties, the section failed to make any impact in relation to sexual history evidence in the vast majority of cases.

Any prospect that the new provision might herald the end of complainants being questioned about their previous sexual history quickly disappeared as section 2 was emasculated by the courts. The distinction between questions going to credit and questions going to the issue had effectively disappeared in rape trials. The previous behaviour of the complainant was almost always seen to be relevant to the issue, usually consent, with the result that the finality rule was overridden. By the late 1980s, it had become apparent that the questioning of rape complainants in court had been largely unaffected by the 1976 Act. Research by Zsuzsanna Adler found that an application to admit sexual history evidence was made under section 2 in 40 per cent of the cases

---

141 Heilbron, R., *Report of the Advisory Group on the Law of Rape*, Cmnd 6352 (HMSO, 1975).
142 Ibid., at p. 15.
143 [1982] 3 All ER 73.

studied, and was admitted in 75 per cent of such applications.[144] The research further suggested that, contrary to the intention behind section 2, such evidence was routinely used with little reference to the concept of relevance. Instead, previous sexual history evidence was used to discredit her character in the eyes of the jury. A more recent study by Lees confirmed these findings: over half of all female rape complainants had been cross-examined about their sexual history with men other than the defendant.[145]

6.2.4.2 Reform: the Youth Justice and Criminal Evidence Act 1999

In 1998, *Speaking Up for Justice* paved the way for a major overhaul of the law regulating sexual history evidence. The subsequent Youth Justice and Criminal Evidence Act 1999 repealed section 2 of the 1976 legislation. The new provision, contained in section 41 of the 1999 Act, is not the easiest to interpret, but it basically prescribes a blanket rule prohibiting the admissibility of any evidence concerning the previous sexual behaviour of the complainant in any trials involving a sexual offence.[146]

This rule is, however, subject to four somewhat narrow exceptions in subsections (3) and (5). Before considering these provisions in detail, it is worth considering what precisely is meant by the term 'sexual behaviour.'

Sexual behaviour is defined in section 42(1)(c) as

> any sexual behaviour or other sexual experience, whether or not involving any accused or other person, but excluding (except in section 41(3)(c)(i) and (5)(a)) anything alleged to have taken place as part of the event which is the subject matter of the charge against the accused.

This definition covers not only physical advances of a sexual nature but also verbal advances.[147]

This issue has confronted the Court of Appeal on a relatively frequent basis. The leading case is that of *R v T; R v H*.[148] In two separate cases, T was charged with rape of his niece and H with indecent assault of his stepdaughter. In both cases, the trial judge had refused to allow cross-examination directed by the defence to one of the complainants alleging past fabrication of such an assault, and the other complainant's failure to mention the alleged assault when complaining of other such assaults. In T's case, it was submitted that the proposed questions were about the failure to mention the allegations and not about sexual behaviour. In H's case, it was argued that the questions were about lies, albeit about sexual matters.

Adopting a purposive approach in interpreting the statute, the court noted that the mischief at which section 41 was aimed was to prevent evidence of the complainant's sexual behaviour being admitted and presented to the jury with the invitation to infer from it that a person with a colourful sexual history is more likely to tell lies, or to have consented to the sexual intercourse subject of the charge. However, in these circumstances, the questions were clearly relevant to the issues in the trial and did not constitute 'evidence of sexual behaviour' for the purposes of section 42(1)(c). The court noted that, as in the past, a distinction had to be drawn between questions about sexual behaviour itself and questions concerning statements *about* such behaviour by the complainant. Such a distinction is pivotal as the 1999 Act was never intended to restrict questions

---

144 Adler, Z., *Rape on Trial* (Routledge, 1987).

145 Lees, S., *Carnal Knowledge: Rape on Trial* (Hamish Hamilton, 1996).

146 YJCEA 1999, s 41(1). A sexual offence is classed as any offence under Part 1 of the Sexual Offences Act 2003 or any relevant superseded offence. For the definition of a 'relevant superseded offence,' see s 62(1A) YJCEA 1999.

147 *R v Hinds* [1979] Crim LR 111.

148 [2002] 1 WLR 632.

that were not 'about' sexual behaviour. While it would be profoundly improper to elicit details of a complainant's previous sexual experience under the guise of previous false complaints, this danger could be counteracted by the intervention of the trial judge to prevent abuse of questioning where there was not an evidential basis for the defence asserting that a previous statement had been made and that it was untrue. The appeal was thus allowed.

Similar reasoning was adopted in *R v Mukadi*,[149] in which the complainant, wearing a short skirt and a vest top, approached a supermarket security officer. They went to a park where they drank a bottle of wine before a sexual encounter took place at the defendant's flat. While the complainant admitted oral sex and kissing were consensual, she claimed intercourse was not. In support of his defence that the complainant had consented, the defence attempted to adduce evidence that before the woman had entered the store that day she was standing on the pavement when a large and expensive car drew up, driven by a much older male. The complainant got in, and they drove to a filling station.

At first instance, the judge refused to admit this evidence since it was not relevant to the issue of consent. The Court of Appeal, however, concluded that he had been wrong to do so, since it would have been possible for the jury to infer that when the complainant got into the car, she had anticipated some sexual activity with the occupant. This evidence could serve to rebut her claim that she went to the defendant's flat merely to get to know him with a view to becoming friends. If the jury had heard about the previous incident, that would have been relevant when assessing that part of her evidence.[150] Subsequent decisions have confirmed that false allegations are not 'evidence about sexual behaviour,' but refer instead to a general propensity to be untruthful.[151] Provided that the defence merely use such evidence to show that a particular statement was likely to be false, section 41 will not prohibit its use in this way. Thus, in *R v E*,[152] the court held that this right is not to be abused as the court must ensure that the defendant is able to 'point to material that is capable of supporting the inference.'

It now appears to be firmly established that section 41 does not cover those cases in which the defence has a 'proper evidential basis' for alleging that the complainant has made an untruthful statement in relation to an alleged act.[153] This was defined in *R v Murray*, as 'less than a strong factual foundation for concluding that the previous complaint was false. But there must be some material from which it could properly be concluded that the complaint was false.'[154] However, even where such a basis exists, the Court of Appeal held in *R v V*[155] that leave must also be obtained under section 100, since allegations of false complaints would constitute evidence of a non-defendant's bad character. Recently in *Ali and Ors v R*,[156] the Court of Appeal warned that counsel should not attempt to use section 100 to admit evidence that would circumvent the operation of section 41. In that case, the defence alleged that the complainant had made a previous false complaint against her father on the basis that the complaint was investigated but never prosecuted. The trial judge, with whom the Court of Appeal agreed, found no evidence to support the allegation that the complaint

149 [2004] Crim LR 373.

150 If this act constituted sexual behaviour, it was admissible under s 41(3)(b) and a refusal of leave under s 41(2)(b) would have had the effect of rendering unsafe a conclusion of the jury on the issue of consent. If it was not sexual behaviour, it was not within s 41 and was relevant and admissible. The Court of Appeal took the view that, in the circumstances, C's behaviour shortly before 'picking up' M probably was 'sexual behaviour' coming close to acting as a prostitute picking up clients for sex and was clearly relevant to the issue of whether C consented to intercourse with M.

151 See also *R v Garaxo* [2005] Crim LR 883; *R v W* [2005] Crim LR 965.

152 [2009] EWCA Crim 2668.

153 *R v E (Dennis Andrew)* [2004] EWCA Crim 1313. In that case, the Court of Appeal expressed the test as whether the complainant had (i) made a statement and if so, (ii) whether that statement was untrue.

154 *R v Murray* [2009] EWCA Crim 618, at [23] (Dyson LJ).

155 [2006] EWCA Crim 1901.

156 [2017] EWCA Crim 1211.

was false and reaffirmed the principle in *R v E* that a 'proper evidential basis' must be identified before the admission of such evidence can be entertained under section 100.

Finally, it is worth noting that 'sexual behaviour … need not involve any other person.'[157] Thus, in *R v Ben-Rejab*,[158] the Court of Appeal held that an indulgence by answering questions in a sexually explicit quiz amounted to sexual behaviour, stating that 'the expression is plainly wide enough, in our view, to embrace an activity of viewing pornography or engaging in sexually-charged messaging over a live internet connection.'[159]

6.2.4.3 The exceptions to the rule

Provided the conduct in question constitutes sexual behaviour, under section 41(2), the court may give leave in relation to any evidence or question only on an application made by or on behalf of an accused, and may not give such leave unless it is satisfied (a) that subsection (3) or (5) applies, and (b) that a refusal of leave might have the result of rendering unsafe a conclusion of the jury or (as the case may be) the court on any relevant issue in the case. Where leave is sought, an application must be made to the court to show that the anticipated line of questioning falls within one of the four exceptions contained within these particular subsections. These will come into play if, under subsection (3), the evidence is relevant to: (a) an issue in the case other than consent; (b) sexual behaviour 'at or about' the time of the incident in question; and (c) previous behaviour is 'so similar … so that similarity cannot be explained by coincidence' or under subsection (5) where the evidence is relevant to rebut the prosecution evidence. Each of these heads is now considered below.

6.2.4.4 Section 41(3)(a): an issue other than an issue of consent

Under section 41(3)(a) of the 1999 Act, the court may grant leave if the evidence or questioning relates to any issue that has to be proved other than an issue as to whether the complainant consented. Section 42(1)(b) defines 'issue of consent' as meaning any issue whether the complainant in fact consented to the conduct constituting the offence with which the accused is charged. Thus, the defendant's *belief* that the complainant was consenting falls within the scope of section 41(3)(a) as relevant to an issue other than consent.

In *R v Y*,[160] one of the first cases to be heard under section 41, the defendant alleged that the complainant had consented to intercourse or, if not, that he believed that she had consented. At a preparatory hearing, the judge refused leave for the defence to cross-examine the complainant about a recent sexual relationship with the accused. This ruling was challenged by the defendant, and the Court of Appeal took the view that such evidence was relevant to any *belief* in consent that the defendant may have had. It was thus admissible pursuant to section 41(3)(a), but could not be used to establish *actual* consent on the part of the complainant. In the view of the court, the previous sexual relationship between the complainant and the accused was clearly relevant to *belief* in consent as a matter of common sense, although this was restricted to sexual behaviour in the recent past prior to events giving rise to the charge. The court did not accept that such an approach stemmed from a sexist view of women; rather, it was said to reflect human nature:

> The trial process would be unduly distorted if the jury were precluded from knowing, if it were the case, that the complainant and the defendant had recently taken part in sexual

---

157 *R v Ben-Rejab* [2011] EWCA Crim 1136, at [35] (Pitchford LJ).

158 [2011] EWCA Crim 1136.

159 Ibid., at [35]. However, questions concerning an abortion are not considered to be questions 'about' sexual behaviour: *R v RP* [2013] EWCA Crim 2331 (McCombe LJ).

160 *The Times* (13 February 2001).

> activity with each other and it might be that a fair trial would not be possible if there could not be adduced in support of the defence of consent, evidence as to the complainant's previous consensual recent sexual activity with the defendant.[161]

This view of human nature, expressed by Rose LJ, was similar to that expressed by Lord Steyn on appeal to the House of Lords,[162] but such a perspective is not universally held. Critics might argue that the entire purpose of the restriction on the use of sexual history is to deny the relevance of the complainant's previous sexual history except in the circumstances indicated in section 41(3). As such, it may well be necessary for the jury to know of the previous relationship, but not for the purpose of inferring that, because the complainant consented to intercourse on previous occasions, she might well have consented on the specific occasion in question. For example, if a wife complains of rape within marriage, it would be nonsensical to hide from the jury the fact that the defendant and complainant are married and have engaged in sexual activity within that marriage.

As in R v Y, the fact that the accused had recently had a sexual relationship with the complainant may give rise to a belief that she will consent to sexual intercourse and may explain why he approached her in the first place, but the previous relationship will not by itself provide grounds for a belief that she was consenting to the intercourse that is the subject of the charge. It is therefore submitted that the sexual behaviour of the complainant with the defendant can be relevant to support a belief in consent if, and only if, it is sufficiently proximate to the act of intercourse.

Additional circumstances may make previous sexual activity between the defendant and the complainant relevant to, and provide reasonable grounds for, the belief that the woman was consenting.

Example 6.3

Suppose that Kenny and Maisy had consensual sexual intercourse in the past as part of a simulated rape fantasy. As part of this simulation, assume that Kenny pretended to force himself upon Maisy, who pretended to resist through vocal protests and physical resistance. If the alleged rape took place in similar circumstances, the accused might well have believed that she was consenting when in fact she was not. The basis for this belief would be the fact that Kenny had had consensual intercourse with Maisy in the past, and that she had displayed a similar reaction in such circumstances. As section 1(2) of the Sexual Offences Act 2003 makes clear, the jury must determine whether the belief was reasonable having regard to all of the circumstances, including any steps taken by the defendant to ascertain whether the complainant was consenting. The fact that Maisy was behaving exactly as she had behaved in the past when the intercourse was consensual is a circumstance providing a reasonable basis for Kenny's belief that she was consenting on this occasion. However, had the previous sexual relationship between Kenny and Maisy not involved simulated rape or any other extraordinary circumstances, that relationship would be unlikely to be relevant to the defence of belief in consent.

161 Ibid., at [31] (Rose LJ).

162 See below.

There are other scenarios that could arise in which the issue is not consent. In the recent case of *Gjoni*,[163] the accused was convicted of raping his friend's girlfriend. He argued that a third party present in the house at the time of the offence had told him that the complainant had intercourse with others on previous occasions with the approval of the boyfriend. The defence contended that evidence of this conversation had been improperly excluded by the trial judge under section 41; and that it should have been allowed under this particular gateway since his *belief* in consent came about as a result of what he had been told. Rejecting the appeal, it was held that in the instant case, it ought to have been clear to the appellant that the complainant was rejecting his advances. The fact that she may have consented to intercourse in the past with another man could not justify any belief that the defendant had that the complainant was consenting. Moreover, this particular type of evidence was expressly prohibited by section 41(4) since the primary purpose of such evidence would be to impugn the complainant's credibility, in that it would infer that a woman who consented to intercourse with one particular stranger would consent to intercourse with another in entirely different circumstances one week later.[164]

In *R v Elahee*,[165] a decision based on section 2 of the 1976 legislation, a 13-year-old girl alleged that she was walking past a takeaway restaurant when the accused, a 43-year-old man, led her into a lobby and raped her. The accused claimed that the complainant had introduced herself and, without invitation on his part, had touched his genital area. He said he had pushed her away and no sexual intercourse took place, the allegations being a complete fabrication. Medical evidence showed that the complainant displayed no injury and that her hymen was not intact. She had told the doctor that she had had full sexual intercourse some 12 months previously with her boyfriend, but that had been edited out of the doctor's statement and the jury were not made aware of what the complainant had said. Counsel for the accused sought leave under section 2 of the 1976 Act to elicit that evidence from the complainant, arguing that it was relevant to show that, contrary to her outward appearance, the complainant was a person capable of the conduct alleged by the accused. The trial judge refused leave and the accused was convicted.

Perhaps predictably, the appeal was allowed. It was held that the issue in this case was not one of consent, but concern about who had made the first approach. The evidence of the complainant's previous sexual experience was a matter that was relevant to an issue in the trial insofar as it enabled the jury to assess the plausibility of the defendant's account. Disallowing such cross-examination gave rise to the clear risk that the jury would have regarded the medical evidence as confirmation of the complainant's evidence, and thus posed a real danger that the jurors may have taken a different view of the evidence had the statement not been edited. The defendant's conviction was found to be unsafe, and a retrial was ordered.

This is a poignant example of how section 2 routinely failed to protect the complainant. The doctor's evidence showed that the complainant's hymen was already broken. The prosecution, after discussion with the judge, put that information on the record lest the jury assume that the accused was responsible. The defence were not satisfied with that and made an application under section 2 to allow the complainant to be questioned about the previous act of intercourse because, without that evidence, the jury might think it unlikely that a 13-year-old would approach and touch a 43-year-old man as alleged. It was also alleged that it would have been unfair, once the jury had been told that the complainant's hymen was already broken, for them not to be told the details. This, it was contended, may have led them to speculate about other ways in which it might have been broken.

---

163 [2014] EWCA Crim 691.

164 Contrast with *Barador* [2005] EWCA Crim 396.

165 [1999] Crim LR 399.

Such arguments, which were routinely put forward in rape cases, are largely spurious. In truth, the evidence of one act of intercourse with a boyfriend 12 months earlier is of no relevance to the issue of who made the initial advance. It may very well be the case that virgins in their early teens do not generally approach middle-aged men and initiate sexual contact, but then neither do the vast majority of women. Recent studies suggest that many teenagers have some sexual experience, and some have a great deal,[166] but sexual experience in itself does not suggest a tendency to approach middle-aged men in the manner suggested. As for the suggested speculation, given that the jury had been told that the hymen was already broken, it would have been clear to them that the accused was not responsible. If they did speculate as to the cause, it would not have been prejudicial or unfair to the accused. Arguably, it would have been better to tell the jury not to speculate, rather than to introduce C's previous sexual history. It is possibly true, as the Court of Appeal suggests, that 'if the jury knew about the complainant's sexual activity on a previous occasion they might take a different view of the case' – but why would they do so? Simply because she was not a virgin? If so, this is precisely the sort of prejudicial reasoning that section 2 of the 1976 Act sought to prevent. Had *Elahee* been heard under the new regime, it is doubtful whether the application of section 41 would have made any difference. Assuming that the court viewed the complainant's previous sexual behaviour as relevant to the issue of who made the first approach, then the refusal of leave to allow C to be questioned about the previous act of intercourse might have the result of rendering unsafe a conclusion of the jury on a relevant issue. It follows that the same result would have been reached under section 41 and the supposed reform will have made no difference.

6.2.4.5 Section 41(3)(b): sexual behaviour 'at or about' the same time

This provision severely restricts evidence or questions about any sexual behaviour of the complainant. The first draft of the Bill only permitted such evidence where the incident in question took place 24 hours either side of the alleged offence. In its enacted form, the legislation adopts the phrase 'at or about the same time,' which certainly provides a greater degree of flexibility. The provision permits evidence such as that in *Viola*, in which the complainant was seen to be drinking and flirting with men before the alleged rape, and afterwards a man, naked but for his socks, was seen sleeping on her couch. The obvious inference the court was invited to draw was that she was drunk and looking for sex, and therefore was likely to have consented to the intercourse that took place some little time later. However, in *R v Stephenson*,[167] the court held that evidence of the complainant kissing other men had no relevance under the 1999 legislation to the issue of consent to intercourse with the accused.

Nevertheless, concerns remain given the ambiguity that is apparent in the phrase 'at or about the same time.' In *R v A (No. 2)*, the House of Lords declined to assign a specific temporal limit to it, but their Lordships were unanimous in holding that a sexual relationship between the defendant and the complainant some three weeks before the alleged rape fell outside the scope of section 41(3)(b). While holding that the test was a flexible one to be determined in the light of the particular circumstances of a case, the sum of the guidance given was somewhat unclear. Lord Slynn thought that the words should be given a narrow meaning, which would restrict evidence and questions to sexual behaviour of the complainant that was 'really contemporaneous' with the event subject of the charge. By contrast, Lord Steyn thought that the complainant's invitation to the

166 See, generally, Brook, *Teenage Sexual Activity*. Available at http://www.brook.org.uk/old/index.php/information/facts-and-figures/sexual-activity (last accessed 1 April 2015); Wellings, K., Field, J., Johnson, A.M., Wadsworth, J., and Bradshaw, S., *Sexual Behaviour in Britain* (Penguin, 1994); Wellings, K., Nanchahal, K., Macdowall, W., McManus, S., Erens, B., and Mercer, C.H., 'Sexual Behaviour in Britain: Early Heterosexual Experience' (2001) 358 *The Lancet* 1843; McManus, S., Field, J., Korovessis, C., Johnson, A.M., Fenton, K., and Wellings, K., *National Survey of Sexual Attitudes and Lifestyles II: Technical Report* (National Centre for Social Research, 2001).

167 [2006] EWCA Crim 2325.

defendant to have sex with her made earlier in the evening would be within the subsection, but he thought the temporal restriction would not extend to days, weeks, or months. For his part, Lord Hope of Craighead referred to the Notes of Guidance, which expected that the phrase should not be interpreted more widely than 24 hours before or after the offence. In the view of Lord Hutton, it was clear that an act one week before the offence was outside the subsection, and Lord Clyde thought it would be difficult to extend the provision to include a period of several days. However, in the years since *A*, there has been a growing consensus that the best interpretation of the phrase refers to a 24-hour period either side of the offence.

6.2.4.6 Section 41(3)(c): previous behaviour that is 'so similar ... that the similarity cannot be explained by coincidence'

Until a very late stage in the passage of the Bill that is now the 1999 Act, section 41(3) contained only two exceptions to the blanket rule of exclusion – those outlined in paragraphs (a) and (b). It was feared, however, that to confine the relevant evidence to a 24-hour period either side of the alleged rape would be unfair to the accused. The potential for such an injustice to arise is demonstrated by the facts of *R v Cox*.[168] Here, the complainant alleged that the defendant had raped her while her boyfriend was in police custody. The defence was granted permission to cross-examine her about alleged intercourse she had had on a previous occasion with another man, while her boyfriend was away. On that occasion, C also complained that she had been raped. The defence contended that she did so, as in the instant case, in order to hide her infidelity. Had the 2003 Bill been enacted in its original form, the previous sexual behaviour in this case would fall well outside the period required under section 41(3)(b). In turn, the accused would have been effectively denied the right to adduce relevant evidence to the court.

To this end, it seems that policymakers took into account the concerns expressed by, among others, the late Judge Andrew Geddes. Geddes argued that there was little evidence that section 2 of the 1976 Act was not working and that the radical change effected by section 41 was unjustified.[169]

He described 'a not uncommon case' in which a former cohabitee of the accused alleges that he came to the house where the complainant lived (often the former matrimonial home) and raped her, whereas the accused claims that the intercourse was consensual. In these circumstances, the defence may often try to allege that, in spite of the fact that the relationship had broken down, the complainant had nonetheless frequently allowed the accused back in the house, and that sexual intercourse had taken place on virtually every occasion with her consent. If the jury is unaware that there has been a long history of the complainant consenting to sexual intercourse with the accused after they had separated, there must be a real danger that they would convict where otherwise they would acquit.

In response to these criticisms, section 41(3)(c) was added to the Bill, which applies when the issue is one of consent. The purpose of the subsection is to allow the defence to cross-examine the complainant about their previous sexual behaviour where such conduct is so similar to that in the instant case that the similarity cannot reasonably be explained as a coincidence. Such similarity may tend to lend credence to any suggestion that the defence may make that the complainant was disposed to having consensual sexual intercourse in a particular or distinctive way. For example, in *R v Tahed*,[170] the Court of Appeal quashed a conviction where the complainant had claimed she was raped on a climbing frame in a public park. It was held that the defence had been improperly

168 (1986) 84 Cr App R 132.

169 Geddes, A., 'The Exclusion of Evidence Relating to a Complainant's Sexual Behaviour in Sexual Offence Trials' (1999) 149 NLJ 1084.

170 [2004] 2 Cr App R 32.

denied the opportunity to cross-examine her about a similar sexual encounter that allegedly took place at the same climbing frame three weeks beforehand. In *R v Harris*,[171] it was noted that, while some cases, such as *Tahed*, are fairly clearly cut since 'the similarity was so clear that it was not disputed,'[172] other cases are not quite so straightforward. The behaviour in *Harris* itself involved the complainant's alleged habit of engaging in casual and risky sexual encounters. The court held that, although the act was similar, it was not 'sufficiently similar' that the complainant was more likely to have done it again. Similarly, in *R v M(M)*,[173] the appellant wished in addition to cross-examine the complainant about previous sexual encounters with the accused (namely, that she had performed oral sex on him in a cinema and that she had sent her younger brother out of the house in order that they could engage in sexual intercourse). While it was accepted that these instances had 'parallels' with the occasion of the alleged rapes, the defence 'came nowhere near establishing a degree of similarity.'[174]

The leading case on the scope of section 41(3)(c) is, however, *R v A (No. 2)*, which is how the case of *R v Y* was reported when the Director of Public Prosecutions was given leave to take the Court of Appeal's decision to the House of Lords. It will be recalled that the accused wanted to cross-examine the complainant on the sexual relationship that he claimed they had been having up until three weeks prior to the alleged rape. The respondent argued that, in restricting cross-examination on the prior consensual sexual relationship between the complainant and the defendant, section 41 of the 1999 Act effectively denied the defendant the means to present an effective defence. It was contended that the legislation thus contravened the defendant's right to a fair trial under Article 6 of the European Convention on Human Rights. The House of Lords dismissed the Crown's appeal and concurred with the view that the absence of evidential material relevant to the issue of consent could infringe the accused's Article 6 rights.

As Lord Steyn recognised, the crux of the conundrum facing the courts was the fact that section 41 imposed the same exclusionary provisions in respect of the complainant's sexual history with the accused as with other men:

> The statute did not achieve its object of preventing the illegitimate use of prior sexual experience in rape trials. In retrospect one can now see that the structure of this legislation was flawed. In respect of sexual experience between a complainant and other men, which can only in the rarest cases have any relevance, it created too broad an inclusionary discretion. Moreover, it left wholly unregulated questioning or evidence about previous sexual experience between the complainant and the defendant, even if remote in time and context. There was a serious mischief to be corrected.[175]

It might be contended that the logic underpinning Lord Steyn's analysis seems sound. It is arguably more likely that a woman will consent to intercourse with a person whom she knows well and with whom she has had a previous sexual relationship than to intercourse with a total stranger. Therefore, this type of previous sexual history between the complainant and the defendant will, on some occasions, be relevant to the issue of consent insofar as it might throw light on the complainant's state of mind. By the same token, however, their Lordships were keen to stress that such evidence would not constitute proof that the complainant consented on the occasion in question: relevance and sufficiency of proof were entirely different matters.

---

171 Ibid.
172 Ibid., at [19] (Thomas LJ).
173 [2011] EWCA Crim 1291.
174 Ibid., at [43] (Pitchford LJ).
175 Ibid., at 12.

However, the difficulty for the court was that a literal interpretation of the Act would lead to the exclusion of this relevant evidence: none of the relevant exceptions to the blanket rule of exclusion applied. Since this effectively amounted to a violation of the accused's fair trial rights under the European Convention, the House of Lords construed section 41(3)(c) of the Act somewhat creatively, through exercising its interpretive obligation under section 3 of the Human Rights Act 1998. This provision requires courts to interpret legislation in a way that is compatible with Convention rights, insofar as it is possible to do so. Thus, it was held that section 41(3)(c) should be read subject to the proviso that the previous sexual history evidence should nonetheless be admitted where it 'is nevertheless so relevant to the issue of consent that to exclude it would endanger the fairness of the trial under Article 6 of the Convention.'[176]

Thus, in future cases in which the defence seeks to admit sexual history evidence that falls outside the literal scope of the exceptions contained within section 41, the court must then apply a further test. Essentially, the trial judge must ask whether the evidence should nonetheless be admitted, where the evidence was so relevant to the issue of consent that to exclude it could violate the fairness of the trial. In this sense, the House of Lords has effectively made the legislation subject to the common law concept of relevance.

The House of Lords held that while the statute pursued desirable goals, the methods adopted amounted to legislative overkill. It was realistic to proceed on the basis that the legislature would not, if alerted to the problem, have wished to deny the right to an accused to put forward a full and complete defence by advancing truly probative material, and that was the basis on which section 3 of the Human Rights Act 1998 came into play. However, the effect of the decision in *A* was to restore to the trial judge some degree of control over the ambit of cross-examination in relation to previous sexual history evidence. The test of admissibility was whether the evidence and questioning in relation to it were nevertheless so relevant to the issue of consent that to exclude them would endanger the fairness of the trial under Article 6. If that test were satisfied, the evidence should not be excluded. Lord Slynn, Lord Hope, Lord Clyde, and Lord Hutton delivered speeches concurring in the result.

However, since their Lordships gave little guidance as to when such questions would be relevant and when they might not, problems could arise in future years because the question of relevance is placed back in the hands of trial judges. In effect, the House of Lords has removed a bar on the exercise of discretion imposed by Parliament. While the logic behind the decision in R v *A* seems sound enough on the basis of those particular facts, the door is now left slightly ajar for future interpretations of the legislation that may stretch well beyond what Parliament had originally intended. As Grohovsky remarked, section 41(3)(c) is 'both vague enough and broad enough to permit almost limitless irrelevant and prejudicial evidence.'[177] Although it seems very unlikely that R v *A* could ever be used as a basis on which to admit previous sexual history evidence in respect of third parties, it remains to be seen whether judicial attitudes have changed sufficiently to sustain this approach in the years to come.

6.2.4.7 Section 41(5): rebutting prosecution evidence

The other occasion on which the judge can give leave for sexual behaviour evidence to be admitted is when the defence wish to dispute evidence that the prosecution has introduced about the complainant's sexual behaviour. This is based on the principle that there should be equality of arms between the parties. Any evidence called in rebuttal must go no further than directly to contradict or explain claims made by or on behalf of the complainant. Thus, if the prosecution

---

176 Ibid., at 15 (Lord Steyn).

177 Grohovsky, J., 'Giving Voice to Victims: Why the Criminal Justice System in England and Wales Should Allow Victims to Speak Up for Themselves' (2000) *Journal of Criminal Law* 421.

evidence states or suggests that the complainant was a virgin before the alleged rape, evidence that she previously had had intercourse with another or others could be adduced.[178]

However, section 41(6) provides that any evidence or questioning about sexual behaviour must relate to a specific instance, or instances, of such behaviour. Intrusive interrogations concerning the complainant's general lifestyle will not be permitted.[179]

The provision was subject to challenge before the Court of Appeal in *R v Soroya*.[180] The appellant had been convicted of raping the 19-year-old complainant. She had claimed that she had tried to put him off having sex with her by telling him she was a virgin. At trial, the complainant admitted that she had intercourse on one previous occasion with a boyfriend. The defence wished to contest this fact by claiming she was much more sexually experienced, but the judge refused leave for them to adduce any previous sexual history evidence. Section 41(5) could not be relied upon in these particular circumstances since the defence was unable to adduce any relevant evidence to rebut the claims of the prosecution.

In summing up, the judge highlighted to the jury that the defence was not permitted to ask any questions about sexual history but indicated that the defence did not accept the complainant's account that she had only had intercourse on one previous occasion. Following his conviction, the appellant contended that section 41 had interfered with the principle of equality of arms and thereby had violated his Convention right to a fair trial. While the prosecution had been allowed to introduce evidence of previous sexual history, the defence had been refused leave. In effect, this meant that section 41 resulted in a fundamentally unbalanced process that operated adversely to the defendant.

Dismissing the appeal, the court held that the object of the legislation was to prevent anyone, prosecution or defence, from asking questions that might cause embarrassment or difficulty to a complainant. In the instant case, the prosecution had not relied, directly or indirectly, on the complainant's previous sexual history. The issue of C's sexual experience had only arisen in the first place as an integral part of the incident, and to avoid the rape, she had made what was admittedly an untruthful claim that she was a virgin. From the prosecution's point of view, it had been important evidence bearing on the issue of consent. No justified complaint could be directed at the admission of that evidence, and, as such, the conviction was safe.

Yet even if the defence had been allowed to introduce evidence under section 41(5), there would still be an arguable case that the additional hurdles placed in their path could interfere with the principle of equality of arms. As David Ormerod states in his note on the case:

> Even where the defence are able to rebut the evidence of the Crown, it might still be argued that s. 41(5) does not provide a complete solution because the defence are not as free to adduce rebuttal evidence as the Crown are to lead it. First, the prosecution are not subject to the notice requirements as are the defence. Secondly, the defence must satisfy the judge as to the requirements of s. 41(5) and 41(2). Thirdly, the defence must point to specific allegations within s. 41(6). The defence position under s. 41(5) is clearly restricted even though such rebuttal is not hedged in by s. 41(4) and the defence may be allowed to impugn the complainant's credibility ... Bearing in mind the restrictions on the defence, is the potential inequality compatible with the Strasbourg jurisprudence recognising that some measures are necessary in sexual cases to protect the private life of the complainant and that equality

178 See *R v L* [2015] EWCA Crim 741.

179 See *R v White* [2004] EWCA Crim 946, where the Court of Appeal held that questions about the complainant being a prostitute did not relate to the specific instance and therefore were inadmissible.

180 [2007] Crim LR 181.

> of arms demands only that a party is not placed at a substantial disadvantage vis-à-vis the opposing party?[181]

No doubt the courts will be confronted again with this issue in the not too distant future.

6.2.4.8 Section 41(4): the additional protection

Section 41(4) also provides a further safeguard for the complainant in providing that evidence will not be regarded as relating to a relevant issue in the case 'if it appears to the court to be reasonable to assume that the purpose ... for which it would be adduced or asked is to establish or elicit material for impugning the credibility of the complainant as a witness.' The judge must also be satisfied under section 41(2)(b) 'that a refusal of leave might have the result of rendering unsafe a conclusion of the jury ... on any relevant issue in the case.' Before leave is granted, the test in section 41(2)(b) must always be met. This is an overriding condition that must be satisfied in every case; however, this hurdle is not particularly high as the court need only be satisfied that a refusal might have the consequences specified, not that such a consequence is probable or even likely. This is an improvement on the test under the 1976 Act and the interpretation of that test in *R v Lawrence*,[182] in which May J stated that questioning about the complainant's relationships with other men should be allowed only when the jury might tend to take a different view had the evidence been adduced or the questions asked. The problem with this stipulation was that juries, on hearing about the complainant's sexual history, often would take a different view based on bias or prejudice resulting from the debasement of the complainant's character.

In respect to section 41, the question of whether the conclusion of a jury might be unsafe is inevitably based on guesswork, given that we cannot ask the jury why they came to a particular conclusion. However, the judgment as to whether a conclusion of the jury might be unsafe if the evidence is not adduced or the questions not asked will again be based on the relevance of the evidence or question to the relevant issue(s) in the case. The difficulty is that, once again, there is no requirement of a substantial degree of relevance to the issue. The phrase in section 41(2)(b), 'the refusal of leave *might* have the result,' suggests a low degree of relevance, allowing sexual history evidence more readily than if the section said 'refusal of leave *would* have the result' (emphasis added).

However, section 41(4) attempts to restore the distinction between credit and the issue, in providing that:

> no evidence or question shall be regarded as relating to a relevant issue in the case if it appears to the court to be reasonable to assume that the purpose (or main purpose) for which it would be adduced or asked is to establish or elicit material for impugning the credibility of the complainant as a witness.

Much will depend on whether the courts are prepared to accept this distinction. The fact that the evidence may be of marginal relevance, but nonetheless may be very damaging to the complainant, makes it reasonable to assume that the purpose (or main purpose) is to impugn credibility, rather than to assist in proving or disproving the relevant issue. On the other hand, if the evidence is highly relevant and highly prejudicial, it cannot be reasonable to assume that the purpose (or main purpose) of adducing the evidence is to impugn credibility, although that is an inevitable consequence of allowing the evidence to be adduced.

---

181 Ormerod, D., 'Case Comment: Sexual History Evidence' [2007] Crim LR 181.

182 [1977] Crim LR 492.

In *R v Martin (Durwayne)*,[183] the Court of Appeal emphasised the distinction between the *main* purpose of adducing the evidence and *one* of the purposes. The defendant alleged that the complainant had pestered him for sex and that it was his rejection of her advances that led to her making a false allegation against him. The trial judge refused to permit cross-examination of the complainant as to the alleged sexual acts on the basis that the main purpose of the cross-examination was to impugn the credibility of the complainant. The Court of Appeal took the view that the judge's ruling was wrong. Although one purpose of the proposed questions was to impugn the credibility of C, this was not the main purpose. The primary reason why the defence had sought to adduce the evidence was to strengthen their case, not to impugn the credibility of the complainant. Accordingly, the judge's ruling was wrong.[184] This briefly reported case suggests that section 41(4) may not provide the intended safeguard against attempts by defence counsel to blacken the complainant's character.[185]

6.2.4.9 Section 41: procedure and practice

It is worth noting briefly the procedure that is used where a party wishes to apply to the court to admit evidence under section 41 (Figure 6.2). Section 43(1) provides that any application will be heard in the absence of the jury, any witnesses (other than the defendant), the public, and the press. Rules of court will require the applicant to specify, in relation to each item of evidence or question to which they relate, particulars of the grounds on which it is asserted that leave should be granted.[186] The court will be able to require from the parties to the proceedings any information it considers will assist in making the decision whether or not to grant leave.[187] Reasons for giving or refusing leave must be stated in open court (but in the absence of the jury),[188] and if leave is granted, the court must indicate the extent to which evidence may be adduced or questions asked in pursuance of the leave.[189] This will give the trial judge more time to consider the application (under the previous law, such applications were made orally during the course of trial) and will require a reasoned argument, in writing, from the defence, to which counsel for the prosecution can respond. It may also put an end to the improper practice of asking questions about the complainant's sexual behaviour that should not be asked, unless and until leave has been given. As noted above, research conducted in relation to the old law suggested that questions about the complainant's previous sexual history were asked without application to the trial judge either because the judge and counsel were unaware of the requirement for leave, or perhaps deliberately to avoid the restriction on such questions. The fact that there are new legislative safeguards and procedures in place should ensure that counsel in rape trials are aware of the restrictions on questions about the complainant's sexual behaviour, and of the need to support any application for leave with reasoned argument.

6.2.4.10 Section 41: is it working?

Despite the safeguards contained in section 41, empirical research suggests that the legislation is not operating as effectively as might be expected. In 2005, Kelly et al. reported that applications to admit sexual history evidence were made in a third of all rape trials, and two-thirds of these were

183 [2004] 2 Cr App R 22.

184 However, the Court of Appeal declined to overturn the conviction on the grounds that the defendant did not give evidence and the judge would have directed the jury that the question, if allowed, did not result in any evidence on which the jury could act.

185 Although see *R v Gjoni* [2014] EWCA Crim 691 on the use of s 41(4).

186 The complete rules are set out and can be found in Pt 22 of the Criminal Procedure Rules 2015, Rules 22.1–22.7.

187 YJCEA 1999, s 43(3)(b).

188 Ibid., s 43(2)(a).

189 Ibid., s 43(2)(b).

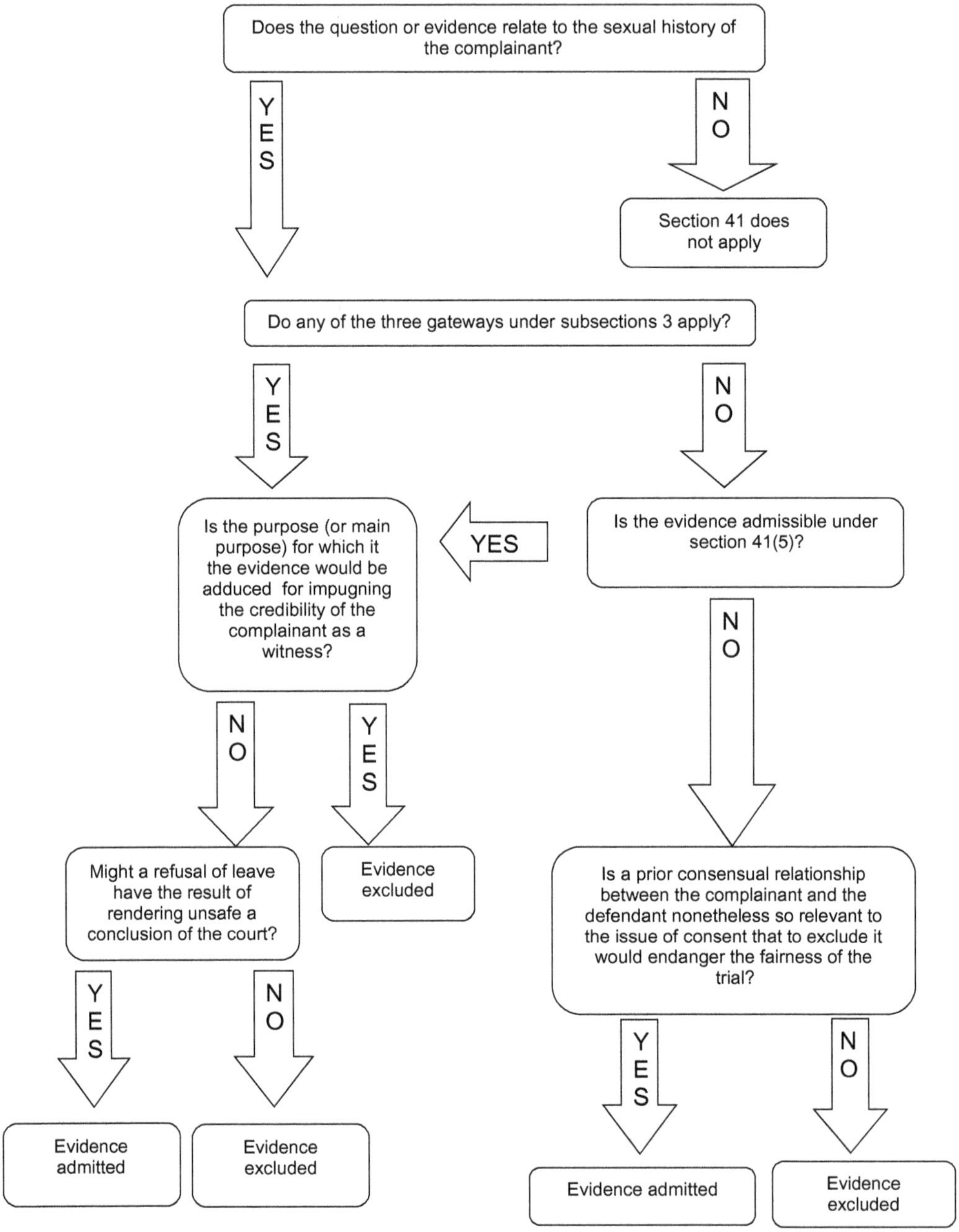

Figure 6.2 The process for determining whether evidence is admissible under section 41

successful.[190] Moreover, interviews with 17 judges revealed that many had very little knowledge of the legislation prohibiting or allowing the use of sexual history evidence. This explains another disconcerting finding: namely, that counsel frequently conducted cross-examinations about the

190 Kelly, L., Lovett, J., and Regan, L., *A Gap or Chasm? Attrition in Reported Rape Cases*, Home Office Research Study No. 293 (HMSO, 2005).

complainant's sexual history without seeking permission from the judge at all. In three-quarters of these cases, the judge failed to intervene to prevent such questioning.

It thus seems that some elements of the judiciary are reluctant to enforce the new rules as Parliament intended. Neil Kibble has observed how judges he interviewed 'were highly sceptical of the argument that sexual history evidence was overwhelmingly prejudicial and should therefore generally be excluded.'[191] The legislation was described by judges as 'an impenetrable maze,' 'a dog's breakfast,' and a 'nightmare.'[192] As a result, irrelevant evidence relating to previous sexual behaviour still emerges in many rape trials. This suggests that even if Parliament had succeeded in formulating a perfectly balanced rule on paper that did not give rise to the need to read down the legislation, the ultimate success of such a provision could be severely hampered by attitudinal resistance on the part of the judiciary. Similar findings have emerged from a recent study of the Scottish rape shield provision.[193] Unless judicial attitudes undergo a fundamental shift in outlook, legislative efforts to protect complainants will surely continue to be undermined.

6.2.4.11 Questioning defendants about their sexual history

A final point worth discussing at this stage is whether it is possible for the prosecution to question the defendant about his own sexual behaviour or adduce evidence of such behaviour in a similar respect to the rules laid out above. As a starting point, section 41 applies solely to 'evidence of' or 'questions asked' about 'any sexual behaviour of the complainant.' No provision, therefore, is made for the prosecution to exercise a similar power against an accused. According to Alison Saunders, the Director of Public Prosecutions, change may be on the horizon. In an interview with the *Evening Standard*,[194] Ms Saunders commented that new guidance will be issued so that in future trials, prosecutors will 'focus on the behaviour of men leading up to alleged rapes, rather than just the incident itself.'[195] Ms Saunders further comments that:

> Prosecutors will be asked to focus on a male suspect's previous conduct in other relationships in order to find any relevant evidence. This may include situations where an alleged rapist exercised controlling or coercive behaviour towards other women, including previous girlfriends.

She envisages that future prosecutions may be heavily based on the use of CCTV images of the defendant examining his conduct and manner, extracts from the defendant's social media accounts, and testimonies from witnesses regarding the defendant's demeanour and behaviour. She is also reported as having said that:

---

191 Kibble, N., *Judicial Perspectives on Section 41 of the Youth Justice and Criminal Evidence Act 1999* (Criminal Bar Association, 2004).

192 Ibid. See further Kibble, N., 'Uncovering Judicial Perspectives on Questions of Relevance and Admissibility in Sexual Offence Cases' (2008) 35(1) *Journal of Law and Society* 91.

193 Burman, M., 'Evidencing Sexual Assault: Women in the Witness Box' (2009) 56(4) *Probation Journal* 1.

194 'Rapists who ply victims with drink or drugs targeted in new clampdown,' *Evening Standard* (9 August 2017) https://www.standard.co.uk/news/crime/rapists-who-ply-victims-with-drink-or-drugs-targeted-in-new-clampdown-a3606336.html (last accessed 9 August 2017).

195 See also 'Rape juries to hear more about men's sexual history to increase chance of conviction,' *Telegraph* (9 August 2017) http://www.telegraph.co.uk/news/2017/08/08/rape-juries-hear-mens-sexual-history-increase-chance-conviction/ (last accessed 9 August 2017); 'Men accused of rape will have their relationship history delved into at trial under new guidance issued by Britain's top prosecutor,' *Daily Mail* (9 August 2017) http://www.dailymail.co.uk/news/article-4774240/Alison-Saunders-says-alleged-rapists-spast-trial.html (last accessed 9 August 2017); 'Prosecutors could examine suspected rapists' past treatment of women to increase conviction rate,' *Independent* (9 August 2017) http://www.independent.co.uk/news/uk/crime/prosecutors-rape-trials-jury-past-behaviour-alcohol-drugs-conviction-rates-alison-saunders-cps-dpp-a7884176.html (last accessed 9 August 2017).

> Some of it will be if you have already been in a relationship, understanding the dynamics of coercive and controlling behaviour and presenting cases in a way that doesn't just look at the individual incident.

A number of observations emerge from this interview. First, no official guidelines have yet been drawn up or issued to prosecutors. The statements from the Director of Public Prosecutions (DPP) form merely part of the review that is being undertaken in relation to the guidance on rape. There is no guarantee that this will be a feature of the criminal justice system.[196] Second, the law presently protects a defendant from being asked questions about, or have evidence adduced, of his bad character.[197] Evidence relating to a defendant's 'controlling or coercive behaviour' is likely, although open for debate, to fall within the definition of bad character under section 98 of the Criminal Justice Act 2003.[198] In this respect, in order for a prosecutor to adduce the evidence that Ms Saunders speaks of, it is likely that an application under section 101 will be required.[199] That application will have to be approved by the trial judge meaning that the admission of such evidence will not be a decision for prosecutors, as Ms Saunders suggests, but rather will be a decision for the trial judge. Third, it is questionable whether evidence of the defendant's 'controlling or coercive' behaviour will be relevant to the criminal trial. Indeed, a prosecutor may attempt to argue that a defendant who is controlling or coercive in his behaviour is also likely to be the sort who could commit a sexual offence. However, it remains the case that unless there is evidence demonstrating from that behaviour that the defendant is more likely to have committed the offence (i.e. the evidence is logically probative to whether he committed the offence), then it is unlikely to be admitted.[200]

In any respect, the complainant's sexual history remains a matter covered by section 41 with no application for defendants. Should a prosecutor wish to adduce evidence of a defendant's sexual conduct or behaviour, this may amount to an attack on his character and be restricted by the provisions in section 101.

6.3 Re-examination

A witness who has been cross-examined may be re-examined by the party who called him. The object of re-examination is, in general terms, to repair any damage that has been done by counsel through cross-examination. The cardinal rule is that questions must be confined to such matters that arise out of the cross-examination.[201] As in examination-in-chief, no leading questions may be asked in re-examination.

---

196 For the most recent guidance on rape from the CPS, https://www.cps.gov.uk/legal-guidance/rape-and-sexual-offences-overview-and-index-2021-updated-guidance (last accessed 5 March 2024). There is a major consultation ongoing in this area, see: Law Commission, *Evidence in Sexual Offence Prosecutions* (Law Com No 259 2023).

197 Criminal Justice Act 2003, s 101. See Ch 11.

198 The definition of bad character is 'evidence of, or a disposition towards misconduct.' 'Misconduct' is defined as 'the commission of an offence or other reprehensible behaviour.' See s 112(1) CJA 2003.

199 See a series of Tweets by 'The Secret Barrister' which criticise the remarks made on the basis that the defendant's character would be called into question by the admission of such evidence.

200 Interestingly, however, a new offence of 'controlling or coercive behaviour in an intimate or family relationship' has been introduced into the Sexual Offences Act 2003, s 15A by the Serious Crime Act 2015, s 78. The introduction of this offence may be a sign that trial judges will be willing to find that evidence of coercive or controlling behaviour, even without conviction, falls within the definition of bad character.

201 *Prince v Samo* (1838) 7 A & E 627.

6.4 Key learning points

- Before giving evidence, all witnesses may refresh their memories from statements or other documents made reasonably close to the events about which they are to give evidence.
- Section 139 of the Criminal Justice Act 2003 creates a presumption that witnesses in criminal proceedings may refresh their memory from a document while giving evidence, subject to certain conditions.
- Witnesses might not seek to bolster their evidence by reference to a previous consistent statement, except in one of the circumstances provided for in section 120 of the 2003 Act.
- Counsel can only ask leading questions in cross-examination or where the court determines that the witness is hostile.
- The finality rule dictates that a witness's answer to a collateral question is final, unless one of the exceptions of the rule applies.
- Evidence of a complainant's previous sexual history is not generally admissible unless one of the four exceptions in section 41 of the Youth Justice and Criminal Evidence Act 1999 applies or the judge feels that it ought to be admitted to ensure a fair trial.

6.5 Practice questions

1 Dan is charged with robbery. It is alleged that he snatched a handbag belonging to Martha, after knocking her to the ground. You are asked to address a number of questions in respect of the following witnesses, who will testify at trial.

(a) Martha, aged 62, is the alleged victim. She identified Dan as the assailant, and told police that he lives in her tenement block. Police are aware that there has been an ongoing feud between Martha's family and Dan's family for some years. In particular, Martha has made some 20 complaints to the police and the local council about noise emanating from the flat occupied by Dan, and has told the police that it was 'time he was locked up once and for all.'

Can the defence cross-examine Martha about this animosity and bring evidence in rebuttal if she denies it?

(b) William lives in the same estate as the victim and the defendant. He will say that he saw the defendant, whom he knows by sight, knock Martha to the ground, snatch the handbag, and run off. The defence has evidence that William has recently been diagnosed as a diabetic, but is refusing to stick to the diet given to him. He insists on eating foods with a high sugar content, which, while not putting him into a hyperglycaemic coma, can affect his eyesight and balance.

Can the defence cross-examine William about his condition and bring medical evidence as to the effect of his condition on him and his ability to identify the accused?

(c) Dan confessed to DC Lyons in the course of a police interview. However, the defence allege that he did so only because DC Lyons threatened to charge his brother with possession of heroin if he did not do so. DC Lyons was recently demoted after the acquittal on appeal of a man convicted of robbery, when it became apparent that the confession had been fabricated.

On the assumption that the confession is admitted, can the defence cross-examine DC Lyons about this acquittal and the subsequent disciplinary proceedings and demotion?

(d) Benjamin, a traffic warden, was on duty on the day of the robbery. He made a statement to the police later that day in which he said that he had chased the assailant, who fitted the description of the defendant. Benjamin says the assailant managed to outrun him, but claims he saw the man enter Flat 222 on the second floor, which is occupied by the defendant's family. The trial took place nearly 10 months after the offence and the prosecution permitted Benjamin to read his statement before going into the witness box. Despite having done so, once Benjamin starts to give evidence he states that he is unable to recall the details of his statement. The prosecution now apply for leave to allow Benjamin to refresh his memory from the statement made to the police. The defence object.

Assuming you are the trial judge, would you permit the witness to refresh his memory?

2 Elliott was engaged to be married to Christine for several months in 2001, during which time full intercourse regularly took place between them consensually. Christine broke off the relationship when she discovered that Elliott was sleeping with another woman. In June 2006, they met again at a party given by a mutual friend. Christine told guests that she felt unwell, and said she was going upstairs to lie down. She then alleges that Elliott entered the bedroom and raped her, despite her struggling and asking him to stop. In defence, Elliott states that Christine had asked him to resume their relationship earlier in the evening and invited him to the bedroom, where intercourse then took place with her consent.

(a) Elliott pleads not guilty to rape. Can defence counsel adduce evidence of his previous relationship with Christine?

(b) Would your answer be any different if the following information were to come to light? It transpires that, during their relationship, the intercourse that took place did so in the circumstances of simulated rape – that is, Christine pretended to resist Elliott by screaming, protesting, and struggling, and Elliott pretended to overcome her resistance using force.

3 'Section 41 has clearly failed in obtaining its legislative goal; the time has come to overhaul the provision in order to ensure that previous sexual history can never be adduced against a complainant in a rape trial.' Do you agree with this statement?

6.6 Suggested further reading

Birch, D., 'Untangling Sexual History Evidence: A Rejoinder to Professor Temkin' (2003) Crim LR 370.

Conaghan, J. and Russell, Y., 'Sexual History Evidence and The Rape Trial' (1st Edn.) Briston University Press.

Durston, G., 'Previous (In)consistent Statements after the Criminal Justice Act 2003' (2005) Crim LR 206.

Henderson, E., 'Best Evidence or Best Interests? What Does the Case Law Say About the Function of Criminal Cross-Examination?' (2016) 20(3) E & P 183.

Kelly, L., Temkin, J. and Griffiths, S., *Section 41: An Evaluation of New Legislation Limiting Sexual History in Rape Trials*, Home Office Online Report No. 20/06 (HMSO, 2006).

Kibble, N., 'Uncovering Judicial Perspectives on Questions of Relevance and Admissibility in Sexual Offence Cases' (2008) 35(1) Journal of Law and Society 91.

Temkin, J., 'Sexual History Evidence: Beware the Backlash' (2003) Crim LR 217.

Tidball, M., *Disabling Criminal Justice: The Governance of Autistic Adult Defendants in the English Criminal Justice System*, (1st Edn), Hart Publishing.

Chapter 7

The Privilege against Self-Incrimination and the Right to Silence

Chapter contents

DOI: 10.4324/9781003416098-7

As a general rule, all witnesses are required to answer questions asked of them in court. A witness who refuses to do so may be found to be in contempt of court. However, there are a number of exceptions to this position, and, in certain circumstances, some witnesses may avoid this obligation through the doctrine of 'privilege.'

Privilege arises in a number of contexts. The focus of the first part of this chapter is the privilege against self-incrimination, which relates to the extent to which suspects and accused persons can be made to produce evidence against themselves and the effects of remaining silent in response to questioning. However, at the outset it is worth noting that privilege may also arise in a number of other forms, which are beyond the scope of this book. For example, lawyers may refuse to answer questions about advice given to clients on the grounds of legal professional privilege,[1] and may also refuse to disclose communications between their clients and any other party that have been prepared for the purposes of litigation. The rationale for this rule is to facilitate honest and frank communication between lawyer and client. Doctors, counsellors, ministers of religion, and other professionals who hold a confidential or fiduciary relationship with their clients do not enjoy a similar privilege. Technically, such persons have no legal right to refuse to answer questions, although in practice most advocates would be reluctant to put such a person in the position of having to breach the moral duty of confidentiality unless absolutely necessary. Journalists cannot normally be required to disclose their source of information, although there is a procedure under section 10 of the Contempt of Court Act 1981 by which they can be required to do so. In that vein, commentators have drawn attention to how the integrity of the criminal process is partly a function of the personal integrity of its key personnel.[2] As discussed above, this primarily includes the lawyer and client. However, defence lawyers also have crucial roles to play, as demonstrated by their roles in the Cardiff Three and Heron case. Within criminal theory, Dixon[3] and Redmayne[4] have previously observed that too little attention is paid to the role and responsibility of the defence lawyer.

While not strictly a form of privilege, public interest immunity (formerly known as Crown privilege) may also allow public servants and representatives of quasi-government bodies to refuse to answer certain questions or disclose material on the grounds that it might harm the national interest. In *Conway v Rimmer*,[5] a police officer sought disclosure of probationary reports written about his work by superior officers to support a claim for malicious prosecution. The Home Secretary claimed that the disclosure of such material would be injurious to the public interest. However, the House of Lords held that it was for the court to decide where the balance of public interest lay: in protecting a government claim for secrecy or in upholding a litigant's right to have all relevant materials available for the proper adjudication of his claim. This was ultimately an assessment that could only be carried out by the court, rather than by a Minister of the Crown.

---

1 The scope of legal professional privilege at common law is contained in s 10 of the Police and Criminal Evidence Act 1984. See also *R v Central Criminal Court, ex p Francis and Francis* [1989] AC 346.

2 Section 58(1) of the Police and Criminal Evidence Act (PACE) provides that 'A person arrested and held in custody in a police station ... shall be entitled, if he so requests, to consult a solicitor privately at any time.'

3 Dixon, D., 'Integrity, Interrogation and Criminal Injustice,' in J. Hunter, P. Roberts, S.N.M. Young, and D. Dixon (eds), *Integrity of Criminal Process: From Theory into Practice* (Hart Publishing, 2016).

4 Redmayne, M., 'Rethinking the Privilege Against Self-incrimination' (2007) 27 *Oxford Journal of Legal Studies* 209, 221.

5 [1968] AC 910. See further Spencer, M. and Spencer, J., 'Coping with *Conway v Rimmer* [1968] AC 910: How Civil Servants Control Access to Justice' (2010) 37(3) *Journal of Law & Society* 387.

However, the focus of the first part of this chapter is the privilege against self-incrimination. In very broad terms, the principle prohibits any form of compulsion on suspects to provide evidence against themselves, and, therefore, no suspect is under any obligation to help the police with their inquiries.[6] As Ho points out, freedom of choice is exhibited in the freedom to either plead guilty or not, within the context of the right to silence in the privilege against self-incrimination and other non-participatory rights.[7]

The principle also envelops a suspect's right not to have adverse inferences drawn from their failure to answer questions, or, once accused, their failure to testify at trial (the so-called right to silence), which will be dealt with in the second half of this chapter. These two aspects of the privilege against self-incrimination are clearly interlinked, since without the latter protection there is an element of indirect compulsion to answer questions or give evidence.[8] The protections afforded by a right to silence have been severely curtailed by sections 34–37 of the Criminal Justice and Public Order Act 1994, so that now 'proper inferences' may be drawn from an accused's failure to answer questions.[9] We will return to consider these provisions later in the chapter. There is little consensus on what the right to silence specifically entails or what the legal significance of the privilege should be. As case law indicates, it has changed over time and has a variety of applications.[10]

7.1 The 'even terms' rule

As a starting point, it may be useful to consider the relatively straightforward position of the common law, which continues to govern those situations in which the parties are on 'even terms' with each other – that is, in which neither person is in a position of authority. The even terms rule basically states that an accusation by X that is unanswered by Y can be said to provide evidence that Y accepted the truth of the allegation.[11] The rule is grounded on the basis that it is a natural and intuitive response to deny a false allegation made by another layperson who does not occupy any position of authority.[12] Thus, at trial, an accused's conduct or demeanour in response to such allegations may be used as evidence of guilt by the prosecution. The rule was summarised by Cave J in *R v Mitchell*,[13] in the following terms:

> Undoubtedly, when persons are speaking on even terms and a charge is made, and the person charged says nothing, and expresses no indignation, and does nothing to repel the charge, that is some evidence to show that he admits the charge to be true.

---

6 *Rice v Connolly* [1966] 2 QB 414.

7 Ho, H.L., 'Liberalism and Criminal Trial' (2010) *Singaporean Journal of Legal Studies* 87, 99.

8 For an examination of evidence obtained under compulsion, see: *Saunders v UK* (1996) 23 EHRR 313; *O'Halloran and Francis v UK* (2008) 26 EHRR 21, in which two motorists invoked the privilege against self-incrimination when contesting convictions for driving in excess of the speed limit; Binding, M., 'Self-Incrimination Goes to Strasbourg: *O' Halloran and Francis v United Kingdom*' (2008) 12 *International Journal of Evidence and Proof* 58; Spencer, J.R., 'Curbing Speed and Limiting the Right to Silence' (2007) *Cambridge Law Journal* 531.

9 The 1994 Act applies to both Crown Court and magistrates' courts equally.

10 For example, see the six immunities identified by Lord Mustill in *R v Director of Serious Fraud Office, Ex Parte Smith*, [1993] AC 1 (HL) 30–31.

11 This principle is preserved under s 34(5) of the Criminal Justice and Public Order Act 1994.

12 See *R v Hall* [1971] 1 WLR 298; *R v Parkes* [1976] 1 WLR 1251.

13 (1892) 17 Cox CC 503, 508.

The principle was applied in *Parkes v The Queen*.[14] Parkes was charged with murder by the stabbing of a young woman. The victim's mother found her bleeding from her wounds and saw the defendant nearby holding a knife. She twice accused him of stabbing her daughter. He did not reply. She then took hold of him saying she was going to hold him until the police arrived. He made to strike her with the knife, cutting her finger. The Privy Council upheld the judge's direction to the jury that they could take the defendant's reaction and his silence into account when determining whether he was or was not guilty of murder.

A more up-to-date, and widely reported, example is to be found in the evidence given by a witness in the trial of Barry George for the murder of television presenter Jill Dando.[15] Lenita Bailey was a customer at a hairdresser near the accused's flat. She knew him and recalled a conversation with him. George came into the salon and claimed police were harassing him over the death of Jill Dando. He complained that they had searched his home and his mother's house. Ms Bailey said to him: 'Did you do it?' George remained silent and stared at the floor. She repeated the question twice more and asked him to look at her. At trial, she said: 'His lips moved as if he was thinking of an answer but none was forthcoming.' Her evidence of the discussion, or lack of it, was admitted, and George was convicted.[16] The defendant and the mother in *Parkes*, and the witness and defendant in the Dando trial, were clearly on equal terms and it was reasonable to expect a denial of the accusation if that was the position. By contrast, a suspect arrested by the police will not usually be seen as being on equal terms with the police, although in *R v Chandler*[17] it was held that a suspect interviewed by police in the presence of his solicitor was on even terms, and therefore a failure to respond to an accusation before caution could be taken into account by the jury. That decision has now been overtaken by events, and in particular the requirement under the Police and Criminal Evidence Act 1984 (PACE) that a suspect be cautioned before the actual arrest when they are suspected of involvement in a crime.[18] Whatever the position might be at common law in relation to the above, it does not apply in situations in which a defendant refuses to leave their prison cell to be interviewed by police and thus remains silent.[19] This is a very different situation from one in which, for example, the defendant fails to offer an explanation for the fact that he was in possession of stolen goods.[20] If the accused's silence is deemed admissible, it may then be inferred from that silence that they have accepted the truth of what is being said.[21]

7.2 The nature and extent of the privilege in court

When the accused came to give evidence, the privilege against self-incrimination at common law prohibited both the prosecution counsel and the judge from making any comment where

14 (1977) 64 Cr App R 25.

15 *The Times* (5 May 2001).

16 On 15 November 2007, the Court of Appeal quashed the conviction and ordered a retrial following fresh evidence that had come to light. See *The Times* (16 November 2007).

17 [1976] 1 WLR 585. However, as a general rule, the accused will never be on even terms with a police officer. The Court in *Chandler* suggested *obiter* that a suspect may be on even terms with the police if a solicitor was present. This has never been followed.

18 Code C [10.1].

19 *R v Gilbert* (1977) 66 Cr App R 237; *R v Johnson* and *R v Hind*, *The Times* (3 May 2005).

20 *R v Raviraj* (1986) 85 Cr App R 93.

21 See *R v Christie* [1914] AC 545.

the accused chose to refuse to give evidence,[22] to remain silent,[23] to fail to answer any specific questions,[24] or not to reveal the nature of their defence in advance of trial.[25] The privilege applied – and in its contemporary form still applies – only to the person making the assertion. Therefore, A cannot rely on privilege on the grounds it would incriminate B. However, the defendants cannot claim privilege when called on their own behalf insofar as the answer relates to the offence then charged against them. Answers given without objection are admissible against the witness on a subsequent charge as to the offence admitted.[26] However, anything a witness is wrongly compelled to say after claiming privilege will be treated as having been said involuntarily and will not be admissible against them subsequently,[27] but the evidence remains admissible in the trial in which it was given.[28]

7.2.1 Statutory exceptions to the privilege

The privilege may be removed by statute, either expressly or by necessary implication. According to the Court of Appeal in *R (Malik) v Manchester Crown Court*,[29] clear language is required to show that Parliament intended to abrogate the privilege. Where clear language does not exist, the courts must be careful to establish the necessary implication. Examples include:

(i) Section 1(2) of the Criminal Evidence Act 1898: a defendant called on their own behalf cannot claim privilege so far as the answer relates to the offence then charged against them.

(ii) Section 172(2)(a) of the Road Traffic Act 1988: the keeper of a motor vehicle must provide the identity of the driver where the driver was involved in a road traffic offence. Failure to do so can amount to an offence, and upon conviction is punishable by way of fine or penalty points.

(iii) Section 98 of the Criminal Justice Act 2003: material which *has* to do with the alleged facts of the matter being tried is not covered by privilege and may be adduced, subject only to the pervasive requirement of relevance, and the accused must deal with questions on it, if they have chosen to give evidence, or else run the risk of being held in contempt.

(iv) Section 1 of the Witnesses Act 1806: the privilege is not available in respect of a risk of liability for debt in civil proceedings.

In the controversial case of *Beghal v DPP*,[30] the Supreme Court arguably took the abrogation of an individual's privilege to a new level. The appellant, Beghal, was stopped at a port for the purpose of questioning by the police in relation to a suspected involvement in the commission, preparation, or instigation of acts of terrorism. Beghal refused to answer the questions asked and was charged with wilfully failing to comply with the requirement to answer questions under Sch 7, para 18 of the Terrorism Act 2000. The appellant pled guilty to the offence. However, she then brought proceedings against the police in the Divisional Court, arguing that Sch 7 had breached her rights under:

22 Section 1(b) of the Criminal Evidence Act 1898 originally forbade comment by the prosecution on the failure of the defendant to give evidence. This provision was later abolished by s 168 of and Sch 11 to the Criminal Justice and Public Order Act 1994.

23 *R v Lecky* [1944] KB 80.

24 *R v Gilbert* (1977) 66 Cr App R 237.

25 *R v Lewis* (1973) 57 Cr App R 860.

26 *R v Sloggett* (1865) Dears 656.

27 *R v Garbett* (1847) 1 Den 236.

28 *R v Kinglake* (1870) 11 Cox 499.

29 [2008] All ER 403.

30 [2016] AC 88.

- Article 5 (right to liberty),
- Article 6 (right to a fair trial), and
- Article 8 (right to privacy).

The Divisional Court dismissed her appeal. In the Supreme Court, a majority of 4:1[31] found against the appellant on the basis that Sch 7, para 2 of the 2000 Act abrogated the privilege against self-incrimination on the basis that Sch 7 would be 'rendered very largely nugatory if privilege applied.'[32] The majority went on to find that the risk of prosecution based on answers to Sch 7 is not a 'real and appreciable one' given that, in practice, section 78 of PACE 1984 would have the effect of rendering such evidence inadmissible.[33] The majority concluded that the appellant had no right to Article 6 in this instance given that it applies only to a 'person charged,' for which Mrs Beghal was not at the point of questioning.[34] Lord Kerr, dissenting, found that the requirement to answer questions under Sch 7, whether abrogated or not, breaches an individual's common law privilege against self-incrimination. In his Lordship's view, the provision was incompatible with Article 6 on the basis that the privilege is designed to protect an individual from the risk of prosecution, not from conviction. Lord Kerr went on to say that:

> It seems to me inescapable that there is a real and appreciable risk of prosecution if the answers to the questions posed prove to be self-incriminating.[35] ... The plain fact is, however, that self-incriminating answers given in response to questions posed under Schedule 7 can form the basis of a prosecution.[36]

Lord Kerr took a different stance from Lord Hughes on the latter's suggestion that section 78 could be invoked to prevent any potential injustice in the face of the prosecution. His Lordship identified two caveats with that approach:

> In the first place, answers to questions posed under Schedule 7 can prompt inquiry which might lead to the obtaining of evidence independent of the material which the responses have supplied. Secondly, it is by no means clear that evidence of those answers will automatically be excluded if there is other evidence which directly implicates the person responding.

Mrs Beghal has indicated her intention to appeal to the European Court of Human Rights (ECtHR), for which, no doubt, Lord Kerr's dissenting judgment will form part of her legal argument.[37]

7.2.2 Summing up to the jury

In *R v Martinez-Tobon*,[38] the Court of Appeal held that judges should abide by the following principles in summing up to the jury.

31 Lord Hughes, Lord Hodge, Lord Neuberger, and Lord Dyson in the majority and Lord Kerr dissenting.

32 It should be noted that there are a number of other authorities proceeding through the courts on the point of Sch 7, particularly: *Malik v UK* (Application no. 32968/11), which was adjourned by the ECtHR earlier this year pending the decision in *Beghal* and *Miranda v Home Secretary* [2014] EWHC 255 (Admin), which will be heard in the Court of Appeal in December 2017.

33 Ibid., at [65]–[66].

34 Ibid., at [69].

35 Ibid., at [115].

36 Ibid., at [116].

37 See n. 27.

38 [1994] 1 WLR 388. See also *R v Jackson* [1953] 1 WLR 591; *R v Sparrow* (1973) 57 Cr App R 352; *R v Hook* [1994] TLR 375.

- The judge should give a direction along the lines of the Judicial Studies Board specimen direction based on *R v Bathurst*:[39]

> The defendant does not have to give evidence. He is entitled to sit in the dock and require the prosecution to prove its case. You must not assume that he is guilty because he has not given evidence. The fact that he has not given evidence proves nothing one way or the other. It does not establish his guilt. On the other hand, it means that there is no evidence from the defendant to undermine, contradict or explain the evidence put before you by the prosecution.

- The essentials of that direction are that the defendant is under no obligation to testify, and the jury should not assume that they are guilty because they have not given evidence.
- Provided that those essentials are complied with, the judge may think it appropriate to make a stronger comment where the defence case involves alleged facts that are at variance with the prosecution evidence, or additional to it and exculpatory, and must, if true, be within the knowledge of the defendant.
- The nature and strength of such comment must be a matter for the discretion of the judge and will depend on the circumstances of the individual case. However, it must not be such as to contradict or nullify the essentials of the conventional direction.

These stipulations have, however, been qualified by changes introduced by the Criminal Justice and Public Order Act 1994 and the Criminal Procedure and Investigations Act 1996. The principal aim behind these two pieces of legislation was to prevent the use of 'ambush' defences at trial, whereby the defendant would remain silent until trial, in the hope that the prosecution would not have time to rebut the defence. Part I of the Criminal Procedure and Investigations Act 1996[40] provides for primary disclosure of prosecution material to the defence that is to be followed by disclosure by the defence of a statement containing the outline of their defence. Section 5 of the Act provides that where the case is to be tried in the Crown Court, the defendant must supply a defence statement to the prosecutor and the court. This is known in the legislation as 'compulsory disclosure.' This is in contrast to proceedings to be tried in the magistrates' court, where section 6(2) of the Act provides that the accused (a) may give a defence statement to the prosecutor, and if he does so, must also give such a statement to the court. This is known as 'voluntary disclosure.'

Section 6A(1)(a) states that such a statement should outline the general nature of the defence, and must include reference to any specific defences to be relied upon. In addition, the statement should give details of any matters about which the defence take issue with the prosecution, and the reasons for doing so (including any relevant points of law).[41] Moreover, where the accused proposes to rely on an alibi defence, the statement should give the name, address, and date of birth of any witness whom the accused believes is able to give evidence in support of the alibi, or as many of those details as possible.[42] Once the defence have complied with these obligations,

39 [1968] 2 QB 99.

40 As amended by Pt 5 of the Criminal Justice Act 2003.

41 Criminal Procedure and Investigations Act 1996, s 6A(1).

42 Ibid., s 6A(2). There appears to be cultural resistance to the Criminal Procedure and Investigations Act scheme with the disclosure protocol calling for 'a complete change in the culture' from defence lawyers: Disclosure: A Protocol for the Control and Management of Unused Material in the Crown Court, 20 February 2006, para 37. Research by Plotnikoff and Woolfson, carried out in 2001, found that 54 per cent of defence statements do not meet the requirements of section 5: Plotnikoff, J. and Woolfson, R., *A Fair Balance? Evaluation of the Operation of Disclosure Law*, RDS Occasional Paper No 76 (London: Home Office, 2001), p. 72.

the prosecution will undertake secondary disclosure of any further material that is relevant in the light of the defence disclosed or issues raised. Section 11 of the Act provides that, where the defence are required to disclose their defence, and the accused

- fails to give the prosecutor a defence statement under section 5,
- gives the prosecutor a defence statement, but does so only after the expiry of the specified period,
- sets out inconsistent defences in the defence statement given under section 5,
- puts forward a defence that is different from that disclosed in the defence statement,
- at his trial adduces evidence in support of an alibi without having given particulars of the alibi in the defence statement, or
- at his trial calls a witness to give evidence in support of an alibi without having provided the prosecution with the name of that witness and any information necessary to trace him,

then the court or any other party (with the leave of the court) may make such comment as appears appropriate, and the court or jury may draw such inferences as appear proper in deciding whether the accused is guilty of the offence concerned.[43]

7.3 The right to silence

In addition to the provisions of the 1996 Act concerning disclosure, the Criminal Justice and Public Order Act 1994 effected radical changes in respect of the suspect's rights to silence.[44] Despite widespread questions about the wisdom of abrogating such a long-standing component of the common law, the Government was persuaded that some amendment to the law was necessary in order to restore the balance following the raft of safeguards for the accused contained in the Police and Criminal Evidence Act 1984.[45] In amending the law to allow inferences to be drawn from the accused's silence, the Government had not only ignored advice of the Bar Council, Criminal Bar Association, and Law Society, but had also rejected the majority recommendation of the Royal Commission on Criminal Justice that the status quo be retained.[46] The decision can, perhaps, be attributed to the political agenda of the day, and the prevailing crime control ethos that prevailed in criminal justice policymaking under the then Home Secretary, Michael Howard.[47] The Government was also keen to draw parallels with the fact that an identical provision had been introduced in Northern Ireland some six years earlier and appeared to have been operating successfully.[48]

---

43 It was held in *Essa* [2009] EWCA Crim 43 that the obligations on the defence did not contravene fair trial rights provided for under Article 6 of the European Convention.

44 For a detailed review of the right to silence, see: Quirk, H., *The Rise and Fall of the Right of Silence* (Routledge, 2016).

45 For further discussion, see Birch, D., 'Suffering in Silence: A Cost–Benefit Analysis of s 34 of the Criminal Justice and Public Order Act 1994' [1999] Crim LR 769.

46 Royal Commission on Criminal Justice, *Report*, Cmnd 2263 (HMSO, 1993) [4.13]. The Commission noted that not only are the circumstances of police interrogation disorientating and intimidating in themselves, but also there can be no justification for requiring a suspect to answer questions when they may be unclear both about the nature of the offence that they are alleged to have committed and about the legal definitions of intent, dishonesty, and so forth on which the indictment may turn. See also Royal Commission on Criminal Procedure, *Report*, Cmnd 8092 (HMSO, 1981); Zander, M., 'Abolition of the Right to Silence, 1972–1994,' in D. Morgan and G. Stephenson (eds), *Suspicion and Silence: The Right to Silence in Criminal Investigations* (Blackstone, 1994).

47 Criminal Law Revision Committee, *The Right of Silence*, Eleventh Report (HMSO, 1972). See also Home Office, *Report of the Working Group on the Right to Silence* (HMSO, 1989).

48 See Criminal Evidence (Northern Ireland) Order 1988 (SI 1988/1987), Arts 3–6. See further Jackson, J.D., 'Recent Developments in Criminal Evidence' (1989) 40 NILQ 105; 'Curtailing the Right of Silence: Lessons from Northern Ireland' [1991] Crim LR 404; Justice, *The Right of Silence Debate: The Northern Ireland Experience* (Justice, 1994). Later research would, however,

Table 7.1 Circumstances in which inferences may be drawn from the silence of the accused

Section	Situation
Section 34	where D fails to mention any facts when being questioned under caution before charge that he later relies upon in his defence at trial
Section 35	where D fails to give evidence at his trial
Section 36	where D fails to account for the presence of any object, substance, or mark on his person, clothing, or footwear, or otherwise in his possession or at any place in which he is at the time of arrest
Section 37	where D fails to account for his presence at a place at or about the time of the commission of an offence

The trier of fact may now draw 'such inferences as appear proper' in four situations pursuant to the Criminal Justice and Public Order Act 1994 (see Table 7.1).

7.3.1 Section 34: a failure to mention facts when questioned

Section 34 affects the defendant's right to silence prior to trial and has been the source of considerable debate both in the appellate courts as well as in academic journals.[49] The provision stipulates:

1. Where, in any proceedings against a person for an offence, evidence is given that the accused –
   (a) at any time before he was charged with the offence, on being questioned under caution by a constable trying to discover whether or by whom the offence has been committed, failed to mention any fact relied on in his defence in those proceedings; or
   (b) on being charged with the offence or officially informed that he might be prosecuted for it, failed to mention any such fact, being a fact which in the circumstances existing at the time the accused could reasonably have been expected to mention when so questioned, charged or informed, as the case may be, subsection (2) below applies.[50]
2. Where this subsection applies –
   (d) the court or jury, in determining whether the accused is guilty of the offence charged, may draw such inferences from the failure as appear proper.

2A. Where the accused was at an authorised place of detention at the time of the failure, subsections (1) and (2) above do not apply if he had not been allowed an opportunity to consult a solicitor prior to being questioned, charged or informed as mentioned in subsection (1) above.

3. Subject to any directions by the court, evidence tending to establish the failure may be given before or after evidence tending to establish the fact which the accused is alleged to have failed to mention.

suggest that the legislation had little impact upon conviction rates in the province: see Jackson, J., Quinn, K., and Wolfe, M., *Legislating Against Silence: The Northern Ireland Experience* (Belfast: Northern Ireland Office, 1995).

49 See *R v Bresa* [2005] EWCA 1414, at [51] (Waller LJ) and his comment that '[s]ection 34 is a very difficult area.'

50 In *R v Dervish and Anori* [2001] EWCA Crim 2789, the trial judge had ruled that the defendants' no comment interviews were inadmissible, but had directed that the jury may draw an adverse inference from silence at charge in accordance with s 34(1)(b). At the Court of Appeal, the defendants had argued that this approach was wrong as the two limbs of s 34 were inextricably linked. The Court of Appeal rejected this argument and approved the judge's approach. The CPS has provided guidance on this point: (1) if faced with a situation of silence on charge and interview, counsel should remind the court of the potential drawing of adverse inference under both subsections, and; (2) if there is any doubt as to the admissibility of the interviews, counsel should be prepared to invite the court to draw an adverse inference under s 34(1)(b) if applicable. See http://www.cps.gov.uk/legal/a_to_c/adverse_inferences/ (last accessed 7 December 2014).

The provision thus places an onus on the suspect to provide explanations in response to police questioning. It should be noted, however, that the nature of this obligation is not absolute. A failure to respond to police questioning cannot of itself prove the defendant's guilt.[51] The section merely allows the trier of fact to consider what, if any, inferences should be drawn; no inferences should be drawn if the fact in question has been shown to be true.[52] In that respect, there is no automatic sanction if the accused opts to remain silent.

In the years after the provision took effect, the appellate courts were quick to formulate a range of additional protections for the suspect. In *R v Argent*,[53] the accused was convicted of manslaughter, and appealed, contending that the trial judge had been wrong to direct the jury that they were free to draw 'such inferences as appear proper' from his failure to answer questions in a police interview. Dismissing the appeal, the Court of Appeal highlighted that the fact that the section could only apply in very specific circumstances was ultimately dependent on a range of safeguards:

- proceedings must be under way against a person for an offence;
- the failure to mention facts must occur before the defendant is charged or on being charged;
- the failure must occur during questioning under caution;
- the questioning must be directed to trying to discover whether or by whom the alleged offence has been committed;
- the defence must actively seek to rely on the omitted facts in the proceedings; and
- the fact that the accused fails to mention must be one that, in the circumstances existing at the time, they could reasonably be expected to mention when questioned.

A number of these issues merit further consideration.

7.3.1.1 The need for a caution

For an inference to be drawn, section 34(1)(a) expressly states that it only applies in the case of an accused 'on being questioned under caution.'[54] The questioning can be conducted by constables or persons who are either charged with the duty to investigate offences or charge offenders. This, for example, might include store detectives (depending on their contract of employment), customs officers, and RSPCA officials. The standard police caution, which had to be amended in response to the legislation, is as follows:

> You do not have to say anything. But it may harm your defence if you do not mention when questioned something which you later rely on in court. Anything you do say may be given in evidence.[55]

---

51 A conviction should not be 'wholly or mainly' based on the inference from the defendant's silence: Criminal Justice and Public Order Act 1994, s 38(3). See further *R v Dolbur* [2000] Crim LR 178; *Bristow and Jones* [2002] EWCA Crim 1571. *Bristow and Jones* illustrates the implications of a defective direction by the judge to the jury on how to approach the drawing of inferences under s 34. This is a painstaking task and is fraught with difficulty and has fallen prey to a large number of appeals: see comments of Buxton LJ in *R v Compton* [2002] EWCA 2835 [37].

52 *R v Webber* [2004] 1 All ER 770.

53 [1997] 2 Cr App R 27.

54 As to what constitutes 'questioning,' see *R v Johnson* [2005] EWCA Crim 971. Here, the Court of Appeal concluded that no question was in fact put to the accused and therefore his failure to respond did not come within the ambit of the phrase 'on being questioned.'

55 PACE, Code C [10.5].

Although we may be accustomed to hearing these words in the context of television dramas, it is a matter of some concern that there is evidence to suggest that not all suspects will understand their full implications. A study by Buckle et al. suggested that both police officers and legal advisers doubted the extent to which suspects understood the caution, even if it were explained in lay terms.[56] The researchers also suggested that the new caution is harder to understand than the old one, which simply said: 'You do not have to say anything unless you wish to do so, but what you say may be given in evidence.'[57]

Minor deviations from the precise wording will not amount to a breach of the PACE Code of Practice C, 'provided the sense of the relevant caution is preserved.'[58] However, where it appears that a suspect does not understand the caution, the officer should then explain it using their own words.[59] Interestingly, where a 'significant silence' has occurred before the start of the interview at the police station, then at the start of the interview, after cautioning the suspect, the interviewer shall put the earlier 'significant silence' to the suspect and ask them whether they confirm or deny it and if they want to add anything.[60] This illustrates that even where the interview has yet to begin, inferences may be drawn from the suspect's silence, providing that they confirm that they understood the caution when asked.

7.3.1.2 Failure to mention facts

In order to prevent adverse inferences being drawn, a suspect's solicitor will sometimes prepare a written statement, which is simply read out to the police or handed to an officer irrespective of whether or not the suspect answers police questions. There is a risk, of course, with such a strategy, in that the defence must take care to ensure that the statement sets out in full the facts of the defence case. If a material fact is omitted and subsequently relied on in court, inferences may be drawn by the trier of fact.[61] This will occur regardless of whether the suspect has refused to answer police questions.[62] Thus, in *R v Knight*,[63] K, who had been arrested on suspicion of indecent assault, presented a written statement to the police, and subsequently declined (on the advice of his solicitor) to answer any questions about his version of events. The trial judge directed the jury that they were still at liberty to draw inferences from K's failure to respond to questioning. However, allowing the appeal, the Court of Appeal noted that since K's statement had contained all of the facts that K later relied on in court, no adverse inferences could be drawn. The objective of section 34(1)(a) was to prevent a suspect from relying on facts in court that should properly have been disclosed to the police during questioning. There was no requirement that suspects submit to police cross-examination, and indeed such a requirement could constitute an even greater intrusion into a suspect's general right of silence than a requirement on the suspect to disclose their factual defence. Had Parliament intended that section 34 should include such a requirement,

---

56 Bucke, T., Street, R., and Brown, D., *The Right of Silence: The Impact of the Criminal Justice and Public Order Act 1994*, Home Office Research Study No. 199 (HMSO, 2000).

57 See also Clare, I.C.H., Gudjonsson, G.H., and Harari, P.M., 'Understanding the Current Police Caution (England and Wales)' (1998) 8 *Journal of Community & Applied Social Psychology* 323; Fenner, S., Gudjonsson, G.H., and Clare, I.C.H., 'Understanding the Current Police Caution (England and Wales) Among Suspects in Police Detention' (2002) 12 *Journal of Community and Applied Social Psychology* 83. None of the 54 suspects and job seekers (of similar intelligence) participating in Fenner's study could explain the caution correctly when it was read to them in its entirety (at p. 89).

58 PACE Code C [10.7].

59 Ibid. [10D].

60 Ibid. [11.4].

61 See *R v Turner* [2004] 1 Cr App R 24 [25]. Here, the Court of Appeal observed the 'dangerous course for an innocent person who subsequently discovers at trial that something significant was omitted' from the pre-prepared statement.

62 See also Choo, A., 'Prepared Statements, Legal Advice and the Right to Silence: *R v Knight*' (2004) 8 *International Journal of Evidence and Proof* 62.

63 [2004] 1 WLR 340.

the legislation would have expressly stated so. Despite the resolution of the case in favour of the appellant, the Court of Appeal was still keen to sound a note of caution in respect of pre-prepared statements:

> The making of a pre-prepared statement is not in itself an inevitable antidote to later adverse inferences. The pre-prepared statement may be incomplete in comparison with the defendant's later account at trial, or it may be, to whatever degree, inconsistent with that account ... We wish to make it crystal clear that of itself the making of a pre-prepared statement gives no automatic immunity against adverse inferences under section 34.[64]

It is thus clear that, in advising this course of action, the legal representative must be very cautious about taking this approach, as the practical line of attack taken by the Court of Appeal in *Knight* could backfire on the defendant if not used correctly.

7.3.1.3 The objective of the questioning

The questioning must be directed to trying to discover whether and/or by whom the alleged offence had been committed.[65] If the questioning officer already has sufficient evidence to charge the suspect, any subsequent questions will not be directed to discovering whether, or by whom, the offence has been committed, and the section will not apply in such circumstances.[66] However, inferences may still be drawn if, in such circumstances, the officer maintains an open mind and is allowing the suspect an opportunity to relate their version of events.[67] Code C of PACE has been amended to this effect.[68]

7.3.1.4 Reliance in court

Inferences can only be drawn by the factfinder if the defence later relies on a fact at trial. For example, an accused may submit an alibi defence, or suggest that they acted in self-defence, having failed to mention any such fact in response to direct questioning by the police. However, a fact must be distinguished from a theory, or speculation, as to what might have happened, as illustrated by the case of *Nickolson*.[69] Here, the defendant was asked in cross-examination if he could explain the existence of semen on the complainant's nightdress. He speculated that perhaps the complainant had picked up the semen from his bathroom. The court held that the accused was not relying on this as a fact, but merely offering a possible explanation, and the failure to mention this explanation at earlier interview was not caught by section 34. Similarly, a failure to mention a trivial fact or small detail will fall outside the scope of the provision.[70]

The fact also need not be established by the defendant's testimony for it to be relied upon in defence. It can be established by other defence evidence, or in cross-examination of a prosecution witness.[71] In *Webber*, the House of Lords went further, holding that a positive suggestion put to a

---

64 Ibid., at [13]. See also *R v Mohammad* [2009] EWCA Crim 1871.

65 Criminal Justice and Public Order Act 1994, s 34(1).

66 See *R v Pointer* [1997] Crim LR 676; *R v Gayle* [1999] Crim LR 502.

67 See *R v McGuinness* [1999] Crim LR 318; *R v Loannou* [1999] Crim LR 586; *R v Odeyemi* [1999] Crim LR 828.

68 See Code C [11.6]. See further Cape, E., 'Detention Without Charge: What Does "Sufficient Evidence to Charge" Mean?' [1999] Crim LR 874; 'The Revised PACE Codes of Practice: A Further Step Towards Inquisitorialism' [2003] Crim LR 355.

69 *R v Nickolson* [1999] Crim LR 61; cf. *Esimu* [2007] EWCA Crim 1380. In *Nickolson*, the Court of Appeal allowed the appeal, as when the defendant was interviewed by police, neither the police nor the defendant were aware of the semen stain, and he could not reasonably be expected to give an explanation for it.

70 *R v Brizzalari* [2004] EWCA Crim 310. Ultimately, this will be a question for the trial judge to determine.

71 See *R v Bowers* [1998] Crim LR 817.

witness by counsel could amount to a fact relied on in the accused's defence for the purpose of section 34, even if the suggestion was not adopted by the witness:

> 'Fact' should be given a broad and not a narrow or pedantic meaning. The word covers any alleged fact which is in issue and is put forward as part of the defence case: if the defendant advances at trial any pure fact or exculpatory explanation or account which, if it were true, he could reasonably have been expected to advance earlier, section 34 is potentially applicable. When directing the jury in this case the trial judge made repeated reference to 'fact or matter', which is consistent with the reference to 'something' in the caution and in our view expresses the meaning of the subsection. There would be a similar reliance, the House held, where counsel adopts on behalf of his client in closing submissions evidence by a co-defendant.[72]

However, the defendant will be deemed to have relied upon a fact if they do no more than admit a fact asserted by the prosecution (i.e. a bare admission), although it seems that denial of the prosecution's alleged fact may be construed as automatic reliance upon any contradictory fact.[73]

Thus, admissions and denials appear to be treated differently by the courts. Furthermore, where the defendant does not testify and does not advance other evidence (i.e. merely tests the prosecution case), then section 34 cannot apply since no evidence will be relied upon in their defence. Quite simply, in that case, the defendant's silence cannot be commented upon.[74]

7.3.1.5 Reasonably be expected to mention ... in the circumstances existing at the time

Section 34 was not intended to capture all failures by the accused to mention relevant facts, only those that they could have been reasonably expected to mention in the circumstances existing at the time. On many occasions, the defence will wish to explain the defendant's silence to the jury and explain why they did not respond to the relevant question(s). Indeed, in *Turner*, the Court of Appeal stated that it was incumbent upon the prosecution to question defendants as to why they chose to remain silent, and give them an opportunity to provide an explanation.

In *Argent*, the Court of Appeal made it clear that the question as to what could be considered reasonable at the time was solely a matter for the jury, and each case was to be decided on its own individual facts. Ultimately, what might be considered reasonable for X in a particular circumstance might not be considered reasonable for Y in a similar situation. The question of reasonableness is thus subjective, and to this end:

> matters such as time of day, the defendant's age, experience, mental capacity, state of health, sobriety, tiredness, knowledge, personality and legal advice are all part of the relevant circumstances; but these are only examples of what may be relevant.[75]

---

72 At [37]. *Webber* was followed in *Esimu*, in which inferences were properly drawn from a failure to explain to police as to how his fingerprints came to be found on false number plates attached to a stolen car, but an explanation was advanced at his trial that he might have removed them while working in a valet business. In addition, s 34 does not require the jury to make a decision about the truthfulness of the fact relied on before considering whether the defendant could reasonably have been expected to mention it. See *R v Gowland-Wynn* [2001] EWCA Crim 2715, at [26] (Lord Woolf CJ), and Lord Bingham's criticism of *R v Mountford* in *Webber*.

73 *R v Betts and Hall* [2001] 2 Cr App R 257.

74 *R v Moshaid* [1998] Crim LR 420.

75 [1997] 2 Cr APP R 2, at [33].

In addition, if the trial judge concludes that the requirements of section 34 are not fulfilled and they cannot leave it to the jury to draw inferences, then the judge must positively direct the jury that they must not hold the accused's failure to answer questions against them.[76]

7.3.2 Section 34 and legal advice

One of the most contentious aspects of the 1994 legislation was the fact that inferences could be drawn from the suspect's silence even where they had not received legal advice. In *Murray v United Kingdom*,[77] the applicant alleged that the failure to allow him access to a lawyer, coupled with the drawing of inferences from his silence, constituted a violation of Article 6 of the European Convention on Human Rights.[78] Significantly, the Court found the UK Government to be in breach of Article 6 in denying the accused access to a solicitor,[79] but found no violation in permitting inferences to be drawn from the failure of the accused to explain his presence at the scene of the crime, or his failure to give evidence at his trial. While the Court recognised that the right to remain silent under police questioning and the privilege against self-incrimination lie at the heart of the notion of a fair trial, the right to silence was not absolute. Provided that certain safeguards were in place, inferences could be drawn where a defendant had failed to provide an explanation in circumstances in which the facts called for such an explanation. However, the Court did find a breach of Article 6(1) in relation to the separate issue of the 48-hour delay in accessing legal advice,[80] and held that adverse inferences should never be drawn where a suspect did not have access to legal advice. In response to the decision, the Government introduced section 58 of the Youth Justice and Criminal Evidence Act 1999, which provides that no inferences can now be drawn if the accused was in police detention and did not have prior access to a solicitor.[81]

A related problem occurs where the suspect is given access to a solicitor, who subsequently advises them to remain silent. In *R v Condron and Condron*,[82] both suspects were heroin users and their solicitor considered that they were unfit to be interviewed. However, the police doctor determined that they were fit to answer questions, and the suspects subsequently remained silent on the advice of their solicitor. At trial, the defendants rebutted the prosecution evidence with various explanations, all of which could have been given in response to police questions. The trial judge rejected a submission that, since their solicitor had given bona fide advice to the defendants to remain silent, no adverse inference could be drawn. The judge directed the jury that it was a matter for them to decide whether any adverse inferences could be drawn against the defendants. The jury convicted, and the Court of Appeal affirmed the convictions stating that the application of section 34 could not ultimately depend upon the nature of the legal advice given to a client. Delivering the judgment of the Court, Stuart-Smith LJ stated: 'It is not so much the advice given by the solicitor, as the reason why the defendant chose not to answer questions that is important. That is a question of fact which may be very much in issue.'[83]

---

76 This is called a '*McGarry* direction': *R v McGarry* [1999] 1 Cr App R 377.

77 (1996) 22 EHRR 29.

78 In Murray's case, inferences were drawn under the Police and Criminal Evidence (Northern Ireland) Order 1989, Arts 3–6 of which are broadly equivalent to ss 34–38 of the Criminal Justice and Public Order Act 1994.

79 The Strasbourg Court has also warned that, for Article 6 to be 'practical and effective,' Member States must allow a suspect access to a lawyer at the initial stage of police interrogation no matter how serious the charge: *Salduz v Turkey* [2008] ECHR 1542.

80 This was permissible under s 15 of the Northern Ireland (Emergency Provisions) Act 1987.

81 For a discussion of the relationship between s 34 CJPOA and s 78 PACE, see Ch 9.

82 [1997] 1 WLR 827.

83 At 833. A similar view was taken by Lord Bingham in *Argent* at [35]–[36]: 'The jury is not concerned with the correctness of the solicitor's advice, nor with whether it complies with the Law Society Guidelines, but with the reasonableness of the defendant's conduct in all the circumstances which the jury have found to exist. A highly relevant circumstance is the advice given to a defendant. The advice given to the defendant is a matter for the jury to consider.'

Following this decision, the appellants took their case to the ECtHR.[84] The Strasbourg Court held that the applicants had not received a fair trial under Article 6(1) since the trial judge had not taken into account the fact that the accused were advised by their lawyer to maintain their silence, and that there may have been good reason why such advice was given. Thus, the judge's direction to the jury had failed to reflect the balance that the Court, in its *Murray*[85] judgment, sought to strike between the right to silence and the circumstances in which an adverse inference may be drawn from silence. The Court in *Condron* reiterated the fact that, provided that appropriate safeguards were in place, an accused's silence could be taken into account in assessing the persuasiveness of the evidence adduced by the prosecution against him. However, as a matter of fairness, the jury should be directed that it should only draw an adverse inference if satisfied that the applicants' silence at the police interview could *only* sensibly be attributed to their having no answer or none that would stand up to cross-examination. If a suspect genuinely remains silent on the basis of legal advice, then inferences should not be attached to them having no answer or none that would stand up to cross-examination as the silence cannot be sensibly attributed to them having no answer. Their silence is attributed to legal advice from their legal adviser to remain silent and not to them having no answer. Ultimately, therefore, the jury should consider the context of any legal advice and take this into account in assessing the overall reasonableness of the suspect's decision to remain silent.

Example 7.1

Bjorn, a recently qualified solicitor, attends the police station in the middle of the night to advise Kamil, who has been arrested on suspicion of criminal damage. Bjorn is given less than 10 minutes to consult with his client before the police ask to interview Kamil and, as the case is considerably more complex than he was led to believe, Bjorn feels that he would like more details of the police case against his client before the interview proceeds. The police wish to interview Kamil immediately, so Bjorn recommends that he remain silent for the time being.

In such circumstances, it may well have been reasonable for Bjorn to have advised Kamil not to answer questions since Bjorn had been given few details of the nature of the case against the defendant and did not have the opportunity to discuss the case properly with him. If the solicitor is not in a position to advise their client usefully, the best course of action is, arguably, to advise silence until the full nature of the material in the hands of the police is made known.

Furthermore, if this material is so highly complex as to require specialist advice or forensic analysis, or relates to matters so long ago, then no immediate response may be feasible.[86] In *R v Betts and Hall*,[87] Kay LJ stated that the key issue was whether the decision to remain silent was motivated by advice that was important, as opposed to the actual content of that advice:

> It is not the quality of the decision but the genuineness of the decision that matters. If it is a plausible explanation that the reason for not mentioning facts is that the particular

---

84 *Condron v United Kingdom* (2001) 31 EHRR 1. See also *Averill v United Kingdom* (2001) 31 EHRR 839 and *Beckles v United Kingdom* (2003) 36 EHRR 162.

85 *Murray v United Kingdom* (1996) 22 EHRR 29.

86 See further comments of Rose LJ in *R v Roble* [1997] Crim LR 449.

87 [2001] 2 Cr App R 257.

> appellant acted on the advice of his solicitor and not because he had no, or no satisfactory, answer to give then no inference can be drawn.
>
> That conclusion does not give a licence to a guilty person to shield behind the advice of his solicitor. The adequacy of the explanation advanced may well be relevant as to whether or not the advice was truly the reason for not mentioning the facts. A person, who is anxious not to answer questions because he has no or no adequate explanation to offer, gains no protection from his lawyer's advice because that advice is no more than a convenient way of disguising his true motivation for not mentioning facts.[88]

At first sight, it appears that there was scope for the *Betts and Hall* dictum to be interpreted as meaning that once it has been shown that the advice has genuinely been relied on, adverse comment is thereby disallowed. However, this is not quite correct. Further clarification on this point was provided by the Court of Appeal in *R v Howell*:[89]

> The premise of such a position is that in such circumstances it is in principle not reasonable to expect the suspect to mention the facts in question. We do not believe that is so. What is reasonable depends on all the circumstances ... The kind of circumstance which may most likely justify silence will be such matters as the suspect's condition (ill-health, in particular mental disability; confusion; intoxication; shock, and so forth – of course we are not laying down an authoritative list), or his inability genuinely to recollect events without reference to documents which are not to hand, or communication with other persons who may be able to assist his recollection. There must always be soundly based objective reasons for silence, sufficiently cogent and telling to weigh in the balance against the clear public interest in an account being given by the suspect to the police. Solicitors bearing the important responsibility of giving advice to suspects at police stations must always have that in mind.[90]

In *R v Hoare and Pierce*,[91] the Court of Appeal held that there was no inconsistency between *Betts and Hall*, on the one hand, and the cases of *Howell* and *Knight*, on the other. The Court commented:

> The section 34 inference is concerned with flushing out innocence at an early stage or supporting other evidence of guilt at a later stage, not simply with whether a guilty defendant is entitled, or genuinely or reasonably believes that he is entitled, to rely on legal rights of which his solicitor has advised him. Legal entitlement is one thing. An accused's reason for exercising it is another. His belief in his entitlement may be genuine, but it does not follow that his reason for exercising it is.[92]

A further attempt to clarify the position was made in *R v Beckles*:[93]

> In our judgment, in a case where a solicitor's advice is relied upon by the defendant, the ultimate question for the jury remains under section 34 whether the facts relied on at the trial were facts which the defendant could reasonably have been expected to mention at interview. If they were not, that is the end of the matter. If the jury consider that the defendant

---

88 Ibid., at [53]–[54].

89 [2003] Crim LR 404. See further Choo, A. and Jennings, A., 'Silence on Legal Advice Revisited: *R v Howell*' (2003) 7 *International Journal of Evidence and Proof* 185; Cape, E., 'Police Station Advice: Defence Strategies After *Condron*' (1997) 17 *Legal Action* 19.

90 Ibid., at [23].

91 [2005] 1 WLR 1804.

92 Ibid., at [54].

93 [2005] 1 WLR 2829.

> genuinely relied on the advice, that is not necessarily the end of the matter. It may still not have been reasonable for him to rely on the advice, or the advice may not have been the true explanation for his silence.

In *Betts and Hall*, Lord Justice Kay was particularly concerned with 'whether or not the advice was truly the reason for not mentioning the facts.'[94] In the same paragraph, he also notes that:

> A person, who is anxious not to answer questions because he has no or no adequate explanation to offer, gains no protection from his lawyer's advice because that advice is no more than a convenient way of disguising his true motivation for not mentioning facts.

If, in the last situation, it is possible to say that the defendant genuinely acted upon the advice, the fact that they did so because it suited their purpose may then mean they were not acting reasonably in failing to mention the relevant facts. Ultimately, however, any question of reasonableness remains to be determined by the jury. If they conclude that the accused was acting unreasonably, they are free to draw an adverse inference from their silence.

One problem with the attempts to clarify this line of case law has been that the courts do not appear to recognise the inconsistency between asking the jury to decide as a question of fact why the defendant had remained silent, and then assessing the quality of that decision.[95] Logically, it would appear to follow that if a defendant kept silent on legal advice and not because they had no story to give or none that would stand up to scrutiny, then it does not matter whether the advice was well grounded or not. From a due process perspective, where defendants genuinely rely on the advice of their legal representatives, they should not be penalised for doing so. If this were not the case, what would be given by way of concession with one hand would effectively be taken away by the other. As Munday observes:

> The paradoxical implication of *Argent* is that the courts consider that, despite the pains Parliament took when enacting PACE to guarantee a suspect a right to legal advice before and during interrogation, it can still be inherently unreasonable for a suspect to take legal advice![96]

7.3.3 Directions to the jury: advice from the Judicial College

The Judicial College (formerly the Judicial Studies Board) in its *Crown Court Compendium*[97] breaks the issue of reasonableness down into distinct issues and, following *Petkar*,[98] states that directions to the jury should include the following key elements.[99]

- The facts that the accused failed to mention, but which are relied on in his defence, should be identified.
- The inferences (or 'conclusions,' as they are called in the specimen direction) that it is suggested might be drawn from failure to mention such facts should be identified, to the extent that they may go beyond the standard inference of late fabrication.

94 *R v Betts and Hall*, op. cit., n. 73 at [54].
95 Dennis, I., 'Silence in the Police Station: The Marginalisation of Section 34' [2002] Crim LR 25, 34.
96 Munday, R., *Evidence*, 7th edn (Oxford University Press, 2013), at 414.
97 Judicial College, *Part I: Jury and Trial Management and Summing Up* (Judicial College 2017).
98 *R v Petkar* [2004] 1 Cr App R 270, at [51] (Rix LJ).
99 At Ch 17–5. It can be added that this form of direction has been expressly approved by the European Court of Human Rights in *Beckles*.

- The jury should be told that if an inference is drawn, they should not convict 'wholly or mainly on the strength of it.'
- The jury should be told that an inference should be drawn 'only if you think it is a fair and proper conclusion.'
- An inference [of guilt] should be drawn 'only if ... the only sensible explanation for his failure' is that he had no answer or none that would stand up to scrutiny. *In other words, the inference canvassed should be drawn only if there is no other sensible explanation for the failure.*[100]
- An inference should be drawn only if, apart from the defendant's failure to mention facts later relied on in his defence, the prosecution case is 'so strong that it clearly calls for an answer by him.'[101]
- The jury should be reminded of the evidence on the basis of which the jury are invited not to draw any conclusion from the defendant's silence. (It is only after a jury has considered the defendant's explanation for his failure that they can conclude that there is no other sensible explanation for it.)
- A special direction should be given where the explanation for silence of which evidence has been given is that the defendant was advised by his solicitor to remain silent.

In *R v Sakyi*,[102] the Court of Appeal provided a statement as to the manner of the judicial direction to the jury as to the possible inferences that they may draw. In that case, the defendant was convicted (*inter alia*) of offences relating to possession of a prohibited firearm and ammunition that had been thrown from a car he was driving in the course of a police pursuit. Upon arrest and interview, the defendant declined to answer questions but handed a prepared written statement following legal advice. The statement contained nothing more than mere denials of the offences. At trial, the defendant's counsel asserted that a passenger in the car had thrown the gun and ammunition out of the window without his knowledge. The trial judge directed the jury according to section 34. The defendant appealed to the Court of Appeal on the basis that a section 34 direction was inappropriate and the trial judge had made inappropriate comments during his direction. The trial judge directed the jury as follows:

> The prosecution say, if this [explanation] is true, he would have wanted the police to know it because it is a 100 per cent defence to the allegations for which he had been arrested and for which he was now being interviewed. Why would he not say it, argue the prosecution?
>
> Examples have been given of similarities between going to see your doctor and your accountant and taking advice but, of course, it will not escape you that those situations are very different in important respects to a defendant sitting in an interview room at a police station ... each of these men knew that, as they were sitting there making no comment, that they were suspected of being in possession of a gun and live ammunition ... and they knew that they were the ones arrested and being charged by the police, actually charged with these offences and brought to the court. The solicitor is not at risk of being charged. He goes home. These two are the ones that run the risk of being charged. They know that and they know that they have the choice as to whether or not to accept the advice given. That, you

100 The italicised words, as noted by the *Bench Book*, exemplify the need to identify legitimate inferences before directing the jury on the statutory test. It is particularly important that the judge's directions are crafted within the context of the facts of the case and the evidence given. It will not assist the jury to repeat the words of the specimen without placing them in their specific factual context: at [265].

101 This has been clarified by the Court of Appeal. See *R v Gill* [2001] 1 Cr App R 11; *R v Chenia* [2002] EWCA 2345; *R v Paton* [2007] EWCA Crim 1572.

102 [2014] EWCA Crim 1784.

may think, is the stark difference between advice being given by a doctor to a patient and a solicitor to a defendant.

The Court of Appeal approved this direction and added:

> A judge is entitled to comment provided he gives the jury the standard directions on functions and does so fairly. He is not obliged sit quiet. ... A defendant cannot escape an adverse inference by stating simply 'I did what my solicitor told me.'

7.3.4 Police disclosure and section 34

There is no requirement for the police to disclose any information to the suspect or their legal adviser at the police station.[103] However, in practice, most officers are prepared to give solicitors some information about the offence. If this were not the case, police interviews would grind to a halt routinely so that the lawyer could take instructions from their client when further information is disclosed.[104] Also, it might be suggested that a small minority of officers may be tempted to lie about information that they have or have not disclosed. Defence solicitors are therefore taught to routinely assess the integrity of the police case, in case the police infer that the evidence is stronger than it later turns out to be.[105] If the police do relay false information to the legal adviser, then any evidence obtained is likely to be excluded.[106] Lack of disclosure, however, may become an issue at trial and provide circumstances from which a jury might conclude that a defendant's silence during questioning by the police was reasonable.[107] As Chen comments, the prosecuting authorities may simply decide not to prosecute an accomplice, if it is in the public interest to do so.[108] As a legal comparative, in Hong Kong, if an accomplice is called as a prosecution witness, immunity is necessary to overcome the privilege against self-incrimination. Without immunity, the accomplice witness would have the 'right' to remain silent in court and refuse to produce any documents that might incriminate them.[109] Therefore, in other common law countries, immunity provides the legal means of circumventing the privilege against self-incrimination, unlike in the English legal system.[110]

---

103 *Imran and Hussain* [1997] Crim LR 754. See also *R v Thirwell* [2002] EWCA Crim 2703, in which there was held to be no duty to disclose provisional medical evidence of how the victim had died. There was limited disclosure in *DPP v Ara* [2001] 4 All ER 559, but only to the extent of imposing a duty on the police to disclose the contents of a previous interview so that the lawyer could advise his client on whether to accept a caution. PACE does, however, exempt the custody record from this. Legal representatives have a right to see the custody record (Code C [2.4]), from which they should read and make careful notes. They are entitled to a copy. The exemption also applies to the initial description of a witness if identification is an issue (Code D [3.1a]).

104 The PEACE method of interviewing used by the police encourages information-giving, but not full disclosure. See further Clarke, C. and Milne, R., *National Evaluation of the PEACE Investigative Interviewing Course*, PRAS/149 (HMSO, 2001).

105 See, generally, Cape, E. and Luqmani, J., *Defending Suspects at Police Stations*, 5th edn (LAG, 2007).

106 *R v Mason* [1987] 3 All ER 481. See further Chapter 9.

107 *R v Roble* [1997] Crim LR 449.

108 Chen, A.H.Y., 'Focus on the Discretion Whether to Prosecute: Prosecutorial Discretion, Independence, and Accountability' (1998) 28 *Hong Kong Law Journal* 406.

109 For example, see Li CJ in *Fu Kin Chi v Secretary of Justice* (1998), HKCFAR 85, 96: 'At common law, a person has the privilege from being compelled to answer questions, the answers to which might tend to expose him to any punishment or penalty.'

110 *HKSAR v Leung Kai Chung* [2002] 1 HKLRD 771, [52], per Stock JA: 'The right against self-incrimination goes once an immunity is granted, because there is then no risk of exposure to criminality in the scene intended by the privilege.'

7.4 Section 35: the effect of not giving evidence

It will be recalled from the discussion above that while accused persons have been competent to testify in their own defence since the end of the nineteenth century, they cannot be compelled to give evidence. One of the reasons why the provisions of the 1994 Act proved so contentious was the fact that section 35 of the legislation effectively means that adverse consequences might well result from a defendant's failure to testify. Section 35(2) provides that the court or jury 'may draw such inferences as appear proper from the failure of the accused to give evidence or his refusal, without good cause, to answer any question.' Section 35(4) provides that the provision 'does not render the accused compellable to give evidence on his own behalf, and he shall accordingly not be guilty of contempt of court by reason of a failure to do so.' Moreover, such inferences may not be drawn where the refusal of the defendant is justifiable (e.g. on grounds of legal privilege, some other statutory exemption, or if the court has ruled that the question need not be answered).[111] In *The Queen v D (R)*,[112] HHJ Peter Murphy held that the defendant was free to wear the niqab during trial. However, he proceeded to direct that the defendant may not give evidence wearing the niqab and, if she refused to remove it beforehand, she would not be permitted to give evidence and the judge should direct the jury about her failure to do so under section 35, albeit with appropriate modifications.

In spite of the outcry among the legal profession and various civil liberties organisations that arose in the immediate aftermath of the legislation, it is arguable that the only significant change to the pre-existing common law is that the prosecution were now able to comment on the failure of the accused to give evidence. It is questionable whether section 35 of the Criminal Justice and Public Order Act 1994 has any real effect on the common law, as set out in *Martinez-Tobon*. The Government clearly *intended* to change the law, but there remains some doubt as to whether it actually succeeded in doing so.

Two further points ought to be emphasised. First, the silence of the accused is not in itself evidence and, as such, a refusal to answer questions adds nothing to the prosecution case. If the defendant is to be convicted, the conviction must be based on all of the evidence presented to the jury. Inferences are drawn from the evidence and the silence of the accused serve only to leave the prosecution evidence unchanged. If it is unchanged, the jury may then infer that it is true, and if they are satisfied beyond reasonable doubt, they may convict. Arguably, it is therefore incorrect to allude to 'inferences from silence'; it may be more accurate (albeit more verbose) to speak of 'inferences from the prosecution evidence and lack of rebutting evidence from the accused.' This accords with one of the core principles laid down in *Martinez-Tobon*: namely, that the silence of the accused adds nothing to the prosecution case, nor does it take anything away.

Second, section 38(3) makes it clear that, *inter alia*, no conviction can be made solely on the inferences drawn under section 35. The inferences, if any, will be drawn from the evidence. It may be that, in certain cases, the only *proper* inference is that the accused is guilty, but that conclusion stems from the fact that the prosecution have presented a strong case that persuades the jury that the accused is guilty beyond any reasonable doubt.[113] In *Murray v DPP*,[114] the trial judge had told the jury that it was remarkable that the accused, in the light of the cumulative strength of circumstantial and forensic evidence against him, had not given evidence, and that it was only common sense to infer 'that he [was] not prepared to assert his innocence on oath because that [was] not

---

111 Criminal Justice and Public Order Act, s 35(5).

112 Unreported (16 September 2013) http://www.judiciary.gov.uk/judgments/thequeenvd/ (last accessed 16 December 2014).

113 See *R v Hawkins* [1997] 1 Cr App R 234; *R v Petkar and Farquar* [2003] EWCA Crim 2668; *R v Adetoro* [2006] EWCA Crim 1716; *Steele, Whomes and Corry* [2006] EWCA Crim 194.

114 [1994] 1 WLR 1 (a decision based on the Northern Ireland legislation). See also *R v Ackinlose* [1996] Crim LR 747; *R v Friend* [1997] Crim LR 817.

the case.'[115] The House of Lords appeared to reject the suggestion that the silence provisions were merely declaratory of the common law, and upheld the conviction for murder. It stated that, in appropriate circumstances, the inference that the person was guilty of the offence with which he was charged is permissible. Put in such stark terms, the decision can be seen as suggesting that the silence of the accused can be used as direct evidence of guilt. However, silence is never direct evidence of anything; rather, it is negative evidence in the sense suggested by the Court of Appeal in *Martinez-Tobon*. If, therefore, the prosecution have produced an overwhelming case against the accused, who does not give evidence, it may well be common sense to infer that they are guilty as charged, but the inference is drawn from the fact that the prosecution case is unchanged and uncontradicted, not from the fact that D has refused to answer questions. The jury then convict on the prosecution evidence, not on the silence of the accused.

At the close of the prosecution's case, the court will ascertain either from defence counsel or, if unrepresented, the defendant herself whether she proposes to give testimony. In *Ebanks v R*,[116] the Privy Council held that where it is decided that the defendant will not give evidence, this should be recorded in writing, along with a brief summary of reasons for that decision which, if possible, should be endorsed by the defendant. The case was taken to Strasbourg, though the complaints were rejected by the Court.[117]

In *Wright v The Queen*,[118] the appellant contended that the trial judge had failed to effectively inform the defendant of his right to give evidence in his defence and to warn him of the effects of failing to testify in court. The Privy Council, hearing the appeal from the Cayman Islands, agreed that the trial judge had erred in law by failing to advise the defendant in open court of these circumstances. Despite this, however, the Privy Council concluded that there was no suggestion that the defendant was not already aware of his right to testify and the effects of his failure to testify. As a result, the conviction was safe.[119] Comparison can be drawn with the US legal framework regulating self-incrimination, confessions, and the values it protects: the Fifth Amendment privilege against self-incrimination prevents the government from compelling a suspect to speak and also affords the legal basis for the much-heralded rule in *Miranda v Arizona*.[120] Under the US constitution, the sixth amendment also prohibits all law enforcement officers from eliciting unconsented written statements from a suspect whose right against self-incrimination has been infringed, unless that right is waived.[121]

In summary, prosecuting counsel is now permitted to comment on the failure of the accused to give evidence, and will doubtless emphasise that the prosecution case is unchallenged and uncontradicted. The trial judge may direct the jury that they may draw proper inferences and indicate what those proper inferences are in the particular case, drawing attention to the fact that the prosecution case has not been changed or contradicted. To this end, the judge may also point out that if the accused had been able to contradict, undermine, or explain the prosecution evidence, they may conclude that the reason why they have not chosen to do so is that they are unable to do so.

---

115 *Murray*, ibid., at 8.
116 [2006] UKPC 16.
117 *Ebanks v United Kingdom*, App. No. 36822/06 (26 January 2010).
118 [2016] UKPC 18.
119 See also *R v Farooqi* [2014] 1 Cr App R 69 (8).
120 *Miranda v Arizona*, 284 US 436 (1966).
121 See *Montejo v Louisiana*, 556 US 778, 786 (2009), where officers seek a waiver of the right to counsel from a suspect for whom the Sixth Amendment right is attacked. See also *Patterson v Illinois*, 378 US 285, 296–98 (1988), on the ability to waive Miranda Rights under the Sixth Amendment for intelligence waiver purposes.

7.4.1 Safeguards under section 35

No inferences may be drawn under section 35 if 'it appears to the court that the physical or mental condition of the accused makes it undesirable for him to give evidence.'[122] It is, however, incumbent on the defence to adduce evidence of such a condition: the court is not free to make inquiries of its own motion.[123] The scope of the provision was considered by the Court of Appeal in *R v Friend*.[124]

The accused, a 15-year-old boy, was on trial for murder and did not wish to give evidence. The trial judge rejected a defence submission that no inferences should be drawn on the grounds that the accused had a mental age of 9. In the judge's view, the fact that D had been able to give a clear account of events in his statements to the police suggested that he was capable of testifying in court. The accused was subsequently convicted, and argued that since the legislation had (at that point) provided for no inferences to be drawn in cases involving a person under the age of 14,[125] the court had applied the wrong test.

Dismissing the appeal, the court stated that it was inappropriate to speak of a 'test' to be applied in this type of situation. Instead, it was for the judge to determine whether or not it was undesirable for a defendant to give evidence. Even though the defendant had a mental age of 9, it did not follow that he had or should have had the same immunity from adverse inference as a person under the age of 14. Instead, it was open to the defence to introduce medical evidence concerning the mental age of the defendant, which could then be taken into account by the jury in determining 'such inferences as appear proper.' In the case of *O'Donnell v United Kingdom*,[126] the ECtHR found that the defendant's right to a fair trial had not been interfered with as a result of the adverse inferences drawn by the court. The ECtHR noted that the jury had been informed of competing expert evidence towards the defendant's alleged mental condition and it was left to them to properly decide whether to draw an inference.

The significance of this particular phrase was considered by the Court of Appeal in *R v Cowan, Gayle and Ricciardi*,[127] in which it was argued by defence counsel that section 35 was so at variance with established common law principles that its operation should be reduced and marginalised as far as possible. Therefore, it was contended that defence counsel ought to be allowed to present reasons or excuses for not drawing inferences from the failure of the accused to testify without the need for evidence. It was proposed, for example, that one reason for not drawing inferences might be the fact that the accused wished to attack the character of a prosecution witness, and then avoid the risk of being cross-examined on their own record by declining to testify.[128] The court rejected this argument, pointing out that this would lead to the bizarre result that a defendant with previous convictions would be in a more privileged position than one with a clean record. The court accepted that, apart from the mandatory provisions of section 35, it would be open to a court to decline to draw an adverse inference from silence at trial and for a judge to direct or advise a jury against drawing such inference if the circumstances of the case justified such a course. However,

---

122 Criminal Justice and Public Order Act 1994, s 35(1)(b). See also *R v Ensor* [2010] 1 Cr App R 18, in which Aikens J made it clear that just because a defendant may find it difficult to give evidence, it does not mean that it is undesirable for them to give evidence (at [35]); *R v Tabbakh* [2009] EWCA Crim 464, in which in assessing whether it is 'undesirable' the judge is entitled to weigh the likely significance of the defendant's evidence to the issues in the case with the nature and consequences of the mental condition revealed by the expert evidence.

123 *R v A* [1997] Crim LR 883.

124 [1997] 1 WLR 1433.

125 Criminal Justice and Public Order Act 1994, s 35(1). These words were subsequently removed from the legislation by the Crime and Disorder Act 1998, Sch 10.

126 [2015] ECHR 357.

127 [1996] QB 373.

128 See Ch 11.

in order for this scenario to arise, there would need to be some evidential basis for doing so, or some exceptional factors in the case.[129]

The Court of Appeal then proceeded to stress that the inferences permitted by section 35 were only such 'as appear proper.' The inclusion of that phrase within the legislation was, in the court's view, intended to confer a broad discretion to a trial judge to decide in all of the circumstances whether any proper inferences were capable of being drawn by the jury. If no such inferences could be drawn, the jury should be instructed not to draw any. Otherwise, it was for the jury to decide what, if any, inferences might be drawn. The court then proposed a number of elements that judicial directions to the jury should contain by way of safeguards to the accused:

(1) The judge must tell the jury that the burden of proof remains upon the prosecution throughout and what the required standard is.
(2) The judge must make clear to the jury that the defendant is entitled to remain silent. That is his right and his choice. The right of silence remains.
(3) An inference from failure to give evidence cannot on its own prove guilt.
(4) The jury must be satisfied that the prosecution have established a case to answer before drawing any inferences from silence. The jury may not believe witnesses whose evidence the judge thought raised a *prima facie* case.
(5) If, despite any evidence relied upon to explain his silence or in the absence of any such evidence, the jury conclude the silence can only sensibly be attributed to the defendant's having no answer or none that would stand up to cross-examination, they may draw an adverse inference.[130]

These safeguards have since been incorporated into the *Crown Court Bench Book*.[131]

It is, of course, impossible to anticipate all of the circumstances in which a judge might think it right to direct or advise a jury against drawing adverse inferences, and it may not even be wise to devise examples, as each case must turn on its own facts.[132] In *Cowan*, it was underlined that the Court of Appeal would not lightly interfere with a judge's exercise of discretion to direct or advise the jury as to the drawing of inferences from silence, nor would it offer any guidance as to the nature, extent, and degree of such inferences. On the one hand, it can be contended that this position merely serves to consolidate the common law (and, perhaps, common-sense) approach that juries had been applying for many years before the 1994 legislation was conceived. Fundamentally, it does not affect the burden of proof, nor does it detract from the accused's right to remain silent and to refuse to give evidence. On the other hand, it may be argued that it is undesirable to leave such a broad measure of discretion in the hands of judges. Perhaps, as far as the drawing of inferences from silence is concerned, the interests of justice are best served through a consistent and certain approach, rather than through the allure of a flexible discretion.

7.5 Section 36 and section 37

The final two circumstances that allow inferences to be drawn from silence are outlined in sections 36 and 37 of the 1994 Act. Section 36 permits inferences to be drawn at trial if the accused fails to account for the presence of objects, substances, or marks on his person, provided that the following conditions are satisfied:

---

129 For example, in *R v McManus* [2001] EWCA Crim 2455, the Court of Appeal conceded that s 35 did not come into play where there was no factual dispute between the parties. The issue in that case was whether particular premises were a 'disorderly house,' and the facts were largely agreed upon between the prosecution and defence.

130 *Cowan*, op. cit., n. 116, at 7 (Lord Taylor CJ).

131 *Crown Court Compendium*, op. cit., n. 97, p. 285.

132 *R v McLernon* (1990) 10 NIJB 91, 102.

- The suspect is under arrest.
- The object, mark, or substance is found on his person, clothing, footwear, or is 'otherwise in his possession.'
- The arresting officer or constable investigating the case reasonably believes that the presence of the object, substance, or mark may be attributable to the participation of the person arrested in the commission of a specified offence.
- The constable informs the person arrested that he so believes, and requests him to account for the presence of the object, substance, or mark using 'ordinary language.'[133]
- The suspect is allowed an opportunity to consult a solicitor prior to the request for an explanation being made.

This is clearly narrower than sections 34 or 35, focusing solely on the failure to account at the point of arrest for objects, substances, or marks. It can also be noted that inferences may be drawn irrespective of whether the accused proposes to rely on an explanation at trial on a fact that was not mentioned at the time of arrest. Of greater significance still is the fact that no requirement of reasonableness applies. While the defence may well put forward an explanation at trial as to why the accused failed to account for the object, substance, or mark, the trier of fact is under no obligation to find that the accused could reasonably have been expected to account for the object, substance, or mark prior to drawing any inferences.

Neither is there any requirement that the defendant be told the specific offence of which they are suspected of having committed. In *R v Compton*,[134] two brothers were convicted of conspiracy to supply both cannabis and heroin. Police had recovered substantial amounts of used banknotes, heavily contaminated with heroin, at each of the brothers' houses. When asked at interview to account for this, both suspects remained silent. The judge accordingly directed the jury that they could draw 'such inferences as appeared to be proper,' and the defendants were convicted. On appeal, it was alleged that section 36 should not apply since the officer had told one of the brothers, when delivering the caution, that he was being investigated for 'drug trafficking.' When charges were brought, they were unrelated to trafficking, and were confined to conspiracy to supply. The Court of Appeal rejected the appellant's contention that this was an inadequately specific description of the offence of conspiracy as required by section 36(1)(b). In the view of the court, it was sufficient that the suspect had been made aware of the general context of the investigation.

Section 37 of the 1994 Act is formulated in very similar terms to section 36, but is concerned with inferences drawn where the accused fails to account for their presence at the scene of the crime. The following conditions must be satisfied.

- The suspect is under arrest.
- The suspect was found at a place at or near the time that the offence is alleged to have been committed.
- The arresting officer or constable investigating the case reasonably believes that the suspect's presence at the scene at the time of arrest may be attributable to the participation of the person arrested in the commission of a specified offence.
- The constable informs the person arrested that they so believe, and requests them to account for the presence of the object, substance, or mark using 'ordinary language.'[135]
- The suspect is allowed an opportunity to consult a solicitor prior to the request for an explanation being made.

---

133 For this purpose, the special caution contained in Code of Practice C [10.11] should be used.

134 [2002] EWCA Crim 2825. See also *R v Abbas* [2010] All ER 79.

135 For this purpose, the special caution contained in Code of Practice C [10.11] should be used.

The case of *R v Martin*[136] provides a useful example of the equivalent Northern Ireland provision in operation. Here, a leading member of Sinn Féin had been arrested next door to a property where a police informer was allegedly being interrogated by the IRA. When asked to account for his presence, the accused remained silent. At trial, the accused admitted that he had been in the house where the alleged informer was being held, but claimed that he had run off to the house next door when he heard the police coming. He told the court that he had no idea that the person in question was being held against his will, and said he had gone to the house to arrange a press conference to publicise the informer's claim that he had been forced to turn informer by the police. When asked why he had refused to provide this explanation at the outset, the defendant replied that he had refused to do so 'out of principle.' In these circumstances, the court was satisfied that it was proper to draw an inference from the accused's failure to account for his presence that the accused was actually present in the house for the purpose of keeping the informer captive against his will.[137]

7.6 The privilege against self-incrimination in civil proceedings

The basic position in the civil courts is relatively straightforward. The common law has traditionally excused witnesses from having to answer certain questions if the answer would, in the opinion of the judge, 'expose the deponent to any criminal charge, penalty or forfeiture which the judge regards as reasonably likely to be preferred or sued for.'[138] The privilege was placed on a statutory footing by section 14(1) of the Civil Evidence Act 1968, which stipulates that a witness may refuse to answer any question or produce any document or thing if to do so would tend to expose that person, or their spouse or civil partner, to criminal proceedings.[139] No inferences may be drawn. In this sense, the privilege is considerably wider than that which exists in the criminal courts.[140]

7.7 Concluding comment

In the law of evidence, there are few issues that as frequently arouse such impassioned debate as the right to silence. For some, permitting adverse inferences to be drawn should not be seen as a step that contradicts the privilege against self-incrimination, as it simply permits the trier of fact to make a common-sense assessment of all the relevant evidence in the case. Ultimately, it may be seen as somewhat foolhardy, if not manifestly unjust, to ignore the fact that most reasonable people who are innocent of allegations will attempt to rebut them at every given opportunity. However, for many human rights and civil liberties campaigners, the fear is that any inferences from silence operate as a backdoor means of coercion. Curtailing the right in any form will effectively amount to shifting the burden of proof from the prosecution to the defence. In simple terms, it could be said that it is nonsensical for the law to guarantee a fundamental right in the form of the privilege against incrimination and then penalise a person who chooses to exercise

136 Unreported (8 May 1991), as cited by Jackson, J., 'Interpreting the Silence Provisions: The Northern Ireland Cases' [1995] Crim LR 587, 592–93.

137 For further guidance and illustration on the directions given to the jury in relation to ss 36 and 37, see *Crown Court Compendium*, op. cit., n. 97, ch 15, pp. 268–71.

138 *Blunt v Park Lane Hotel Ltd* [1942] 2 KB 253, at 25 (Goddard LJ).

139 See further Pt 34.20 CPR 1998 and Burns, S., 'A Very Limited Privilege' (2007) 151 *Solicitors Journal* 1014.

140 See further comments of Lord Diplock in *Rio Tinto Zinc Corporation v Westinghouse Electric Corporation* [1978] AC 547, 637.

it.[141] As Duff, Farmer, and Marshall recently concluded, despite the numerous bars to effective communication and participation for many defendants, it is no longer accurate to state that, in England and Wales, 'it is regarded as a central principle of criminal trials that the defendant can sit back and wait for the prosecution to prove the case against him.'[142] As a recent development, the way prosecutors have used rap music and videos reveals one of the underlying assumptions of 'rap on trial': that rap music 'somehow reflects the true thoughts, beliefs, and character of the person performing it.' Given this development, an important consideration would be if a defendant can afford to remain silent during the trial when this form of evidence is pitted against him.[143]

In considering the merits of such arguments, it is clear that the 1994 legislation undoubtedly constitutes a significant inroad to the right, at least as regards pre-trial silence. Certainly, in the common law world, few jurisdictions have sought to mirror the English approach, which arguably constitutes the thin end of the wedge. In the United States, the right to silence is enshrined in the Fifth Amendment, and it is similarly entrenched in the legal systems of Canada, South Africa, and India.[144]

This is, perhaps, unsurprising given that the legislation has not affected the conviction rate,[145] although it has resulted in a slightly higher level of response to police questions. In contrast to 77 per cent of suspects attempting all questions posed to them in the interview before the measures took effect, 84 per cent attempted to answer all questions once the provisions were in force.[146] To some extent, this small rise may be attributed to the fact that solicitors are now wary of advising clients to remain silent,[147] knowing that they could be blamed for any adverse inference that might be drawn when the case comes to court. As a comparative, in New Zealand, the Evidence Act 2006[148] defines self-incrimination succinctly as 'the provision by a person of information that could reasonably lead to, or increase the likelihood of, the prosecution of the person for a criminal offence.' As Choo illustrates, adopting this might be a useful working definition, where the logical implication of recognising a privilege against self-incrimination is that 'a person cannot be legally required or legally compelled to provide information which could reasonably lead to, or increase the likelihood of that person's prosecution for a criminal offence.'[149]

Although there is no shortage of opposition from both academic and civil liberty groups to the 1994 provisions,[150] there is currently no significant pressure on the political platform for either repeal or amendment. However, as Dennis points out, the case law that has emanated from Strasbourg and the consequential statutory amendments that have followed have already resulted in a significant change to the practical operation of the provisions.[151] However, as Dennis himself acknowledges, the legislation has survived the advent of the Human Rights Act 1998, and it has not to date been declared incompatible with Article 6 of the European Convention on Human

---

141 See further Michael, J. and Emmerson, B., 'Current Topic: The Right to Silence' (1995) 1 *European Human Rights Law Review* 4.

142 Duff, A., Farmer, L., Marshall, S., and Tados, V. (eds), *The Trial on Trial: Towards a Normative Theory of the Criminal Trial* (Hart Publishing, 2007), 199.

143 Neilson, E. and Dennis, A.L., *Rap on Trial: Race, Lyrics, and Guilt in America* (The New Press, 2019).

144 See s 11(c) of the Canadian Charter of Rights, s 35 of the Constitution of the Republic of South Africa, and Art 20(3) of the Constitution of India, respectively. Section 89(1) of the Uniform Evidence Acts in Australia also prohibits the drawing of any inferences from an accused's failure to respond to questioning.

145 Jackson and others, op. cit., n. 48.

146 Bucke, Street, and Brown, *The Right of Silence*, op. cit., n. 56.

147 Ibid.

148 Evidence Act 2006 (NZ), S.4.

149 Choo, A.L-T., *The Privilege Against Self-Incrimination and Criminal Justice* (Hart Publishing, 2013), p. 180.

150 See e.g. Leng, R., 'Silence Pre-Trial, Reasonable Expectations and the Normative Distortion of Fact Finding' (2001) 5 *International Journal of Evidence and Proof* 240; Birch, op. cit., n. 45; Justice, op. cit., n. 48; Easton, S., *The Right to Silence*, 2nd edn (Ashgate, 1998).

151 Dennis, op. cit., n. 95.

Rights.[152] For the time being, at least, we can be fairly confident that the current regime permitting adverse inferences is here to stay.

7.8 Key learning points

- The principle against self-incrimination prohibits any form of compulsion on suspects to provide evidence against themselves. The principle also envelops the suspect's right not to have adverse inferences drawn from their failure to answer questions, or, once accused, their failure to testify at trial.
- Where the parties are on 'even terms' with each other, an accusation by X that is unanswered by Y can be said to provide evidence that Y accepted the truth of the allegation.
- The Criminal Justice and Public Order Act 1994 effected radical changes in respect of the suspect's rights to silence. The trier of fact may now draw 'such inferences as appear proper' in four situations.
- A failure to respond to police questioning cannot of itself prove the defendant's guilt.
- These provisions are subject to a number of safeguards both within the legislation and as developed by the appellate courts.
- No inferences can now be drawn if the accused was in police detention and did not have prior access to a solicitor.
- Where the suspect is given access to a solicitor who subsequently advises them to remain silent, the jury should consider the context of any legal advice and take this into account in assessing the overall reasonableness of the suspect's decision to remain silent.

7.9 Practice questions

1. 'The danger is that the less responsive an accused is, the more difficult it will be for the court or jury to make any inference that it can be satisfied is correct. They are left to speculate about what people in the accused's position might be expected to do if guilty or innocent.' Consider the issues raised in this statement. Does authorising the drawing of inferences encourage a court or jury to be less cautious than it otherwise might be in such situations?
2. 'When the decision was taken in 1994 to introduce legislation formally enabling the tribunal of fact, if it thought fit, to draw an adverse inference from the defendant's failure to respond to questioning, the Act had to thread its way through a veritable minefield of motivational and procedural considerations. The relevant provisions are predictably complex.' Critically discuss the issues arising in this quotation.
3. Pauline is stopped outside a local clothes shop by Tansey, a fellow shopper, who accuses her of placing a T-shirt in her bag without paying for it. Pauline shrugs her shoulders and walks on. Later that evening, the police arrest Pauline on suspicion of theft. At the police station, Pauline's solicitor advises her not to answer any questions since she 'will just end up in more trouble.' Pauline remains silent at the interview, but at trial testifies that the T-shirt was placed in her bag by her 4-year-old daughter without her knowledge. Discuss the evidential issues arising.

---

152 The 'right to silence' is not mentioned expressly in Art 6. However, it is well established that it is a standard that lies at the heart of the generic provision laid down in Art 6(1). See further *Delcourt v Belgium* (1970) 1 EHRR 355; *Moreira de Azvedo v Portugal* (1992) 13 EHRR 731; *Funke v France* (1993) 16 EHRR 297; *Murray v United Kingdom* (op. cit., n. 85); *Saunders v United Kingdom* (1997) 23 EHRR 313; *Heaney and McGuinness v Ireland* App. No. 34720/97 (21 December 2000); *Averill v United Kingdom* (op. cit., n. 84); *Condron v United Kingdom* (op. cit., n. 84); *Beckles v United Kingdom* (2003) 36 EHRR 162; *Salduz v Turkey* [2008] ECHR 1542.

7.10 Suggested further reading

Allen, R.J., 'Theorizing about Self-Incrimination' (2008–2009) 30 Cardozo Law Review 729.
Brooks, J., *You Might Go to Prison, Even Though You're Innocent* (University of California Press, 2023).
Bucke, T., Street, R. and Brown, D., *The Right of Silence: The Impact of the Criminal Justice and Public Order Act 1994*, Home Office Research Study No. 199 (HMSO, 2000).
Dennis, I., 'Silence in the Police Station: The Marginalisation of Section 34' (2002) Crim LR 25.
Godsey, M., *Blind Injustice: A Former Prosecutor Exposes the Psychology and Politics of Wrongful Convictions* (University of California Press, 2017) 76.
Jackson, J., 'Silence and Proof: Extending the Boundaries of Criminal Procedure in the UK' (2001) 5 E & P 145.
Jennings, A., Ashworth, A. and Emmerson, B., 'Silence and Safety: The Impact of Human Rights Law' (2000) Crim LR 879.
Owusu-Bempah, A., 'How to Reinstate the Right of Silence' in JJ Child and RA Duff (eds.) *Criminal Law Reform Now: Proposals & Critique* (Hart, 2018) pp 270–278.
Quirk, J., *The Rise and Fall of the Right of Silence: Principle, Politics and Policy* (Hart Publishing, 2016).
Redmayne, M., 'Rethinking the Privilege Against Self-Incrimination' (2007) 27(2) Oxford Journal of Legal Studies 209.
Roberts, P. and Zuckerman, A., *Criminal Evidence*, 2nd edn (Oxford University Press, 2010): see Ch 13, in particular pp 547–563.
Seet, M., 'Suspected Terrorists and the Privilege Against Self-incrimination' (2015) 74(2) CLJ 208.
Stewart, H., 'The Privilege Against Self-Incrimination: Reconsidering Redmayne's Rethinking' 20(2) E & P 95.

Chapter 8

Confession Evidence

Chapter contents

DOI: 10.4324/9781003416098-8

One of the key factors that may influence the outcome of the trial is the manner in which the accused has responded to police questions. The interrogation of suspects remains one of the primary investigative techniques for the police, and the most desirable outcome in virtually every interview will be an incriminating statement from the suspect under questioning. If the prosecution have such an admission to rely upon at trial, their task in proving the accused's guilt beyond reasonable doubt is likely to be considerably more straightforward.

However, the use of confessions in court in this manner *prima facie* constitutes an infringement of the rule against hearsay, but a confession is admissible at common law as evidence of the truth of its contents since people do not generally make untrue statements that are against their own interests.[1] During the 1990s, false or unreliable confessions were the source of several high-profile miscarriages of justice.[2] This led to calls in some quarters to impose corroboration requirements, to make it impossible for a defendant to be convicted solely on the basis of their confession. Although the Royal Commission on Criminal Justice rejected this option,[3] in practice there have been sufficient examples to caution courts against the ready acceptance of confessional evidence alone, and to remind the police and Crown Prosecution Service of the desirability of supporting evidence.[4]

The modern test for the admissibility of a confession is contained in sections 76 and 76A of the Police and Criminal Evidence Act (PACE) 1984.[5] Section 76(1) provides that a confession made by an accused person is admissible insofar as it is relevant to any matter in issue in the proceedings and is not excluded by the court in pursuance of that section. Subject to passing the relevance threshold, a confession may be used as evidence of any issue, including any matter favourable to its maker.

Section 76(2) provides that the prosecution can be required to prove, beyond reasonable doubt, that the confession that it proposes to introduce in evidence was not obtained by oppression (section 76(2)(a)) or in circumstances of unreliability (section 76(2)(b)). Section 76A makes similar provisions for the admissibility of a confession made by an accused person on behalf of a co-accused,[6] although a co-accused need only prove on the balance of probabilities that the confession was not obtained by oppression or in circumstances of unreliability.

---

1 Confessions are also known as 'informal admissions' in contrast to a statement made by the accused while giving evidence or in more formal circumstances under s 10 of the Criminal Justice Act 1925. For a historical overview of the law relating to confessions, see Mirfield, P., *Silence, Confessions and Improperly Obtained Evidence* (Oxford University Press, 1997).

2 See further Gudjonsson, G., 'Unreliable Confessions and Miscarriages of Justice in Britain' (2002) 4 *International Journal of Police Science and Management* 332. The cases of the Guildford Four, Birmingham Six, and Judith Ward are perhaps the most notorious in respect of the emphasis placed on confessions by the prosecution at trial.

3 Royal Commission on Criminal Justice, *Report*, Cmnd 2263 (HMSO, 1993) [13.10]. See further Pattenden, R., 'Should Confessions Be Corroborated?' (1991) 107 *Law Quarterly Review* 317.

4 However, see the case of *R v K (Julie)* [2010] EWCA Crim 914, where a murder conviction was upheld by the Court of Appeal, even though the Crown's only evidence consisted of confessions which K later either denied making or denied were true. Principle (b) of the *Principles of Investigative Interviewing* (Home Office Circular 22/1992) encourages police to seek supportive evidence, and stresses that the courts look for it in respect of mentally disordered defendants. However, see Clarke, C. and Milne, R., *National Evaluation of the PEACE Investigative Interviewing Course* (HMSO, 2001). The authors of this report found poor transfer of information and skills from the classroom to the workplace, poor use of interviewing techniques for obtaining an interviewee's account, little evidence of routine supervision of interviews in the workplace, and misunderstandings about the PEACE model of interviewing. See further Bull, R. and Milne, R., 'Attempts to Improve Police Interviewing of Suspects,' in G.D. Lassiter (ed.), *Interrogation, Confessions and Entrapment* (Kluwer/Plenum, 2004).

5 Before PACE 1984 came into force, a trial judge who found that a confession had been obtained by oppression or as a result of threats or inducements from a person in authority, which rendered it involuntary, would exclude it as a matter of law (*Ibrahim v R* [1914] AC 599). There was also a discretion to exclude a confession obtained in breach of the Judges' Rules, the precursor of what is now Code C.

6 Inserted by CJA 2003, s 128.

Even if the prosecution successfully clears these hurdles, section 78 provides for a broad judicial discretion to exclude prosecution evidence if it would have such an adverse effect on the fairness of the proceedings that it ought not to be admitted. These provisions are examined below in some detail. First, however, the question of how the law of evidence defines a 'confession' will be considered.

8.1 What constitutes a confession?

Section 82(1) of PACE 1984 defines a confession as 'any statement wholly or partly adverse to the person who made it, whether made to a person in authority or not and whether made in words or otherwise.' A confession may thus be made orally, in writing, by conduct, or in any other way that information may be communicated. Thus, if the defendant, by words or conduct, indicates that they accept an accusation made by the victim of a crime, or by someone else who is on an equal footing, then to the extent that they have accepted it, the statement becomes their own.[7] The re-enactment of a crime by an accused that is video-taped by the police is clearly a confession within section 82(1) insofar as it is adverse to the accused. In the same way, a suspect may make a confession by demonstrating how they picked a lock, or how they stabbed a victim.[8]

The definition will encompass any informal admission made out of court, and it is immaterial to whom the confession is made. Although the great majority of confessions are made to the police, or other investigative bodies such as HM Revenue and Customs,[9] this is not a requirement of the legislation. Under section 82(1), a confession made to anyone such as a spouse, friend, social worker, or police is subject to the same test of admissibility under section 76. In *Rumping v DPP*,[10] a letter written by the defendant to his wife was held to constitute a confession, and the same reasoning would apply to a letter of apology written by the defendant to the alleged victim.

A further example can be found in a report on the murder of British student Isabel Peake, which was in *The Times* in 2000.[11] A murder suspect in Portugal, Sid Ahmed Rezala, was said to have confessed to a journalist that he took part in the killing of three girls in France, including the British student. That statement, although made to a journalist in the context of an interview, would be a confession for the purposes of section 82(1).[12] The same edition of *The Times* reported the conviction for murder, by an American court, of a mother and son, despite the fact that the prosecution failed to find the body. The son had kept detailed notes of the plot to kill the victim, a Manhattan socialite, in order to gain control of her US$7 million town house using forged documents. These notes were admitted as confession evidence in that trial, and would also constitute a confession for the purposes of section 82(1).

---

7 *R v Christie* [1914] AC 545.

8 *Li Shu-Ling v R* [1989] AC 270.

9 See e.g. *Seelig v Spens* (1991) 94 Cr App R 17. The case of *R v Bayliss* (1994) 98 Cr App R 235 involved a confession made to in-store detectives.

10 [1964] AC 814.

11 *The Times* (20 May 2000).

12 If introduced in evidence in an English criminal trial, the admissibility of this statement may well be the subject of a challenge under s 76(2)(b) of the 1984 Act since Rezala had been paid for his story.

Similarly, in the trial of four youths for the murder of Damilola Taylor in March 2002, the prosecution adduced evidence of confessions made to other inmates at a detention centre in the presence of a member of staff. In that case, these confessions were challenged under section 76(2)(b) as being unreliable, but were nevertheless admitted. However, in *Benedetto v The Queen; Labrador v The Queen*,[13] the Privy Council warned that juries must be cautious before accepting a cell confession allegedly made by the accused to a fellow prisoner, particularly if they are held together on remand. Such prisoners might well have something to gain from assisting the prosecution and their evidence was inherently unreliable.

In *R v Ellaray*,[14] the defendant was convicted of rape solely on the basis of admissions made to a probation officer preparing a pre-sentence report. The appellant alleged that the judge was wrong to admit the statements, given the nature of the relationship between an offender and his probation officer. The Court of Appeal held that, before proceeding in a case such as this, the prosecution should carefully consider whether it was right to rely upon evidence provided by conversations between a probation officer and an offender, and should rely upon it only if it was in the public interest to do so. The court should bear in mind the contrast between an interview involving the police and the offender, and an interview between a probation officer and the offender. A number of key differences should be taken into account: there was a need for frankness between the offender and the probation officer; there might not be a reliable record of what was said; and the offender had not been cautioned and was not legally represented. Section 78 of PACE 1984 was available to ensure no unfairness occurred,[15] but in the instant case such factors were taken into account and the appeal was dismissed.

8.1.1 Content of the confession

The content of a confession can take various forms. The confession may constitute a full, signed admission of guilt, or it may simply constitute one potentially incriminating comment that the suspect has inadvertently made under the pressure of interrogation. By confining the definition of 'confession' to 'adverse' statements, section 82(1) does not cover wholly exculpatory statements, but it will cover so-called mixed statements – those that contain both inculpatory and exculpatory elements.

Example 8.1

Charlie is arrested on suspicion of taking part in a bank robbery. In response to police questioning, he admits his involvement by stating that he drove the getaway car, but had no idea that the others implicated were intent on committing a robbery. Such a statement is a confession insofar as its maker admits being the driver of the getaway car. By the same token, it is also exculpatory as the maker states he had no idea he was involved in a robbery. In order to avoid potential unfairness to the accused, the whole statement should be admitted in evidence.[16]

However, the evidential value of self-serving extracts from a confession may be slight, and the judge may well comment on their lack of weight. Similarly, statements that are overly vague will

13 [2003] 1 WLR 1545.
14 [2003] 2 Cr App R 11.
15 See discussion below.
16 *R v Sharp* [1988] 1 All ER 65.

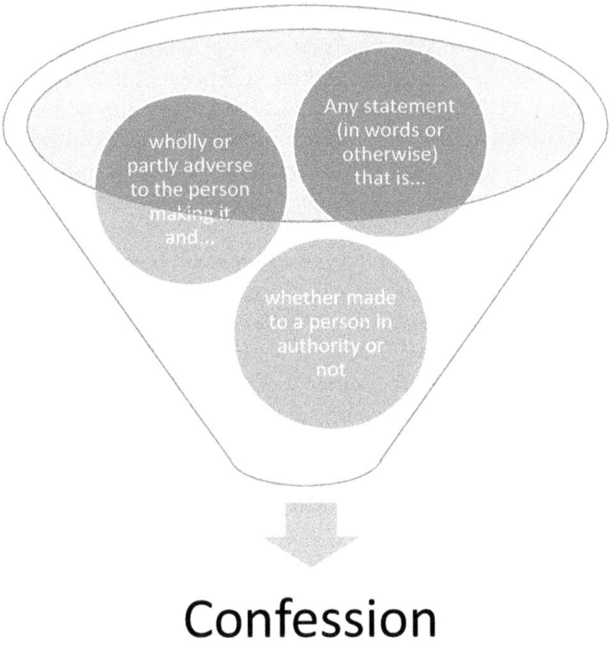

Figure 8.1 Meaning of a confession

not be considered as confessions,[17] and similarly those that are wholly exculpatory, such as 'I had nothing to do with it,' are not covered by section 82(1). Such a statement may be admissible to show the suspect's reaction when accused of the offence and arrested, but should not be treated as confession evidence for the purposes of PACE.

This principle was confirmed by the House of Lords in *R v Hasan*.[18] The appellant was convicted of aggravated burglary, which he admitted subject to the defence of duress. At trial, the prosecution were permitted to cross-examine him and to call rebuttal evidence concerning a confidential 'off-the-record' conversation with the police, which took place after the suspect had been charged. Although the conversation was entirely exculpatory, the appellant argued that it should have been treated as a confession since the prosecution had used it against him at trial to show that it was inconsistent with his testimony in some material respects.

The Court of Appeal agreed that the conversation should not have been admitted. Statements made by Hasan during that conversation later transpired to be adverse to him within the meaning of section 82(1), and thus constituted a confession for the purposes of section 76(2). Since the original conversation took place in circumstances that might have made the confession unreliable, the prosecution should have been obliged to prove that it did not. However, this decision was subsequently reversed by the House of Lords. In the view of Lord Steyn, the conversation was not adverse to the accused at the time it took place. Thus, it was entirely exculpatory and could not qualify as a confession for the purposes of section 82(1).

17 See e.g. *R v Schofield* (1917) 12 Cr App R 191, in which the defendant exclaimed: 'Just my luck!'
18 [2005] 2 WLR 709.

In *R v Sliogeris*,[19] the appellant (D1) had been convicted of murder alongside one of his co-defendants (D2). A third defendant (D3) was acquitted and did not give evidence at trial but had made an out-of-court statement to a witness that he was present at the scene of the murder but blamed co-defendant D1 for the killing. D2 (whose defence was that D1 committed the offence alone) attempted to rely on this statement at trial. The trial judge admitted the evidence under section 76A of PACE 1984 on the basis that the statement was a 'mixed statement' and under section 114(1)(d) of the Criminal Justice Act 2003 (hearsay in the interest of justice). The Court of Appeal was tasked with considering whether the evidence had been lawfully admitted. Elias LJ found that:

> We accept that the statement by [D3] that he was present is a statement against interest and may be said to fall under the terms of section 82. However, that is not the statement which the co-accused, [D2], wishes to have admitted in evidence. He is relying upon another comment made by [D3], which is logically quite distinct from his admission of his presence, namely that the appellant [D1] had committed the offence. That is an exculpatory statement and does not itself amount to a confession; nor is it so inextricably linked with the (partial) confession to justify it being treated in that way.[20]

Elias LJ thus found there not to be one mixed statement, but rather, two statements (one inculpatory and one exculpatory). His Lordship thus found that the evidence should not have been admitted under section 76A, but did go on to find that the evidence was, however, admissible under the interest of justice provisions in the CJA 2003.[21]

8.2 The principle of exclusion

Section 76(1) of PACE provides that:

> In any proceedings a confession made by an accused person may be given in evidence against him insofar as it is relevant to any matter in issue in the proceedings and is not excluded by the court in pursuance of this section.

Breaches of PACE 1984 and Code of Practice C,[22] which govern the detention and questioning of suspects, and Code of Practice E,[23] which requires the tape-recording and/or the video-taping of interviews with suspects, tend to be the grounds on which the defence will most commonly seek the exclusion of a confession. The custody record, which is created in respect of every person arrested and taken to a police station, details every action in respect of the suspect. This record, together with the tape-recording and/or the video-recording of interviews with the suspect, may provide the defence with evidence of any violation, which they can then use to put the prosecution to proof that section 76 or section 78 of the 1984 Act has not been breached.

Any breach of procedure outside the police station may also be grounds for excluding a confession. In these circumstances, there are two overriding principles that must be applied. First, as soon as a police officer has grounds to suspect that a person has committed an offence and wishes to question them, a caution must be given in the following terms:

---

19 [2015] EWCA Crim 22.
20 Ibid., at [30].
21 Ibid., at [44].
22 Last updated 23 February 2017.
23 Last updated 26 January 2016.

> You do not have to say anything. But it may harm your defence if you fail to mention when questioned something which you later rely on in court. Anything you do say may be given in evidence.

Second, an interview with a suspect should normally take place in a police station soon after arrest, where the suspect will have all of the protections of the 1984 Act and Codes of Practice (particularly Codes C and E), which include access to legal advice and an audio- or video-recording of the interview.

The importance of these two principles stems from the fact that an arrest (and caution) should only take place where the officer has 'reasonable grounds to suspect' involvement in an offence.[24] It follows that the on-street questioning that precedes an arrest should only be of the kind that provides the reasonable grounds for arrest. The questioning should cease once the arrest takes place, and any further interrogation should take place at the police station in accordance with Codes of Practice C and E. As noted below, any deliberate attempt to circumvent the protections provided by the Act and Codes is likely to be met by exclusion of any evidence obtained in this way. However, it should be underlined that the courts will not necessarily automatically exclude anything said by the suspect outside the interview room, so anything that the defendant may have said spontaneously following his arrest may still be given in evidence if it is not ruled out by section 76.

8.2.1 The scope of section 76(2)

Section 76(2) provides:

> If, in any proceedings where the prosecution proposes to give in evidence a confession made by an accused person, it is represented to the court that the confession was or may have been obtained –
>
> (a) by oppression of the person who made it; or
> (b) in consequence of anything said or done which was likely in the circumstances existing at the time, to render unreliable any confession which might have been made by him in consequence thereof,
>
> the court shall not allow the confession to be given in evidence except insofar as the prosecution proves to the court beyond reasonable doubt that the confession (notwithstanding that it may be true) was not obtained as aforesaid.

A virtually identical provision is contained in section 76A(2) in respect of the co-accused.[25]

The provision thus provides two separate grounds under which a confession may be excluded: oppression and unreliability. The onus lies on the defence to 'represent' to the court that either one of these grounds applies. The defence will usually intimate its intention to challenge the admissibility of the confession before counsel for the prosecution make the opening address; the

24 PACE, ss 24(1), (2), and (3).

25 Section 76A(2) is identical, except for the reference in the first line to 'a co-accused' rather than the prosecution and the final clause, which reads as follows: 'The court shall not allow the confession to be given in evidence for the co-accused except insofar as it is proved to the court on the balance of probabilities that the confession (notwithstanding that it may be true) was not so obtained.' It follows from the lower standard of proof that a confession that is ruled inadmissible for the prosecution could be admitted for a co-defendant.

prosecution will then make no reference to it at this stage.[26] It is then for the court to determine the question of admissibility within a *voir dire*.[27] If the defence has not raised the question, the court of its own motion may require the prosecution to prove that it was not obtained by the methods described in exercising its power under section 76(3).

8.2.2 The *voir dire*

The *voir dire* can take two main forms. Sometimes this will take place before the trial proper, but more often the jury will be sent out at the point at which the prosecution intends to call the police officer(s) or other persons to whom the confession was made. However, in many cases it will be more convenient to hear the argument as to admissibility at an earlier stage of the trial, for example, prior to the opening to the jury. In *R v Murray*, the court justified this approach on the basis that prosecuting counsel would be unable otherwise to explain the case for the Crown in opening.[28] It is for the prosecution to prove beyond reasonable doubt that the confession was not obtained in breach of the legislation. This was the decision in *R v Sat-Bhambra* [1988] Crim LR 453. If counsel fails to discharge this burden, the trial judge must exclude the evidence and has no discretion in this matter. However, as a starting point in the *voir dire*, the defence will need to produce some *prima facie* evidence to suggest that the confession was or may have been so obtained. This evidence may appear on the face of the custody record, which should reveal any prolonged periods of questioning or lack of entitlements under the PACE 1984 or Codes of Practice. Alternatively, violations may be apparent from the recording of the interview. Often, the judge will seek evidence from the police officers or other law enforcement officials who conducted the interview.

The defendant may also testify, but cannot be compelled to do so.[29] In practice, however, there will be many cases in which the accused must testify if they are to stand any chance of getting the confession excluded. In the *voir dire*, the sole issue for the court is the admissibility of the confession. It may be declared inadmissible even if it is true, since the section is concerned only with the question of whether it was obtained by oppression or in circumstances of unreliability. This is understandable where oppression has been applied, but arguably less so when the issue is the reliability of the confession. The question of whether or not a confession is likely to be true is perhaps the best measure of its reliability, but the truth is not in issue within the *voir dire*. Evidence led, or cross-examination conducted, by the prosecution designed to show that the confession is true will ultimately be irrelevant to the issue of admissibility. Thus, in *R v Cox*,[30] the defendant, who had a learning disability, was interviewed in the absence of an 'appropriate adult,' which constituted a violation of Code C.[31] During the interview, he admitted being involved in two burglaries. At the *voir dire*, the defendant gave evidence and admitted his involvement in one of the burglaries, which persuaded the judge that the confession was reliable and should be admitted. The Court of Appeal held that the trial judge had applied the wrong test. The essential question was not whether the confession was true, but whether the breach of the Code was likely in the circumstances to produce an unreliable confession.

The admissibility and relevance of a confession are thus questions of law to be decided by the judge prior to the confession being admitted in evidence. By contrast, the question of how

---

26 Depending on the importance of the confession to the case, the issue of its admissibility may be decided before the prosecution gives any evidence at all. Indeed, if a confession is central to the prosecution case but is excluded, the trial judge may then withdraw the case from the jury and direct an acquittal as empowered by s 17 of the Criminal Justice Act 2003.

27 *R v Millard* [1987] Crim LR 196.

28 [1950] 34 Cr App R 203.

29 *R v Davis* [1990] Crim LR 860.

30 [1991] Crim LR 276.

31 An 'appropriate adult' is an independent person who must be present to protect the interests of juveniles and the mentally handicapped as required by Code C [3.6]–[3.14].

much weight ought to be placed on it is for the jury to decide. Even if the prosecution successfully discharges its burden in the *voir dire* and the confession is admitted, the defence may still raise the issue again in the course of the trial. Counsel would still be free to intimate to the jury that the confession was not reliable and should be disregarded, despite that question having been already determined for the purposes of admissibility by the trial judge. In *Mushtaq*,[32] Lord Roger made clear the factors that should be taken into account by the jury: unreliability, the privilege against self-incrimination, and the behaviour of the police towards the suspect.[33]

Therefore it is quite possible, for example, for counsel to elicit new information from police officers, when conducting a cross-examination, that might lead the confession to be viewed in a different light. The jury would then be free to attach little weight to the confession, or to disregard it altogether. Alternatively, the trial judge may choose to revisit their decision to admit the evidence. In these circumstances, section 76 and section 78 of PACE are prospective, and cannot be used to exclude the confession where it has already been admitted in evidence. The judge will, however, be able to apply the common law discretion and instruct the jury that they are to disregard the evidence entirely.[34]

8.2.3 The confessions of co-defendants

In *R v Beckford*,[35] section 76 was held to apply only to confessions tendered by the prosecution. This was confirmed by the House of Lords in *R v Myers*,[36] in which it was held that D1 could make use of a confession made by D2, even if D2's confession was inadmissible against him on behalf of the prosecution having been excluded under section 76. Arguably, this decision was fundamentally unfair to D2,[37] whose confession had been excluded as against the prosecution either because it was obtained by oppression or because it was potentially unreliable.

This problem was acknowledged by policymakers, and section 128 of the Criminal Justice Act 2003 amended the law to prevent any potential unfairness arising by inserting a new section 76A into PACE. As section 76A now makes clear, a confession made by an accused may be admissible on behalf of a co-accused where the provisions of that section are satisfied. If D1 seeks to rely on a confession made by D2, counsel for D1 will have to prove on the balance of probabilities that neither of the grounds within section 76A(2)(a) or (b) applies. It is thus possible that the prosecution may fail to prove beyond reasonable doubt that a confession was not obtained in breach of these provisions, while a co-accused, bearing the lower standard of proof, may well succeed. In these

---

32 [2005] UKHL 25. See further Clare, A., 'Confessions' (2006) 70 *Journal of Criminal Law* 7. See also *R v Pham* [2008] EWCA Crim 3182. As Cross and Tapper point out, it is questionable whether such a direction will really make any difference: Tapper, C., *Cross and Tapper on Evidence*, 12th edn (Oxford University Press, 2010), p. 640.

33 However, since the appeal was dismissed by the House of Lords, these comments are effectively *obiter*. For information on the rules governing the editing of a confession, see *Weaver* [1967] 1 All ER 277; *Silcott* [1987] Crim LR 765; *Hay* (1983) 77 Cr App R 70.

34 *Sat-Bhambra* (1988) 88 Cr App R 55. The scope of the common law is discussed in Chapter 9. That discretion is distinct from the discretion contained in s 78 PACE, and is expressly preserved by s 82(3). It should also be noted that, unlike s 76, s 78 and the common law discretion apply only to prosecution evidence. In *R v Dhorajiwala (Bhavna)* [2010] 2 Cr App R 21, it was held that the court should have exercised its power under PACE. The prosecution did not prove beyond reasonable doubt that the confession contained in the interview fell foul of s 76(2); the court should not have permitted the confession to be given in evidence, and this procedural irregularity impugned the fairness of the trial. See also Cotton, T., 'Confession Evidence and the Circumstances Requiring a *Voir Dire*' (2010) 74 *Journal of Criminal Law* 400. See also the Judicial College website for alternative directions to the jury: http://www.judiciary.gov.uk (last accessed 18 July 2017).

35 [1991] Crim LR 833. See also *R v Rogers and Tarran* [1971] Crim LR 413.

36 [1997] 3 WLR 552.

37 See Hartshorne, J., 'Defensive Use of a Co-accused's Confession and the Criminal Justice Act 2003' (2004) 8(3) *International Journal of Evidence and Proof* 165, who argues that the exclusion of a co-defendant's statement is manifestly unfair, given that in many cases it will be true, and is contrary to the right contained in Article 6. See also Hirst, M., 'Confessions as Proof of Innocence' [1998] *Cambridge Law Journal* 146.

circumstances, the confession may then be relied upon by the co-accused and will be evidence against the defendant who made it. Although the evidence was not adduced by the prosecution, it will nonetheless serve to assist the prosecution in proving its case against that particular defendant. Simultaneously, however, it may also act to undermine the case of the prosecution against the co-accused in whose favour the confession was admitted.

Since an accused is generally neither competent nor compellable for the prosecution, an out-of-court statement by D1 *against* D2 is inadmissible as evidence. However, this is subject to the requirements imposed by the House of Lords in *R v Hayter*.[38] Three defendants were charged with murder and jointly indicted as principals in proceedings relating to a contract killing. The first defendant, Bristow, wanted to arrange a contract killing of her husband. The second defendant, Hayter, was the go-between who engaged and paid the third defendant, Ryan, to kill the husband. Bristow's husband was shot in the head at point-blank range, dying instantly. The evidence against Ryan, the killer, was solely based on a confession that he allegedly made to his girlfriend. The trial judge directed the jury to consider in logical phases the case against Ryan, the alleged killer, then against Bristow, the woman who allegedly procured the killing, and finally against the middleman, Hayter.

The judge also directed the jury in clear terms that the confession that Ryan allegedly made to his girlfriend was only evidence against him and not evidence in the separate cases against Bristow and Hayter. The jury were also told that they should consider the case against Ryan first. If they found him guilty of murder, they could then use that finding of guilt in their consideration of the case against Bristow and Hayter, while taking care not to allow anything in the girlfriend's evidence of Ryan's confession to play any part in their consideration of the case against either. The jury found all three guilty and the House of Lords dismissed the appeal, holding that where the prosecution case against D1 is dependent upon the prosecution proving the guilt of D2, and the evidence against D2 consisted solely of his own out-of-court confession, then such a confession would be admissible against D1. However, this could only be used insofar as it went to proving the guilt of D2. If D1 then chooses to testify and admits his part in the offence and incriminates his co-defendant, that can then be taken as evidence against D2. Similarly, if D1 ceases to be a defendant, where, for example, the prosecution offers no evidence against D1 or files a *nolle prosequi*, D1 can then give evidence for the prosecution against D2.[39]

8.3 Criteria for admissibility

The prosecution may be required to jump up to three hurdles before a confession can be admitted in evidence (Figure 8.2). The first hurdle is 'oppression' under section 76(2)(a); the second is

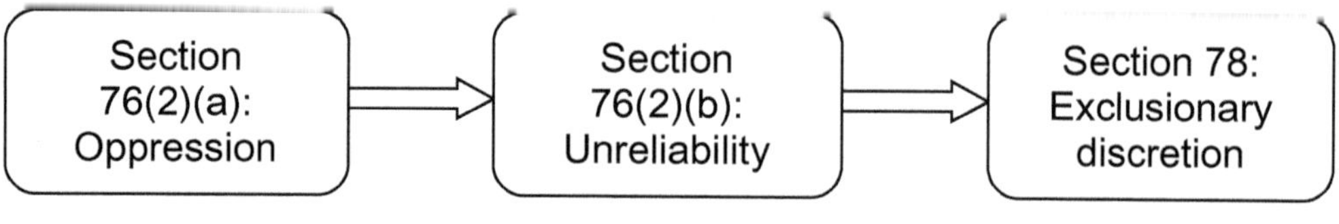

Figure 8.2 Hurdles to admitting a confession

38 [2005] 1 WLR 605. See further McGourlay, C., 'Is Criminal Practice Impervious to Logic?' (2006) 10 *International Journal of Evidence and Proof* 128. See also *R v Johnson* [2007] EWCA Crim 1651; *R v Finch* [2007] 1 WLR 1645; *Persad v State of Trinidad and Tobago* [2007] UKPC 51; *R v Nazir* [2009] EWCA Crim 213. In *Persad*, Lord Browne made it clear that *Hayter* does not apply unless the defendants were charged with a joint offence for which they were alleged to be jointly liable.

39 See *R v Sliogeris* [2015] EWCA Crim 22.

'unreliability' under section 76(2)(b). The third hurdle is the general discretion provided for by section 78, where the trial judge must be satisfied that admitting the confession would not have 'such an adverse effect on the fairness of the trial that the court ought not to admit it.'

Usually, a defendant will allege a breach of section 76(2)(a) and/or (b). Occasionally, the defence look solely to section 78. Exceptionally, a defendant might represent that a confession ought to be excluded under all three heads by representing, first, section 76(2)(a), then, if that should fail, alleging a violation of section 76(2)(b). As a last resort, the defence may urge the court to exclude in the interests of a fair trial under section 78. However, the Court of Appeal has held that if the prosecution succeeds in discharging the burden under section 76(2)(a) and (b), *prima facie* there are no grounds for exclusion under section 78.[40]

8.3.1 Oppression

The defence may represent to the court that the confession 'was or may have been obtained ... by oppression of the person who made it.' This reflects the views of the Criminal Law Revision Committee,[41] and those of the Royal Commission on Criminal Procedure,[42] that society's abhorrence of methods of investigation amounting to oppression should be signalled by the automatic exclusion of a confession obtained thereby, even if the confession turns out to be true. It also reflects the pre-PACE position of the common law.[43]

8.3.1.1 Defining 'oppression'

At common law, the test for the admissibility of a confession was that it was voluntary and not forced from the mind by pressure of threats or inducements.[44] The characteristics of the accused were of particular significance, and it was recognised that conduct that might not have been oppressive in the case of an experienced person (e.g. someone with a criminal record and well used to police interrogatory methods) might well be deemed to be oppressive in the case of an inexperienced young man or woman, or a person who is vulnerable for other reasons. As noted below, such characteristics are similarly relevant to the statutory test under PACE.

Section 76(8) offers a non-exhaustive statutory definition of the term. 'Oppression' includes 'torture, inhuman or degrading treatment and the use of threat of violence (whether or not amounting to torture).' In *R v JA*, however, Burnton LJ stated that 'while subsection (8) is not a definition of that term [oppression], it indicates what kind of conduct may amount to oppression.'[45]

The phrase 'torture or inhuman or degrading treatment' is derived from Article 3 of the European Convention on Human Rights. This is undoubtedly a high threshold: torture is widely recognised in international law as the most severe form of oppression and, according to a resolution of the United Nations in 1975, 'constitutes an aggravated and deliberate form of cruel, inhuman or degrading treatment or punishment.'[46] It suggests a systematic and premeditated course of action rather than a spontaneous act of violence: in the 1984 United Nations Convention against Torture and Other Cruel, Inhuman and Degrading Treatment or Punishment, torture is defined as 'any act by which severe pain or suffering, whether physical or mental, is intentionally

---

40 See *Halawa v Federation against Copyright Theft* [1995] 1 Cr App R 21; *R v Dhorajiwala (Bhavna)* [2010] 2 Cr App R 21.

41 Criminal Law Revision Committee, *Eleventh Report: Evidence (General)*, Cmnd 4999 (HMSO, 1972).

42 Royal Commission on Criminal Procedure, *Report*, Cmnd 8092 (HMSO, 1981).

43 Oppression was first established as a ground of inadmissibility in *Callis v Gunn* [1964] 1 QB 495. This was then incorporated, but not defined, in the revised Judges' Rules of 1964.

44 *R v Priestly* (1965) 51 Cr App R 1.

45 [2010] EWCA Crim 1506 at [25].

46 GA/RES/3452 (1975).

inflicted on a person for such purposes as obtaining from him or a third person information or a confession.'[47]

'Inhuman treatment' has been described by the European Commission of Human Rights as covering 'at least such treatment as deliberately causes severe suffering, mental or physical.'[48] In *Ireland v United Kingdom*,[49] the European Court of Human Rights described the interrogation techniques (prolonged wall-standing, hooding, subjection to white noise, deprivation of sleep, and rationing of food and drink) employed by British security forces in Northern Ireland as 'degrading' because they were 'such as to arouse in their victims feelings of fear, anguish and inferiority capable of humiliating and debasing them and possibly breaking their physical or moral resistance.'[50]

It is thus clear that psychological, as well as physical, acts are included within the ambit of the statute, and the alleged maltreatment of 'illegal combatants' at Guantánamo Bay and at Abu Ghraib prison, Baghdad, would also fall within the definition of 'inhuman treatment,' if not 'torture.' It would clearly constitute 'oppression' under section 76(2)(a), and may explain why the United States was initially reluctant to allow the British prisoners held at Guantánamo Bay to be repatriated and tried in the United Kingdom. Any confession evidence obtained from these prisoners while in custody would almost certainly be excluded by an English court.

However, it should be noted that over the recent decades, the European Courts have shown a leniency towards accepting evidence of confessions obtained by using 'fruits of the poison tree.' In the infamous 2011 case of *Gafgen v Germany*,[51] the court confirmed that the use of confessions would always render proceedings unfair. However, in a controversial aspect of the judgment, the court found that real evidence would not breach the convention on the fairness of the trial if it was only compromised by inhumane treatment as opposed to torture, and the admission of the impugned evidence had a significant bearing on the outcome of justice and proceedings of the defendant. Therefore, there seems to be an acceptance by the human rights courts of situations where there can be evidence obtained illegally that will not violate the privilege against self-incrimination.[52]

The definition of oppression within section 76(8) is not, however, exhaustive, and the drawing of subtle distinctions within the terminology is unnecessary. Indeed, the expansive view of oppression taken by the Court of Appeal in *R v Fulling* has meant that the narrow terms of section 76(8) are virtually redundant.[53] Fulling was convicted of obtaining property by deception. The defendant staged a burglary at her flat along with her boyfriend, and then claimed some £5,000 from an insurance company. In seeking to exclude a confession made after a number of interviews, the defendant claimed that, during a break in the final interview, a detective had told her that her boyfriend had been having an affair with a girl called Christine, who had also been arrested and was in the cell next to her. This, she said, caused her distress and, she claimed, amounted to oppression. The police denied telling her this. The trial judge made no finding as to whether she or the police were telling the truth, but was prepared to assume for the purpose of argument that the defendant's version was true. Ruling that the confession was admissible, the trial judge remarked:

---

47 UN Doc. A/39/51 (1984), Art. 1.

48 *The Greek Case* (1969) 12 Yearbook ECHR 1.

49 (1978) 2 EHRR 25.

50 See also *Soering v UK* (1989) 11 EHRR 439.

51 (2011) 52 EHRR 1

52 On the relationship between Article 6 and Article 3, see Ashworth, A., 'The Exclusion of Evidence Obtained by Violating a Fundamental Right: Pragmatism Before Principle in the Strasbourg Jurisprudence,' in P. Roberts and J. Junter (eds), *Criminal Evidence and Human Rights: Reimagining Common Law Procedural Traditions* (Hart Publishing, 2012).

53 [1987] QB 426.

> Bearing in mind that whatever happens to a person who is arrested and questioned is by its very nature oppressive, I am satisfied that in section 76(2)(a) of the Police and Criminal Evidence Act 1984 the word oppression means something above and beyond that which is inherently oppressive in police custody and must import some impropriety, some oppression actively applied in an improper manner by the police. I do not find that what was done in this case can be so defined and, in those circumstances, I am satisfied that oppression cannot be made out on the evidence I have heard in the context required by the statutory provision.[54]

The Court of Appeal adopted this part of the ruling, and held that 'oppression' in section 76(2)(a) should be given its ordinary dictionary meaning, taking the third definition of that word in the *Oxford English Dictionary*, which reads as follows:

> the exercise of authority or power in a burdensome, harsh, or wrongful manner; unjust or cruel treatment of subjects, inferiors etc.; the imposition of unreasonable or unjust burdens.

Such a wide definition more than encapsulates everything within section 76(8) and extends oppression well beyond that partial definition. The Lord Chief Justice also added that the court found it 'hard to envisage any circumstances in which such oppression would not entail some impropriety on the part of the interrogator.'[55] Furthermore, he implicitly adopted the trial judge's ruling that 'oppression' means something above and beyond that which is inherently oppressive in police custody, and must import some degree of impropriety on the part of the police.

The requirement of impropriety initially focuses the court's attention on what the investigator has done rather than on the effect of their conduct on the suspect. It will be noted that the prosecution must prove beyond reasonable doubt that the suspect was not oppressed. If the court is persuaded that the confession was or *may* have been obtained by oppression of the person who made it, the confession is inadmissible. It follows that there is no need to prove that the suspect was *actually* oppressed. Instead, the prosecution must prove beyond reasonable doubt that they were not oppressed or, if they were, that there was no causal connection between the conduct alleged to have been oppressive and the obtaining of the confession. As noted above, if a co-accused seeks to rely on a confession by another co-accused, they must do so on the balance of probabilities.

In order for section 76(2)(a) to be triggered, *Fulling* suggests that there should be some serious impropriety on the part of the police or other investigatory authority. This will often occur within the confines of the police station, but it should be borne in mind that questioning or conduct that occurred at the time of arrest or while the person was being conveyed to a police station may be similarly relevant. In any event, the court will wish to hear an account of the whole proceedings that took place between the police and the accused before deciding whether there has been oppression. While a breach of the Code of Practice may be seen as wrongful, it is unlikely to amount to oppression unless it amounts to an accumulation of breaches, which together form a gross breach.[56]

Lesser impropriety is more likely to come within section 76(2)(b). This would usually include the application of tricks, such as covert tape-recording of a suspect, which will not per se amount to oppression.[57]

Lord Lane seemed to suggest in *Fulling* that 'impropriety' is a synonym for 'wrongful,' as used in the definition, but arguably it instead refers to serious wrongdoing and does not encompass

54 Ibid., at 429–30.
55 Ibid., at 432.
56 See *R v Davison* [1988] Crim LR 442.
57 *R v Parker* [1995] Crim LR 233.

minor breaches of procedure. Nevertheless, it remains apparent that a number of lesser breaches may take a cumulative toll on the suspect, and together may amount to oppression. This was held to be the case in *R v Davison*, which contained a catalogue of improprieties. The defendant was arrested at 6.25 am for handling a stolen ring. At the police station, he agreed to be interviewed in the absence of a solicitor, but made no admissions. The judge found that, by 11 am, the police had no evidence against the defendant and should have released him under section 34 of PACE. In fact, the suspect remained in custody, and an entry in the custody record at 1.15 pm purported to authorise further detention to allow further interviews to take place. That was a breach of section 37 of the Act. By 3 pm, the police had learnt that the defendant had provided information to a third party that led to a serious robbery, and then the police had sought the authority of a superintendent to delay access to a solicitor under section 58(8) of PACE 1984.[58] When the defendant asked to see a solicitor, this was denied, although there were then no grounds in section 58(8) under which delay could be lawfully authorised.

At 4.30 pm, a confrontation took place between the defendant and the robbery suspects, followed by a 'conversation' in which the police told the defendant he was being questioned about an armed robbery. He was not, however, arrested for that offence, as required by section 31, thus constituting yet another breach of PACE. Both the confrontation and the conversation were recorded in the police officers' notebooks, but no attempt was made to show the defendant the notes and to obtain his confirmation. This was a breach of Code of Practice C. At 5.10 pm, the suspect was interviewed in the absence of a solicitor and made admissions. The trial judge found that the defendant had been unlawfully detained from 11 am, and that there was a total failure to arrest him for the armed robbery. The police were found to have been exercising their powers in a 'wrongful manner,' which was found to amount to oppression under the terms of *Fulling*. The judge therefore excluded all of the evidence after the first interview under section 76(2)(a).

8.3.2 The method of questioning

Overly zealous or aggressive questioning of suspects may also amount to oppression, as defined in *Fulling*. In *R v Mason*,[59] the defendant was falsely told that forensic evidence had been found linking him to the crime. Although the Court of Appeal felt that this fell short of the dictionary definition of oppression, it did state that it was possible to envisage circumstances in which such conduct may fall within the remit of section 76(2)(a). For example, if a suspect were falsely told that a parent was close to death, and that they should confess to get home, this could amount to oppressive treatment.

Nevertheless, the deliberate abuse of power would seem to be essential, as *Fulling* stipulates that oppression must be 'actively applied.' In *R v Miller*,[60] a paranoid schizophrenic confessed to killing his girlfriend. The confession contained delusions mixed with facts. A psychiatrist testified that the questioning had triggered delusions. The judge's decision was that the questioning was not oppressive, as it was not deliberately designed to induce delusions. However, had the police been aware of the defendant's mental state and deliberately set out to induce delusions, that might well have passed the threshold for oppression.

There is, however, no doubt that persistent, heavy-handed, or bullying questioning interspersed with misrepresentations could qualify. For example, in *R v Beales*,[61] a confession extracted during a 35-minute interview was excluded because the officer had invented evidence against the defendant and forcefully confronted him with it. In addition, he repeatedly misrepresented the

58 See discussion below.

59 [1987] 3 All ER 481.

60 (1986) 83 Cr App R 192. This decision was, however, based on the law before PACE took effect.

61 [1991] Crim LR 118.

defendant's answers and 'hectored and bullied [him] from first to last.' Similarly, in *R v West*,[62] there was oppression when the interviewing officer interrupted the suspect on a large number of occasions before he had finished his reply, often vigorously and rudely with a raised voice, and used obscenities to indicate that he was lying. It was clear to the court that the officer had made up his mind that the defendant had committed the offence, and would continue to question him until he admitted this. However, the extent of oppression will always be a matter of degree, and it should be borne in mind that the very purpose of police interrogations is to gather further information, which may involve applying pressure to the interviewee. In *R v Emmerson*,[63] a police officer lost his temper, shouted, and swore at the suspect, but this was deemed to fall short of the required threshold.

Much more clearly oppressive than any of the above cases was the conduct of the interviewing officers in *R v Paris, Abdullahi and Miller*,[64] often dubbed the Cardiff Three. The three defendants were accused of the murder of a prostitute, Lynette White, who was stabbed some 50 times. After a trial in which the prosecution relied on the evidence of two discredited witnesses and admissions made by Miller after exhaustive interviews, all three were convicted. Miller was described by a defence doctor as 'on the borderline of mental handicap' with an IQ of 75, a mental age of 11, and a reading age of 8. The officers shouted at Miller, and told him what they wanted him to say, despite his denying involvement some 300 times. The following extract, taken from one of 19 taped interviews totalling 13 hours, and recorded over five days, may provide something of the flavour of the type of questioning the suspect faced. What the extract below cannot convey, however, is that the questioner was shouting in a frustrated manner, thumping the table, and spluttering in his indignation so much that he failed to finish sentences:

Miller: I wasn't there.
DC Greenwood: How can you ever ...?
Miller: I wasn't there.
DC Greenwood: How you ... I just don't know how you can sit there ...
Miller: I wasn't ...
DC Greenwood: Really don't ...
Miller: I was not there, I was not there.
DC Greenwood: Seeing that girl, your girlfriend, in that room that night like she was ... I don't know how you can sit there and say it.
Miller: I wasn't there.
DC Greenwood: You were there that night.
Miller: I was not there.
DC Greenwood: Together with all the others, you were there that night.
Miller: I was not there. I'll tell you already.
DC Greenwood: And you sit there and say that.
Miller: They can lock me up for 50 billion years, I said I was not there.
DC Greenwood: Cause you don't wanna be there.
Miller: I was not there.
DC Greenwood: You don't wanna be there because if ...
Miller: I was not there.
DC Greenwood: As soon as you say you were there you know you're involved.
Miller: I was not there.
DC Greenwood: You know you were involved in it.
Miller: I was not involved and wasn't there.
DC Greenwood: Yes you were there.
Miller: I was not there.

---

62 Unreported (2 May 1988).

63 (1990) 92 Cr App R 284.

64 (1993) 97 Cr App R 99.

> *DC Greenwood*: You were there, that's why Leanne is come up now ...
> *Miller*: No.
> *DC Greenwood*: Cause her conscience is ...
> *Miller*: I was not there.
> *DC Greenwood*: She can't sleep at night.
> *Miller*: No. I was not there.
> *DC Greenwood*: To say you were not there that night ...
> *Miller*: I was not there.
> *DC Greenwood*: Looking over her body seeing what she was like ...
> *Miller*: I was not there.
> *DC Greenwood*: With her head like she had and you have got the audacity to sit there and say nothing at all about it.
> *Miller*: I was not there.
> *DC Greenwood*: You know damn well you were there.
> *Miller*: I was not there.

Having heard the entire tape, the court had no doubt that this constituted oppression within the meaning of section 76(2)(a). The convictions were quashed,[65] and a damning judgment was delivered by Lord Taylor CJ who expressed the view that, short of physical violence, it was hard to conceive of a more hostile and intimidating approach by police officers to a suspect.[66] One of the factors that concerned him most was that a solicitor was present for the vast majority of the interviews, but had failed to intervene. The solicitor's failure to protect his client was subject to particularly heavy criticism, which was instrumental in leading to a change in the training and authorisation of solicitors who attend police stations.[67] The police were also prompted to retrain their officers in interrogation (interviewing) techniques so that this kind of questioning is unlikely to be repeated. For that reason, where the defence seek to exclude a confession on the grounds of aggressive questioning alone, they may be more likely to be successful in arguing their case under the 'unreliability' head in section 76(2)(b).

It is always going to be a matter of degree whether aggressive and hostile questioning amounts to oppression. It is evident that it is more likely to cross the threshold where a suspect is a weak or vulnerable person, so in that sense there is a subjective element to the test for oppression. Although initially the trial judge is likely to be concerned with the conduct of the police, the characteristics of the person on the receiving end of that conduct are also important, as are the particular circumstances in which the questioning takes place.[68] While, unlike the common law test, the *Fulling* test of oppression excludes the inherent oppression involved in arrest and custody, the characteristics of the suspect can be considered in determining whether a confession was obtained by oppression and in determining the related question of whether the conduct was 'burdensome,' 'harsh,' or 'cruel' within the definition of oppression. In *Paris, Abdullahi and Miller*, the fact that one of the suspects was below normal intelligence and on the borderline of learning disability was taken into consideration, although the method of questioning in that case may still have been deemed oppressive for a person of average intelligence. Similarly, in *R v Seelig*,[69] the Court of Appeal

---

65 *The Times* (5 July 2003) reported the conviction of Jeffrey Gafoor for the murder of Lynette White. After the conviction, South Wales police announced that they would hold another inquiry, overseen by the Independent Police Complaints Commission. In May 2005, this investigation into the original conviction of the Cardiff Three resulted in five retired police officers finally being arrested on suspicion of false imprisonment, conspiracy to pervert the course of justice and misconduct in public office after an investigation into this conviction. See *The Times* (19 May 2005).

66 Op. cit., n. 64, at 103.

67 See further Skinns, L., '"Let's Get It Over With": Early Findings on the Factors Affecting Detainees' Access to Custodial Legal Advice' (2009) 1 *Policing and Society* 58; Skinns, L., 'I'm a Detainee, Get Me Out of Here' (2009) 49 *British Journal of Criminology* 399.

68 Other factors that the judge may take into account include the weakness of the overall case against the defendant and any initial failure to allow access to a solicitor. See *R v L* [1994] Crim LR 839.

69 [1991] 4 All ER 429.

held that the trial judge was correct to take into account the fact that the defendant was an experienced and intelligent merchant banker in determining whether he had been subject to oppression.

8.3.2.1 The requirement for a causal link

As a final point in relation to oppression, it is necessary that a causal link be established between the oppressive conduct and the suspect's confession.[70] If the defendant confesses before being subjected to oppressive treatment, section 76(2)(a) does not apply. More realistically, there may be occasions on which the police have used oppression, but the accused confesses for other reasons unconnected with it, for example after a night in a cell, following oppressive treatment, when he or she has decided to get the 'matter off their chest,' or simply wants to be released from custody. In practice, the defence will in all probability raise the issue of oppression, in which case it will be extremely difficult for the prosecution to rebut the alleged causal connection between the police conduct and the confession. Indeed, the night in the cell may be seen as an opportunity for the oppressive treatment to take effect by giving the accused time to think over the options.

While some form of causal link must be established, the oppressive conduct in question need not emanate from the police. The defendant's confession will be excluded if it is shown that the oppression caused them to confess. For example, a defendant, a suspected paedophile, is severely beaten by enraged neighbours, and confesses to police who arrive on the scene that he has committed a number of serious sexual offences against children. Although the police have done nothing improper within this scenario, the members of the public have committed an assault against the defendant. In these circumstances, the defence would be entitled to represent that his only reason for confessing was to appease his attackers. The prosecution would thus be put to proof on the issue.

It is, of course, possible that the defendant will make a second confession that is not induced by oppression, but that will be a question of fact for the court to determine. It may be legitimately determined that a period in custody away from the threats of others may break the chain of causation, in which case the court would find that the subsequent confession was not tainted by the oppressive conduct of those who attacked the accused.

If, however, the police are responsible for the oppressive conduct within custody, it will be much more difficult for the court to find that the chain of causation has been broken. If, for example, a confession has been elicited through oppression in one interview, all subsequent interviews will be deemed to be tainted by the original oppressive conduct. Thus, if the suspect repeats a confession on a number of occasions, the general rule states that each confession will be deemed to be inadmissible.[71] If that were not the case, PACE and the Codes of Practice could be endlessly flouted until a confession was obtained, provided that at least one interview was conducted properly.

It is, however, a question of fact and degree in each case as to whether a later unobjectionable interview should be excluded. Much will depend upon the objections raised to the earlier interview, and whether those objections were of a fundamental and continuing nature. Occasionally, it may be possible for the Crown to prove that there is no link at all between interviews. This might occur where, for example, the defendant confesses subsequent to oppressive conduct. They are released on bail, but several days later return to the station with their lawyer and confess again.[72] In such a case, the chain of causation may well be broken. In *R v Conway*,[73] the defendant alleged that, during a visit to his cell by a police officer, he had been promised that if he admitted the

---

70 In *R v Alagaratnam* [2010] EWCA Crim 1506, it was held that there is no basis for excluding a confession where pressure to make it came from the suspect's legal representative rather than from police officers.

71 *R v Blake* [1991] Crim LR 119; *R v Ismail* [1990] Crim LR 109.

72 *R v Gillard and Barrett* (1991) 92 Cr App R 61.

73 [1994] Crim LR 838.

offence, he could go home to his sick mother. There was no record of the visit in the custody record, no caution was given and no note of the conversation was made. The defendant then confessed in an interview some 20 minutes later. The prosecution did not seek to rely on the interview in the cell, but the defence sought to exclude the later interview upon which the prosecution did rely. The trial judge's decision that there was no oppression or unreliability was overturned on appeal. The cell interview would have been excluded as unreliable, and there was nothing in the intervening 20 minutes to suggest that the effect of the earlier breaches had ceased to have any effect on the defendant.

Similarly, in *R v Neil*,[74] police took a witness statement from the defendant in which he admitted giving a knife to the man who stabbed the deceased before driving him from the murder scene. Immediately afterwards, Neil was arrested, cautioned, and kept in custody overnight, before being interviewed as a suspect when he made the same admission. The original witness statement was excluded under section 78, but the second interview was admitted. The Court of Appeal reversed this decision, and stated that the defendant had no opportunity to seek legal advice before being interviewed as a suspect, and may well have felt bound by the admissions in the earlier statement.

Other factors may come into play that would make it difficult in practice to rectify breaches in a later interview. In *R v Wood*,[75] the defendant, who was of limited mental capacity, was charged with manslaughter of a child by striking him a heavy blow. During an interview with no solicitor, no caution, and no contemporaneous record, he admitted striking the boy on the day before his death. In a second, properly conducted, interview, he repeated this admission. The medical evidence, however, suggested that the blow that killed the boy had been delivered on the day of his death, not on the previous day. This in itself suggested that the defendant's confession was unreliable and, in the absence of a record of the earlier interview, it was impossible for the prosecution to prove that the second interview was not tainted by the first.

8.3.3 Unreliability

Section 76(2)(b) of PACE 1984 stipulates that a confession will be inadmissible if:

> [It] was or may have been obtained … in consequence of anything said or done which was likely, in the circumstances existing at the time, to render unreliable any confession which might be made [by the person] in consequence thereof.

As with section 76(2)(a), once it is represented that the confession was or may have been given in circumstances of unreliability, the burden passes to the prosecution to prove beyond reasonable doubt that it was not so obtained. While the trial judge must initially determine the question of unreliability, if the confession is admitted, the jury will also do so in reaching their verdict. In order to avoid potential embarrassment to the jury who may, in effect, overrule the trial judge by reaching a different conclusion, the judge will be primarily concerned with the factors that led the suspect to confess as opposed to the *content* of the incriminating statement.

In order to determine the ambit of section 76(2)(b), close attention should be paid to the precise wording of the legislation. As a starting point, it can be noted that the phrase 'anything said or done' is potentially very broad in scope, and will certainly encompass conduct that amounts to oppression under section 76(2)(a). It will, however, stretch well beyond these circumstances, and may include threats, inducements, or some form of promise. Everything said or done before, and

74 [1994] Crim LR 441.
75 [1994] Crim LR 222.

during, the period of detention must be considered, and the court will seek to gain an insight into the whole picture surrounding the incriminating statement rather than focus on selective parts of it. In *R v Barry*,[76] the defendant was interviewed over two days. On the first day, he was told that it would be 'beneficial' for him to assist the police to recover certain property. On the second day, he was interviewed and confessed. The judge's conclusion that the statement on the first day had no effect on the confession made on the second day was rejected by the Court of Appeal. The court stipulated that judges should follow a three-stage test to determine whether a confession should be excluded on grounds of unreliability.

1. The first step is to identify what was said or done and this should include everything said or done.
2. The next step is to decide whether what was said or done was likely to render a confession unreliable; all of the circumstances should be taken into account. The test is hypothetical.
3. Finally, the judge should ask whether the prosecution had proved beyond reasonable doubt that the confession had not been made as a result of what was said or done.

In the context of this case, the promise of some benefit on the first day was 'something said' that had to be taken into account. It was likely to render any confession made unreliable, and the fact that the defendant had some time to think about it made it more likely that he would be influenced by it. This is not to say that something 'said or done' cannot be rendered ineffective by time: much depends on what was said or done and the particular circumstances. A connection, or causal link, must be established between what was 'said or done' and the obtaining of the confession; any delay in time may weaken that connection.

Something 'said or done' can also embrace conduct that is directed towards a person other than the suspect. Notable examples include a promise to take another offence into consideration at the trial rather than prosecute separately for that offence;[77] a threat to, or promise not to, prosecute the accused's spouse or mistress or other close relation;[78] and a threat to prosecute the defendant on a charge unrelated to the one under investigation.[79] Other possible circumstances would include threats to have children put into care, or to report the suspect's or a related person's income to HM Revenue and Customs or the Department of Work and Pensions. While such actions in themselves are not illegal, and may even be appropriate courses of action in certain circumstances, they should not be used as means to induce the suspect to confess.

The courts have established that things 'said or done' by the accused must arise from external factors that exert some form of pressure on the accused to confess. This external pressure need not emanate from the police.[80] In *R v Roberts*,[81] the defendant confessed to the shop manager where he worked that he had stolen an iPod. The manager had told him that if he admitted taking the device, he would take the matter no further, but that if he did not admit it, he would contact the police. The defendant admitted taking the iPod but the manager, nevertheless, called the police. The Court of Appeal allowed the appeal because the untrue inducement made the confession unreliable. Given the emphasis placed on the requirement that there be 'external pressure,' it should not show that the court will not consider the motives of the person making the confession as 'something said or done'; neither, it seems, will it consider self-inflicted drug addiction,

---

76 (1992) 95 Cr App R 384.

77 *R v Northam* (1968) 52 Cr App R 97.

78 *R v Middleton* [1974] 2 All ER 1190. However, it should be underlined that the more remote the relationship, the less likely it is that there will be a causal connection between the threat/promise and the making of the confession.

79 *Commissioners of Customs and Excise v Harz and Power* [1967] 1 AC 760.

80 It could be someone in prison with you (*R v Samuel* [2005] EWCA Crim 704) or your own legal representative (*R v M*, 12 June 2000, unreported).

81 [2011] EWCA Crim 2974.

which could prompt the defendant to agree to anything in order to be released from custody to feed an addiction. In *R v Goldenberg*,[82] a heroin addict was convicted on a charge of conspiracy to provide diamorphine. Following a search of the defendant's premises, where heroin and some £1,600 in cash were found, he was arrested and remanded in custody. Five days later, the defendant requested another interview and confessed. According to the defence, his motive in doing so was to obtain credit for helping the police, which would increase his prospects of obtaining bail. Subsequently, he would be able to satisfy his craving for a 'fix.'

On appeal, the defence contended that these circumstances fell within section 76(2)(b), and should thus render the confession unreliable. The Court of Appeal rejected this argument:

> In our judgment the words 'said or done' in section 76(2)(b) of the 1984 Act do not extend so as to include anything said or done by the person making the confession. It is clear from the wording of the section and the use of the words 'in consequence' that a causal link must be shown between what was said and the subsequent confession. In our view it necessarily follows that 'anything said or done' is limited to something external to the person making the confession and to something which is likely to have an influence on him.

The court was thus concerned more with the motives of a suspect for making a confession rather than the condition of the suspect who was suffering the immediate effects of withdrawal. However, in *R v Crampton*,[83] the court was faced with a defendant who was a drug addict more immediately affected by withdrawal symptoms, and who, it was alleged, was prepared to say anything in order to get out of the police station and 'get a fix.' The defendant was convicted of conspiracy to supply heroin. The police were aware that he was an addict and postponed interviewing him until the day after his arrest. Having rejected the offer of a solicitor and confirmed that he was feeling well enough to be questioned, the suspect made a number of incriminating remarks under interrogation. Afterwards, however, he complained that he was suffering withdrawal symptoms. A doctor was called, and deemed the defendant to be lucid despite showing some symptoms. Sometime later, a second doctor examined the suspect, who noted that withdrawal symptoms were subjective, appearing 8–16 hours after the last dose, and potentially worsening for up to 24 hours. However, in his opinion, at all times the sufferer would be lucid with no mental confusion, although there was a possibility that he may attempt to manipulate or lie to the police in order to obtain more drugs.

In the *voir dire*, the defence argued that the confession should be excluded as unreliable under section 76(2)(b) or as unfair under section 78, relying on the fact that the defendant had been interviewed while suffering from withdrawal symptoms. However, the judge admitted the confession and the defendant was convicted. On appeal, counsel for the defence sought to distinguish *Goldenberg* on the basis that, in this case, the police decided when the interview should be conducted and it was not at the request of the appellant. The Court of Appeal doubted that the mere holding of an interview at a time when the appellant was experiencing symptoms of withdrawal from heroin addiction was something 'said or done' within section 76(2)(b), but was prepared to assume that it was for the purposes of the appeal. The reason for the court's doubt was that section 76(2)(b) is concerned with the nature and quality of the words spoken, or things 'said or done, which are likely, in the circumstances existing at the time, to render the confession unreliable in the sense that it is not true.' The court went on to uphold the decision of the trial judge that the confession had been correctly admitted:

---

82 (1989) 88 Cr App R 285.

83 (1991) 92 Cr App R 369.

> It is plain that the experienced officers, who dealt with drug addicts, considered that he was fit to be interviewed. More important, perhaps, Dr Koppel [the first doctor to see the defendant] said that when he saw the appellant he considered he was then fit to be interviewed. It follows a fortiori that the appellant would have been fit at the time of his interview which occurred earlier ... In our judgement, the position is this. Whether or not someone who is a drug addict is fit to be interviewed, in the sense that his answers can be relied upon as being truthful, is a matter for judgement of those present at the time.[84]

The court also referred to the provisions of Code C, which stipulates the need to call a doctor if the police are in any doubt as to whether or not the defendant is well enough to be interviewed:[85]

> If the police had summoned Dr Koppel, and he had seen the appellant before the interview, the doctor would have certified that he was fit to be interviewed. That is the evidence that he effectively gave and the evidence which the trial judge accepted. It is then for the judge at the trial within a trial to decide whether the assessment of those present at the time was correct. The mere fact that someone is withdrawing, and may have a motive for making a confession, does not mean the confession is necessarily unreliable.[86]

The court then proceeded to cite with approval the observations of the Lord Chief Justice in *Rennie*:[87]

> Very few confessions are inspired solely by remorse. Often the motives of an accused are mixed and include a hope that an early admission may lead to an earlier release or a lighter sentence. If it were the law that the mere presence of such a motive, even if prompted by something said or done by a person in authority, led inexorably to the exclusion of a confession, nearly every confession would be rendered inadmissible. This is not the law. In some cases the hope may be self-generated. If so, it is irrelevant, even if it provides the dominant motive for making the confession. In such a case the confession will not have been obtained by anything said or done by a person in authority. More commonly the presence of such a hope will, in part at least, owe its origin to something said or done by such a person. There can be few prisoners who are being firmly but fairly questioned in a police station to whom it does not occur that they might be able to bring both their interrogation and their detention to an earlier end by confession.

The decision in *Crampton* does not exclude the possibility that the fact that the defendant is withdrawing can be a circumstance within section 76(2)(b) that could render any confession made in consequence unreliable. The important question is whether the confession was made in consequence of the withdrawal symptoms. As should be apparent from the discussion below, the test is to be applied objectively. It is not a question of what the police *believe* to be the facts, but what the facts actually are (or would have been), as ascertained by a doctor who examines the suspect.

In *Beeres v Crown Prosecution Service*,[88] the court held that interviewing a suspect who is not fit to be interviewed may lead to the exclusion of the interview under section 76 of the 1984 Act. The court emphasised that while paragraphs 2(b) and 3 of Annex G of the Code of Practice focus primarily on physical or mental unfitness, they can apply equally in relation to incapacity resulting

84 Ibid., at 372.
85 Code C, Notes 9A–9C.
86 *Crampton*, op. cit., n. 83, at 374.
87 (1982) 74 Cr App R 207, 212.
88 [2014] 2 Cr App R 8.

from alcohol or sleep deprivation. Therefore, if a detainee is materially under the influence of alcohol, then there is an obvious risk that answers given may not be rational or logical; and the same applies to a detainee who is sleep-deprived. If the ability of a detainee to perform properly in interview may be impaired for such reasons, then the evidence that they do give may be unreliable. This argument was raised by the appellant in her appeal; however, the court concluded (in addition to the above) that there was simply no evidence that B was affected by alcohol when interviewed, nor that her ability to function was affected by sleep deprivation, and thus it followed that B's confession evidence was reliable and fair and that neither section 76 nor section 78 applied to exclude it.

In *R v Everett*,[89] the defendant, aged 42, had a mental age of 8 and an IQ of 61 when he pleaded guilty to indecent assault. He lived with a family who had known him for some years, and was left alone with a 5-year-old boy and a 6-year-old girl. The mother returned to find that the boy's tracksuit bottoms were pulled down and his underpants crumpled. She told the police, describing the defendant as slightly mentally defective and slow in speech. He was arrested, and on the way to the police station he told police that he had touched the boy and had then touched himself. The police, however, failed to appreciate that he had a mental disability, and subsequently interviewed him on tape in the absence of an appropriate adult or solicitor. In the course of this interview, the defendant admitted indecently touching the boy, and the tape of the interview was the only evidence at his trial. Had the police been aware of the fact the suspect was mentally impaired, they would have been obliged by the Code of Practice to call an appropriate adult to look after his interests while at the police station and while being interviewed. In spite of this, the trial judge decided to admit the interview tapes. However, the Court of Appeal quashed the conviction on the grounds that the judge had paid insufficient attention to the 'circumstances existing at the time,' which obviously included the mental condition of the suspect. Even if the police were unaware of the suspect's disability, the test was essentially objective and the medical evidence adduced at the *voir dire* should have meant that the confession was excluded.

Thus, while a self-inflicted addiction to narcotics will normally mean that a case falls outside the scope of section 76(2)(b), there is no doubt that the mental condition of the suspect is a relevant circumstance to be taken into account. Indeed, in *R v Walker*,[90] the Court of Appeal had to consider the case of a suspect with a personality disorder and a drug habit. The defendant, a prostitute, was convicted of robbery. It was alleged that she had taken the car keys from a man and demanded money for their return, while showing the man a knife concealed in her waistband. At the police station following her arrest she was seen by a police doctor. She told him she was a heroin addict and was taking methadone, which she was duly prescribed. In an interview, she denied having a knife, but admitted that she had tried to frighten the victim into giving her money.

The defence sought to exclude the confession, alleging that the defendant had smuggled crack cocaine into the police station and was under its influence when she was interviewed. Psychiatric evidence was also called to the effect that the defendant suffered from a severe personality disorder. Having listened to the tapes of the interview, the psychiatrist expressed the opinion that the suspect's condition might render her admissions unreliable. In particular, the suspect would have been prone to embellishing her account without understanding the implications, and this effect was likely to be exacerbated if she was a user of crack cocaine. For their part, the prosecution claimed that her condition remained the same throughout the suspect's time in custody, and rebuked the suggestion that her personality disorder would have rendered the interview

---

89 [1988] Crim LR 826.

90 [1998] Crim LR 211. See also *R v O'Brien, Hall and Sherwood* (2000), *The Times* (16 February 2000); O Brien, M., *The Death of Justice* (Ceredigion, 2008).

unreliable. On that ground, the judge refused to exclude the confession and stated that he disbelieved the defendant's evidence that she had smoked crack cocaine in the police station.

On appeal, it was argued, first, that the trial judge had adopted the wrong approach to section 76(2)(b), and second, that there was new evidence from the duty solicitor that the defendant had smoked crack cocaine earlier in the day. Allowing the appeal, the Court of Appeal noted that the evidence of the psychiatrist was uncontradicted. In his analysis of the evidence, the trial judge appeared to limit the question of whether the defendant's personality disorder was such as to render the confession unreliable, by reference to previously decided cases of what he termed 'mental impairment' or of 'impairment of intelligence or social functioning.' This was the wrong approach to section 76(2)(b), and there was no requirement for any wrongdoing by the police. Moreover, relying on *Everett*, the court emphasised that the defendant's mental condition was one of the circumstances to be taken into account. Nothing in the *Everett* case limited or defined the particular form of mental or psychological condition or disorder upon which the defendant could rely to show that the confession was unreliable; any mental or personality abnormalities may be of relevance.

Having come to that conclusion, it was not necessary to rule on the new evidence, although the court made it clear it still had considerable reservations as to whether there had been a reasonable explanation for not adducing the evidence at trial. Had it been available to the judge, it would have been influential on his decision on the factual issue of whether or not the defendant took the drug. However, that issue was not central to the evidence of the psychiatrist, which was principally concerned with the pre-existing disorder.

It is unfortunate that the court did not consider the effect of the new evidence, which might have led to a clarification of the question of whether, and if so in what circumstances, self-administration of drugs and/or the symptoms of withdrawal can be a relevant consideration. *Goldenberg* was not considered in *Walker*. Therefore, *Goldenberg* remains authority for the proposition that 'anything said or done' in section 76(2)(b) does 'not extend so as to include anything said or done by the person making the confession,' but rather these words are 'limited to something external to the person making the confession' and to something that is likely to have some role in inducing the confession.

While *Goldenberg* was not directly concerned with a suspect under the influence of drugs or suffering withdrawal symptoms, there is no doubt that the taking of a narcotic substance and its subsequent effect do constitute 'something done' by the person making the confession and are not to be regarded as something external. There is some dispute among the medical fraternity as to whether withdrawal from drugs has any effect on cognitive function. In *Crampton*, one doctor said that withdrawal did not affect intelligence, while the other stated that the sufferer would be lucid with no mental confusion, but manipulative and lying in order to get more drugs. *Crampton* appears to assume that interviewing a heroin addict in withdrawal can be something 'said or done which was likely in the circumstances existing at the time' to render the suspect's confession unreliable. If the doctor's evidence had been that the defendant was a heroin addict in withdrawal and that those symptoms could influence him in such a way that any confession would be unreliable, there seems little doubt that it would fall within the scope of section 76(2)(b).

In her commentary on the decision in *Walker*, Professor Birch notes that:

> In order to give effect to the purpose of the subsection, which (as the present case acknowledges) is not to attach penalties to police misconduct at interview, but rather to prevent reliance on potentially unreliable material, the better approach would be to include the drugged (or drug-dependent) state of D as potentially relevant 'circumstances', and to concede that even the perfectly ordinary interviewing of somebody in such a state might be 'something said or done' which is conducive to the making of an unreliable confession. This

> seems to be the approach taken in the present case (though without consideration of the effect of Goldenberg) and it would seem, with respect, to be right.[91]

In a Home Office survey published in 1998,[92] 61 per cent of arrestees had taken at least one illegal drug: 46 per cent tested positive for cannabis; 18 per cent for opiates/heroin; and 10 per cent for cocaine/crack. Nearly half of the arrestees across all five areas surveyed said that their drug use was connected with their offending. Therefore, given that the number of people arrested while on drugs is so high, there may be an element of policy behind the decision to exclude confessions since the suspect's impaired state of mind is self-induced. However, if the medical evidence is correct in stating that the intelligence of drug-dependent suspects is not affected by withdrawal, then it is arguable that the drug-dependent suspect is in no different position from the suspect who is desperate to get bail for other, equally compelling reasons. Where a suspect confesses in the self-generated hope of some benefit, then the confession should not be excluded under section 76(2)(b). Moreover, where a defendant confesses in the hope or belief that they will get bail, but without any threat, encouragement, or inducement on the part of the police, this will also fall outside the remit of the statute.

There may be other conditions that, perhaps coupled with impaired intelligence, might constitute a 'circumstance' that could result in an unreliable confession. In *R v McGovern*,[93] a woman aged 19, six months pregnant and with a mental age of 10, was arrested on a charge of murder. She was interviewed twice. On the first occasion, she was improperly denied access to a solicitor and confessed under questioning. She was then interviewed for a second time with a solicitor present, when she again incriminated herself. The Court of Appeal held that the confessions in both interviews were inadmissible because the first interview had tainted the second. However, the absence of legal counsel by itself was not the sole ground on which the evidence was excluded: this factor interacted with the facts that she was young, pregnant, and mentally impaired. Together, the combined effect of these elements meant that the confession was unreliable.

8.3.3.1 Something 'said or done' need not emanate from the police

The most obvious external event that might constitute something 'said or done' is the conduct of the police. However, this need not necessarily be the case. In *R v Harvey*,[94] the defendant confessed to a murder. The previous day, she had heard that her lover had confessed to the same offence. The defendant was mentally impaired, and two psychiatrists had suggested that she might have confessed in a child-like attempt to protect her lover. Although the police had acted properly throughout, the prosecution was unable to prove beyond reasonable doubt that hearing her lover confess did not cause her to confess. On these grounds, the confession was considered to be unreliable.

In *R v Wahab*,[95] the accused was arrested for conspiracy to supply drugs together with members of his family. He was interviewed in the presence of his solicitor and, after the third interview, he asked his solicitor to approach the police to see whether the members of his family who were also in custody would be released if he confessed. The solicitor did so, but the police made it clear that no such guarantee could be given. The solicitor then told his client that if he confessed, police would look at the whole picture and, if the evidence against his family was 'borderline,' they would be released. The suspect confessed to playing the role of a 'middleman' shortly afterwards.

---

91 [1998] Crim LR 211.

92 Bennett, T., *Drugs and Crime: The Results of Research on Drug Testing*, Home Office Research Study No. 183 (HMSO, 1998). See also, *Drug-Misusing Offenders: Results from the 2008 Cohort for England and Wales* (HMSO, 2010) http://www.drugscope.org. uk/Resources/Drugscope/Documents/PDF/Good%20Practice/offenderstats2010.pdf (last accessed 6 October 2011).

93 (1991) 92 Cr App R 228.

94 [1988] Crim LR 241.

95 [2003] 1 Cr App R 15.

At his trial, the accused challenged the admissibility of the confession on the basis that he had been incompetently advised by his solicitor. He called another solicitor to show that the conduct of the first solicitor had fallen below the proper standard of professional competence. However, this evidence was rejected by the trial judge, who admitted the confession.

Dismissing the appeal, the Court of Appeal noted that advice properly given by a solicitor did not normally provide a basis for exclusion of a subsequent confession under section 76(2)(b). Although one of the duties of a legal adviser was to give the client realistic advice, that emphatically did not mean that the advice had to be directed to 'getting the client off' or simply making life difficult for the prosecution. In the instant case, the cross-examination of the second solicitor was not relevant to the reliability of Wahab's confession. Applying *Goldenberg*, the court held that the conduct of the solicitor did not ultimately influence the suspect's decision to confess.

Other forms of conduct that are 'external' to the police may include: a threat by a parent towards a child that the latter had better tell the truth or they will be beaten; a promise by an employer to an employee that if they admit the misconduct they will not be dismissed; or a threat by a headteacher to a pupil that unless the latter tells the truth to a police officer, they will be disciplined. However, by the same token, it should be emphasised that there must be a causal connection between what was said or done and the obtaining of the confession. It may be that, in many such cases, the prosecution would be able to prove that there was no such connection, particularly where the police are aware of what was said or done, and have taken steps to ensure that the suspect is no longer influenced by it when interviewed.

8.3.3.2 Improper conduct by the police

It will be recalled that, in *Fulling*, the inherent sense of oppression involved in arrest and custody is not enough to trigger section 76(2)(a). In the same way, it is clear that the phrase 'anything said or done' implies something out of the ordinary, beyond the proper exercise of normal police powers and procedures under section 76(2)(b). However, in contrast to oppression under section 76(2)(a), no impropriety on the part of the police is required under section 76(2)(b).[96] This is clearly the correct approach, since section 76(2)(b) focuses on the likely reliability of the confession and not the propriety of police conduct per se. The fact that 'something said or done' includes almost anything external to the suspect, and does not require any impropriety on the part of the police, may, however, encourage the defence to raise the issue of unreliability in many more circumstances than were possible in the pre-PACE era under the common law. Certainly, there is a narrow dividing line that separates legitimate police responses from illegitimate ones. Difficulties arise, for example, in relation to how the police ought to respond to questions from the suspect concerning the prospect of bail or the nature of any charges that might be brought.[97]

Code of Practice C seeks to sidestep these issues by providing that the police should give 'proper and warranted' responses to these sorts of questions.[98] Notwithstanding this provision, it still remains within the power of the court to decide whether a proper response to a suspect's question was likely to induce an unreliable confession. In practice, however, it is unlikely that the courts will find that a proper response could be used as the basis for exclusion. As the case law discussed above illustrates, it may often be the case that the suspect is merely seeking support for their own motives for confessing, having recognised that a confession will bring an end to the interrogation and to their release on bail. Nonetheless, a police officer would still be well advised to think twice before responding to a suspect's questions lest the answer be seen as improper and an inducement to confess.

---

96 See *R v Harvey* op. cit., n. 94 and *R v Morse* [1991] Crim LR 195.

97 See, respectively, *R v Barry* (1992) 5 Cr App R 384; *R v Phillips* (1988) 86 Cr App R 18.

98 PACE Code of Practice C [11.5].

This danger was seemingly ignored by the interviewing officer in *R v Howden-Simpson*,[99] who promised the defendant that he would be charged with only two offences if he confessed, but many more if he failed to do so. This evidence was excluded, although the court relied on section 78, rather than section 76(2)(b). The latter provision is really the appropriate tool for excluding this type of evidence since the conduct of the police clearly impacted upon the reliability of the admission. Indeed, the behaviour of the interviewing officer in this case is precisely the type of inducement that section 76(2)(b) was intended to address. In relying on section 78 in such cases, the court risks excluding inadmissible evidence that should automatically be excluded under section 76.[100]

Even in relation to more serious breaches of the Codes of Practice, the courts have demonstrated a preference for section 78 above section 76. For example, in *R v Sparks*,[101] a failure to caution and to record the interview were breaches of Code C, but were held not to be likely per se to affect reliability. Instead, the court held that they should have been excluded under section 78. Similarly, the latter provision is favoured in cases involving the improper denial of access to legal advice.[102]

To some extent, this is understandable, since failure to allow access to a solicitor will not necessarily lead to unreliability. However, in order to gauge whether or not unreliability has resulted, the court should first take into account a range of factors, including the seriousness of the offence under investigation. Undoubtedly, the protective presence of a solicitor will be seen as even more necessary where the suspect is being questioned about serious offences. Moreover, if the suspect is vulnerable, a juvenile, or mentally disordered, or, as in *McGovern*, young, of low intelligence, and pregnant, it may do so and almost certainly will do so, especially if coupled with a failure to provide an appropriate adult.[103] Indeed, if such an adult is not present, this in itself may amount to grounds for exclusion.[104]

The provisions within Code C that concern the accurate keeping of records in connection with the interview are designed to protect the accused against abuse by 'verballing,' which refers to the act of attributing words to the suspect that they never said, or taking them out of context to attribute to them a different meaning.[105] If the police failed to record the interview,[106] or to show it to the suspect for approval, and the suspect later disagrees with the officer's recollection of the record, this will effectively amount to an allegation that the police have fabricated or misrepresented the confession. The failure to record, coming after the confession was made, in itself may not be regarded as 'something said or done' within section 76(2)(b), but the alleged fabrication or doctoring of the confession would certainly qualify. Crucially, a failure to record deprives the prosecution of evidence that might be used to rebut the allegation. In practice, this may mean that the prosecutor may find it difficult to convince the trial judge that the burden of proof has been successfully discharged. In comparison, American judges must read the confession in the written records of police interviews and also formally endorse a plea-bargaining procedure, which is the procedure applied in the vast majority of the Anglo-American Criminal Justice System.[107]

99 [1991] Crim LR 49.

100 See the comments of Ralph Gibson LJ in *Halawa v Federation Against Copyright Theft* [1995] 1 Cr App R 21, 33.

101 [1991] Crim LR 128.

102 See discussion below.

103 PACE Code of Practice C [11.15]; see *R v Moss* (1990) 91 Cr App R 371.

104 *DPP v Blake* (1989) 89 Cr App R 179; *R v Cox* [1991] Crim LR 276. See also *R v Morse* [1991] Crim LR 195, in which the 'appropriate adult' himself was incompetent.

105 The requirement to tape-record interviews reduces the importance of the Code C requirement that written records of the interview be kept. That provision was directed at the pre-tape-recording era when the requirement was that the interview be recorded in writing, read to the suspect, and signed by them.

106 For example, *R v Waters* [1989] Crim LR 62; *Doolan* [1988] Crim LR 447.

107 Jedick, J., 'A Change in the Environment of Plea Bargaining: Using the Inspiration of Administration Procedural Safeguards like NEPA to Add Process Protections' (2014) *Washington University Law Review* 136.

Following an amendment to Code F introduced in June 2002,[108] many police interviews are now routinely video-recorded. This adds an additional protective dimension for the suspect and, indeed, for the police officers conducting the interview. It is not unusual for the defendant to allege that physical intimidation took place, and this could potentially be evidenced by recordings of shouting or screaming. Alternatively, such a recording might also help in exonerating the police by showing that the interview was conducted in conformity with PACE and the relevant Codes of Practice. The advent of video-recording means that the court will now have an opportunity to view the whole picture of what took place, which should – in theory at least – avoid words or noises on the audio-recording being taken out of context.

8.3.3.3 The method of questioning

The tape-recording or video-recording of interviews has meant that police officers must now take considerable care to ensure that the method of questioning does not fall foul of section 76. For this reason, cases that are likely to cross the oppression threshold of section 76(2)(a), such as *Paris, Abdullahi and Miller*, are now very rare in practice.

However, there is no doubt that the unreliability head under section 76(2)(b) clearly encompasses a much wider range of conduct. Such conduct may well lack the gravity of oppression, but it may still have an effect on the particular suspect that might induce an unreliable confession. Therefore, in practice, the defence will often plead both limbs of section 76. This may encourage a court to decide that even if section 76(2)(a) does not apply, the lower threshold of section 76(2)(b) might nonetheless be crossed. In *R v Beales*,[109] for example, the suspect was subjected to a course of aggressive and persistent questioning, which included a number of misrepresentations by the officer. Although this conduct was found to fall short of oppression, it was enough to suggest a state of confusion or hopelessness on the part of the suspect to such an extent that it might have resulted in an unreliable admission.

There remains some doubt about how far the parameters of section 76(2) extend; a key issue will often be the extent of the causal connection between the conduct in question and the circumstances in which the confession was made. In practice, this requires that the court look carefully at the circumstances of the detention, and take into account the characteristics of the particular suspect. If the judge, putting herself in the position of the suspect, decides that any confession made in those circumstances is likely to be unreliable, it is then for the prosecution to prove the converse beyond reasonable doubt.

Clearly, the method of questioning may produce an unreliable confession in that the suspect may speak for a variety of motives other than that of telling the truth. As some of the cases discussed have illustrated, the suspect may want to protect someone, may be keen to leave the police station and be prepared to say anything in the hope of retracting it later, may be suggestible and anxious to appease the interrogator, may be induced by threats or promises, or may become confused and mistakenly make an incriminating statement.

In *Fulling*, the Lord Chief Justice decided that the following definition of oppression, laid down in *R v Priestly*,[110] was insufficient for section 76(2)(a), but suggested that it may include the type of conduct for section 76(2)(b):

> [Q]uestioning which by its nature, duration or other attendant circumstances (including the fact of custody) excites hope (such as the hope of release) or fears, or so affects the mind

108 The most recent amendment came on 25 February 2022.
109 [1991] Crim LR 118.
110 (1965) 51 Cr App R 1.

> of the subject that his will crumbles and he speaks when otherwise he would have stayed silent.[111]

Of course, this definition places the court (and initially the prosecution) in a very difficult position in trying to fathom the defendant's motives for speaking. It is easier if the defendant falls within a group identified by PACE 1984 and the Code as vulnerable (e.g. juveniles, the mentally handicapped). Such persons may be suggestible or readily manipulated, with the consequence that certain styles of questioning are likely to produce unreliable confessions. In these types of cases, the prosecution can face an uphill task. Thus, in *R v Delaney*,[112] the interviewing officer had throughout suggested to the defendant that he really needed psychiatric help, and that if he owned up, people would help him. The officer played down the significance of the criminal offence and falsely aroused the defendant's hopes of treatment. As Lord Lane CJ put it, 'he might, by the same token, be encouraging a false confession.'[113] In less extreme circumstances, such as those present in *Harvey*, the evidence of psychiatrists or psychologists as to the likely effect of police conduct on the defendant could readily sow sufficient seeds to raise a reasonable doubt.

As regards non-vulnerable suspects, the court must consider all of the circumstances of the interrogation and what was said by the police, or any other relevant person. Such a person may include a parent, friend, or a co-accused; even a solicitor who suggests that the accused plead guilty in order to obtain a lesser sentence and could potentially fall within section 76(2)(b). In addition, the court should take into account the likely effect of what was said on the mind of the accused, taking into account their personal characteristics. However, the task of reconstructing the picture of what actually took place at the police station will not necessarily be a straightforward task, since the judge will be required to place herself in the suspect's shoes at the time of the interrogation. Few judges are likely to have gained personal experience of the pressures that a police interrogation might engender.[114]

Section 76(2)(b) may also be triggered where police tricks or misrepresentations are practised on the suspect in the course of questioning. The difficulty here, however, is that deceptions that suggest that there is conclusive evidence of guilt may lead to a reliable confession, rather than an unreliable one. For example, in *R v Blake*,[115] the confession was ruled out as unreliable after the defendant was falsely told that his voice had been recognised on a tape. However, this decision can be contrasted with *Mason*, in which the defendant was falsely told that his fingerprints had been found on a part of a bottle used as a petrol bomb. Here, section 76(2)(b) was not argued, presumably because in the circumstance the confession was, in fact, reliable. Instead, the defence invoked section 78 on the basis that the deceit practised on the solicitor led him to advise his client on the basis of false facts.

Brooks identifies the case of Amanda Knox[116] as highly illustrative of the problems faced by various defendants who have described their interrogations as resulting in distress, trauma, and their being implicitly coerced into confessing.[117] These feelings correlate with the contemporary research by Ofshe and Leo[118] which found that an innocent suspect is likely to experience considerable shock and disorientation during the interrogation process, given how wholly unprepared

---

111 *Fulling*, op. cit., n. 53, at 430. Cited with approval in *Prager* [1972] 1 All ER 1114.

112 (1989) 88 Cr App R 338.

113 Ibid., at 344.

114 See the observation of the Lord Chief Justice in *Rennie* (op. cit., n. 87); see also *Goldenberg* (op. cit., n. 82) and *Crampton* (op. cit., n. 83).

115 [1991] Crim LR 119.

116 Knox, A., *Waiting to Be Heard* (Harper Collins, 2013), 74.

117 See Brooks, J., *You Might Go to Prison, Even Though You're Innocent* (University of California Press, 2023).

118 Leo, R.A. and Ofshe, R.J., 'The Decision to Confess Falsely: Rational Choice and Irrational Actions' (1997) 74(4) *Denver University Law Review* 989.

for the confrontation and accusations they are during the process and not understanding how the investigator could possibly suspect them.[119] In America, one of the most famous instances of innocent incarceration showcasing this phenomena in practice is the case of the Fourbanks Four, which was successfully proven to be a false confession by Bill Oberly and his team at the Alaska Innocence Project.[120]

Steven Drizin,[121] co-founder of the Center on Wrongful Convictions, has published contemporary commentary distinguishing interviews from interrogations. He argues that the goal of interviewing is to obtain the truth through non-accusatorial, open-ended questioning to find the 'truth' of the matter in the early stages of the criminal investigation, whereas interrogations are techniques elicited by the police force with a purpose trained to interrogate only suspects whom they already suspect are guilty.[122]

8.3.4 Facts discovered subsequent to an excluded confession

Section 76(4)–(6) deals with the conundrum that arises in relation to evidence discovered as a consequence of an excluded confession.[123]

Example 8.2

Beverly has been charged with theft. Under questioning, she is subjected to a hostile and aggressive interrogation, and there is also evidence to suggest that she was threatened with physical violence if she failed to confess. She eventually does so, and tells the police where they can find a quantity of designer handbags that she had stolen. Although her confession is subsequently excluded at the *voir dire*, police have uncovered the handbags exactly where Beverly had told them they would be. Can the prosecution (a) produce the goods at Beverly's trial, and (b) link their discovery to what she has told the police? The Criminal Law Revision Committee had unanimously recommended an affirmative answer to (a) and, by a majority, to (b).[124] However, the 1984 Act opted for a halfway house. On the one hand, the prosecution can use in evidence 'any facts discovered as a result of the confession' even if the confession is itself inadmissible.[125] On the other hand, proof that those facts were discovered as a result of a wholly or partly inadmissible confession is not admissible, unless the accused themself gives evidence that they were so discovered.[126]

The policy underlying this rule is that it is unfair for the inadmissibility of a confession to be negated by the admissibility of the 'fruits of the crime,' unless the accused so chooses. Such an approach seems wholly justifiable where confessions are obtained by oppression. However, it appears somewhat illogical where a finding of unreliability is involved. In the above scenario, the discovery of the stolen goods at the place where she said they would be seems to indicate that the confession was reliable in the first

119 See also Nirider, L., '13 Years After Disproven Confessions, Dassay Must Be Freed,' *OnMilwaukee* (2 May 2020).

120 McDaniel, M., 'False Confessions and the Lessons of the Fairbanks Four,' *Anchorage Daily News* (3 January 2016).

121 Drizin, S.A. and Leo, R.A., 'The Problem of False Confessions in the Post-DNA World,' *North Carolina Law Review* (May 2008).

122 Akehurst, L. et al., 'Lay Persons and Police Officers Beliefs Regarding Deceptive Behaviours,' (1996) 10(6) *Applied Cognitive Psychology*.

123 It should be highlighted that the principles contained in subss (4) and (5) are applicable only to a confession excluded under s 76. There is no equivalent provision in s 78.

124 Criminal Law Revision Committee, *Eleventh Report, Evidence (General)*, Cmnd 4999 (HMSO, 1972).

125 PACE 1984, s 76(4)(a).

126 Ibid., s 76(5)–(6). This places the old common law rule in *R v Berriman* (1854) 6 Cox CC 388 upon a statutory footing.

instance. Nonetheless, the law states that the prosecution can produce the stolen goods at trial, but cannot show that they were discovered as a result of the defendant's confession. The difficulty thus arises for the prosecution when a link to the defendant can be established only by specific reference to the confession. So, for example, if Beverly had told the police that they were concealed in a ditch on a country lane, it may be impossible to connect the goods to her in any way. If, however, such stolen goods could be linked to her without the aid of the confession (e.g. they were found on her premises, or there was forensic evidence connecting her to the goods), there is no difficulty for the prosecution given that no reference to the confession need be made.

It should also be underlined that where only a part of a confession is excluded, evidence found as a result of the admissible part may still be admissible.[127] It is perfectly possible, for example, for the court to exclude only one interview if the suspect has confessed on a number of different occasions. Moreover, those parts of a confession that are relevant as showing that the accused 'speaks, writes or expresses himself in a particular way' are still admissible for that purpose.[128] The object of this exception is illustrated by *R v Voisin*,[129] in which the body of a murder victim had been found alongside a piece of paper bearing the words 'Bladie Belgiam.' The accused was asked by the police to write the words 'Bloody Belgian' and he happily wrote 'Bladie Belgiam.' This evidence was held to be admissible, and would now be admissible under section 76(4)(b), even if the confession itself were to fall within section 76(2)(a) or (b).

This rule was applied in the unreported case of *R v Nottle*.[130] Here, the defendant had been charged with criminal damage to a vehicle. It was alleged that he scratched an obscene message on to the paintwork, referring to the owner of the car, whose name was 'Justin,' as 'Jutin.' The suspect was then asked by the police to write the same phrase, which he did, and wrote 'Jutin' instead of 'Justin.' In this particular case, this was held to constitute a confession that was not found to be unreliable. However, had there been some incidence of oppression or something said or done to make that statement unreliable, the prosecution would still be able to use a sample of handwriting in evidence to identify the characteristics mentioned in section 76(4)(b). Similarly, where the defendant is charged with kidnapping and the victim states that the kidnapper spoke

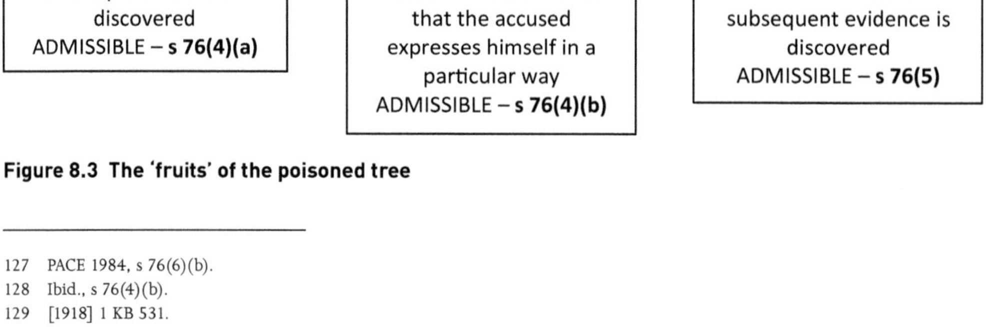

Figure 8.3 The 'fruits' of the poisoned tree

127 PACE 1984, s 76(6)(b).
128 Ibid., s 76(4)(b).
129 [1918] 1 KB 531.
130 [2004] EWCA Crim 599.

with a local accent and stammered, the non-incriminating parts of the defendant's excluded tape-recorded confession can be used for voice comparison.[131]

8.3.5 Confessions by the 'mentally handicapped'

Section 77 of PACE 1984 provides:

> Where at such a trial (on indictment) –
>
> (a) the case against the accused depends wholly or substantially on a confession made by him; and
> (b) the court is satisfied;
>
> (i) that he is mentally handicapped; and
> (ii) that the confession was not made in the presence of an independent person,

the court shall warn the jury that there is a special need for caution before convicting the accused in reliance on that confession.

In addition, Code C provides that no interview with a juvenile, 'mentally disordered,' or 'mentally handicapped' person should take place unless an 'appropriate adult' is present.[132] In respect of juveniles, the appropriate adult may be a parent, friend, or anyone else deemed appropriate. However, in other cases, the appropriate adult referred to in section 77 must be independent of the person by whom the confession is made. Thus, they may not be a friend or relative; the 'independent person' must be entirely non-aligned with the police, the solicitor, and the mentally disordered/handicapped suspect.[133]

The function of the appropriate person is to advise the vulnerable suspect, to see whether or not the interview is being conducted fairly and properly, and to facilitate communication between the suspect and police.[134] On that basis, any confession made in the absence of an independent person is likely to fall foul of section 76(2)(b) and should be excluded as unreliable. Therefore, section 77 should apply only in exceptional circumstances. For example, in *R v Moss*,[135] a 'mentally disordered' person was interviewed nine times over a long period before confessing. The trial judge admitted the confession and gave a section 77 warning, but the Court of Appeal thought that it should have been automatically excluded under section 76(2)(b).

The court further suggested that the section was directed at two types of case: first, those in which the interview had been in the emergency circumstances envisaged in paragraph 11.1 of Code C; and second, those in which the interview was in breach of the Code requirements, but consisted of no more than one interview, conducted over a short period of time. The second set of circumstances envisaged by the court may be doubted, as there is no reason why an appropriate adult should not be in attendance, however short the interview. It is sometimes difficult for the police to determine that a suspect suffers from a condition that could trigger the additional protections in section 77, but the test is objective. It does not matter what the police think (if indeed they give the issue any thought); what is important is any information that has subsequently been ascertained from medical experts.[136]

---

131 See *R v Robb* (1991) 93 Cr App R 161. See further *R v Deenick* [1992] Crim LR 578 for the admissibility of voice recognition evidence by a non-expert such as a police or customs officer.

132 PACE Code of Practice C [11.15].

133 *R v Bailey* [1995] Crim LR 723.

134 PACE Code of Practice C [11.16].

135 (1990) 91 Cr App R 371.

136 See *Everett*, op. cit., n. 89.

In *R v McKenzie*,[137] a defendant with a personality disorder was convicted of two offences of manslaughter and two of arson. The prosecution case on the manslaughter charge depended almost entirely on his unsupported confession, while the arson charges were supported by other evidence. Quashing the convictions for manslaughter, the Court of Appeal held that where the defendant suffers from a 'significant degree' of mental illness and the case against him depends wholly upon confessions that are 'unconvincing to the point where a jury properly directed could not convict upon them,' then the trial judge (assuming that they have not already excluded the confessions) should withdraw the case from the jury. In this case, the confessions were particularly unconvincing since they lacked the incriminating details that would have made them reliable, and because the defendant had confessed to 12 other killings that no one believed he had committed. There was also the possibility that the defendant had confessed to ensure that he stayed in the secure hospital where he was detained.[138]

In *R v Law-Thompson*,[139] the suspect suffered from Asperger's syndrome, which is characterised by marked obsessiveness, extreme rigidity of thought, and strict adherence to rules and rituals. One manifestation in this particular case was that the suspect thought his mother was evil. One morning he attacked his mother with a meat cleaver, shouting: 'I'm going to kill you!' He was restrained and the police were called. On being asked what the cleaver was for, the accused replied: 'It's my duty to kill her.' On being arrested and cautioned, he then told the police: 'I won't harm you. I only intend to kill my mother.' At the police station, a psychiatrist found him fit to be interviewed, and the police had arranged for an appropriate adult to be present. However, a social worker advised that it was not necessary, and consequently the suspect was then interviewed in the presence of a solicitor, but without an appropriate adult. In the interview, he again made it clear that his intention had been to kill his mother and he would try again given the opportunity.

At trial, the remark made to the police before caution was excluded, although the interview itself was admissible. A psychiatrist stated that, although the defendant had a personality disorder, he was not mentally ill. He understood the nature and quality of his actions, but did not comprehend that they were wrong. However, the defendant refused to plead insanity and was duly convicted of attempted murder. He then appealed, one ground being the absence of an appropriate adult (independent person) at the interview, which, according to the defence, rendered the interview inadmissible.

Dismissing the appeal, the Court of Appeal held that it was not easy to apply section 76(2) to these facts, since there was nothing to suggest that the confession was obtained *in consequence* of the absence of an appropriate adult, or that such absence rendered the confession unreliable. The focus was then on section 78, which gave the judge a discretion to exclude that was at least as wide as that at common law. In support of exclusion, defence counsel argued that the prosecution was in breach of Article 6 of the European Convention on Human Rights. While accepting that the trial judge would have been entitled to consider Article 6 had his attention been drawn to it, the court said that his focus had to be on section 76 and section 78. Even if there had been a breach of Article 6, it did not lead to the conclusion that evidence thus obtained must be excluded. Section 77 was not argued in this case, presumably because the case did not depend wholly or substantially on his confession. Had the case for exclusion been argued, it would have been highly improbable that the prosecution would have proceeded relying solely on a confession obtained in the circumstances envisaged by section 77.[140]

---

137 (1993) 92 Cr App R 369.

138 See also *Wood*, op. cit., n. 75.

139 [1997] Crim LR 674.

140 See also *R v Campbell* [1995] 1 Cr App R 522; *R v Scott (John Kevin Joseph)* [2010] EWCA Crim 3212.

8.3.6 Section 78: discretionary exclusion

Section 78 of PACE provides for any evidence to be excluded if it appears to the court that, 'having regard to all the circumstances, including the circumstances in which the evidence was obtained, the admission of the evidence would have such an adverse effect on the fairness of the proceedings that the court ought not to admit it.'

Although the provision is sometimes simply labelled as 'unfairness' as a form of academic shorthand, the section actually requires more than showing this. Establishing some adverse effect to the accused will not be enough; the word 'such' imports a degree of adverse effect over and above the baseline of 'adverse effect.' As Spencer argues, a fair trial does not mean a trial that is free from all possible detriment or disadvantage to the accused.[141] Thus, in exercising its discretion under section 78, the question of whether a particular method or technique used to gather evidence will amount to unfairness should always be considered by the judge as a matter of extent and degree.[142]

It should be noted, however, that, unlike the exclusionary rules contained in section 76(2), the concept of burden of proof has no part to play under section 78. In *R (Saifi) v Governor of Brixton Prison*,[143] the Divisional Court noted that the situation in which a judge is considering whether or not to exercise his discretion under the section is distinct from any other decision-making process related to the trial proper. The judge must be satisfied, after hearing evidence from both sides, that a decision to admit the evidence would have such an adverse effect on the fairness of the trial that it ought not to be admitted. The decision to exclude is thus a question to be determined by the court and does not require 'proof' by either side, although the defence should normally first present an argument that the evidence ought not to be admitted.[144]

Although this provision confers a discretion on the court, it does not impose a duty. Since section 78 took effect, trial judges at first instance have traditionally enjoyed a considerable degree of latitude in determining in what circumstances evidence should be excluded. Provided that the judge interprets the 1984 Act and the Codes correctly, and professes to consider all of the circumstances of the case, they will be the final arbiter as to when the evidence in question should be excluded. The prospects of a successful appeal on the grounds that the discretion was improperly exercised are slight.[145] In *R v Dures and others*,[146] the trial judge's refusal to exclude evidence of interviews held in the cell, which were neither contemporaneously recorded nor confirmed and signed by the second appellant, was upheld on the basis that it was not a decision that no reasonable judge could have reached. The standard is thus, effectively, that of *Wednesbury* unreasonableness.[147]

The broad nature of the discretion also means that it should not be fettered by the erection of rules, since each decision rests on its own particular facts.[148] If an appellate court concludes that the discretion has been wrongly exercised (or not exercised at all), it may be able to put itself in the position of the trial judge and consider if or how the discretion should have been exercised.[149] Nonetheless, the general unwillingness of the appellate courts to uphold appeals based on section

141 Spencer, J.R., 'Orality and the Evidence of Absent Witnesses' [1994] Crim LR 628.

142 Most cases under s 78 involve confessions made to the police, but this is not essential. Section 78 can be used to exclude a confession made to others (e.g. a doctor, as in *R v McDonald* [1991] Crim LR 144, or a probation officer, as in *R v Ellaray* [2003] 2 Cr App R 11).

143 [2000] 1 WLR 1134.

144 *R v Raphaie* [1996] Crim LR 812.

145 *R v O'Leary* (1988) 87 Cr App R 387.

146 [1997] 2 Cr App R 247.

147 As outlined by Lord Taylor CJ in *R v Quinn* [1995] 1 Cr App R 480, 487: 'Before this Court could reach the conclusion that the judge was wrong [to exercise his discretion under s 78 as he did] we would have to be satisfied that no reasonable judge, having heard the evidence that this learned judge did, could have reached the conclusion that he did.'

148 *R v Canale* [1990] 2 All ER 187; *R v Gillard and Barrett* [1991] Crim LR 280.

149 *R v Mason* [1987] 3 All ER 481.

78 has not held defence counsel back from using it as a ground of appeal across a wide range of circumstances, albeit with varying degrees of success.

The terse terms of section 78 give little help as to the proper interpretation of the section, and the courts have displayed a range of approaches. Three general points can be made. First, the section is to be construed widely.[150] Second, the test is fairness of the proceedings, not fairness to the defence. In other words, fairness to the prosecution and to the court (that it be able to hear all of the relevant evidence) must also be considered.[151] Third, as Auld J remarked in *R v Jelen and Katz*:[152]

> The circumstances of each case are almost always different, and judges may well take different views in the proper exercise of their discretion even where the circumstances are similar. This is not an apt field for hard case law and well-founded distinctions between cases.[153]

In *R v Oliphant*,[154] the Court of Appeal further emphasised the need to consider the facts of each case against the statutory language of PACE 1984 when it stated *per curiam*: 'It is important, in deciding admissibility of evidence under PACE, not to be diverted by other decisions of the court, often on different facts, from considering the statutory language.'[155]

8.3.6.1 Section 78 and confession evidence

It was initially thought that, in light of the relatively stringent exclusionary requirement contained in section 76(2), section 78 might not apply to confessions. This was not, however, a view that was shared by the courts, and as such it is difficult to draw a neat dividing line between case law that is strictly relevant to confession evidence and that which is relevant to the application of section 78 in respect of more general issues arising from improper police conduct. In the discussion that follows, we aim to highlight some of the key features of the provision insofar as it may apply to confession evidence.[156]

One of the first cases in which the Court of Appeal applied section 78 to confession evidence was that of *Mason*. The court made it clear that the word 'evidence' in section 78 included a confession, and held that the trial judge had wrongly exercised his discretion under section 78 by failing to take account of the deceit practised on the appellant and his solicitor. Despite failing to explain *how* that deceit had an adverse effect on the fairness of the trial, the court made it clear that the conviction should nonetheless be quashed:

> It is obvious from the undisputed evidence that the police practised a deceit not only on the appellant, which is bad enough, but also on his solicitor, whose duty it was to advise him. In effect, they hoodwinked both solicitor and client. That was a most reprehensible thing to do. It is not however because we regard as misbehaviour of a serious kind conduct of that nature that we have come to the decision soon to be made plain. This is not the place to discipline the police. That has been made clear here on a number of previous occasions. We are concerned with the application of the proper law. The law is, as I have already said,

---

150 *R v Keenan* [1990] 2 QB 54.

151 *DPP v Marshall* [1988] 3 All ER 683; *R v Quinn* [1990] Crim LR 581.

152 (1990) 90 Cr App R 456.

153 Ibid., 465. Approved in *R v Roberts* [1997] 1 Cr App R 217.

154 [1992] Crim LR 40.

155 Ibid.

156 However, this discussion should not be read in isolation from that which follows in the next chapter (i.e. in respect of other forms of improperly obtained evidence). In order to understand the full context of how s 78 operates in practice, it is vital that both aspects of this discussion are taken into account.

> that a trial judge has a discretion to be exercised of course upon right principles to reject admissible evidence in the interests of a defendant having a fair trial. The judge in the present case appreciated that ... So the only question to be answered by this Court is whether, having regard to the way the police behaved, the judge exercised that discretion correctly. In our judgment he did not.[157]

Although one may take issue with the court's view that it had no role to play in disciplining the police,[158] the use of section 78 can be justified in these circumstances on the basis that the provision of false information led the defendant's solicitor to misadvise him. This effectively amounted to a denial of the defendant's fundamental right to legal advice based on the true facts.

8.3.6.2 Improper denial of access to legal advice

The case law on section 78 abounds with many examples of improper denial of access to legal advice. Section 58 of PACE confers all suspects with the right to consult a solicitor in the police station, both before and during the interview. This right was significantly bolstered by the decision of the Court of Appeal in *R v Samuel*,[159] in which the accused had been charged with burglary. At first, the suspect denied any involvement. He was then interviewed again and denied access to a solicitor. On this occasion, he confessed to robbery. The Court of Appeal held that refusal of access to a solicitor after the first charge constituted a breach of section 58 of PACE. Noting that it was 'one of the most important and fundamental rights of the citizen,' it was held that the judge should have at least considered the question as to whether the confession ought to be excluded under section 78. Since he had failed to do so, the conviction for robbery was unsafe and was quashed. It is, however, somewhat lamentable that the Court of Appeal chose to ignore entirely the question of reliability of the confession, turning immediately to section 78 and ignoring section 76(2)(b). As suggested in the previous section, the courts have largely continued this approach, with the result that refusing access to a solicitor is seldom considered to lead to unreliability where the suspect is an adult and not vulnerable for any reason.

The decisions in both *Mason* and *Samuel* serve to emphasise that denial of legal advice per se is not enough; it must also be shown that the denial produced an adverse effect. To some extent, the complexity of the offence under investigation may increase the need for legal advice and exacerbate the potential adverse effect stemming from its improper denial.[160] However, much will depend upon the individual character and experiences of the accused. This latter point was addressed in *Alladice*,[161] in which the confession was admitted, notwithstanding the wrongful denial of access to a solicitor. The Court of Appeal noted that the defendant, having been regularly accustomed to police interviews, was already aware of his rights. Therefore, the solicitor's presence would not have made a difference, and there was no unfairness to the proceedings. Similarly, in *R v Chahal*,[162] the defendant said that he did not want a solicitor and later confirmed this. However, unknown to Chahal, his family had instructed a solicitor who attended, but was refused access by the police on the grounds that the defendant did not want a solicitor. His appeal against conviction was dismissed. The defendant was a capable and mature businessman, who knew the consequences of his initial decision to refuse legal advice. As such, he had suffered no prejudice.

---

157 *Mason*, op. cit., n. 149 at 484.

158 For further discussion, see Ch 9.

159 [1988] QB 615.

160 See *R v Guest* (unreported, 20 January 1988) and *Salduz v Turkey* [2008] ECHR 1542. In *Salduz*, the Grand Chamber of the European Court of Human Rights concluded that for Article 6 to be 'practical and effective,' Member States must allow a suspect access to a lawyer at the initial stage of police interrogation, no matter how serious the charge.

161 (1988) 87 Cr App R 380.

162 [1992] Crim LR 124.

As *Alladice* and *Chahal* illustrate, suspects who are familiar with the criminal justice system, or those who are considered capable of handling police interrogation effectively themselves, will not generally be prejudiced to any great extent by the absence of a legal representative.[163]

However, the courts have tended to take a much dimmer view of the improper denial of legal advice to vulnerable suspects. In *R v Franklin*,[164] the defendant, a young unemployed man, initially said that he did not want a solicitor. Ten minutes later, he asked that his father be informed of his arrest, so that he could obtain a solicitor for him. However, the suspect nonetheless agreed to be interviewed without a solicitor present, and made admissions. In the meantime, the defendant's father had instructed a solicitor, who attended at the police station, but was told that the defendant would not be informed because he did not want legal advice.[165] Two further interviews followed at which the defendant was reminded of his right to legal advice, but was not told that a solicitor had attended. The trial judge admitted the evidence of all four interviews, believing he was bound by *Chahal*.

The Court of Appeal disagreed, and noted that there were significant differences between the two cases. In *Chahal*, the solicitor had merely telephoned, and, furthermore, the suspect was a mature businessman. In this case, the solicitor actually attended and the defendant was a young unemployed man who had never been in a police station before. The trial judge had therefore exercised his discretion wrongly. However, the case against the defendant was overwhelming, and notwithstanding the error, the appeal was dismissed.[166] Similarly, in *R v Sanusi*,[167] it was held that a confession made by a foreign suspect with no understanding of the English legal system should have been excluded under section 78, because he was wrongly denied access to a solicitor. Arguably, however, the absence of a solicitor in both *Franklin* and *Sanusi* may well have produced *unreliable* confessions, which should, accordingly, have been dealt with under section 76(2)(b) as opposed to section 78.[168] These decisions again highlight the judicial tendency to ignore section 76 altogether, which means that, in practice, judges are exercising a discretion to exclude evidence that should really be automatically inadmissible.

The potential for inferences to be drawn from silence under the Criminal Justice and Public Order Act 1994 also increases the need for legal advice in the police station, and increases the likelihood of an adverse effect to result from its improper denial. Even the Alladices of this world may not fully appreciate the potential effect of remaining silent under police interrogation. As noted in Chapter 4, the Youth Justice and Criminal Evidence Act 1999 has amended the Criminal Justice and Public Order Act 1994 so that inferences cannot be drawn under those sections unless the defendant has had access to a solicitor.[169] This statutory intervention, together with the decisions in *Samuel* and *Salduz*, means that any decision to deny a suspect immediate access to a solicitor will only be lawful in the most exceptional of circumstances. This laid the foundations for the

163 See also *R v Dunford* (1990) 91 Cr App Rep 150, in which the improper denial of legal advice was balanced by the defendant's knowledge of his rights and his ability to cope on his own.

164 *The Times* (16 June 1994).

165 See now PACE Code of Practice C [6.15], which requires that the defendant be informed that the solicitor has attended.

166 Other cases in which denial of access to legal advice led to exclusion of the confession include: *R v Vernon* [1988] Crim LR 445, in which the defendant was not told of the duty solicitor scheme or that a solicitor was on the way; *R v Absolam* [1989] Cr App R 332, in which the defendant was not told of his right to legal advice and proceeded to make damaging admissions; *R v Beycan* [1990] Crim LR 185, in which D was wrongfully denied a solicitor, being told 'we usually interview without a solicitor' (this decision seems particularly unfair since the suspect was a foreigner with poor English and therefore vulnerable).

167 [1992] Crim LR 43.

168 See also *R v Beycan* [1990] Crim LR 185.

169 YJCEA 1999, s 58. See further Ch 9.

decision in *Cadder v HM Advocate*,[170] which was a devolution appeal from Scotland.[171] In Scotland, a suspect has no right of access to a lawyer, although the police often allow it.[172] In *Cadder*, at no time was there legal advice given, although there was an offer that a solicitor could be informed of his detention. Cadder appealed on the basis that there was a breach of Article 6(1) and (3)(c) of the European Convention on Human Rights in that he had not been given the opportunity to obtain legal advice. The Supreme Court unanimously allowed the appeal in this case. Dennis argues that *Cadder* will 'have a clear impact on English law' and that it must now be the case that where a suspect makes a confession after requesting legal advice but fails to obtain it, the fair trial jurisprudence as interpreted in *Cadder* will require the judge to exclude the confession under section 78 of PACE except in the most compelling circumstances. As Dennis further observes, the message for any police officers tempted to use ploys to discourage requests or delay consultations until after the interview is unmistakable.[173]

8.3.6.3 Other breaches of PACE

In relation to other violations of PACE or the Codes of Practice, each case will turn on its own particular facts, with particular emphasis being placed on the nature and extent of the breach. If the procedure is regarded by the court as an important one, it does not matter whether lack of adherence to it was wilful or inadvertent; the degree of adverse effect on the proceedings is the key issue that the court will need to determine.[174]

The case of *R v Canale*[175] offers some guidance as to when a failure to record interviews at the police station might give rise to exclusion. Here, the defendant was suspected of assisting in a robbery. He allegedly confessed in two interviews, although no recording of these confessions was made, nor was any reason given for a failure to record. In two subsequent interviews, the defendant repeated the admissions, which were then contemporaneously recorded. At trial, the judge admitted the evidence of the four interviews. D appealed, contending that the first two interviews should not have been admitted since he had been tricked and induced into making the confessions. Allowing his appeal and quashing his conviction, the Court of Appeal stated that the lack of a contemporaneous note of the initial interviews meant that the judge was deprived in the *voir dire* of the very evidence that enabled him to decide whether the admissions were admissible. The contemporaneous notes of the subsequent interviews did not cure the initial breaches of Code C, since their admissibility depended on whether the admissions on the unrecorded interviews were properly obtained. Importantly, it was also noted that since the police officers had flagrantly and deliberately breached Code C, the judge should have exercised his discretion to exclude the evidence.

By contrast, in *R v Dunn*,[176] the accused was charged with aggravated burglary. Following an interview in a police station, there was a conversation during the signing of the interview notes, and in the presence of the solicitor's clerk, when D allegedly confessed to the offence. The conversation was not recorded contemporaneously and no note of it was ever shown to the appellant.

---

170 [2010] UKSC 43. This case was in effect an appeal against a decision of the High Court of Justiciary (*HM Advocate v McLean* (2010) SLT 873). This appeal came about despite the ruling in *Salduz*, op. cit., n. 160. *Salduz* has been repeatedly followed by the European Court of Human Rights. This applies even to countries that were in the same legal position as Scotland before the ruling: the Netherlands, France, Belgium, and Ireland.

171 This appeal was under the terms of the Criminal Procedure (Scotland) Act 1995.

172 The Thomson Committee feared this would hinder criminal investigations: *Criminal Procedure in Scotland: Second Report*, Cmnd 6218 (HMSO, 1975).

173 Dennis, I., 'Legal Advice in Police Stations: 25 Years On' [2011] Crim LR 1. See also a very different outcome in the Canadian case of *R v Sinclair* (2010) SCC 35.

174 *R v Kerawalla* [1991] Crim LR 252. See Ch 9.

175 [1990] 2 All ER 187.

176 (1990) 91 Cr App R 237.

The defendant and the solicitor's clerk denied that any such conversation took place. Dismissing the appeal, the Court of Appeal held that although there were clear breaches of Code C, this was counterbalanced by the presence of the defendant's legal adviser during the interview. Similarly, in *R v Matthews*,[177] the defendant's alleged admissions were noted after the interview ended, but the note was not subsequently shown to her. Here, the Court of Appeal accepted that there had been a clear breach of the Code C, but did not disturb the trial judge's refusal to use section 78, apparently on the basis that he had considered all of the circumstances and his discretion could not be challenged.[178]

Since the advent of tape- and video-recording of interviews under Code E, the failure to record interviews in police stations is rare, with much of the relevant case law pre-dating PACE. Nowadays, any failure to record will usually relate to statements made outside the interview room. In *R v Maloney and Doherty*,[179] interviews outside and inside the station were not contemporaneously recorded, notes of the interviews were not shown to the suspects, and, although they could not read, no lawyer or third party was made available to assist them. It was held that these interviews should have been excluded. In *RSPCA v Eager*,[180] the accused was interviewed in her home by RSPCA inspectors, who drew up their record of the interview in their car at a later point in time, giving her no opportunity to verify it. Again, the court held that this should have been ruled out. By contrast, in *R v Courtney*,[181] customs officers intercepted parcels of herbal cannabis and one posed as a postman to deliver them to the defendant's address. A note of the defendant's comments on the doorstep was made, but was not shown to the defendant. In this instance, the breach was not significant or substantial, and the note was admitted.

Exclusion under section 78 is more likely if the breach is flagrant,[182] or wilful,[183] or in bad faith.[184] Ultimately, however, the key question for the trial judge is when the breach is so substantial that it interferes with the fairness of proceedings. In the case of *Walsh*,[185] the denial of legal advice, omitting to note the reason for not recording an interview contemporaneously, and failure to show the defendant the record of interview were regarded as significant and substantial breaches that were not cured by good faith. This case has become a standard reference point for cases involving breach of PACE 1984 and the Codes, particularly those involving wrongful exclusion of a solicitor but, as Woolf LJ pointed out in *Oliphant*, the words 'significant' and 'substantial' are not terms of art, but are simply offered as guides to ruling out of consideration those merely technical breaches that have no adverse consequences. In *R v Quinn*,[186] it was further suggested that any act that was deliberate would automatically render proceedings unfair. Since this particular case concerned the inadvertent breaches of Code C on the conduct of an identity parade, it was held that the judge had been correct not to exclude the evidence. However, as Mark George QC points out, the modern practice of the appellate courts increasingly seems to brush over procedural defects in a prosecution so as to avoid having to quash the conviction of an apparently guilty person because of a 'mere' procedural hiccup. On that basis, the decision in *Charles v DPP*,[187]

177 [1990] Crim LR 190.

178 See also *Gill* [2004] 1 WLR 469.

179 [1988] Crim LR 523.

180 [1995] Crim LR 59.

181 [1995] Crim LR 63.

182 In *R v Canale* [1990] 2 All ER 187, the Lord Chief Justice found a cynical disregard for the rules governing the contemporaneous recording of interviews.

183 *R v Nagah* (1991) 92 Cr App R 344, in which, although the defendant agreed to an identification parade, he was released so that a street identification could more easily be made.

184 See the remarks by Lord Lane CJ in *R v Alladice* (1988) 87 Cr App R 380, that a court might find it easier to employ s 78 if bad faith on the part of the police is proved.

185 (1990) 91 Cr App R 161.

186 [1990] Crim LR 581.

187 [2010] RTR 402 DC; [2009] EWHC 3521.

in which the court found two breaches of Code C to have occurred,[188] is to be welcomed. When questioned about having been driving with excess alcohol, the defendant made admissions that he had been driving. The court held that the admission should have been excluded under section 78 of PACE on account of the two breaches of the Code, saying: 'The provisions of the 1984 Act and Code C are important protections that impose significant disciplines upon the police as to how they are to behave.'[189]

The presence of other evidence against the defendant should not affect the decision regarding unfairness.[190] However, where there is enough other evidence to convict the defendant, the court might be more easily persuaded to exclude the peripheral and disputed evidence while still allowing the rest to go before the jury.[191] By contrast, the absence of other evidence, apart from the disputed area, could be crucial to the fairness of the trial. For example, in *R v Cochrane*,[192] the interviews were the only evidence against the defendant and, since section 58 had been transgressed, it would have been unfair to use them. A further problem is that such other evidence that does exist may even be linked to and tainted by the improper conduct. In *Beycan*,[193] it was held that, once admissions at the station had been excluded under section 78, it was unfair to admit statements made in the car en route there. Indeed, as with section 76, an earlier improper interview may affect a subsequent one conducted properly to such an extent that the exclusion of all of the interview evidence is warranted. As in *Canale*, this may be because the impropriety still influences the later interview, or because the court is determined not to let the police flagrantly flout the rules and then attempt to offset the previous impropriety by conforming to the rules on subsequent occasions.[194]

8.3.6.4 Section 78 and the right to silence

One of the seminal cases concerning breach of the Codes of Practice is that of *Keenan*,[195] in which the defendant was charged with possessing an offensive weapon. He challenged the admissibility of statements made in the course of interviews with the police, alleging that no proper record had been kept in contravention of paragraphs 11 and 12 of the Code of Practice. Although the trial judge acknowledged that the police had breached the Code, he refused to rule the evidence out, and said that the defendant could counteract the effect of the breaches by testifying himself in court. Having opted to exercise his right to silence, the accused was convicted and appealed. Quashing the conviction, the Court of Appeal held that the function of Codes of Practice was to provide safeguards against the police inaccurately recording or inventing words, and to make it difficult for unfounded allegations to be made against the police. It was stressed that, as in the instant case, where there had been 'significant and substantial' breaches of these provisions, evidence should 'frequently' be excluded.[196] Furthermore, it was stressed that it could not be

---

188 The first was that the defendant was interviewed after being informed that he was to be charged with an offence of being in charge while unfit, where there was no 'specified purpose' under Code C [16.5]. The second was that he was then erroneously cautioned in terms of C [10.5] rather than C [16.5]. (He was informed that a failure to answer might harm his defence, rather than simply that he was entitled to remain silent.)

189 Garden Court Chambers, *Criminal Law Update*, Issue 28 (25 January 2011).

190 That aspect is the preserve of s 2(1) of the Criminal Appeals Act 1968, the proviso to which can counterbalance any refusal to exclude evidence under s 78: see further *Walsh*, op. cit., n. 185.

191 See *Waters*, op. cit., n. 106; *Keenan*, op. cit., n. 150.

192 [1988] Crim LR 449.

193 [1990] Crim LR 185.

194 See *Canale* [1990] 2 All ER 187. However, the court, in exercising its discretion, may find that the later interview is not so tainted and can simply refuse to exercise its discretion to exclude. See *R v Gillard and Barrett* (1991) 92 Cr App R 61. The distinction between this case and *Canale* is narrow and seems to depend on the degree of flagrancy of the misconduct.

195 [1990] 2 QB 54.

196 Ibid., at 69.

assumed that any unfairness to the defendant could be remedied by his testimony at court, since the defendant was entitled to rely on his right to silence. The evidence should therefore have been excluded.

In *R v Roberts*,[197] the accused was arrested on suspicion of robbery of a building society and two banks. Roberts was interviewed over a number of days and, although he remained silent, was nevertheless charged with two of the robberies. C was arrested on suspicion of involvement in one of the robberies with Roberts. He was also interviewed a number of times and implicated himself in a number of offences, including conspiracy to rob, supplying drugs, large-scale shop-lifting, and escaping from police custody, but he denied involvement in the robbery for which he had been arrested.

When visited by a police officer in his cell, and without prompting, C asked to move in with Roberts in order to persuade him to admit the robbery. This, he said, would clear him of any involvement. A note was made of this conversation, but, in breach of Code C, it was not read to or signed by C. Both men were duly placed in a cell together, and a listening device was covertly installed. In a recorded conversation, C was heard pressing Roberts to clear him of the robbery, and Roberts also admitted participating in two further robberies after being questioned about them by C. Evidence of the conversations was admitted at his trial and Roberts was convicted of all of the offences to which he had admitted in the recorded conversation.

On appeal, Roberts claimed that there had been a material irregularity in the trial insofar as the judge had wrongly permitted the prosecution to adduce evidence of the covert tape-recordings of the conversation in the police cell where C, a police stooge, was placed to obtain admissions from Roberts in breach of the Code of Practice. No solicitor was present and he alleged that he had been deceived into believing his conversation to be in private. However, dismissing the appeal, the Court of Appeal held that it was not part of the purpose of the Code of Practice to protect an accused in relation to breaches of the Code in respect of another suspect. Accordingly, since there had been no causal link between the breaches of the Code and the appellant's subsequent spontaneous admissions, the judge was right to regard those breaches as insignificant in relation to the appellant. Furthermore, each case of this kind was to be decided on its own facts and it was inappropriate to draw a distinction between mere eavesdropping and putting a person in the cell with the suspect. The true test was whether the conduct of the police, either wittingly or unwittingly, led to unfairness or injustice, and in the instant case the trial judge's application of this test could not be faulted.

Unfortunately, the precise basis on which discretion is exercised is not always so clearly articulated. Indeed, sometimes the courts, despite what was said in *Walsh*, proceed almost automatically to apply section 78 where improprieties have been established, without first considering the statutory language.[198] Thus, it is difficult to elicit any overriding principles. The best that can be done is to survey the existing cases and try to gauge the types of factors that are likely to warrant exclusion and those that are not. Clearly, some forms of breaches are more likely to result in exclusion than others.

8.4 Admissions in civil proceedings

The preceding content in this chapter has dealt solely with the law relating to confessions in criminal proceedings. The reason for this is that in civil litigation, there are no 'confessions' per se. Rather, a person who wishes to 'confess' to a civil wrong can make an 'admission.'

---

197 [1997] 1 Cr App R 217.

198 See further *R v Hughes* [1988] Crim LR 519.

Part 14 of the Civil Procedure Rules 1998 contains detailed guidance on the procedure that must be followed should a party wish to make an admission. A defendant who admits the claim against him is best advised to complete the admission form included in the response pack.[199]

Rule 14.1

(1) A party may admit the truth of the whole or any part of another party's case.
(2) A party may do this by giving notice in writing (such as in a statement of case or by letter).

Rule 14.1(2) does not require an admission to be in any particular form, merely that it be 'in writing.' If it is not in writing, it may still be admissible in evidence, but it is not a formal admission for the purposes of Part 14. Rule 14.2(1) states that the period for returning an admission is (a) where the defendant is served with a claim form which states that particulars of claim will follow, 14 days after service of the particulars; and (b) in any other case, 14 days after service of the claim form. An admission may be made for a specified amount of money[200] or an unspecified amount of money.[201]

Whether an admission may be withdrawn will depend on when it was made. Should it be made after proceedings have begun, an admission may only be withdrawn with permission of the court.[202] On the other hand, should a pre-action admission have been made, a person may, by giving notice in writing, withdraw a pre-action admission before commencement of proceedings, if the person to whom the admission was made agrees; or after commencement of proceedings, if all parties to the proceedings consent, or with the permission of the court.[203] Where an admission stands, however, Rule 14.1(4) allows for the claimant to enter judgment, as of right (the exception to this being where the defendant is a child or protected party).

8.5 Key learning points

- Confession evidence may be excluded on three grounds: oppression, unreliability, or through the exercise of judicial discretion.
- If there is serious impropriety in the criminal process that may amount to oppression, section 76(2)(a) should be relied upon in the first instance.
- If the impropriety amounts to something said or done (or not done) that was likely, in the circumstances, to lead to an unreliable confession, section 76(2)(b) should be relied upon. This is likely to involve conduct that falls short of the threshold for section 76(2)(a).
- If either of these circumstances applies, the court must exclude the evidence.
- Facts obtained as a result of an excluded confession are admissible, provided that no connection is made in court with the suspect having confessed.
- Where section 76(2) does not apply, the defence may ask the court to use its discretion to exclude the evidence under section 78.
- The exercise of the exclusionary discretion under section 78 is a matter for the trial judge. Generally, breaches of PACE will have to be 'significant and substantial' before they are likely to give rise to exclusion.

---

199 The Response Pack is the N9 Form and must be served on the defendant when the Claim Form or the Particulars of Claim are served. The Response Pack consists of forms of acknowledgement of service, admission, defence, and counterclaim.

200 As to the rules, see Rule 14.4 of the Civil Procedure Rules 1998 and the N9A Form.

201 See the N9C Form.

202 CPR 1998, r 14.1(5).

203 CPR 1998, r 14.1A(3).

- In civil proceedings, a party wishing to confess to a civil wrong is required to make an 'admission.'
- Such admissions must be in writing to be legally binding, otherwise they are merely evidence to be used against a party.

8.6 Practice questions

Consider whether the trial judge should exclude the following confessions.

1. Aaron is a mature businessman, a director of a number of companies and former mayor. He was arrested on a charge of corruption at 6.30 am on Monday in the presence of his wife and taken to a police station. He was refused access to a solicitor by a superintendent who stated that, in reliance on section 58(8)(b) of the Police and Criminal Evidence Act 1984, he had reasonable grounds to believe that others suspected of involvement in the offence and not yet arrested would be alerted. He was interviewed three times. During the course of these interviews, he made it clear that he knew his rights and refused to answer a number of questions. However, during the third interview, he admitted that he had corruptly received money from a number of contractors in return for ensuring that council contracts went to them.
2. Ben is a heroin addict who was arrested for burglary. The police realised he was a drug addict and made no attempt to interview him until 18 hours after his arrival at the police station. Before being interviewed he was asked if he wanted to see a solicitor. He said he did not and signed the custody record to that effect. Ben made no complaint during the 18 hours of detention, and told the police he felt able to answer questions. He was subsequently interviewed by two police officers, having again refused a solicitor. During the interview, he admitted involvement in a number of burglaries, which, he said, he did to get money to feed his habit. After the interview, he complained that he was suffering withdrawal symptoms. A doctor then attended him, and, on finding a high pulse rate, prescribed medication. However, he expressed the opinion that Ben was otherwise fit to be detained. Ben now says the confession was false. He was suffering from withdrawal symptoms and was prepared to say anything in order to get out and obtain a 'fix.'
3. Julie is a 21-year-old medical student. During her training on a hospital ward, a young boy died after his oxygen equipment had been tampered with and a tube detached. Police arrested Julie on suspicion of murder. She was detained for a total period of 49 hours. Owing to an administrative error, the last 13 hours were not properly authorised in accordance with PACE and the Code of Practice. Julie was interviewed in the presence of a solicitor six times, for periods of two hours over two days. On the tape-recording of the interview, the interviewing officer can be heard repeatedly telling Julie in an aggressive voice that she killed the boy. Despite Julie's denial, the officer repeated the accusation some 30 times over the six interviews. Towards the end of the fifth interview, a police officer showed Julie a picture of the little boy taken during the post-mortem and told her to take it to her cell and reflect on what she had done. During the final interview, the interviewing officer could be heard shouting at Julie and demanding that she tell the truth. Julie then made a series of statements in which she accepted responsibility for the boy's death. Julie's solicitor said nothing during the interviews.
4. Ahmed and his girlfriend were arrested on suspicion of making a fraudulent claim on their insurance in respect of an alleged burglary of their flat. Ahmed refused a solicitor and signed the custody record to that effect. During a taped interview, Ahmed asked the interviewing officer what was likely to happen to his girlfriend. The officer told him that she would be interviewed and, if found to be involved, she would be charged. Ahmed then made a confession in which he said he was totally to blame and that the girlfriend was not involved.

Would your answer to (4) above differ if the interviewing officer had told Ahmed that if he admitted the offence, his girlfriend would not be prosecuted?

8.7 Suggested further reading

Clare, A., 'Confessions' (2006) 70 Journal of Criminal Law 315.
Cotton, T., 'Confession Evidence and the Circumstances Requiring a Voir Dire' (2010) 74 Journal of Criminal Law 400.
Gudjonsson, G.H., *The Psychology of Interrogations and Confessions: A Handbook* (Wiley, 2003).
Hartshorne, J., 'Defensive Use of a Co-accused's Confession and the Criminal Justice Act 2003' (2004) 8(3) E & P 165.
Hirst, M., 'Confessions as Proof of Innocence' (1998) 57 CLJ 146.
Jackson, J. and Summers, S., *Written Records of Statements and Fairness in Criminal Proceedings: Individual Rights and Institutional Forms* (Hart Publishing, 2020).
Kassin, S.M., 'The Psychology of Confession Evidence' (1997) 52 American Psychologist 221.
Memon, A., Vrij, A. and Bull, R., *Psychology and Law: Truthfulness, Accuracy and Credibility*, 2nd edn (Wiley, 2003) 78.
Mirfield, P., *Silence, Confessions and Improperly Obtained Evidence* (Oxford University Press, 1997).
Munday, R., 'Adverse Denial and Purposive Confession' (2003) Crim LR 850.

Chapter 9

Improperly Obtained Evidence

Chapter contents

DOI: 10.4324/9781003416098-9

Aside from confessions, convictions based on other forms of evidence obtained by allegedly illegal or unfair means are regularly challenged in the appellate courts. Such evidence may take a variety of forms, but commonly falls into three main areas: (1) cases dealing with failure to abide by the protocols laid down by the Police and Criminal Evidence Act (PACE) 1984 and the Codes of Practice; (2) cases involving covert surveillance; and (3) cases involving tricks or so-called entrapment evidence.

There is no barrier at common law that excludes the use of improperly obtained evidence, but the courts have frequently expressed their disapproval of such practices. In *Brannan v Peek*,[1] Lord Goddard CJ described an attempt by undercover police officers to uncover unlicensed gambling establishments by involving themselves in illegal betting rings as 'wholly wrong.'[2] Although courts have always held a discretion to exclude evidence that was obtained unfairly or as a result of the actions of an agent provocateur, it is only in more recent times that statutory intervention has begun to regulate such evidence in a closer manner than has previously been the case. Indeed, in the wake of the Human Rights Act 1998, it increasingly appears that the police and Crown Prosecution Service (CPS) need to exercise considerably more caution in basing prosecutions around evidence that might be regarded as suspect. In addition, academic commentators have cited a variety of rationales for the exclusion of evidence, and these may be broadly grouped into four categories.

First, it is arguably morally unfair to make use of evidence that was not obtained according to the law. Even if improperly obtained evidence is highly cogent and highly relevant to the charge, it must be questioned whether it should nevertheless be excluded on the grounds that it would be fundamentally unfair to the accused. As Duff et al. have argued, a court – as a state institution – cannot morally be seen simultaneously to condemn the wrongdoing of the accused and condone that of the police – another state institution.[3] Previously, it was once thought that a general power of the court to exclude otherwise admissible evidence and relevant evidence was contrary to the principles of a fair trial and carried the risk of miscarriages of justice.[4] However, as will be discussed later, it is now accepted that there are important reasons towards safeguarding a free and fair trial that include the exclusion of improperly obtained evidence. The Gross Report did anticipate that, subject to the interests of justice, late disclosure within criminal proceedings was capable of resulting in the exclusion of such evidence; however, it showed no enthusiasm for a general exclusionary rule when there has been a disclosure failure.[5]

Second, it is the proper duty of the court to restore the victim of police wrongdoing to the position in which they would have been had that evidence not been collected. In effect, this 'remedial' stance means that the case against the accused should proceed only if the rest of the evidence (that which was properly gathered) is strong enough. While this approach clearly prioritises helping the victim, it also may serve to exclude evidence that is otherwise reliable.

1 [1948] 1 KB 68.
2 Ibid., at 72.
3 Duff, R., Farmer, L., Marshall, S.L., and Tadros, V., *The Trial on Trial, Vol.* 3 (Hart Publishing, 2007), p. 244.
4 Lord Justice Gross and Lord Justice Treacy, 'Further Review of Disclosure Failure' (London, Judiciary of England and Wales, 2012).
5 Lord Justice Gross, 'Review of Disclosure in Criminal Proceedings' (London, Judiciary of England and Wales, 2012) 9.

Example 9.1

Stuart and Jimmy are suspected of dealing in Class A drugs. They are held together in the cell of a magistrates' court while waiting for committal proceedings. Unbeknown to them, a covert CCTV device has been installed in the cell and the two men are overheard discussing a number of drug deals. It is illegal to install such devices in court precincts under section 41 of the Criminal Justice Act 1925. Should the trial judge opt for a remedial approach (thereby excluding the evidence) in these circumstances? On the one hand, there can be no doubt that the rights of the suspects have been very clearly violated and that the law has been violated. On the other hand, there is nothing unreliable about this evidence, since the men did not know they were being filmed. So should cogent and reliable (although illegally obtained) evidence be admitted? These facts bear some resemblance to those of *R v Loveridge*,[6] discussed below. In that case, the court found that while the evidence had been illegally obtained, it was nevertheless admissible.

Third, it is widely acknowledged among commentators that the fairness of the process impacts upon the accuracy of the verdict. As noted in Chapter 2, Goodpaster argues that truth and justice are 'intimately connected' and cannot be clinically separated. Just as fair procedures are conducive to accurate fact-finding, unfair procedures may lead to erroneous fact-finding.[7] In Goodpaster's final analysis, fair outcomes are fundamentally dependent upon fair processes. As we saw in Chapter 8, police investigations will occasionally stray into the territory of illegality, with 'facts' being constructed, evidence being tampered with or fabricated, suspects being intimidated into confessing, or disclosure procedures not being fully complied with. During the late 1980s and early 1990s, there were a number of high-profile acquittals by the Court of Appeal, including the Birmingham Six, the Guildford Four, the Bridgewater Four, the Cardiff Three, Judith Ward, and Derek Bentley. Although PACE 1984 was intended to safeguard personal liberties by placing tighter controls upon the exercise of police powers, it would be naïve to believe that it has been effective in eradicating corruption within the investigative process. It is self-evident that a failure to follow formal procedures and to respect due process requirements carries risks to the fact-finding process. If left unchecked, evidence obtained improperly may then be admitted as 'facts' and may comprise part of the case against the accused in court. The 2011 Gross Report also endorsed a strong participatory role for the defendant. It suggested that, provided that the prosecutorial party has a grip of its disclosure obligations from the onset, 'there is also much to be said for the proposal that in appropriate cases the court should press for involvement from the defendant personally – not merely from his legal representatives.'[8]

The third rationale for the exclusionary principle is to deter future wrongdoing by the police and other investigatory authorities. This is what is frequently termed the disciplinary approach since it involves the courts effectively punishing the investigating authorities for straying outside the law by ensuring that they cannot rely on the evidence in court. In doing so, they should deter

6 *The Times* (3 May 2001). See p. 252.
7 Goodpaster, G., 'On the Theory of the American Adversary Criminal Trial' (1987) 78(1) *Journal of Criminal Law and Criminology* 118.
8 Lord Justice Gross, 'Review of Disclosure in Criminal Proceedings' (London, Judiciary of England and Wales, 2011) 75.

the future collection of evidence outside the law. As we shall see, English courts have traditionally rejected the disciplinary approach, although it is readily accepted in many other jurisdictions, including most of the United States. Of course, whether or not such a stance *actually* deters the gathering of illegal evidence in practice is not known.[9]

Fourth, the integrity of the criminal justice system arguably hangs on its ability to remain pure and untouched by instances of illegality. On this view, all improperly obtained evidence ought to be excluded, irrespective of how it relates to the broader question of the fair trial, since to do otherwise would result in the administration of justice being brought into disrepute. This view also links to the wider question of the legitimacy of the process in the eyes of the public. Clearly, faith in the criminal justice system would be greatly undermined if illegal material were routinely admitted in the course of criminal trials. By the same token, however, there is also widespread distaste for the notion that serious criminals might simply be allowed to walk free if procedural technicalities are not followed to the letter.

Notwithstanding these objections to the use of illegal evidence, those strongly in favour of a free model of proof might advance the argument that it is ultimately for the factfinder, not the judiciary or indeed Parliament, to accept or reject the nature of the evidence in criminal trials. Arguably, all evidence that is logically probative or disprobative of the facts in issue should be put before the court. If, for instance, we hold the principle of trial by jury as sacrosanct, is there any reason for distrusting the juror with certain aspects of evidence? Such arguments are widely used in respect of evidence of previous convictions and hearsay evidence,[10] and it could equally be argued in the case of improperly obtained evidence that it should be for counsel to explain to the jury why they should not attach any weight to it instead of the judge simply excluding such evidence at the outset. Arguably, victims of police wrongdoing have other means to access justice (such as filing a complaint to the Independent Police Complaints Commission or pursuing a separate action for damages under the Human Rights Act 1998). Given the pressure on time and resources within criminal trials, it is arguable that the behaviour of those charged with gathering the evidence is simply not the concern of the criminal trial except insofar as it impacts on the reliability of the evidence. Students should always keep in mind that foundationally, the proposition that improperly obtained evidence should be excluded from court proceedings is grounded in the autonomy and dignity afforded to citizens in a liberal democracy, and not as mere 'objects for the extraction of information.'[11]

9.1 Exclusion at common law (criminal cases)

Unlike many other jurisdictions, there is neither any defence of entrapment in English law nor any rule that evidence that has not been obtained in accordance with the law cannot be used in court. In other words, the question as to how evidence was obtained will usually not affect its admissibility; courts have never seen it as their function to police the police or the CPS. In the words of Crompton J: 'It matters not how you get it, if you steal it even, it would be admissible in evidence.'[12]

This position largely continues to reflect modern criminal practice, although some notable exceptions have evolved. In Chapter 8, it was noted that confessions obtained through oppression

9 See Ashworth, A. and Redmayne, M., *The Criminal Process*, 4th edn (Oxford University Press, 2010). As the authors point out, there is very little empirical evidence to support the idea that the exclusionary principle carries a deterrent effect in practice.

10 See Chs 11 and 12, respectively.

11 See McCrudden, C., 'Human Dignity and Judicial Interpretation of Human Rights' (2008) 19 *European Journal of International Law* 655. See also Barroso, L.R., 'Here, There and Everywhere: Human Dignity in Contemporary Law and in the Transitional Disclosure' (2012) 35 *Boston College International and Comparative Law Review* 331.

12 *R v Leatham* (1861) 8 Cox CC 498, 501.

or in circumstances likely to make the content unreliable cannot be used in evidence. Similarly, privileged documents may not be used if the party seeking to adduce them has obtained them from the opposing side using trickery or deception.[13] Evidence obtained through torture is never admissible, even if the torture took place abroad or was not directly attributable to the state.[14] In addition to these mandatory exclusions, the courts always have a general discretion to exclude evidence obtained unfairly. For example, in *Jeffrey v Black*,[15] two police officers arrested the accused on suspicion of theft of a sandwich from a pub. Having charged him, they proceeded to search his accommodation without a warrant, where they found a quantity of cannabis. The Divisional Court held that the evidence was properly admitted. In Lord Widgery's view, the court's duty was to evaluate the relevance of the evidence; the manner in which it was obtained was of no concern. Although Lord Widgery acknowledged that there was a common law discretion to exclude evidence obtained in circumstances of trickery or oppression by the police, the facts of the present case did not justify its exercise here. In sum, the willingness of the courts to apply the common law discretion in favour of the accused was rare, and it was even rarer for the failure to use that discretion to result in a successful appeal.[16]

The leading case on the scope of the common law discretion is *R v Sang*.[17] Here, a currency counterfeiter had arranged a meeting with someone claiming to be interested in forged banknotes, only to discover that the person in question was an undercover police officer. Having failed to persuade the trial judge that the evidence should have been excluded, the defendant pleaded guilty, but duly appealed, contending that the judge should have exercised his discretion to disallow the evidence since the offence was instigated by an agent provocateur. His appeal was rejected first by the Court of Appeal, and then by the House of Lords. Their Lordships accepted that a judge in a criminal trial has a general discretion to refuse to admit evidence where its probable prejudicial effect so outweighed its probative value as to make its admission unfair to the accused, but ruled that the evidence must in some way impact upon the fairness of proceedings. As Lord Diplock famously surmised:

> Save with regard to admissions and confessions and generally with regard to evidence obtained from the accused after the commission of the offence, [the judge] has no discretion to refuse to admit relevant admissible evidence on the ground that it was obtained by improper or unfair means. The court is not concerned with how the evidence was obtained.[18]

Thus, according to Lord Diplock, the potential scope of any such discretion is extremely limited, and it cannot be used merely to reprimand the police or any other investigatory authority for reprehensible conduct. Only in instances that were already well defined by the law (including evidence of similar facts, previous convictions, and breaches of the Judges' Rules) should a judge exclude evidence that was otherwise relevant. While Viscount Dilhorne largely concurred with Lord Diplock's speech, a slightly less restrictive view was expounded by the other Law Lords. In the opinions of Lords Fraser, Salmon, and Scarman, it was incorrect to limit judicial discretion to predefined areas since the overall duty of the trial judge was to ensure that both sides receive a fair trial. Despite the lack of unanimity in their analyses, it was clear that all of their Lordships agreed

---

13 See e.g. *ITC Film Distributors v Video Exchange Ltd* [1982] Ch 431.

14 *A v Secretary of State for the Home Department (No. 2)* [2005] WLR 1249.

15 [1978] QB 298.

16 See also *Kuruma v R* [1955] AC 197 and *King v R* [1969] 1 AC 304. A rare exception was *R v Payne* [1963] 1 WLR 637, a drink-driving case in which the court excluded the evidence of a doctor since the driver had been told that the doctor would only examine him to ascertain whether he was suffering from any illness or disability.

17 [1980] AC 402.

18 Ibid., at 437.

that there was no defence of entrapment in English law. However, little guidance was provided in the speeches as to the circumstances in which judges could feel free to rule out evidence on the grounds that its probative value was outweighed by its prejudicial effect. Indeed, the subsequent decisions in Trump[19] and Fox[20] did little to clarify the scope of the common law discretion.

As a comparative, in the US legal system, it is important to note that an interrogation is less about investigating the truth and discovering new evidence than it is a concerted effort to get the suspect to accept and adopt the investigator's truth; their version of events. Over the last few years, there has been much concentrated academic debate on the 'Reid Techniques'[21] and its implications of improperly obtained evidence. According to the technique of interrogation, investigators should only interrogate subjects whom they already believe to be guilty.[22] By comparison, the Australian legal system treats interrogations as inquisitorial processes to enquire on the truth of the matter.[23] As Professor Andrew Choo comments, another illustration of the differences in responding towards improperly obtained evidence comes from New Zealand, where the legislature codified an integrity-based power to exclude improperly obtained evidence after more than a decade of jurisprudence under the New Zealand Bill of Rights Act 1990.[24] Section 30 of the Act confers a judicial power to exclude 'improperly obtained evidence' based on a balancing of listed public interest considerations.[25]

9.2 Exclusion under PACE

It was thus clear that the common law discretion to exclude evidence was very restrictive in scope. It was concerned not with how the evidence was obtained but with the effect of the evidence on the fairness of the trial. In practice, however, the effect of the decision in *Sang* was to be short-lived. Parliament's enactment of section 78 of PACE placed the judicial discretion to exclude evidence on a statutory footing.[26] As noted in Chapter 8, under this provision a court may exclude the evidence if it appears that 'having regard to all the circumstances, including the circumstances in which the evidence was obtained, the admission of the evidence would have such an adverse effect on the fairness of the proceedings that the court ought not to admit it.'

It may *prima facie* appear that the statutory provision simply codifies the position of the common law. Certainly, as the Court of Appeal noted in *Christou*,[27] the standard of unfairness is essentially the same. However, the exclusionary discretion at common law applied only to prosecution evidence and was concerned not with the manner in which it was obtained but rather with its overall effect on the fairness of the trial. Section 78 now provides a broad discretion to exclude any evidence, including confessional evidence obtained in a manner that, while not rendering it unreliable, would have an adverse effect on the fairness of the trial if admitted.[28] It is broader than the common law discretion for a number of reasons. First, it can take into account the manner in which the evidence was obtained in determining its effect on the fairness of the trial. Thus, unlike the common law discretion, it may cover instances of entrapment by agents provocateurs.[29] Second, it applies not only to confessions and evidence obtained after the commission of the

19 (1980) 70 Cr App R 300.
20 (1986) 82 Cr App R 295.
21 Dixon, D., 'Questioning Suspects: A Comparative Perspective' (2010) 26 *Journal of Contemporary Criminal Justice* 426.
22 Inbau, F.E., Reid, J.E., Buckley, J.P., and Jayne, B.C., *Criminal Interrogation and Confessions*, 5th edn (Jones and Bartlett, 2013).
23 For a comparative, see Australia's Evidence Act 1995, S.138(3).
24 See Butler, A. and Butler, P., *The New Zealand Bill of Rights Act: A Commentary* (Lexis Nexis, 2005) ch 29.
25 See Evidence Act 2006 (NZ), S.30(3); see also application in the case of *Omar Hamed v R* [2011] ZSC 101.
26 It should be stressed, however, that PACE expressly preserved the common law discretion under s 82(3).
27 [1992] 2 QB 979.
28 *Mason* [1987] 3 All ER 481.
29 See discussion below.

offence, but also to *any* form of evidence on which the prosecution proposes to rely. This may include hearsay and bad character, notwithstanding other statutory provisions that may *prima facie* appear to allow their admission. However, both the statutory and the common law discretions are concerned with the *effect* that the evidence has on the fairness of the trial. As recognised by the Court of Appeal in *Smurthwaite and Gill*,[30] the statutory provision did not change the rule of substantive law that entrapment does not per se afford a defence to a criminal charge.

In light of the strong similarities between the two forms of discretion, it might be asked whether there is any role left for the common law discretion in contemporary criminal practice. Arguably, the drafters of PACE envisaged that there would be: section 82(3) preserves any power of a court to exclude evidence. One use was suggested in *R v Sat-Bhambra*.[31] Like the use of section 76 in relation to confession evidence, section 78 is incapable of applying retrospectively. In this case, the defendant's confession had been admitted following a *voir dire*, but later, on hearing further medical evidence, the judge changed his mind. In these circumstances, it was recognised that the common law discretion allows the court to remedy earlier unfairness to the accused by excluding a previously admitted confession. The common law discretion thus remains as a separate head for excluding evidence, but in almost all cases in which evidence could properly be excluded at common law it can be excluded under section 78 before it is actually admitted.[32]

It may also be the case that where the improperly obtained evidence, other than confessional evidence, would not be excluded at common law, it will not be excluded either under section 78. This was the case in *R v Stewart*,[33] in which it was argued that evidence of tampering with an electricity meter should be excluded under section 78 because of breaches of section 16 of PACE and Code B concerning entry to the premises.[34] In dismissing the appeal, the Court of Appeal found it unnecessary to decide whether PACE 1984 or the Code applied, or even whether the entry was unlawful. In the view of the court, there was simply no unfairness in admitting the evidence, which was there for all to see, whether the entry was effected properly or not. This is consistent with the common law's approach to the exclusion of real evidence. There is no question of unreliability, the evidence speaks for itself, and while admitting it may operate unfortunately for the accused, it does not operate unfairly.

9.2.1 The discretion to hold a *voir dire*

When section 78 is raised, the court has a discretion as to whether to hold a *voir dire*,[35] although it remains unclear how it should exercise that discretion. In *R v Keenan*,[36] Hodgson J offered the following guidance:

- Sometimes, evidence of police irregularity is plain for all to see (e.g. on the custody record, officers' notebooks, or through witness statements).
- Where there is *prima facie* evidence of irregularity, this must be justified by evidence from the prosecution. An order refusing access to a solicitor can only be justified by compelling evidence from the senior police officer who made the order.

30 [1994] 1 All ER 898.

31 (1988) 88 Cr App R 55.

32 See further comments of Lord Lane CJ in *R v Delaney* (1988) 88 Cr App R 338, and those of May LJ in *R v O'Leary* (1988) 87 Cr App R 387. See also *Matto v Wolverhampton Crown Court* (1987) RTR 337.

33 [1995] Crim LR 500.

34 Code B was most recently updated on 23 October 2013.

35 *Carlisle v DPP* (unreported, 9 November 1987).

36 [1990] 2 QB 54.

- In some (albeit rare) cases, the defence will need to adduce evidence from the accused himself or herself to support the case for exclusion.

Hodgson J also acknowledged the problem that, in many cases, when the application to exclude is made at an early stage, the judge is unlikely to know the nature of the accused's likely defence. This means that the judge is ill-equipped to determine the potential degree of adverse effect, since they will only have access to a limited version of the facts. This observation highlights the underlying problem with the Court of Appeal decision in *R v Bailey*,[37] in which it was stated that all of the circumstances of the case should be taken into account, including the amount of other evidence against the accused and the characteristics of the accused. The provisions of the Criminal Procedure and Investigations Act 1996, which require that the defence provide the prosecution with a statement setting out the general nature of their defence, operate to overcome this difficulty to some extent, but in the absence of a closer understanding of the case, the question of adverse effect may have to be resolved on a fairly minimalist evidential basis. The alternative is to require more from the defence at the *voir dire*. Indeed, if the defence case is thin, the onus then lies on the defence to establish the alleged adverse effect.[38]

9.2.2 Breaches of PACE and the codes of practice

In *R v Samuel*,[39] Hodgson J stated that, because of the infinite variety of circumstances, it was undesirable to attempt any general guidance as to how the judge's discretion under section 78 or their inherent powers should be exercised. However, the most common examples of breaches of PACE which often lead to exclusion include, *inter alia*:

- Confession evidence
- Evidence obtained as a result of an unlawful search of a person or their property
- Evidence obtained by entrapment
- Identification evidence by an unlawful search or by unlawful surveillance
- Evidence obtained by deception or trickery
- Evidence obtained in violation of legal professional privilege.

In the vast majority of cases, the defence will seek to show that there has been a breach of PACE 1984 or the Codes of Practice. The Codes of Practice, introduced subsequent to section 66 of PACE, stipulate the parameters under which the police must conduct themselves in the investigation of crime. In *Jelen and Katz*,[40] it was emphasised that the overriding purpose of the Codes was 'the protection of those who are vulnerable because they are in the custody of the police.'[41] Observations of a similar effect were made in *Elson*.[42] There are now a total of eight separate Codes annexed to the Act.[43] Although the Codes are not legally binding in themselves, compliance with them is obviously expected in order to safeguard the civil liberties of the suspect and to ensure the

---

37 [1995] 2 Cr App R 262.

38 See the commentary to *Rajakuruna* [1991] Crim LR 458.

39 [1988] QB 615.

40 (1990) 90 Cr App R 456.

41 Ibid., at 465 (Auld J).

42 *The Times* (30 June 1994).

43 The Codes were substantially revised following a Home Office review in 2004. Code A deals with stop and search powers; Code B deals with the searching of premises and seizure of property; Code C concerns the detention, treatment, and questioning of suspects; Code D lays down requirements regarding identification and accurate record-keeping; Code E refers to the tape-recording of interviews; Code F concerns audio-visual recording; Code G (introduced in January 2006) concerns statutory powers of arrest; and Code H (introduced in July 2006) concerns the detention of terrorism suspects.

moral integrity of the criminal process. On the other hand, it can be contended that occasional misconduct, particularly if unintentional or if it is of little consequence, should not undermine the strong public interest in the prosecution process. Certainly, such arguments seem stronger in cases involving serious crime where public policy dictates that the protection of the public should not be jeopardised by single instances of human error.

In practice, most police officers involved in the interrogation of suspects are highly trained and intentional illegality is thus exceedingly rare. However, inadvertent mistakes are still made in the application of the Codes of Practice, and the appellate courts have had to face calls for the use of section 78 to exclude evidence in such circumstances. It has been clearly established that not every breach of correct procedures will be greeted with exclusion of evidence. Thus, in *R v Walsh*,[44] it was said that a breach of Code C meant that, *prima facie* at least, the standards of fairness set by Parliament have not been met and any evidence admitted in such circumstances must have an adverse effect on the fairness of the trial. However, it was underlined that this did not mean that exclusion should be automatic: 'The task of the court is not merely to consider whether there would be an adverse effect on the fairness of the proceedings, but such an adverse effect that justice requires the evidence to be excluded.'[45]

Certainly, the courts have remained loyal to their historical reluctance to use the exclusionary discretion as a sword to discipline the police.[46] However, it is suggested that such reasoning is disingenuous, for, no matter how the court expresses it, an inevitable consequence of exclusion of evidence is that the police are disciplined by the collapse of a prosecution. Hodgson J arguably came closer to the mark in *Samuel* when he described police disciplinary procedures as 'a much less secure method of ensuring compliance' with PACE 1984 than sections 76 and 78.[47] Thus, in practice, the courts are increasingly prepared to use the discretionary exclusion where the police have acted in bad faith. In *Matto v Wolverhampton Crown Court*,[48] for example, it was held that evidence of the defendant's blood alcohol level should have been ruled out after police conducted a breath test on the accused's driveway, despite his protests that they were on private property. Section 78 has also been used to condemn the tactics and content of police questioning. In fact, this was the concern of the first leading case on the section, *R v Mason*.[49] It will be recalled from the previous chapter that the Court of Appeal was enraged that the defendant's solicitor had been hoodwinked, thereby affecting the advice he gave his client. On that basis, section 78 was used to exclude the defendant's confession.

It is thus evident that the courts do see themselves as exercising *some* power in using the provision to discipline or punish the police. That may be no bad thing, but an honest acceptance of that principle would assist in understanding the application of the section. In theory, at least, the question whether or not evidence should be excluded will be determined by looking at the extent of any departure from the standards contained within PACE and the impact that this has upon the fairness of proceedings as a whole. This means that some degree of uncertainty as to the consequences of a breach is likely to arise when the requirements laid down in the Codes are not followed.

Many cases in which section 78 arises involve confession evidence. These were considered in Chapter 8, but it should be borne in mind that there is a considerable degree of overlap between

---

44 (1989) 91 Cr App R 161.

45 See also *Keenan*, op. cit., n. 36; *Delaney*, op. cit., n. 32; *R v Waters* [1989] Crim LR 62.

46 See e.g. *Delaney*, op. cit., n. 32; *Mason*, op. cit., n. 28; and *R v Fennelly* [1989] Crim LR 142.

47 [1988] QB 615, at 628. See also the trenchant criticism of police conduct by Lord Lane CJ in *R v Canale* [1990] 2 All ER 187, and of officers of Customs and Excise whose disregard of Code C caused the Court in *R v Weerdesteyn* [1995] 1 Cr App R 405 some concern.

48 [1987] RTR 337.

49 For further discussion, see Ch 8.

the principles that apply in cases concerning confession evidence and those that do not. In the discussion below, we have attempted, where possible, to avoid repeating what has already been discussed in the previous chapter. However, in some cases, it will be necessary to refer back to some of the case law that has already been covered.

Irrespective of whether a confession is involved, it will be recalled that courts tend to take a particularly dim view of those cases in which a suspect was improperly denied access to legal advice.[50]

In *Walsh*, for example, there were a multitude of violations of PACE, including improper denial of access to legal advice under section 58. In addition, the police had failed to note the interview contemporaneously, had failed to keep a record of the reasons for not recording the interview, and had failed to give the suspect an opportunity to read and sign the interview record that they later compiled. In the *voir dire* at first instance, the judge accepted that none of the officers had acted in bad faith, and held that access to a solicitor would have made no difference. Therefore, he refused to rule out any of the evidence under section 78. Allowing the appeal, the Court of Appeal held that this series of breaches were indeed 'significant and substantial' and failed to measure up to the benchmark of fairness set down by Parliament in passing the legislation.[51]

Similarly, the absence of a caution is often considered a sufficiently serious breach of Code C that may lead to exclusion. In *R v Sparks*,[52] the failure of the police to issue a caution and to record the interview was regarded as a substantial breach of Code C and warranted exclusion of the conversation under section 78. The Court of Appeal also found a substantial breach in *R v Saunders*,[53] in which the key component of a caution (that the defendant need not say anything) was omitted. On the other hand, failure to tell or remind suspects that they are volunteers and are free to leave is not necessarily a substantial breach,[54] particularly where they are under the impression that they were a suspect in an investigation.[55] Indeed, there are many provisions in the Code that are generally considered to be of lesser importance, including stipulations on the precise timing to provide meals or drinks, recording the times at which interviews commenced and finished, and the mandatory eight-hour period of continuous rest. A failure to abide rigidly with these requirements did not weigh particularly heavily in the view of the court in *R v Deacon*,[56] and the courts have frequently remarked that not every breach of the Code will lead to automatic exclusion under section 78. As suggested in *Walsh* and in many subsequent cases, the breaches must be significant and substantial to justify exclusion. Those provisions that are mandatory are more likely to be so than those that are directory.[57] Also, there may be an accumulation of minor breaches of procedure, which together justify the exercise of the section 78 discretion.[58]

It will be recalled from Chapter 8 that, in *Keenan*,[59] the Court of Appeal stated that the primary function of Codes of Practice was to provide safeguards for the accused against the abuse of police power. Thus, where breaches of the Codes were 'significant and substantial,' the evidence should 'frequently' be excluded.[60] However, the decision in *Keenan* was distinguished in *Sanghera*.[61] The defendant, a postmaster, appealed against his conviction for theft on the ground that evidence

---

50 See Ch 8.
51 Compare *R v Williams* [1989] Crim LR 66.
52 [1991] Crim LR 128.
53 [1988] Crim LR 521.
54 See PACE Code of Practice C [10.2].
55 *R v Rajakuruna* [1991] Crim LR 458.
56 [1987] Crim LR 404.
57 *R v Grier* (1989) LAG (14 April 1989).
58 See e.g. *R v Moss* (1990) 91 Cr App R 371.
59 [1990] 2 QB 54.
60 Ibid., at 69.
61 [2001] 1 Cr App R 299.

obtained as a result of a police search should have been ruled out since he had failed to give the necessary consent required by Code B. Although the Court of Appeal acknowledged that the search was unlawful, evidence found as a result of that search was not unreliable. However, the court differentiated the nature of the breaches that occurred here from those that arose in *Keenan*: they were fundamentally different and less serious in nature. It was emphasised that each case should turn on its own particular facts to determine whether the fairness of the trial had been adversely affected. A similar approach was taken by the High Court in *DPP v Wilson*,[62] where the fact that a defendant suspected of driving with excess alcohol was arrested unlawfully (because he was a patient in hospital) did not mean the subsequent blood-testing procedure was inadmissible. The court concluded that an arrest was not a prerequisite for the test to be carried out and the unlawful arrest itself did not invalidate the subsequent procedure.

Thus, considerable care needs to be taken in generalising about the nature of the case law relating to breaches of the Codes of Practice. The overarching test is, as per the wording of section 78, whether the admission of the evidence would have such an adverse effect on the fairness of proceedings.[63] The concept of 'adverse effect' is open to interpretation and is therefore somewhat nebulous, but it is possible to identify a number of factors that may sway courts either towards, or against, admissibility. One of the key factors will certainly be the particular type of PACE procedure that has been breached. It should be noted that 'the mere fact that there has been a breach of the Codes of Practice does not of itself mean that evidence has to be rejected.'[64] A link between the breach and fairness to the proceedings must be established.[65] If the PACE procedure is an important safeguard for the suspect, an adverse effect on the fairness of the proceedings is inevitable and that effect is likely to be so adverse that justice demands the exclusion of any evidence thus obtained. In this context, most important are the provisions designed to prevent 'verballing' of the suspect – that is, concocting admissions through unfair means.[66] Transgression of these standards often leads to exclusion under section 78 because it is unfair to deprive the defendant of their rights, it is unfair to the court since it is deprived of a more accurate record of an interview, and it is dangerous to the overall integrity of the criminal process since it would essentially allow the prosecution to win by foul play.

Thus, even actions by the police where there is no intention to mislead or violate the Codes of Conduct may still lead to exclusion. In *Nathaniel*,[67] N, who had been convicted of rape, appealed on the ground that DNA evidence presented at his trial should have been excluded. This evidence was obtained primarily from a blood sample he had given four years previously, while under investigation for two other rape offences. He had agreed to give this sample only after assurances were given by police that the sample would be destroyed if he were acquitted of those crimes (in accordance with section 64 of PACE). Owing to an administrative error, this was not done, and the samples relating to the previous offences were used to connect N with the offence in question. Allowing his appeal, the court held that, since the police had both misled N as to the use of the sample and had failed to comply with their statutory obligation to destroy it, it would have been proper to exclude it under section 78 of the 1984 Act.

However, many other cases suggest that mistaken conduct on the part of the police carried out in good faith may tilt against the use of section 78, or at very least be a neutral factor in the

62 [2009] EWHC 1988.

63 This has been reiterated by the courts in numerous cases. See especially *R v P* [2002] 1 AC 146 and *R (CPS) v Wolverhampton Magistrates' Court* [2009] EWHC 3467.

64 *Delaney*, op. cit., n. 32, at 341 (Lord Lane CJ).

65 *R v Hughes* [1988] Crim LR 519; *R v Dunford* (1990) 91 Cr App Rep 150.

66 See e.g. *Keenan*, op. cit., n. 36.

67 [1995] 2 Cr App R 565.

equation. Examples include: *R v Clarke*,[68] in which the officers did not realise that the defendant was deaf, but the breach of what is now Code C, para 13.5, could still be considered; *R v Younis*,[69] in which the suspect 'volunteered' most of the remarks in the police car and there was no evidence of deliberate police prompting; and *R v Kerawalla*,[70] in which the absence of bad faith was considered to be one of a number of relevant factors that could be taken into account. However, it should be borne in mind that, unlike section 76(2)(a), impropriety is not essential for the section 78 discretion to be exercised,[71] and good faith will not serve to remedy a significant or substantial breach of PACE procedures.

Section 78 may also be used to exclude real evidence, although the courts seem reluctant to apply it in this fashion. The only recorded case in which real evidence had been excluded was *R v Fennelly*,[72] which concerned a failure to comply with the stop-and-search requirements of PACE 1984. A quantity of heroin was seized from the underpants of the defendant, but this evidence was excluded on the basis that, in the view of the court, it would have been unfair to admit it.

That decision was, however, doubted in the case of *R v Khan, Sakkaravej and Pamarapa*.[73] Pamarapa, a Thai diplomat, was convicted of importing around £5 million of drugs into the United Kingdom. Having had his diplomatic immunity waived by the Thai Government, he was subsequently convicted. His appeal centred on the argument that the search of his suitcase (which had taken place in the hold of the aircraft) was in breach of Article 36(2) of the Vienna Convention on Diplomatic Relations 1961, which provided that any searches should take place in Pamarapa's presence and then only if the customs/police had serious grounds to believe that the case contained prohibited goods. It was also argued that the arrest was unlawful and the subsequent search of his bag also unlawful. The Court of Appeal upheld the decision of the trial judge to refuse to exclude the evidence. There were grounds to believe the bags contained drugs, and the only actual illegality was the absence of Pamarapa when the search took place. The Convention provided a right to search, which implied a right to detain; therefore, there was no unlawful arrest. While acknowledging that section 78 had enlarged the judge's discretion to exclude evidence obtained by unfair means, it remained the effect on the fairness of the trial that was relevant, and only if this was subject to interference should the court conclude that the evidence should not be admitted. The trial judge correctly found that the search did not taint the quality of the evidence, or the fairness of admitting it into evidence.

9.2.3 Covert surveillance

A second major area in which section 78 is often triggered concerns eavesdropping or covert electronic bugging. A number of cases have come before the Court of Appeal in recent years concerning covert surveillance both in custodial and non-custodial settings. Where the surveillance takes place in custody, it seems unlikely that the courts will be keen to exclude the evidence. In *Bailey and Smith*,[74] two suspects, charged with robbery, chose to remain silent when questioned by police. Unknown to the men, their cell had been bugged, and incriminating evidence was recorded. Dismissing their appeal, it was held that the police were under no duty to protect prisoners from making incriminating statements to one another, even in circumstances in which they had exercised their right to silence.

---

68 [1989] Crim LR 892.

69 [1990] Crim LR 425.

70 [1991] Crim LR 252.

71 *O'Leary*, op. cit., n. 23; *Samuel*, op. cit., n. 39.

72 [1989] Crim LR 142.

73 [1997] Crim LR 508.

74 (1993) 97 Cr App R 365.

As noted at the outset of this chapter, *R v Loveridge and Others*[75] raised a very similar issue. Here, three defendants were convicted of robbery after the prosecution had relied on a covert video-recording of them waiting in the holding area of a magistrates' court. An expert witness compared the video-recording with film taken by a surveillance camera at the scene of the robbery, and concluded that the defendants were those depicted in the surveillance camera. The trial judge accepted that the recording contravened section 41 of the Criminal Justice Act 1925, which makes filming in the precincts of a court unlawful. However, while not approving or encouraging the tactics adopted by the police, the judge determined that the admissibility of the video film would not have an adverse effect on the fairness of the trial.

The Court of Appeal agreed. It was accepted that filming in the court was unlawful, being a breach of section 41 of the 1925 Act, and that there may also have been a breach of the Codes of Practice or Article 8 of the European Convention on Human Rights. However, insofar as the outcome of the appeal was concerned, such breaches were only relevant if they interfered with the right of the defendants to a fair hearing. Satisfied that the fairness of the hearing had not been subject to interference, the Court of Appeal ruled that the judge had been entitled to admit the evidence. Collectively, the evidence of the involvement of each of the defendants was overwhelming. The trial was fair and the convictions were not in any way unsafe.

However, bugging a meeting between solicitor and client, which is legally privileged, is considered much more reprehensible. As stated by Lord Taylor in *R v Derby Magistrates' Court, ex p B*:[76] 'Legal privilege is ... much more than an ordinary rule of evidence ... [i]t is a fundamental condition on which the administration of justice rests.'[77] The Court of Appeal confirmed this principle in *R v Grant*.[78] The common law largely mirrors the jurisprudence of the European Court of Human Rights.[79] Thus, a breach of Article 6 of the European Convention on Human Rights can be found if there was an infringement of the right to confidential advice, even if it cannot be proved that the accused did not have a fair trial. In *R v Sutherland and others*,[80] Mr Justice Newman held that the prosecution of five men for murder could not proceed owing to an abuse of process. Here, the police in Grantham had long suspected that the defendants had been involved in a murder. The police were granted permission under the Regulation of Investigatory Powers Act (RIPA) 2000 to place listening devices in the cells and communal areas at two police stations.[81] In the event, a listening device was also placed in the exercise area and conversations between the defendants and their solicitors were also recorded in breach of the defendants' right to legal privilege. The prosecution did not seek to use these conversations in evidence, and therefore section 78 could not be relied upon. However, although the police denied listening to the taped conversations between lawyer and client or making any use of them, the trial judge did not accept this. He held that knowledge of the conversations must have informed their decisions and their use of the privileged conversations prejudiced the defendants, and that this amounted to an abuse of process. The trial judge concluded that justice had been 'affronted in a grave way' and said he was satisfied that there could be no fair trial given the nature of the issues which had arisen at the trial.

Outside of custodial settings, eavesdropping on suspects is becoming increasingly commonplace as technology advances and bugging devices become smaller. In *R v Chalkley and Jeffries*,[82] the prosecution sought to rely on covertly obtained tape-recordings of conversations between the

75 See above.

76 [1996] AC 487, at 507.

77 Ibid., at 507.

78 *The Times* (12 May 2005).

79 See *Lanz v Austria* (App. No. 24430/94, 31 January 2002); *S v Switzerland* (1992) 14 EHRR 670; *Niemitz v Germany* (1992) 16 EHRR 97; *Brennan v UK* (2002) 34 EHRR 18.

80 Unreported (29 January 2002).

81 See discussion below on the Regulation of Investigatory Powers Act 2000.

82 [1998] 2 All ER 155.

defendants, charged with conspiracy to rob. In order to obtain the recordings, police arrested Chalkley and his partner on unrelated charges and, in their absence, entered their house and planted a listening device. The defence, contending that it would be fundamentally unfair to admit the recordings, argued that they should be excluded using section 78. The trial judge concluded that he was obliged to conduct a balancing exercise between the interests of justice, the effective prosecution of offences, and the wider public interest in discouraging the abuse of police power. He concluded that, in this particular case, the balance lay with the effective prosecution of offences and admitted the evidence. The defendants then changed their plea to guilty.

On appeal, the court concluded that there was no basis for the defence submission that admission of the taped conversations would have such an adverse effect on the fairness of the proceedings that they ought to have been excluded. Moreover, the court noted that the reference in the provision to 'the circumstances in which the evidence was obtained' was not intended to widen the common law rule stated by Lord Diplock in *Sang* to the effect that the judge has 'no discretion to refuse to admit relevant and otherwise admissible evidence solely on the ground that it was obtained by improper or unfair means.'[83] The quality and reliability of the evidence had to be considered; therefore, the trial judge had been wrong to apply the balancing process applicable to abuse of process cases in relation to section 78.[84]

Nevertheless, the importance of the human rights dimension to cases involving covert surveillance cannot be overstated. Article 8 of the European Convention seeks to protect privacy and the right to a family life. Although a right to privacy never evolved under the common law, the desirability of such a concept has received a considerable degree of attention in recent years, particularly in the post-Human Rights Act 1998 era. With respect to covert surveillance, the leading case is *R v Khan*,[85] which was heard by the House of Lords before the Human Rights Act 1998 was even drafted. Police were suspicious of the behaviour of the appellant, who had recently arrived in the United Kingdom from Pakistan. Covert listening devices were placed at the home of a third party, a suspected drug dealer, which recorded K making a number of incriminatory statements concerning the supply of heroin. K was convicted of being knowingly concerned in the importation of a Class A-controlled drug; he appealed, alleging that the evidence obtained by the listening device should have been excluded under section 78.

The defence contention was that a private conversation in a private house was analogous to a private telephone call, the interception of which is governed by the Interception of Communications Act 1986 and the decision of the European Court of Human Rights in *Malone v United Kingdom*.[86]

Section 9 of the 1986 Act forbade the use in evidence of material obtained by the interception of communications and a similar restriction should be applied to materials obtained by aural surveillance devices. The House of Lords rejected this argument because it required the formulation of two new principles: (a) that the appellant enjoyed a right of privacy in respect of the taped conversation; and (b) that evidence of a conversation obtained in breach of that right was inadmissible. There was no such right of privacy in English law, and even if there were, evidence obtained improperly or even unlawfully remained admissible, subject to the trial judge's power to exclude it at his discretion.

Turning to the issue of whether the judge should have exercised his discretion to exclude the evidence in the exercise of his common law discretion or under section 78, Lord Nolan stated that

---

83 See also *Khan*, discussed in depth below.

84 The appellant took his case to the European Court of Human Rights claiming a breach of Article 6(1), but the Court found that proper procedure had been followed and it had not been unfair to admit the surveillance evidence: *Chalkley v United Kingdom* [2003] Crim LR 51.

85 [1997] AC 558.

86 (1984) 7 EHRR 14.

the only relevant element of the common law discretion was that part which authorised the judge 'to exclude evidence if it is necessary in order to secure a fair trial for the accused.'[87] It was unnecessary to consider the common law position separately from that under section 78, since both are concerned with securing a fair trial. Liberty contended that if the evidence had been obtained in breach of the European Convention (which, under Article 8, does include a right to privacy) then that should be regarded as grounds for excluding what was otherwise admissible evidence.

In Lord Nolan's view, while the principles reflected in the European Convention could hardly be irrelevant to the exercise of the section 78 power under English law, there was nothing unlawful about a breach of privacy (note that the case was decided well before the Human Rights Act 1998 took effect). The appellant's case rested wholly upon the lack of statutory authorisation for the particular breach of privacy (it then being authorised under administrative guidelines laid down by the Secretary of State) and the consequent infringement of Article 8. In these circumstances, the appellant could no more succeed on this second issue than he could on the first. Even if the evidence had been obtained in breach of Article 8 or, for that matter, in breach of the law of another jurisdiction, that fact would be of no greater significance per se than if it constituted a breach of English law. Dismissing the appeal, their Lordships considered that the judge was fully entitled to hold that the circumstances in which the relevant evidence was obtained, even if they constituted a breach of Article 8, were not such as to require the exclusion of the evidence. Lord Nolan went on to say that it would be a strange reflection of our law if a man who had admitted his participation in the illegal importation of a large quantity of heroin should have his conviction set aside on the ground that his privacy had been invaded. This was a serious criminal offence, and the police had acted within Home Office protocols, notwithstanding the absence of any statutory regulation. While the US exclusionary principle permits an accused to walk free if their privacy or other rights are infringed, the English common law rule, and the statutory power under section 78, carry no such effect.

Although unsuccessful in the domestic courts, Khan took his case to Strasbourg and was successful in alleging a breach of Article 8.[88] The Strasbourg Court found that since domestic law did not regulate the use of covert listening devices at the time of the applicant's conviction, the actions of the police did constitute a violation of Article 8. The Court went on to state that not only should some form of regulation have been in place, but also 'the law must be sufficiently clear in its terms to give individuals an adequate indication as to the circumstances in which and the conditions on which public authorities are entitled to resort to such covert measures.'[89] Importantly, however, the failure of the judge at first instance to exclude the evidence was found not to constitute a violation of Article 6. The discretionary mechanism to exclude evidence if it would lead to substantive unfairness (section 78) was sufficient to protect the right of a fair trial.

Khan was reviewed by the Court of Appeal in a case of the same name, but not the same defendant: *R v Khan*.[90] In this later case, a bugging device was placed into a police transport in breach of the RIPA 2000.[91] The Court of Appeal was required to consider whether such evidence ought to have been excluded from the trial per section 78 of PACE 1984. McCombe LJ ruled that:

> It is accepted that there was a failure to observe the limits of the authorisation obtained. ... The result was a breach of two appellants' rights of privacy, contrary to Article 8 of the Convention. In our judgment, on the facts of this case, it says nothing about the fairness of

87 Ibid., at 578, citing Lord Griffiths in *Scott v The Queen* [1989] AC 1242, at 1256.

88 *Khan v United Kingdom* App. No. 35394/97 (12 May 2000).

89 Ibid., at [26].

90 [2013] ECA Crim 2230.

91 Importantly, authorisation was obtained to bug the transport before the appellants were charged with the offence, but the device was used post-charging (when authorisation had technically ended).

> the appellants' trial. As in *Plunkett*[92] there was no misrepresentation, entrapment or trickery. The police had simply made use of the opportunity afforded to the two appellants to talk to each other. As the recordings themselves demonstrate, the two men were well aware of the possibility that their conversation might be bugged. There was no oppression or coercion. Nothing limited the appellants' right to challenge the evidence or to explain it.[93]

As the decisions in both *Khan* cases suggest, Article 8 is not an absolute right. Interferences with the right can be justified by signatory states, provided that it is shown that such an interference

> is in accordance with the law and is necessary in a democratic society in the interests of national security, public safety or the economic well-being of the country, for the prevention of disorder or crime, for the protection of health or morals, or for the protection of the rights and freedoms of others.[94]

However, any state seeking to rely on Article 8(2) as a defence must first illustrate that the interference is prescribed in law: this was not the case either in *Khan* or in the earlier case of *Malone*. Even if such a privacy law is in place, the state must then show that it is proportionate for the purposes of achieving one of the objectives in Article 8(2). This was a hurdle that Germany failed to overcome in *Klass v Germany*.[95] The law in question permitted the police to intercept mail in certain circumstances. The court found that this situation constituted a 'menace of surveillance' for all citizens who made use of the postal service. This was a 'menace' that violated the freedom of communication between individuals and constituted a breach of Convention requirements. The Court noted: 'Powers of secret surveillance of citizens, characterizing as they do the police state, are tolerable under the Convention only in so far as strictly necessary for safeguarding the democratic institutions.'[96]

There has been relatively little discussion of the suspect's right to privacy in a police station, even by the Strasbourg Court. It did, however, arise in the case of *PG and JH v United Kingdom*,[97] in which the use of covert listening devices in a police station was held to violate Article 8. Here, B was suspected of preparing for a robbery, and authorisation was then given for listening devices to be placed in his flat. However, after B and others discovered the bugs, they left the flat and the police began to think that the robbery had been called off. Several days later, B and others were arrested in a stolen car containing two black balaclavas, five black plastic cable ties, two pairs of leather gloves, and two army rucksacks. In order to obtain speech samples to compare with the tapes from the flat, police were granted authorisation to use covert listening devices in the cells and on the police officers who were to be present when B and others were charged. Evidence derived from the listening devices was admitted at their trial for conspiracy to rob. They were convicted and their appeal was rejected.

The Strasbourg Court, applying its own decision in *Khan v United Kingdom*, held that the use of a covert listening device in B's flat was not in accordance with the law existing at the time, as there was no statutory provision for surveillance. Similarly, the Court held that there was a breach of Article 8 in respect of the use of covert surveillance devices in the police station. However, no breach was found in respect of Article 6, the right to a fair trial. The taped evidence was not the only evidence against B and the others. There was ample opportunity to challenge both the

---

92 *R v Plunkett* [2013] 1 WLR 3121.

93 At [55]. See also *R v Mahmood* [2013] EWCA Crim 2356 in relation to the blanket recording of prisoner phone calls.

94 Article 8(2).

95 (1978) 2 EHRR 214.

96 Ibid., at [3f].

97 App. No. 44787/98 (25 September 2001).

authenticity and the use of the recordings. Even though the domestic courts had declined to exclude the evidence, the Court further considered that there was no unfairness in leaving it to the jury, on the basis of a thorough summing-up by the trial judge, to decide where the weight of the evidence lay. The defence claim that the use of voice samples to compare with other recordings was a breach of their right not to incriminate themselves was rejected by the Court, which saw these as akin to the use of blood or other samples used in forensic analysis, to which that right did not apply. This decision is consistent with those considered above where the fact that the evidence was obtained unlawfully does not necessarily mean that admitting it will have such an adverse effect on the fairness of the trial that it ought not to be admitted.

The interaction between Articles 6, 8, and section 78 of PACE was considered again in *Allan v United Kingdom*.[98] The applicant, who had been arrested for robbery, contended that his Article 8 rights had been infringed when police tapped his cell and the prison visiting area in order to obtain evidence that he had been responsible for a murder. Following his arrest, Allan chose to remain silent, but the prosecution relied upon three statements he had made to his cellmate, to his friend who had visited him, and to another police informant briefly placed in the cell alongside him. His application to the European Court of Human Rights rested on the argument that the judge should have ruled out the statements as they were unfairly obtained and infringed his right to privacy. The Government accepted, on the basis of *Khan*, that the lack of any regulatory regime did mean that Article 8 had indeed been infringed. However, it contested the allegation that use of the evidence interfered with the fairness of proceedings, contrary to Article 6. In relation to the first two statements, made to his cellmate and to his visiting friend, the Court held that there was nothing inherently contrary to Article 6 in the way in which the evidence was used. The judge had taken a decision to admit them at the *voir dire* and, taking into account all relevant factors, had concluded that the evidence was reliable and its use would not result in an unfair trial. However, the Court came to a different conclusion in relation to the evidence obtained by the police informer. Inculpatory statements made by the applicants were not made voluntarily, but instead had been induced by persistent questioning by the informer. As such, these statements were unreliable and thus affected the fairness of the trial.

In summary, then, from the perspective of European human rights law, covert surveillance of any type is likely to fall foul of Article 8 if it is not regulated by legislation. Where some form of regulation is in place, each alleged interference must be considered on the particular facts and circumstances of each case, taking into account the clarity of the relevant law, the basis for surveillance, and whether the actions of the state can be regarded as proportionate. That use of surveillance is an interference with rights protected by Article 8 of the European Convention on Human Rights and is *prima facie* a violation of those rights unless the interference is in accordance with the law, is in pursuit of one or more of the legitimate aims established by Article 8(2) and is 'necessary in a democratic society.'

In response to these decisions, the use of electronic surveillance is now much more closely regulated in the United Kingdom. The Police Act 1997 stipulates that the use of covert listening devices by the police in private places, such as homes, offices, and hotel bedrooms, first requires prior authorisation by a Commissioner, unless the need for surveillance is urgent, in which case a Commissioner must be informed as soon as practicable. Forms of surveillance not covered by the Police Act are mostly regulated by the RIPA 2000, which covers 'directed surveillance,' 'intrusive surveillance,' and the use of covert human intelligence sources.

Directed surveillance is a type of covert surveillance where police, intelligence agencies, and other public authorities observe an individual in public and record their actions. It is not intrusive, and is undertaken for the purposes of a specific investigation in such a manner as is likely to result

98 (2002) 36 EHRR 12.

in the obtaining of private information about a person (whether or not specifically identified for the purpose of the investigation or operation).[99]

'Intrusive surveillance' would include surveillance by an individual or device on residential premises or in a private vehicle (i.e. an observation point), but observing activity elsewhere would be directed surveillance.[100] The main issue is that the surveillance is carried out in relation to anything taking place on any residential premises or in a private vehicle and involves the presence of an individual on residential premises or in a private vehicle, etc. This is considerably more contentious than directed surveillance, since it involves interference with privacy, and a potential *prima facie* breach of Article 8 of the Convention. If any public authority wishes to engage in intrusive surveillance, authorisation must be sought from either the Secretary of State or a senior authorising officer.[101] Permission may be granted provided that the surveillance is considered proportionate,[102] and if such action is necessary:

(a) in the interests of national security;
(b) for the purpose of preventing or detecting serious crime; or
(c) in the interests of the economic well-being of the United Kingdom.[103]

In addition to authorisation by the authorising officer, the grant (or renewal) of an authorisation for intrusive surveillance must be approved by a Surveillance Commissioner unless the case is one of urgency.[104]

The conduct of covert human intelligence sources is also dealt with in the legislation. Under section 26(8), a person is considered a covert human intelligence source of the Act if he or she:

(a) establishes or maintains a personal or other relationship with another person for the covert purpose of facilitating the doing of anything falling within paragraph (b) or (c) below;
(b) covertly uses such a relationship to obtain information or to provide access to any information to another person; or
(c) covertly discloses information obtained by the use of such a relationship or as a consequence of the existence of such a relationship.

Covert human intelligence sources would therefore include informants, whistleblowers, or undercover police officers. Examples would be placing a police informer in a cell, as in *Allan v UK*, or the use of officers as part of an operation to apprehend those dealing in drugs or stolen goods, as in *Looseley* or *Christou* (see below). An authorisation to use a covert human intelligence source must be made on the same grounds as for directed surveillance set out above. It must therefore be proportionate and, in addition, meet one of the statutory criteria stipulated in section 29(3).

---

99 RIPA 2000, s 26(2). Directed surveillance can be ordered by a superintendent, or, if a superintendent is not available, an inspector. Authorised surveillance must be proportionate to what is sought to be achieved by carrying it out, and must meet one of the grounds set out in subs 3. These are: (a) the interests of national security; (b) for the purpose of preventing or detecting crime or of preventing disorder; (c) in the interests of the economic well-being of the United Kingdom; (d) in the interests of public safety; (e) for the purpose of protecting public health; (f) for the purpose of assessing or collecting any tax, duty, levy or other imposition, contribution or charge payable to a government department; or (g) for any purpose (not falling within paragraphs (a) to (f)) which is specified for the purposes of this subsection by an order made by the Secretary of State. The authorisation must be granted by the Chief Constable where the likely consequence of the directed surveillance would be for any person to acquire knowledge of confidential material.

100 RIPA 2000, s 26(3).

101 In the case of the police, this will usually be a chief constable.

102 RIPA 2000, s 32(3).

103 Ibid., s 32(3).

104 Ibid., s 35.

9.2.4 Undercover operations and entrapment

Operations involving covert 'human intelligence sources' have traditionally been referred to in straightforward layman's terms as 'undercover' or 'sting' operations. *R v Christou*[105] is a classic case. A mock shop, Stardust Jewellers, was set up by the police in a high crime area of London. Staffed by undercover officers, they let it be known that they would be prepared to deal in stolen property. All of the transactions were recorded by covert video cameras and sound equipment, and sellers were asked to sign receipts for the money that they had received. The defendants, who had sold stolen items to the shop on a number of occasions, were convicted of burglary and handling stolen goods. They appealed, alleging that the evidence of the undercover operation should have been excluded either at common law or under section 78.

The Court of Appeal agreed with the decision at first instance to admit the evidence. Although the police had practised a form of trickery, they had not acted as agents provocateurs, in the sense that they did not encourage the commission of a crime that had not already taken place. In the words of Lord Taylor: 'The trick was not applied to the appellants; they voluntarily applied themselves to the trick.'[106] The trial judge, by considering the operation as a whole, had exercised his discretion correctly. Code C was primarily devised to protect potentially vulnerable parties from the abuse or pressure from police officers under questioning, and did not apply in these circumstances, in which the suspects were not aware of the true identity of the police officers. As such, they interacted on equal terms. By way of a caveat, it was added that it would be wrong for police to use such an undercover operation simply to evade the Code of Practice's provisions and evidence obtained in that way should normally be excluded. Observations were also made on the nature of the bases for exclusion under common law and the 1984 Act. Both thresholds were essentially the same; it would be illogical to have differing standards in place.

The *Christou* test, which seemed to hinge upon whether or not the defendants had voluntarily applied themselves to the trick, was applied in three subsequent Court of Appeal decisions that followed shortly afterwards. In the first of those decisions, *Bryce*,[107] it was held that evidence of the conversations between the appellant and an undercover police officer should have been excluded because these conversations went directly to the crucial issue of guilty knowledge. They were hotly disputed, and, in contrast to *Christou*, there was no contemporary record of them. As noted in Chapter 8, however, a preferable avenue for their exclusion should have been section 76(2)(b), since the decision seemed to be based more on concerns about the reliability of the statements rather than the potential impact upon the fairness of the proceedings.

In the second case, *MacLean and Kosten*,[108] D was found to be carrying cannabis through customs concealed in a car. Anxious to catch the importer as well as the courier, a story was concocted whereby the courier was said to be in hospital following a road accident. Subsequently, and according to plan, the importer arranged to recover the car in order to obtain his order of cannabis. He appealed against conviction on the grounds that the evidence should have been excluded since it had been unfairly obtained through trickery. Dismissing the appeal, it was held that there had been nothing unfair about the means adopted to make D incriminate himself since he had already committed the crime in question.

The third case to follow on the heels of *Christou* concerned the more contentious circumstances that arose in *Williams and O'Hare*.[109] The defendants were charged with interfering with a motor vehicle with intent to commit theft. Police had left an unlocked and unattended van in a busy high street where there had been a high rate of vehicle crime. Imitation cigarette cartons

---

105 [1992] 2 QB 979.
106 Ibid., at 989.
107 [1992] 4 All ER 567.
108 [1993] Crim LR 687.
109 (1994) 98 Cr App R 209.

were visible through its rear window. The appellants were observed walking around the van and removing cartons from it. Following conviction, it was contended that the evidence against them should have been excluded by the trial judge under section 78 of PACE on the ground of entrapment. Dismissing the appeal, the court found in favour of the Crown. Applying *Christou*, the court underlined that the police did not act as agents provocateurs because they made no communication with the defendants and did not set out to catch any particular thieves when they placed the van. Central to the court's decision was the fact that the appellants committed the crime 'voluntarily, of their own free will.'[110] They had, according to Farquharson LJ, committed the act as a result of their inherent 'criminal instincts' rather than as a result of the actions of the police.[111] As Geoffrey Robertson contends,[112] the proper application of the *Christou* test was highly questionable, since there was no basis (as there was in *Christou*) for suspecting that they would have committed the act in question had the sting operation not been put in place. While the court highlighted the absence of any verbal act of incitement or encouragement, no explanation was given as to why the physical act of tempting persons to commit a crime is fundamentally different from the verbal one:

> This decision appears to allow section 78 to operate in cases where the incitement to crime comes from the mouth of an agent provocateur but not where the temptation, however hard to resist, results from a carefully laid trap which contains its own lure. The distinction is artificial, but it has permitted police to take 'crime initiatives' which initiate crime, yet which are described as 'entirely legitimate enterprise.'[113]

Following these cases, it appeared questionable as to whether circumstances of entrapment would ever give rise to an obligation to exclude evidence.[114] In *Smurthwaite and Gill*,[115] however, the Court of Appeal made clear that it could do so, subject to the application of a number of factors by the trial judge in the exercise of his section 78 discretion. Both appellants (in two separate cases) were convicted of soliciting a contract killer to murder their spouses. In each case, the police sent undercover officers to pose as contract killers and recorded the conversations. Arguing that the police should be considered to be acting as agents provocateurs, the appellants contended on appeal that all of the covert recording should have been excluded. Echoing the House of Lords' decision in *Sang*, the Court of Appeal repeated that the fact that the evidence was obtained by entrapment, or by agent provocateur, or by a trick did not place the judge under an obligation to exclude it. Although such actions were not entirely irrelevant, any decision to exclude the evidence on that basis had to be made in accordance with the statutory test. In deciding whether such actions might have an adverse effect on the fairness of proceedings, Lord Taylor proceeded to list a number of 'relevant factors' that should be taken into account by the trial judge in arriving at his decision:

> Was the officer acting as an agent provocateur in the sense that he was enticing the defendant to commit an offence he would not have otherwise committed? What was the nature of any entrapment? Does the evidence consist of admission to a completed offence or does it consist of the actual commission of an offence? How active or passive was the officer's role in obtaining the evidence? Is there an unassailable record of what occurred or is it strongly corroborated? Further consideration for the judge in deciding whether to admit an

---

110 Ibid., at 213.

111 Ibid., at 215.

112 Robertson, G., 'Entrapment Evidence: Manna from Heaven, or Fruit of the Poisoned Tree?' [1994] Crim LR 805.

113 Ibid., at 811.

114 This was the view of Stocker LJ in *Harwood* [1989] Crim LR 285, who stated that s 78 could not be used as a basis for exclusion in entrapment cases.

115 [1994] 1 All ER 898.

> undercover officer's evidence is if he has abused his role as a police officer to ask questions and if they are in accordance with the codes.[116]

The Court of Appeal thus departed from *Sang* in acknowledging that entrapment may give rise to procedural unfairness that might warrant exclusion. The court suggested a series of guidelines as to when section 78 might come into play, but the decision stopped short of offering any solid, guiding principle that would add any element of predictability as to how entrapment evidence would be treated at first instance.

Entrapment may not only produce circumstances that require the exclusion of evidence under section 78, but may also lead the court to stay a prosecution on grounds of abuse of process. Such a scenario arose in *R v Latif and Shahzad*,[117] which concerned a plan to import heroin from Pakistan. The plan was partly instigated and organised by a police informer, along with officers from Customs and Excise. Despite acknowledging that the offence would probably never have been committed but for the role played by the authorities, the House of Lords acknowledged that the case posed something of a conundrum. If, on the one hand, prosecutions were always to be stayed in such circumstances, this would have an inevitable knock-on effect on the protection of the public. If, on the other hand, courts were to refuse blankly to stay proceedings, then that would undermine public confidence in the criminal justice system. It was thus required to chart a middle course between these two extreme options. The proper approach advocated by their Lordships comprised a two-pronged test. First, it should be asked whether the conduct in question rendered a fair trial impossible. If the answer were 'yes,' it would be appropriate to stay proceedings at that point. If the answer were 'no,' the second limb of the test asked whether, despite a fair trial being possible, proceedings should be nonetheless stayed on the grounds of 'an affront to the public conscience.' Applying this test to the scenario before the court, their Lordships held that the judge had rightfully declined to stay proceedings. He had properly taken into account all of the relevant considerations, including the fact that Shahzad was a major importer in the heroin trade and had initially proposed the operation.

In the aftermath of the decision, judges at first instance were thus left with a choice of what to do in cases in which an unfair trial might be the result of entrapment by the authorities. They could either exclude the evidence under section 78 of PACE where the evidence-gathering adversely affected the fairness of the case, or stay proceedings for abuse of process by executive authorities. Furthermore, courts faced an additional challenge in that the Human Rights Act 1998 was shortly to come into force. Increasingly, therefore, jurisprudence from Strasbourg on the matter had to be taken into account.

The leading Strasbourg case was that of *Teixeira de Castro v Portugal*.[118] The case concerned an offer to purchase drugs made by undercover police operators to a suspected dealer. The applicant, who was previously unknown to the police, had been introduced to the officers by a third party. Unaware of the identity of the undercover officers, the applicant was offered cash in the back of a car in exchange for a quantity of heroin. Having obtained it for them, he was arrested and convicted on the basis of the undercover operation.

The applicant contended that he had not had a fair trial, since he had been incited to commit the offence by the plain-clothes officers. He maintained that he had no previous convictions and would never have committed the offence had it not been for the intervention of the police as agents provocateurs. In addition, he argued that the police officers had acted on their own initiative, without any supervision by the courts, and without any preliminary investigation. The

116 Ibid., at 903.
117 [1996] 1 WLR 104.
118 (1998) 28 EHRR 101.

court agreed that there had been a violation of his fair trial rights. The key basis for the decision was the fact that the officers had taken on an active role in procuring the offence. A distinction was made with those cases in which the police attempted to purchase drugs from known suppliers, which would not ordinarily amount to a breach of Article 6.

The impact of the decision on domestic law was considered in *Nottingham City Council v Amin*,[119] which provides a useful illustration of the distinction between causing the commission of the offence and providing an opportunity for its commission. The defendant had been charged with running a taxi within an area in which it was not licensed to ply for hire. The taxi was hailed by two plain-clothes officers, who duly paid their fare before charging the driver with plying for hire without a licence. At first instance, the magistrate excluded the evidence on the ground that the police had acted as agents provocateurs, and accepted the argument of the accused that he would not have committed the offence in question but for the actions of the officers. Reversing the decision of the magistrate, and distinguishing the case from *Teixeira*, the Divisional Court found that there had been no incitement or pressure placed on the defendant to commit the offence. As Lord Bingham observed:

> On the one hand it has been recognised as deeply offensive to ordinary notions of fairness if a defendant were to be convicted and punished for committing a crime which he only committed because he had been incited, instigated, persuaded, pressurised or wheedled into committing it by a law enforcement officer. On the other hand it has been recognised that law enforcement agencies have a general duty to the public to enforce the law and it has been regarded as unobjectionable if a law enforcement officer gives a defendant an opportunity to break the law, of which the defendant freely takes advantage, in circumstances where it appears that the defendant would have behaved in the same way if the opportunity had been offered by anyone else.[120]

For Lord Bingham, the fact that this particular fare involved two undercover police officers did not provide a basis for abuse of process, since they had acted as ordinary members of the public. They did not wave £50 notes or pretend to be in distress, and this suggested that the defendant would have provided a fare for anyone else who flagged him down. Each case must turn on its own facts, and crucial to this decision was the fact that the police did not take on any active role in applying pressure.

The same approach is to be followed where the alleged entrapment emanates from a non-state actor (as opposed to the police or other law enforcement authority). In *Shannon*,[121] the accused, a popular television actor, was convicted of supplying cocaine and cannabis resin to an undercover reporter from the *News of the World*. The purpose of the investigation had been to expose the actor as a drugs supplier. It had been argued that since the prosecution evidence had been obtained by an agent provocateur, it should be excluded under section 78 and, moreover, reliance on the unfairly obtained evidence was contrary to the Human Rights Act 1998 in that it deprived the defendant of a right to a fair trial. The judge ruled the evidence admissible and C was convicted. On appeal, it was held that the judge had acted correctly; there was no indication here that there had been actual incitement or instigation to commit the drugs offences. The discretion would only have come into play if the prosecution evidence was unreliable or tainted in some other way.

119 [2001] 1 WLR 1071.
120 Ibid., at 1076–77.
121 [2001] 1 WLR 51.

The leading case on entrapment is now *R v Looseley; AG's Reference* (No. 3 of 2000).[122] This joined case brings together many of the different strands of the above cases, and provides a relative degree of clarity on the position of entrapment in domestic law post-Human Rights Act. Looseley, a known heroin dealer, contended that he had been lured into supplying drugs by an undercover police officer. In the second case, the defendant, G, had been acquitted, following the trial judge's decision to stay proceedings for abuse of process. The facts here were somewhat different. The prosecution contended that undercover officers supplied the defendant with contraband cigarettes, and one then asked the defendant whether he could 'sort out any brown.' The defendant, it seems, took some persuading, and told the officers that he 'wasn't really into heroin.' He eventually obtained it from another source, and duly supplied it, but in the police interview he told them that he had 'nothing at all' to do with heroin, and only agreed to supply it as a favour after the two men had approached him offering cheap cigarettes.

The House of Lords acknowledged the absence of any doctrine of entrapment in English law, but also stated that proceedings should be stayed where the actions of the police were so seriously improper as to bring the administration of justice into disrepute. To that end, a useful guide was to consider whether the police 'did no more than present the defendant with an unexceptional opportunity to commit a crime.'[123] In the view of Lord Nicholls, four factors ought to be taken into account in deciding whether conduct should be classified as 'seriously improper.'

1. *The nature of the offence.* The use of proactive techniques is more needed, and, hence, more appropriate, in some circumstances than others. The secrecy and difficulty of detection, and the manner in which the particular criminal activity is carried on, are relevant considerations.
2. *The reason for the particular police operation.* It goes without saying that the police must act in good faith and not, for example, as part of a malicious vendetta against an individual or group of individuals. Having reasonable grounds for suspicion is one way in which good faith may be established, but having grounds for suspicion of a particular individual is not always essential. Sometimes, suspicion may be centred on a certain place, such as a particular public house. Sometimes, random testing may be the only practicable way of policing a particular trading activity.
3. *The nature and extent of police participation in the crime.* The greater the inducement held out by the police, and the more forceful or persistent the police overtures, the more readily may a court conclude that the police overstepped the boundary: their conduct might well have brought about the commission of a crime by a person who would normally avoid crime of that kind. In assessing the weight to be attached to the police inducement, regard is to be had to the defendant's circumstances, including his vulnerability. This is not because the standards of acceptable behaviour are variable; rather, this is a recognition that what may be a significant inducement to one person may not be so to another. For the police to behave as would an ordinary customer of a trade, whether lawful or unlawful, being carried on by the defendant will not normally be regarded as objectionable.
4. *The defendant's criminal record.* The defendant's criminal record is unlikely to be relevant unless it can be linked to other factors grounding reasonable suspicion that the defendant is currently engaged in criminal activity.[124]

As a general principle, it would be acceptable for police officers to provide a person with an unexceptional opportunity to commit a crime and, if that person proceeded to do so freely, then there would be no grounds for exclusion of evidence or abuse of process. However, if a person were to commit an offence that they would not have ordinarily committed following some form

---

122 [2001] 1 WLR 2060.

123 Ibid., at 2069.

124 Ibid., at 2070.

of inducement or allurement, this would serve to undermine the need for the police to carry out their work in good faith. This position was in line with the decision of the European Court of Human Rights in *Teixeira* and, where a violation had resulted, the appropriate remedy was a stay of proceedings under the abuse of process doctrine. In relation to the two cases before the court, it was acceptable in *Looseley*, since L was a known dealer, for an officer to pose as an addict looking for drugs. By contrast, in relation to the other case, the officers had overstepped the boundary since they had incited and encouraged G to commit an uncharacteristic offence. Their actions were so seriously improper as to bring the administration of justice into disrepute, and thus the proceedings had been properly stayed. The abuse of process doctrine, rather than section 78, was the appropriate remedy in this type of situation. The latter provision was directed 'primarily at matters going to fairness in the actual conduct of the trial; for instance, the reliability of the evidence and the defendant's ability to test its reliability.'[125] However, even if the threshold for abuse of process were not met, it would seemingly remain open for the evidence to be excluded under the statute.

The decision in *Looseley* was applied in the unreported case of *Moon*.[126] Following considerable persuasion by an undercover policewoman, the accused had supplied her with a small quantity of heroin, which the accused obtained from a dealer. While she pleaded guilty to an offence of possession, she contested the charge of supply on the ground that she had been entrapped. The judge refused her application to stay the prosecution because, although procedural errors were made, the undercover operation was found to be largely bona fide since, in his opinion, the defendant would have committed the offence even if the errors had not been made. However, the appellant's conviction was quashed on appeal. While the court agreed that the undercover police operation had been bona fide, there was no evidence that she would have been prepared to supply any would-be purchaser. Moon had no predisposition to deal and had no previous history of dealing. Furthermore, it was the police officer who made the first approach. Taking these factors into account, the court concluded that the appellant had been lured into committing the offence, and, following *Looseley*, the proceedings should have been stayed.

Looseley, *Teixeria*, and *Christou* were all considered by the Court of Appeal in *R v Palmer*.[127] The facts were remarkably similar to those of *Christou*; police officers had conducted a covert operation, in line with the RIPA 2000, in which they posed as the operators of a dishonest pawnshop in which local criminals could sell stolen property (and thus incriminate themselves for offences). With over 100 arrests, the covert operation was an apparent success; however, concerns were raised that the police had seduced individuals with no prior criminal propensity to commit offences they might not have otherwise committed and as a result the operation had given rise to an affront to justice or an abuse of process. Rejecting the appeal, the Court of Appeal found the operation to be fair and just in the circumstances and the trial judge's directions on the matter to be 'impeccable.'[128] Specifically, Hallett LJ ruled that:

> 75. [The trial judge] found as a fact that the designated officers who granted the authorisations had good reason to believe that the operation was necessary and proportionate. ... Burglary was particularly prevalent in the targeted areas ... and conventional methods were not working. A less conventional approach was adopted with the legitimate aims of preventing and detecting burglary offences in the area; and it was to a significant degree successful.

---

125 Ibid., at 2066.
126 [2004] EWCA Crim 2872.
127 [2014] EWCA Crim 1681.
128 Ibid., at [79] (Hallett LJ).

> 76. Whereas other boroughs saw yet another increase in burglary of 8–10%, Barnet saw an increase of just 3%. A large number of people were arrested (of which the vast majority pleaded guilty) and many hundreds of items of stolen property were recovered and returned to their owners. The fact that many of those items were identity documents and not all of them stolen does not undermine the integrity of the whole operation. As the judge observed, the undercover officers could not refuse to buy identity documents and maintain their credibility as fundamentally dishonest. In any event, many of the identity documents were undoubtedly stolen ... and because identity documents are generally easier to trace, the officers thereby gathered useful evidence.
>
> 77. Further, the judge rejected in clear terms and on good evidence that the applicants were in any way vulnerable or enticed by the officers' conduct into committing crimes they would not otherwise have committed. He saw and heard the applicants on the surveillance tapes. Their only vulnerability was their greed. There was nothing exceptional about the opportunity presented to them. In the words of Lord Taylor CJ in *Christou* they 'voluntarily applied themselves to the trick.'[129]

Certainly, in light of *Looseley* and *Palmer*, a considerable degree of clarity has been shed on the law. In determining whether proceedings should be stayed on grounds of entrapment, each case will continue to turn on its own facts. However, it is now clear that a defendant who commits an offence that they would not have otherwise committed as a consequence of the actions of the authorities should normally have proceedings stayed. In those cases in which conduct does not meet this threshold, section 78 remains available, although in such circumstances the courts are more concerned with the reliability of any statements made than the conduct of the police. However, there continues to be some degree of uncertainty as to when precisely actions of the police that fall short of the *Looseley* requirements may give rise to the adverse effect required for section 78 to be invoked.

9.3 Exclusion of evidence in civil cases

The power to exclude evidence, both under common law and PACE, was originally confined to criminal cases; no such discretion existed in respect of civil proceedings.[130] The provisions of PACE, of course, similarly apply only to criminal proceedings. An exclusionary discretion in civil proceedings was, however, introduced in the Civil Procedure Rules 1998.[131] Rule 32.1 provides:

> (1) The court may control the evidence by giving directions as to –
>   (a) the issues on which it requires evidence;
>   (b) the nature of the evidence which it requires to decide those issues; and
>   (c) the way in which the evidence is to be placed before the court.
>
> (2) The court may use its power under this rule to exclude evidence that would otherwise be admissible.

This is a broad-ranging provision that is designed to ensure that cases are managed both more efficiently and cost-effectively than had been the case prior to the introduction of the Rules.

The leading case relating to the discretionary exclusion is *Jones v University of Warwick*.[132] The claimant had sought damages for a wrist injury sustained while working for the defendant employer. The defendant had instructed private investigators to probe claims concerning the

---

129 See also *R v Harmes* [2006] EWCA 928 as to the proper limits of undercover operations under the RIPA 2000.

130 *Helliwell v Piggott-Sims* [1980] FSR 582.

131 Civil Procedure Rules 1998 (SI 1998/3132).

132 [2003] 1 WLR 954.

extent of the injury. Posing as market researchers, the investigators had subsequently entered the claimant's home on two separate occasions and covertly recorded her movements. At trial, the defence then produced an expert witness who testified, on the basis of the recordings, that she appeared to have normal hand functioning.

The claimant applied for the evidence to be excluded on the grounds that her right to privacy under Article 8 of the European Convention had been infringed. For the Court of Appeal, however, this was one of 'two conflicting public interests' that had to be balanced by the court. The other public interest element was the desirability of admitting evidence that was clearly relevant to the case. In the end, it was the latter concern that prevailed. Lord Woolf explained the decision to uphold the original decision of the trial judge to admit the video evidence in the following terms:

> It would be artificial and undesirable for the actual evidence, which was relevant and admissible, not to be placed before the trial judge. To exclude the evidence would create a wholly undesirable situation. Fresh medical experts would have to be instructed on both sides. Evidence which was relevant would have to be concealed from them, perhaps resulting in a misdiagnosis; and it would not be possible to cross-examine the claimant appropriately. For those reasons the court did not consider it would be right to interfere with the judge's decision not to exclude the evidence.[133]

Notwithstanding, Lord Woolf proceeded to criticise the conduct of the defendant's insurers as 'improper and not justified.' Such conduct, he said, should not go unpunished and exclusion was not 'the only weapon in the court's armoury.'[134] To discourage this type of conduct in the future, costs were awarded against the defendant.

While the exclusionary regimes governing criminal and civil proceedings differ substantially, it is clear that in both fora there are no hard-and-fast tests that can be applied to determine when exclusion might be appropriate. In *Jones*, it was clear that the evidence in question was cogent and reliable, and the conduct of the defence, while improper, was not *so* outrageous that it would have justified the defence being struck out. It is thus perfectly possible to envisage more extreme scenarios in which less reliable evidence – or more intrusive surveillance techniques – might be excluded under Rule 32.

9.4 Key learning points

- Improperly obtained evidence (other than confessions) may or may not be admissible in English law.
- The judge will have a discretion both at common law and in statute as to whether the evidence should be admitted.
- For both forms of discretion, the key test will be whether the actions of the police have resulted in unfairness at the trial.
- Breaches of PACE and the Codes may have this effect if they are 'significant and substantial.'
- Covert surveillance will not normally be grounds for exclusion, although it should be properly authorised under the Police Act 1997 or the Regulation of Investigatory Powers Act 2000.
- There is no defence of entrapment in English law. However, where the actions of the police are so seriously improper as to bring the administration of justice into disrepute, proceedings should be stayed.
- In civil proceedings, the court enjoys a broad-ranging discretion to exclude evidence.

---

133 Ibid., at [28].

134 Ibid., at [30].

9.5 Practice questions

1 In *Sang* [1980] AC 402, Lord Diplock stated that a trial judge 'has no discretion to refuse to admit relevant admissible evidence on the ground that it was obtained by improper or unfair means' (at 437). Is this still an accurate summary of the law?

2 Critically evaluate how serious violations of PACE and the Codes of Practice have to be before evidence will be ruled out under section 78.

3 Police suspect that Joe and Dave are dealing in cannabis. Having kept them under close surveillance, two officers break into the flat one night after seeing the two men leaving. Without the appropriate authorisation, they install covert listening devices in the kitchen. Over the next two weeks, a number of incriminating statements are transmitted by the devices, but police fear that they still do not have enough evidence to charge them. Consequently, Jemima, an undercover officer, is sent to a local pub where the two men have allegedly dealt cannabis on previous occasions. She approaches them in the car park and asks whether they could supply her with some heroin. Joe tells her he 'doesn't do hard stuff,' but Jemima says that if he could get hold of a large quantity for her, she would 'make it worth his while' and would pay 'through the roof.' A week later, the two men meet Jemima and supply her with the requested amount of heroin. Both men are arrested and prosecuted. The prosecution now seeks to use both the recordings transmitted by the listening devices and the heroin offered to Jemima as evidence against Joe and Dave. Advise Joe and Dave.

9.6 Suggested further reading

Ashworth, A., 'Redrawing the Boundaries of Entrapment' (2002) Crim LR 161.

Choo, A. and Nash, S., 'Improperly Obtained Evidence in the Commonwealth: Lessons for England and Wales?' (2007) 11(2) E & P 75.

Hyland, K. and Walker, C., 'Undercover Policing and Underwhelming Laws' (2014) Crim LR 555.

Levanon, L., 'The Law of Police Entrapment: Critical Evaluation and Policy Analysis' (2016) 27(1) Crim LR 35.

Murphy, B. and Anderson, J., 'Confessions to Mr Big: A New Rule of Evidence?' (2016) 20(1) E & P 29.

Ormerod, D., 'ECHR and the Exclusion of Evidence: Trial Remedies for Article 8 Breaches?' (2003) Crim LR 61.

Ormerod, D. and Birch, D., 'The Evolution of the Discretionary Exclusion of Evidence' (2004) Crim LR 767.

Ormerod, D. and Roberts, P., 'The Trouble with Teixeira: Developing a Principled Approach to Entrapment' (2002) 6(1) E & P 38.

Squires, D., 'The Problem with Entrapment' (2006) 26(2) OJLS 351.

Chapter 10

Suspect Evidence

Corroboration and Identification

Chapter contents

DOI: 10.4324/9781003416098-10

This chapter focuses on two particular topics within the law of evidence that are often labelled 'suspect' or 'hazardous': uncorroborated evidence and identification evidence. These areas have been treated by the courts with particular caution since they are regarded as considerably less reliable than other types of evidence. As will become apparent in the course of this chapter, recent shifts towards broader freedom of proof have meant that suspect evidence – like hearsay and bad character – is now much more readily admissible in court. In practice, it is generally recognised that on many occasions such evidence may be highly relevant. Thus, the general rule is that suspect evidence will be admissible, but, in practice, may be accompanied by some form of judicial warning to the jury.

10.1 Corroboration

The Latin maxim *testis unus testis nullus* (one witness is no witness) continues to form the basis of most continental legal systems. In effect, it means that a conviction should not be secured on the basis of one person's testimony alone. This also reflects the position in Scottish criminal law. Under the English common law, however, the general rule is that the trier of fact may convict on the uncorroborated testimony of one witness, and there is no requirement for the judge to warn the jury of the dangers of convicting on such evidence. In practice, however, the lack of corroboration may mean that the case is too weak to prosecute or, if prosecuted, it may be difficult to persuade the jury of the defendant's guilt. At the outset, it is worth highlighting the distinction between corroboration evidence and supporting evidence.

Corroboration was defined in the following terms by Lord Reading CJ in *R v Baskerville*:

> We hold that evidence in corroboration must be independent testimony which affects the accused by connecting or tending to connect him with the crime. In other words, it must be evidence which implicates him, that is, which confirms in some material particular not only the evidence that the crime has been committed, but also the prisoner committed it.[1]

At its simplest, corroboration may thus entail no more than another independent witness giving similar testimony, so that each witness supports the other. Supporting evidence, by contrast, may derive from the same person/source as the evidence for which support is being sought (for example, an alleged rape victim, speaking of an attack, with supporting medical evidence or evidence of distress). Of course, both corroboration and supporting evidence may be provided in many other forms – including the use of documents, scientific evidence, and computer or machine printouts. Thus, in *Connell v CPS*,[2] a police officer was entitled to corroborate his opinion that a motorist had travelled at a speed that exceeded the statutory limit by reference to the speed reading given by a speed-measuring device that was a prescribed device, but not of an approved type.[3] Evidently, the use of such supporting evidence can add considerable weight to a case that might otherwise appear weak in the event that it hinges on one person's testimony.

---

1 [1916] 2 KB 658, 667.

2 (2011) EWCH 158 (Admin); (2011) 175 JP 151.

3 The use of such devices continues to be a contentious area of focus within corroboration. See also *Roberts v DPP* (1994) RTR 31; *DPP v Thornley* (2006) 170 JP 385; *Iaciofano v DPP* [2011] RTR 15.

An example of such a fatal weakness can be found in the civil case of *Hedges v Mahendran*.[4] The court was required to assess damages due to the claimant after he sustained injuries in a road traffic accident for which the defendant was solely liable. The defendant contended that the claimant's evidence could not be relied upon unless there was some clear corroboration for it, since the evidence was so tainted and unreliable that it was unbelievable. The defendant pointed to the lack of medical evidence and that, at the time that the claimant was supposedly injured, he had carried out a serious sexual assault upon a young woman to which he pleaded guilty and received a custodial sentence. The court accepted that there were real inconsistencies in the claimant's evidence and that it could not be relied upon without clear corroboration from an independent party.

In the modern criminal trial, forensic evidence increasingly provides corroboration, although DNA evidence is now seen as direct, and often conclusive, evidence. In appropriate cases in which it is alleged that the defendant committed the same offence against a number of victims, such as multiple rapes, the jury may take the evidence of other victims into account when considering the count in relation to a particular victim, so that each victim supports the evidence of the other victims, thus providing mutual corroboration.[5]

10.1.1 Mandatory corroboration

With the exception of a small number of statutory offences, it has never been the case in English criminal law that a party be *required* to produce corroborating evidence.[6] As Mirfield notes, these provisions 'do seem to change the climate – as they were intended to – such that in law, the suspect is recruited as an active part of the investigation process.'[7] One such exception is perjury: section 13 of the Perjury Act 1911 stipulates that 'a person shall not be convicted ... solely upon the evidence of one witness as to the falsity of any statement alleged to be.' Indeed, in *R v Carroll*,[8] it was said that a judge is required to make express reference to section 13 in their summing-up. However, the provision came under scrutiny in *R v Cooper*.[9] C had been convicted of using a mobile phone while driving in May 2008. It had been a critical factor in C's defence that his vehicle had been fitted with a hands-free system so there was in fact no need for him to handle the phone while driving. In support of this, C produced a letter signed by the manager of a motor accessories store, T, confirming that C had indeed had a hands-free system installed in his car, in April 2008. Following C's conviction, additional police enquiries revealed that when C had asked T to confirm that his vehicle had been fitted with a hands-free system, T had agreed to do this, but could not recall the date of the fitting. Rather than check his records, T took the word of C that it was installed in April 2008. When T subsequently checked his records, it became apparent that the system had in fact been installed in July 2008. C was charged with wilfully making a false statement at his trial. At C's trial for perjury, T confirmed that his records were correct and the judge directed the jury that if they accepted the evidence of T's records, they could rely upon those in addition to the oral evidence of T as to the date on which the system was actually fitted.

4 Unreported, Bournemouth County Court, 28 June 2010. Full report available on Westlaw.

5 [1994] 1 WLR 788; (1994) 9 CLY 97.

6 For a full account on how mandatory corroboration affects the right to silence and a culture of 'police control' more generally from the 1990s onwards, see Garland, D., *The Culture of Control: Crime and Social Order in Contemporary Society* (Oxford University Press, 2001).

7 Mirfield, P., 'Two Side Effects of Section 34 to Section 37 of the Criminal Justice and Public Order Act 1994' (1994) (1995) Crim LR 612, 616.

8 (1993) 99 Cr App R 381.

9 [2010] 1 WLR 2390.

Allowing the appeal, the court held that the statutory provision made it clear that the evidence of one witness as to the falsity of a statement given in evidence was not enough to establish a perjury conviction. There had to be at least two pieces of evidence and at least one of those must be independent of the witness called to establish the falsity of a statement. In this particular case, the evidence of falsity had not been supported by business records made and prepared within the business independently of the key prosecution witness, as he had prepared them. Indeed, in *R v Rider*, the court held that where corroboration of the main witness's evidence is not possible, the judge ought to direct an acquittal.[10]

A further mandatory corroboration requirement is contained in section 89 of the Road Traffic Regulation Act 1984. This provides that a person may not be convicted of speeding on the basis of the uncorroborated evidence of one witness who has expressed an opinion that the vehicle in question was exceeding the required limit.[11] This provision applies only to evidence of *opinion*; it does not cover evidence of *fact*. In *Crossland v DPP*,[12] a police constable testified to the court that, having examined the scene of an accident and carried out a number of tests, he had concluded that the car's speed at the point of impact was no less than 41 mph. On appeal, it was held that this evidence had been rightly admitted since it did not merely constitute the opinion of one witness: it had described in some detail the 'objectively detectable phenomena' on which his expert opinion was based. Evidence obtained through police radars and other speed-tracking devices that have been properly calibrated will similarly be assumed to constitute evidence of fact.[13]

Treason and charges of attempt are also subject to mandatory corroboration requirements.[14]

10.1.2 Mandatory warnings

Although corroboration is only *required* in relation to a very small number of offences, until recently trial judges were nonetheless under an obligation to warn the jury of the danger of convicting the accused on the uncorroborated evidence of certain categories of witnesses. Such a warning was required in relation to accomplices who testified on behalf of the prosecution, complainants in sexual cases, and child witnesses.

10.1.2.1 Accomplices

As regards accomplices, the motives of those who agreed to testify for the Crown against their erstwhile partner(s) in crime were often called into question. Naturally, many such witnesses might exaggerate the role of others, while minimising their own role in the offence, in the hope of a lighter sentence. *In R v Beck*,[15] it was held that although a judge was required to warn a jury of the need for caution where a witness's evidence may be tainted by some purpose of his own, he was only required to give an accomplice direction where there are grounds for believing that the witness was in some way involved in the crime that is at trial. Moreover, the corroborating evidence need not directly relate to some specific piece of evidence of an accomplice. Where an accomplice provided evidence against a defendant, the corroborating evidence that the common

---

10 (1986) 83 Cr App R 207.

11 Road Traffic Regulation Act 1984, s 89(2).

12 [1988] 3 All ER 712.

13 *Darby v DPP*, *The Times* (4 November 1994).

14 See respectively the Treason Act 1795, s 1, and Criminal Attempts Act 1981, s 2(2)(g).

15 [1982] 1 WLR 461.

law required was corroboration in the form of a particular material tending to show that the accused committed the crime. It was not enough that the corroboration simply showed that the witness has told the truth in irrelevant matters.[16]

It was, however, somewhat inconsistent that the warning was required only where the accomplice was called as a witness for the Crown; no similar warning was needed where the accused was implicated as part of the accomplice's own defence. Thus, the appeal was dismissed in *R v Prater*,[17] in which no warning was given despite D1 having implicated D2 while giving evidence on his own behalf. While the court recognised the desirability of a warning in such circumstances, its absence did not constitute a miscarriage of justice.

10.1.2.2 Complainants in sexual offences

Corroboration warnings were also mandatory in relation to complainants testifying in sexual cases. The requirement that a specific warning be given in these circumstances can be traced back to the writings of the jurist Sir Matthew Hale in the seventeenth century, who warned of the danger of false accusation in rape cases, observing that the charge was 'an accusation easy to be made and hard to be proved, and harder to be defended by the party accused, tho' never so innocent.'[18] He proceeded to state that if the complainant was of good character and reported the crime promptly, the greater her credibility; if she were of ill repute and slow to complain, the less credible her testimony. Hale's observations became the stock-in-trade of defence lawyers, and some judges included them in their summing-up. In the 1910 case of *R v Graham*,[19] the Court of Appeal laid down a requirement that the judge should warn the jury that it is dangerous to act on the unsupported evidence of the complainant in sexual cases. The warning thus became mandatory and soon developed a life of its own,[20] with judges often justifying the warning through reference to the ill-perceived likelihood of false accusation based on sexual neurosis, spite, or shame at having consented to intercourse, which the victim now regretted.

10.1.2.3 Child witnesses

The final circumstance in which a warning was necessary was where the prosecution sought to rely on the evidence of a child. Under section 38(1) of the Children and Young Persons Act 1933, the accused could not be convicted in the absence of corroborating evidence where the child's evidence had been given unsworn, whereas in those cases in which a child had been sworn, the judge was required to issue a warning to the jury. The rationale was that children were perceived to be more prone to fantasy and suggestibility, and their evidence was therefore inherently less credible than that of an adult witness.

Over the years, the mandatory warning evolved into an excessively technical requirement that contributed greatly to the difficulties experienced in prosecuting alleged rapists and child abusers. The 'full' warning comprised four requirements:

(a) the warning to the jury that it was dangerous to convict on the uncorroborated evidence of the particular witness, although they might convict despite the absence of any corroboration;

---

16 *R v Baskerville* [1916] 2 KB 658.
17 [1960] 2 QB 464.
18 Sir Matthew Hale, *The History of the Pleas of the Crown* (1736), pp. 635–36.
19 (1910) 4 Cr App R 218.
20 No warning was necessary where the identification of the accused was in issue but not the commission of the offence itself: *R v Chance* [1988] 3 All ER 225.

(b) an explanation of 'corroboration,' which had developed a technical meaning;
(c) a direction as to what evidence was, or was not, capable of amounting to corroboration; and
(d) a direction that it was for the jury to decide whether that evidence did in fact constitute corroboration.

The rise – and subsequent fall – of the corroboration requirements during the nineteenth and twentieth centuries illustrates how many of our evidential rules developed as a form of protection for the accused, based on what may have been a mistaken belief that such rules were essential to a fair trial. The mistrust of evidence given by an accomplice was understandable, but the mistrust of victims of sexual offences and children was less so. Towards the end of the twentieth century, the mandatory corroboration warnings were perceived as being outdated and ill-founded. As policy-makers became increasingly aware of the plight of victims of sexual offences and child witnesses, they were gradually dismantled. The corroboration requirement in respect of children was the first to be abolished. Section 34 of the Criminal Justice Act 1988 abrogated the requirement of a warning in respect of children giving sworn evidence and the requirement of actual corroboration in respect of children giving unsworn evidence. An attempt to require judges to give a cautionary warning, and in effect continue the old law, notwithstanding the statutory intervention, was rejected by the Court of Appeal in *R v Pryce*.[21] Similarly, in *R v MH*,[22] where the complainant was just 3 years old, the Court of Appeal firmly rejected a suggestion that the judge should have directed the jury that children may imagine or fantasise or misunderstand a situation, may be easily coached, may say what they think their mother wants to hear, or may merely repeat that which has been said on a previous occasion. Moreover, the Court rejected that they should have warned the jury not to be lured by the attractiveness of the child and to bear in mind his extreme youth. It would, the Court said, have been quite wrong for the judge to have engaged in generalisations remote from the facts of the case.

The other two requirements (in respect of sexual complainants and accomplices) were abolished by section 32 of the Criminal Justice and Public Order Act 1994. Inevitably, that was not the end of the matter. While the statute abolished the need for 'obligatory' warnings, it remained possible for a judge to warn a jury in a particular case that it might be dangerous to convict on the uncorroborated evidence of a particular witness where there was a particular reason to do so. In *R v Makanjuola*,[23] counsel for the defendant tried unsuccessfully to reimpose the common law rule when he argued on appeal that, where a judge does exercise his discretion to warn the jury, he had to give the full warning ((a)–(d) above). Lord Taylor CJ, speaking for the Court of Appeal, rejected this submission and stated that section 32(1) abrogated entirely the requirement to give a corroborative direction in respect of an alleged accomplice or a complainant of a sexual offence simply because the witness falls into one of those categories. It was for the judge alone to determine what, if any, warning was necessary in such cases, taking into account the circumstances of the case, the issues raised, and the content and quality of the witness's evidence. Where the judge did decide to issue a warning, this should not be done solely because the witness is a complainant of a sexual offence or an accomplice. There would need to be an evidential basis for suggesting that the evidence of the witness may be unreliable, which would not include mere suggestions by cross-examining counsel. The new position following *Makanjuola* is summarised in the following terms:

21 [1991] Crim LR 379.
22 [2013] Crim LR 849.
23 [1995] 3 All ER 730.

(a) Section 32(1) abrogates the requirement to give a corroboration direction in respect of an alleged accomplice or a complainant of a sexual offence simply because a witness falls into one of those categories.
(b) It is a matter for the judge's discretion what, if any, warning he considers appropriate in respect of such a witness, as indeed in respect of any other witness in whatever type of case.
(c) In some cases, it may be appropriate for the judge to warn the jury to exercise caution before acting upon unsupported evidence of a witness.
(d) If any question arises as to whether the judge should give a special warning in respect of a witness, it is desirable that the question be resolved by discussion with counsel in the absence of the jury before final speeches.
(e) Where the judge does decide to give some warning in respect of a witness, it will be appropriate to do so as part of the judge's review of the evidence rather than as a set-piece legal direction.
(f) Where some warning is required, it will be for the judge to decide the strength and terms of the warning.
(g) Attempts to reimpose the straitjacket of the old corroboration rules are strongly to be deprecated.
(h) The Court of Appeal will be disinclined to interfere with a trial judge's exercise of his discretion save in the case where the exercise is unreasonable.

While warnings are no longer mandatory, they may still be considered desirable in certain circumstances. In *R v M*,[24] a young complainant told her grandmother that she had been sexually abused by her father, and the grandmother then relayed this information at trial. The defendant was convicted and appealed to the Court of Appeal on the basis that the trial judge had failed to direct the jury that the grandmother's evidence was not independent from the evidence of the complainant – the grandmother had simply relayed what she had been told (i.e. it was hearsay). The Court of Appeal dismissed the defendant's appeal on the basis that there was never any suggestion that the grandmother's evidence was independent to that of the complainant and there was no real risk of the jury assuming such.[25] However, the Court of Appeal did warn that in cases such as this, it was appropriate that the jury should be directed as to the weight that may be attached to such evidence.[26] The conviction remained safe.

It is now clear that the common law rules have finally been laid to rest. The judge retains a discretion to warn the jury in terms appropriate to the facts of a particular case, and research suggests that it is still relatively common for judges to warn the jury about the dangers of convicting on the basis of uncorroborated evidence in sex cases or in cases involving children.[27] Where a witness has been shown to be unreliable, the judge may consider it necessary to urge caution. In a more extreme case, if the witness is shown to have lied, to have made previous false complaints, or to bear the defendant a grudge, a stronger warning may be appropriate and the judge may suggest that it would be wise to look for supporting material before acting on the impugned witness's evidence.[28]

---

24 CACD (14 March 2017) (unreported).
25 See *R v A* [2011] EWCA Crim 1517.
26 See *R v AA* [2007] EWCA Crim 1779.
27 Davies, G., Hoyano, L., Keenan, C., Maitland, L., and Morgan, R., *An Assessment of the Admissibility and Sufficiency of Evidence in Child Abuse Prosecutions* (HMSO, 1999), p. 68.
28 For a reaffirmation of the principles set out in *Makanjuola*, see *R v Muncaster* [1999] Crim LR 409 and *R v Causeley* [1999] Crim LR 572.

10.1.3 Cases with a special need for caution

Notwithstanding the abrogation of the formal corroboration requirements, the courts have identified certain other cases where some form of warning as to a special need for caution should be given to a jury. These cases came to be known as the 'analogous cases.'[29] In *R v Muncaster*,[30] it was held that the guidance of the Court of Appeal in *Makanjuola* was still relevant for witnesses who fell within three analogous categories, despite the fact that the corroboration requirements no longer applied.

10.1.3.1 Co-defendants

In *R v Knowlden*,[31] it was held that in exercising his discretion as to what to say to the jury, the judge is at least expected to give a clear warning to the jury, where defendants have given evidence against one another, to examine the evidence of each with care because each has or may have an interest of his own to serve. This approach was confirmed in *R v Cheema*.[32]

10.1.3.2 Witnesses tainted by improper motives

Giving the judgment of the Court of Appeal *R v Beck*,[33] Ackner LJ concluded that there may be an 'obligation upon a judge to advise a jury to proceed with caution where there is material to suggest that a witness's evidence may be tainted by an improper motive.' The strength of that advice would vary according to the facts of the case. This position extends to other improper motives, including jealousy, spite, levelling of an old score, and hope of financial advantage.

10.1.3.3 Witnesses of bad character

In *R v Spencer*,[34] the court referred to the fact that judges always warn juries about the evidence of witnesses of 'admittedly bad character,' 'in whatever terms they think appropriate to the case.'

10.2 Identification evidence

Eyewitness identification evidence implicating the accused is often highly cogent, and consequently a high degree of weight may be placed upon it by the factfinder. Where it serves merely to corroborate other evidence, it is not generally problematic. However, there is greater cause for concern where it is used as the sole or primary basis for the prosecution's case.

Eighteenth- and nineteenth-century lawyers were well aware of the fallibility of identification evidence, but the fact that such evidence was a frequent source of false convictions failed to lead to any formal safeguards. However, many judges, perhaps personally aware of the risk of false conviction, took to warning the jury of the possible dangers of convicting on identification evidence alone, or even went so far as to direct an acquittal where they thought the identification was too poor to sustain a conviction. Indeed, it was the notorious case of Adolf Beck, who had been mistakenly identified by a number of victims of theft and fraud,[35] which led to the creation of the Court of Appeal in 1907.

---

29 *R v Spencer* [1987] AC 128.
30 [1999] Crim LR 409.
31 (1983) 77 Cr App R 94.
32 [1994] 1 WLR 147.
33 [1982] 1 WLR 461, at 469.
34 [1985] QB 771.
35 See generally Coates, T., *The Strange Case of Adolph Beck* (HMSO, 2001).

10.2.1 The *Turnbull* guidelines

Despite the clear miscarriage of justice in Beck's case, it was not until 1977 that the Court of Appeal laid down guidelines relating to possible mistaken identification. The Court of Appeal was responding to the Devlin Report,[36] which recommended that there should be no conviction in a case in which the prosecution relied wholly or mainly on the evidence of visual identification by one or more witnesses. While stopping short of implementing the recommendations in full, in *R v Turnbull*[37] the Court of Appeal did issue guidelines that required the lower courts to bear in mind the possible dangers of identification evidence and to take a number of factors into account. Key questions that jurors ought to consider include the following:

- How long was the suspect under observation?
- At what distance?
- In what light?
- Was the observation impeded?
- Had the witness seen the suspect before? (Is the identification one of pure recognition rather than the identification of a stranger?)
- How often? If only occasionally, had the witness any special reason for remembering the accused?
- How long elapsed between the original observation and the subsequent identification to police?
- Were there any particular reasons for noting the suspect?

It was added by the court that a failure to follow these guidelines – and to give the *Turnbull* direction in full – was likely to result in a conviction being quashed. In *R v Curry; Keeble*,[38] the judge had instructed the jury that they should bear in mind that there was a risk of mistaken identification. They should thus evaluate the extent of that risk, taking into account the fact that it would be much higher where the identification had been based upon a fleeting glance. The defence appealed, contending that a full *Turnbull* warning should have been given. Dismissing the case, the Court of Appeal stated that the warning in *Turnbull* was not intended to deal with every case involving a minor identification problem, but was only intended to deal with cases of fleeting encounters. Since the identification evidence in this case was not based on a fleeting glance, the full warning was not necessary.

At the conclusion of the prosecution evidence, the defence has the opportunity to make a submission of no case to answer (also known as a half-time submission). Generally, such submissions are governed by *R v Galbraith*;[39] however, the principles of *Turnbull* apply in cases where the prosecution relies heavily on identification evidence. There are three major circumstances that arise in a case concerning identification. For each of these circumstances, the judge's action will vary.

10.2.1.1 No identification

Where there is no identification evidence at all, the judge's discretion is simple: the submission of no case to answer succeeds.

---

36 Lord Devlin, *The Report of the Committee on Evidence of Identification in Criminal Cases*, Cmnd 338 (HMSO, 1976).

37 [1977] QB 224.

38 [1983] Crim LR 737.

39 (1981) 73 Cr App R 124. For further discussion, see Ch 2.

10.2.1.2 Poor quality and unsupported

When the quality of the identifying evidence is poor and unsupported, the trial judge should be under a duty to invite submissions and, if appropriate, to withdraw the case from the jury.[40] The quality of the identification evidence, and the extent to which it is supported, should be assessed both at the close of the prosecution's case and at the close of the accused's case.[41] If the judge is minded to withdraw the case, they ought to direct the jury to acquit, as opposed to merely withdraw the evidence.[42]

10.2.1.3 Poor quality but supported

Where the identification evidence is poor but there is other supporting evidence, the jury should be instructed that it is for them to decide, if they accept that evidence, whether in fact it does support the identification. Essentially, the jury should not be told that the identification evidence is of poor quality and that the case would have been withdrawn if there was no supporting evidence.[43] If evidence is based on a fleeting glance and there is no other supporting evidence, then it is the duty of the judge to direct an acquittal. This means that a serious objective decision must be made by the judge on whether or not the quality of the identification evidence alone justifies leaving the case to the jury.[44] In *Daley v R*,[45] a shopkeeper claimed to have identified the defendant as the murderer of his wife. However, it was decided that he had not had adequate opportunity to view the killer from where he was hiding. There was no other evidence implicating the defendant in the murder and the Privy Council held that, in these circumstances, the judge should withdraw the case from the jury.

This problem is not exclusive to single individual witnesses, and the identifying evidence of more than a single witness may turn out to be unreliable. The Court of Appeal made the following observation in *Weeder*:[46]

> The identification evidence can be poor, even though it is given by a number of witnesses. They may all have had only the opportunity of a fleeting glance or a longer observation made in difficult conditions, e.g. the occupants of a bus who observed the incident at night as they drove past.[47]

By contrast, the appellant in *Andrews*[48] was successful in arguing that a full form of the *Turnbull* warning should have been given. The victim was violently attacked by three men who ran off on being approached by the police. A short time later, the defendant was discovered in a nearby street, and was aggressive and uncooperative. A police officer identified him as one of those involved in the attack a short time earlier. The judge had declined to give a full *Turnbull* warning, and had even told the jury that the officer's description 'quite plainly' identified the accused. Allowing the appeal, the Court of Appeal stated that the judge had effectively usurped the function of the jury in determining whether the identification was accurate. Furthermore, since the issue of identity was central to the case, a full *Turnbull* warning should have been given.

---

40 *R v Fergus (Ivan)* (1994) 98 Cr App R 313.
41 *Turnbull*, op. cit., n. 37.
42 Ibid.
43 *R v Akaidere* [1990] Crim LR 808.
44 *Shervington* [2008] EWCA Crim 658, esp. at [20].
45 [1994] 1 AC 117.
46 [1990] Crim LR 50.
47 Ibid., at 231.
48 [1993] Crim LR 590. See also *R v Thornton* (1995) 1 Cr App R 578.

Similarly, a direction should be given even where the eyewitness believes they recognise the accused from a previous encounter. In *R v Ryan*,[49] such a direction was deemed to be appropriate even though the eyewitness recognised the accused as being the brother of a school friend. Although the Court of Appeal conceded in *Turnbull* that 'recognition may be more reliable than identification of a stranger,' it proceeded to stress that the jury should always be reminded that mistakes in recognition of close relatives and friends are sometimes made.[50]

In *R v Slater*,[51] the Court of Appeal made a fine distinction between identification evidence that places the accused at the scene of the offence, and identification evidence that relates to their particular actions. The case concerned an assault that took place in a nightclub. The defendant had admitted that he had been present, and had witnessed the disturbance, but denied any involvement. The victim had, however, described his assailant as a 'very big man' – a description that matched the defendant, who was 'a man of unusually large size.' The accused was convicted and appealed on the ground, *inter alia*, that the judge should have given a full *Turnbull* direction. Dismissing the appeal, the court held that the need for such a direction arose where there was a possibility of mistaken identification. This possibility would generally arise when the issue was whether the defendant was present and a witness claimed to identify him on the basis of a previous sighting. Where, however, there was no issue as to the defendant's presence at or near the scene of the offence, but the issue was as to what he was doing, it did not automatically follow that such a direction had to be given. Whether such a direction was necessary would ultimately turn on the individual facts of a particular case. In the instant case, the appellant was of wholly unusual size, and there was no evidence to suggest that anyone else in the nightclub was remotely similar in height to him. The issue was not really one of identification, but instead concerned what the appellant had done, and it would be 'contrary to common sense' to require the direction in all cases in which presence is admitted, but conduct disputed. Accordingly, the judge was not required to give a full *Turnbull* direction.

In *Capron v R*,[52] the trial judge had summed up without a proper *Turnbull* warning. He had, however, directed the jury that they had to be sure that the witnesses were telling the truth and that they were not mistaken about the identity of the person who had shot the victim. The Privy Council held that the nature of the warning in the instant case was insufficient:

> [E]ven in a recognition case, the trial judge should always give an appropriate Turnbull direction unless, despite any defence challenges, the nature of the eyewitness evidence is such that the direction would add nothing of substance to the judge's other directions to the jury on how they should approach that evidence.[53]

It is therefore apparent that a *Turnbull* warning need not be given in every case that involves identification evidence.[54] However, if a warning was not given where it ought to have been, the conviction will normally be quashed.[55]

49 [1990] Crim LR 50.
50 Ibid., at 228. See also *Beckford v R* (1993) 97 Cr App R 405.
51 [1995] Crim LR 244.
52 [2006] UKPC 34.
53 Ibid., at [16] (Lord Rodger of Earlsferry).
54 There is no need, for example, to give it where a witness identifies a vehicle: see *R v Browning* (1992) 94 Cr App R 109.
55 See e.g. *R v Hunjan* (1979) 68 Cr App R 99; *Reid v R* (1990) 90 Cr App R 121.

10.2.1.4 Voice identification evidence

The courts also now require trial judges to give an even more stringent version of the *Turnbull* warning in cases in which the prosecution seeks to rely on voice identification, though no precise form of words need be used provided that all the key elements of the warning are in place.[56]

Voice identification is fundamentally split into two different forms: expert advice, given by specialists who have extensive knowledge in the necessary field; and non-expert evidence, provided by people who have merely familiarised themselves with the target's voice. As the case of *R v Flynn and St John*[57] highlights, the admissibility of non-expert voice identification evidence is particularly problematic. The prosecution had sought to rely on voice identification evidence provided by two police officers. The officers had interviewed the defendants during and after their arrest on suspicion of conspiracy to commit robbery, and stated that they were able to recognise their voices from a covert recording device that had been concealed within the van that they had been driving.

In determining whether the evidence should have been excluded, the Court of Appeal identified a number of factors, which included:

(a) the quality of the recording of the disputed voice;
(b) the gap in time between the listener hearing the known voice and their attempt to recognise the disputed voice;
(c) the ability of the individual to identify voices in general (research showing that this varies from person to person);
(d) the nature and duration of the speech which is sought to be identified; and
(e) the familiarity of the listener with the known voice; and even a confident recognition of a familiar voice by a lay listener may nevertheless be wrong.

Applying these to the facts at hand, the court noted that the officers' familiarity with the appellants' voices was gained over comparatively short periods of time, nothing was known of the ability of any of the police officers to recognise voices, and there was no evidence that any of them had undergone any training in auditory analysis. Moreover, expert evidence showed that lay listeners with considerable familiarity of a voice and listening to a clear recording could still make mistakes.

10.2.2 The role of Code of Practice D

Code of Practice D, issued under the Police and Criminal Evidence Act (PACE) 1984, is a backup means of preventing any miscarriages of justice arising from mistaken identifications. The latest version of this Code came into force on 23 February 2017, and it lays down the rules and procedures relating to police conduct in pre-trial identification procedures.[58] The specific provisions of Code D are designed to test the ability of the witness to identify the person seen on a previous occasion and to provide safeguards against mistaken identification.[59] The Code applies to three kinds of suspects.

---

56 *Shand v The Queen* [1996] 1 WLR 67; *Phipps v The Queen* [2012] UKPC 24.
57 [2008] 2 Cr App R 266.
58 Code of Practice D [3.12].
59 Ibid., at [1.2].

10.2.2.1 Suspects known and available to the police (Code D: [3.4])

The Code imposes specific identification procedures in respect of suspects known and available to the police. A suspect is 'known' if there is sufficient information known to the police to justify the arrest of a particular person for suspected involvement in the offence.

A suspect is 'available' if they are immediately available or will become available within a reasonably short time and are willing to take an effective part in at least one of the following identification procedures which it is practicable to arrange.

The options available in this case include:

- video identification,
- identification parade, or
- group identification.

10.2.2.2 Suspects known but not available to the police (Code D: [3.21])

When a known suspect is not available or has ceased to be available, the officer may make arrangements for a video identification or may use still images if necessary. These may be obtained covertly if necessary. Alternatively, the officer may make arrangements for a group identification.

10.2.2.3 Suspects whose identity is not known to the police (Code D: [3.2])

In these circumstances, a witness may be taken to a particular neighbourhood or place to see whether they can identify the person they saw on a previous occasion. The requirement that, where practicable, a record shall be made of any description of the suspect given by the witness is not mere bureaucracy; it affords the best safeguard against the possibility of auto-suggestion. Importantly, the Code is not breached if it is impracticable to make such a record.

This pre-trial identification process would then be admitted at trial in support of the prosecution's case as to the identity of the accused. In-court identifications (i.e. where a witness points out the accused in the dock) are generally frowned upon and could invite a defence application to exclude this evidence on grounds of unfairness under section 78 of PACE 1984.[60] In cases relating to driving offences, it is more acceptable for the prosecution to seek and rely upon an in-court identification of the defendant. The rationale for this change of approach in relation to these cases was in response to the all-too-familiar story of those charged with instances of careless driving, who have made no statement to the police, simply sitting back and submitting that no evidence has proven that they were in fact in control of the vehicle at the time of the offence being committed.[61]

10.2.2.4 Exclusion for breaches of Code D

It is widely accepted that, like the other PACE Codes of Conduct, Code D is critically important in preventing contamination of evidence and optimising the reliability, validity, and also fairness of the identification process. Where insufficient regard is paid to these key factors, then the court may exercise its discretion under section 78 of PACE to exclude the evidence.[62] For example, where a less reliable form of identification has been used in preference to a much better and much more reliable alternative, then this will side in favour of exclusion. Such were the facts of *R v Nagah*,[63] in which the police deliberately released the defendant from a police station in order

---

60 *R v Johnson* [2001] 1 Cr App R 26; *R v John* [1973] Crim LR 113; *R v Tido* [2011] 2 Cr App R 336. See further Tain, P., 'In the Dock' (2005) 149 *Solicitors Journal* 739.

61 *Barnes v Chief Constable of Durham* (1997) 2 Cr App R 505, 512.

62 See *R v Popat* (1998) 2 Cr App R 208, 224.

63 (1990) 92 Cr App R 344.

that the complainant could identify him in the street, despite the defendant's willingness to partake in an identification parade. The Court of Appeal decided that exclusion was justified in these circumstances.

Exclusion is not, however, automatic, and the nature of the breach and the quality of the identification evidence will be of crucial importance. Indeed, in *R v Quinn*,[64] it was held that the trial judge had been entitled to admit the evidence, but should have issued a direction to the jury concerning the nature of the breach and its circumstances. The jury could then rely on this information as part of their fact-finding process. In *R v Forbes*,[65] the police had failed to hold an identification procedure in line with Code D, and had instead sought to rely on a street identification by the victim of an attempted robbery. Moreover, the trial judge had failed to properly explain the breach to the jury. However, in the view of the House of Lords, the evidence was 'compelling and untainted'; although proper procedure had not been followed, it was felt that a reasonable jury, having been properly directed, would nonetheless have convicted the accused.[66]

Forbes was applied by the Court of Appeal in *R v Byrne*,[67] where the Court of Appeal concluded that evidence need not be excluded simply because the proper procedure had not been followed.[68] The trial judge had been right to leave the evidence before the jury and allow them to determine how much weight was to be attached to the evidence. The Court commended the trial judge for his summing up where he pointed out that 'best practice' had not been followed and further directed the jury as to how they may address the reliability of the evidence. Given these statements and the safeguards in place, the conviction was safe.

Neither did breaches of the Code prove fatal in *R (on the application of Pierre Wellington) v DPP*.[69] The defendant had fled the scene of a police checkpoint, and, around two weeks later, one of the officers recognised his picture during a briefing session at the police station. Approximately eight weeks after that, the same officer again identified him at the police station, whereupon he was charged with driving a vehicle while disqualified, driving a vehicle without insurance, and wilfully obstructing a police officer in the execution of his duty. These offences had all allegedly been carried out at the time that the vehicle had first been stopped, some 10 weeks earlier. His appeal to the High Court was dismissed; despite the Code having been breached, it was virtually inevitable that the police officer would have correctly identified the suspect had proper identification procedures been followed.[70]

10.2.3 Photographs and video-recordings

With the increased presence of technology such as CCTV, along with the increased use of video equipment during police operations (for example, at football matches and other major public events), it is now commonplace for these methods to be used in the identification process at trial. Photographs and video-recordings are now commonly presented to the jury as a process of identifying a defendant. Nevertheless, there are still question marks over the reliability of this type of evidence.[71] In *R v Dodson*,[72] the Court of Appeal held that it is imperative that a jury is warned of the perils of deciding whether or not a defendant has committed a crime based on this form

---

64 [1995] 1 Cr App R 480.

65 [2001] 1 AC 473.

66 See also *R v Lewis* [2006] EWCA Crim 2895; *R v Lariba* [2015] EWCA Crim 478; *R v Byrne* [2016] All ER (D) 129.

67 [2016] All ER (D) 129.

68 In this case, a police officer failed to conduct a formal identification procedure in accordance with PACE, Code D [3.12].

69 [2007] EWHC 1061.

70 For guidance on breaches of Code D, see *R v Lariba* [2015] EWCA Crim 478.

71 See Laurance, J., 'Security Cameras "Distorting Justice",' *The Independent* (27 March 1998) p. 10; and Worsley, K., 'Closed-Circuit Cameras Short Circuit Justice,' *The Times Higher Education Supplement* (27 March 1998) p. 23.

72 [1984] 1 WLR 971.

of evidence alone. In particular, they should be directed to bear in mind that the visual appearance of the accused might have changed over a period of time. However, in *R v Blenkinsop*,[73] it was decided that, while the jury should be made aware of the risk, there is no requirement for a full *Turnbull* warning. *Blenkinsop* was called into question by the Court of Appeal in *R v Lariba*.[74] Pitchford LJ explained that, in many cases, the quality of CCTV images is so poor that juries will rely on another person to make the identification:

> The danger in such a case is that the jury will simply take on trust a convincing assurance from the witnesses when they are unable to make the judgement themselves; hence, the importance of directions to the jury as to the caution with which they must approach their task.[75]

Referring back to *R v Selwyn*,[76] the Court noted that a *Turnbull* warning would ordinarily be required in these circumstances.

There are no rules regarding whether or not a video-recording should be the original or a copy. However, if a particular video-recording is no longer available, then a person who previously viewed the recording is permitted to give evidence of what they saw on the recording. It is in these instances that a full *Turnbull* warning would be required.

The legal position on photographic evidence was summarised in *AG's Reference (No. 2 of 2002)*.[77] It was held that there were at least four circumstances in which the jury could rely upon photographic evidence in deciding whether or not the defendant committed the offence:

1. Where the photographic image is sufficiently clear, the jury can compare it with the defendant sitting in the dock.
2. Where a witness knows the defendant sufficiently well to recognise that he or she is the offender depicted in the photographic image.
3. Where a witness does not know the defendant, but spends substantial time analysing photographic images, the witness will have acquired special knowledge that the jury does not have. This relies on the photographic evidence also being made available to the jury.
4. A qualified facial mapping expert can give opinion evidence of identification based on a comparison between images taken at the time of the crime and a reasonably up-to-date photograph of the defendant. Again, this is reliant on the photographic evidence also being made available to the jury.

10.3 Key learning points

- Criminal courts may convict on the uncorroborated testimony of one witness.
- There is no requirement for the judge to warn the jury of the dangers of convicting on the basis of uncorroborated evidence, although in practice such warnings may still be given.
- Where eyewitness identification evidence is disputed, the judge should issue the jury with a *Turnbull* direction in full. Failure to do so may form the basis of a successful appeal.
- An even more stringent warning is required in cases in which voice identification evidence is disputed.
- The requirements of Code D are designed to prevent contamination of evidence. Failure to abide by these requirements may result in the evidence being excluded.

---

73 [1995] 1 Cr App R 7, 12.
74 Ibid.
75 Ibid., at [40].
76 [2012] EWCA Crim 2968.
77 [2003] 1 Cr App R 321 at [19].

- Judges should make juries aware of the dangers of convicting the accused on the basis of photographs or video evidence alone.

10.4 Practice questions

1 'Since the mandatory warnings have now been abrogated, the English law of evidence need no longer concern itself with the issue of corroboration.' Discuss the issues arising in the above quotation.

2 In its 1972 report, the Criminal Law Revision Committee expressed the view that mistaken identification was 'by far the greatest cause of actual or possible wrong conviction.' How satisfactory has the response of the courts been in terms of addressing this problem?

3 Darren, Len, and Martyn are charged with causing grievous bodily harm with intent. It is alleged by the prosecution that Darren, the leader of a local criminal gang, was furious that the victim, Jeff, was having an affair with his wife. As Jeff was leaving his work at a local pub late one summer's evening, he was set upon by three men, who beat him with baseball bats and an iron bar. All were wearing balaclavas at the time of the attack.

Kitty, a witness who was standing outside the pub, informs police that she saw one of the men remove his balaclava as they ran off, and she identifies one of the assailants as Len, an ex-boyfriend.

Melanie, who was also standing outside the pub, recorded the attack on her mobile phone. During the recording, one of the attackers can be heard shouting: 'That'll teach you to mess with my missus.' PC Brown, who has arrested and interviewed Darren on a number of previous occasions, immediately identifies the voice as that of Darren.

A short distance away, Peter, who was walking his dog in the vicinity, bumped into a man whom he described as being out of breath and carrying a balaclava and an iron bar. Police ask Peter to attend the station, and show him a one-way screen, through which he can see Martyn being interviewed by detectives. PC Hunt asks, 'Was this the man who ran into you?,' to which Peter responds 'yes.'

Discuss the admissibility of the relevant evidence.

10.5 Suggested further reading

Bogan, P. and Roberts, A., *Identification: Investigation, Trial and Scientific Evidence* (Jordans, 2011).

Davidson, F.P. and Ferguson, P.R., 'The Corroboration Requirement in Scottish Criminal Trials: Should it be Retained for Some Forms of Problematic Evidence?' (2014) 18 E & P 1.

Davies, G. and Griffiths, L., 'Eyewitness Identification and the English Courts: A Century of Trial and Error' (2008) 15 Psychiatry, Psychology and Law 435.

Hartshorne, J., 'Corroboration and Care Warnings after Makanjuola' (1998) 2 E & P 1.

Leahy, S., 'The Corroboration Warning in Sexual Offence Trials: Final Vestige of the Historic Suspicion of Sexual Offence Complainants or a Necessary Protection for Defendants?' (2014) 18 E & P 41.

Lewis, P., 'A Comparative Examination of Corroboration and Caution Warnings in Prosecutions for Sexual Offences' (2006) Crim LR 889.

Ormerod, D., 'Sounds Familiar? – Voice Identification Evidence' (2001) Crim LR 595.

Roberts, A., 'Pre-Trial Defence Rights and the Fair Use of Eyewitness Identification Procedures' (2008) 71 MLR 331.

Valentine, T., Memon, A., Roberts, A. and Davis, J.P., 'Should We be Concerned about Street Identifications?' (2014) Crim LR 633.

Chapter 11

Character Evidence

Chapter contents

DOI: 10.4324/9781003416098-11

This chapter examines the admissibility of the accused's previous good or bad character in evidence. As a starting point, it is worth underlining that the rules relating to this topic are clouded by a number of definitional issues. For the most part, as far as its usage within the law of evidence is concerned, 'character' refers to the tendency of a person to act, think, or feel in a particular way. 'Disposition' and 'propensity' are alternative terms with the same meaning, and you will find that they are widely used in case law and academic commentary on the subject. Thus, a person with previous convictions for violence may be described as being of a 'violent disposition' or having a 'propensity towards violence,' whereas someone of good character may be described as 'a person of integrity.'

There are many ways in which a person's character may be made known to a court, although it is most commonly revealed through reference to any previous convictions. However, not all convictions carry the same stigma: a minor motoring offence, for example, is unlikely to influence a jury in the same way as a serious sexual offence. As we shall see, bad character can also be acquired by the commission of criminal acts for which a person has been acquitted, or where a prosecution does not proceed for lack of evidence. Similarly, good character can be shown by the absence of convictions, or by association with good people or causes, such as being a churchgoer or undertaking work for voluntary or charitable organisations. Yet, by the same token, it is worth bearing in mind that much of the evidence of good or bad character stems from a reputation that may or may not be a true reflection of the person's character. For example, a local priest may appear to be of good character, having a very good reputation among his parishioners, but may be abusing choirboys. The bank employee may appear to be the epitome of respectability, but may be stealing from customer accounts or using bank facilities to launder money. A footballer or Olympic athlete may be widely admired in the national press, but may be battering a partner behind closed doors. Nevertheless – and as a corollary of the presumption of innocence – all persons are treated before the courts as being of good character until the contrary is proved. Recently, academics such as Farmer[1] have expressed concern regarding the role of innocence, especially in the context where there is great emphasis on the rights of the victim and justified punishment of the guilty, described by Lacey as a 'resurgence of character.' Lacey[2] also argued that contemporary criminal law is marked by a form of culpability that is grounded in a 'capacity' of responsibility that is based on the character of the defendant, pointing out the resurgence of character evidence to provide context to the *mens reas* requirement and in judgments of reasonableness or motive, which often collapses into judgments of character.[3]

Recently, popular discourse about criminal justice has been dominated by debate over the role of criminals versus victims. On this, Edwards notes that the criminal law climate is now characterised by the maxim 'the defendant's gain is the victim's loss,' where the political logic has been established wherein being 'for' victims equals being tough on defendants.[4] As Hoyano

1 'Innocence, The Burden of Proof and Fairness in the Criminal Trials: Revisiting Woolmington v. DPP (1935).'

2 Lacey, N., 'The Resurgence of Character: Responsibility in the Context of Criminalization,' in R.A. Duff and S. Green (eds), *Philosophical Foundations of Criminal Law* (Oxford University Press, 2011).

3 See also Lacey, N., *In Search of Criminal Responsibility, Ideas, Interests and Institutions* (Oxford University Press, 2016), Ch 2.

4 Edwards, I., 'An Ambiguous Participant: The Crime Victim and Criminal Justice Decision Making' (2004) 44 *British Journal of Criminology* 967, 969–970.

evaluates, this logic implies that affording greater protections to an alleged victim or a witness necessarily means removing rights from the defence.[5]

Traditionally, evidence of the accused's previous misconduct has been inadmissible in criminal proceedings on grounds that it was both irrelevant and overly prejudicial. However, from the late nineteenth century, the courts and legislature came to accept the fact that there were certain circumstances in which it would be in the interests of justice for this evidence to be made known to the trier of fact. From that point in time until the early part of this century, the law developed in a haphazard fashion, given the fact that the use of such evidence against a defendant would often be highly contentious. While there were certain perceived advantages in moving towards a system of free proof that would allow all incidents of previous misconduct to be admitted in every case, there has also been a great deal of scepticism concerning the true value of such evidence. In criminal proceedings, it was the latter position that held sway until the enactment of the Criminal Justice Act 2003, which clearly marked a shift towards the former approach. In the years since the Act took effect, there has been a considerable body of case law surrounding the use of character evidence in criminal trials that has emerged from the higher courts.

11.1 The rationale for exclusion

The primary rationale for excluding character evidence stems from the fear that evidence of bad character might have a disproportionately prejudicial effect on the jury. It is, perhaps, something of an irony that, despite the supposedly revered status of the jury as an institution of English criminal justice, many remain sceptical about the ability of jurors to assess the impact of previous convictions in an objective and rational manner. The primary fear has always been that the jury may attach too much weight to such evidence, and thereby embark on what Lord Hailsham termed 'the forbidden chain of reasoning' by inferring guilt from general disposition or propensity.[6]

In spite of this mistrust, there is no hard evidence of such prejudice among jurors, as section 8 of the Contempt of Court Act 1981 prevents research into the deliberations of juries. However, research conducted with 'shadow' or 'mock' juries has tended to show that the admission of previous convictions increased the chance of a guilty verdict only in those cases in which the offence was similar to that charged.[7] It has also been suggested that juries may be more likely to convict if told that the defendant has previous convictions of indecent assault on a child, regardless of the nature of the offence with which they are charged. Such convictions are understandably viewed with a greater degree of revulsion than most, and it is probably dangerous to draw wider conclusions about the ability of juries to deal with potentially prejudicial evidence. Importantly, Lloyd-Bostock's survey also suggests that juries do give real weight to an instruction to disregard relevant previous convictions wrongly admitted.[8] If it is indeed the case that juries are able to follow judicial directions carefully, perhaps the apparent decline in the exclusionary rules relating to character evidence is to be welcomed as a sign of a greater degree of trust now being placed in the jury to evaluate the evidence fairly. Treschel has recently suggested that the right to a fair trial is a 'fuzzy panacea,

5 Hoyano, L.,'What Is Balanced in the Scales of Justice? In Search of the Essence of a Right to a Fair Trial' (2014) Crim LR 4, 6.

6 *DPP v Boardman* [1975] AC 421, at 453.

7 Cornish, W. and Sealey, A., 'Juries and the Rules of Evidence: The LSE Jury Project' [1973] Crim LR 208; Lloyd-Bostock, S., 'The Effects on Juries of Hearing about the Defendant's Previous Criminal Record' [2000] Crim LR 734. For an overview of further research conducted into juries, see generally Sanders, A. and Young, R., *Criminal Justice*, 3rd edn (Oxford University Press, 2010), pp. 593–602.

8 Ibid., Lloyd-Bostock.

a cluster of rights, not exclusively reserved for the accused, a vague ideal, more a shell than a guarantee of substances,' suggesting that the concept of fairness[9] is a nebulous one.[10]

The second reason for the traditional tendency to exclude bad character evidence was that it is broadly considered irrelevant. There is no reason why a defendant who committed a criminal act in the past will be guilty of the offence with which they are charged in a future case. However, by the same token, the law of evidence has long accepted that an exception to this principle arises where the accused has a conviction of a very similar nature. In such instances, such past behaviour might provide evidence of a particular character trait that would make it more probable that they committed the offence charged. This is what is commonly referred to as 'evidence of disposition.' As the Criminal Law Revision Committee explained in 1972:

> Evidence of other misconduct of the accused tending to show that he has a disposition to commit the kind of offence charged may clearly be highly relevant in the sense of making it more probable that he committed the offence charged; and this is the sense in which relevance must be understood for the purpose of the law of evidence. Obviously if there is no other evidence at all to connect the accused with the offence charged, the fact that he has a disposition to commit this kind of offence, then evidence of disposition must be of greater or lesser value according to the circumstances.[11]

The Committee thus emphasised that there must be evidence linking the defendant to the crime with which they are charged, and the previous conviction should form only *part* of the prosecution case. It is therefore suggested that it is fundamentally misguided to speak of juries being 'prejudiced' by the introduction of such evidence. Arguably, it is correct that previous convictions *should* make the jury more likely to convict since it adds something of value to the prosecution case. In this sense, the prospect of conviction will then be increased, not because the jury are prejudiced by hearing of the previous conviction(s), but because of the increased weight of the evidence that supports the defendant's guilt.

Historically, the common law recognised this fact but demanded a high degree of relevance in the previous convictions, which in turn outweighed any possible prejudice resulting from the admission of the convictions. The fact that its use may serve to increase the likelihood of the defendant being found guilty ought not really to be termed 'prejudicial,' since *all* prosecution evidence is arguably directed to this end.

Indeed, it can be added that 'disposition evidence' normally forms part of the investigating judge's dossier in most inquisitorial systems, where there is a considerably higher degree of faith placed in the factfinder. Although continental factfinders are likely to consist partly, or entirely, of professional judges, there is no reason per se that a legally qualified judge should be less open to prejudice than a member of the general public. Many professional people were previously exempt from it, meaning that juries were often extremely unrepresentative of society at large. However, the Criminal Justice Act 2003 removed most of the previous exemptions, making jury service compulsory for a wide range of professionals, including those connected with the legal system, such as judges, barristers, solicitors, and police officers.

Whether this broadening of representation will lead to a greater trust in the ability of future juries to handle potentially prejudicial material remains to be seen. A recent case saw a retired

9 See also McDermott, T., *Fairness in International Criminal Trials* (Oxford University Press, 2016), 44.

10 Weissbrodt, D. (2007), *Human Rights in Criminal Proceedings*. By Stefan Trechsel, Oxford, New York: Oxford University Press, 2005, pp. cx, 611, *American Journal of International Law*, 101(3), 701–703.

11 Criminal Law Revision Committee, *Eleventh Report: Evidence (General)*, Cmnd 4999 (HMSO, 1972), [72].

police officer seeking to be excused from jury service on the grounds of his own inevitable bias. He wrote to the court in response to receiving his jury summons claiming he was incapable of fairly deciding the case:

> I was deluded in believing that I could come to an unbiased decision.
>
> Thirty years' service as a police officer (I retired ten years ago) has left me with the unshakeable belief that if both the investigating police officers and the Crown Prosecution Service feel that the evidence is sufficient to charge, then the individual is most definitely guilty of the offence(s).
>
> I suspect that my time in the jury room after the evidence has been heard will be spent just persuading the other jurors of the defendant's guilt.
>
> I am willing to answer the summons and perform jury service, but believe it is only fair that I point out the bias that I now realise I hold.[12]

The trial judge refused to excuse him from jury service in advance of the trial, having questioned him and obtained from him an assurance that he would comply with the terms of his affirmation to faithfully try the defendant and return a true verdict. A later appeal by the defendant on the ground that the conviction was unsafe due to the juror's apparent bias was dismissed by the Court of Appeal. It may well be that this was seen as a rather obvious attempt to evade jury duty, but it may be suggested that the Court of Appeal was somewhat optimistic in concluding that 'the fair minded and informed observer would not think it a real possibility that Juror 11 remained biased.'[13]

11.2 The evolution of the law

Until very recently, the admissibility of evidence of bad character was governed both by the 'similar fact' rule at common law and by the rules laid down in the Criminal Evidence Act 1898. As much of the case law continues to have a bearing on the contemporary regime contained in the Criminal Justice Act 2003, it is worth recounting some of the main features of the law as it previously stood.

11.2.1 The 'similar fact' rule

The main exception to the rule excluding bad character evidence was known (somewhat misleadingly) as the 'similar fact' rule. It was laid down in *Makin v Attorney-General for New South Wales*,[14] in which a husband and wife were convicted of murdering a foster child, whose body was found buried in their garden. During their trial, the Crown had introduced evidence of 12 further bodies of babies and young children that had been discovered at their previous residences. The question for the Privy Council was whether this evidence had been rightly admitted. In the words of Lord Herschell:

> It is undoubtedly not competent for the prosecution to adduce evidence tending to show that the accused has been guilty of criminal acts other than those covered by the indictment, for the purpose of leading to the conclusion that the accused is a person likely from his criminal conduct or character to have committed the offence for which he was being tried.

12 Hernandez [2023] EWCA Crim 814.

13 Ibid.

14 [1894] AC 57.

> On the other hand, the mere fact that the evidence tends to show the commission of other crimes does not render it inadmissible if it be relevant to an issue before the jury, and it may be so relevant if it bears upon the question whether the acts alleged to constitute the crime charged in the indictment were designed or accidental, or to rebut a defence which would otherwise be open to the accused.[15]

The first paragraph of this excerpt sets out the general rule that evidence of previous criminal conduct cannot be adduced in order to show that the defendant is a person likely from their criminal conduct or character to have committed the offence charged. In the second paragraph, Lord Herschell explains the exception to that rule, in stating that such evidence is admissible if it is relevant to an issue in the case, such as rebutting a defence of accident, or any other defence open to the accused.[16]

Over the years, the rule was refined so that the basis of the admissibility of evidence of bad character was that it had to be not merely relevant to an issue in the case, but *so* relevant that its probative value outweighed any prejudice that might arise. One of the most straightforward ways of establishing relevance was to show a similarity between the manner and circumstances in which the previous offences were committed and the manner and circumstances in which the offence charged had been committed. It was this comparative exercise that led to the description of such evidence as 'similar fact evidence.' Perhaps the most infamous example of its application came in *R v Smith*,[17] popularly known as the Brides in the Bath case, in which the defendant was accused of drowning his wife in the bath. Having run the defence of death by accident, the prosecution adduced evidence that two previous wives had arrived at an unfortunate end in a remarkably similar fashion. In all three cases, the accused stood to gain financially from their deaths, and all three women had drowned in the bath shortly after having wed him.

In *Boardman v DPP*,[18] there was a shift in emphasis from adducing the similar fact evidence to the amount of relevance that it bore to the matter in issue. In this case, the House of Lords developed the idea that, in order to be admissible, the similar fact evidence should have 'striking similarity' with the facts of the instant case. In the years that followed, this was interpreted as imposing a mandatory requirement upon the prosecution to show how any evidence they sought to adduce under this head bore a striking similarity to the manner and circumstances in which the offence charged was committed. Merely committing the same offence in a manner that was the stock in trade of persons committing such an offence was not sufficient to make evidence of the previous offences admissible. Instead, there had to be some 'unique and striking similarity' in the manner in which the previous offences had been committed. Consequently, the courts began to refuse to admit such evidence unless it was strikingly similar to the way in which the offence charged had been committed. Inevitably, this rendered the task of the prosecution considerably more difficult. Increasingly, similar fact evidence was ruled inadmissible, and the Court of Appeal seemed ever more willing to quash convictions where the extent of similarity could not be described as 'striking.'[19]

The House of Lords sought to remedy this problem in *DPP v P*.[20] In this case, a father was accused of rape and incest with his two daughters. As in *Boardman*, the question was whether the evidence in relation to each daughter was cross-admissible. The common features were that, in each case, there was evidence to indicate that the father had exercised dictatorial power over each

---

15 Ibid., at 65.
16 *Makin* was approved by the Privy Council in *Phillip v St Christopher and Nevis* [2017] UKPC 14.
17 (1915) 11 Cr App R 229. See also *R v Z* [2009] 1 Cr App R 34.
18 [1975] AC 42.
19 See e.g. *Inder* (1977) 67 Cr App R 143; *Clarke* (1977) 67 Cr App R 398; *Scarrott* [1978] QB 1016; *Brooks* (1990) 92 Cr App R 36.
20 [1991] 2 AC 447.

girl and that, in each case, he had paid for an abortion. The Court of Appeal had held that although the cases bore similarities, they could not be said to be striking. On that basis, the evidence should not have been admitted. However, this decision was reversed by the House of Lords, which concluded that striking similarities ought not to be the determining criteria of admissibility. Their Lordships stated that striking similarities were merely one method of establishing the probative force of the evidence, particularly in cases in which the identity of the accused was at issue. In the instant case, the issue was not identity, but whether an offence had actually been committed. There were therefore other ways of deriving probative force:

> When a question of the kind raised in this case arises I consider that the judge must first decide whether there is material upon which the jury would be entitled to conclude that the evidence of one victim, about what occurred to that victim, is so related to the evidence given by another victim, about what happened to that other victim, that the evidence of the first victim provides strong enough support for the evidence of the second victim to make it just to admit it notwithstanding the prejudicial effect of admitting the evidence. This relationship, from which the support is derived, may take many forms and while these forms may include 'striking similarity' in the manner in which the crime was committed, consisting of unusual characteristics in its execution the necessary relationship is by no means confined to such circumstances. Relationships in time and circumstances other than those may well be important relationships in this connection. Where the identity of the perpetrator is in issue, and evidence of this kind is important in that connection, obviously something in the nature of what has been called in argument a signature or other special feature will be necessary. To transpose this requirement to other situations where the question is whether a crime has been committed, rather than who did commit it, is to impose an unnecessary and improper restriction on the principle.[21]

As a result of this decision, the rule in *Boardman* concerning 'striking similarity' was subject to a broader interpretation. In practice, this meant that similar fact evidence became more frequently admissible, particularly in cases involving sexual abuse of children by carers or parents. However, overall, the rule will be remembered by many as a device that was overly narrow in scope and which served to impede the flow of information to the jury. This paternalism led to much relevant evidence being excluded, and, arguably, many travesties of justice followed.

In August 1992, the jury at the Old Bailey acquitted Simon Berkowitz of the burglary of a solicitor's office and the theft of personal documents belonging to Paddy Ashdown, the then leader of the Liberal Democrats.[22] Berkowitz was caught in possession of the stolen documents, which he was trying to sell to the media. He admitted possession of them, but claimed that they had been given to him by a man in a pub. The jury was not, however, told that Berkowitz had 240 previous convictions, 230 of which were for burglary, and a majority of these for burglary of solicitors' offices and the theft of documents. The prosecution had applied to the trial judge to allow these convictions to go before the jury as evidence of guilt, but the judge refused on the ground that it would be too prejudicial to do so. It is, at the very least, arguable that a man found in possession of goods stolen in the burglary of a solicitor's office, who has some 200 convictions for burglary of a solicitor's office, committed the burglary in question. That is not to say that one merely jumps from the fact of previous convictions to conviction on the present charge – there must be other evidence linking the defendant to the present burglary. However, this was indeed the case with Berkowitz (the stolen documents were found in his possession), and it seems odd

21 Ibid., at 462.
22 *The Times* (13 August 1992).

that the evidence of his previous convictions for burglaries was somehow found to be insufficiently relevant to be placed before a jury.

An even more serious case arose in 1987 when one William Beggs was convicted of murder at Teesside Crown Court. Beggs admitted the killing, but claimed that he acted in self-defence. However, the Court of Appeal found that evidence was incorrectly introduced by the prosecution to rebut his defence,[23] which concerned his past tendencies to attack sleeping young men and inflict grievous wounds with sharp instruments. In the view of the Court, these incidences were insufficiently similar, and the conviction was quashed. In 2001, Beggs was back at court in Edinburgh, and found guilty of sexually assaulting and murdering a young man whose body had been dismembered and decapitated, and the police began further investigations after traces of blood belonging to 17 other men were uncovered at his flat.[24] We may never know how many deaths or serious assaults could have been prevented had the Court of Appeal taken a less restrictive view of the evidence of his disposition towards violence 12 years earlier.

There is no doubt that the fact that a person has a disposition to commit particular offences can be highly relevant evidence in certain cases.[25] In view of the ongoing difficulties surrounding the uneven application of the similar fact rule, it is perhaps unsurprising that the Government took the decision to abolish it in the Criminal Justice Act (CJA) 2003.[26] However, as we shall see below, section 101(1)(d) of the legislation provides for the admissibility of 'bad character' evidence if it is relevant to an important matter in issue between the defendant and the prosecution. Such an issue may include a propensity to commit the kind of offence charged or to be untruthful, and such a propensity may be established by evidence that the defendant has been convicted of offences of the same description as, or in the same category as, the offence with which they are charged. Thus, although the formulation of the rule has entirely changed, the new statutory provision should encapsulate those types of case to which the similar fact rule would previously have been applied.

11.2.2 The Criminal Evidence Act 1898

Alongside the similar fact rule at common law, the Criminal Evidence Act 1898 also permitted evidence of bad character to be adduced in certain circumstances. It should be underlined, however, that evidence admitted under this legislation went to the question of credibility only; juries would be instructed not to use it as evidence of guilt. Prior to enactment of the 1898 Act, defendants were not permitted to give evidence in their own defence; thereafter they were able to do so upon application to the court, which meant that accused persons could choose to give evidence, but could not be compelled to do so. Policymakers were faced with two problems resulting from the decision to make the accused a competent witness in their own defence:

- whether the accused should be entitled to claim the privilege against self-incrimination in respect of the offence charged; and
- whether, and to what extent, defendants should be open to cross-examination about their previous bad character for the purpose of either proving their guilt on the offence charged or attacking their credibility as witnesses.

---

23 (1989) 90 Cr App R 430.

24 *The Times* (15 October 2001).

25 See further the remarks of the Criminal Law Revision Committee, op. cit., n. 11, at p. 149.

26 Criminal Justice Act 2003, s 99.

The Act represented a compromise by providing that while the defendant could be cross-examined as to any matter concerning the offences with which he was charged,[27] he was also given a 'shield against cross-examination as to his bad character,' which prevented such cross-examination unless one of the circumstances set out in section 1(3) of the Act applied.

Section 1(3) provided for three circumstances in which the shield could be lost. The first, contained in section 1(3)(a), was resorted to least often and provided that 'proof that he has committed or been convicted of such other offence is admissible evidence to show that he is guilty of an offence with which he is then charged.' In effect, this provision allowed the accused to be cross-examined about his previous bad character when it was exceptionally admissible at common law (as similar fact evidence) or by statute to prove his guilt on the offence charged (e.g. on charges of driving while disqualified).

Second, the shield would be lost where the accused:

> has personally or by his advocate asked questions of the witnesses for the prosecution with a view to establish his own good character, or has given evidence of his own good character, or the nature or conduct of his defence is such as to involve imputations on the character of the prosecutor or the witnesses for the prosecution, or the deceased victim of the alleged crime.[28]

This provision thus protected the accused from cross-examination about previous bad character unless the accused asserted their own good character by giving or calling character evidence,[29] or attacked the character of prosecution witnesses or the deceased victim of the offence charged.[30]

The subsection was essentially founded on the tit-for-tat principle, in that it was intended to be an automatic response so that the jury, who had to decide whom they were going to believe, knew the character of the person casting the imputations. One exception to the rule arose in rape cases in which the defendant alleged consent.[31] This was regarded as an attack on the character of the complainant, and thus defence counsel was at liberty to probe issues relating to the complainant's lifestyle and sexual history without the shield being lost.

The result was that comparatively minor imputations resulted in a long history of previous convictions being admitted, even when the imputation was seen as necessary to the defence. For example, in *R v Bishop*,[32] the defendant, charged with burglary, sought to explain the presence of his fingerprints in the burgled premises by alleging a homosexual relationship between himself and the occupier. As the occupier was a witness for the prosecution, this was seen as an imputation on his character, thereby entitling the prosecution to cross-examine the defendant on his previous convictions. In the lower courts, some judges felt that this was unfair and had been exercising their discretion for some years to exclude attacks on the accused's character where they felt such cross-examination would unfairly prejudice the jury. However, this was outside the remit of the statute and in *Selvey v DPP*[33] the House of Lords rejected what it described as a 'fetter' on the exercise of the discretion and held that the discretion should only be used to disallow cross-examination on bad character in the most exceptional of cases.

A final circumstance in which the defendant's shield could be lost was provided by section 1(3)(c) of the Act. This applied where a co-accused ran a 'cut-throat' defence and attacked the

27 Criminal Evidence Act 1898, s 1(2).

28 Ibid., s 1(3)(b).

29 See e.g. *Samuel* (1956) 40 Cr App R 8, in which the accused was charged with stealing a camera. In his defence, he alleged that he was going to return it to the police as lost property, and proceeded to give evidence of two other occasions on which he had returned lost property. In these circumstances, his shield was lost, and cross-examination was permitted about previous thefts.

30 See e.g. *Rappolt* (1911) 6 Cr App R 156, in which the defendant said that the prosecution witness was such an awful liar that his own brother would never believe him.

31 *R v Turner* [1944] KB 463.

32 [1975] QB 274.

33 [1970] AC 304.

character of another co-accused to suggest that they were more likely to have committed the offence in question.[34] In these circumstances, the co-accused was permitted to cross-examine another co-accused as to their previous convictions. The trial judge had no discretion to prevent such cross-examination, but they were obliged to direct the jury that the cross-examination went only to the credibility of the co-accused and was not to be used in order to determine the co-accused's guilt.[35]

11.2.3 The road to reform

A range of practical and conceptual difficulties plagued the application of both the similar fact rule at common law and the 1898 Act. In particular, there were concerns that the rules were open to abuse by corrupt police officers who invented confessions or planted evidence that they knew the defendant could not dispute without being seen to cast imputations on them. In such circumstances, the defendant's often lengthy list of convictions would be put before the jury. In a 2001 report, the Law Commission recommended that the law be entirely overhauled.[36]

It recommended that a radically different regime be introduced, which would cover the use of character evidence relating to both defendants and non-defendants. Accepting that bad character evidence did have the potential to be prejudicial, it recommended that a general rule of exclusion be put in place, but made subject to a number of statutory exceptions that would partially reflect, but would also serve to clarify, aspects of the law as it stood. In relation to the similar fact rule, the Commission believed that overall it worked fairly well and needed only a clearer statutory formula to clarify the difficult borderline between similar fact evidence and background or explanatory evidence. However, the 1898 Act was viewed as being entirely out of date, and was in need of being repealed and reworked to enable the defendant more readily to challenge the central features of the case against them, without making their previous convictions or bad character admissible.

While broadly accepting the Law Commission's recommendations, the Government issued a White Paper, *Justice for All*,[37] which outlined its legislative proposals. It was clear that the Government intended to go further and admit the defendant's bad character and previous convictions in a greater range of circumstances than the previous regime had permitted, and which the Law Commission had proposed. The White Paper's proposals were expanded upon in the CJA 2003 (sections 98–113), which now govern the admissibility of evidence of the bad character of a defendant and non-defendant. For example, section 100 of the CJA 2003 restricted the admissibility of evidence of a witness's previous bad character, while section 101 extended the realm of admissible bad character evidence adduced against the defendant.[38]

11.3 What constitutes 'bad character'?

Section 98 of the 2003 Act defines 'bad character' as 'evidence of, or a disposition towards misconduct.' The term 'misconduct' is subject to further definition in section 112(1) where it is

---

34 See e.g. *Murdoch and Taylor* [1965] AC 574.

35 This was also the case under s 1(3)(b). But see *R v Randall* [2004] 1 WLR 56. Here, the House of Lords held that where two defendants are jointly charged with a crime, and each blames the other for its commission, thus permitting both to cross-examine the other as to his previous convictions under s 1(3)(c) of the 1898 Act, one accused may rely on the criminal propensity of the other. Furthermore, the trial judge was not required to direct the jury that the bad character revealed went only to the credibility of the other accused.

36 Law Commission, *Evidence of Character in Criminal Proceedings*, Report No. 273 (HMSO, 2001).

37 Home Office, *Justice for All*, Cmnd 5563 (HMSO, 2002).

38 Ashworth, A., and Redmayne, M., *The Criminal Process*, 4th edn (Oxford University Press, 2010) 44.

labelled 'the commission of an offence or other reprehensible behaviour.' It will be apparent that this description was intended to be broad and to encapsulate any evidence that shows that a person has committed an offence or has acted in a reprehensible way, as well as evidence from which such conduct may be inferred. Even if past criminal charges are relatively minor in nature, they will still constitute misconduct under section 112(1).[39] Similarly, such evidence may include: previous convictions; charges being tried concurrently; evidence relating to offences for which a person has been charged, but with which prosecution opts not to proceed;[40] formal cautions;[41] and charges of which the defendant has been acquitted at a previous trial.[42] Note, however, that fixed-penalty notices are excluded from this list.[43]

On a literal reading, and possibly contrary to the intention of the drafters, the phrase 'other reprehensible conduct' is potentially wide enough to cover a broad range of conduct, including that which is not criminal.[44] However, some of the early decisions suggest that the courts are reluctant to interpret the provision in such a broad manner. In *R v Renda*,[45] an absolute discharge following a finding that the defendant was unfit to plead was held not to constitute 'misconduct' for the purposes of the Act. In the view of Judge LJ, the term 'reprehensible' 'carries with it some element of culpability or blameworthiness.'[46] In the consolidated appeals reported as *R v Weir*,[47] the Court of Appeal had to determine whether two separate instances of behaviour amounted to 'bad character' for the purposes of section 98. In *Manister*, in which the accused was charged with indecent assault on a 13-year-old girl, the fact that he had a previous relationship with a 16-year-old girl was deemed inadmissible. So too was a comment that he had made to the 15-year-old sister of that girl, where he allegedly asked her: 'Why do you think I am still single? If only you were a bit older and I a bit younger.' Both of these comments were deemed by the Court of Appeal to fall outside the scope of section 98. Strictly speaking, there was nothing that was per se reprehensible about a relationship between a 34-year-old man and a young woman above the age of consent. Some additional feature would be required to make such conduct reprehensible, such as evidence of grooming her as a minor or disapproval by the girl's parents. As regards his comment to the girl's sister, this was 'unattractive,' but not said to be reprehensible.

In *Osbourne*,[48] the Court of Appeal rejected the proposition that shouting at one's partner in the presence of a child, while 'not to be commended,' did not cross the threshold and could not be classed as reprehensible. By contrast, however, in *Saint*,[49] the Court of Appeal took a much dimmer

---

39 Furthermore, s 108 of the CJA 2003 repeals the previous prohibition on the use in evidence of offences committed by the defendant while a child, but in order for these to be admitted, both the offence for which the defendant is being tried and the offence for which the defendant was convicted must be indictable, and the court should be satisfied that the interests of justice require the evidence to be admissible. A similar approach is taken on 'spent convictions' under the Rehabilitation of Offenders Act 1974. Although admissible in criminal proceedings, Part 35 of the *Criminal Practice Directions* [2013] EWCA Crim 1631 recommends that advocates should not refer to a spent conviction when such reference can reasonably be avoided. However, where the prosecution does wish to adduce such evidence, leave should be obtained and the judge should then exercise his or her discretion to ensure that there is no unfairness to the defendant.

40 *R v Edwards* [2006] 1 WLR 1524. See also *R v Ali* [2010] EWCA Crim 1619, in which the Court of Appeal judged that photos of the appellant holding firearms in Pakistan were admissible. In Pakistan, handling guns as photographic props is not illegal, but the Court of Appeal judged the criminality of the appellant's conduct according to English law, and the evidence was thereby held to be evidence of misconduct on his part.

41 See *S (Stephen Paul)* [2006] 2 Cr App R 23 (Rose LJ).

42 See *R v Z (Prior Acquittal)* [2000] 2 AC 483, discussed below.

43 See *R v Hamer* (2011) 175 JP 19. Fixed-penalty notices were held not to be admissions of guilt or proof that a crime has been committed and do not blacken an accused's character.

44 See further Munday, R., 'What Constitutes "Other Reprehensible Behaviour" under the Bad Character Provisions of the Criminal Justice Act 2003?' [2004] Crim LR 533.

45 [2006] 1 Cr App Rep 380.

46 At [24].

47 [2006] 1 WLR 1885. See also *V* [2006] EWCA Crim 1901.

48 *Osbourne* [2007] Crim LR 712.

49 [2010] EWCA Crim 1924.

view of the defendant's interest in 'swinging parties' and 'dogging' in camouflage wearing night vision goggles. In *Saleem*,[50] it was held that violent images and rap lyrics found in the possession of the accused were admissible as they made specific reference to the defendant's plan to commit violent acts on his 17th birthday (the day on which he was allegedly party to a violent assault). Similarly, in *R v D (N)*,[51] it was deemed that evidence of possession of indecent photographs of children was capable of being admitted as bad character evidence to demonstrate a sexual interest in children. Proof of propensity was not limited to the commission of the same kind of offence, but could include any evidence that the defendant had behaved as charged.

In the light of these decisions, we are still unclear as to when non-criminal conduct might be considered reprehensible enough in order to fall within the ambit of the legislation.[52] Indeed, some of the decisions discussed above might legitimately be questioned. It seems particularly odd, for example, that a clear expression of sexual attraction by a 34-year-old man to a 15-year-old girl was not considered to be sufficiently reprehensible, whereas lyrics to a rap tune composed by a teenager and voluntary attendance at a swingers' party were. As the law currently stands, no clear principle or test has emerged as to when previous behaviour might cross the threshold. Some measure of clarity on this point is urgently required, and, hopefully, the issue will be addressed by the Supreme Court in the not-too-distant future.

11.3.1 Previous acquittals and allegations

The inclusion of acquittals within the ambit of bad character evidence reflects the previous law and preserves the decision of the House of Lords in *R v Z*.[53] Here, the House of Lords held that there was no special rule that required the exclusion of evidence that a person had been involved in earlier offences, even if he had been acquitted of those crimes at a previous trial. Z was charged with a single count of rape committed in 1998. The prosecution sought leave to adduce evidence of four previous incidents involving Z and four different women, who complained of rape in 1984, 1985, 1989, and 1993. Z was tried on a charge of rape in respect of each of these incidents. In each case, it was admitted that intercourse had taken place and the central issue was whether the complainant consented. Only in one case was Z convicted; in the other three, he was acquitted.

The trial judge accepted the Crown's case that the four incidents involved circumstances sufficiently similar to those of the present case for them to have been admissible under the principles established in *Boardman* and *P*. However, the judge held that the fact of the prior acquittals in respect of three of the complainants meant that the Crown could not adduce evidence involving those incidents as similar fact evidence in respect of the present charge of rape. Standing by itself, one conviction did not present a sufficiently cogent picture of similar incidents to be admissible.

The Crown's appeal was rejected by the Court of Appeal, but it referred the case to the House of Lords, certifying that a question of general public importance was involved in its decision – namely:

> Other than in cases of *autrefois acquit*, (a) is evidence admissible on behalf of the Crown in a trial of offence A which also proves guilt in respect of one or more prior incident (B, C and D)

---

50 [2007] EWCA Crim 1923. See also *Tirnaveanu* [2007] EWCA 1239, in which it was held that a nexus in time is needed between the offence and previous misconduct.

51 *The Times* (1 July 2011).

52 But see *R v Palmer (Terri-Marie)* [2016] EWCA 2237, in which evidence, in the form of three social media messages sent by the defendant in which she stated her anger at her boyfriend and that she might stab him (which she eventually did), was admitted.

53 Op. cit., n. 32; although the common law rules have been abolished, the courts continue to adopt the approach in *R v Z*. See *R v Harrison* [2004] EWCA Crim 1792; *R v Barney* [2005] EWCA Crim 1385. By contrast, see *R v Woodhead (Peter Edmund)* [2011] EWCA Crim 472, in which it was held that it was not necessary to regard the law that pre-dated the CJA 2003 when considering whether bad character evidence should be admitted.

in respect of each of which the defendant has been tried and acquitted; and (b) is evidence so admissible if its nature and purpose is to show guilt in respect of offence A on the basis that offence A was not an isolated offence, but one in a series of similar incidents (including those in respect of which the defendant was tried and convicted)?

The House of Lords found in favour of the Crown. Lord Hutton, giving a speech with which all of their Lordships agreed, came to the following conclusions.

- The principle of double jeopardy operated to cause a criminal court in the exercise of its discretion to stop a prosecution where the defendant was being prosecuted on the same or substantially the same facts as had given rise to an earlier prosecution that had resulted in his acquittal or conviction.
- Provided that a defendant was not placed in double jeopardy in that way, evidence that was relevant on a subsequent prosecution was not inadmissible because it showed or tended to show that the defendant was, in fact, guilty of an offence of which he had earlier been acquitted.
- It followed from this that a distinction should not be drawn between evidence that showed guilt of a previous offence of which the defendant had been acquitted and evidence that tended to show guilt of such an offence or that appeared to relate to one distinct issue rather than the issue of guilt of such an offence.

In this instance, the defendant was not placed in double jeopardy because the facts giving rise to the present prosecution were different from those that had given rise to the earlier prosecution. The evidence of the earlier complainants was accepted to be relevant and to come within the ambit of the similar fact rule, and therefore it was not inadmissible because it showed that the defendant was, in fact, guilty of the offences of which he had earlier been acquitted. The admissibility of previous acquittals would be subject to the judge's discretion to exclude them after weighing the evidence's prejudicial effect against its probative value.

Under the 2003 Act, Z is still good law, and furthermore it may apply to convictions in respect of any offence. Thus, if there were a series of robberies, and the defendant were acquitted of involvement in them, evidence tending to show that he had committed those earlier robberies could be given in a later case involving a similar charge. This may be particularly likely if such evidence showed that the previous incidents took place in similar circumstances to those in the case at hand. The issue of previous acquittals and their use in a criminal trial has been addressed by the Court of Appeal in *R v Preko*.[54] The defendant, tried with money laundering for the second time, attempted to introduce evidence of previous acquittals in an attempt to demonstrate his innocence in this case. Rafferty LJ emphasised that acquittals have never been considered proof of innocence and noted that:

> In our view it would achieve nothing to speculate *ad infinitum* on the range of potential explanations for these acquittals. That one jury in one trial did not find the Crown's case proved to the criminal standard is of no relevance to the decision of the jury in the retrial.

In *R v Smith (David)*,[55] the Crown successfully relied on the decision in Z to argue for the admissibility of previous allegations that had never come to court. At Smith's original trial for nine different counts of rape and other sexual offences, the judge stayed proceedings in relation to three of

---

54 [2015] EWCA Crim 42.

55 This was one of the consolidated appeals reported as *R v Edwards* [2006] 1 WLR 1524. See also *R v O'Dowd* [2009] 2 Cr App R 16.

the charges as the police had previously told the accused that no further action would be taken. However, the prosecution then succeeded in obtaining leave to admit the evidence as tending to show the defendant's propensity to commit the kinds of offences charged. The Court of Appeal rejected the appellant's contention that the evidence had been improperly admitted. In the view of the court, there was no difference in principle between evidence on which a defendant had previously been acquitted and evidence relating to allegations that had never been tried. The court proceeded to state that, as a general rule, all evidence that is relevant to the question of whether the accused is guilty or innocent of the offence charged will be admissible under the bad character provisions of the 2003 Act.[56]

The Supreme Court revisited the issue of allegations amounting to bad character in the case of *R v Mitchell*.[57] In *Mitchell*, the defendant was charged with murder following a fatal stabbing to her partner. The prosecution adduced evidence of several alleged incidents involving the defendant and the use of knives in threatening situations. On the use of allegations as a form of bad character evidence, Lord Kerr stated that:

> The jury is not asked to return a verdict on any previous allegations relied upon, and indeed should be reminded that the defendant is not on trial for them. It should be told to focus on the indicted offence(s). Reliance on cumulative past incidents in support of a case of propensity may indeed illuminate the truth of the currently indicted allegations, but excessive recourse to such history may skew the trial in a way which distracts attention from the central issue.[58]

In *Johnson*,[59] the trial judge ruled that previous convictions of a similar nature were not propensity evidence, but were still relevant to whether or not the defendant would participate in a conspiracy to burgle. The Court of Appeal rejected this notion and properly labelled the convictions as propensity evidence.

The provision would thus be potentially broad enough to cover the previous history of Ian Huntley, who was convicted in December 2003 of the infamous murder of Holly Wells and Jessica Chapman in Soham two years previously. Between 1995 and 1999, Huntley had been investigated for four alleged rapes, four cases of sex with underage girls, and one indecent assault on an 11-year-old girl. A charge was preferred in respect of only one of these allegations, but the Crown Prosecution Service discontinued the prosecution because there was no reasonable prospect of conviction. No charges were brought in respect of the other allegations and no record was kept of them. However, even if records had been kept, the allegations would have remained unproven and Huntley's record would have remained unblemished.

11.3.2 'Evidence of the facts of the offence charged'

Section 98 does not affect the admissibility of evidence that (a) 'has to do with the alleged facts of the offence' or (b) 'evidence of misconduct in connection with the investigation or prosecution of that offence.' These fall outside the definition of bad character provided in section 98. Thus, if the defendant were charged with burglary, the prosecution evidence of the facts of the offence, which tends to show that the accused is guilty of the offence charged, including any witnesses to the crime and any forensic evidence gathered, would be admissible outside the terms of these provisions.

56 Compare *R v Bovell; Dowds* [2005] 2 Cr App R 401.
57 [2016] UKSC 55.
58 Ibid., [53].
59 [2009] 2 Cr App R 7 [15], [19].

It is also important to bear in mind that many offences will inherently contain elements of certain other offences. For example, a person committing robbery may have a weapon in their possession, or a burglar may commit criminal damage in the course of the burglary. These will all be accepted by the courts as facts that are directly relevant to the charges at hand. Evidence that the defendant had tried to intimidate prosecution witnesses would also be admissible as evidence of misconduct in connection with (as appropriate) the investigation or the prosecution of the offence, as would allegations by the defendant that the evidence had been planted. Nevertheless, it is important to draw the distinction between these types of facts and facts that relate to another episode entirely. Thus, for example, evidence that the defendant had committed a burglary on another occasion, or that a witness had previously lied on oath, would not be evidence to do with the facts of the offence or its investigation or prosecution, and would therefore fall within the scope of section 98. In *R v Mullings*,[60] the prosecution wanted to adduce evidence of letters received by the defendant while on remand in prison in order to prove his affiliation to a street gang. The prosecution argued that this 'had to do with the alleged facts of the offence' within the meaning of section 98 of the 2003 Act and was therefore admissible without having to be admitted through one of the section 101 gateways. In an *obiter* observation, the Court of Appeal doubted that this was correct,[61] and held that section 98 of the Act should be narrowly interpreted so that the words 'has to do with the alleged facts of the offence' are construed in a way that means that a close temporal relation must exist between the incident and the alleged facts of the case. Indeed, this was the view in *Tirnaveanu*,[62] where the Court of Appeal held in this case that to come within section 98(a), the evidence must have some nexus in time with the offence charged. However, this decision has been doubted in *R v Sule*,[63] where the Court of Appeal held that section 98(a) includes no temporal qualification. *Sule* has been considered in two further Court of Appeal cases, namely *R v Lunkulu*[64] and *R v Ditta*.[65] In *Lunkulu*, the defendant was charged with a gang-related murder and the prosecution sought to introduce evidence of the defendant's previous conviction for gang-related violence. The trial judge admitted the evidence without reference to section 101 on the basis that the evidence had to do with the alleged offence. Specifically, the prosecution, as agreed with by the trial judge, felt that the evidence demonstrated the defendant's involvement in a long-standing feud between the gangs concerned in the offence. The Court of Appeal upheld this decision and affirmed the wording of the trial judge in his summing up to the jury:

> It is for you to decide whether these offences were to do with the facts of the present offence, as showing his involvement in the feud between the two gangs in general and in this offence in particular. If they were, the prosecution submit that his commission of these offences shows that he had a leading position within the Tottenham Turks and makes it more likely that he was a party to the commission of this murder.

Interestingly, the Court of Appeal did note that this sort of evidence is generally covered by section 101(1)(c), given that it will provide some sort of explanation or context for the defendant's conduct. Despite this, the Court affirmed that such evidence has to do with the alleged facts, and the bad character provisions could thus be avoided.[66]

---

60 [2010] EWCA Crim 2820.
61 The observation being *obiter* owing to the fact that the Court agreed that the letters were admissible on other grounds.
62 [2007] 2 Cr App R 23.
63 [2013] 1 Cr App R 3.
64 [2015] EWCA Crim 1350.
65 [2016] EWCA Crim 8.
66 See also *R v Stewart* [2016] EWCA Crim 447.

In *Ditta*, the Court of Appeal clarified that the meaning of the phrase 'to do with' should be wide enough to cover conduct prior to the offence, which provided a reason for the commission of the alleged offence. The defendant, a solicitor, was charged with perverting the course of justice by passing on to his drugs supplier information about police drugs operations. The evidence admitted was that the defendant was a user of the drugs supplied by the dealer.

11.4 Conditions for admissibility

Section 101(1)(a)–(g) of the 2003 Act sets out seven circumstances in which the prosecution, or in certain cases a co-defendant, can adduce evidence of bad character. These are:

(a) where all parties agree to the evidence being admissible;
(b) where the evidence is adduced by the defendant himself, or is given in answer to a question asked by him in cross-examination and intended to elicit it;
(c) where it is important explanatory evidence;
(d) where it is relevant to an important matter in issue between the defendant and the prosecution;
(e) where it has substantial probative value in relation to an important matter in issue between the defendant and a co-defendant;
(f) where it is evidence to correct a false impression given by the defendant; or
(g) where the defendant has made an attack on another person's character.

Each head of admissibility is then expanded upon by a number of sections, which provide additional definitional material.[67] It should also be noted that two of these heads of admissibility, sections 101(1)(d) and 101(1)(g), are subject to a judicial discretion to refuse to admit the evidence if, on application by the defendant, the trial judge is of the opinion that it would have such an adverse effect on the fairness of the proceedings that it ought not to be admitted. Figure 11.1 illustrates the process that is now used to determine whether evidence of bad character is admissible.

Although evidence admissible under section 101 of the 2003 Act will primarily go to the credit of the defendant and allow their character to be known by the jury, there is no strict rule (as there was in the 1898 legislation) that prevents the jury from taking the character of the accused into account when adjudicating the issue of guilt. This was the core issue that confronted the Court of Appeal in one of the most important cases to date on the character provisions, *R v Campbell*.[68] The defendant had been convicted of false imprisonment and assault occasioning actual bodily harm. At trial, the prosecution applied under section 101(1)(d) of the Act to adduce evidence of two previous convictions that the defendant had for violence against women. Permission was granted on the grounds that the convictions showed a propensity to commit acts similar to those that were the subject of the current charge. The judge proceeded to explain the relevance of these convictions to the jury, in line with the then Judicial Studies Board's specimen directions.[69] He also told them that the convictions were not only relevant to the accused's propensity to commit acts of violence towards women, but also to the question of whether the defendant had told the truth to the court.[70]

The defendant was convicted, and argued on appeal that the jury should not have been told that his previous convictions were relevant to his propensity not to tell the truth. Applying the

67 Criminal Justice Act 2003, ss 102–106.

68 [2007] 1 WLR 2798. See also *R v Jordan* [2009] EWCA Crim 953.

69 Now the *Crown Court Compendium. Part I: Jury and Trial Management and Summing Up* (Judicial College, 2017).

70 See also *Wallace* [2007] 2 Cr App R 30. *Wallace* is significant insofar as any evidence against the defendant in respect of other offences listed in the same indictment amounts to evidence of bad character.

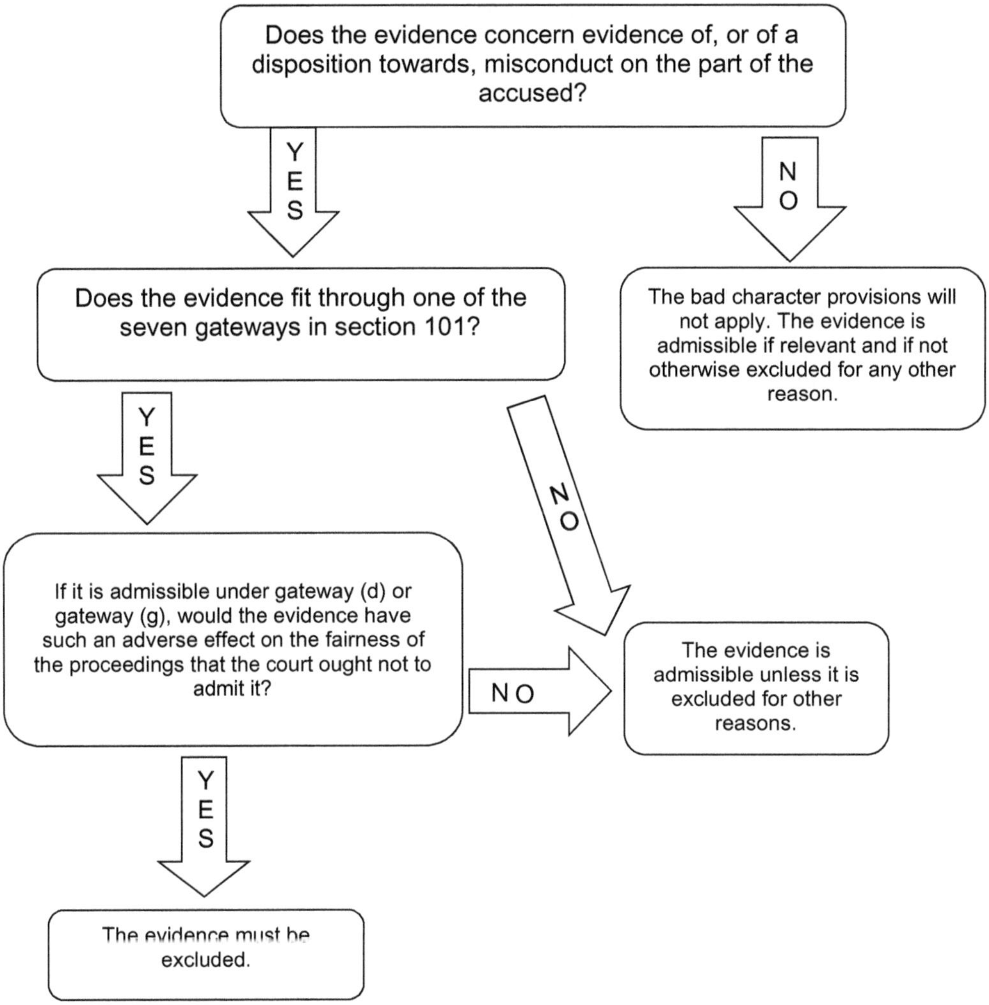

Figure 11.1 Admissibility of the defendant's bad character

earlier decision of *R v Highton*,[71] the court dismissed this argument and stated that once evidence of bad character was introduced, it was for the jury to determine in what respect it was relevant. In the view of the court, it was unhelpful for the judge to draw a distinction between propensity to commit the type of offence charged and matters pertaining to credibility. As a matter of common sense, where the jury learn that a defendant had shown a propensity to commit criminal acts, they may in turn conclude that he was less likely to be telling the truth while testifying:

> The summing up that assists the jury with the relevance of bad character evidence will accord with common sense and assist them to avoid prejudice that is at odds with this ... It is open to the jury to attach significance to it in any respect in which it is relevant. To direct them

71 [2005] 1 WLR 3472. See also *Amponsah* [2005] EWCA Crim 2993.

> only to have regard to it for some purposes and to disregard its relevance in other respects would be to revert to the unsatisfactory practices that prevailed under the old law.[72]
>
> In considering the inference to be drawn from bad character the courts have in the past drawn a distinction between propensity to offend and credibility. This distinction is usually unrealistic. If the jury learn that a defendant has shown a propensity to commit criminal acts they may well at one and the same time conclude that it is more likely that he is guilty and that he is less likely to be telling the truth when he says that he is not.[73]

However, it was underlined that the question of whether a defendant had a *propensity* for being untruthful would not normally be capable of being described as 'an important matter in issue' unless dishonesty was actually an element of the offence in question. Even when such circumstances did arise, the propensity to tell lies was only likely to be relevant if the lying was done in the context of committing criminal offences. In the rare case in which propensity to be untruthful was an important issue, the judge should always warn the jury that a propensity for untruthfulness would not, of itself, go very far to show that the accused had committed the offences charged.[74]

11.4.1 Gateway (a): evidence admitted by agreement

The first two gateways under the legislation are probably the least contentious and are fairly self-explanatory. Under both of these provisions, the defence must be content to have the evidence adduced before the court. In practice, they will rarely adopt such tactics unless they form part of the overall strategy to reveal previous convictions or other character traits. An illustration as to why a defendant would ever agree to their own character going into evidence can be seen in *R v Hussain*,[75] where the parties agreed to the bad character of both accused and co-accused being admitted as it would have been admitted through one of the other gateways regardless. According to the court, this case is a positive reflection of a saving of time and money. However, where evidence is adduced under this gateway, the judge must be informed by counsel that such an agreement has been reached.[76]

11.4.2 Gateway (b): evidence adduced by the defence

There are a number of potential scenarios in which the defence may wish to adduce their own character for strategic reasons if, for example, they wish to launch an attack on the character of a prosecution witness. In all probability, the trial judge would then allow evidence of the defendant's bad character to be introduced under section 101(1)(g).[77] In such a case, it may be more tactical for counsel to be frank with the jury, rather than having the prosecution adduce evidence or ask questions about such bad character under section 101(1)(g). In addition, a defendant may wish to adduce evidence of their own bad character where the evidence is of comparatively minor misconduct as jurors may speculate that their character is worse than it is, especially those jurors who have experience. This was the case in *R v Harper*,[78] where the defendant was charged with wounding with intent and affray. To boost his credibility, he 'came clean' to the jury regarding

---

72 *Highton*, ibid., at [24–25].

73 Ibid., at [28].

74 See also *R v Davis* [2008] EWCA 1156. In this case, the Court of Appeal appears to have tried to modify the effect of *Campbell*. The Court pointed out that what was said in *Campbell* was said in relation to gateway (d), and such an approach was not so easily applied to gateway (c).

75 [2008] EWCA Crim 1117.

76 *R v DJ* [2010] EWCA Crim 385.

77 See discussion below.

78 [2007] EWCA Crim 1746.

his previous conviction for affray. Alternatively, such a ploy may be adopted where the defendant is charged with an offence involving violence, but has convictions only for non-violent offences.

Example 11.1

Ralph is charged with armed robbery, but his previous convictions are for shoplifting and theft from cars. Those previous convictions might well be disclosed to the jury in an effort to persuade them that the defendant is a small-time criminal and not into major-league crime involving violence of the kind charged. In *R v Shaw*,[79] the accused pleaded self-defence to a charge of assaulting police officers. In order to support this defence, he sought to adduce evidence of his bad relationship with the police, including an arrest for murder, in order to show his state of mind as being more likely to imagine he was under threat from police officers. The Court of Appeal held that the bad character of the defendant was properly admitted on behalf of the defendant for that purpose. Once bad character evidence is properly revealed to the jury, the prosecution can cross-examine the defendant in detail on the matters raised, although the trial judge should prevent counsel from dwelling on the evidence too much, lest the jury be given the impression that it is of greater importance than is the case. Cross-examination may also follow bad character evidence revealed by the defendant inadvertently or by other witnesses, provided that such evidence is properly adduced.

Similarly, in *Jones v DPP*,[80] the accused had been arrested following the rape of a Girl Guide and the murder of a second girl just one month later. He was first tried for the rape and was convicted. He was then tried for the murder of the second girl. The circumstances of the murder resembled those of the rape in many respects, but the prosecution made no attempt to admit them as similar fact evidence to avoid putting the victim through the ordeal of giving evidence again. When giving evidence at his murder trial, Jones attempted to explain a false alibi he had given to the police on being questioned by stating that he had been 'in trouble with the police' on a previous occasion. He then put forward a new alibi, in which he said he had been with a prostitute in London at the time. He gave an account of his return home and an account of a conversation with his wife, in which he assured her that his late return home had nothing to do with the crime that had been reported in the newspapers. The prosecution was then given leave to cross-examine him about a previous occasion on which he had claimed to have had exactly the same conversation with his wife, again after supposedly visiting a prostitute in London. Counsel did not indicate what that previous occasion was, but it must have been obvious to the jury, given the notoriety of the case, that it was the occasion on which he had been charged with the rape of the Girl Guide. The cross-examination was directed at discrediting the new alibi given by Jones, and placed an emphasis on how unlikely it was that Jones and his wife should repeat an earlier conversation word for word.

The appeal against conviction, which argued that leave should not have been given to cross-examine, went to the House of Lords. Their Lordships interpreted the words of section 1(3) of the 1898 Act, which prohibited questions 'tending to show that he has committed or been convicted of or been charged with any offence,' as meaning 'tending to show the jury for the first time matters which had not been already disclosed to them.' Since Jones himself had revealed the facts upon which the cross-examination was based, the cross-examination was properly allowed.

79 [2003] Crim LR 278.
80 [1962] AC 655.

In the earlier case of *R v Chitson*,[81] the defendant was convicted of unlawful sexual intercourse with an underage girl. The girl was allowed to give evidence that the defendant had boasted to her of his sexual relationship with another girl. The Court of Appeal held that he was properly cross-examined about these claims on the basis that, if they were true, it would strongly corroborate the young girl's evidence that he had had sexual intercourse with her.[82] The Court of Appeal's decision that it was admissible under section 1(2) of the 1898 Act was disapproved of by the House of Lords in *Jones*, but the basis for this distinction is not particularly clear, given that it would appear to be caught by the principle enunciated by their Lordships in that very case: namely, that the statement was already before the court, and therefore the prohibition in section 1(3) did not apply. However, section 99(1) of the 2003 Act abolishes the common law rules governing the admissibility of evidence of bad character, and the prosecution must seek leave to admit the evidence of bad character under section 101.[83] The *Jones* case is likely to fall under section 101(1)(b), but if *Chitson* were tried under the 2003 rules, the previous conviction for underage sexual intercourse might not be admissible given that the defendant did not directly adduce the evidence. Nevertheless, it might still be admissible under section 101(1)(d) as relevant to an important matter in issue between the defendant and the prosecution since it includes the question of whether the defendant has a propensity to commit the kind of offence charged.[84] The case of *R v Speed*[85] illustrates the relationship between this gateway and that of section 101(1)(g). Here it was held that where a defendant puts his own bad character in evidence pursuant to section 101(1)(b) of the CJA 2003 but where the evidence could also have been admitted via section 101(1)(g) (attack on another person's character), the judge may give the conventional direction to the jury as to the approach to bad character evidence appropriate to a case where such evidence is in fact admitted via gateway (g).

11.4.3 Gateway (c): important explanatory evidence

For evidence to be admissible as important explanatory evidence, it must be such that, without it, the factfinder would find it impossible or difficult to understand other evidence in the case.[86] If, therefore, the facts or account to which the bad character evidence relates are largely understandable without this additional explanation, the evidence should not be admitted.[87] The explanation must also give the court some substantial assistance in understanding the case as a whole. In other words, it will not be enough for the evidence to assist the court to understand some trivial piece of evidence.

At common law, explanatory (or background) evidence was always admissible as an exception to the rules that excluded evidence of bad character. In the Australian case of *O'Leary v R*,[88] a number of men employed at a timber camp went on a drunken rampage for several hours, during which time several serious assaults were committed. After the rampage, one of the men, who had been seriously assaulted, was found dying. At the trial for murder, it was held that the episode should be treated as one event, which included the other assaults that had occurred:

---

81 [1909] 2 KB 945.

82 In *Chitson*, the defendant's statement made to the girl was properly admitted as an exception to the rule against hearsay. See Ch 12.

83 In the event that the prosecution fails to seek leave, the trial judge nevertheless retains a discretion to admit such evidence: see *Lawson* [2007] 1 WLR 1191.

84 See below. See also *R v B* [2011] EWCA Crim 1630.

85 [2013] EWCA Crim 1650.

86 Criminal Justice Act 2003, s 102.

87 See *R v MP* [2015] EWCA Cm 924.

88 (1946) 73 CLR 566.

> The evidence disclosed that, under the influence of the beer and wine [the prisoner] had drunk and continued to drink, he engaged in repeated acts of violence which might be regarded as amounting to a connected course of conduct. Without evidence of what, during that time, was done by those men who took any significant part in the matter and especially evidence of the behaviour of the prisoner, the transactions of which the alleged murder formed an integral part could not be truly understood and isolated from it, could only be presented as an unreal and not very intelligible event. The prisoner's generally violent and hostile conduct might well serve to explain his mind and attitude and, therefore, to implicate him in the resulting homicide.[89]

The difficulty in providing the essential background information is contained in the phrase 'to implicate him in the resulting homicide.' As in *O'Leary* itself, it could include evidence of other offences committed by the defendant, or evidence of other misconduct on his part. In *R v Sidhu*,[90] the defendant was charged with conspiracy to possess explosives in England. It was held that the trial judge had rightly admitted a video-tape, which appeared to show the defendant leading a band of armed rebels in Pakistan. Although the evidence suggested to the jury that the defendant had been involved in other criminal activities, it was justified as being necessary to explain the background to the defendant's activities in England and the motives for his activities.

Similar reasoning was applied in *R v Sawoniuk*,[91] in which the accused was charged with the murder of Jews during the Nazi occupation of Belorussia in 1942. Evidence was admitted that, during that period, the accused had been a member of a group of police officers who had carried out search and kill operations for Jewish survivors of an earlier massacre. In this case, background evidence was necessary to enable the jury properly to understand the circumstances that prevailed such a long time ago in a foreign country. The court recognised that it would have been highly unlikely that any of the jurors had an understanding of the particular atmosphere in which ethnically based war crimes were committed, and noted that criminal charges cannot fairly be judged in a factual vacuum. Evidence describing the context and circumstances in which the offences were said to have been committed was deemed to be necessary. In *Phillip v St Christopher and Nevis*,[92] the Privy Council dismissed an appellant's appeal against conviction for the murder of his estranged wife. At trial, the prosecution adduced evidence of previous violence to the wife as important explanatory evidence. The board held that the evidence was admissible to show that the defendant felt some general ill-will towards his wife and also went to his motive.

In *R v M (T)*,[93] the defendant had been charged with raping his sister. The Court of Appeal held that a long history of sexual and physical abuse within the household was rightly admitted as essential background evidence to explain why the victim had not turned to her parents for help when her brother allegedly raped her. The evidence was that daughters and sons were raped and buggered by the father, and the sons were forced to watch him abuse their sisters. In one particular instance, M was forced to watch the abuse and later made to copy what his father had done. By the time he had reached the age of 16, he was abusing his 10-year-old sister on a regular basis. Without this evidence, the court felt that the jury would have received an incomplete and incomprehensible account. However, it was solely for this purpose that the evidence was admitted – explanatory evidence may not be used by the jury as evidence of propensity tending to show guilt. On the other hand, in *R v Lee*,[94] the defendant had been charged with numerous sex offences

89 Ibid., at 577 (Dixon J).
90 (1994) 98 Cr App R 59.
91 [2000] 2 Cr App R 220.
92 [2017] UKPC 14.
93 [2000] 1 WLR 421.
94 [2012] All ER (D) 106.

against his stepdaughter X and her friend Y. The prosecution wanted to rely on evidence from X that when she was 16 the defendant had planted a video-recorder in her bathroom to film her bathing. The judge admitted the evidence but the appeal was allowed. The court held that while those pieces of evidence were highly damaging for the defendant, X's evidence was 'perfectly comprehensible' without the need for reference to the defendant's bad character. It is questionable whether the evidence could be adduced under gateway (d).

Although some critics fear that the use of explanatory evidence is sometimes used as a backdoor means of admitting evidence of the defendant's bad character, the courts have put in place very stringent guidelines as to when precisely such evidence can be used, and how it ought to be evaluated by the jury.[95] Certainly, in the cases above, it can be clearly seen how the facts in question may have appeared incomplete or incomprehensible without such evidence being given. However, by the same token, one can readily see that such evidence may be a useful tool in the prosecutor's war chest in proving the guilt of the defendant. For example, in *Davis*,[96] Rix LJ talked at length about the different rationales for using gateways (c) and (d), and stressed that the manner of the defence and nature of judicial direction would both depend on which gateway had been used. The commentary by Mirfield in the Criminal Law Review following the case of *R v Leathem and Mallett*[97] strongly argues that while cases involving the overlap of these gateways are often difficult and complex, and may present real practical difficulties for the court, it is unacceptable for gateway (c) to be misused and it should be remembered that when dealing with questions of probative value and prejudicial effect 'the proper territory'[98] was to be found in section 101(1)(d) and (3).

11.4.4 Gateway (d): relevance to an important matter in issue between prosecution and defendant

This subsection roughly equates with the similar fact principle applied at common law, and is the primary gateway under the bad character evidence admitted under the Act. Such evidence will be admissible if it is relevant to an important matter in issue between the defendant and the prosecution. Section 112(1) defines such a matter as 'a matter of substantial importance in the context of the case as a whole' and section 103(1) states that, for the purposes of section 101(1)(d), matters in issue between the defendant and the prosecution include the question 'whether the defendant has a propensity to commit offences of the kind charged, except where his having such a propensity makes it no more likely that he is guilty of the offence.' Section 103(2) provides that such a propensity can be established by evidence that the defendant has been convicted of offences of the same description, or of the same category. Section 103(4)(a) makes clear that 'two offences are of the same description as each other if the statement of the offence in a written charge or indictment would, in each case, be in the same terms.' Therefore, the 'description' of an offence simply relates to its given name within the criminal law – that is, theft, burglary, driving while disqualified, handling stolen goods, etc. The 'category' in which a particular offence falls will be prescribed by the Secretary of State.[99]

On that basis, it can be assumed that the scope of 'propensity' under the 2003 Act is considerably wider than what it had been under the similar fact rule at common law. However, a number

95 See *R v West* [2003] EWCA Crim 3024; *R v Dolan* [2003] 1 Cr App R 18; *R v Pronick* [2006] EWCA Crim 2517; *R v Beverley* [2006] Crim LR 1064; *R v Osbourne* [2007] EWCA Crim 481; *R v Davis* (2008) 172 JP 358; *R v Saint* [2010] EWCA Crim 1924.

96 *R v Davis* (2008) 172 JP 358.

97 [2017] EWCA Crim 42

98 [2017] Crim LR 10, 788–93

99 Criminal Justice Act 2003, s 103(4)(b). As at December 2014, two such orders are in place, one categorising offences related to 'theft,' and another related to 'sexual offences involving persons under the age of 16': see Criminal Justice Act 2003 (Categories of Offences Order) 2004.

of caveats apply to this observation. First, section 103(3) provides that evidence of a conviction of the same description or category is not to be admitted 'if the court is satisfied, by reason of the length of time since the conviction or for any other reason that it would be unjust for it to apply in his case.' The judge must therefore approach each case on its own facts, and consider carefully the precise nature of the previous offences, any underlying reasons for the offender's behaviour, and the time that has since elapsed. In *R v McGarvie*,[100] it was deemed that the defendant's two previous convictions of rape were too old to satisfy the requirements of the Act since they had occurred 32 and 18 years ago, respectively. However, see the case of *R v Royston Jackson*,[101] where although the defendant's previous conviction for murder was 20 years old, the fact that the previous and current murder were both done by strangulation, the victims were both male, and certain other factors were similar meant that the defendant's propensity was admissible.

Second, the discretion in section 101(3) also applies to this gateway: the court may exclude the evidence if it appears that its admissibility would have such an adverse effect on the fairness of the proceedings that the court ought not to admit it. Here, the judge may pay particular attention to the seriousness of the previous offence(s). The more serious they are, the more weight the jury may attach to them. As suggested above, this is not necessarily unfair to the accused, but it does mean that the judge should consider carefully the potential consequences of allowing the prosecution to use such evidence. It was suggested in the case of *R v Olu, Wilson and Brooks*[102] that where the prosecution seeks to cite evidence of the acceptance by a defendant of a caution as evidence of bad character, the court must contemplate its discretion to exclude the evidence under section 101(3) with specific care. This duty is all the more important in relation to a situation in which the defendant did not receive legal advice at the time. As important context, it has been argued that previous legislation was based on the view that the accused have too many rights and should cede some of them in 'fairness' to the prosecution. This re-balancing narrative reinforced the 'populist punitiveness' of criminal justice policy that subsequently took hold.[103]

Third, it should be borne in mind that evidence of a propensity to act in a particular way is not admissible if 'the existence of such a propensity makes it no more likely that the defendant is guilty of the offence charged'.'[104] It follows that the trial judge must determine that the particular propensity evidence is sufficiently relevant to make it more likely that the defendant is guilty of the offence charged. In *R v O'Dowd*,[105] the appellant appealed against his conviction for rape, sexual assault, false imprisonment, threatening to kill, and poison. He submitted that the trial judge had incorrectly instructed the jury in his approach to the balancing exercise required by section 101(3). There were a number of difficulties with the bad character evidence that the Crown had adduced, which had included the age of the incidents relied upon, one of which had occurred over 22 years ago. It is also important to note that only one of the previous incidents had resulted in a conviction, which was a necessary foundation for establishing propensity.[106] Without this foundation, a trial of the collateral issues was necessary. The important factor in the appeal being allowed was the nature and complexity of the bad character allegations and the time frame required to put them before the jury where they would be contested. The trial judge had failed to consider

---

100 [2011] EWCA Crim 1414. See also *Urushadze* [2008] EWCA Crim 2498; *R v Bullen* [2008] 2 Cr App R 25; *R v Woodhouse* (2009) 173 JP 337. With regard to foreign convictions, see *R v Kordansinki* [2007] 1 CR App R 17, in which it was held that such convictions may be admissible where the offences have been authenticated in accordance with the Crime (International Co-operation) Act 2003.

101 [2011] EWCA Crim 1870.

102 [2010] EWCA Crim 2975.

103 Bottoms, A.E., 'Philosophy and Politics of Punishment and Sentencing,' in C. Clarkson and R. Morgan (eds), *The Politics of Sentencing Reform* (Oxford University Press, 1995), 17–49.

104 Criminal Justice Act 2003, s 103(1).

105 [2009] 2 Cr App R 16.

106 *R v McKenzie (Mark Anthony)* [2008] EWCA Crim 758, [2008] 172 JP 377.

properly the consequences of introducing three separate contested issues on the overall length of the trial and on the jury. He had also failed to consider directing the Crown to select the best of the three allegations, rather than risking confusing the jury with details of all three.

Finally, it should also be underlined that section 103(2) states that showing an offence falls within the same category or description is only one means of illustrating propensity; it may be proved in any other way. This could potentially include someone with a history of being subject to previous criminal investigations in similar offences where charges were never brought or were later dropped. This information may still be regarded by the court as carrying some form of probative value. Unfortunately, there is still relatively little guidance from the courts on how these various provisions will dovetail with each other in practice. The leading case to date is still *R v Hanson*,[107] in which the Court of Appeal stated that essentially there are three questions to be considered.

- Did the history of the defendant's convictions establish a propensity to commit offences of the kind charged?
- Did that propensity make it more likely that the defendant had committed the offence charged?
- Was it just to rely on the convictions of the same description or category, and, in any event, would the proceedings be unfair if they were admitted?

Therefore, such evidence might be relevant to a number of issues in the case. For example, it might assist the prosecution to prove the defendant's guilt by establishing his involvement or state of mind, or by rebutting a defence or explanation of his conduct. Previous convictions for offences that are of the same description or category as those charged are admissible to prove a propensity to commit that kind of offence, or to be untruthful when either of these matters are in issue. Notwithstanding this, the Court of Appeal did issue a warning that there should not be a presumption of admissibility merely because a particular offence falls within the same category or description. In highlighting the broad nature of the theft category of offences, noting that it encapsulated both handling stolen goods and aggravated vehicle-taking,[108] the court stated that these offences were significantly different from each other and, furthermore, that neither would show a propensity to burgle or steal on the part of the defendant.

In determining probative value, the judge should assess each case on its own facts, carefully examining the degree of similarity between the offences in question before arriving at a decision. Furthermore, as the Court of Appeal observed in *R v Edwards*,[109] the direction given to the jury on how to treat such evidence is of the utmost importance. The Court of Appeal underlined that judges should take care to direct the jury carefully about the degree of weight they should place on previous convictions. In particular, judges should issue a clear warning to the jury against placing undue emphasis on previous convictions and should remind them that, by themselves, they cannot prove guilt. In addition, the judge should explain precisely the purpose of the evidence and the ways in which it is relevant to their decision. In *R v Gourde*,[110] it was decided that there was not an error of law when the judge directed the jury that they would be allowed to consider the defendant's previous convictions in deciding whether or not he had committed the offence charged. The defendant's appeal was dismissed on the basis that the judge had given a careful and balanced direction throughout.

---

107 [2005] 1 WLR 3169. See also *R v Campbell* [2007] 1 WLR 2798; *R v O'Dowd (Kevin)* [2009] 2 Cr App 16. See further Redmayne, M., 'Recognising Propensity' [2011] Crim LR 117.

108 *Hanson*, ibid., at 3176.

109 [2006] 1 WLR 1524.

110 [2009] EWCA Crim 1803.

11.4.4.1 Propensity to be untruthful

Propensity to commit the offence in question is only one ground on which evidence may be admitted under section 101(1)(d). Section 103(1)(b) provides that evidence relating to whether the defendant has a propensity to be untruthful can also be admitted. However, such evidence will not be relevant to the question of guilt, and can only be used by the jury in determining whether or not the accused is to be regarded as a credible witness.[111] According to the Explanatory Notes under the Act, this provision 'is intended to enable the admission of a limited range of evidence such as convictions for perjury or other offences involving deception (e.g. Obtaining property by deception).'[112]

It is not, however, intended that a conviction for any criminal offence should be admissible by virtue of this provision, only those that show a propensity to be untruthful where it is suggested that the defendant's case is untruthful in one particular respect. As the Court of Appeal noted in *Hanson*, a propensity to untruthfulness is not the same as a propensity to dishonesty.[113] In practice, this provision is likely to be relied on most frequently where the defendant and the prosecution are agreed on the facts of the alleged offence and the question is whether all of the elements of the offence have been made out.[114]

Example 11.2

Joe is charged with burglary and theft of a CD player from his neighbour's house. Joe admits that he entered the property and took the CD player, but claims that it belongs to him. The only issue in the case is whether the property alleged to have been stolen 'belonged to another' as required by the definition of 'theft' in the Theft Act 1968. Here, evidence that Joe has been untruthful in his claims could well be supported were the prosecution to adduce evidence of a previous conviction for perjury.[115]

11.4.4.2 Other matters in issue between the prosecution and defence

It should be underlined that propensity to commit the kind of offence charged and propensity to be untruthful are only two examples of common issues that may be contested between the parties. The application of gateway (d) is not, however, limited to questions of propensity. Evidence that does not establish propensity under section 103(1)(a) or (b) may still be admissible to prove any

---

111 *R v Highton* [2006] 1 Cr App R 7.

112 Explanatory Notes to the CJA 2003, at [374].

113 Ibid., at 3173.

114 Precisely what is meant by 'agree' is discussed in *Williams v VOSA* (2008) 172 JP 328 and *R v Marsh* [2009] EWCA Crim 2696, [46].

115 See also *S (Andrew)* [2006] EWCA Crim 1303 and *R v Brewster (Neil)* [2011] 1 WLR 601. Both are cases about the relevance of the credibility of non-defendants under s 100 of the 2003 Act rather than defendants under s 101. There is an important difference. *Hanson* has more or less ruled out inclusion of a defendant on previous offences unless the offences were ones such as perjury or obtaining by deception in which the conduct behind the offence itself was intrinsically untruthful. The same principle does not apply to non-defendants. The issue in the case of non-defendants is whether the proposed evidence is relevant to their creditworthiness. *Brewster* is an interesting case because it seems to have widened the legitimate area of inquiry beyond offences such as perjury and obtaining by deception. The same applies to offences in which there has been a guilty plea. The point made in *R v S (Andrew)* was that if a non-defendant had pleaded guilty to the offence, he was thereby demonstrating his honesty and therefore the fact of the previous conviction did not reflect on his truthfulness. That always seemed a rather questionable assumption and *Brewster* has now laid that notion to rest. *Brewster* was applied in *R v Harvey (Shelton)* [2014] EWCA Crim 54.

other fact in issue.[116] For example, in *R v Tirnaveanu*,[117] the defendant was charged with a number of offences in relation to people trafficking. It was alleged by the Crown that he had posed as a solicitor in order to obtain money from illegal immigrants from Romania by offering them dishonestly forged entry documents. At trial, he denied the offences, contending that another person had stolen his identity and had framed him for the alleged acts. The prosecution was then granted leave to introduce evidence to show that the defendant had, in the past, entered into a number of dealings with other illegal entrants. This evidence was accepted by the Court of Appeal as being relevant to an important matter in issue between the defendant and the prosecution: namely, whether it was the defendant who committed the offences and not some other person.[118]

11.4.4.3 Section 101(1)(d) in operation: some practical scenarios

Although there has been no shortage of reported case law relating to gateway (d) since the CJA 2003 took effect, it may still be useful to pause to consider how section 101(1)(d) might be applied in practice through contemplating a number of fictional scenarios. Consider the following situations.

Example 11.3

Michael is charged with obtaining property by deception, having sold a necklace which he said he had inherited from his grandmother. He falsely represented to the buyer that it was a diamond necklace when in fact it was glass. His defence is that he honestly believed it was a diamond necklace, and the issue before the court is whether he genuinely held that belief.

Six months previously, Michael had been arrested and charged with a similar offence in which he sold a glass necklace inherited from a relative, which he had also represented as a diamond necklace. He was acquitted, with the jury having accepted his defence that he honestly believed that it was made from diamonds. The similarity of the offences and the fact that Michael had made the same false representation previously suggest that he now knows the difference between diamonds and glass, and this would be admissible to prove that, contrary to his defence, he knew the necklace was glass. The previous acquittal is thus relevant to an important matter in issue between the defendant and the prosecution, and is admissible under section 101(1)(d), subject to the exercise of the discretion in section 101(3).

Example 11.4

Olivia has two previous convictions, one for obtaining property by deception and one for obtaining a pecuniary advantage by deception. In the first instance, she had used a cheque drawn on a closed account to obtain goods, and later claimed she did not know the account had been closed. In the second case, she used a credit card to purchase goods after being told by the credit card company that she had exceeded her limit and was not to use the

116 See *R v Hesse and Anor* [2015] EWCA 884, where the Court of Appeal explained that gateway (d) covered circumstances 'beyond a mere propensity' and also includes an 'enhanced capability of proving a matter in issue between the two appellants.'

117 [2007] 1 WLR 3049.

118 See also *R v Isichei* (2006) 170 JP 753; *R v Saleem* [2007] EWCA Crim 1923; *R v PB* [2016] EWCA Crim 1462.

card. Here, the convictions are relevant to the issue of whether the defendant was dishonest, and whether she has a propensity to commit the kind of offence charged.[119] The convictions are for offences of the same description (the offence of dishonestly obtaining property by deception) and thus would be admissible under section 101(1)(d) to establish the propensity to commit an offence of the kind charged.

Example 11.5

Norman is charged with rape, during which the victim was threatened with a knife. The victim's description of her assailant fitted that of the accused. Norman denied being in the area, and claimed to be away on holiday at the time. However, Norman was arrested the day after the rape while trying to sell stolen goods at a car boot sale. It transpired that some of these items had been stolen from a car parked near the scene of the rape, which had been broken into shortly before the incident took place.

Norman was convicted of the offence of theft from the vehicle, and has previous convictions for violence involving the use of a knife and a number of convictions for theft from cars. Unusually for a rape case, the issue here is whether the defendant was the rapist, or whether, as he states, he was elsewhere at the time. Norman's previous convictions would be admissible under section 101(1)(d), the issue being not whether he has a propensity to commit an offence of rape, but whether he has a propensity to be untruthful. The possession of the stolen items and his convictions for theft from the car put him at the scene of the rape and rebut his story that he was elsewhere at the time, and his propensity to violence using a knife assists in identifying him as the rapist.

Example 11.6

An example of bad character that fell short of criminal conduct is to be found in the case of *R v Barrington*.[120] Barrington was convicted of indecently assaulting three young girls. They gave evidence to the effect that they had been invited into his house on separate occasions to babysit, and were shown pornographic pictures and persuaded to pose nude. At that point, it was alleged that the accused touched the girls inappropriately. Barrington's defence was that the girls were lying and had got together to concoct the charges. Three other young girls were permitted to give evidence of being induced to enter Barrington's house to babysit, and being subsequently shown pornographic pictures and invited to pose nude. All three had refused and no offence was committed against them. The Court of Appeal noted that the fact that they did not include evidence of the commission of offences similar to those with which the appellant was charged does not mean that they are not logically probative in determining the guilt of the appellant. Indeed, the Court was of the

119 Criminal Justice Act 2003, s 103(1)(a).
120 (1981) 72 Cr App R 280.

opinion that, taken as a whole, they are inexplicable on the basis of coincidence and are of positive probative value in assisting to determine the truth of the charges against the appellant, in that they tended to show that he was guilty of the offences with which he was charged.[121] How, then, would the provisions of the 2003 Act apply to Barrington's scenario if it were to come before the courts today? The issue between the defendant and the prosecution would be whether the defendant had indecently assaulted the young girls, or whether they had concocted a false story. Here, although the conduct is not criminal, it may well be viewed as some form of misconduct or reprehensible behaviour under section 112 given that it seems relatively close to an attempt at indecent assault. If the defendant had previous convictions for indecent assault, those convictions would also be admissible under section 101(1)(d), since the issue between the defendant and the prosecution would include the question of whether he has a propensity to commit the kind of offence charged.

11.4.4.4 The distinction between section 101(1)(c) and section 101(1)(d)

There is often a fine line between important explanatory evidence, admitted under gateway (c), and evidence of a propensity, admitted under gateway (d). Explanatory evidence is intended to enable the court and jury better to understand the evidence and the case as a whole. Unlike evidence admitted under section 101(1)(d), it is not intended to demonstrate a propensity to commit the kind of offence charged, although it is questionable whether juries are capable of using such evidence only for the intended purpose.

The difficulty is illustrated by the decision in *R v Dolan*,[122] in which the defendant was charged with the murder of his 3½-month-old son by shaking him to death. Evidence of the defendant's tendency to lose his temper with inanimate objects and react violently towards them was wrongly admitted as what we now call 'important explanatory evidence' because it did not show a tendency to lose his temper with human beings. As such, it served no useful function, and diverted the jury from the real and important issue before them. It would seem to follow that had there been evidence of the defendant's tendency to lose his temper with human beings, and of his violent reaction towards them, that would have been admissible as important explanatory evidence.

However, had the defendant's loss of temper resulted in violence towards persons, it might well be admissible under gateway (d) in terms of the current law. Suppose the facts of *Dolan* were slightly different. The defendant has been charged with the murder of his young child by shaking him to death. There is evidence that he is quick to lose his temper when criticised or on the losing side of an argument. In addition, he has a number of convictions for assault occasioning actual bodily harm, and there is a history of violence towards his wife, which has resulted in the police and paramedics being called to the property on various occasions.

If the defendant pleads not guilty to the murder charge and claims that the death was accidental, such evidence of bad character would appear to be admissible under section 101(1)(d) as relevant to an important matter in issue between the defendant and the prosecution, the issue being accident or deliberate assault. That issue would include, as section 103(1)(a) makes clear, the question of whether the defendant has a propensity to commit an offence of the kind charged. His tendency to lose his temper without provocation, his convictions for assault and his violence towards his wife combine to suggest that the accused has a propensity to commit the kind of

121 Ibid., at 290.
122 [2003] 1 Cr App R 18.

offence charged (murder is basically a serious assault resulting in death). As such, the evidence of bad character is likely to be admitted under section 101(1)(d) and is unlikely to be excluded under section 101(3). If the evidence were to be admitted as important explanatory evidence under gateway (c), the emphasis would have to be on the explanatory nature of the evidence (i.e. the circumstances of the accused's home life), rather than its tendency to suggest a propensity to commit the kind of crime charged.

This issue was addressed in *R v D, P and U*,[123] where Hughes LJ made a number of important statements regarding gateways (c) and (d). His Lordship emphasised that gateway (c) is not a substitute for gateway (d): 'It is not possible to dress up a failed case of gateway (d) as gateway (c).' The Crown sought to adduce evidence of child pornography as important explanatory evidence, as it showed the defendant had an interest in sexual activity with underage girls. The Court of Appeal held that this evidence was relevant to gateway (d) but not (c). The Court of Appeal stated that gateway (c) is concerned with 'the situation in which a jury cannot properly understand the case without hearing evidence ... of bad character,' but in this case, there would 'not be the slightest difficulty' in understanding the case without the bad character evidence.[124]

11.4.4.5 Co-accused taking advantage of bad character evidence

Section 103(6) makes it clear that only prosecution evidence is admissible under section 101(1)(d). Therefore, D1 cannot rely on this section to adduce evidence of the bad character of D2. Instead, D1 must rely on section 101(1)(e), discussed below. However, once the evidence has been admitted, there is no reason why D1 cannot take advantage of the prosecution's use of such evidence and cross-examine D2 on the issues that it raises. At common law, where evidence of the propensity of a co-accused to commit the kind of offence was relevant to a fact in issue between the prosecution and a co-accused, the trial judge was required to direct the jury that they were to ignore that evidence in considering the case against another co-accused. However, in *R v Randall*,[125] Lord Steyn stated:

> For the avoidance of doubt I would further add that in my view where evidence of the propensity of a co-accused is relevant to a fact in issue between the Crown and the other accused it is not necessary for the trial judge to direct the jury to ignore that evidence in considering the case against the co-accused. Justice does not require such a direction to be given. Moreover, such a direction would needlessly perplex a jury.[126]

Example 11.7

Suppose Jackie and Ted are charged with robbery at a local off-licence. Ted denies that he was involved in the robbery, and claims that Jackie was acting on her own. The prosecution applies successfully for leave to introduce Jackie's previous convictions for robbery, in order to prove a propensity to commit offences of this type. The jury, when considering Ted's liability, can take account of the fact that Jackie has previous convictions for robbery, which might be instrumental in persuading them that Ted was not involved.

123 [2013] 1 WLR 676.
124 Ibid., at 686.
125 [2003] 2 Cr App R 442.
126 Ibid., at 451. See also *R v Javis* [2008] EWCA Crim 488.

11.4.5 Gateway (e): substantial probative value in relation to an important matter in issue between defendant and co-defendant

According to section 104(2), this gateway may only be used by a co-accused. The question as to what constitutes an 'important matter in issue' between co-defendants will differ according to the circumstances of the case. As in the scenario described above in Example 11.7, often it will simply boil down to which one of the accused committed the offence charged. This scenario arose in the important House of Lords case of *Randall*, in which Randall and Glean were jointly charged with murder. Each raised a cut-throat defence, claiming that the other had killed the deceased. Each had given evidence of his own bad character during his evidence-in-chief. While Randall had minor convictions for driving offences and disorderly behaviour, Glean had convictions for theft and nine separate convictions for burglary, the most recent of which involved burglary of a dwelling house by an armed gang who threatened the owner with hammers and screwdrivers.

At the time of the murder, Glean was on the run from the police following another robbery, committed by a gang armed with knives. One of the robbers held a knife to the victim's throat and Glean admitted threatening a witness, saying: 'If they get me for this, I will get you.' Counsel for each defendant told the jury that the propensity of the other accused to use violence was relevant to the likelihood of that accused having attacked the deceased. However, the trial judge directed the jury that the previous convictions were relevant only to the credibility of each defendant and were irrelevant to the likelihood of his having attacked the deceased. Randall was convicted of manslaughter and Glean was acquitted. Randall appealed, arguing that evidence of Glean's bad character was relevant to the issue of who, as between Randall and Glean, was more likely to have inflicted serious violence on the deceased.

The Court of Appeal agreed that evidence of propensity was relevant to guilt, not just credibility, and ordered that Randall be retried. However, the court certified a question of law for the House of Lords as follows: 'Where two accused are jointly charged with a crime, and each blames the other for its commission, may one accused rely on the criminal propensity of the other?' Their Lordships unanimously answered the question in the affirmative, and cited with approval the dictum of Kennedy LJ in the Court of Appeal:

> [I]n the particular circumstances of the present case, where there was a cut throat defence, the antecedent history of Glean was relevant not only in relation to the truthfulness of Glean's evidence but also because of the imbalance between that history and the antecedents of Randall ... the evidence tended to show that the version put forward by one co-accused was more probable than that put forward by the other.[127]

Although this case was heard before the 2003 Act came into force, there is little doubt that the previous convictions of Glean and Randall could be admitted under section 101(1)(e), the important matter in issue between them being which of them was more likely to have been responsible for the death of the deceased. Glean's propensity to commit crimes that involved violence would make it more likely that he killed the deceased.[128] Randall could, as he did in the above case, adduce his own bad character under section 101(1)(b) with a view to demonstrating the lack of a propensity to violence. If Glean had convictions for offences of the same description or of the same category, the prosecution could adduce them under section 101(1)(d), but offences of burglary, or aggravated burglary and robbery, are not of the same description or category as murder, which was not committed in the course of either of those offences. *Randall* has, however, been doubted

127 [2003] 2 Cr App R 442, at 451.
128 See also *Price* [2005] Crim LR 304.

by the Court of Appeal in *R v Platt*.[129] The Court of Appeal held that the test of admissibility under gateway (e) was a strict one, and different from that which was applicable under the old test of relevance considered in *Randall*. Lord Thomas CJ emphasised that the test under section 101(1)(e) was a 'strict one' and was different to the test applied by the pre-2003 authorities (i.e. *Randall*). Lord Thomas CJ stated:

> Although the decision in *Randall* and other common law cases are referred to ... they are not relevant to the determination of the admissibility, which is governed by the statutory provisions. It is particularly important that the test set out in the CJA 2003 is the test solely applied for admissibility as, unlike the position between the prosecution and the defendant, the court has no discretion to refuse the admission of the evidence where the statutory conditions for admissibility are met. ...
>
> It seems to us that ten years after the coming into force of the CJA 2003 and with all the new authority on the new statutory code provided for in the bad character provisions of that Act as to the admissibility of the bad character evidence, there should be no need to refer to the old law on admissibility of such evidence.

Section 104 also limits the admissibility of evidence of the defendant's propensity to be untruthful to circumstances in which the defendant has undermined his co-defendant's evidence. Under section 1(3)(c) of the Criminal Evidence Act 1898, a co-defendant was permitted to cross-examine another defendant on their previous convictions or bad character when that defendant gave evidence against the co-defendant. This was interpreted as evidence that directly supported the prosecution case against the co-defendant, or indirectly undermined the co-defendant's defence. Section 101(1)(e) and section 104 replace that provision. These sections relate to evidence that is relevant to an issue between the defendant and a co-defendant. Section 104(1), while covering evidence that is relevant to the question of whether the defendant has a propensity to be untruthful, states that such evidence is only admissible if 'the nature and conduct of his defence is such as to undermine the co-defendant's defence.'

In *R v Varley*,[130] the Court of Appeal gave the following guidance as to the meaning of 'evidence against a co-defendant' under the 1898 Act:

> 1 If it is established that a person jointly charged has given evidence against a co-defendant, that defendant has a right to cross-examine the other as to previous convictions and the trial judge has no discretion to refuse an application.
> 2 Such evidence may be given either in-chief or during cross-examination.
> 3 It has to be objectively decided whether the evidence either supports the prosecution case in a material respect or undermines the defence of the co-accused. A hostile intent is irrelevant.
> 4 If consideration has to be given to the undermining of the other's defence, care must be taken to see that the evidence clearly undermines the defence. Inconvenience to or inconsistency with the other's defence is not of itself sufficient.
> 5 Mere denial of participation in a joint venture is not of itself sufficient to rank as evidence against a co-defendant. For the [provision] to apply, such denial must lead to the conclusion that if the witness did not participate, then it must have been the other who did.
> 6 Where the one defendant asserts or in due course would assert one view of the joint venture that is directly contradicted by the other, such contradiction may be evidence against the co-defendant.[131]

129 [2016] EWCA Crim 4.
130 [1982] 2 All ER 519, at 519.
131 See also *R v Davis* [1975] 1 All ER 233; *R v Crawford* [1998] 1 Cr App R 338.

Under section 101(1)(e), the courts are likely to take a similar view of the meaning of the words 'the nature and conduct of his defence is such as to undermine the co-defendant's defence.' However, the 1898 Act allowed cross-examination on any aspect of the co-defendant's bad character only if the co-defendant had given evidence against the other co-defendant. Under the 2003 Act, the requirement that the co-defendant undermines the defence of the other co-defendant is confined to the situation in which a co-defendant seeks to adduce evidence of the other defendant's propensity to be untruthful. Other evidence that is of substantial probative value in relation to an important matter in issue between the defendants is admissible whether or not the nature or conduct of the other's defence is such as to undermine the co-defendant's defence.

Evidence of a propensity to be untruthful may include offences of dishonesty and convictions for perjury that suggest that the defendant is not a credible witness. However, as the Law Commission envisaged, it is not confined to such convictions:

> D1 (who has previous convictions for robbery) and D2 are jointly charged with robbery. D1's defence is that D2 did it on her own. In order to get D1's criminal record admitted under the co-defendant exception on the basis that D1 has undermined D2's case, D2 must show that his convictions show that he is likely to lie on oath. What is in issue is D1's propensity to tell the truth not his propensity to rob.[132]

The Law Commission accepted that such evidence is less likely to be admitted as being relevant to credibility than under the then-existing law and recognised that previous convictions for robbery will be more directly relevant to the issue of who committed the robbery. In such circumstances, the prosecution will seek to adduce those convictions under section 101(1)(d). However, if the trial judge were to exclude those convictions under section 101(3), D2 in the above scenario could seek to adduce them under section 101(1)(e). The discretion to exclude does not apply to section 101(1)(e), but D2 must demonstrate that the convictions are of substantial probative value in relation to an important issue between her and D1.[133]

11.4.5.1 'Important issue' vs 'substantial probative value'

Under section 101(1)(e), evidence is admissible only if it has substantial probative value in relation to an important issue between a defendant and co-defendant. In *R v Lawson*,[134] it was held that while there is an element of overlap in the evaluation of whether evidence has substantial probative value and a consideration of the importance of the matter in issue, it is necessary that the questions 'be addressed seriatim' (i.e. separately). This was affirmed in *R v Phillips*,[135] where the Court of Appeal held that although the elements of s101(1)(e) may overlap, a separate assessment of each question is required, particularly 'where the bad character evidence relates not to the bare fact of a conviction but to detailed allegations of previous behaviour, and where there are multiple factual issues arising between the defendants.'[136] The test is as follows. First, did the evidence that the co-accused wished to adduce have substantial probative value? Second, was the matter in respect of which the evidence was substantially probative a matter of substantial importance in the context of the case as a whole?

---

132 Law Commission, op. cit., n. 36 [14.49].

133 See also *De Vos* [2006] EWCA Crim 1688; *R v Lawson* [2007] 1 Cr App R 11; and *R v Rosato* [2008] EWCA Crim 1243, in which the court made it clear that an appellate court is unlikely to interfere with a trial judge's decision unless it is plainly wrong or unreasonable.

134 [2007] 1 WLR 1191.

135 [2012] 1 Cr App R 25.

136 Ibid., at [39], citing *R v Apabhai* [2011] EWCA Crim 917.

The two conditions, 'substantial probative value' and 'an important issue,' make it clear that evidence that has marginal or trivial value will not be admissible; neither will it be admissible if the issue to which it relates is marginal or trivial in the case as a whole. The Explanatory Notes under the Act state exactly this,[137] and in *R v Scott*,[138] Aikens LJ expressed the view of the court that 'the word "substantial" must mean that the evidence concerned has something "more than trivial probative value but it is not necessarily of conclusive probative value."'[139]

Scott was doubted, however, by the Court of Appeal in *R v Phillips*,[140] where the Court of Appeal noted that any attempts to 'add the gloss of "more than merely trivial" are potentially misleading.' Lord Thomas CJ affirmed this view in the Court of Appeal where his Lordship explained that 'substantial' is an 'ordinary word and needs no gloss.'[141]

Under the 1898 Act, a denial of guilt by one defendant was not evidence against the other unless the circumstances were such that in denying guilt the defendant was inevitably accusing the other. For example, in *R v Davis*,[142] the circumstances were such that a stolen necklace could only have been taken by the defendant or his co-accused. The defendant's denial that he had taken the necklace was then inevitably evidence against the co-accused. Such circumstances are rare, and an ordinary denial of guilt was not evidence against the other defendant and would not raise an issue between the defendants under this head.

In *R v Bruce*,[143] Bruce, M, and another were charged with robbery. The prosecution case was that they had frightened a passenger on a train into giving them money. M gave evidence that there had been a prior agreement to commit a robbery, but claimed that he played no part in the offence. Bruce denied that there had been any such plan. The trial judge ruled that this claim constituted evidence against his co-defendants, who were then permitted to cross-examine Bruce on his past record. However, this decision was reversed by the Court of Appeal. Although Bruce had contradicted part of M's evidence, he had not specifically challenged M's statement that he took no part in the robbery. Indeed, Bruce's evidence did more to contradict the prosecution case, and gave M an additional line of defence. In the view of the court, if a defendant contradicts his co-defendants but in doing so gives the co-defendant a better defence, it ought not to be viewed as evidence against the co-defendant. This is also likely to be the position under the 2003 Act.

At common law, and under the 1898 Act, the courts had no discretion to exclude defence evidence. Their task was confined to ensuring the defence evidence was relevant and, in the context of the 1898 Act, that the defendant had 'given evidence against a co defendant.' Similarly, under the new scheme, the discretion under section 101(3) is confined to gateways (d) and (g). Therefore, under section 101(1)(e), the task of the trial judge is confined to determining whether the evidence has substantial probative value in relation to an important issue in the case.[144]

11.4.6 Gateway (f): evidence to correct a false impression

For section 101(1)(f) to apply, the defendant must have been responsible for an assertion that gives a false or misleading impression about their character. This might be done expressly, for example

137 Explanatory Notes to the Criminal Justice Act 2003, at [375].

138 [2009] EWCA Crim 2457.

139 Ibid., at [45].

140 [2012] 1 Cr App R 25.

141 *R v Platt* [2016] EWCA Crim 4.

142 (1974) 60 Cr App R 157.

143 [1975] 1 WLR 1252.

144 See further *R v Lawson* [2007] 1 WLR 1191. Each accused alleged that the other was lying, but counsel for D1 cross-examined D2 about a previous conviction for assault without giving notice to the court. The appeal on this ground has, however, been dismissed, since the judge had power to dispense with notice requirements Criminal Procedure Rules 2020, r 21.6(1)(c).

by claiming to be of good character when this is not the case, or impliedly, through conduct in court, or through appearance or dress.[145]

The provision largely reflects the old law contained in section 1(3) of the Criminal Evidence Act 1898, which permitted the prosecution to cross-examine a defendant about his previous convictions or bad character if 'he has personally or by his advocate asked questions of the witnesses for the prosecution with a view to establishing his own good character or has given evidence of his good character.' Although the courts never devised a definitive test, the cases under the 1898 Act suggest that an accused gives evidence of his good character if he: gives evidence that he has previously handed lost property back to its owner;[146] gives evidence that he is a religious man who has attended church services for years;[147] asserts that for the past four years he has been carrying on an honest living;[148] or asserts that he is a married man, with a family and in regular work.[149] Such cases are likely to continue to be seen as examples of a direct assertion of good character, which, if true, may be rebutted by evidence admissible under gateway (f) of the 2003 Act.[150]

By contrast, however, giving evidence of general relations with customers with a view to negating a charge of fraud was not found to be an attempt to assert good character,[151] and neither was the wearing of a regimental blazer in court.[152] Furthermore, it is perhaps obvious to state that a mere attempt to assert innocence or repudiate guilt could not constitute evidence of good character. Otherwise, it would be impossible for any defendant to mount a successful defence without risking losing their shield.[153]

It is likely to be those cases that involve an implied assertion of good character that will trouble the appellate courts most frequently in the years to come. Indeed, it was recognised by the Criminal Law Revision Committee back in 1971 that such implications are necessarily subjective, and are not always clear-cut.[154] One example cited by the Committee was drawn from a case tried at the Old Bailey in 1968. One of two men charged with conspiracy to rob (both of whom had long criminal records) went into the witness box wearing a dark suit and looking every inch the respectable businessman. When asked by his counsel when and where he met his co-defendant, he replied: 'About eighteen months ago at my golf club. I was looking for a game and the secretary introduced us.' The Committee had no doubt that this was an imputation of good character, as was the suggestion in another case that the defendant, who lived on crime, was negotiating the purchase of a substantial property. However, it is questionable whether the same conclusions would be drawn in the twenty-first century. The Committee appeared to assume that golf clubs admit only persons of good character as members. This might have been the case in the 1960s, but in the modern era membership of a golf club, or even the purchase of a substantial property, are unlikely per se to be indicative of good character in the minds of the general public.

The Explanatory Notes to the 2003 Act suggest an example of asserting good character by dress or conduct: a defendant who wears a clerical collar to which he is not entitled. Such extreme

---

145 Criminal Justice Act 2003, s 105(4)–(5).

146 *R v Samuel* (1956) 40 Cr App R 8. The charge here was theft.

147 *R v Ferguson* (1909) 2 Cr App R 250.

148 *R v Baker* (1912) 7 Cr App R 252.

149 *R v Coulman* (1927) 20 Cr App R 106. The charge here concerned indecency with young boys – the stable family relationship suggested he was unlikely to have committed such an offence.

150 In *Renda* (op. cit., n. 45), however, the court seemingly disapproved of citing pre-2003 Act cases, and stated that they are merely 'factual examples of occasions when it was decided that an individual defendant had put his character in issue' (at 2952).

151 *R v Ellis* [1910] 2 KB 746.

152 *R v Hamilton* [1969] Crim LR 486. This case might now be decided differently given that s 105(5) makes it clear that 'conduct' in s 105(4) includes appearance or dress. It would, of course, be only a *false* impression if the defendant is not *entitled* to wear that regimental blazer.

153 *R v Rouse* [1904] 1 KB 184.

154 Criminal Law Revision Committee, op. cit., n. 11, p. 135 ff.

scenarios are likely to be rare, but this comes fairly close to the manner in which the accused presented himself in Z.[155] In a television dramatisation of the trial,[156] the defendant stood in the dock dressed in a dark suit, white shirt, and tie, clutching a Bible with both hands as though in prayer. That might now be seen as asserting a false good character, given that he had a conviction for rape and had been acquitted of rape a number of times.

The circumstances were somewhat similar in *R v Robinson*.[157] The defendant, a rather difficult witness, gave evidence at his trial for theft while holding a small Bible in his hand and gesticulating, so that it could be clearly seen by the jury. The trial judge said that this was a cynical and manipulative action calculated to make the jury think that he was a religious person and likely to tell the truth, and accepted the prosecution's argument that he had put his character in issue. However, the Court of Appeal disagreed, and held that he did not put his character in issue by taking the oath, or by reminding the jury of the oath he had sworn on the Bible. Ultimately, there was no evidence that the impression he gave of himself was false, so the conviction was unsafe and a retrial was ordered. There is nothing within section 105(4) that would suggest that the court would arrive at a different conclusion under the new law.

Section 105(2) sets out the circumstances in which a defendant is to be treated as being responsible for an assertion. These will usually occur through the defendant making the assertion themselves while giving evidence. A relatively straightforward example can be found in *R v Renda*, which was decided under the 2003 Act. Here, the defendant claimed to have suffered a head injury while serving with the armed forces, and also stated that he was employed as a security guard at the time of the alleged offence. This information was false, and the prosecution were thus entitled to introduce evidence of his previous involvement in a serious assault. Similarly, in *R v Garrett*,[158] a claim by the defendant that he had been involved in cases 'where I've been a victim and [the police] have not helped me,' or where he had been 'stitched up' by the police was held to be a false impression. The Court of Appeal concluded that this impression 'did not sit at all well with the actuality of the totality of his antecedent history.'[159]

Alternatively, the defendant may now make such an assertion while being questioned under caution or being charged with the offence. This circumstance represents a change to the previous law, which took the view that any assertion had to be made by the defendant in evidence. Thus, in *R v Holman*,[160] the accused was charged with stealing two necklaces, which were found in his possession. He told the police he had found them in the garden of a house when he went to recover a car, and intended to telephone the police and tell them. It was held that he had given evidence of his good character and the prosecution was allowed to cross-examine him under section 1(3)(b) of the 1898 Act. The Court of Appeal held that the judge should not have allowed counsel to do so since the accused did not state this in direct testimony to the court.

That is no longer the position under the 2003 Act. If the defendant makes any assertion while being questioned under caution before charge, or on being charged with the offence, and that statement is then admitted in evidence, they will now be seen as being responsible for it.[161] Furthermore, the defendant is also seen as being responsible for assertions made by defence witnesses, those made by any other witness in response to questions by the defendant that were intended (or likely to) elicit them, and out-of-court assertions made by anybody if adduced in evidence by the defendant.

---

155 *R v Z*, op. cit. n. 42. See discussion above.
156 *Dispatches*, 'Still Getting Away with Rape,' Channel 4 (16 March 2000).
157 [2001] Crim LR 478.
158 [2015] EWCA Crim 757.
159 Ibid., at [21] (Davis LJ).
160 *The Times* (9 September 1992).
161 Criminal Justice Act 2003, s 105(2)(b)(i)–(ii).

11.4.6.1 Correcting the false impression

In correcting the impression, the prosecution may introduce evidence of the defendant's misconduct that has a probative value in correcting it.[162] Exactly what evidence is required in order to do this will turn on the facts of each specific case and, in particular, the nature of the misleading impression that has been given. Evidence is admissible under section 105(6) only if it goes no further than is necessary to correct the false impression. This reverses the common law rule that character was indivisible.[163] Thus, where a defendant is charged with theft, and asserts their reputation for honesty, convictions for offences of dishonesty will be admissible to correct that false impression, but a conviction for a sexual offence would be excluded. If, however, the defendant gives the impression, either verbally in evidence or by their conduct and dress, that they are an upstanding citizen, convictions for any and all offences would be admissible as necessary to correct that false impression. An interesting example of this came before the Court of Appeal in *R v Stokes*.[164] In *Stokes*, the trial judge admitted the defendant's previous convictions for possession of a Class A drug in order to correct what the prosecution alleged to be a 'misleading impression of naivety' put forward by the defendant. Although dismissing the defendant's appeal against conviction, the Court of Appeal did note that the defendant had not put forward any such misleading impression about himself and the adduced previous convictions would not have corrected such an impression in any respect. McCombe LJ was clear that the court must be sure that the defendant made a false impression before attempting to correct it. As a final point in relation to gateway (f), it is worth noting that defendants may withdraw or disassociate themselves from a false or misleading impression by correcting the impression through their own testimony or through cross-examination of witnesses.[165] Evidence to correct the false impression will not then be admissible. However, the Court of Appeal was keen to stress in *Renda* that, for the shield to be restored, the defendant's renunciation of their claims must be unequivocal:

> There is a significant difference between the defendant who makes a specific and positive decision to correct a false impression for which he is responsible, or to dissociate himself from false impressions conveyed by the assertions of others, and the defendant who in the process of cross-examination is obliged to concede that he has been misleading the jury. A concession extracted in cross-examination that the defendant was not telling the truth in part of his examination-in-chief will not normally amount to a withdrawal or dissociation from the original assertion for the purposes of section 105(3).[166]

Given that the defendant can prevent bad character evidence from being admitted by such withdrawal or disassociation, the opportunity to apply under section 101(3) to have such evidence excluded through judicial discretion does not apply to this subsection.[167] Any residual discretion can only be exercised under section 78 of the Police and Criminal Evidence Act 1984.

---

162 Note that only the prosecution may correct a false impression under s 105(7). A co-defendant is not able to do so.

163 This position has been confirmed by the Court of Appeal in *R v Somanathan* [2006] 1 WLR 1885. For an example of the operation of the former common law rule, see *R v Winfield* (1939) 27 Cr App R 139. See *RB* [2008] EWCA Crim 1850, which provides an example of why the prosecution must take care to avoid unfairly manipulating or trapping a defendant into triggering gateway (f).

164 [2015] EWCA Crim 1911.

165 Criminal Justice Act 2003, s 105(3).

166 *Renda*, op. cit., n. 45, 2952.

167 As made clear by McCombe LJ in *R v Stokes* [2015] EWCA Crim 1911.

11.4.7 Gateway (g): attacks on another person's character

Under the final gateway, a defendant's own bad character will become admissible when there has been an attack on another person's character. This is deemed to occur where the accused gives evidence that a particular individual committed an offence (either the one charged or a different one) or has behaved or is disposed to behave in a reprehensible way.[168] This is a continuation of the tit-for-tat principle that applied under section 1(3)(b) of the Criminal Evidence Act 1898. However, the nature of the provision in the 2003 legislation is significantly wider, since there is no longer any requirement that the rule will only be triggered where the character of a prosecution witness or the prosecutor is attacked; section 101(1)(g) simply refers to 'another person.' To some extent, it is understandable why an attack on the character of someone involved in the trial should result in the defendant's bad character being put before the court or jury: in determining whether a witness or the defendant is to be believed, it is only right that the character of the person who has attacked the credibility of the witness or deceased victim be known, so that their credibility can be properly judged. However, by the same token, casting the net so widely under the new law seems somewhat unnecessary.

Example 11.8

Gary is charged with assault occasioning actual bodily harm on Gerry. He alleges that he has been the victim of a mistaken identity and that his twin brother Steve (who is not a witness in the trial) was the real culprit. Gary has two previous convictions for burglary.

In these circumstances, it is not entirely clear why gateway (g) should apply. If the accused has a propensity to be untruthful, evidence to show such a characteristic is admissible under section 101(1)(d). Adducing his previous convictions for burglary on a tit-for-tat basis here would make little sense, and would arguably be grossly unfair to the accused.

The definition of 'attacking another person's character' for the purposes of gateway (g) is similar to the generic definition of bad character in section 98, but includes evidence relating to the facts of the offence charged and its investigation and prosecution. Thus, a defendant would be attacking a prosecution witness if they were to claim that the witness was lying while giving evidence or was in some way biased or motivated by animosity to give false evidence. Indeed, the provision will apply to any evidence whatsoever of previous misconduct that has been introduced to undermine the witness's credibility. The defence will also be regarded as having attacked another person's character where questions are put to opposing witnesses that are likely to elicit evidence of this sort or if the defendant makes an allegation of this nature when questioned under caution or on being charged with the offence.[169] Where an attack occurs, unlike section 101(1)(f), there is no provision to allow the defendant to withdraw or disassociate themselves from the attack.

---

168 CJA 2003, s 106(1)(a) and (2). See *Lamaletie and Royce* (2008) 172 JP 249 in which the Court of Appeal indicated how gateway (g) might function. Underhill J made it clear that where a defendant has impugned the character of a prosecution witness, the jury will be assisted in deciding who to believe by knowing of the defendant's character in a broad general sense beforehand. See also O (2009) 173 JP 616.

169 Criminal Justice Act 2003, s 106(1). Provided that the statement is then admitted in evidence – this may occur, for example, where a police officer gives evidence of an interview with the defendant or of the accused's response on being charged.

It might be asked whether it matters if such an attack or imputation is true or false. Under the 1898 Act, the veracity of such an attack did not affect the loss of the shield. In *R v Bishop*,[170] it was said that 'an imputation on character covers charges of faults or vices whether reputed or real.'[171]

Similarly, in *R v Wainwright*,[172] the court rejected the submission that there can only be an imputation if the facts are disputed. It would seem to follow that the attack on another person's character, or an imputation about the other person, need not be untrue for the purposes of gateway (g).

Many cases under the 1898 Act arose from claims by the defence that a prosecution witness had fabricated a confession or obtained it through duress. In practice, however, corrupt police officers were essentially able to use the 1898 Act as a shield for their misconduct. The introduction of tape-recording of interviews, and now video-recording, has largely brought an end to such allegations. However, it is still not unusual for police officers and other law enforcement officials to have their characters attacked. It could be alleged, for example, that evidence was obtained through an illegal search, or that real evidence had been tampered with. All such attacks will fall within the ambit of section 101(1)(g). However, an assertion of innocence or emphatic denial of guilt will not trigger the provision, provided that it does not constitute a direct attack on a prosecution witness. As the facts of *Bishop* demonstrate, there is a thin line between an emphatic denial of guilt and attacks on the veracity of the prosecutor or their witnesses. The outright denial of having given a confession, or disclaiming knowledge of an article found during a search by police, is one thing; to claim that the police concocted the confession or planted the evidence is another. Whether such evidence constitutes a mere denial of guilt or an attack on the character of an opposing witness will turn on the facts of each case.

The discretion to exclude evidence of bad character under section 101(3) applies to section 101(1)(g). At common law, the purpose of the discretion was to prevent an overly harsh application of section 1(3)(b) of the 1898 Act. In *R v Burke*,[173] the Court of Appeal accepted that 'cases must occur in which it would be unjust to admit evidence of a character gravely prejudicial to the accused, even though there may be some tenuous grounds for holding it technically admissible.'[174] Nonetheless, it concluded that:

> In the ordinary and normal case the trial judge may feel that if the credit of the prosecutor or his witnesses has been attacked, it is only fair that the jury should have before them the material on which they can form their judgement whether the accused person is any more worthy to be believed than those he has attacked. It is obviously unfair that the jury should be left in the dark about an accused person's character if the conduct of his defence has attacked the character of the prosecutor or the witnesses for the prosecution within the meaning of section 1(3)(b) of the Act of 1898.[175]

The same approach is likely to be taken under the 2003 Act, as the Court of Appeal has already declared that the old case law relating to the 1898 Act should still apply.[176] The discretion could be used to limit the application of the subsection in cases in which the accused had attacked the character of a person not involved in the trial. Although technically admissible, such evidence

---

170 [1975] QB 274. See also *R v Rouse* [1904] 1 KB 184; *R v Williams* [2007] EWCA Crim 1951.
171 Ibid., at 282.
172 [1998] Crim LR 665.
173 (1986) 82 Cr App R 156.
174 Ibid., at 161.
175 Ibid.
176 *Hanson*, op. cit., n. 107, at 3173. This is not, however, the case with gateway (f). See further *Renda* (op. cit., n. 45). See also *R v Nelson* [2006] EWCA Crim 3412; *RB* [2008] EWCA Crim 1850.

might be seen as having such an adverse effect on the fairness of the trial that it ought not to be admitted. However, if the defendant makes a deliberate attack on a prosecution witness, the judge is likely to share the opinion of the Court of Appeal in *Burke* that it is 'obviously unfair that the jury should be left in the dark about [the] accused person's character.'[177]

11.4.8 Procedural matters

11.4.8.1 Offences committed by the defendant when a child

Section 108(2) of the 2003 Act provides that in proceedings for an offence committed or alleged to have been committed by the defendant when aged 21 or over, evidence of his conviction for an offence when under the age of 14 is not admissible unless (a) both of the offences are triable only on indictment, and (b) the court is satisfied that the interests of justice require the evidence to be admissible. These conditions were not satisfied in *R v Valencia*[178] in which the defendant, charged with affray and unlawful wounding, had committed offences of robbery and wounding when he was 14 and 15, respectively. These former convictions were adduced at trial and the defendant was convicted. On appeal against the conviction, the Court of Appeal noted that the defendant's bad character ought not to have been admitted as the conditions under section 108(2) had clearly not been satisfied. Despite this, however, the Court of Appeal noted that the introduction of the evidence was not automatically unfair.[179]

Section 109 provides that

> (1) Subject to subsection (2), a reference in this Chapter to the relevance or probative value of evidence is a reference to its relevance or probative value on the assumption that it is true.
> (2) In assessing the relevance or probative value of an item of evidence for any purpose of this Chapter, a court need not assume that the evidence is true if it appears, on the basis of any material before the court (including any evidence it decides to hear on the matter), that no court or jury could reasonably find it to be true.

Subsection (2) was reaffirmed in *R v Dizaei*,[180] where it was held that a court and a jury are not bound to assume that the evidence is true.

11.4.8.2 Court's duty to give reasons for rulings

Section 110 provides that:

> (1) Where the court makes a relevant ruling –
> (a) it must state in open court (but in the absence of the jury, if there is one) its reasons for the ruling;
> (b) if it is a magistrates' court, it must cause the ruling and the reasons for it to be entered in the register of the court's proceedings.
> (2) In this section 'relevant ruling' means –
> (a) a ruling on whether an item of evidence is evidence of a person's bad character;
> (b) a ruling on whether an item of such evidence is admissible under section 100 or 101 (including a ruling on an application under section 101(3));
> (c) a ruling under section 107.

177 *Burke*, op. cit., n. 173, at 157.
178 [2015] All ER (D) 146.
179 See *R v DM* [2016] EWCA Crim 674.
180 [2013] EWCA Crim 88.

Rule 21.5 of the Criminal Procedure Rules 2020 also sets a requirement on the trial judge to give reasons, in absence of the jury, for a decision to admit or refuse to admit character evidence.

11.4.8.3 Rules of court

In this section, we shall deal with the procedure for adducing a defendant's character and with the procedure for non-defendants below. Part 21 of the Criminal Procedure Rules 2020 deals with the procedure for applying for a person's bad character to be admitted. Rule 21.2 (Content of application or notice) provides that:

(1) A party who wants to introduce evidence of bad character must –
  (a) make an application under rule 21.3, where it is evidence of a non-defendant's bad character;
  (b) give notice under rule 21.4, where it is evidence of a defendant's bad character.
(2) An application or notice must –
  (a) set out the facts of the misconduct on which that party relies,
  (b) explain how that party will prove those facts (whether by certificate of conviction, other official record, or other evidence), if another party disputes them, and
  (c) explain why the evidence is admissible.

The importance of making an application to adduce a defendant's bad character was demonstrated in *Barnard v DPP*,[181] where the High Court held that a judge should not question a witness as to the potential bad character of the defendant where there has been no application by the parties. Further to this, section 111(4) CJA 2003 provides that in considering the exercise of its powers with respect to costs, the court may take into account any failure by a party to comply with a requirement of Part 21.

Rule 21.4 (Notice to introduce evidence of a defendant's bad character) provides that:

(1) This rule applies where a party wants to introduce evidence of a defendant's bad character.
(2) A prosecutor must serve any such notice not more than –
  (a) 28 days after the defendant pleads not guilty, in a magistrates' court; or
  (b) 14 days after the defendant pleads not guilty, in the Crown Court.
(3) A co-defendant who wants to introduce such evidence must serve the notice –
  (a) as soon as reasonably practicable; and in any event
  (b) not more than 14 days after the prosecutor discloses material on which the notice is based.
(4) A party who objects to the introduction of the evidence identified by such a notice must –
  (a) apply to the court to determine the objection;
  (b) serve the application on –
    (i) the court officer, and
    (ii) each other party not more than 14 days after service of the notice; and
  (c) in the application explain, as applicable –
    (i) which, if any, facts of the misconduct set out in the notice that party disputes,
    (ii) what, if any, facts of the misconduct that party admits instead,
    (iii) why the evidence is not admissible,
    (iv) why it would be unfair to admit the evidence, and
    (v) any other objection to the notice.
(5) The court –
  (a) may determine such an application –
    (i) at a hearing, in public or in private, or
    (ii) without a hearing;

181 [2011] ACD 108.

(b) must not determine the application unless the party who served the notice –
 (i) is present, or
 (ii) has had a reasonable opportunity to respond;
(c) may adjourn the application; and
(d) may discharge or vary a determination ...

(6) A party entitled to receive a notice may waive that entitlement by so informing –
(a) the party who would have served it; and
(b) the court.

(7) A defendant who wants to introduce evidence of his or her own bad character must –
(a) give notice, in writing or orally –
 (i) as soon as reasonably practicable, and in any event
 (ii) before the evidence is introduced, either by the defendant or in reply to a question asked by the defendant of another party's witness in order to obtain that evidence; and
(b) in the Crown Court, at the same time give notice (in writing, or orally) of any direction about the defendant's character that the defendant wants the court to give the jury under rule 25.14 (Directions to the jury and taking the verdict).[182]

11.5 Collusion and contamination

11.5.1 Trials involving multiple victims

As indicated above, many cases involving similar fact evidence at common law were cases in which the defendant was charged with the commission of the same type of crime against several victims. In such cases, several counts (charges) were joined in the same indictment and all were tried together rather than in several separate trials. The normal rule applying to such trials was that the jury must consider the evidence on each count separately, and in determining the defendant's guilt on one count, they were not permitted to take into account the evidence on the other counts. The similar fact principle operated to override this rule and permit the evidence of each of the other victims to be cross-admissible, and possibly to be taken into account by the jury when considering the evidence on a charge against another victim. The practical effect was that each victim became a witness for the other victims, greatly increasing the likelihood of conviction on all charges.

The exclusion from the definition of 'bad character' of 'evidence of the facts of the offence charged' would seem at first sight to put trials involving multiple victims outside the framework of the new law. However, section 112(2) of the 2003 Act provides that

> where a defendant is charged with two or more offences in the same criminal proceedings, this Chapter ... has effect as if each offence were charged in separate proceedings; and references to the offence with which the defendant is charged are to be read accordingly.

The effect of this subsection is that, in trials in which the defendant is charged with a number of offences in the same indictment, the evidence of the alleged facts of each individual offence, together with evidence of misconduct in connection with the investigation or prosecution of that offence, is admissible without seeking leave under section 101. However, if the prosecution wants the jury, when considering the guilt of the defendant on one count, to take into consideration the evidence of the witnesses and victims of other counts, leave must first be sought.

The intention is that this part of the Act will provide a new basis for the admissibility of previous convictions and other misconduct. Accordingly, section 99 abolishes the common law

182 Inserted by the Criminal Procedure (Amendment) Rules 2016 (SI 2016 No. 120).

rules governing the admissibility of such evidence. Statutes dealing with admissibility are also repealed,[183] although this abolition does not extend to the rule that allows a person's bad character to be proved by his reputation. At common law, it was held in *R v Rowton*[184] that character evidence should be confined to reputation in the community. Reputation referred to the accused's reputed disposition or propensity to act, think, or feel in a given way, as opposed to their actual disposition or propensity to act, think, or feel in a given way. Evidence of opinion, or of particular acts or other examples of conduct, should not be given, but the decision in *Rowton* (although never overruled) was often ignored in practice and, as an indulgence to the accused, such evidence was frequently admitted. This common law rule is preserved as a category of admissible hearsay in section 118(2).[185]

11.5.2 The risk of collusion or contamination

Where the accused faces a trial involving more than one victim, it is not uncommon for the defence to allege that the victims have collaborated in concocting a joint story, thereby destroying its corroborative value. Such allegations were commonplace in cases involving multiple victims of sexual abuse, particularly when the victims were known to each other. Police and prosecutors are well aware of the possibility of collusion in such cases and would rarely prosecute if there were a likelihood of contamination. Witnesses who have yet to give evidence are not allowed in the court while others give evidence, but they often sit together outside the courtroom, and there have been cases in which a witness who has given evidence has been seen talking to a witness who has yet to do so. It follows that while such collusion or contamination is rare, it is not entirely unknown.

The leading case prior to the 2003 Act was that of *R v H*,[186] in which the House of Lords held that the admissibility of similar fact evidence should be approached on the basis that the evidence is true. Here, the defendant was charged with a number of sexual offences against his adopted daughter and stepdaughter between 1987 and 1989. At the defendant's trial, the judge directed the jury that they had to consider whether the girls had colluded and invented a false story against their father, and whether they, as the defence claimed, might have fantasised about the assaults. He further directed that it was for the prosecution to satisfy the jury that the girls were in fact telling the truth, and that the evidence of one girl could support the evidence of the other only if the jury were sure that the girls had not collaborated to concoct a false story.

The defendant was convicted and appealed, contending that the judge had misdirected the jury on the risk of collusion. The House of Lords dismissed the appeal and advocated a two-stage approach where the question of witness collusion arose. First, the judge should consider whether the similar fact evidence, if true, was so probative of the crime of which the defendant was accused that it ought to be admitted notwithstanding the prejudicial effect of disclosing that the defendant had committed other crimes. If the evidence was admitted, it was then for the jury to determine its credibility as a question of fact. The judge should direct them that they could not properly rely on the evidence as corroboration unless they were satisfied that it was reliable and true and not tainted by collusion or other defects. Only when it was obvious that no reasonable jury could accept the evidence as free from collusion or contamination should the judge direct the jury that they should not rely on the evidence at all.

Section 107 of the CJA 2003 now deals with the circumstances in which bad character evidence has been admitted, but it later emerges that the evidence is contaminated through collusion of prosecution witnesses. It is still for the jury to decide whether or not to believe the evidence

---

183 Criminal Justice Act 2003, Sch 37.

184 (1865) Le & Ca 520 CCR.

185 See Ch 12.

186 [1995] 2 AC 596.

and decide on the weight to be placed on it, but an additional duty is conferred on the judge to stop the case if the contamination is such that, considering the importance of the evidence to the case, a conviction would be unsafe. Having stopped the case, the judge may then consider that there is still sufficient uncontaminated evidence against the defendant to merit his retrial or may consider that the prosecution case has been so weakened that the defendant should be acquitted.[187]

The provision has featured in two cases before the Court of Appeal. In the first, *R v Chopra*,[188] a dentist appealed against his conviction of indecently touching two teenage patients. He had been acquitted of indecently touching a third. Each of the three complainants alleged that C had squeezed her breast during an examination. The girls did not know each other, and the incidents allegedly took place over a 10-year period. As such, the trial judge ruled that all of the evidence should be cross-admissible. The defendant was convicted, and argued on appeal that the judge should have directed the jury that an acquittal on the counts relating to one complainant would undermine the likelihood that the complaints of the other girls were likely to be true. The appeal was, however, dismissed, with the court stressing that the critical question for the judge was whether or not the evidence of one complainant was relevant as going, or capable of going, to establish a propensity to commit offences of the kind charged. In this case, there was sufficient similarity between the allegations to make them cross-admissible, and the fact that three girls were making the same allegation made it more likely to be true than if only one of them had made it.

Chopra was considered some months later by the Court of Appeal in *R v Lamb*.[189] The defendant had been convicted of sexual activity as an abuse of his position of trust with two 17-year-old students at the school where he taught. The girls had alleged that the accused made sexual advances towards them at two separate leavers' balls. A key difference between this case and that of *Chopra* was that the two complainants here admitted that they had discussed their experiences, and one prompted the other to make her complaint. While stopping short of alleging that the girls had maliciously concocted their stories, the appellant alleged that each account had been subject to some degree of 'innocent contamination,' which should have been explained to the jury. In this case, the appeal was allowed.

In the view of the Court of Appeal, the trial judge had materially misdirected the jury. Although he had explained that they should consider the potential for false fabrication, this was not appropriate in the case at hand. Instead, he should have directed them as to the possibility of innocent contamination, as there was some evidence that the girls may have either consciously or unconsciously influenced each other's account. Therefore, not only was the necessary point not made, but the wrong point was emphasised.

In summary, then, section 107 requires that the trial judge must not only be alert to the possibility of collusion but should also actively consider the form and extent of such collusion. If they suspect that collusion has taken place and that cross-admissibility is central to the case, the trial should be halted. Otherwise, the direction to the jury should contain some form of warning about the risk of possible contamination of the evidence.

---

187 Section 107(1) provides for the judge to take either of these courses. If, however, an acquittal is ordered, then the defendant is also to be acquitted of any other offence for which they could have been convicted, if the judge is satisfied that the contamination would affect a conviction for that offence in the same way (s 107(2)). Section 107(3) extends the duty to the situation in which a jury is determining, under the Criminal Procedure (Insanity) Act 1964, whether a person who is deemed unfit to plead did the act or omission charged. Section 107(4) makes it clear that s 107(3) does not affect any existing court powers in relation to ordering an acquittal or discharging a jury.

188 [2007] 1 Cr App R 16. See also *R v Weir* [2005] EWCA Crim 2866.

189 [2007] EWCA Crim 1766.

11.6 The bad character of non-defendant witnesses

The 2003 Act not only regulates the types of questions that can be asked of the accused but also puts in place new hurdles to prevent unfounded or irrelevant character attacks on non-defendant witnesses. Section 100(4) provides that 'except where sub section (1)(c) applies, evidence of the bad character of a person other than the defendant must not be given without the leave of the court.' Bad character carries precisely the same meaning as it does in respect of the accused; the section 98 definition applies. It is thus not limited to previous criminal offences, but may also include evidence that shows that a person has acted in a reprehensible way.

Under section 100(1), the court may only grant leave for such evidence to be adduced if one of three circumstances applies:

(a) it is important explanatory evidence,
(b) it has substantial probative value in relation to a matter which –
  (i) is a matter in issue in the proceedings, and
  (ii) is of substantial importance in the context of the case as a whole,
 or
(c) all parties to the proceedings agree to the evidence being admissible.

11.6.1 Important explanatory evidence

The term 'explanatory evidence' carries the same meaning as it does under section 101(1)(c). If, therefore, the facts or account to which the bad character relates are largely understandable without this additional explanation, the evidence will not be admitted.

11.6.2 Substantial probative value

Evidence is of probative value, or relevant, to a matter in issue where it helps to prove that issue one way or the other. In respect of non-defendants, such evidence is most likely to be relevant where a question is raised about the credibility of the victim or witness, as this is likely to affect the court's assessment of the issue on which the witness is giving evidence. It might also cover attempts by the defence to engage in so-called victim-blaming tactics, which are particularly well documented in cases involving rape and domestic violence.[190] In order for such evidence to be admitted, it must satisfy the 'enhanced relevance' test set out in section 100(1)(b). This means that the evidence must be of substantial probative value and the matter to which it relates must be of substantial importance in the context of the case. Thus, evidence that goes only to a trivial or minor issue in the case will be inadmissible.[191]

Section 100(3) directs the court to take into account a number of factors when assessing the probative value of evidence of a non-defendant's bad character. These include the nature and number of the events to which it relates and when those events occurred. When considering evidence that is probative because of its similarity with evidence in the case (e.g. where the defence suggests that another person was more likely to have committed the offence), the court should take into account the nature and extent of the similarities and dissimilarities.[192] Similarly, where the evidence is being tendered to suggest that a particular person was responsible, the court must

190 See e.g. Adler, Z., *Rape on Trial* (Kegan Paul, 1987); Abrams, D., Viky, G., Masser, B., and Gerd, B., 'Perceptions of Stranger and Acquaintance Rape: The Role of Benevolent and Hostile Sexism in Victim Blame and Rape Proclivity' (2003) 84 *Journal of Personality and Social Psychology* 111.

191 Mere assertions of a victim's bad character with no probative value will most certainly be inadmissible. See *R v Alyson (Mark Stuart)* [2016] EWCA Crim 2253.

192 Criminal Justice Act 2003, s 100(3)(c).

consider the extent to which the evidence shows or tends to show that the same person was responsible on each occasion.[193]

The Court of Appeal warned (*obiter*) in *R v Burchell*[194] that, where evidence passes through the strict hurdles laid down by section 100, the fact that it may then give rise to unwelcome satellite litigation is not 'a basis for refusal to admit the evidence.'[195]

Prior to the 2003 Act, evidence of the victim's or witness's past would be routinely adduced in order to challenge their credibility as a witness, particularly where the defendant did not have any previous convictions. The defence is now required to enunciate precisely how the evidence meets the required threshold as part of the enhanced relevance test. Under this scheme, attacks on the character of a witness must be justified in terms of substantial relevance to credibility. In its 2001 report on character evidence, the Law Commission provided examples of how such a scheme might operate in practice:[196]

> D is charged with theft. W, who was D's employee at the time of the alleged offence, is a witness who will give incriminating evidence which a jury could hardly accept without convicting D. The bad character evidence in question is the fact (not disputed by the prosecution) that, in her previous job, W was dishonest in her expenses claims. D says that the witness is incompetent and therefore mistaken. It is hard to conceive that the evidence would be admissible under our enhanced test.
>
> Alternatively, D is charged with theft, and wishes to ask W about an allegation that she was dishonest in her previous job. In this example, D's case is that W is lying, not incompetent. The fact that in the relatively recent past she has been guilty of dishonesty at the workplace might well surmount the test of enhanced relevance.
>
> A third variation: D is charged with theft and wishes to ask W about an allegation of dishonesty 10 years previously, or in a non-work context. The court might well take the view that it did not pass the enhanced relevance test (applying section 100(3)(b)).[197]

As the Law Commission proceeded to note, before the 2003 Act the evidence of the victim's or witness's past might well be put in or allowed in all three of the above scenarios, or at least under the last two. The basis for this was that since there was a general dispute about the reliability of a witness's evidence, any evidence that might reflect on their credibility as a witness should be admitted, especially if the defendant did not have any previous convictions. Under the enhanced relevance test, the court would force the advocate to consider and articulate why it is that the evidence ought to be admitted as satisfying that test. The outcome might be that a witness will be saved a public humiliation for a cause that could not sensibly have been thought to advance the defendant's case. At the very least, the defence will be forced to sharpen up the focus of their attack.

However, where the 'bad character' in question is regarded as a central issue in the case, section 100 is unlikely to prevent its admissibility. As the Court of Appeal stated in *R v S (Andrew)*,[198] a 'matter in issue' may include not only a disputed fact but also whether or not a particular witness is telling the truth. Here, the accused was charged with indecent assault. He alleged that the complainant, a prostitute, had informed him that she would accuse him of rape if he did not give her an additional payment on top of the £10 they had agreed upon for sexual services. She denied

---

193 Ibid., s 100(3)(d).

194 [2016] EWCA Crim 1559.

195 See also *R v Phillips* [2012] 1 Cr App R 332.

196 Law Commission, *Evidence of Character in Criminal Proceedings*, Report No. 273 (HMSO, 2001).

197 Ibid., at [9.32].

198 See e.g. [2006] 2 Cr App R 31.

having made such a demand, but the court held that defence counsel should have been allowed to cross-examine her in relation to previous convictions related to theft and burglary since they showed a propensity to act dishonestly. Such a propensity had substantial probative value in relation to whether the complainant had tried to blackmail the defendant. In *R v Yaxley-Lennon*, one of the conjoined appeals in *R v Weir and Others*,[199] the appellant was convicted of assault occasioning actual bodily harm and assault with intent to resist apprehension. He appealed against conviction on two grounds. The first ground was that evidence that a defence witness had been cautioned by the police for the possession of cocaine should have been inadmissible since it went to credibility alone and therefore fell outside the scope of section 100. In the alternative, the appellant argued that even if credibility was encompassed by the provision, the evidence did not pass the test of admissibility since it was not of substantial importance in the context of the case as a whole.

The first ground of appeal was rejected: the court stated that it was clear that section 100 was capable of applying to matters pertaining solely to the credibility of a witness. However, the court accepted the appellant's submissions in respect of the second ground of appeal. Accepting that the caution did not relate to an offence of dishonesty nor did it constitute evidence of untruthfulness, the court also noted that it related to an incident after the events in issue, that the witness, by agreeing to be cautioned, had accepted her guilt, that the witness was frank about her caution in evidence, and that there was no suggestion that she was under the influence of drugs during the incident itself. For these reasons, the evidence should not have been admitted and the jury should have been discharged.[200]

Section 100 also proved to be of no assistance to the stepfather of murdered schoolgirl Milly Dowler. Milly had disappeared on her way home from school in March 2002 and her body was recovered some six months later. Eight years later, Levi Bellfield was charged with her murder and was put on trial at the Old Bailey the following year. In June 2011, the media widely reported how the defence cross-examined her stepfather about pornographic magazines that his daughter had discovered prior to her death, and also put questions to him concerning bondage paraphernalia found in his loft. Both he and the girl's mother were accused of favouring their other daughter over Milly. The object of such questioning was – apparently – to suggest that the girl had become so distraught by her parents' attitudes and her stepfather's sexual deviancy that she might have run away and met a tragic end somewhere other than the accused's backyard. This theory – which was somewhat fanciful given the overwhelming nature of the case against the defendant – was nonetheless allowed to be played out before open court and the eyes of the national media. Following Bellfield's conviction, Milly Dowler's stepfather read a statement on the steps of the Old Bailey, which recounted the trial experience as a 'truly mentally scarring experience on an unimaginable scale.'[201]

While section 100 may offer some degree of additional protection for victims and other non-defendant witnesses, its overall impact against the backdrop of the gladiatorial combat of the adversarial arena is difficult to ascertain. The nature of the Milly Dowler case and the much less publicised decision in *S* suggest that the courts may veer towards admissibility where the line between material issues and credibility is blurred. The attack on the characters of victims and other non-defendant witnesses is still relatively commonplace in English criminal proceedings, and may well continue to be the predominant approach in cases of sexual and domestic violence in which it is commonly alleged that the defendant's behaviour is often precipitated by the victim's conduct.[202]

---

199 [2006] 1 WLR 1885.

200 However, the Court of Appeal declined to quash the conviction, having reviewed the evidence as a whole.

201 *The Guardian* (24 June 2011).

202 See e.g. Fielding, N., *Courting Violence* (Oxford University Press, 2006), in which a number of such instances are recorded (at pp. 104–105).

11.6.3 Admitted by agreement

Under section 100(1)(c), evidence of the bad character of a person other than the accused may be admitted by the agreement of 'all parties to the proceedings.' Importantly, in *Williams (t/a Williams of Porthmadog) v Vehicle and Operator Services Agency* [2008] EWHC 849 (Admin), the court held that the word 'agreement' is not to be interpreted in the manner of a contract law analysis of offer and acceptance.

11.6.4 Rules of court

In addition to those stated above at 11.4.8.3, the law lays down certain rules to be followed when a party wishes to admit bad character evidence of a non-defendant witness. Rule 21.3 provides that:

(1) This rule applies where a party wants to introduce evidence of the bad character of a person other than the defendant.
(2) That party must serve an application to do so on –
  (a) the court officer; and
  (b) each other party.
(3) The applicant must serve the application –
  (a) as soon as reasonably practicable; and in any event
  (b) not more than 14 days after the prosecutor discloses material on which the application is based (if the prosecutor is not the applicant).
(4) A party who objects to the introduction of the evidence must
  (a) serve notice on –
    (i) the court officer, and
    (ii) each other party not more than 14 days after service of the application; and
  (b) in the notice explain, as applicable –
    (i) which, if any, facts of the misconduct set out in the application that party disputes,
    (ii) what, if any, facts of the misconduct that party admits instead,
    (iii) why the evidence is not admissible, and
    (iv) any other objection to the application.
(5) The court –
  (a) may determine an application –
    (i) at a hearing, in public or in private, or
    (ii) without a hearing;
  (b) must not determine the application unless each party other than the applicant –
    (i) ic procont, or
    (ii) has had at least 14 days in which to serve a notice of objection;
  (c) may adjourn the application; and
  (d) may discharge or vary a determination where it can do so under –
    (i) section 8B of the Magistrates' Courts Act 1980 (ruling at pre-trial hearing in a magistrates' court), or
    (ii) section 9 of the Criminal Justice Act 1987 (ruling at preparatory or other pre-trial hearing in the Crown Court).

11.7 The defendant's good character

Where defendants are of good character, the common law has traditionally allowed them to put their character in issue either by giving or calling evidence of good character or by drawing the issue out from a prosecution witness or witnesses during cross-examination. It is for the defendant to raise the issue of good character and not the judge. Ironically, even before defendants were competent to testify in their own defence, the courts recognised the desirability of informing the jury that the accused had a clean slate.[203]

203 See e.g. *R v Stannard* (1837) 7 C & P 673.

The 2003 Act has not altered the common law rules, and if the defendant places their character in issue, such evidence will be deemed relevant to both credibility and guilt.[204] The Court of Appeal conducted a 'very thorough review' of the case law and principles concerning a defendant's good character in the case of *R v Hunter*.[205] Composed of a specially constituted five-member panel,[206] the Court of Appeal was tasked with considering the question of in what circumstances a good character direction is required, the effect on the safety of convictions where a direction is required but is not given, and the impact of the Criminal Justice Act 2003 on the relevance of good character. *Hunter* was concerned with five conjoined appeals; in each case the appellants had previous convictions and adduced those convictions at trial in the hope that the trial judge could give some form of modified good character direction. The ability for the court to make a modified direction has been evident throughout a number of judicial precedents on the matter. The Court took the time to identify the relevant legal principles as laid down by the courts in *R v Vye*[207] and *R v Aziz*[208] before then laying down concrete guidelines for future cases to apply. Before we consider the approach of the Court of Appeal in *Hunter*, it will be first useful to establish and discuss the guiding principles laid down in the previous case.[209]

11.7.1 *R v Vye*

Prior to *Hunter*, the leading case in this area was that of *R v Vye*. According to the Court of Appeal, a trial judge has an obligation to issue a specific two-limb direction to the jury where the defendant is of 'good character.'[210] The court expressed the two-limb direction in the following way:

- 1st limb: The trial judge must instruct the jury that they are to accept the defendant's good character when assessing the *credibility* of their testimony.
- 2nd limb: The trial judge must instruct the jury that they ought to consider the defendant's good character when determining whether they had a disposition to committing the offence in question (i.e. they had a propensity to commit the offence).

Whether a defendant was entitled to these limbs ultimately depended on the circumstances of their individual case. We shall consider each limb and its availability in turn.

What these limbs should show is that where a defendant of good character has neither given evidence nor made pre-trial answers or statements, no issue as to his credibility arises and no direction relating his good character to such issue is required.

The Court of Appeal in *Vye* found no hardship in identifying a defendant as being able to rely on both limbs of the direction, but stressed the need for the defendant to be of 'good character.' Later cases, however, established that before the second limb of the direction may be given, some representation from the defence will usually be necessary, and the judge must be sure that there is relevant information that can properly and safely be relied upon.[211] The effect of *Vye* was clear: a direction from the trial judge is mandatory in all cases, and failure to give it is likely to amount to

---

204 *R v Aziz* [1996] AC 41. See also *R v Anderson* [1990] UKPC 36; *R v Durbin* [1995] 2 Cr App R 84; *R v Shaw* [2001] WLR 1519.

205 [2015] EWCA Crim 631.

206 Thomas CJ, Sir Brian Leveson P, Hallett LJ, Coulson and Globe JJ.

207 [1993] 3 All ER 241.

208 [1995] 3 All ER 149.

209 Which was the exact approach adopted by the Court of Appeal in *Hunter*.

210 Understood to mean no criminal record or any form of misconduct covered by section 98, although see the meaning of good character post-*Hunter*.

211 *Thompson v R* [1998] AC 811. See also *Sealey and Headley v The State* [2002] UKPC 52; *R v Maye* [2008] UKPC 36; *Campbell v R* [2010] UKPC 26 (Lord Mance).

a material irregularity, which will normally constitute good grounds for an appeal.[212] The Court of Appeal did note, however, that a specific form of words need not be used, and that the judge should feel free to tailor a direction to the specific circumstances of each case.[213] The issuing of such a direction usually poses few problems where defendants have no previous criminal convictions. However, the situation becomes more complex where a defendant has a few convictions for minor offences in the distant past, or where there is evidence to suggest involvement in some form of criminality, despite the absence of formal convictions.[214]

11.7.2 Post-*Vye*

It was the view of the Court of Appeal in *R v Nye*[215] that good character directions in cases in which the defendant had spent convictions were contrary to both the language and spirit of the law. This advice appeared to be heeded in *Bailey*,[216] in which a defendant with four spent convictions, the most recent of which was 25 years old, was refused leave to present himself as a person of good character. In later years, however, the courts appeared to become more generous to the accused. For example, in *R v Timson and Hales*,[217] the Court of Appeal held that the trial judge should have given a good character direction in favour of the appellant, despite a conviction five years previously for drink-driving. Similarly, in *R v Durbin*,[218] the Court of Appeal, with the leading judgment being provided by Evans LJ, found that a number of what the court referred to as 'blemishes' should not have prevented a good character direction.[219] In *R v Fulcher*,[220] the Court of Appeal emphasised that a good character direction will always be of some value to a defendant and is therefore capable of having some effect in every case in which it is appropriate for such a direction to be given. In *Harmer*,[221] the Court of Appeal held that an accused who had no previous convictions or cautions but who had been issued with a fixed penalty notice for disorder (PND) was entitled to an 'unfettered' *Vye* direction.

11.7.3 *R v Aziz*

The House of Lords in *Aziz* took the opportunity to review the law post-*Vye* having been asked the following certified question from the Court of Appeal:

> Whether directions in accordance with *Vye et al* (1993) 97 Cr. App. R. 134, must be given in all cases in which a defendant has adduced evidence of previous good character, and if not, in what circumstances must such a direction be given.

---

212 *R v Fulcher* [1995] 2 Cr App R 251. See also *R v Lloyd (David)* [2000] 2 Cr App R 355, CA (Crim Div), which states that a judge is required as a matter of law to give the full good character direction, and *Scarnage* [2001] EWCA Crim 1171. However, see now *R v Hunter* [2015] EWCA Crim 631 in which Hallett LJ stated that '[t]here can be no fixed rule or principle that a failure to give a good character direction or a misdirection is necessarily or usually fatal' (at [89]).

213 *Vye*, op. cit., n. 207, at 477.

214 See e.g. *R v M* [2009] EWCA Crim 158, in which the appeal was allowed due to M submitting that the judge had misdirected the jury in relation to the defendant's previous convictions.

215 (1982) 75 Cr App R 247.

216 [1989] Crim LR 723.

217 [1993] Crim LR 58. See also *R v Wood* [1996] 1 Cr App R 207 (Lord Staughton LJ); *Jagdeo Singh v Trinidad and Tobago* [2006] 1 WLR 146; *Bhola v Trinidad and Tobago* [2006] UKPC 9.

218 [1995] 2 Cr App R 84.

219 *Durbin* was criticised by Munday, R. ('What Constitutes Good Character?' [1997] Crim LR 247, and, importantly, in *R v Hunter* Hallett LJ commented that *Durbin* had taken 'a wrong turn' (at [20])).

220 [1995] 2 Cr App R 251.

221 [2010] EWCA Crim 2053.

In explaining that the court retains a residual discretion to withhold a *Vye* direction in certain circumstances, Lord Steyn took the opportunity to explain the present state of the law:

> A good starting point is that a judge should never be compelled to give meaningless or absurd directions. And cases occur from time to time where a defendant, who has no previous convictions, is shown beyond doubt to have been guilty of serious criminal behaviour similar to the offence charged in the indictment. A sensible criminal justice system should not compel a judge to go through the charade of giving directions in accordance with *Vye* in a case where the defendant's claim to good character is spurious. I would therefore hold that a trial judge has a residual discretion to decline to give character directions in the case of the defendant without previous convictions if the judge considers it an insult to common sense to give directions in accordance with *Vye*...
>
> That brings me to the nature of the discretion. Discretions range from the open-textured discretionary powers to narrowly circumscribed discretionary powers. The residual discretion of a trial judge to dispense with character directions in respect of a defendant of good character is of the more limited variety. *Prima facie* the directions must be given. And the judge will often be able to place a fair and balanced picture before the jury by giving directions in accordance with *Vye* and then adding words of qualification concerning other proved or possible criminal conduct of the defendant which emerged during the trial. On the other hand, if it would make no sense to give character directions in accordance with *Vye* the judge may in his discretion dispense with them. Subject to these views, I do not believe that it is desirable to generalise about this essentially practical subject which must be left to the good sense of trial judges. It is worth adding, however, that whenever a trial Judge proposes to give a direction, which is not likely to be anticipated by counsel, the judge should follow the commendable practice of inviting submissions on his proposed directions.[222]

While the House of Lords suggested that it would be an 'insult to common sense' to give the direction where it would be clearly misleading, it was unfortunate that their Lordships did not take the opportunity to clarify the precise circumstances in which a direction was required. This task was left to the Court of Appeal in *R v Gray*.[223]

11.7.4 *R v Gray*

In *Gray*, the Court of Appeal took the opportunity to summarise the principles of good character. Rix LJ set out the following seven propositions as key guiding principles. These are:

> (1) The primary rule is that a person of previous good character must be given a full direction covering both credibility and propensity. Where there are no further facts to complicate the position, such a direction is mandatory and should be unqualified.
>
> (2) If a defendant has a previous conviction which, either because of its age or its nature, may entitle him to be treated as of effective good character, the trial judge has a discretion so to treat him, and if he does so the defendant is entitled to a *Vye* direction; but
>
> (3) Where the previous conviction can only be regarded as irrelevant or of no significance in relation to the offence charged, that discretion ought to be exercised in favour of treating the defendant as of good character. In such a case, the defendant is again entitled to a *Vye* direction. It would seem to be consistent with principle (4) below that, where there is room for uncertainty as to how a defendant of effective good character should be treated, a judge would be entitled to give an appropriately modified *Vye* direction.

222 *Aziz* at 488B.

223 [2004] 2 Cr App R 30.

(4) Where a defendant of previous good character, whether absolute or, we would suggest, effective, has been shown at trial, whether by admission or otherwise, to be guilty of criminal conduct, the *prima facie* rule of practice is to deal with this by qualifying a *Vye* direction[224] rather than by withholding it; but

(5) In such a case, there remains a narrowly circumscribed residual discretion to withhold a good character direction in whole,[225] or presumably in part where it would make no sense, or would be meaningless or absurd or an insult to common sense, to do otherwise.[226]

(6) Approved examples of the exercise of such a residual discretion are not common. Lord Steyn in *Aziz* appears to have considered that a person of previous good character who is shown beyond doubt to have been guilty of serious criminal behaviour similar to the offence charged would forfeit his right to any direction. On the other hand, Lord Taylor's manslaughter/murder example in *Vye* shows that even in the context of serious crime it may be crucial that a critical intent separates the admitted criminality from that charged.

(7) A direction should never be misleading. Where, therefore, a defendant has withheld something of his record so that otherwise a trial judge is not in a position to refer to it, the defendant may forfeit the more ample, if qualified, direction which the judge might have been able to give.[227]

These principles should thus be seen as a valuable guide where aspects of the defendant's past appear somewhat murky. However, in *R v Payton*,[228] it was stated that they should not be taken as prescribing precisely what a judge must do; it was vital that each case turned on its own facts, and the overriding duty of the judge was to ensure fairness to the parties in the particular case. In short, the trial judge will have discretion as to the nature and form of any direction that is given.

11.7.5 *R v Hunter*

In *Hunter*, Hallett LJ warned that, although the *Vye* and *Aziz* principles 'began life as good practice,'[229] her Ladyship concluded that the good character principles have 'been extended too far and convictions have been quashed in circumstances we find surprising.'[230] In the next section, we shall address the 'conclusions' of the Court of Appeal and the approach the court lays down to be adopted by future courts.

Table 11.1 The *Vye* limbs

Limb	Availability
1st Limb	Where the defendant testifies directly of their own good character, or calls witnesses to that effect, they are entitled to the first limb of the direction.
2nd Limb	All accused persons of good character are entitled to the second limb of the direction whether or not they have testified or made pre-trial answers or statements.

224 See also *R v Remice* [2010] EWCA Crim 1952, at [11] (Kay LJ). Here, it was made clear that even if the defendant has a criminal record for 'old or irrelevant offences,' the court may ignore them.

225 Also see *R v Lawson* [2007] 1 WLR 1191, in which Hughes LJ refused to accept that a good character direction ought to be given in every case where evidence relating to a defendant's bad character had been deemed inadmissible: 'The good character direction is appropriate to those who are, or who the judge rules may be treated as if they are, those without known bad character of any kind' [at 41].

226 With regard to defendants of good and bad character, see *R v Doncaster* (2008) 172 JP 202.

227 *Aziz* at [57].

228 [2006] Crim LR 997.

229 At [66].

230 At [70].

11.7.5.1 Impact of *Vye* and *Aziz*

The Court of Appeal felt it necessary to emphasise that it was bound by the judgments of the Court of Appeal in *Vye* and the House of Lords in *Aziz*.[231] In relation to the impact of *Vye* and *Aziz*, the Court divided their discussion into what *Vye* and *Aziz* did decide and what the courts in those cases did not decide. These are clarified in Table 11.2.

The Court of Appeal proceeded on this basis to ensure that it would be 'unnecessary in future for other courts to [conduct a review of the law]. Reliance on this judgment, *Vye* and *Aziz* should suffice.'[232]

Table 11.2 Comparing *Vye* and *Aziz*

What *Vye* and *Aziz* did decide:[a]	What *Vye* and *Aziz* did not decide:[b]
The general rule is that a direction as to the relevance of good character to a defendant's credibility is to be given where a defendant has a good character and has testified or made pre-trial statements.	A defendant with no previous convictions is always entitled to a full good character direction whatever his character.
The general rule is that a direction as to the relevance of a good character to the likelihood of a defendant's having committed the offence charged is to be given where a defendant has a good character whether or not he has testified or made pre-trial answers or statements.	A defendant with previous convictions is entitled to good character directions.
Where defendant A, of good character, is tried jointly with B who does not have a good character, the above rules still apply.	A defendant with previous convictions is entitled to the propensity limb of the good character directions on the basis that he has no convictions similar or relevant to those charged.
There are exceptions to the general rule, for example where a defendant has no previous convictions but has admitted other reprehensible conduct, and the judge considers it would be an insult to common sense to give directions in accordance with *Vye*. The judge then has a residual discretion to decline to give a good character direction.	A defendant with previous convictions is entitled to a good character direction where the prosecution does not seek to rely upon the previous convictions as probative of guilt.
A jury must not be misled.	The failure to give a good character direction will almost invariably lead to a quashing of the conviction.
A judge is not obliged to give absurd or meaningless directions.	

[a] *Hunter*., at [68] per Hallett LJ.

[b] Ibid., at [69] per Hallett LJ.

231 *Hunter*, at [68] (Hallett LJ).
232 Ibid., at [101].

11.7.5.2 Availability of a direction of the categories of good character

The Court of Appeal took its chance to explain the circumstances in which a good character direction was available. The Court emphasised the need to clarify the principles of good character given the fact that the law had been 'extended to the point where defendants with bad criminal records or who have no right to claim a good character [were] claiming an entitlement to a good character direction.'[233]

Hallett LJ made it clear that:

> [O]nly defendants with a good character or deemed to be of effective good character are entitled to a good character direction. A defendant who has a record of previous convictions or has a bad character of some other kind is not entitled as of right to a good character direction … It does not follow from the fact that the bad character is not considered probative of guilt that a defendant is entitled to be treated as if he had a good character. Once evidence of bad character is admitted, a judge cannot ignore it and give directions to a jury which would make no sense.[234]

The Court then proceeded to lay out the 'categories' of good character which are outlined in Figure 11.2 and in the accompanying text.

11.7.5.2.1 Category (i): absolute good character

According to the Court of Appeal, a defendant has 'absolute good character' if he has 'no previous convictions or cautions recorded against them and no other reprehensible conduct alleged, admitted or proven.'[235] Hallett LJ made it clear that a defendant is under no obligation to adduce evidence of a positive good character and in any event, this category of defendant is entitled to both limbs of the *Vye* direction.

11.7.5.2.2 Category (ii): effective good character

A defendant *may* be said to have 'effective good character' if they have 'previous convictions or cautions recorded which are old, minor and have no relevance to the charge.'[236] The word 'may' has been used and emphasised intentionally to demonstrate that a defendant will not be entitled, per se, to be treated as of effective good character. Rather, the Court of Appeal, following *Aziz*, has provided the trial judge with a discretion, as opposed to an obligation, as to whether or not to treat the defendant as a person of effective good character. This does not, of course, mean that a trial judge should attempt to avoid handing out good character directions; however, the Court of Appeal did emphasise that the trial judge should 'be vigilant to ensure that *only those defendants* who merit an "effective good character" are afforded one.'[237] In deciding whether a defendant ought to be entitled to a good character direction, the trial judge must make a judgment 'by assessing all the circumstances of the offence/s and the offender, to the extent known, and then deciding what fairness to all dictates.'[238] It should not be a matter for the jury.

---

233 Ibid., at [68].
234 Ibid.
235 Ibid., at [77].
236 Ibid., at [79].
237 Ibid., at [79] (emphasis added).
238 Ibid.

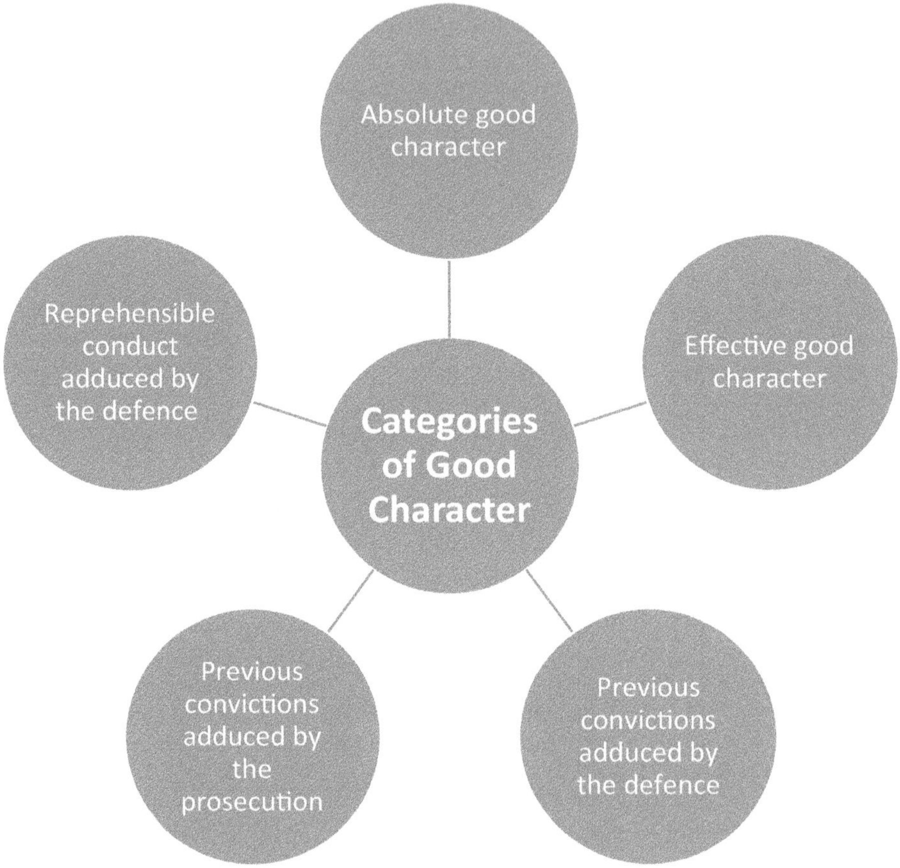

Figure 11.2 Categories of good character

In the circumstances where the trial judge does find the defendant to be a person of effective good character, he is obligated to provide both limbs of the *Vye* direction modified, as necessary, to reflect the other matters and thereby ensure the jury is not misled.[239]

11.7.5.2.3 Category (iii): previous convictions/cautions adduced under section 101 by the defence

In many cases, defendants will introduce their own bad character[240] in an attempt to persuade the jury that those convictions, or reprehensible conduct, do not reflect the situation within the present trial. For example, the defence may adduce previous convictions which are not relevant to the present case (for example, convictions for theft in a rape trial) in an attempt to convince the jury that the defendant does not commit the type of offences alleged in the present trial (i.e. the defendant would hold his hands up in the air and admit that he is a thief but was not a rapist). Other cases may be where the defendant was convicted of relatively minor or old offences and he wishes to adduce those convictions to 'come clean' to the jury and demonstrate that he is not

239 Ibid., at [80].
240 In accordance with the CJA 2003, s 101(1)(b). See above.

the person he used to be. Regardless of the reason for their admission, defence counsel has been prone to argue that a defendant, in such circumstances, ought to be entitled to a modified good character direction.

This category specifically concerns defendants with previous convictions or cautions[241] who adduced their own bad character under section 101(1)(b) of the CJA 2003. The Court of Appeal expressed that in such circumstances 'a defendant with previous convictions or cautions to his name has no entitlement to either limb of the good character direction.'[242] The Court did note, however, that although the defendant had no *entitlement* to a direction, the trial judge did maintain a *discretion* to give such a direction. The Court explained that the direction was 'a broad one of the "open textured variety" ... It is not narrowly circumscribed. The judge will decide what fairness dictates.'[243] The Court concluded their explanation of this category by making clear that this court (i.e. the Court of Appeal) would have 'proper regard'[244] to the trial judge's discretion should any matter come before them on appeal.

11.7.5.2.4 Category (iv): bad character adduced under section 101 and relied on by the prosecution

This category concerns the circumstances where the defendant has no previous convictions or cautions, but there is evidence of some misconduct or other reprehensible behaviour. In such cases where the prosecution rely on this bad character, the Court of Appeal had made clear that the judge is obliged to give a bad character direction.[245] Understanding the possibility of unfairness in this approach, the Court of Appeal has granted trial judges a narrow discretion to apply, as a matter of fairness, a modified good character direction. However, the Court was quick to warn that such directions will often 'offend Lord Steyn's absurdity principle'[246] and such a discretion must be left to the 'good sense of trial judges.'[247]

11.7.5.2.5 Category (v): bad character adduced by the defence under section 101 and not relied on by the Crown

The final category of good character concerns defendants who have no previous convictions or cautions but admit some other form of misconduct or reprehensible behaviour under section 101(1)(b) which is not relied upon by the prosecution as probative of guilt. In this circumstance, the trial judge has an 'open-textured' discretion as to whether to give a direction. The Court emphasised that, as a result of the 2003 Act, there was no longer a presumption that a good character direction would be given in these circumstances. Hallett LJ reasoned that it is:

> preferable to leave the decision as to what directions to give in this situation to the good sense of the trial judge. He or she will be far better placed to assess what fairness demands and we would, therefore, allow them the usual generous ambit of discretion.[248]

---

241 As opposed to mere misconduct or other reprehensible behaviour (for which see Category (v) below).
242 *Hunter*, at [82] (Hallett LJ).
243 Ibid.
244 Ibid.
245 Ibid., at [83].
246 Ibid., referring to Lord Steyn's remarks in *R v Aziz*.
247 Ibid.
248 Ibid., at [88].

11.7.6 Post-*Hunter*

Hunter has already been applied and considered in subsequent cases before the Court of Appeal.[249] One of the most interesting post-*Hunter* cases is that of *R v Mittal*.[250] Here, the defendant, a general practitioner, was charged with theft of money from a patient's bag. The defendant wished for the trial judge to direct the jury that she was of good character; however, the trial judge warned counsel for the defence that if any attempt was made by the defence to present the defendant as of good character, the prosecution would be entitled to respond by adducing evidence of an alleged shoplifting incident that took place a number of years previous. No evidence of character was admitted and the defendant was convicted. On appeal, McCombe LJ in the Court of Appeal dismissed the appellant's case on the basis that the trial judge had been right to warn the defence of the right of the prosecution to rebut any evidence of good character following the principles enunciated in *Hunter*.[251]

In *R v B*,[252] the Court of Appeal considered the effect of a bind over on a defendant's ability to secure a good character direction.[253] The Court of Appeal concluded that neither a bind over, nor the conduct leading to it, 'must necessarily deprive a defendant of his entitlement to an unqualified good character direction.'[254] However, a defendant should not expect a bind over to simply be ignored when such a direction is given. They considered that 'in certain circumstances it may be appropriate to treat a defendant who has in the past been bound over as a person of "effective good character", and therefore entitled to a full good character direction.'[255] Ultimately, however, this would remain a matter for the trial judge to consider in their discretion and the Court of Appeal would be slow to interfere. The failure of the trial judge to give a good character direction was, therefore, not fatal to the safety of the defendant's conviction.

11.7.6.1 The *Crown Court Compendium*

Following *Hunter*, the Judicial College (formerly the Judicial Studies Board) amended the *Crown Court Bench Book* and replaced it with the *Crown Court Compendium*. Chapter 11 of the Compendium is concerned with good character directions, and para 11 stipulates the wording that must be used when directing the jury accordingly. Paragraph 11 states that:

A full good character direction is as follows:

(1) Good character is not a defence to the charge.

(2) However, evidence of good character counts in D's favour in two ways:

  (a) his good character supports his credibility and so is something which the jury should take into account when deciding whether they believe his evidence (the 'credibility limb'); and

  (b) his good character may mean that he is less likely to have committed the offence with which he is charged (the 'propensity limb').

(3) It is for the jury to decide what weight they give to the evidence of good character, taking into account everything they have heard about the defendant.[256]

---

249 See *R v Fitzpatrick (Shane)* [2015] EWCA Crim 1286; *R v Benjamin (Mark Edward)* [2015] EWCA Crim 1377; *R v Goorani (Mohammed)* [2015] EWCA Crim 1855; *R v Coulter (William Ernest)* [2015] NICA 73; *R v AB* [2015] NICA 70; *R v Pacurar (Adrian)* [2016] 1 WLR 3913; *R v Martin (Graham)* [2016] EWCA Crim 474; *R v Abidi (Syed)* [2016] EWCA Crim 1119; *R v Ay (Ender)* [2016] EWCA Crim 1605; *Phillip v St Christopher and Nevis* [2017] UKPC 14.

250 [2016] EWCA Crim 451.

251 On the practice of issuing judicial warnings, see *R v Cojan* [2014] EWCA Crim 2512.

252 [2017] 1 Cr App R 31.

253 An order from the magistrates' court that the defendant will be of good behaviour or keep the peace (akin to a promise or undertaking to refrain from certain conduct).

254 Ibid., at [46].

255 Ibid.

256 Between 11.5 and 11.8 of the *Compendium*, examples are given as to how the jury are to be directed in specific circumstances.

11.7.7 Commentary

The effect of *Hunter* is to clear up the uncertainty that roamed this area of law for a number of years. The Court of Appeal issued clear guidance on the circumstances when a defendant would and would not be entitled to a good character direction. In addition, the Court ensured that the law remained flexible and adaptive by granting the trial judge an 'open-textured' discretion to determine some of the more difficult cases. The judgment is to be commended in this respect; however, it remains the case that granting a margin of discretion to a trial judge will continue to result in potentially inconsistent results given the potentially complex, or unique, set of facts that may come before the trial courts (as evident in *R v B* discussed above). In the words of Scott Ivill, '[t]he doors remain fully open only to the unblemished.'[257]

Matthew Stanbury in his blog 'Bad News for Good Character'[258] argues that it was 'particularly dispiriting' that the Court of Appeal found against Hunter in his appeal. Stanbury reasons that the trial judge had agreed at the time to give the full character direction; however, it was only at the time of summing up that the trial judge failed to deliver a direction on the first limb (the credibility limb). The Court of Appeal appeared to take no course of response in relation to this other than to point out that defence counsel had failed to raise this issue at the time.[259] Stanbury contends that such failure of defence counsel is of 'doubtful relevance' and, in general, the approach of the Court of Appeal seemed to be 'more concerned with stemming out-of-time appeals than with fairness to defendants.' Further, Stanbury remarks that the Court of Appeal ultimately concluded that Hunter was not entitled to a good character direction at all – despite the trial judge finding that there was such a direction available. Stanbury concludes that the lesson to be learned from *Hunter* is as follows:

> [W]here a judge declines to give the direction his or her discretion will rarely, if ever, be interfered with. Conversely, if he/she deems the direction appropriate, but comes up short, this will not carry any weight unless the Court agrees that a direction was required, only then if objections have been raised by trial counsel, and only if it renders the conviction unsafe having regard to the wider facts.[260]

Contemporarily, Mirfield has noted that all the provisions discussed above, 'seem[ed] to change the climate – as they were intended to – such that in law, the suspect is recruited as an active part of the investigation process.'[261] Similarly, as Young, Cameron, and Tinsley[262] have observed, it is one thing to encourage questions about evidence that has been admitted, and another to encourage the court to question perceived gaps in the evidence from a character standpoint. In the United States, judges often tell jurors not to speculate about missing evidence. Yet, as academics have observed, it appears that jurors are often alive to gaps in the evidence of a case.[263]

---

257 Ivill, S., 'Character: the Good, the Bad and the Somewhere In-between', *2 Hare Court*, http://www.2harecourt.com/training-and-knowledge/character-the-good-the-bad-and-the-somewhere-in-between/ (last accessed 24 July 2017).

258 Stanbury, M., 'Bad News for Good Character', *Appeals Barrister*, https://appealsbarrister.com/2015/04/16/bad-news-for-good-character/ (last accessed 27 July 2017).

259 *Hunter*, at [156] (Hallett LJ).

260 See also 'Trial Good Character Vye Direction No Obligation to Give Such a Direction in Favour of a Defendant with Previous Convictions' (2016) 3 *Archbold Review* 3; Stockdale, M., 'Revised Guidance on Good Character Directions' (2015) 79(5) *Journal of Criminal Law* 317; Monaghan, M., 'Reconceptualising Good Character' (2015) 19(3) *International Journal of Evidence and Proof* 190.

261 Mirfield, P., 'Two Side Effects of Section 34 to Section 37 of the Criminal Justice and Public Order Act 1994' (1995) Crim LR 612, 616.

262 Young, W., Cameron N., and Tinsley, Y., *Juries in Criminal Trials Part Two – A Summary of the Research Findings*, Preliminary Papers 37, Volume 2 (NZ Law Commission, 1999) [4.8]–[4.11]

263 For an example of this observation, see Ho, H.L., *A Philosophy of Evidence Law* (Oxford University Press, 2008), which is also discussed in *Roberts*.

11.8 Character evidence in civil cases

The use of character evidence is generally much less contentious in the civil arena, in which the defendant will not face being blighted with a criminal record or the loss of liberty in the event that the court has been unduly prejudiced by such evidence. Counsel is free to attack the credit of a witness, and may do so by making reference to previous convictions in cross-examination. There is no regime equivalent to that contained in Part 11 of the Criminal Justice Act 2003 to regulate the admissibility of such evidence, although spent convictions under the Rehabilitation of Offenders Act 1974 cannot normally be raised.[264]

Evidence of previous conduct – including (although not limited to) previous bad character – may also be adduced through the common law similar fact principle. Although the rule was abolished in criminal cases by virtue of the 2003 Act, the House of Lords confirmed that it continues to apply in the civil courts. The claimant in *O'Brien v Chief Constable of South Wales Police*[265] sought damages from South Wales Police following the quashing of his murder conviction. He sought to introduce evidence indicating that, as part of the original murder investigations, police officers had relied on specific operational methods that were oppressive, dishonest, and unprofessional. He sought to support his allegations through adducing evidence to show that the same officers had used the same or similar methods in two earlier cases. Counsel for the Chief Constable objected on the grounds that such evidence did not meet the test of admissibility, that it should be reasonably conclusive of an issue in the case or have enhanced relevance or substantial probative value, and that, in any event, if admitted, it would add unjustifiably to the length and complexity of the trial. The appeal was dismissed first by the Court of Appeal, then by the House of Lords. Lord Bingham clearly felt that the previous conduct of the officers was directly relevant to the issue before the court:

> That evidence of what happened on an earlier occasion may make the occurrence of what happened on the occasion in question more or less probable can scarcely be denied. If an accident investigator, an insurance assessor, a doctor or a consulting engineer were called in to ascertain the cause of a disputed recent event, any of them would, as a matter of course, inquire into the background history so far as it appeared to be relevant. And if those engaged in the recent event had in the past been involved in events of an apparently similar character, attention would be paid to those earlier events as perhaps throwing light on and helping to explain the event which is the subject of the current inquiry. To regard evidence of such earlier events as potentially probative is a process of thought which an entirely rational, objective and fair-minded person might, depending on the facts, follow. If such a person would, or might, attach importance to evidence such as this, it would require good reasons to deny a judicial decision-maker the opportunity to consider it.[266]

His Lordship then proceeded to outline a two-stage test that should be followed in the civil courts:

> [T]he question of admissibility turns, and turns only, on whether the evidence which it is sought to adduce, assuming it (provisionally) to be true, is in Lord Simon's sense probative. If so, the evidence is legally admissible. That is the first stage of the inquiry ... The second stage of the inquiry requires the case management judge or the trial judge to make what will often be a very difficult and sometimes a finely balanced judgment: whether evidence

---

264 Although, under the Rehabilitation of Offenders Act 1974, s 7(3), the court may permit evidence of spent convictions to be given in evidence if satisfied that 'justice cannot be done in the case' without such evidence being admitted.

265 [2005] 2 AC 534.

266 Ibid., at 540–41.

> or some of it (and if so which parts of it), which ex hypothesi is legally admissible, should be admitted. For the party seeking admission, the argument will always be that justice requires the evidence to be admitted; if it is excluded, a wrong result may be reached ... The strength of the argument for admitting the evidence will always depend primarily on the judge's assessment of the potential significance of the evidence, assuming it to be true, in the context of the case as a whole.

The general rule is thus relatively clear-cut: character evidence is admissible if it is deemed relevant to the matters in issue, subject to the broad discretion of the court to control or exclude evidence that is otherwise admissible as set out in Part 1 of the Civil Procedure Rules.[267] Other occasions on which the courts have seen fit to rely on such evidence include *Mood Music Publishing Co Ltd v De Wolfe Publishing Ltd*[268] (an action for copyright infringement, concerning the close similarity of the defendant's previous music compositions) and *Jones v Greater Manchester Police* Authority[269] (concerning the propensity of a sex offender to reoffend).[270]

11.8.1 Good character in civil cases

In contrast to the criminal courts, the good character of any party in civil proceedings is generally regarded as irrelevant and will not be admissible. Thus, in *Hatton v Cooper*,[271] which concerned a road traffic accident, the Court of Appeal held that the trial judge had been wrong to admit evidence from the claimant's employer to the effect that he was an excellent driver, and would have been unlikely to have caused the accident.[272]

11.9 Key learning points

- Prior to the 2003 Act, evidence of the accused's bad character could be admitted only under the similar fact rule at common law, or under the Criminal Evidence Act 1898.
- This regime has now been abandoned and replaced by the provisions contained in sections 98–113 of the Criminal Justice Act 2003.
- Evidence of bad character will be admissible only if it falls under one of the seven 'gateways' in section 101.
- Where it is clear that evidence has been contaminated, the judge must stop the case if the contamination is such that, considering the importance of the evidence to the case, a conviction would be unsafe.
- Where the defendant has no previous record of misconduct, the judge is under an obligation to issue a good character direction following *Vye*.
- Section 100 of the 2003 Act aims to protect all non-defendant witnesses from character attacks.
- In civil cases, bad character evidence is admissible if it is deemed relevant to the facts in issue and is subject to the broad discretion of the court to control or exclude evidence in Part 1 of the Civil Procedure Rules 1998.
- Evidence of good character is not usually admissible in civil proceedings.

---

267 Civil Procedure Rules, r 32.1.
268 [1976] Ch 119.
269 [2001] EWHC Admin 189.
270 See also *Scott v Sampson* (1881) 8 QBD; *Sattin v National Union Bank Ltd* (1978) 122 *Solicitors Journal* 367.
271 [2001] RTR 544.
272 See further Ch 13.

11.10 Practice questions

1. Consider whether the bad character of the defendant is admissible at trial in the following circumstances.
   (a) Mandy is charged with theft from the person. It is alleged that she stole a handbag from a woman after showing her a purse and asking if it was hers. When the woman took her handbag out from her shopping bag to check, Mandy snatched it and ran off. Mandy has two previous convictions for theft from the person using the same trick.
   (b) Gerry is charged with causing grievous bodily harm to Julian, with whom he had an altercation after allegedly being 'cut up' on a slip road. Julian, who sustained bruises and a broken shoulder, says that Gerry punched him and he fell to the ground, breaking his shoulder. Gerry claims that Julian, who had stopped at the roadside, fell while trying to avoid a heavy goods vehicle that overtook as he was climbing out of his car. Gerry has three previous convictions for assault, one of which followed a road rage incident.
   (c) Eric is charged with causing actual bodily harm to Victor. In his evidence, Eric says that he was walking in the park when a young girl complained to him that Victor had made indecent suggestions to her. Eric claims that he then challenged Victor, who responded with violence. In his evidence, Victor said that he went to the park with his children. While in the play area, other children told him that Eric, who had been hanging around, had asked several of them if they wanted to come with him to feed the ducks. When Victor approached Eric to ask him about this, Eric punched him a number of times. Eric has two previous convictions for indecently assaulting young girls and is on the Sex Offenders Register.
   (d) Les is charged with assault occasioning actual bodily harm on Leeroy. The arresting officer gave evidence that, on being charged, Les said: 'Well, he's gay, and he told me he wanted to take me into the toilets for some fun, so I thumped him.' Les has two convictions for burglary, three for taking a motor vehicle without consent, and one for indecent assault on a female.
   (e) Mervyn is charged with indecent assault. In his evidence-in-chief, he told the jury that he was a respected member of the community, he regularly attended church, and he had been a verger. There is evidence that he had attended church regularly and had been a verger until December 2002. However, following an investigation by the church authorities into allegations that he had touched choirboys inappropriately in the vestry, he had been required to resign from his position as verger and he no longer attended church.
   (f) Two of Mervyn's alleged victims, Marcus and Maurice, are friends with Mervyn's 12-year-old son, Alan. The defence alleges that the two boys have known each other all of their lives and concocted their stories together as revenge against Mervyn because he had banned them from seeing his son.
2. 'Evidence of the accused's previous misconduct can be highly prejudicial to the case of the defence and should only be admissible in the most exceptional of circumstances. The current rules, contained in the Criminal Justice Act 2003, too readily allow for such evidence to be admitted.' Critically evaluate the above statement.
3. 'As the number of reported cases on the topic makes clear, similar fact evidence has proved a contentious and uncertain area of the law, particularly in criminal cases but also in civil cases like that before the House. But such evidence may be very important, even decisive. It is undesirable that the subject should be shrouded in mystery.' Critically evaluate the above statement made by Lord Bingham in *O'Brien v Chief Constable of South Wales Police* [2005] 2 AC 534, 539.

11.11 Suggested further reading

For a broad overview of the contemporary study of rap music within evidentiary findings, see the University of Manchester Center for Prosecuting Rap <https://sites.manchester.ac.uk/prosecuting-rap/home/about/> (last accessed 5th March 2024).

Branston, G., 'A Reprehensible Use of Cautions as Bad Character Evidence?' (2015) Crim LR 594.
Coen, M., 'Hearsay, Bad Character and Trust in the Jury: Irish and English Contrasts' (2013) 17 E & P 250.
Law Commission, *Evidence of Character in Criminal Proceedings: Previous Misconduct of a Defendant*, Report No. 273 (HMSO, 2001).
Lloyd-Bostock, S., 'The Effects on Juries of Hearing about the Defendant's Previous Criminal Record: A Simulation Study' (2000) Crim LR 734.
Monteith, K., Quinn, E., Dennis, A., Joseph-Salisbury, R., Kane, E., Addo F. and McGourlay, C., 'Racial Bias and the Bench: A response to the Judicial Diversity and Inclusion Strategy (2020–2025)', University of Manchester, November 2022.
Munday, R., 'What Constitutes a Good Character?' (1997) Crim LR 247.
Munday, R., 'What Constitutes "Other Reprehensible Behaviour" under the Bad Character Provisions of the Criminal Justice Act 2003?' (2005) Crim LR 24.
Munday, R., 'Case Management, Similar Fact Evidence in Civil Cases, and a Divided Law of Evidence' (2006) 10 E & P 81.
Munday, R., 'Misconduct that "Has to Do with the Alleged Facts of the Offence with which the Defendant is Charged" . . . More or Less' (2008) Journal of Criminal Law 214.
Munday, R., 'Single-Act Propensity' (2010) Journal of Criminal Law 128.
Owusu-Bempah, A., 'Prosecuting Rap: What Does the Case Law Tell Us?' (2022) 41(4) Popular Music 427–445.
Owusu-Bempah, A., 'The Irrelevance of Rap' (2022) 2 Crim. L.R. 130–151.
Quinn, E., White, J. and Street, J., Introduction to Special Issue: Prosecuting and Policing Rap (2022) 41(4) Popular Music 419–426.
Redmayne, M., 'Recognising Propensity' (2011) Crim LR 117.
Spencer, J.R., *Evidence of Bad Character*, 3rd edn (Hart Publishing, 2016).
Waterman, A. and Dempster, T., 'Bad Character: Feeling Our Way One Year On' (2006) Crim LR 614.

Chapter 12

Hearsay Evidence

Chapter contents

DOI: 10.4324/9781003416098-12

Hearsay may be defined as any oral or written statement, made by a person other than the maker, which is offered in evidence to prove the truth of the matter asserted. Put more simply, it is evidence that aims to establish the existence of a fact not through the witness's first-hand knowledge, but through what a third party has stated out of court. The rule against the admissibility of hearsay evidence has traditionally been regarded as one of the defining features of the Anglo-American trial. Until recently, such statements, whether in oral or written form, were inadmissible at common law unless they fell within a common law or statutory exception.

Various rationales have been cited for the rule.[1] The most common justification, however, tends to centre around concerns over the potential unreliability of such evidence. Just as in the game of Chinese whispers, a statement can become increasingly distorted or misconceived as it passes along the chain of communication. A second reason for excluding hearsay, which is arguably of equal importance, is that the adversarial system places a high value on oral evidence given on oath before a jury. In theory, at least, this enables the trier of fact to observe the demeanour of the witness and evaluate the strength of the evidence under cross-examination. Cross-examination is a tool by which weaknesses of the opposing party's case are exposed. The hearsay rule was thus a necessary corollary of the adversarial paradigm: admitting such evidence would have undermined basic tenets of the system.[2]

For much of the twentieth century, the hearsay rule was stringently enforced. Judges had no discretion to admit hearsay evidence, even where the evidence was seemingly extremely reliable. As illustrated below, this resulted in a number of manifest injustices, to both the prosecution and the defence. Gradually, the courts, and later Parliament, sought to counteract these effects by crafting a large number of exceptions; on occasions, courts simply sidestepped the rules by interpreting what was quite plainly hearsay as real evidence. By the end of the twentieth century, the parameters of the hearsay rule had become so uncertain, and its rationale so dubitable, that the common law regime was abandoned; it was abolished in the civil courts by the Civil Evidence Act 1995 and replaced in the criminal sphere with a new statutory scheme contained in the Criminal Justice Act (CJA) 2003.

12.1 Evolution of the modern law

12.1.1 What is hearsay?

In *Subramaniam v Public Prosecutor*,[3] it was stated that:

> Evidence of a statement made to a witness by a person who is not himself called as a witness may or may not be hearsay. It is hearsay and inadmissible when the object of the evidence is to establish the truth of what is contained in the statement. It is not hearsay and is admissible when it is proposed to establish by evidence, not the truth of the statement, but the fact that it was made.[4]

1 See generally Choo, A., *Hearsay and Confrontation in Criminal Trials* (Oxford University Press, 1996), Ch 1.
2 See comments of Lord Normand in *Teper v R* [1952] AC 480, 486.
3 [1956] 1 WLR 965.
4 Ibid., at 970.

It follows from the above statement that, in order to identify a statement as hearsay, the purpose for which such evidence is adduced has to be ascertained.[5] This is not always a straightforward task and, as indicated above, there are many cases in which the courts treated real evidence as hearsay when it was not, and vice versa. Thus, in *Woodhouse v Hall*,[6] the defendants were charged with managing a brothel at premises described as a 'sauna and massage parlour.' Magistrates refused to allow police officers who had posed as customers to give evidence of conversations between them and the masseuses, giving details of the availability and cost of sexual services, stating that the conversations were hearsay. The Divisional Court allowed the prosecution appeal against this refusal. Donaldson LJ had some sympathy with the magistrates, whom he thought had been misled by *Subramaniam*, but he stated that there was no question of the hearsay rule applying to these conversations. The relevant issue here was not the content of the statements, but the fact that offers of sexual services were actually made.

Similarly, in *Roberts v DPP*,[7] the question arose as to whether certain documents were hearsay. The accused was charged with assisting in the management of a brothel and running an unlicensed massage parlour. He had been seen entering the premises, and a search of the office of the company of which he was the managing director revealed a number of documents relating to the company's ownership of the premises used as a brothel, including a telephone account for the premises in the accused's name, documents relating to goods and services supplied to the premises, and adverts placed for the premises, invoiced to the company. A search of the accused's home revealed other documents relating to the premises, including a gas bill. He was convicted and appealed, arguing that these documents should not have been admitted. Dismissing the appeal, the court accepted that the documents were not admissible to show the truth of their contents, but were admissible as circumstantial or 'real' evidence, to which the hearsay rule did not apply. The prosecution did not seek to rely on the truth of the contents of the documents, but on the fact that they were in the accused's possession, from which the inference could be drawn that he was involved in the management of the premises. His knowledge that the premises were being used as a brothel was an easy inference to draw from the fact that he had visited the premises, as well as from the letter requesting adverts in a magazine. There was therefore ample evidence to convict.

12.1.1.1 Direct and indirect hearsay

Hearsay may be direct (or first-hand) or indirect (second-hand or multiple).

Example 12.1

Alex sees a robbery taking place; he notes the registration number of the getaway car and the physical features of one of the robbers who removed his mask. He immediately makes a statement to the police in which he states what he saw, but he dies before the case is brought to trial. In such circumstances, the prosecution may seek to rely on the statement Alex made to the police before his death. However, since the purpose of adducing the

---

5 The Court of Appeal emphasised that a statement cannot be hearsay unless it is intended to be relied upon as being true (*R v Amjad* [2016] EWCA Crim 1618).

6 (1980) 72 Cr App R 39.

7 [1994] Crim LR 926.

statement would be to prove the truth of the facts asserted (that is, the identity of a particular person/vehicle), then this would constitute hearsay evidence. Moreover, it would be classed as direct or first-hand hearsay, because the witness perceived the events directly before communicating them to the police. In these circumstances, this statement would have been inadmissible at common law unless it fell within one of the established exceptions to the rule of exclusion.

Now imagine a slightly different set of facts.

Example 12.2

What if Alex had seen the above events unfold, but had decided not to report it to the police at all? Instead, he told his friend Bryan what he had seen. Unable to convince Alex to go to the police, Bryan relays the account to DC Rollins. Now, when the case comes to trial, not only is Alex dead but Bryan also has emigrated and cannot be traced. If the prosecution now wish to seek to rely on Bryan's statement, by calling DC Rollins as a witness, his evidence will be second-hand or multiple hearsay, since it has passed through one further conduit before reaching the court.

Traditionally, multiple hearsay has been seen as the least reliable form of hearsay, given the possibility of distortion, which increases as the chain of communication grows longer. For that reason, multiple hearsay was generally inadmissible at common law. As we shall see below, however, there are certain circumstances in which it may well be admissible under the new statutory arrangements.[8]

12.1.2 Reliable evidence excluded

One of the problems of the common law regime was that it was extremely rigid and operated to exclude evidence no matter how reliable. In *Myers v DPP*,[9] the prosecution wished to adduce microfilm records from a car manufacturer, showing the different vehicle identification numbers (VINs) that had been assigned to the stolen cars at the time of manufacture in the factory. The purpose of adducing this evidence was to show that the numbers corresponded with those of certain stolen vehicles that had been seized. The manufacturer operated a system under which the VIN passed through several operators in the production line before being recorded in a log. It was, however, impossible to determine who those persons were. The House of Lords, while accepting

8 Multiple hearsay was also inadmissible under s 23 of the Criminal Justice Act 1988 if contained in a document. However, it is relatively commonplace in business, and s 24 of the 1988 Act (and now s 117 of the Criminal Justice Act 2003) allowed such a statement in a document to be admitted provided that the statement was created or received by a person in the course of a trade, business, profession, etc., and the information contained in the statement was received by each person in the chain of communication in the course of a trade, business, profession, etc. Under the 2003 Act, multiple hearsay remains inadmissible if it is in oral form, but is now subject to discretionary admissibility under s 114(1)(d) (see discussion below).

9 [1965] AC 1001.

that the evidence of the VIN was reliable and recommending major statutory change to the law, upheld the decision of the trial judge to refuse to admit the evidence because it was hearsay.[10]

Myers was not the only case that resulted in an obvious injustice. In *Sparks v R*,[11] the defendant, who was white, was convicted of indecently assaulting a 3-year-old girl. Since the child was not competent to give evidence, the trial judge ruled that a statement by the girl that her assailant was 'a coloured boy' was inadmissible hearsay. The Privy Council upheld this ruling, despite it serving to show that the accused was innocent. Similarly, in *R v Thompson*,[12] the accused was charged with using an instrument to procure an abortion. The woman died before trial from an unrelated cause. The trial judge ruled that two statements from the woman – the first, made before the operation by the defendant, that she intended to operate on herself, and the second, made after the operation, that she had in fact done so – were inadmissible hearsay. The Court of Appeal upheld this ruling as correct.

The esoteric nature of the rule against hearsay and its potential inconvenience to the criminal justice system was again illustrated in *R v Hussain*,[13] in which the accused was convicted of the murder of his sister-in-law. It was alleged that he drove over her several times, killing her. Four men, including the defendant, were regular drivers of the car that killed her. A witness, X, identified the accused as the driver at the time and as a person he had seen driving the car previously. He knew him as H because the deceased had told him that the person he recognised as H was her brother-in-law. H's appeal against conviction was allowed on the basis that X's evidence was hearsay and should not have been admitted. The Crown was seeking to rely on X's evidence to prove two facts: (1) X recognised the man he had previously seen; and (2) the man X had previously seen was H. The only basis on which they could establish the second fact was by relying on the hearsay statement of the deceased. The Court of Appeal expressed some sympathy with the trial judge in that this ought to be a matter of weight rather than admissibility, but it was not for the court to seek to legislate in relation to the long-established hearsay rule, to which the present situation was not an exception. A retrial was ordered, at which H pleaded guilty to manslaughter.

12.1.3 Avoiding the rule

It should be underlined that the courts will not always deem that a statement constitutes hearsay. For example, if the purpose of the evidence is to establish the state of mind of the maker of a statement, then the rule will not apply. In *Ratten v R*,[14] the defendant was convicted of murdering his wife by shooting her. His defence was that the gun had gone off accidentally while he was cleaning it. The time of death was put at between 1.12 and 1.20 pm. A telephonist was permitted to give evidence that at 1.15 pm she had received a telephone call from Ratten's house made by a sobbing and hysterical woman, who had said: 'Get me the police please.' The Privy Council held that this was correctly admitted. Holding that there was no element of hearsay, the Privy Council held that the evidence was relevant, first, to show that, contrary to Ratten's evidence denying that his wife had made the call, the call had been made, and, second, to show the state of mind of the wife as being fearful at an existing or pending emergency, which was capable of rebutting the accused's defence that the shooting was an accident. The Privy Council held that the exact words

10 It was not until the enactment of s 68 of the Police and Criminal Evidence Act 1984 (later replaced by s 24 of the Criminal Justice Act 1988, and now covered by s 117 of the Criminal Justice Act 2003) that such evidence became admissible as a statutory exception to the hearsay rule.

11 [1964] AC 964.

12 [1912] 3 KB 19.

13 [1998] Crim LR 820.

14 [1972] AC 378.

used by the wife in the call were hearsay (that the maker wanted the police) but were admitted to show that she made the call and was hysterical in doing so.[15]

In a similar vein, statements are also admissible to prove the state of mind of the witness who heard the statement. In *Subramaniam*, the accused had been charged with unlawful possession of ammunition. He ran the defence of duress, alleging that he had been threatened by a terrorist organisation. Although the trial judge excluded the evidence of the threats as hearsay, the conviction was quashed on appeal. In the view of the Court of Appeal, the central issue was whether the defendant held a genuine belief that he would be killed if he refused to follow the orders of the terrorist group. Since there was no other way to establish this belief, other than admitting evidence that threatening words were actually spoken, the statement should have been admitted. As the decisions in *Ratten* and *Subramaniam* demonstrate, the courts concern themselves primarily with the *effect* of the statement, rather than the truth of its actual contents. If a statement is tendered for any purpose other than proving the truth of its contents, it should thus be regarded as direct evidence.

However, sometimes it can be difficult to draw such a stark dividing line. In *R v Blastland*,[16] the defence sought to draw a distinction between the use of a statement to prove the truth of its contents and its use to prove a state of knowledge of particular facts. Here, the accused was convicted of the buggery and murder of a 12-year-old boy. He gave evidence that he had attempted to bugger the boy, but stopped when the boy said it was too painful. Shortly afterwards, he had seen M nearby and, afraid that he had been seen trying to commit a serious offence, he had run off and gone home. He sought to adduce evidence from a number of witnesses that M had, before the death of the boy had been made public, told them that the boy had been murdered. M had also confessed to the police that he had killed the boy, but later withdrew that statement, so the defendant applied to call M and treat him as a hostile witness. Both applications were refused and the accused was convicted on both counts. His appeals to the Court of Appeal and to the House of Lords were both dismissed, both courts holding that the evidence had been correctly excluded. Lord Bridge pointed out that to admit statements of third parties, not called as witnesses, confessing to the crime for which the defendant was being tried, would be to create a significant and (many may think) a dangerous new exception to the hearsay rule.

12.1.4 Hearsay 'fiddles'

The cases discussed thus far indicate that the hearsay rule can mean that cogent and reliable evidence may be excluded. While, over the years, the courts and Parliament developed exceptions to the rule, judges and counsel often sought ways in which to sidestep it altogether. Hearsay 'fiddles' arise when the court deems that evidence that is plainly hearsay is not, in order to avoid an inconvenient result. Using somewhat creative judicial reasoning, the courts have displayed a willingness to admit clearly reliable and relevant evidence when there is no hearsay exception to fit the circumstances.

In *Glinski v McIver*,[17] Lord Devlin roundly condemned the practice of attempting to evade the rule by disguising the nature of the evidence being adduced. He was particularly scathing about the common device that involves counsel attempting to avoid the rule by enticing the content of the statement from the witness through a series of carefully thought-out yes or no questions.

---

15 Note, however, that the House of Lords in *R v Kearley* [1992] 2 AC 228 took the view that the evidence of the telephonist was hearsay, but that it was admissible as an exception to the rule as being part of the *res gestae*. Evidence of the state of mind of a person is admissible as an exception to the rule against hearsay under the *res gestae* principle, discussed below.

16 [1986] AC 41.

17 [1962] AC 726.

Example 12.3

Counsel: Did you go to see Peter?
Witness: Yes.
Counsel: Don't tell us what he said, but as a result of what Peter told you, did you do something?
Witness: Yes.
Counsel: What did you do?

Such questioning thinly disguises the fact that the witness is responding to what a third party said, but by the letter of the law, such a practice is just as inadmissible as repeating what the third party actually said. This is illustrated by the case of *R v Saunders*,[18] in which the prosecution sought to prove that the defendant, charged with obtaining by deception, had not carried on a genuine business. Counsel asked a witness whether he had made any enquiries as to whether any trade had been done by the defendant. The witness replied that he had made the enquiries. Counsel then asked whether, as a result of those enquiries, he had found that any trade had been done, to which the witness had replied that he had not. The Court of Appeal quashed the conviction because the line of questioning was intended to circumvent the hearsay rule.

There was an even more blatant attempt at evasion of the rule in *Jones v Metcalfe*.[19] An eyewitness to a road accident memorised the number of the lorry he thought responsible, and later dictated it to a police officer. The officer made a note of it, but the witness did not verify the note as correct. At trial, the witness could not remember the number and, because he had not verified the note made by the officer, he was not permitted to refresh his memory from that note. However, another officer (not the one to whom the witness had dictated the note) was allowed to give evidence that he had interviewed the accused and had put the allegation to him that he was responsible for the accident. Quashing the conviction, Diplock LJ pointed out that although the inference that the appellant was the driver of the lorry at the time of the accident was irresistible as a matter of common sense, what the witness had said to the police was inadmissible hearsay and the inference was based on that evidence.

Similarly, courts have also strained the concept of 'real' evidence to cover what really ought to have been considered hearsay. This has been a particularly common ploy where strict application of the rule would have resulted in the exclusion of highly cogent evidence. An example can be found in *R v Rice*.[20] Part of the prosecution case on a charge of conspiracy was that Rice had taken a flight to Manchester on a particular date, in the company of a co-accused, H, who had already given evidence to this effect. To rebut Rice's denial of this, the prosecution produced an airline ticket to Manchester on the date in question in the names of Rice and another co-accused, M. Rice denied all knowledge of the ticket, but it was nonetheless admitted in evidence and shown to the jury as an exhibit. On appeal, it was argued that the ticket should not have been admitted. Since it was tendered by the prosecution to show that Rice had flown to Manchester on the date in question with a co-accused, it was plainly hearsay and should have been excluded. The Court of Appeal rejected that argument, holding that the ticket was relevant and admissible circumstantial evidence from which the jury would be entitled to draw the inference that Rice had taken the flight. Such reasoning was certainly guileful on the part of the court: an inference can be drawn only if one assumes that the statement on the ticket is true; so it follows that the purpose of adducing the ticket was to prove the truth of the facts asserted and thus the ticket should really have fallen

18 [1968] 1 QB 490.
19 [1967] 1 WLR 1286.
20 [1963] 1 QB 857.

under the reach of the hearsay rule. Such reasoning was similarly advanced in *R v Lilley*,[21] in which the Court of Appeal held that a notebook bearing the inscription 'Sharon's notebook,' containing practice signatures, was not hearsay when used to connect the accused, one Sharon Lilley, with a conspiracy to obtain benefits using stolen benefit books.

In *R v Shone*,[22] it was established that hearsay statements can be used to prove the non-existence of a fact, provided that an officer in charge of the records comes to testify as to the non-existence of a particular fact. Here, a stock clerk and a sales manager gave evidence to the effect that workers in a firm would have made an entry on record cards if certain items had been disposed of lawfully. However, since there were no such entries, the jury were deemed free to draw the inference that the items in question must therefore have been stolen. In the view of the court, it seems that if an inference was drawn from what a document said, the document was hearsay; if an inference was drawn from what it did not say (or from the fact that no document existed), then it was a form of direct evidence.

12.2 The erosion of the rule

As the above cases demonstrate, the courts were becoming increasingly frustrated with the operation of the rule against hearsay in the second half of the last century. There was an increasing willingness among judiciary in the lower courts to allow hearsay evidence to slip through the net and a corresponding reluctance of the appellate courts to interfere with these decisions. The enactment of sections 23–30 of the CJA 1988 made most hearsay statements in documentary form admissible, subject to certain conditions and judicial discretion.[23] Thus the airline ticket in *Rice* would have been admissible under section 24 of the 1988 Act, and would still be admissible today under section 117 of the 2003 Act without the need for the court to try to justify it as a form of real evidence. By the end of the century, exceptions to the rule had been created either by common law or by statute in the following areas:

- admissions and confessions of parties and their agents;
- statements by deceased persons:
  - declarations against interest;
  - declarations in the course of duty;
  - declarations as to public interests;
  - dying declarations (in the case of homicide);
  - declarations as to pedigree;
  - declarations by testators as to their wills;
  - testimony given in a previous trial;
- reputations or family traditions:
  - of bad character (reputations only);

---

21 [2003] All ER (D) 143.

22 (1983) 76 Cr App R 72. See also *DPP v Leigh* [2010] EWHC 345 (Admin).

23 The written statement was admissible if the maker of the statement was unable to give oral evidence because they were dead, mentally or physically unable to give oral evidence, out of the country, or in fear. In addition, business documents not made for the purposes of criminal proceedings were admissible without proof that the maker was unavailable for one of the above reasons. Admissibility was subject to judicial discretion, but that discretion was seen as being overly concerned with whether admitting the document would be unfair to the defendant, who could not cross-examine on it, and failed to take account of the interests of the prosecution. There were also wide powers under the Criminal Procedure and Investigations Act 1996 to admit at trial depositions taken by magistrates from witnesses at committal proceedings or statements admitted at such proceedings. They were inadmissible if either party to the trial objected, but the objection could be overridden if the court considered it to be in the interests of justice to do so. There was, however, no guidance as to how this wide discretion should be exercised.

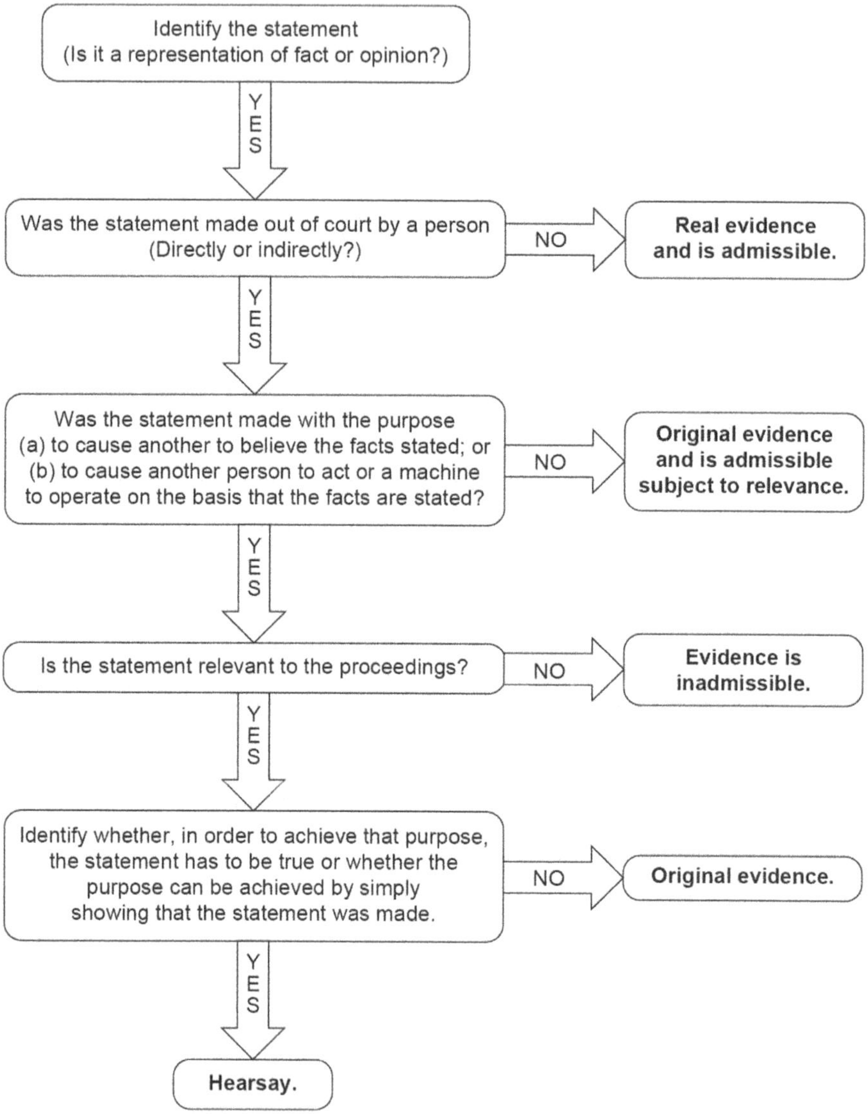

Figure 12.1 Identifying hearsay

  - of pedigree;
  - of the existence of a marriage;
  - of the existence or non-existence of any public or general rights;
  - to identify any person or object;
- public documents;
- statements admitted as part of the *res gestae* (see below);
- statements made by a party to a common enterprise, admitted against another party to the enterprise as evidence of any matter stated.

12.2.1 Reform of the rule

In the criminal arena, reform came much more slowly than its civil counterpart, which is discussed below at 12.4. In a 1998 article, John Jackson likened the rule to a sacred cow that could not be slaughtered.[24] Yet, by the beginning of that decade, it was already apparent that the law had become 'exceptionally complex and difficult to interpret.'[25] In recommending major reform, the Royal Commission on Criminal Justice concluded that:

> In general, the fact that a statement is hearsay should mean that the court places less weight on it, but not that it should be inadmissible in the first place. We believe that the probative value of relevant evidence should in principle be decided by the jury for themselves, and we therefore recommend that hearsay evidence should be admitted to a greater extent than at present.[26]

At the suggestion of the Royal Commission, the Law Commission considered the scope of criminal hearsay shortly after concluding its work into the operation of the rule in civil proceedings. It recommended a programme of far-reaching reform in its final report, *Evidence in Criminal Proceedings: Hearsay and Related Topics*.[27] These recommendations, along with those contained in Sir Robin Auld's *Review of the Criminal Courts*,[28] formed the basis of legislative reform proposals that the Government outlined in the following terms in its White Paper, *Justice for All*:[29]

> Another area ripe for change is the principle that evidence must be given by witnesses in person to the court. This is based on the idea that seeing and hearing the evidence of a witness in the witness box is the best means of getting at the truth. Whilst reported evidence, or 'hearsay', is generally less satisfactory than first hand, there may be some cases where this is not so and others where it is all that is available and should therefore be considered by the court. The strict application of the rules also means that the previous statements of witnesses are not admissible as evidence even on long forgotten issues of detail, and that video recorded evidence is only admissible in a limited range of specified cases.
>
> We believe that the right approach is that, if there is a good reason for the original maker not being able to give the evidence personally (for example, through illness or death) or where records have been properly compiled by businesses, then the evidence should automatically go in, rather than its admissibility being judged. Judges should also have a discretion to decide that other evidence of this sort can be given. This is close to the approach developed in civil proceedings.
>
> We believe it is important to ensure that when witnesses are testifying, rules of evidence do not artificially prevent the true and full story from being presented to the court. Justice is not served if important information is excluded for no good reason. Therefore we propose to legislate to make it easier for witnesses to give their evidence by making their previous and original statements, often made at the time or shortly after the incident, more widely admissible at trial and allowing witnesses to refer to them when they give their

24 Jackson, J., 'Hearsay: The Sacred Cow That Won't Be Slaughtered' (1998) 2(3) *International Journal of Evidence and Proof* 166.

25 Royal Commission on Criminal Justice, *Report*, Cmnd 2263 (HMSO, 1993), Ch 8 [26].

26 Ibid.

27 Law Commission, *Evidence in Criminal Proceedings: Hearsay and Related Topics*, Report No. 245 (HMSO, 1997).

28 Sir Robin Auld took the view that the Law Commission had not gone far enough in its proposed relaxation of the rule. He proposed that the strict rule against the admission of hearsay evidence in criminal proceedings should be abandoned. Instead, a more flexible approach should be adopted where evidence was admitted on a much more widespread basis, and trust was placed in factfinders to evaluate the weight of such evidence fairly: Auld, Sir R., *Review of the Criminal Courts of England and Wales*, Cmnd 9376 (HMSO, 2002) [95]–[104].

29 Home Office, *Justice for All*, Cmnd 5563 (HMSO, 2002).

> evidence in court. We also propose to extend the scope for witnesses to give evidence on tape or by TV link.[30]

On the basis of this proposal, the Government introduced a new Criminal Justice Bill into Parliament, which would radically overhaul the existing scheme by substituting the old common law rules with a new statutory framework.

12.3 The Criminal Justice Act 2003

With the exception of eight of the common law exceptions to the rule against hearsay, which were preserved, Part 11 of the CJA 2003 abolished the entire hearsay regime. Section 114 of the Act stipulates that there is still a general rule that excludes hearsay evidence.[31] However, such a statement may be admissible provided that it falls under one of the heads set out in section 114(1):

(a) it is admissible under any statutory provision (including the 2003 Act itself);
(b) it is admissible under a common law rule preserved by the 2003 Act;
(c) the parties agree that it should be admitted;[32] or
(d) the court gives leave to admit the statement.

12.3.1 Section 114(1)(d): the inclusionary discretion

For the most part, these headings are fairly self-explanatory, and the circumstances within the Act under which hearsay can be admitted are considered in depth below.[33] However, as a start-

Figure 12.2 Hearsay under the Criminal Justice Act 2003

30 Ibid., at [4.60]–[4.62].

31 As was emphasised by the Court of Appeal in *R v Bhagchandka* [2016] EWCA Crim 700.

32 See *Emlyn Williams t/a Williams of Porthmadog v Vehicle and Operator Services Agency* (2008) 172 JP 328, where it was held that, for the purposes of subsection (1)(c), 'agreement' does not require a contract law analysis of offer and acceptance, nor does it require some formal recording of the position by the court, nor does it necessarily require express agreement. In *R v J (D.C.)* [2010] 2 Cr App R 2, it was held that even where hearsay could properly be put before the court by agreement, the court should be informed as to the nature of the agreement and how it was proposed to put the evidence before the jury. In *R v Bhagchandka* [2016] EWCA Crim 700, the Court of Appeal hinted that a failure to object to hearsay evidence being admitted is not the same thing as agreeing to it being admitted for the purpose of s 114(1)(c).

33 Note also that s 114(3) provides that out-of-court statements may still be excluded even if they fulfil the requirements of the 2003 Act. For example, confessions must meet the additional requirements of ss 76, 76A, and 78 of the *Police and Criminal Evidence Act 1984* (see Ch 8). If the out-of-court statement includes evidence of the bad character of a witness or defendant, the statement must also satisfy the requirements of ss 100 or 101 of the CJA 2003, and may be excluded under s 101(3) of the Act (see Ch 11).

ing point, it may be useful at this juncture to highlight the radical nature of circumstance (d). Effectively, this provision confers an inclusionary discretion on the court to admit *any* hearsay evidence, even if its admissibility is not expressly provided for elsewhere within the statute. However, before the court can grant leave to admit such a statement under section 114(1)(d), it must be satisfied that, despite the difficulties that there may be in challenging the statement, it would not be contrary to the interests of justice to admit the evidence. The intention is therefore that the court should be able to admit an out-of-court statement that does not fall within any of the other categories of admissibility, but only where such evidence is cogent and reliable. The discretion extends to multiple hearsay (where the statement passes through more than one person before it is recorded), as well as first-hand hearsay (where a statement is made by a person who directly perceived the facts of which the evidence is being given).

Section 114(2) sets out a number of factors that the court must consider when deciding whether to grant leave under the discretion in section 114(1)(d):

(a) how much probative value the statement has (assuming it to be true) in relation to a matter in issue in the proceedings, or how valuable it is for the understanding of other evidence in the case;
(b) what other evidence has been, or can be, given on the matter or evidence mentioned in paragraph (a);
(c) how important the matter or evidence mentioned in paragraph (a) is in the context of the case as a whole;
(d) the circumstances in which the statement was made;
(e) how reliable the maker of the statement appears to be;
(f) how reliable the evidence of the making of the statement appears to be;
(g) whether oral evidence of the matter stated can be given and, if not, why it cannot;
(h) the amount of difficulty involved in challenging the statement;
(i) the extent to which that difficulty would be likely to prejudice the party facing it.

This list is not intended to be exhaustive[34] but underlines the importance of the circumstances in which the statement was made. The key question for the judge will be whether these circumstances indicate that the statement ought to be treated as sufficiently reliable to enable it to be considered by the trier of fact, even if it will not be subject to cross-examination. In *R v Taylor*,[35] the Court of Appeal made clear that, in weighing up the above factors, a judge is not under an obligation to reach a specific conclusion on each one. They must simply bear them in mind in determining whether it would be in the interests of justice to admit the evidence. In *R v Fox*,[36] the Court of Appeal held that section 114(1)(d) of the CJA 2003 does not allow for the admission of anonymous hearsay evidence.[37]

The relationship between section 114(1)(d) and section 116 was considered by the Court of Appeal in *R v Z*,[38] in which the accused had been convicted of rape and a number of indecent assaults stretching back many years. The trial judge had admitted a written statement by one of the complainants who had been physically able – but reluctant – to testify in court that tended to implicate the defendant in a previous assault. Allowing the appeal, the Court of Appeal held that the statement had been wrongly admitted. This was important and potentially prejudicial evidence, and, in allowing the evidence under section 114(1)(d), the judge had effectively circumvented the restrictions contained in section 116. This was clearly undesirable since the application

34 *R v M* [2007] All ER (D) 21.
35 [2006] 2 Cr App R 14.
36 [2010] EWCA Crim 1280.
37 See also *R v Ford* [2011] Crim LR 475.
38 [2009] 1 Cr App R 34.

of the broad and somewhat elusive 'interests of justice' test could effectively mean that section 114(1)(d) could become a catch-all mechanism to circumvent the more restrictive conditions within section 116, thereby rendering it redundant over time. A warning of a similar nature was also issued by the Court of Appeal shortly afterwards in *R v C; R v T*.[39]

Yet the Court of Appeal in *R v Seton* was prepared to read the admissibility requirements of section 114(1)(d) in much more flexible terms.[40] The accused allegedly owed V around £24,000 for drugs, and was convicted of murdering him. There was considerable circumstantial evidence linking the defendant to the offence, but he maintained that another man, P, was responsible for the murder. P, who was in prison for a separate murder, refused to be interviewed, but was recorded making a number of phone calls to his family in which he denied any involvement in the murder of V. The recordings were admitted into evidence at the trial under section 114(1)(d), despite the fact that no attempt had been made to call P as a witness. The trial judge stated that it was evident that P would not testify, and that defence objections to the evidence could be taken into account by the jury in assessing the weight they ought to attach to the phone calls, but this should not preclude their admission into evidence. The Court of Appeal confirmed the conviction, noting that the judge had already found that P would not have been willing to testify and that, were he compelled to testify, there was no prospect of him giving any sensible evidence to the court. As such, the judge had given appropriate consideration to the factors in section 114(2), and the evidence was rightly admitted.

The case of *Seton* arguably set the admissibility bar too low, and it is submitted that the more restrictive approach of the Court of Appeal in Z and C is to be preferred.[41] This was also the view of the Court of Appeal in *R v ED*.[42] Here, the appellant had been convicted of a number of historical sexual offences of rape, attempted rape, and indecent assault. The offences were committed against family members, all of whom were under 16 years of age at the time. The statement of one witness (M), which incriminated the accused, had been admitted under section 114(1)(d) after she had failed to attend to give evidence, citing personal reasons. Given that none of the circumstances contained in section 116 applied, D appealed, contending that section 114(1)(d) had been unfairly used to circumvent the provisions of section 116. In particular, it was contended that the judge had failed to give appropriate weight to section 114(2)(g) (whether oral evidence of the matter stated can be given and, if not, why it cannot) in deciding to admit the evidence.

The Court of Appeal was keen to emphasise that section 114(1)(d) should not be used to circumvent the requirements of admissibility gateways higher up the section 114(1) hierarchy. In this particular case, the judge had been correct in determining that M's evidence had significant probative value relating to an issue of some importance to the trial, but had also made the mistake of assuming that M was unavailable through no fault of the prosecution. Although the defence were able to cross-examine the complainant, they were unable to directly challenge the maker of the statement about her evidence. As such, M's evidence should not have been admitted under section 114(1)(d).[43] Comparatively, in Hong Kong, the court in the case of *Kissel*[44] found that in most cases where special care is taken to counteract the effect of possibly prejudicial publicity, a properly directed jury can be trusted to deliver its verdict on a fair basis. A similar decision was reached by the High Court in Australia in *Dupas*.[45]

---

39 [2010] Crim LR 858.

40 [2010] EWCA Crim 450.

41 Although note that Seton appealed unsuccessfully to the ECtHR, which found that the defendant's right to a fair trial had not been infringed (*Seton v UK* [2016] ECHR 55287/10).

42 [2010] Crim LR 862.

43 However, the appeal itself was dismissed since the Court of Appeal found that the admission of the statement did not have such a prejudicial effect upon the nature and conduct of the defence that the safety of the jury's verdicts was affected.

44 *HKSAR v Kissel* (Stay: Media) [2011] 3 HKLRD 1, 10.

45 *Dupas v R* (2010) 241 CLR 237.

It is likely that the issue will surface again before the appellate courts in the not-too-distant future, and it may well be that a decision of the Supreme Court will be required in due course to clarify the precise nature of the relationship between the inclusionary discretion in section 114(1)(d) and the admissibility requirements of section 116.[46]

12.3.2 The exclusionary discretion

In addition to the new inclusionary discretion, it can be noted that the Act also provides for an exclusionary discretion. Thus, even if a hearsay statement is admissible under section 114, the court may then refuse to admit it under section 126, which allows trial judges to exclude out-of-court statements if the court is satisfied that the case for excluding it (taking into account the danger that it would cause an undue waste of time) substantially outweighs the case for admitting it (taking into account the value of the evidence).[47] This is a relatively broad discretion, with references to 'undue waste of time' and 'value of the evidence.'[48]

Furthermore, section 126(2) preserves both the existing common law power for the court to exclude evidence where its prejudicial effect outweighs its probative value, and the discretion contained in section 78 of the Police and Criminal Evidence Act (PACE) 1984 regarding the exclusion of evidence that would have such an adverse effect on the fairness of the trial that it ought not to be admitted. In *R v Cole and Keet*,[49] it was stated that this test would be unlikely to yield a different result from the test for inclusionary discretion contained in section 114(1)(d). While both section 126 of the 2003 Act and section 78 of PACE may be used to exclude improperly obtained evidence,[50] the 2003 Act clearly envisages that they may also be used to exclude hearsay evidence where it would result in unfairness to the accused. Roberts and Zuckerman observed, in relation to the changes that have been made to the admissibility of bad character evidence in the Criminal Justice Act 2003, a notable shift in focus from evidentiary exclusion to judicial directions as the principal institutional mechanism for neutralising potential prejudice.[51]

12.3.3 Implied assertions and direct evidence

Section 115 of the Act is concerned with the distinction between assertions and direct evidence, and seeks to resolve the difficulties created by certain common law decisions. There are two basic ways of proving a fact in issue. First, it may be proved by proving some other fact that renders it more likely to be true; the other fact is directly probative of the fact to be proved. Second, it may be proved by a person's assertion that it is true. The hearsay rule applies only to the latter form of proof.

An assertion can consist of words or conduct or both. Nonetheless, merely because a person's words or conduct are relied upon as evidence of a fact, it does not follow that they constitute an assertion of that fact. For example, a person's words may betray guilty knowledge without amounting to a confession of that person's guilt. Often, it will be apparent when a person's words or conduct are adduced as proof of a fact on the basis that they are directly probative of it; as illustrated below, this will not always be clear to the court. In *Wright v Doe d Tatham*,[52] the issue was whether letters in which the writers appeared to assume the sanity of their intended recipient

---

46 See the Court of Appeal's discussion in *R v Sliogeris* [2015] EWCA Crim 22.

47 For discussions of the use of section 126, see *R v Drinkwater* [2016] 4 WLR 42 and David Ormerod's commentary in Crim LR (2016) 9, 647–49. See also *R v Hengari-Ajufo* [2016] All ER (D) 47.

48 *R v C and K* [2006] Crim LR 637.

49 [2008] 1 Cr App R 5.

50 See Ch 9.

51 Roberts, P. and Zuckerman, A., *Criminal Evidence*, 2nd edn (Oxford University Press, 2010) 662–63.

52 (1837) 7 Ad & E 313.

could be admitted as evidence of his sanity. It was held that the letters were hearsay since they were not directly probative of the facts to be proved but only an assertion of it. The decision was explained by the example of a sea captain who boards his ship and sets sail, from which a court might be tempted to infer that the ship was seaworthy. It was said that the hearsay rule would apply to such conduct, and evidence of it would be inadmissible.

In *R v Harry*,[53] the accused and his flatmate P were charged with possession of a controlled drug with intent to supply. The accused's defence was that P was the sole supplier. He sought to prove this by calling police officers to give evidence that, while they were at the flat after arresting Harry and P, the police officers had answered a number of telephone calls from persons who could not be traced, but who had asked for P and enquired whether P had drugs for sale. The trial judge refused to allow evidence of the content of the calls to go before the jury because it was hearsay, on the ground that the callers impliedly alleged P to be the supplier. Harry was convicted and P acquitted. The Court of Appeal upheld the judge's ruling, while recognising that Harry felt a justifiable grievance.

That decision was approved of by a bare majority of the House of Lords in *R v Kearley*.[54] The issue here was whether, on a charge of possessing drugs with intent to supply, a prosecutor could rely on evidence by the police that, on a search of D's property, they had taken a number of telephone calls (and received seven callers at the door) asking for the defendant and asking whether he had any drugs for sale. A majority held that the hearsay rule applied where it was sought to draw an inference of a fact from words or conduct that were intended to be assertive of some other fact, or not intended to be assertive at all. As evidence of the fact that the defendant dealt in drugs, the callers' words were hearsay; being unable to find any applicable exception to the rule, the majority of the House held them inadmissible.

Lord Browne-Wilkinson and Lord Griffiths dissented on the basis that while a single call asking for P and requesting drugs would be of little probative value and would cause great prejudice to P's case if the jury were to draw the wrong inference, they saw no reason why the evidence of multiple calls should not be admitted. Lord Browne-Wilkinson thought that *Harry* had been wrongly decided; the words 'Can I have some drugs?' were not, in his view, a statement making an assertion, but a fact, and therefore a form of direct evidence. In both cases, the property in question was being used to supply drugs, and the only issue was the identity of the supplier. Since the words of the callers were clearly directed at P, they constituted direct evidence that P was supplying drugs. Lord Browne-Wilkinson thought that the inference to be drawn by the jury was not from the *words* used by the callers, but from the *fact* that there were callers who were seeking to acquire drugs.

Evidence of the kind that was excluded in *Wright* and *Kearley* was commonly referred to as an 'implied assertion,' and came to vex both criminal lawyers and academics alike for some time. Section 115(3) seeks to resolve these difficulties by giving effect to the Law Commission's recommendation that a person's words or conduct should not be caught by the hearsay rule unless the purpose, or one of the purposes, of that person appears to cause the hearer to believe that the matter stated is true, or to act on the basis that it is true. Thus, the evidence of police officers in *Kearley* that they received 17 calls from persons asking for drugs would not be a matter to which the 2003 Act applies unless it could be shown that the purpose, or one of the purposes, of the callers was to cause the police officers to believe that the accused was a drug dealer. Indeed, this was the focus of the case of *R v Billy Nathan Midmore*.[55] In that case, the defendant had thrown sulphuric acid into the face of the victim. The trial judge admitted into evidence a text message sent by the

53 (1986) 86 Cr App R 105.

54 1992] 2 AC 228.

55 [2017] EWCA Crim 533.

defendant which contained a photograph of the acid alongside the caption 'this is the one face melter.' The defendant appealed alleging that the text message amounted to hearsay and ought to have been excluded. The Court of Appeal concluded that the text message did satisfy the definition of a 'statement' in section 115(2) but did not satisfy the requirement in section 115(3) in that there was nothing within the text message to make the recipient believe that the acid was actually designed or intended to be used to melt a face.[56]

Section 115 thus appears to constitute a statutory reversal of *Kearley*, and R v Singh[57] and R v N,[58] both reported in 2006, seemed to confirm that this was also the view of the Court of Appeal. However, the case of *Leonard*[59] cast doubt on whether this was so. Here, the prosecution were permitted to introduce two text messages sent to the accused, which complained about either the quantity or quality of drugs that he had supplied. In the view of the Court of Appeal, these text messages should never have been introduced since they were hearsay rather than implied assertions. Four reasons were cited: the texts were not made in oral evidence; they were statements of fact or opinion within the meaning of section 115(2); the reason for the statements being adduced in evidence was to establish as facts the matters stated in the texts in order to invite the jury to infer that the defendant had supplied drugs to the senders of the texts; and, finally, the purpose of each message was to make the receiver believe the matter stated, as required by section 115(3). This decision was somewhat odd in that it appears to assume that the prosecution was attempting to prove the particular contents of the text messages (i.e. the matters stated relating to quality and the quantity of the drugs supplied) rather than the inference that could be drawn from the receipt of the text messages (namely, that the defendant was in the business of supplying drugs). The Court of Appeal in *Bains*[60] adopted similar reasoning, thus creating a new grey area as to what precisely constituted a 'matter stated' for the purposes of section 115.

Aware of the potential of such issues to muddy the waters of an already complex area of law, the Court of Appeal sought to clarify matters in *R v Twist*[61] Four cases were joined for consideration by the Court of Appeal, and all concerned the admissibility of text messages found on the appellants' mobile phones. Here, the Court of Appeal upheld the decision of the trial judge that these messages did not constitute hearsay since they did not contain any direct statement that the defendant was involved in the supply of drugs. While it might be reasonable from the content of the messages to imply that he was a dealer, the application of section 115(3) meant that such implied assertions now fell outside the scope of the rule.

In a rigorous review of the authorities, Hughes LJ noted that references to 'implied assertions' are no longer helpful since the legislation had clearly reversed the effect of the decision in *Kearley*. Indeed, the principal underlying reason why hearsay evidence is admissible only in limited circumstances lies in the danger of concoction and the difficulty of testing or contradicting it when the speaker is not in court to be examined upon it. Citing the Law Commission,[62] his Lordship highlighted that no such danger arose where the person from whose conduct a fact is to be inferred can safely be assumed to have believed that fact to be true. In determining whether the hearsay rules will bite in future cases, a three-stage approach was suggested:

1 Identify what relevant fact (matter) it is sought to prove.

---

56 See also *R v Lam Hai Vo* [2013] EWCA Crim 2292 on the status of a text message as hearsay.

57 [2006] 1 WLR 1564.

58 [2006] EWCA Crim 3309.

59 [2009] Crim LR 802.

60 [2010] EWCA Crim 873.

61 [2011] 2 Cr App R 17.

62 See n. 27 above.

2 Ask whether there is a statement of *that matter* in the communication. If not, then no question of hearsay arises (whatever other matters may be contained in the communication).
3 If there is, ask whether it was one of the purposes (not necessarily the only or dominant purpose) of the maker of the communication that the recipient, or any other person, should believe *that matter* or act upon it as true. If yes, it is hearsay. If no, it is not.

While *Twist* certainly provides considerable clarity on the long-standing problem of implied assertions, the possibility that the issue might again raise its head before the Court of Appeal cannot be discounted. It may be that the responsibility for putting the matter to rest will eventually fall to the Supreme Court.

12.3.3.1 Machine-generated statements

Section 115(3)(b) of the 2003 Act preserves the common law position whereby statements that are not based on human input fall outside the ambit of the hearsay rule. Provided that the machine computes the information automatically and without human input, it will not be considered hearsay, but will qualify as direct evidence. The hearsay rule does not therefore apply to tapes, films, or photographs that record disputed incidents actually taking place, or to documents produced by a machine that automatically recorded an event or circumstances. Thus, surveillance cameras in stores or streets,[63] as well as devices used to analyse specimens of breath or blood,[64] are seen as direct evidence and not hearsay. In *Spiby*,[65] an automatic computer log of telephone calls made from a hotel bedroom was viewed as real evidence, as was a computer log of mobile phone calls in *R v Robson, Mitchell and Richards*.[66]

By contrast, in *R v Wood*,[67] the prosecution sought to prove, by adducing evidence of tests, that metal found in the possession of the accused was of the same type as a stolen consignment. The results of these tests had been produced by a computer, but the information had been fed into the computer by chemists. This scenario was therefore distinct from the cases discussed above, since the computer analysis had been dependent upon human input. In this particular case, it was admissible only because the chemists themselves were able to give oral evidence of the results.[68]

However, had they been unable to do so, the computer analysis would have been excluded under the hearsay rule. Thus, to qualify as real evidence, the computer must merely be used as a calculator or collator of information.[69]

12.3.3.2 Photofit identification

Witnesses to a crime are often asked to provide a description of the criminal. This used to be done by a sketch artist, who drew a likeness of the person based on the description given. In modern times, computer-generated images have largely replaced the artist, but the process and

63 See e.g. *Taylor v Chief Constable of Cheshire* [1987] 1 All ER 225; *Attorney General's Reference (No. 2 of 2002)* [2003] Crim LR 192.

64 *Castle v Cross* [1984] 1 WLR 1372.

65 *R v Spiby* (1990) 91 Cr App R 186.

66 [1991] Crim LR 362.

67 (1982) 76 Cr App R 23.

68 In this respect, it is also worth noting that s 129 is relevant. It provides that where a statement generated by a machine is based on information relayed to the machine by a human, the output of the device will be admissible only where it is proved that the information was accurate. Section 129(2) preserves the common law presumption that a mechanical device has been properly set or calibrated. See further Pattenden, R., 'Machinespeak: Section 129 of the Criminal Justice Act 2003' [2010] Crim LR 623.

69 See also *R (O) v Coventry Magistrates Court* (2003), *The Times* (22 April 2003), in which the Queen's Bench Divisional Court held that a computer printout recording successful and unsuccessful attempts to enter a website was admissible as real evidence, applying *Spiby* and the above line of cases. The case involved attempts to download child pornography from an American company. The printout in question was obtained from the database of the company running the website, and contained a breakdown of the defendant's successful and unsuccessful attempts to access the website, and charges made to his credit card.

underlying principles remain the same. Typically, the witness describes the person's features, and the computer operator then selects the facial characteristics most closely fitting the description. At common law, sketches and photofits were held to fall outside the scope of the hearsay rule, since they had effectively been made by the witness, who merely directed the hand of the artist or the person compiling the photofit.[70]

A literal reading of section 115(2) appears to contradict the idea that such evidence is direct evidence, in defining a statement as inclusive of 'a representation made in a sketch, photofit or other pictorial form.' Since sketches, photofits, and computer-generated images are all intended to cause another person to believe that they accurately depict the characteristics of the suspect, it appears to fall within section 115(3), and the hearsay rule will thus apply. Moreover, such evidence is not covered by any of the common law exceptions preserved by section 118, and since section 118(2) abolishes all other common law rules governing the admissibility of hearsay evidence, it would appear that photofits and sketches are now to be considered as hearsay for the purposes of the 2003 Act.

However, it may be recalled from the discussion in Chapter 6 that section 120 of the Act will provide an alternative avenue under which such evidence may be admitted. It provides that a previous statement of a witness may be admissible under certain conditions. Section 120(4) provides as follows:

> A previous statement by the witness is admissible as evidence of any matter stated of which oral evidence by him would be admissible, if
>
> (c) any of the following three conditions is satisfied, and
> (d) while giving evidence the witness indicates that to the best of his belief he made the statement, and that to the best of his belief it states the truth.

The first condition, as laid down in section 120(5), is that the statement identifies a person, an object, or a place. The photofit statement (and section 115(2) makes it clear that it is a statement) identifying the person seen by the witness is a previous statement made by the witness that satisfies the terms of section 120(4) and meets this condition in section 120(5). Subject to the specific facts in each case, a photofit or computer-generated image is also capable of meeting the other two conditions referred to in section 120(4). The second condition, contained in section 120(6), is that the statement was made by the witness when the matters stated were fresh in their memory, but they do not remember them, and cannot reasonably be expected to remember them, well enough to give oral evidence in the proceedings. The third condition, in section 120(7), lays down a number of separate stipulations that must be satisfied before the evidence is admitted.[71] Although at common law such evidence could be admitted only as evidence of consistency, it is now admissible as evidence of the truth of the matters stated pursuant to section 120. This provision is dealt with in detail in Chapter 6,[72] and will therefore not be subject to any further discussion here.

---

70 See further *Smith (Percy)* [1976] Crim LR 511; *Okorodu* [1982] Crim LR 747; *Cook* [1987] QB 417.

71 These are: (a) that the witness claims to be a person against whom an offence has been committed; (b) the offence is one to which the proceedings relate; (c) the statement consists of a complaint made by the witness; (d) [repealed] … (e) the complaint was not made as a result of a threat or a promise; and (f) before the statement is adduced, the witness gives oral evidence in connection with its subject matter.

72 See Ch 6.

12.3.4 Section 116: where the witness is unavailable

Section 116 of the 2003 Act replaced sections 23–26 of the CJA 1988, and is primarily concerned with statements made by persons who would have been witnesses in criminal cases, but are unable to attend court. The provisions apply to any first-hand hearsay statement, in either oral or documentary form. By contrast, section 117, considered below, is concerned with statements made by persons in the course of a trade or business, and concerns only written statements. Thus, where a statement in a document is involved, the statement may be admissible under both sections 116 and 117. However, where the statement was prepared for the purposes of criminal proceedings (usually a witness statement), there will seldom be any advantage in arguing for admission under section 117. Where the statement was made orally, it may be admitted only under section 116 or one of the exceptions preserved by section 118 (see below). In practice, circumstances will dictate which head of admissibility can be best argued.

A statement made out of court may be admissible under section 116(2) (subject to the additional conditions to be considered below) if the person who made the statement: (a) is dead; (b) is physically or mentally ill; (c) is outside the United Kingdom; (d) cannot be found despite taking reasonably practicable steps; (e) does not give oral evidence through fear. Each of these heads of admissibility will be examined below. However, before proceeding, it is important to note that two further conditions must be satisfied before evidence can be admitted in any of these circumstances.

Section 116(1)(a) requires that oral evidence given in the proceedings by the person who made the statement would be admissible as evidence of that matter. It follows that, before admitting any hearsay statement under this section, the court must ask whether the original maker of the statement would have been able to give oral evidence if they had been available to do so. There are three main reasons why such oral evidence might not be admissible. First, like all forms of evidence, the matter contained in the statement may not be relevant to any issue in the case. Second, the person who made the statement may not have been a competent witness, by reason of age or cognitive capability.[73] Third, the matters stated may be excluded by an exclusionary evidential rule. They may, for example, contain evidence of bad character, or the matters themselves may constitute hearsay. While first-hand hearsay is admissible under section 116, multiple hearsay is not.[74]

Example 12.4

On answering her front door one December evening, Doris is stabbed and knocked to the ground by an intruder. She staggers to her neighbour, Bill, to tell him that Ivanna stabbed her. Shortly afterwards, Doris dies from her wound. Although Doris will be unavailable to testify at Ivanna's trial, section 116 will enable Bill to give evidence of what she told him concerning the identity of her attacker.[75] However, if Bill is also unavailable, the cumulative use of the hearsay statement will not permit Bill's statement to be admitted to the court by anyone else under section 116.

---

73 It will be recalled that s 53 of the Youth Justice and Criminal Evidence Act 1999 states that a person is not competent to give evidence in criminal proceedings if it appears to the court that he is not a person who is able to understand questions put to him as a witness and give answers to them that can be understood. This position is confirmed by s 123 of the CJA 2003.

74 See further below.

75 The section provides a replacement for the provision in s 28(2) of and Sch 2 to the CJA 1988.

The second condition under section 116(1)(b) requires that the person who made the statement is identified to the satisfaction of the court. This will enable the opposing party to challenge the absent witness's credibility under section 124, which allows the opposing party to put before the jury any evidence relevant to the credibility of that witness that counsel could have used as part of any cross-examination had the witness testified in person.[76]

Provided that these two conditions in section 116(1) are met, the party adducing the hearsay evidence must then show the court that one of the circumstances within section 116(2) is satisfied.

12.3.4.1 Where the relevant person is dead

Section 116(2)(a) stipulates that a hearsay statement may be admitted if the relevant person is dead. This head is largely self-explanatory, although it should be noted that evidence of a dying declaration may be admitted under this head.[77] A death certificate will generally be necessary as proof.

12.3.4.2 Relevant person is physically or mentally ill

Section 116(2)(b) applies where the relevant person is unfit to be a witness because of their physical or mental condition. Medical evidence will be necessary to prove the unfitness to attend by reason of physical or mental condition, and this may also be in documentary form if such evidence is uncontested. However, in *R v Elliott and Others*,[78] in which the prosecution sought to rely on a written statement rather than his oral testimony on the ground that the witness was unfit through illness, it was held that the defence should ordinarily be given an opportunity to cross-examine the relevant doctor who was providing support for the application. In a disputed case, it would not be sufficient for the prosecution merely to provide a written statement recording the doctor's views.

A physical disability will not affect the competence of the witness, but a mental condition may do so, depending on its severity and whether that condition was present before the statement was made. In *R v Setz-Dempsey*,[79] an important identification witness was mentally unfit to give evidence at the time of trial and his written statement was admitted under section 23 of the CJA 1988. Allowing the appeal, the Court of Appeal held that the trial judge should not have admitted the written statement. He had failed to take into account the effect of medical evidence about the witness's state of mind on the quality of the identification evidence and the unfairness to the defendant in being unable to cross-examine the witness. This suggests that the witness was mentally incapable when the identification and subsequent statements were made. If so, the witness was not competent to give evidence and would not have satisfied the requirements of section 23, and neither would they now satisfy the condition in section 116(2)(b).

12.3.4.3 Relevant person is outside the United Kingdom

Section 116(2)(c) deals with the scenario in which the relevant person is outside the United Kingdom and it is not reasonably practicable to secure their attendance. It is worded in almost exactly the same terms as the previous provision under the 1988 Act.[80] These provisions were considered in *R v Case*.[81] Here, the defendant was charged with theft, having allegedly taken a

---

76 One presumes that the absent witness will be protected against the admission of bad character evidence to the same extent as a witness who gives oral evidence in person. See further the discussion in Ch 11, dealing with a non-defendant's bad character.

77 Note that a death certificate itself is admissible as a public document (a common law exception to the hearsay rule preserved by s 118(1)(b)).

78 *The Times* (15 May 2003).

79 (1994) 98 Cr App R 23.

80 See CJA 1988, s 23(1)(b)(i)–(ii).

81 [1991] Crim LR 192.

purse from S's handbag. S was a Portuguese tourist, holidaying at the time with her friend, G. The defendant's defence was that S and G were either mistaken or lying, and that he was put under pressure to admit the offence while in custody to secure the release of his companion. The prosecution sought leave to admit in evidence the statements of the two tourists. G had given a Portuguese address, but she had made no mention of where she normally lived, nor of the length of time she had been in Britain or how long she intended to stay. S's statement was similarly vague, and she made it clear that she was living temporarily in a hotel. That was the only evidence that the witnesses were outside the United Kingdom, and there was no evidence that any attempt had been made to find out if either was willing to attend court. The trial judge inferred from the statements that they would be unwilling to attend and that it would not be reasonably practicable to secure their attendance given the expense involved. He therefore admitted the statements, and the defendant was convicted.

However, in quashing his conviction, the Court of Appeal found that there was no evidence before the court that the witnesses were outside the country. Even if it had been permissible to look at the contents of the statements, in the circumstances of this case there was still insufficient evidence. While the word 'reasonably' implied that financial implications could be considered, there was no evidence whatsoever as to whether it was practicable for them to attend court on the day. Given that the criminal standard of proof had to be satisfied, there was no evidence upon which the trial judge could have been satisfied that the conditions had been made out. This amounted to a material irregularity, requiring the quashing of the conviction.[82]

It should normally be possible for a party to prove the existence of a condition under section 116(2) by another document admissible under sections 116 or 117. In *R v Castillo*,[83] the Court of Appeal, applying the 1988 Act, held that it was permissible to prove that a witness was unable to attend by using a statement of another person admitted under section 23 of the Act. That case involved the importation of cocaine from Venezuela and the prosecution sought to admit the statement of M, an airline official, about tickets from a destination in Venezuela that had been issued to Castillo. At the *voir dire*, evidence was given about enquiries made of one Tyler, the drugs liaison officer in Venezuela, as to the ability of M to attend. The judge ruled that it was not reasonably practicable for Tyler to attend and admitted his statement under section 23(2)(b). He also ruled that, having admitted Tyler's statement, it revealed that attendance was not practicable, so that M's statement was also admissible.

It was argued on appeal that it was not open to the trial judge to apply section 23 twice: first, as to the statement of M; and second, as to the statement of Tyler. Section 23, it was argued, applied to first-hand hearsay, and this was, in fact, multiple hearsay. This argument was rejected. In the view of the court, there was no reason why the inability of M to attend should not be proved by the statement of Tyler, whose own inability to attend had already been proved and whose statement had been admitted in evidence under section 23(2)(b). The court also pointed out that although it might well be possible for a witness to attend, that did not necessarily mean that it was 'reasonably practicable' to do so. In order to determine this question, the court had to consider a number of facts. First, it had to question the importance of the evidence the witness could give and whether or not it was prejudicial, and how prejudicial, to the accused if he did not attend. In this case, the evidence of Tyler was concerned only with what M had told him, and it was M's evidence with which the court was concerned. Second, there were considerations of expense and inconvenience in securing attendance. That should not be a major consideration, but in this case it would be a matter of considerable expense for Tyler to travel from Venezuela simply to give

82 Even if the lesser burden of proof is applied to s 116, it is suggested that there would still be insufficient evidence to satisfy the trial judge that the condition had been satisfied.

83 [1996] Crim LR 193.

evidence that could not seriously be challenged in cross-examination. Third, the judge had to consider reasons put forward as to why it was not reasonably practicable for the witness to attend. Those were findings of fact with which their Lordships would not lightly interfere, and they had not been persuaded in this case that the judge's ruling was wrong. It is likely that the courts would take a similar approach if the above facts were to reoccur under the 2003 Act.

It should, therefore, be underlined that what is deemed to be 'reasonably practical' does not necessarily equate to what is physically possible. In *R v Maloney*,[84] the trial judge admitted the written statements of two Greek cadets after hearing that they were either at sea or on leave in Cyprus. The Court of Appeal held that there was evidence from which the judge could find that it was not reasonably practicable to secure their attendance. While the term 'practicable' must be construed in the light of the normal steps that would be taken to arrange the attendance of a witness at trial, the phrase 'reasonably practicable' involved a further qualification of the duty, to secure attendance by taking the reasonable steps that a party would normally take to secure a witness's attendance having regard to the means and resources available to the parties.

This was obviously a consideration of the court in *R v Jiminez-Paez*.[85] Here, the appellant was arrested at Heathrow en route from Colombia to Italy. Customs officers found cocaine with a street value of £50,000 secreted on her person. At trial, the accused claimed that she had thought she was smuggling emeralds, which she had illegally exported from Colombia before. To this end, she sought to introduce in evidence a letter from a Colombian Embassy official, which stated that there was a black market in emeralds in Colombia and that they were frequently illegally exported, and one method of concealment was the type used in the appellant's case.

For its part, the defence sought to rely on a provision similar to section 116(2)(c), arguing that the consular official, who had diplomatic immunity and was therefore immune from process, was effectively outside the United Kingdom, despite the fact that the defendant was physically present but unwilling to give evidence. Not surprisingly, the trial judge rejected the argument and excluded the letter as hearsay. The Court of Appeal held that he was right to do so. The defence contention would not give effect to the two distinct requirements that the person was outside the United Kingdom and that it was not reasonably practicable to secure his attendance. Had the letter been sent from an official in Colombia itself (rather than from an embassy), it would have satisfied the subsection and would thus be admissible under section 116(2)(c).

12.3.4.4 Relevant person cannot be found

Under section 116(2)(d), a statement may be admissible where the relevant person cannot be found although such steps as it is reasonably practicable to take have been taken. The above discussion of 'reasonably practicable' applies with equal measure to this provision. It is not uncommon for witnesses to leave the area without informing the police or lawyers in order to avoid having to give evidence, and, on occasions, a witness will be kept out of the way by persons acting for the defendant. The question of what steps are reasonably practicable to take to find such witnesses will depend on the individual circumstances of each case, and it will be for the party seeking to have the statement admitted to satisfy the court that they have taken all such steps as are reasonable in the particular circumstances.[86]

Thus, in *R v Adams*,[87] it was held that it was not sufficient to leave contacting a witness (who had been informed of the fixed date of trial four months earlier) to ensure his attendance at court on the fixed day until the last working day before that day, nor was it sufficient simply to leave a

84 [1994] Crim LR 525.

85 [1993] Crim LR 596.

86 See *Price v UK* [2016] ECHR 15602/07 at 12.5.

87 [2008] 1 Cr App R 35.

voicemail message when he did not answer his mobile telephone. Those responsible for getting witnesses to court should take account of the fact that it is notorious that witnesses are not invariably organised people with settled addresses who respond promptly to correspondence and messages; that often they do not want to come to court; that, even if they are willing, they may not accord the commitment the priority it warrants; but that even if they do, 'it is only too foreseeable' that something (holidays, work, illness being routine examples) may intervene to push the matter out of their minds or to cause a clash of commitments.

12.3.4.5 Relevant person is in fear

Section 116(2)(e) may apply where a person is reluctant to give oral evidence through fear.[88] For the purposes of this provision, 'fear' is to be widely construed and (for example) includes fear of the death or injury of another person or of financial loss,[89] although the court may only give leave to admit evidence under this head if it considers that the statement ought to be admitted in the interests of justice, having regard to a range of factors set out in section 116(4).[90] The provision replaces section 23 of the CJA 1988, which gave the trial judge discretion to allow a written statement to be used where a witness would 'not give oral evidence through fear.' Use of the section was, however, confined to written statements on which the prosecution sought to rely. Moreover, such statements had to be made to the police or other investigatory authority. The new provision under section 116(2)(e) is broader, insofar as it applies to both written or oral statements, and is available to defence and prosecution witnesses.

The case law stemming from the old law, section 23 of the CJA 1988, continues to guide the courts in their application of the current provisions. For example, in *R v Acton Justices, ex p McMullen*,[91] the Divisional Court rejected the argument that the witness's fear had to be based on reasonable grounds. Dismissing the appeal, the court stated that it was

> not helpful in the context to speak of the objective or subjective approach. It would be sufficient that the court, on the evidence, was sure that the witness was in fear, as a consequence of the material offence or of something said or done subsequently in relation to it and the possibility of the witness testifying as to it.[92]

Like its predecessor, section 116(2)(e) thus requires a causal connection between the fear of the witness and the prospect of giving evidence.[93] However, the fact that the average witness would not be in fear or that the fear of the witness in question is wholly unreasonable is irrelevant. The fact that the witness is timid or vulnerable because of age or another factor is relevant, but the test can still not be said to be subjective in nature. It is simply that it is easier to prove that such witnesses are in fear as a result of the crime or the possibility of testifying as to it. It should nonetheless be underlined that the provision is not limited to protecting those witnesses traditionally viewed as being at heightened risk of reprisals, such as those testifying in cases involving terrorism or organised crime. It is perfectly conceivable that the measure could also protect the young,

88 See *R v Harvey and Others* [2014] EWCA Crim 54.

89 Whether financial loss would have sufficed for the purposes of the 1988 Act was never raised, but one can readily see that the threat to fire bomb a witness's business or home could be as effective as, if not more effective than, a threat to their person. Precisely how much financial or proprietary loss will be sufficient to satisfy s 116(2)(e) and justify the admission of a hearsay statement remains to be seen.

90 See discussion below.

91 (1991) 92 Cr App R 98.

92 Ibid., at 105.

93 See also *Neill v North Antrim Magistrates' Court* (1993) 97 Cr App R 121.

the elderly, or the infirm who have been psychologically damaged by the crime and are fearful of giving evidence in open court in front of their assailants.

The wording of section 23(3) of the 1988 Act, 'does not give evidence through fear,' raised the question of whether the provision would apply where a witness came to court, took the oath, and started to give evidence, but refused to continue, or simply took the oath and then declined to give any evidence at all. It was argued in *ex p McMullen* that the wording of the subsection meant that it did not apply when a witness who had started to give evidence stopped through fear. As soon as the witness uttered one word of testimony, the section ceased to apply. The court, however, rejected this argument, holding that the better interpretation of the section was that the witness 'should not have given evidence of any significant relevance to the case.' The wording of section 116(2)(e), 'does not give (or does not continue to give) oral evidence,' ensures that the wide interpretation placed on the wording of the old statute continues to apply.

A further issue that vexed the courts was how, precisely, the extent of the fear was to be ascertained. Few, if any, witnesses are likely to relish the prospect of giving evidence under adversarial circumstances.[94] Therefore, the vast majority, to some extent, are likely to be fearful about testifying. Clearly, the legislation was not designed to cover all witnesses: something over and above the baseline apprehension that affects most witnesses is clearly required. The most straightforward manner in which the judge can assess the degree of fear is through questioning the witness in person, while observing their demeanour. In *R v Ashford and Tenterden Justices, ex p Hilden*,[95] the accused was committed for trial on a charge of causing grievous bodily harm to his girlfriend, after the magistrates allowed a written statement of the girlfriend to be admitted under section 23 of the 1988 Act. The defendant's girlfriend had managed to get as far as taking the oath, but then simply said she could not remember anything or had no comment to make when questioned. The prosecution thus applied to the magistrate to have the statement admitted under section 23, since the witness was clearly in fear. The magistrate noted that it was obvious from the girl's conduct in the witness box that she was in a genuine state of fear, and accordingly admitted the statement. The Divisional Court refused D's application for judicial review on the basis that the magistrate had satisfied herself from the demeanour of the witness and her responses that the witness was refusing to give evidence through fear.

Similarly, in *R v Greer*,[96] there had been a serious assault by three men on C and G, both employees in a kebab shop. The sole issue in the case was identification. The Crown sought leave to admit statements of three witnesses, C, D, and G, under section 23 of the 1988 Act on the basis that they were afraid to give live evidence. The recorder dismissed the application in respect of D since he had no opportunity to assess his state of mind. However, since C and G were both present in court and explained, without being sworn, why they could not give evidence, their statements under section 23 were admitted. On appeal, it was argued that since C and G had been able to come to court to explain their fear to the judge, section 23 should not apply. Dismissing this contention, the Court of Appeal held there was no reason, either as a matter of practice or on the wording of the statute, why the recorder should not hear from the persons concerned of their actual fear. C and G were not giving evidence as they had not been sworn as witnesses; they had come to court to explain to the judge why they were reluctant to do so. Indeed, this was a helpful and sensible course of action since it allowed the court to determine the matter before the time came for the witnesses to give evidence.

94 See further Ch 5.

95 (1993) 96 Crim App R 92.

96 [1998] Crim LR 572.

However, where a witness is unable or unwilling to personally satisfy the judge of his or her state of mind, major difficulties may arise. In *Neill v North Antrim Magistrates' Court*,[97] police officers recounted what the two witnesses, who did not give evidence through fear, had told their mother. This was clearly hearsay, being a third-hand account of the witnesses' apprehension. Since there was no other evidence given of their fear, the House of Lords held that the statements should not have been admitted. However, Lord Mustill, delivering a speech with which all of their Lordships agreed, pointed out that the police officers could have given evidence of what the witnesses had said about their fear, since it had been long established that a declaration as to a contemporaneous state of mind constitutes an exception to the hearsay rule. It was emphasised that the evidence must *not* be that the witnesses were afraid (that is an inference for the court to draw), but that the witnesses *said* they were afraid and that their demeanour was consistent with what they had said.

Once the court has established that the witness is genuinely in a state of fear, it must then determine whether the statement ought to be admitted in the interests of justice. Under section 116(4), the court should take a range of factors into account in making this assessment:

(a) the statement's contents;
(b) any risk that its admission or exclusion would result in unfairness to any party to the proceedings (and in particular to how difficult it will be to challenge the statement if the relevant person does not give oral evidence);
(c) whether, in appropriate cases, a special measures direction could be made under section 19 of the Youth Justice and Criminal Evidence Act 1999; and
(d) any other relevant circumstances.

It will be noted that section 116(4) applies only to section 116(2)(e), the statement of a fearful witness: this test is not applied to any of the other heads under section 116. It is particularly noteworthy that section 116(4)(b) refers to any risk that the admission or exclusion of the statement will result in unfairness to *any* party to the proceedings; this is a clear departure from the criteria contained in the CJA 1988, which referred only to any unfairness to the defendant.

In the leading case under the 1988 Act, *R v Cole*,[98] the defendant was convicted of an assault on a security guard. The prosecution applied for the statement of a deceased witness to be admitted under section 23. The defence, who disputed the circumstances of the assault as described in the witness's statement, resisted the application. The trial judge ruled that, in relation to section 26(b)(ii), which referred to the possibility of 'controverting' the statement, the defendant might, if he chose, controvert the statement by his own evidence or that of other witnesses.[99] On appeal, it was contended that the trial judge had erred on this point, since this effectively placed an improper pressure on the defence to call witnesses. The trial judge, it was argued, should have had particular regard to the words 'any risk' of unfairness arising, particularly given the importance of that specific statement to the outcome of the proceedings.

Dismissing the appeal, the Court of Appeal noted that the court was not required to disregard the likelihood of the possibility of controverting the statement by the evidence of the accused or of witnesses called on his behalf. The overall purpose of the statutory provisions was to widen the power of the court to admit documentary hearsay evidence, while ensuring that the accused received a fair trial. In determining the issue of fairness, a balance had to be struck between the interests of the public in enabling the prosecution case to be properly presented and the interests of a particular defendant in not being put in a disadvantageous position. The matters to which the court must have regard included any risk of unfairness, having regard to the possibility of

97 (1993) 97 Cr App R 121.
98 [1990] 1 WLR 866.
99 'To controvert' simply means 'to challenge.' Thus, s 116(4)(b) of the 2003 Act refers to inability to 'challenge' the statement.

controverting the statement. However, there was no reason to imply any such restriction upon the plain meaning of the words as counsel for the appellant had suggested. If Parliament had intended the question to be considered on such a narrow basis, express words would have been used to that effect.

This position seems to have prevailed under the 2003 Act; the courts will generally seek to achieve a balance between the contents of the statement and the risk of unfairness to any party from any inability to cross-examine. To this end, the quality of the evidence in the statement will be the crucial factor: the higher the quality, the more probative the statement is likely to be to the issues in the case, and the interests of justice would therefore be more likely to demand that such evidence be admitted. It will be noted that, in *Cole*, the Court of Appeal approved the warning given to the jury by the trial judge that the hearsay statement had not been subjected to cross-examination. This was seen as a counterbalance to any possible unfairness, and such a warning became normal practice in all cases in which such a statement was admitted. This is now seen as a standard requirement, and continues to apply where statements are admitted under section 116 of the 2003 Act. Ashworth and Redmayne describe this 'balancing exercise' as a rhetorical device of which society should be wary, considering how particular values and interests are being observed in the criminal law.[100]

The leading case under the current legislation is *R v Shabir*,[101] which provides an effective summary of the principles discussed above and confirms that – while many of them developed under the old law – they continue to govern the operation of the current provisions. The accused was convicted of a number of offences, including attempted murder, various firearms offences, and assault. A key part of the prosecution case was evidence from a CCTV recording, which showed the appellant threatening a man who was chased in a car and shot at later that evening. The prosecution also sought to rely on a number of statements the victim had given to the police, along with his testimony at an earlier trial that had collapsed. At the second trial, the victim (who was in prison at the time) refused to testify on the basis that he was afraid of the accused and that he had been attacked three times in prison in connection with his impending evidence at the second trial. His original statements to the police along with his testimony at the earlier trial were then admitted as hearsay evidence pursuant to section 116(2)(e).

Allowing the appeal, the Court of Appeal held that the judge's finding that the witness would not give evidence 'through fear' was itself based largely on hearsay evidence of transcripts of an earlier trial and accounts by others of the witness's state of mind. The court concluded that the judge must be satisfied, to the criminal standard:

(i) That there is a causative link between the fear and the failure or refusal to give evidence;
(ii) That every effort must be made to get the witness to court to test the issue as to his fear;
(iii) That a witness alleging fear may be cross-examined by the defence, if needs be on a *voir dire*, and if necessary using 'special measures' to assist the witness;
(iv) That if testing by the defence is properly refused, then it is incumbent on the judge to take responsibility rigorously to test the evidence of fear and to investigate all the possibilities of the witness giving oral evidence in the proceedings; in this regard, it is particularly important that no indication, let alone assurance, is given to a potential witness that his evidence will or may be read if he says he is afraid, because that can only give rise to an expectation that this will indeed happen.[102]

100 Ashworth, A. and Redmayne, M., *The Criminal Process*, 4th edn (Oxford, Oxford University Press).
101 [2012] EWCA Crim 2564.
102 or may be read if he says he is afraid, because that can only give rise to an expectation that this will indeed happen.

Shabir thus confirms the statutory preference inherent in section 116(4) that live evidence with the assistance of special measures will always be preferable to admitting a hearsay statement, since the opposing party is then able to test the evidence through cross-examination. In *R v Davies*,[103] the defendant was convicted of causing actual bodily harm and possession of an offensive weapon. Three complainants had made written representations to the judge that they were frightened of the accused and did not wish to give evidence in court. Thus, written statements were read, pursuant to section 116(2)(e). The appellant argued that there had been insufficient evidence of their fear, and the trial judge had failed to take proper steps to assess the basis for the complainants' assertions. This contention was rejected:

> In our judgment, the judge was perfectly entitled to reach a conclusion as to the genuineness of the witnesses' fears on the basis of the evidence to which we have referred. It must always be recalled that fear is to be widely construed ... and that it was the purpose of this part of the 2003 Act to alter that which had previously been the law under section 23 of the Criminal Justice Act 1988. The law previously referred to, particularly in *R v H*, is no longer that which should guide the courts under the new regime. Indeed, courts are ill-advised to seek to test the basis of fear by calling witnesses before them, since that may undermine the very thing that section 116 was designed to avoid.
>
> Of course, judges must be astute not to skew a fair trial by a too ready acceptance of assertions of fear since it is all too easy for witnesses to avoid the inconvenience and anxiety of a trial by saying they do not want to come. But having said that, in the instant case there was ample evidence to justify the course that the judge took. In those circumstances, there is no basis for the suggestion that he was wrong to do so. Normally a judge will have a much better feel of the truth or otherwise of the assertions of fear than this court could ever do, but we accept that the judge made his ruling at the outset and in those circumstances based it purely upon the written assertions of the witnesses. Had we thought he was plainly wrong, then there would have been merit in this appeal, but, on the contrary, we take the view that he was right.[104]

12.3.4.6 Where the accused is responsible for any of the conditions in section 116(2)

Section 116(5) of the Act provides that the hearsay statement will be rendered inadmissible if a party, or any person acting on their behalf, causes the original maker of the statement to be unavailable. Thus, for example, if the defendant has an alibi witness whom they think will not stand up to cross-examination, they may encourage the witness to be absent, maybe by offering them a holiday or demanding that they stay out of the way during the trial. The provision applies to both the prosecution and defence, and it will be for the party opposing the admission of the statement to satisfy the court that the other side is responsible for the operation of the particular condition.

Similarly, it would be difficult for a defendant to argue against the admission of the statement of a witness who is physically unable to attend if he had been shown to be responsible for an attack on the witness, who was subsequently unable to attend the trial. In *R v Moore*,[105] the appellant challenged his conviction on the ground that the trial judge had erred in admitting the statement of an 82-year-old woman who was not fit to attend court. The witness had let a garage to the defendant, in which he stored his car. It was subsequently alleged that the vehicle had been stolen in order to

---

103 [2007] 2 All ER 1070.

104 Ibid., at [14]–[15].

105 [1992] Crim LR 882.

claim on his insurance. The trial took place five years after the committal because the defendant had absconded. He argued that the only way in which he could effectively challenge it would be through his own direct testimony, and that it would be fundamentally unfair to force him to give evidence in this way. Applying *Cole* and dismissing the appeal, the Court of Appeal noted that the more important the evidence, the greater the damage it may do to the defendant. However, there was no general principle that it would be unfair and contrary to the interests of justice to admit a statement if the only way of controverting the statement is for the defendant to testify in person. In this particular case, the court paid particular attention to the fact that the defendant had evaded trial for so long that the prosecution's elderly witness was no longer fit to give evidence. As was stated in *Cole*, fairness required a balance between the prosecution and the defence, and the prosecution should not be put in a disadvantageous position by the illness of a witness, especially where the defendant's conduct contributed to this state of affairs.

12.3.5 Section 117: use of business and other documents

Section 117 of the 2003 Act replaces sections 24 and 25 of the CJA 1988, and provides for the admissibility of documentary hearsay created or received in the course of trade, business, or a profession, subject to certain conditions. Section 24 of the 1988 Act was worded in similar terms, and it was broadly accepted that statements in business documents were likely to be reliable and less susceptible to challenge by cross-examination. It must be emphasised that while section 116 is concerned with both oral and written statements, section 117 is concerned only with written statements. It will be apparent from the discussion below that there will be circumstances in which a statement in a document will be admissible under either section 116 or section 117. However, all statements admitted under section 116 must satisfy one of the conditions in section 116(2). Under section 117, the document will have had to have been created or received in the course of business.[106]

Section 117(1) refers to 'a statement contained in a document' and section 117(2)(b) refers to 'information contained in the statement.' Before proceeding further, however, it may also be useful to clarify what precisely the three key terms used in these provisions – 'document,' 'statement,' and 'information' – actually mean. As defined by section 134(1), a 'document' means 'anything in which information of any description is recorded,' and is therefore merely a container for a statement that has been reduced to writing or another form.[107] It may therefore apply to tape-recordings or any other form of recording, including data entered on a computer.[108] The Court of Appeal, in *R v Carrington*,[109] held that a document may contain more than one statement, and this is implicitly accepted by section 117(2)(a), which refers to 'the document or part containing the statement.' Every statement contains 'information,' and in this context, the supplier of that information must have had, or be reasonably supposed to have had, personal knowledge of the matters in question. For the purposes of section 117(5), the supplier of the information is thus deemed to be the 'relevant person.'

---

106 In practice, there will rarely be any advantage to be gained in using s 117 rather than s 116. The rare occasion on which it might be advantageous to use s 117 is when a party seeks to rely on s 117(5)(b) (see below).

107 As noted above, 'statement' is widely defined by s 115(2) as 'any representation of fact or opinion made by a person by whatever means; and it includes a representation made in a sketch, photofit or other pictorial form.'

108 See e.g. *Wellington v DPP* [2007] EWHC 1061 (Admin), in which it was held that a record in the police national computer that a person had used a particular alias may be admitted under s 117.

109 [1994] Crim LR 438.

12.3.5.1 The conditions of admissibility

Documents created or received in the course of a trade, business, profession, etc. are admissible under section 117(1) if three conditions are satisfied:

> (a) oral evidence given in the proceedings would be admissible as evidence of any matter stated;
> (b) the requirements of section 117(2) are satisfied; and
> (c) the requirements of section 117(5) are satisfied, in a case in such section 117(4) requires them to be.

The condition contained in section 117(1)(a) is the equivalent criterion as that laid down by section 116(1)(a).[110] The court must ask whether oral evidence of the information within the statement would otherwise be admissible (i.e. it would be relevant, and would not be subject to any other exclusionary rule).

In addition, section 117(1)(b) requires the statement to satisfy three further conditions laid down in section 117(2):

> (a) the document was created or received by a person in the course of a trade, business, profession, or other occupation, or by the holder of a paid or unpaid office; and
> (b) the person who supplied the information in the statement (the relevant person) had or may reasonably be supposed to have had personal knowledge of the matters dealt with in the statement; and
> (c) each person through whom the information was supplied ... received the information in the course of a trade, business or profession, or as the holder of a paid or unpaid office.

While section 117(2)(a) requires that the document was created or received by a person in the course of a trade, business, profession, etc., the particular industry in question need not have any connection with the statement in the document, nor with the maker of that statement or the supplier of the information.

Example 12.5

A robbery occurs in a corner grocery shop, which is witnessed by Andrea, the shop assistant. She tells the driver of a delivery truck what she saw, and the driver writes it down. The driver then passes the statement, now contained in documentary form, to a police officer. In the meantime, Andrea has left the area and cannot be found. However, the prosecution will be able to rely on section 117 in seeking to admit the documentary statement in evidence. Since Andrea, the person who supplied the information, had personal knowledge of the matters contained in the statement, and it was created by the truck driver in the course of business, and received by the police officer in the course of business, it should be *prima facie* admissible. However, had she simply given the details to her next-door neighbour, section 117 would not apply as the neighbour would not have created the document in the course of business.[111]

---

110 See above.

111 In this scenario, s 117(4) requires that the additional requirements of s 117(5) must be satisfied (see below). Thus, one of the conditions in s 116(2) must be satisfied, which will be in this instance since A cannot be found. Therefore, although the statement *may* be admitted under s 117, there is no advantage in seeking to admit it under that section given that s 116 applies.

These facts were not entirely dissimilar to those of *Maher v DPP*,[112] one of the first cases to be decided on the new provisions. The accused had collided with the vehicle and driven off. His actions were observed by a passer-by, who recorded his registration on a slip of paper and left it under the windscreen wiper of the damaged vehicle. The injured party subsequently contacted the police, who took a note of the registration and subsequently arrested and charged the defendant. The Divisional Court held that the trial judge had improperly admitted the evidence under section 117, since the owner of the damaged vehicle had not received the information in the course of business.[113]

Even if the evidence in *Maher* had been received by a third party in the course of business (for example, if the passer-by had left the note at the front desk of a police station), a further hurdle would have to be overcome before the prosecution could rely on the evidence in court. As with Andrea in the fictional scenario above, the passer-by in *Maher* clearly prepared the note of the registration in order that the injured party could contact the police. This will therefore amount to a statement prepared for the purposes of contemplated criminal proceedings, and thus the requirements of section 117(5) must also be satisfied. The statement must either satisfy one of the five conditions in section 116(2), or, alternatively, the additional condition set out in section 117(5)(b), where 'the relevant person cannot reasonably be expected to have any recollection of the matters dealt with in the statement.'

The facts of *R v Carrington*[114] provide an example of the circumstances in which this latter provision might apply. The accused attempted to use a stolen credit card in a supermarket. The cashier called a supervisor, B, who called another supervisor, S, who was about to go off duty. B told the customer that she was going to check on the card. At that point, the defendant left the store and was spotted by S as she walked to her car. She noticed that he was driving a white Peugeot car, which left the car park at high speed. S made a note on a magazine of the make of the car, the registration number, and a brief description of the man. She went back into the store and, using the internal telephone, passed the description of the man and the car to B, who subsequently noted it on her memo pad. S then went home without checking that the memo was correct, and did not keep the magazine.

At trial, the memo written by B was admitted as a business document under what would now be section 117 (formerly section 24 of the CJA 1988). Dismissing the appellant's arguments that the memo should not have been admitted, the Court of Appeal held that the key issue was whether the requirements of section 24(4)(iii) (now section 117(5)(b)) were satisfied. In these particular circumstances, S could not reasonably be expected, having regard to the time that had elapsed since she made it and to all of the circumstances, to have any recollection of the matters dealt with in the statement. The parties had been incorrect to agree among themselves that B was the maker of the statement in the memo. Although B recorded the statement, the supplier of the information was S. She could remember passing on the information about the man and the car and giving the registration number, but could not recall the registration number when giving evidence in court. The fact that S was available to give direct evidence, and did give direct evidence, was the basis of the defence objection to the admissibility of the memo under section 24. In other words, the argument being put forward here by the appellant was essentially that if a person was present and did give evidence, they should not fall within section 24. Rejecting that predication, the court held that a document consists of a number of statements; therefore, parts of the document may be admissible as independent statements notwithstanding that the maker has a clear recollection of

112 [2006] EWHC 1271.

113 However, the Court declined to quash the conviction on the basis that it would have been admissible in the interests of justice under s 114(1)(d). It can also be noted that such a statement would not have been admissible under s 116 since subs (1)(b) would not be satisfied: the person making the statement would not have been identified to the court's satisfaction.

114 [1994] Crim LR 438.

some parts of the document. The prosecution were therefore entitled to treat the part of the memo that contained the registration number of the car as an independent statement for the purposes of section 24.

Were the facts of *Carrington* to arise under the current law, the outcome would be the same. It will be noted that B received the information during the course of her trade, and the statement in the document was created by her from information supplied by supervisor S, who clearly had personal knowledge of the matters therein. In this case, the statement was prepared for the purposes of a criminal investigation; therefore, section 117(4) requires that a condition in section 116(2), or the additional condition in section 117(5), be satisfied. Since S was present and able to give evidence, none of the conditions in section 116(2) could be satisfied. However, section 117(5)(b) would apply. However, it is worth noting that, in these circumstances, the legislation provides for an additional safeguard: the judge could still potentially refuse to admit the evidence under subsections (6) and (7) if they are not satisfied as to its reliability given its contents, the source of the information contained in it, or the way in which, or the circumstances in which, the information or document itself was supplied or received.

12.3.5.2 Where the creator and recipient of the document are the same person

Section 117(3) allows for the possibility that persons mentioned in section 117(2)(a) and (b) may, in some cases, be the same person. It would not be an infrequent occurrence in the course of business for an individual to put information that has come to light into written form for a formal record. In such circumstances, that person will be both the creator of the document and the supplier of the information that it contains. If, for the sake of argument, that same person then posted the document addressed to themselves, the creator and maker of the document would, in due course, also become the recipient of the document.

12.3.6 Section 118: preservation of common law exceptions

It will be recalled that the common law originally developed a number of exceptions to mitigate the harsh operation of the rule against hearsay in practice. Section 118 preserves some of the categories of hearsay evidence that were admissible at common law. Some of these exceptions, concerning certain forms of documentary evidence such as public documents,[115] works of reference,[116] maps, and plans, are now of less importance, and their admissibility is largely accepted without contention. Further exceptions apply in relation to matters concerning reputation or family tradition. However, this form of evidence is now extremely rare in practice, and, as such, its scope will not be considered any further here.

Several of the common law exceptions do, however, continue to play a prominent role in contemporary practice. Foremost among these are confessions, which continue to be viewed as an exception to the hearsay rule by virtue of section 118(1)5. These are considered in Chapter 8. Similarly, experts are frequently permitted to cite out-of-court evidence in support of their opinions. This, too, is a preserved common law exception to the rule against hearsay,[117] and we consider this issue in greater depth in Chapter 13. For the purposes of this chapter, we will focus for the most part on the scope of the *res gestae* exception, although a brief comment will also be made on the use of hearsay in respect of common enterprises. Before proceeding, however, it should be borne in mind that all common law exceptions were decided on a case-by-case basis

115 For example, entries on the Register of Births, Marriages & Deaths, Land Registry, Company Registry, etc.
116 This category includes any relevant published work dealing with any matter of a public nature.
117 Criminal Justice Act 2003, s 118(1)8.

and, inevitably, some are more developed than others. For that reason, some of the common law exceptions continue to be uncertain in their scope and still require some further clarification by the appellate courts.

12.3.6.1 Res gestae

This exception, preserved by section 118(1)4, is in fact an umbrella term that encapsulates a number of distinct, albeit similar, exceptions. The expression *res gestae* is a corruption of a longer Latin phrase meaning 'part of a story.' The basis of this exception is that human conduct consists of words and actions, and often the actions cannot be understood without the words. Looking at actions in isolation may serve to decontextualise events and thereby give a false impression. By contrast, taking account of both actions and words should, in theory at least, give us a clearer picture of what happened in the past, and why. To that end, we may have a better prospect of uncovering the truth about past events. It should be pointed out that, because section 116 of the 2003 Act provides for the admissibility of a statement where a witness is unavailable, it will not be uncommon for there to be a considerable degree of overlap in the types of situation in which both sections 116 and 118 may apply. In particular, reliance may be placed on either section where, as will often be the case, the maker of the statement is dead or otherwise unavailable. In practice, however, it will generally be more straightforward for a party wishing to adduce a hearsay statement to rely on section 116, although section 118 remains a viable alternative in certain circumstances.

Under section 118(1)4, there are three forms of statement that are considered to form part of the *res gestae*:

(a) statements made by a person so emotionally overpowered by an event that the possibility of concoction or distortion can be disregarded;
(b) statements accompanied by an act that explain the act of the maker; and
(c) statements of a person's own contemporaneous state of mind.

12.3.6.2 Section 118(1)4(a): statements made by a person so emotionally overpowered

This head constitutes the most common application of the *res gestae* principle. American lawyers sometimes describe it as the 'excited utterance rule,' since the statement must be made spontaneously and contemporaneously with the events that are the subject of the trial. This will usually occur in a scenario involving a serious and violent offence, since it will depend upon an instinctive and spontaneous reaction on the part of the maker of the statement. The exception has been traditionally justified on the basis that a sudden and emotional reaction to an unusual event will effectively rule out the possibility of fabrication or concoction by the maker. A good example can be found in *R v Fowkes*.[118] Here, a witness to a murder was heard to shout, 'There's Butcher!' (the name by which the defendant was known), just as a face appeared at the window from which the fatal shot had been fired. The policeman who had heard this exclamation was allowed to relay it to the court in evidence. A further example can be found in the case of *Ratten*, in which the Privy Council held that if, contrary to its decision, the telephone call from the victim had been hearsay rather than evidence of state of mind, it would have nonetheless fallen under the *res gestae* exception.[119]

The requirement that the statement be made contemporaneously with the relevant act does not mean that the statement and act must exactly coincide in point of time. At one time, the

---

118 *The Times* (8 March 1856).
119 See above.

common law did require exact contemporaneity. In *R v Bedingfield*,[120] the victim staggered out of a room in which she had been with the accused, with her throat cut. Pointing to the wound, she said to her aunt: 'Oh dear Aunt, see what Harry has done to me!' This was excluded because '[i]t was not part of anything done, nor something said while something was being done, but something said after something was done.'[121] However, this decision no longer represents the law.

The leading case is now *R v Andrews*.[122] The accused was charged with murder. Immediately after a savage knife attack, the victim staggered downstairs to the flat of a neighbour, seeking assistance. Shortly afterwards, the police arrived, and the victim made a statement identifying the accused as one of his assailants. He died some two months later of his injuries. The police officers were allowed to give evidence of what the victim told them as part of the *res gestae*. The House of Lords held that this evidence had been properly admitted as evidence of the truth of the facts asserted. Lord Ackner, with whom all of their Lordships agreed, summarised the relevant principles to be applied when admitting evidence under the *res gestae* doctrine, as follows:

> 1 The primary question which the judge must ask himself is: can the possibility of concoction or distortion be disregarded?
>
> 2 To answer that question, the judge must first consider the circumstances in which the particular statement was made, in order to satisfy himself that the event was so unusual or startling or dramatic as to dominate the thoughts of the victim, so that his utterance was an instinctive reaction to that event, thus giving no real opportunity for reasoned reflection. In such a situation, the judge would be entitled to conclude that the involvement or pressure of the event would exclude the possibility of concoction or distortion, providing that the statement was made in conditions of approximate but not exact contemporaneity.
>
> 3 In order for the statement to be sufficiently 'spontaneous' it must be so closely associated with the event which has excited the statement that it can fairly be stated that the mind of the declarant was still dominated by the event. Thus, the judge must be satisfied that the event which provided the trigger mechanism for the statement was still operative. The fact that the statement was made in response to a question is but one factor to consider under this heading.
>
> 4 Quite apart from the time factor, there may be special features in the case, which relate to the possibility of concoction or distortion. In the instant appeal, the defence relied on evidence to support the contention that the deceased had a purpose of his own to fabricate or concoct, namely a malice ... The judge must be satisfied that the circumstances were such that, having regard to the special feature of malice, there was no possibility of any concoction or distortion to the advantage of the maker or the disadvantage of the accused.
>
> 5 As to the possibility of error in the facts narrated in the statement, if only the ordinary fallibility of human recollection is relied on, this goes to the weight to be attached to and not the admissibility of the statement and is therefore a matter for the jury. However, here again, there may be special features that may give rise to the possibility of error. In the instant case there was evidence that the deceased had drunk to excess. Another example would be where the identification was made in circumstances of particular difficulty or where the declarant suffered from defective eyesight. In such circumstances the trial judge must consider whether he can exclude the possibility of error.[123]

Thus, while *approximate* contemporaneity is required, the emphasis is on the reliability of the statement. The shorter the time gap between the event and the statement, and the more dramatic and unusual the event is, the less likely it will be that the court will find the statement to have been

---

120 Ibid.

121 The trial judge contrasted this with a cry such as 'Don't, Harry!' uttered while the act was done, which, if heard by the aunt, would have been admissible.

122 [1987] AC 281. For an application of *Andrews*, see *Barnaby v DPP* (2015) 179 JP 143 and *Ibrahim v DPP* (unreported 18 May 2016).

123 Ibid., at 300–301.

concocted or distorted. In *Andrews* itself, the relevant time gap was some 15 minutes. It was, however, emphasised that the *res gestae* doctrine should not be used to avoid calling witnesses who can give direct evidence of the matter.[124] In *Tobi v Nicholas*,[125] the accused was convicted of failing to stop after an accident. The evidence was that the accused's car had collided with a coach and had failed to stop. Some 20 minutes after the accident, a police officer went to a house where the damaged car was parked, and there heard the coach driver identify the accused as the driver of the car that had collided with him. The officer was allowed to give evidence of this oral identification, the court ruling that it was admissible under the *res gestae* doctrine. The conviction was quashed on the ground that the coach driver was available but had simply not been called to give evidence. It was also said that, in this particular case, the event in question was not so dramatic as to have dominated the mind of the maker of the statement. This, together with the fact that the statement was made some 20 minutes after the event, did not rule out the possibility of error or concoction. It should be underlined, however, that this decision should not be read as an authority that states that a time lapse of 20 minutes is the upper limit of approximate contemporaneity. Had the event been more dramatic or unusual, the mind of the maker might still have been dominated by it. However, a minor road accident will generally not fall into this sort of category.

In *R v Carnall*,[126] the accused was charged with the murder of V. Two witnesses had seen V in the street outside their house. He was bleeding and asking for help. He claimed that he had been attacked with knives and a baseball bat, and it had taken him about an hour to crawl from his home to the house. The witnesses asked him who had attacked him, and he subsequently named the defendant. At the hospital, before V died, he gave a statement to a police officer, again naming the accused as the attacker. The trial judge admitted both the statement to the witnesses and that given to the police officer as part of the *res gestae*. On appeal, it was argued that he had been wrong to do so. It was alleged that the time that had elapsed between the attack and the making of the statements (over an hour between the attack and the first statement, and nearer two hours in respect of the second statement), coupled with the fact that the statements had been made only in response to questions, meant that they were not sufficiently contemporaneous. Moreover, the appellant also contended that the statements were inherently unreliable, since the victim had lost a lot of blood, which could have resulted in a confused state of mind.

Dismissing the appeal, it was held that the crucial question was whether there was any real possibility of concoction or distortion, or whether the judge felt confident that the thoughts of the maker of the statements were at the time so dominated by what had happened that what the speaker said could be regarded as unaffected by any *ex post facto* reasoning or fabrication. In answering this question, the trial judge had taken account of the appalling nature of the attack itself, the horrific injuries that were inflicted, the pain that the victim was undergoing, and the obsession he had at the time with getting help and trying to stay alive. The time factor was not conclusive. As to the question of the loss of blood, the judge had rightly taken the view that this was merely speculative on the part of the appellant. Thus, the central issue for the court was not a question of a lapse of time but whether there was a real possibility of concoction or distortion as a result of the lapse of time or any other proven factor.

In *R v Newport*,[127] the facts were similar to those in *Ratten*. The defendant's wife left the house after an argument, pursued by N wielding a bread knife. The victim was subsequently stabbed, and later died of her wounds. The prosecution case was that the accused deliberately stabbed her to death. He denied this, and claimed that the death was an accident. Evidence was admitted of a

---

124 See also *Edwards and Osakwe v DPP* [1992] Crim LR 576.
125 [1987] Crim LR 774.
126 [1995] Crim LR 944.
127 [1998] Crim LR 581.

telephone call made by the wife to a friend on the evening of her death. The friend said that the deceased was in an agitated and frightened state, and had asked if she could come to her friend's house if she had to flee in a hurry. This evidence was admitted as part of the *res gestae* and the accused was convicted.[128] The Court of Appeal found that the evidence of the telephone call had been admitted on the basis that it had been made immediately before the wife left the house, when in fact it had been made 20 minutes earlier. In view of that, it was held that the evidence was not a spontaneous and unconsidered reaction to an immediate impending emergency and should not have been admitted. However, on taking into account the weight of the other evidence before the jury, the conviction was not considered unsafe.

As these cases make clear, the admissibility of spontaneous exclamations as *res gestae* is governed by the test laid down in *Andrews*. There is no longer a strict requirement of contemporaneity between the event and the exclamation. What is essential is that the trial judge is satisfied that the 'possibility of concoction or distortion can be disregarded,' which involves considering whether the event was so unusual or startling or dramatic as to dominate the thoughts of the declarant.

In *Attorney General's Reference (No. 1 of 2003)*,[129] the defendant was charged with causing grievous bodily harm to his mother. Prosecuting counsel told the court that he thought the accused's mother might not give reliable evidence, and sought the court's permission to call a number of witnesses who heard her shouting and identifying the accused as her attacker. The trial judge refused to admit this evidence as *res gestae*, since the victim was prepared to testify. The Court of Appeal held that there was no rider to the *res gestae* exception to the effect that the rule was not applicable where better evidence was available. Nonetheless, while the prosecution had not sought to disadvantage the defence by not calling the victim, it was fundamentally unfair to the accused not to call her and to rely instead on *res gestae* evidence.[130]

While most statements admitted under the *res gestae* principle are made by victims who are not able to give evidence, the rule applies to statements made by the accused as well. Where those statements are inculpatory in nature, they will be admissible as a confession. However, the *res gestae* principle could apply to statements not amounting to an admission. In *R v Glover*,[131] the accused assaulted another man and was forcibly restrained by other persons present. He shouted, 'I am David Glover,' and then made threats to shoot the man and his family. There was a possibility that the man was not David Glover, but, having considered that possibility and discounted it, the judge admitted evidence from witnesses who were present at the scene. If we return briefly to the facts of *Bedingfield*, had the accused been heard to say, 'I'm Harry Bedingfield and I've come for you,' that would have been admissible as part of the *res gestae*.

12.3.6.3 Section 118(1)4(b): statements that accompany and explain acts of the maker

In order to be admissible under this head, a statement must relate to, accompany, and explain the act, which must itself be relevant and must be made contemporaneously.

---

128 [2003] Crim LR 547.

129 The relevance of this evidence lies in the deceased's agitated and frightened state and the claim that she might need to flee her husband. Since he claimed the death was an accident, evidence that the wife was in fear and preparing to flee contradicted this and was clearly relevant.

130 However, had the prosecution not called the victim, the court noted that the trial judge could have excluded the *res gestae* evidence under s 78 of the Police and Criminal Evidence Act 1984 as being in breach of the fair trial provisions of Art 6(1) of the European Convention on Human Rights. One way around this kind of problem might have been to call the victim and, if she did not give the expected evidence, to call the other witnesses, whose evidence would then be admissible under the *res gestae* exception.

131 [1991] Crim LR 48.

A simple example is that of a person who runs off on the approach of a police officer. In isolation, it may look like a guilty act; however, if it is accompanied by the words, 'Sorry, I must run, the last bus leaves in two minutes,' it takes on a different meaning. Most examples of this exception are to be found in the civil law. Thus, in order to prove that money was a gift, a witness would be allowed to say in evidence that she heard the claimant say, on handing over money, 'This is for your birthday.' However, the principle was applied within a criminal context in *R v McCay*.[132]

Here, a witness, who had viewed a pre-trial identification parade through a one-way glass screen, said to the police officer: 'It's number 8.' However, he could not remember which number he had said when he came to give evidence at trial. The police officer was permitted to give evidence that the witness had said 'It's number 8,' because those words were deemed to accompany and explain a relevant act.[133]

12.3.6.4 Section 118(1)4(c): statements of the maker's own contemporaneous state of mind

Statements by a person that constitute evidence of their physical or mental state are admissible on the basis that only that person knows how they feel, and there would be no way of proving such emotions unless that statement were admissible. The rule regarding contemporaneity is more flexible in this area. It may, for example, include a statement about the person's physical or mental condition at some earlier point in time. Statements have been admitted on matters such as a person's political opinion, marital affection, the dislike of a child, and to prove (for the purposes of what is now section 116(2)(e)) that a witness who will not give evidence was in fear. It also seems that this head will cover statement of intentions, and that such a statement is admissible to support an inference that the intention referred to existed at a time prior to or after that statement had been made. However, where the statement expresses an intention to do an act, the authorities conflict as to whether it can be relied upon to prove that the act in question was actually committed.

In *R v Buckley*,[134] the defendant was charged with the murder of a police officer. A statement made by the deceased officer to a senior officer, that he intended to watch the accused's movements on the night he was killed, was admitted to prove that the accused had committed the offence. In *R v Moghal*,[135] the accused, who was charged with aiding and abetting a murder, alleged that his mistress, S (who had already been tried and acquitted), had committed the murder alone. The Court of Appeal expressed the opinion that a tape-recorded statement made some six months before V's death, in which S was heard to say that she intended to kill V, should have been admissible in evidence. This decision was, however, doubted in *R v Blastland*,[136] in which the House of Lords questioned whether it was really relevant to the issue as to whether Moghal aided and abetted S. Had S said that she planned to kill V alone, then it would clearly have been relevant in that it would have tended to suggest that D had no part in the murder. Indeed, in *R v Wainwright*,[137] a

---

132 [1990] 1 WLR 645.

133 The same means could have been used in *R v Osbourne and Virtue* [1973] QB 678. An eyewitness had identified Osbourne at an identification parade, but at trial claimed that 'she did not remember that she had picked out anyone on the last parade.' The prosecution had to call a police inspector to confirm the positive identification. The Court of Appeal upheld the trial judge's decision to admit the evidence, although it preferred a somewhat doubtful application of the *res gestae* principle as the basis of its decision. The decision compares unfavourably with that in *Kearley*, in which the House of Lords stated that telephone calls and words of the personal callers could have fallen within the *res gestae* exception if the offence was seen as continuing during the time the officers were in the flat: thus the words of the callers who had effectively accompanied the continuing act of the defendant. Unfortunately, however, that possibility was not considered by the court.

134 (1873) 13 Cox CC 293.

135 (1977) 65 Cr App R 56.

136 [1986] AC 41. See also *R v Callender* [1998] Crim LR 337.

137 (1875) 13 Cox CC 171.

statement by the murder victim that she was going to the accused's premises was held to be inadmissible because it was only a statement of intention, which she might or might not have carried out. Similarly, in *R v Thompson*,[138] the statement by a woman that she intended to abort herself, and the statement after her miscarriage that she had caused it herself, were both held to be inadmissible hearsay on a charge against the accused of using an instrument to procure an abortion. The difference may lie in the fact that the police officer in *Buckley* was seen to be more reliable than the murder victim in *Wainwright* and the woman whose pregnancy had been terminated in *Thompson*.

Had any of these statements been in documentary form, they might now be admissible under section 116 of the CJA 2003. In *R v Gilfoyle*,[139] the defendant had been convicted of the murder of his wife, who had been found hanging from a beam in the garage of her house. There was a note in her handwriting, in which she said she was going to take her own life. At first, her death was thought to have been suicide. However, sometime later, a friend of the deceased made a statement to the police in which she said that the deceased had told her that her husband, who was an auxiliary nurse, was doing a project on suicide at work. He had asked his wife to help him out by writing examples of suicide notes. Two other friends made similar statements to the police. Although these three statements had been ruled inadmissible by the trial judge, the defendant was convicted. The Court of Appeal ruled that all three statements ought to have been admitted. The statements attributed to the deceased by her three friends threw light on her state of mind, which was one of the principal issues in the case. Accordingly, their Lordships were satisfied that the statements should have been used to show that the deceased was not in a suicidal frame of mind when she wrote the notes, instead believing that she was assisting the appellant in a project.[140]

As a final point, it is worth noting that evidence of the telephone call made by the deceased in *Newport* should also have been admissible under this head.[141] Here, the deceased's husband claimed that the stabbing was an accident, but the wife's telephone call to a friend suggested an ongoing argument, which had made her so agitated and frightened that she was contemplating almost immediate flight from the matrimonial home. Evidence of this state of mind was then clearly relevant to rebut the defence of accident.

12.3.6.5 Section 118(1)7: statements made by a party to a common enterprise

Where two or more persons conspire to commit an offence, an out-of-court statement of one may be admissible in evidence against the other, and also against the maker of the statement.[142] If the statement contains facts upon which the prosecution proposes to rely, those facts are admissible as an exception to the rule against hearsay. However, a condition of admissibility is that the statement must have been made in pursuance of the conspiracy subject of the charge. Where there is more than one conspiracy charged, as where A is alleged to have conspired with B and B is alleged to have conspired with C, a statement made by A in pursuance of his conspiracy with B is not admissible in relation to the alleged conspiracy between B and C.

The leading case in this area is *R v Blake and Tye*.[143] The defendants were convicted of fraudulent conspiracy to evade payment of customs duties. The prosecution case was that Blake, a customs official, and Tye, an agent for an importer, falsified documents, by declaring a smaller amount of goods than was actually imported to avoid paying duty. The conspiracy was largely proved by

---

138 [1912] 3 KB 19.

139 [1996] 3 All ER 883.

140 In a second appeal in *R v Gilfoyle* [2001] 2 Cr App R 5, the Court of Appeal rejected evidence of what was described as a 'psychological autopsy' of the deceased's wife in order to show that she was, in fact, suicidal. See further Ch 13.

141 See above.

142 For an example, see *R v Platten* [2006] Crim LR 920.

143 (1844) 6 QB 126.

entries in a book kept by Tye, which showed the true quantity of goods imported. It was held that these entries were properly proved against both conspirators, being statements made in pursuance of the conspiracy. However, entries on cheque book stubs by Tye, recording the division of spoils between Tye and Blake, were not admissible, because they were made after the offence had been completed. They could not, therefore, have been made in pursuance of the conspiracy.

The decision regarding the cheque book stubs in the above case may be compared with that in *R v Davenport*.[144] Here, a document dealing with the proposed division of the proceeds from the alleged conspiracy was held to be admissible against all of the parties concerned, on the basis that it was compiled before the conspiracy was complete and was made in pursuance of it. In *R v Jenkins and Starling*,[145] the defendants, directors of a company, were found guilty of conspiracy to defraud a local authority by falsely claiming a refund of business rates. It was alleged that they had conspired either with a council employee or with an employee of a computer servicing company. At the trial, Exhibit 1 was a document bearing the word 'refund request' with the word 'overpayment' endorsed on it. The signatories of the document were not called as witnesses. On appeal, the prosecution conceded that the document was hearsay, but argued that it was admissible as a document made in pursuance of a conspiracy. The Court of Appeal disagreed. Allowing the appeal, it was held that, in order for such evidence to be admissible, there had to be an assertion by the signatory that he knew the contents to be true. Additionally, there was no evidence as to when the document had been prepared. If prepared after the refund had been received, it was not made *in pursuance* of the conspiracy, since by then the fraud would have already been completed.

The principle that a statement made by a party to a common enterprise is admissible against the maker and the other participants is not confined to those offences that involve a conspiracy. In *R v Gray*,[146] the Court of Appeal approved and adopted the dictum of Dixon CJ in the Australian case of *Tripodi v R*,[147] to the effect that the rule also applied to substantive offences committed by two or more persons with a common purpose. The court attempted to define the application of the rule on the basis of a statement found in *Phipson on Evidence*:

> Where two [or more] persons engage in a common enterprise, the acts and declarations of one in pursuance of that common enterprise are admissible against the other(s). The principle applies to the commission, by one or more people acting in concert, of a substantive offence or series of offences, but is limited to evidence which shows the involvement of each of the defendants in the commission of the offence or offences.[148]

As with conspiracies, the acts or declarations must be made in pursuance of the common enterprise, so that statements made after the completion of the enterprise are admissible only against the maker.[149]

12.3.7 Hearsay and previous inconsistent statements

Section 119(1) of the CJA 2003 clarifies the relationship between hearsay evidence and previous statements. This provides that, once it has been proved that a witness has made a previous

144 [1996] 1 Cr App R 221.

145 [2003] Crim LR 107.

146 [1995] 2 Cr App R 100.

147 (1961) 104 CLR 1.

148 14th edn (Sweet & Maxwell, 1990) [25].

149 Some writers argue that statements by the parties to common enterprises involving substantive offences are admissible under other exceptions either as part of the *res gestae* or as informal admissions. *Cross and Tapper on Evidence* classify them as 'admissions by agents,' while *Andrews and Hirst on Criminal Evidence* see them as a species of *res gestae*.

inconsistent statement, such a statement is not only evidence that undermines the witness's credibility, but, in contrast to the previous law, can also be used as evidence of the truth of its contents.[150] Section 119(2) provides:

> If in criminal proceedings evidence of an inconsistent statement by any person is given under section 124(2)(c) (to attack the credibility of the person), the statement is admissible as evidence of any matter stated in it of which oral evidence by the witness would be admissible.

The provision envisages the following type of situation.

Example 12.6

Amanda makes a statement to the police that she saw Thelma 'outside the jewellers at midday on Monday.' Amanda is unavailable to testify at trial, but her statement is admitted under section 116. Evidence may then be introduced to attack the credibility of Amanda, including the fact that she made another statement inconsistent with this account (for example, if Amanda had earlier told Mark that she did not see Thelma at all on Monday).[151] In these circumstances, section 119(2) provides that if there is such an inconsistent statement, it not only goes to the credibility of A, but also is admissible as to the truth of its contents (that is, that Amanda did not, in fact, see Thelma on Monday).

12.3.8 Multiple hearsay

As noted above in this chapter, multiple hearsay arises where information passes through more than one person before it is recorded. Traditionally, the law of evidence has been extremely restrictive in its approach to admitting such evidence, since it is seen as highly unreliable. Under the 2003 Act, different rules apply to multiple hearsay, depending on the form and context in which it is used at trial.[152] Section 121 provides:

> 1 A hearsay statement is not admissible to prove the fact that an earlier hearsay statement was made unless –
> (a) either of the statements is admissible under section 117, 119 or 120,
> (b) all parties to the proceedings so agree, or
> (c) the court is satisfied that the value of the evidence in question, taking into account how reliable the statements appear to be, is so high that the interests of justice require the later statement to be admissible for that purpose.
>
> 2 In this section 'hearsay statement' means a statement, not made in oral evidence, that is relied upon as evidence of the matter stated in it.

It will be apparent from the above excerpt that multiple hearsay will not be admissible for the purposes of section 116. This provision is based on the recommendation of the Law Commission, which noted:

150 See Ch 6.

151 Criminal Justice Act 2003, s 124(2)(c).

152 See *R v Williams (Ochaine)* [2014] EWCA Crim 1862.

> Suppose, for example, that A said that event x had occurred, and that A knew this because B had seen it happen and had told A about it immediately afterwards, in such circumstances that A could have given oral evidence of B's statement under the *res gestae* rule. But A is dead. Should A's statement be admissible as evidence of x?
>
> The statement is multiple hearsay, since A has no personal knowledge of the fact stated. The unavailability exception should not apply because A had no such knowledge, A would have been unable to give oral evidence of that fact. But in this case A could have given such evidence – by virtue not of personal knowledge, but of the res gestae exception. The question is: should it be sufficient for the purposes of the unavailability exception that the declarant could have given oral evidence of the fact stated, even if that evidence would have been (admissible) hearsay? Or should it be necessary that the declarant could have given oral evidence without resort to a hearsay exception?
>
> We have concluded that the answer should depend on which hearsay exception would have rendered A's oral evidence admissible – in other words, how B's statement (the statement on which the statement of the unavailable declarant A is based) itself comes to be admissible. If B gives evidence then the fact that B is available for cross-examination is in our view sufficient to compensate for the fact that A's statement is multiple hearsay. And if B's statement is admissible on the ground that it was made in a business document, we think the presumed reliability of such documents is again sufficient to outweigh the drawbacks of multiple hearsay.
>
> If, however, B's statement is only admissible on the basis that B is unavailable to testify, or under one of the common law exceptions (such as res gestae) that we recommend should be preserved (section 118), we think it would be going too far to permit B's statement to be proved by another hearsay statement merely because the maker of that other statement is unavailable to testify. Our reasons are essentially those that we have given for excluding multiple hearsay in general from the unavailability exception – namely that with each additional step in the chain, the risk of error or fabrication increases.[153]

The scope of section 121 was the subject of the appeal in *R v Xhabri*.[154] The accused here was charged with kidnapping a Latvian woman, and subjecting her to rape and forced prostitution. One of the statements on which the prosecution proposed to rely was the testimony of a police officer who had spoken to two unidentified men who had come to the police station to report that a woman had told them that she was being held at a particular address against her will. Since the men did not have personal knowledge of this, the only way in which it could be admitted in evidence was if it complied with one of the three requirements set down in section 121(1). In this particular case, since the victim had already given evidence of what she had told the men, section 120(7) applied.[155] The statement was thus admissible under section 121(1)(a). However, the Court of Appeal pointed out that, even if it had not been admissible by virtue of section 120, this was the type of case in which it would have been appropriate for the court to exercise its discretion and admit the evidence in the interests of justice under section 121(1)(c). This provision allows the court to admit multiple hearsay if it is highly reliable and the interests of justice require that it be admitted, and if it is similar to the generic discretion contained in section 114(1)(d). Although there is no formal requirement under section 121 to consider the factors contained in section 114(2), the Divisional Court stated in *Maher v DPP*[156] that these same factors should be taken into

---

153 Law Commission, op. cit., n. 27, at [8.19–22].

154 [2006] 1 Cr App 26.

155 That is, her statement related to a previous complaint about the offence charged.

156 (2006) 170 JP 441.

Figure 12.3 Original evidence, first-hand hearsay, and multiple hearsay

account where the court was considering whether to exercise its discretion under section 121(1)(c) to admit multiple hearsay.[157]

Section 121(1)(c) was again the focus of attention in *R v Thakrar (Miran)*.[158] The appellant had been convicted of the murder of three men, whom he had shot during a dispute over a drug deal. The appellant fled to Northern Cyprus, but was arrested shortly afterwards and returned to the United Kingdom. However, it emerged that, during his time abroad, the appellant had admitted to three local people that he had been involved in the killings. These persons were unwilling to give evidence in the United Kingdom, but did give statements to the police in Northern Cyprus that implicated the accused.

The prosecution sought to make use of these statements at trial. Although the basic requirements of section 116(2)(c) appeared to be satisfied, the fact that they constituted multiple hearsay meant that they could be admitted only if the requirements in section 121(1)(c) were satisfied. The trial judge concluded that, notwithstanding issues relating to reliability, the value of the evidence was so high that the interests of justice required that the statements of the absent

157 Alternatively, the court may choose to admit the statement directly under s 114(1)(d) without relying on s 121 at all.
158 [2011] Crim LR 399.

witnesses be admitted. The defendants were convicted, and appealed, contending that the judge had failed to weigh up the appropriate factors properly in conducting the interests of justice test.

The appeals were rejected. The Court of Appeal held that the trial judge had properly admitted the statements given their value to the case. Moreover, the statements appeared to be reliable insofar as all of the statements contained facts that were consistent with unchallenged evidence, which could only have been known to an eyewitness since it was not in the public domain. There was no apparent motive for the witnesses to have invented the defendant's admissions. It is also worth noting that, in arriving at its decision, the Court of Appeal referred to the list of factors set out in section 114(2), even though those were not directly relevant to the separate interests of justice test under section 121.

Section 121(1)(c) aside, multiple hearsay is inadmissible for the statements of absent witnesses or unavailable witnesses. It may, however, be adduced in relation to evidence falling under section 117, subject to certain conditions. The rationale for the differentiation according to the form of the hearsay statement is based on the assumption that, since the chain of communication will be contained within a business context, the risks of distortion or fabrication are considerably reduced. Furthermore, section 117 contains a further safeguard, in that the court may give a direction under section 117(6) that the statement is not admissible if it believes the statement to be unreliable.

Relevantly, the decision of Musone[159] is framed in terms of ensuring fairness to sanction defence non-cooperation where efficiency and managerialism are at stake. Similarly to expert evidence, which can be excluded when the party has not complied with requirements under Part 19 of the Criminal Procedure Rules 2020, likewise, hearsay evidence can be excluded where notice to introduce the evidence can be excluded where the party has not complied with requirements of Part 20 of the Criminal Procedure Rules.[160]

Example 12.7

Jason, an assembly worker on a car production line, allocates a specific number to a cylinder block. He tells his foreman, Amir, who tells the line manager, Emma, who tells the records clerk, Julie, who enters the information on to a computer. The document (that is, the data file or printout) was created in the course of a business by Julie from information originally supplied by Jason. Thus section 117(2)(c) is satisfied and the evidence would be admissible. The 'relevant person' in this chain of communication is the assembly worker, who allocated the number to the cylinder block and who passed the information to the foreman. Under the previous legislation, there was some confusion as to who actually constituted the 'maker' of the statement, but this was resolved in *R v Deroda*,[161] in which it was made clear that the maker was the person who first compiled the statement as a representation of fact. Thus, where A passes information to B, who passes it to C, who writes it down or otherwise records it, A will be regarded as the relevant person for the purposes of these sections.

However, it is worth bearing in mind that section 123(2) provides that a statement may not be admitted under section 117 if any person who supplied or received the information, or created or

159 *R v Musone* [2007] EWCA Crim 1237, [2007] 1 WLR 2467 [60].

160 Criminal Justice Act 2003, S132(5).

161 [2000] 1 Cr App R 41.

received the document, did not have the required capability or, where that person cannot be identified, cannot reasonably be assumed to have had the required capability to testify. It follows that if anyone who supplied or received the information that is the subject of an application under section 117 was not capable of 'understanding questions put to him about the matters stated, and giving answers to such questions which can be understood,'[162] the information cannot be admitted.

12.4 The Civil Evidence Act 1995

Reform of the hearsay rule in civil cases began much earlier and went substantially further than concurrent developments in the criminal arena. In part, the pace of reform was dictated by the declining role of juries in civil proceedings (and thus the perceived need to 'shield' them from such evidence), and the increased tendency to rely on documentary evidence. The Civil Evidence Act 1968 permitted the use of hearsay evidence in a wide range of circumstances, although the rules were subject to a complex notice procedure that was widely criticised. As pressure from both academics and practitioners mounted on the courts and government to reform the rule, the Law Commission sealed the fate of the rule in its 1993 report, *The Hearsay Rule in Civil Proceedings*.[163] The Commission recommended that the rule be abolished, but that parties intending to rely on out-of-court statements should be obliged to give notice and seek leave from the court.

These recommendations were enacted in the Civil Evidence Act 1995. Section 1(1) lays down the general rule: evidence shall not be excluded on the ground that it is hearsay.[164] Hearsay is defined in section 1(2) as 'a statement made otherwise than by a person while giving oral evidence in the proceedings which is tendered as evidence of the matters stated and ... references to hearsay include hearsay of whatever degree.' This definition mirrors the common law approach to defining hearsay, and, as the Law Commission made clear, pre-existing case law would continue to guide the courts in delineating the scope of the new statutory definition. Section 13 of the Act defines a 'statement' as 'any representation of fact or opinion, however made,' which is wide enough to cover oral, written, and other forms of hearsay previously covered by the common law.[165]

There are, however, a number of caveats that apply. First, the maker of the statement must have been competent to testify at the time the statement was made. A person is deemed to be not competent for the purposes of the Act if they are

> suffering from such mental or physical infirmity, or lack of understanding, as would render a person incompetent as a witness in civil proceedings; but a child shall be treated as competent as a witness if he satisfies the requirements of section 96(2) (a) and (b) of the Children Act 1989.[166]

Thus the statements of very young children or severely mentally disabled witnesses may be ruled inadmissible. Second, the party against whom the hearsay evidence is adduced has a right to call the maker of the original statement for the purposes of cross-examination.[167] If the witness is unavailable to testify, evidence may be adduced to attack their credibility, including evidence of

162 Criminal Justice Act 2003, s 123(3).

163 Law Commission, *The Hearsay Rule in Civil Proceedings*, Report No. 216, Cmnd 2321 (HMSO, 1993).

164 However, this will not prejudice the exclusion of evidence on any other ground: Civil Evidence Act 1995, s 14.

165 It remains moot whether this definition covers the problems posed by implied assertions, discussed above. In *Manchester Brewery Company Ltd v Combs* (1901) 82 LT 347, Farwell J stated *obiter* that such evidence remained admissible.

166 See corresponding discussion in Ch 4.

167 Civil Evidence Act 1995, s 3.

any previous inconsistent statements.[168] Where this occurs, the finality rule will apply and the party relying on the hearsay statement will not be permitted to introduce evidence in rebuttal.[169]

The Act also directs the court as to the weight that ought to be attached to hearsay evidence. Section 4 provides:

> (1) In estimating the weight (if any) to be given to hearsay evidence in civil proceedings the court shall have regard to any circumstances from which any inference can reasonably be drawn as to the reliability or otherwise of the evidence.
> (2) Regard may be had, in particular, to the following –
> (a) whether it would have been reasonable and practicable for the party by whom the evidence was adduced to have produced the maker of the original statement as a witness;
> (b) whether the original statement was made contemporaneously with the occurrence or existence of the matters stated;
> (c) whether the evidence involves multiple hearsay;
> (d) whether any person involved had any motive to conceal or misrepresent matters;
> (e) whether the original statement was an edited account, or was made in collaboration with another or for a particular purpose;
> (f) whether the circumstances in which the evidence is adduced as hearsay are such as to suggest an attempt to prevent proper evaluation of its weight.

These factors are self-explanatory, and were included to ensure that hearsay evidence is not routinely admitted on a free-for-all basis. Despite its apparent abolition in civil cases, the 'best evidence' rule continues to dictate that civil courts prefer to receive direct oral evidence as opposed to out-of-court statements.

12.5 Hearsay and human rights

One of the greatest concerns about the use of hearsay evidence is that it denies the opposing party the opportunity to cross-examine the maker of the statement. Even in the years before the provisions of the 2003 legislation took effect, there was an upsurge in academic concern that there was an increasing array of circumstances in which the use of hearsay evidence may interfere with the fair trial rights of the accused.[170]

These concerns became more acute in the years following the passage of the Human Rights Act 1989, given that Article 6(3)(d) of the European Convention provides that everyone charged with a criminal offence has the minimum right to examine or have examined witnesses against him and to obtain the attendance and examination of witnesses on his behalf under the same conditions as witnesses against him. While the parameters of this right remain somewhat vague, there have been a number of instances in which the use of hearsay evidence in domestic courts was found by the Strasbourg Court to fall foul of this provision.[171] Indeed, such arguments became more commonplace in the higher courts of England and Wales.[172] In *R v M(KJ)*,[173] the accused was charged with murder, but was found unfit to plead. Subsequently, a hearing was convened to determine whether he had committed the acts alleged by the prosecution. The statement of the

---

168 Ibid., s 5(2).

169 See Ch 6.

170 See e.g. Osborne, C., 'Hearsay and the European Court of Human Rights' [1993] Crim LR 255; Friedman, R., 'Hearsay and Confrontation: Thoughts from Across the Water' [1998] Crim LR 697; Prithipaul, R., 'Observations on the Current Status of the Hearsay Rule' (1996) 39 *Criminal Law Quarterly* 84.

171 See e.g. *Kostovski v Netherlands* (1990) 12 EHRR 434; *Windisch v Austria* (1991) 13 EHRR 281; *Van Mechelen v Netherlands* (1997) 25 EHRR 647; *PS v Germany* (2003) 36 EHRR 61.

172 See e.g. *R v Gokal* [1997] 2 Cr App R 266; *R v Thomas* [1998] Crim LR 887; *R v Radak* [1999] 1 Cr App R 187.

173 [2003] 2 Cr App R 21.

sole prosecution witness was admitted under section 23 of the 1988 Act, as the court had found him to be in fear of giving evidence in person. M appealed, arguing that the statement should not have been admitted and that its admission was incompatible with Article 6(3)(d).

In support of this contention, counsel relied upon the decision of the European Court of Human Rights (ECtHR) in *Luca v Italy*,[174] in which it was stated that:

> If the defendant has been given an adequate and proper opportunity to challenge the depositions either when made or at a later stage, their admission in evidence will not in itself contravene Article 6. The corollary of that, however, is that where a conviction is based solely or to a decisive degree on depositions that have been made by a person whom the accused has had no opportunity to examine or to have examined, whether during the investigation or at the trial, the rights of the defence are restricted to an extent that is incompatible with the guarantees provided by Article 6.[175]

In spite of a relatively clear stipulation that Article 6 was likely to be breached where a conviction was based solely or to a decisive extent on untested statements made out of court, in *M(KJ)* the Court of Appeal stated that this rule had to be subject to certain exceptions, since a blanket exclusion of such evidence would simply encourage witness intimidation and operate to prevent convictions in cases involving serious and organised crime. Thus, where the witness gave evidence that he would not give live testimony because threats had been made, and the judge drew the inference that the threats were made by or at the instigation of the accused or with his approval, a hearsay statement could normally be admitted without infringing Convention rights.

Notwithstanding the decision in *M(KJ)*, the English courts have been careful to warn that the problem of witness intimidation should not be used as a smokescreen for prosecutors to prioritise hearsay statements over live evidence. This note of caution was first sounded by the Court of Appeal in *R v Arnold*,[176] and later endorsed in *R v Sellick*.[177] In the latter case, the accused was charged with a murder that had allegedly stemmed from a botched drug deal in the criminal underworld. Strong evidence was presented that associates of the accused had attempted to intimidate two key prosecution witnesses, and so the prosecution sought to adduce their evidence in hearsay form. The defendant was subsequently convicted, and appealed, contending that his right to cross-examine opposing witnesses under Article 6(3)(d) of the Convention had been breached. Following a thorough survey of the Strasbourg case law, the Court of Appeal put forward four main propositions.

> (i) The admissibility of evidence is primarily for the national law.
> (ii) Evidence must normally be produced at a public hearing and, as a general rule, Article 6(1) and (3)(d) require a defendant to be given a proper and adequate opportunity to challenge and question witnesses.
> (iii) It is not necessarily incompatible with Article 6(1) and (3)(d) for depositions to be read, and that can be so even if there has been no opportunity to question the witness at any stage of the proceedings. Article 6(3)(d) is simply an illustration of matters to be taken into account in considering whether a fair trial has been held. The reasons for the court holding it necessary that statements should be read and the procedures to counterbalance any handicap to the defence will all be relevant to the issue, whether, where statements have been read, the trial was fair.

174 (2001) 36 EHRR 807.
175 Ibid., at [40].
176 [2005] Crim LR 56.
177 [2005] 1 WLR 3257.

(iv) The quality of the evidence and its inherent reliability, plus the degree of caution exercised in relation to reliance on it, will also be relevant to the question whether the trial was fair.[178]

Adopting this framework of analysis, the court noted the high degree of probability that the witnesses had been intimidated by the defendant in the instant case, but warned that section 116(2)(e) should not be viewed by the prosecution as an open door through which hearsay evidence could automatically be admitted in every case in which a witness was in fear. In each instance, the court should take care to balance the potential merits and risks of admitting such evidence. Crucial to the final decision will be the extent to which counterbalancing measures are in place for the accused. In this particular case, it was observed that the evidence of both witnesses was credible, and the defence had been able to challenge their credibility. Moreover, the trial judge had given a clear warning to the jury about the potential shortcomings of hearsay evidence compared with live evidence. Since the defendant was the author of his own inability to examine the witnesses in question, the statement was rightfully admitted.[179]

However, in the landmark decision of *Al-Khawaja and Tahery v UK*,[180] the Strasbourg Court delivered a momentous blow to the hearsay provisions of the 2003 Act and the manner in which Article 6(3)(d) had thus far been considered by the courts. Al-Khawaja, a consultant in rehabilitative medicine, had been convicted of two counts of indecent assault on two female patients while they were allegedly under hypnosis. One of the patients had committed suicide prior to the trial, and the prosecution sought to rely on a statement made to the police several months previously. It was accepted that the statement was central to the prosecution case. For his part, Tahery had been convicted of wounding with intent. One of the key prosecution witnesses had informed the court that he was too frightened to give evidence. The prosecution thus sought to rely on an out-of-court hearsay statement as a central plank of their case, and Tahery was duly convicted.

In both cases, the court found a violation of Article 6 on the grounds that there was no realistic way in which the defence would have been able to rebut the hearsay evidence effectively. Since the hearsay statements constituted either the sole or, at the very least, the decisive evidence against them, any conviction that followed would be in breach of Article 6(1) and 6(3)(d).

The decision came as something of a surprise to the Government, as well as many members of the criminal bar. However, it did not take long for the Court of Appeal – and shortly afterwards, the Supreme Court – to state in no uncertain terms that they rejected the Strasbourg analysis. The matter was first addressed by the Court of Appeal in *Horncastle and Others*,[181] which concerned three joined cases of grievous bodily harm, kidnap, and the distribution of indecent photographs of children. Each conviction was based solely, or to a decisive extent, on hearsay evidence, admitted under the provisions of the CJA 2003. However, the Court of Appeal concluded that the Strasbourg Court had misapplied the Convention in *Al-Khawaja and Tahery*. In its view, the hearsay regime under the 2003 Act was consistent with Article 6 rights and there was no need to automatically exclude the evidence of certain absent witnesses just because the conviction was based to a sole or decisive extent on their evidence. One of the most important factors here was that the evidence had come from identifiable witnesses. The Court recognised that there was a need to treat evidence of anonymous witnesses differently from cases in which the witness was simply absent. Moreover, a hearsay statement that stemmed from an anonymous source would not be admissible under the

178 Ibid. [50].
179 *Sellick* was followed in *Campbell and Others* [2005] EWCA Crim 2078.
180 (2009) 49 EHRR 1.
181 [2009] 4 All ER 183.

2003 Act.[182] This view was subsequently accepted by the Supreme Court in *Horncastle*.[183] On this occasion, the Court noted that the 2003 Act contains a 'crafted code,' carefully designed to protect Article 6 rights, but which did not include a 'sole or decisive' rule and rendered such a rule unnecessary. If the provisions of the legislation are applied in a proper fashion, no breach would occur. The President of the Court, Lord Phillips, summarised his decision in the following terms:

> 1 Long before 1953 when the Convention came into force, the common law had, by the hearsay rule, addressed that aspect of a fair trial that Article 6(3)(d) was designed to ensure.
> 2 Parliament has since enacted exceptions to the hearsay rule that are required in the interests of justice. Those exceptions are not subject to the sole or decisive rule. The regime enacted by Parliament contains safeguards that render the sole or decisive rule unnecessary.
> 3 The continental procedure had not addressed that aspect of a fair trial that Article 6(3)(d) was designed to ensure.
> 4 The Strasbourg Court has recognised that exceptions to Article 6(3)(d) are required in the interests of justice.
> 5 The manner in which the Strasbourg Court has approved those exceptions has resulted in a jurisprudence that lacks clarity.
> 6 The sole or decisive rule has been introduced into the Strasbourg jurisprudence without discussion of the principle underlying it or full consideration of whether there was justification for imposing the rule as an overriding principle applicable equally to the continental and common law jurisdictions.
> 7 Although English law does not include the sole or decisive rule, it would, in almost all cases, have reached the same result in those cases in which the Strasbourg Court has invoked the rule.
> 8 The sole or decisive rule would create severe practical difficulties if applied to English criminal procedure.
> 9 *Al-Khawaja* does not establish that it is necessary to apply the sole or decisive rule in this jurisdiction.[184]

With battle lines between the domestic courts and Strasbourg clearly marked, the tension culminated in December 2011 when the Grand Chamber considered the United Kingdom's appeal in *Al-Khawaja and Tahery*.[185] Ruling in the appellant's favour, the European Court of Human Rights conceded, somewhat begrudgingly, that even in those circumstances where the hearsay in question was the 'sole or decisive' evidence, there would be no 'automatic' breach of Article 6. Keen to underline the inherent dangers of convictions based on sole or decisive hearsay and explicitly rejecting many of Lord Phillips' criticisms of the 'sole or decisive' rule, the Grand Chamber nevertheless stressed that Strasbourg had always sought to interpret Article 6(3) by referencing the question whether proceedings as a whole could be considered fair. Taking into account the protections that existed under the common law, PACE, and the 2003 Act itself, the English system had sufficient protections in place that were capable of counterbalancing any unfairness to the accused. In a judgment of similar tenor, the Strasbourg Court found no violation in *Horncastle v United Kingdom*[186] and reiterated that the safeguards in the 2003 Act, if properly applied, were capable of providing sufficient counterbalancing measures to offset any unfairness to the accused.

---

182 This position was reiterated by the Court of Appeal in *R v Ford* [2011] Crim LR 475, where it was held conclusively that there was no power to admit anonymous hearsay, either at common law, or under the 2003 Act, or under Part III of the Coroners and Justice Act 2009.

183 [2010] 2 AC 373.

184 Ibid., at 432–33.

185 (2012) 54 EHRR 23.

186 *Horncastle v United Kingdom*, App. No. 4184/10 (16 December 2014).

The practical ramifications of the fallout between Strasbourg and the Supreme Court were afforded thoughtful consideration in *R v Ibrahim*.[187] It was said that while there may be differences in approach as between the Supreme Court and the Grand Chamber, these differences may be more of form than of substance, and that the practical effect of them might be summarised as follows:

(i) There must be proper justification for admitting the evidence of an absent witness, which, under English law, depends on whether the conditions in section 116 of the 2003 Act are satisfied;
(ii) There must be an inquiry as to whether that evidence can be shown to be reliable; it is therefore a precondition that untested hearsay is shown to be potentially safely reliable before it can be admitted; that is a matter for the judge to rule on, either at the admission stage or after the close of the prosecution case, pursuant to section 125;
(iii) There must be 'counterbalancing measures,' including all the statutory safeguards in the 2003 Act and any common law safeguards (e.g. proper directions in the summing-up).

While approving the general approach in *Ibrahim*, it was explained in *R v Riat*[188] that there is no general rule that hearsay has to be shown to be reliable before it can be admitted, or before it can be left to the jury. It was emphasised that, under the framework of the 2003 Act, a court is concerned at several stages with both (a) the risk of unreliability and (b) the extent to which the reliability of the evidence can be tested. These tests could be effected by reference to five central propositions:[189]

(i) The first matter to be considered is whether there is a specific statutory justification ('gateway') for admission of the evidence; the general principle underlying the preliminary gateway question in section 116 (witness unavailable) is that the necessity for resort to second-hand evidence must be demonstrated;
(ii) The next issue is what material there is that can help to test or assess the hearsay; section 124 (credibility) is critical to this; if it is the prosecution seeking to adduce the evidence, the judge is entitled to expect that full inquiry will have been made as to the witness's credibility and all relevant material disclosed; that will not be confined simply to a check for convictions; if it is the defendant seeking to adduce the evidence, the judge is entitled to expect the defendant to supply sufficient information about the witness to enable such checks to be made;
(iii) The court continued by saying that the next issue will be as to whether there is a specific 'interests of justice' test; in a 'fear' case, the judge must, under section 116(4), be satisfied that the admission of the evidence is in the interests of justice, having due regard to, in particular, the contents of the statement and the difficulty in challenging it;
(iv) If there is no specific justification or gateway, the next matter to be decided is whether the evidence should be admitted on the ground that its admission is, despite the difficulties, 'in the interests of justice' under section 114(1)(d);
(v) Finally, the judge should consider whether, even if *prima facie* admissible, the evidence ought to be excluded pursuant to either section 78 of PACE 1984, which applies to evidence that the prosecution wish to adduce, or section 126 of the 2003 Act, which applies to all tendered hearsay; and the non-exhaustive list of factors in section 114(2), directly applicable to an application under section 114(1)(d), is useful as an aide memoire for any judge considering admissibility, whether under that subsection, under the 1984 Act, or otherwise.

187 [2012] 2 Cr App R 32.
188 [2013] 1 WLR 2592.
189 Ibid., at 2597.

The court added that hearsay must not simply be 'nodded through'; a focused decision must be made,[190] involving a careful assessment of (a) the importance of the evidence to the case, (b) the risks of unreliability, and (c) whether the reliability of the evidence can properly be tested and assessed. It follows that matters such as the circumstances of the making of the statement, the interest or disinterest of the maker, the existence of supporting evidence, what is known about the reliability of the maker, and the means of testing such reliability are all directly material at this point, as is any other relevant circumstance; if the evidence is admitted, then the remaining question, the court said, will be whether the case should be stopped under section 125. This provision confers a power on the judge to stop a trial that is based wholly or partly on hearsay evidence that is 'so unconvincing that, considering its importance to the case of the defendant, his conviction of the offence would be unsafe.' It was further stated that whether, and in what circumstances, any such issue might arise would depend on the circumstances of the individual trial; the exercise involves an overall appraisal of the case; and it may often, therefore, best be dealt with after the court had heard all the evidence.[191]

The ECtHR had the opportunity to once more review the judgments of *Al-Khawaja and Tahery* in *Price v UK*.[192] The court found that the lack of a good reason for the non-attendance of a witness was not, in itself, conclusive that the defendant did not receive a fair trial. The court did note, however, that such an absence remains an important factor to weigh in the balance when determining the overall fairness of the trial. The court noted that the prosecution did make a number of attempts to secure the attendance of the witness, who resided in Guyana and refused to attend trial. Further, the legal framework under the CJA 2003 provided sufficient procedural safeguards which could counterbalance an argument of lack of fairness.

In summary, then, the latest position is that applications to admit hearsay evidence in English courts will be governed by the rules laid down in *Horncastle*, especially given the rejection of the applicant's case in Strasbourg. This means that even where such evidence forms the sole or decisive basis of the prosecution's case, it need not necessarily be excluded to prevent a breach of Article 6. The guidance laid down by the Court of Appeal in *Ibrahim* and *Riat* should provide useful practical guidance to the parties as they prepare their cases, in that those purporting to rely on hearsay evidence will need both to take steps to establish its reliability and to bear in mind the extent to which the opposing party will be able to test its reliability. In any event, however, it seems inevitable that we will, in time, hear more from the higher courts on the interplay between hearsay and fair trial rights.

12.6 Key learning points

- The rule against hearsay has long been regarded as a lynchpin of the common law criminal trial.
- Hearsay evidence is now readily admissible in most circumstances in civil courts under the Civil Evidence Act 1995.
- Hearsay evidence is only admissible in criminal courts if one of the four circumstances outlined in section 114(1) of the Criminal Justice Act 2003 apply.
- Statements of absent witnesses may be admitted under section 116, subject to certain conditions.
- Statements contained in a document created in the course of business, trade, or any profession may be admissible under section 117.

---

190 Ibid., at 2601.

191 See also comments of Aiken LJ in *Shabir*, op. cit., n. 102.

192 [2016] ECHR 15602/07.

- Several common law categories of admissibility are preserved under section 118. The most important of these is the *res gestae* rule.
- Multiple hearsay is not admissible under section 116, but may be admissible under section 117. It may also be admitted at the discretion of the court under section 121(1)(c) or section 114(1)(d).
- Recent years have witnessed a growing tension between the English courts and the European Court of Human Rights concerning the impact of hearsay evidence on the fair trial rights of the accused.

12.7 Practice questions

1 Albert was killed in a brutal attack as he left a London nightclub. He was stabbed and kicked by two men and died of his injuries two days later. Duncan Davies and Eric Evans are charged with his murder. Consider whether the following statements can be admitted at their trial.

(a) Albert's girlfriend, Mattie, who had attended the nightclub with him, told the police that, just before leaving the club on the night of his death, Albert told her he had been threatened by Davies and Evans and said he was going to leave to avoid any trouble.

(b) Albert was unconscious when the ambulance arrived, but revived briefly on his way to the hospital. He told Kelly, the paramedic attending him: 'It was Davies and Evans. Make sure they don't get away with it.'

(c) Stanley, the barman at the nightclub, made a statement to the police on the night of the assault in which he said that he was taking a cigarette break outside the main entrance when he saw Davies and Evans, who were frequent visitors to the club and were well known to him, leave the club and pass between them what appeared to be a knife. The barman has since emigrated from England to Australia and, in response to a request from the prosecution that he should return to give evidence, wrote that he had no intention of doing so.

(d) The defence have notified the prosecution that Davies and Evans had an alibi for the night of the assault. They claim to have written statements from James and Paul Murray, who both claim they were at home playing cards with Davies and Evans at the time of the attack. Police officers have tried to contact both men, but were unable to find them. The defence solicitor states that, a week before trial, she received a telephone call from James Murray in which he said that the police were looking for him and his brother, and that they were too scared to give evidence. There is no evidence of any efforts by the defence to find the two witnesses.

2 Akram, Boris, and Chardonnay are charged with conspiracy to evade the duty on cigarettes and tobacco. Police and customs officers raided a warehouse, and found several thousand packs of cigarettes and tobacco on which duty had not been paid. All three defendants deny involvement in the conspiracy and each denies knowing the other alleged conspirators. Consider the following pieces of evidence that the prosecution wish to adduce at their trial and indicate whether they are likely to be admissible in evidence at their trial.

(a) A container of cigarettes and tobacco had been taken from a bonded warehouse by two men claiming to represent the exporting agency. One had driven a tractor to which the container had been attached; the other drove a white car that followed the container. Michael, a customs officer leaving the warehouse having completed his shift, saw the container leaving and, being suspicious of the direction taken, rang Chris, his supervisor, and gave him the registration number of the white vehicle that proved to be owned by Akram. The supervisor made a note of the number on a memo pad and attached it to his statement. Michael made no note of the number and cannot remember it.

(b) The owners of the warehouse had leased the premises to a private company known as Enterprize North on the basis that gas, electricity, and water supplies would be arranged and paid for by Enterprize North. Following a search of Boris's home, police found letters addressed to Enterprize North acknowledging the request for the supply of gas, electricity, and water to the warehouse and bills for their supply.

(c) Telephone bills were obtained from a mobile telephone company that were automatically produced by a computer. These showed regular calls made to and from mobile telephones owned by the three defendants to each other over a period of two years.

(d) Following the arrest of Chardonnay, a police officer conducting a search of her property received five telephone calls from persons asking for her and requesting further supplies of cigarettes. The prosecution wish to call the officer to give evidence of receiving the calls in order to prove the involvement of Chardonnay in the unlawful supply of cigarettes.

3 'Both the civil and criminal courts of England and Wales now admit hearsay evidence too readily.' To what extent do you agree with this comment?

12.8 Suggested further reading

Biral, M., 'The Right to Examine or Have Examined Witnesses as a Minimum Right for a Fair Trial' (2014) 22 Eur J Crime Cr L Cr J 331.

Birch, D., 'Hearsay: Same Old Story, Same Old Song?' (2004) Crim LR 556.

Callen, C., 'Interdisciplinary and Comparative Perspectives on Hearsay and Confrontation' in P. Roberts and M. Redmayne (eds), *Innovations in Evidence and Proof* (Hart Publishing, 2007).

Clapham, N., 'Hearsay Evidence and the Demise of Absolute Rules' (2016) 80(4) J Crim L 220.

Jackson, J. and Summers, S., 'Confrontation with Strasbourg: UK and Swiss Approaches to Criminal Evidence' (2013) Crim LR 114.

Law Commission, *Evidence in Criminal Proceedings: Hearsay and Related Topics*, Report No. 245 (HMSO, 2001).

Pattenden, R., 'Conceptual versus Pragmatic Approaches to Hearsay' (1993) 56 MLR 138.

Pattenden, R., 'Machinespeak: Section 129 of the Criminal Justice Act 2003' (2010) Crim LR 623.

Spencer, J., *Hearsay Evidence in Criminal Proceedings* (Hart Publishing, 2008).

Taylor, G., 'Two English Hearsay Heresies' (2005) 9(2) International Journal of Evidence & Proof 110.

Wallace, S., 'The Empire Strikes Back: Hearsay Rules in Common Law Legal Systems and the Jurisprudence of the European Court of Human Rights' (2010) 4 European Human Rights Law Review 408.

Chapter 13

Opinion Evidence

Chapter contents

DOI: 10.4324/9781003416098-13

The role played by opinion evidence in both criminal and civil trials has been the source of considerable consternation. 'Opinion' has been defined by the Australian courts as 'an inference drawn or to be drawn from observed and communicable data,'[1] and this definition, although seemingly broad, would appear to be widely accepted. As a general rule, witnesses should only give evidence of facts, since it will be the opinion of the judge or the jury, and not the witnesses, that will determine the end result. However, it is not possible to draw a neat dividing line between fact and opinion, and, therefore, the law of evidence has developed two different sets of rules for experts and lay witnesses.

Before proceeding to examine these in depth, it may be worth explaining why the use of opinion evidence has provoked such public debate. Effectiveness in disposing of cases, witness experience, and judicial acceptance all play a more 'conspicuous role' in the admission of expert opinion than formal scientific evaluation, transparency, and attention to jury comprehension.[2] The controversy has largely been triggered by a number of high-profile miscarriages of justice. The first of these concerned a former solicitor, Sally Clark, who was convicted of murdering her two young children in November 1999. Both infants were found dead in their cots in 1996 and 1997, having seemingly suffered cot deaths. Evidence against her was largely circumstantial, although the prosecution sought to rely on the expert opinion of the paediatrician Professor Sir Roy Meadow. The expert stated his opinion that one cot death was a tragedy, two were suspicious, and three were murder, unless proven otherwise. More controversially, he proceeded to state that there was a 1:73 million chance that two children in the same family would die of cot death. This was despite the fact that the expert had no specialist knowledge of statistics. The jury convicted Mrs Clark, but the conviction was quashed by the Court of Appeal in January 2003 on grounds that Professor Meadow's presentation of the statistics and interpretation of them was misleading.[3]

Sally Clark's appeal was followed shortly afterwards by that of Angela Cannings.[4] Like Mrs Clark, she had been convicted the previous year of murdering two infant children who had apparently suffered cot deaths. Again, the prosecution relied upon the evidence of Professor Meadow. Once more, the appeal succeeded. Not long afterwards, a third high-profile case with very similar facts, involving Donna Anthony, was again the subject of a successful appeal.[5] Together, these cases provoked a backlash in the press, and resulted in a review of 297 other cases in which convictions had been based on expert witness opinion. In February 2006, the Attorney General announced that three of these cases should be reconsidered by the courts, but that the majority did not give cause for concern.[6]

The potential for expert witnesses to clash with each other was also catapulted to the forefront of the media spotlight following the high-profile inquest into the death of Ian Tomlinson. Mr Tomlinson was in the vicinity of the Royal Exchange in London while large-scale protests took place at the G20 summit of industrialised countries in April 2009. Film footage was widely circulated of Mr Tomlinson (who himself was not a demonstrator) being struck with a police baton and being shoved to the ground by a police officer. Shortly afterwards, Mr Tomlinson collapsed and

---

1 *All-State Life Insurance Co Ltd v Australian and New Zealand Bank Group Ltd* (No. 36) (1996) 136 ALR 627, at 629.
2 See e.g. Special Issue, 'Impressions and Expressions' (2013) 45 *Australian Journal of Forensic Science* 248.
3 [2003] 2 FCR 447.
4 [2004] 1 WLR 2607.
5 [2005] EWCA Crim 952.
6 See the *Daily Telegraph* (22 December 2004).

died. His death was to be the subject of three different expert reports. The first, prepared by a Dr Patel on instruction of the coroner, attributed his death to natural causes (coronary artery disease). The second report, prepared by a Dr Carey, came to a different conclusion. This report stated that, when Mr Tomlinson fell, his elbow had impacted in the area of his liver causing an internal bleed, which had led to his death a few minutes later. The third report by Dr Shorrock, which was commissioned by the Metropolitan Police Directorate of Professional Standards, concurred with the findings of the second report.

Despite the Crown Prosecution Service (CPS) and the Independent Police Complaints Commission organising a series of meetings between the experts, they remained irreconcilable in their views. As the sole medical expert who conducted the first post-mortem, it would have been Dr Patel who would have had to testify at trial as a prosecution witness. Subsequently, the CPS would have been unable to prove beyond reasonable doubt that Mr Tomlinson's death was caused by the blow to the abdomen. Thus, no police officer was prosecuted.[7]

Media coverage of such cases has prompted increased discussion among lawyers, and expert witnesses themselves, as to how the opinion of experts should be presented in court and the weight that ought to be attached to it. Traditionally, a desire to uphold maximum freedom of proof by the parties has meant that both policymakers and the courts have been reluctant to become overly involved in regulating what expert witnesses say. Under the basic tenets of the adversarial system, where one party calls an expert who presents unreliable data or questionable evidence, the other party should be able to rebut it with expert evidence of their own. However, as the above-noted series of miscarriages has underlined, unfettered freedom of proof may no longer be quintessentially a 'good thing' if it results in innocent defendants being convicted in court.[8] As Edmond and San Roque[9] comment, however, while the scope of rebuttal is important in adversarial contexts, we should not assume that allowing or expecting the defence to rebut the opinions of experienced investigators represents an appropriate counter to insufficiently reliable expert evidence or an effective way to facilitate the evaluation of expert evidence.

Academically, Zander also proffers that within the 'reasonable exceptions' of disclosure and expert evidence, 'it is wrong to require the defendant to be helpful by giving advance notice of his defence, and to penalise him by adverse comment if he fails to do so.'[10] Similarly, Owusu Bempah argues that a critique of defence disclosure is that it reflects a 'non-assistance' approach to the defendant's role in the criminal process; the defendant should not be required to actively participate in a way that may assist the prosecution in establishing its case.[11] As Dror comments, when an expert called by the defence from calling rebuttal experts or explaining a methodology or technical problems, prosecutors should not seek to trivialise the issue unfairly. As Dror correctly points out, the fact that these experts may be research scientists, often from different disciplines presenting the state's incriminating opinion evidence, should make little material difference.[12]

---

7 CPS, 'The Death of Ian Tomlinson: Decision on No Prosecution,' at 7 http://www.cps.gov.uk/news/articles/the_death_of_ian_tomlinson_decision_on_prosecution/ (last accessed 12 April 2011).

8 See further Wilson, A., 'Expert Witness in the Dock' (2005) *Journal of Criminal Law* 330.

9 Edmond G. and San Roque, M., 'The Coal Crucible: Forensic Science and the Fairy of the Criminal Trial' (2002), 24 *Current Issues in Criminal Justice* 51.

10 Royal Commission on Criminal Justice Report (CM 2263, 1993), 221.

11 Owusu-Bempah, A., 'Defense Participation through Pre-trial Disclosure: Issues and Implications' (2013) 17 Ex Parte 183, 197.

12 Dror, I.E., 'The Paradox of Human Expertise: Why Experts Get it Wrong,' in N. Kapur (ed.), *The Paradoxical Brain* (Cambridge University Press, 2011).

Section 6D of the Criminal Procedure and Investigations Act 1996, which requires disclosure of the names and addresses of experts consulted by the defence, as Zander contends, is presumably intended to prevent the defence from 'shopping around' for experts to support its case (which rarely occurs in practice).[13] It is particularly unlikely in cases which are publicly funded under the Legal Aid scheme as funding would not be extended to cover additional experts. However, as Dennis comments, defendants may be prejudiced by disclosing the fact that numerous experts were approached. In the United States, Dennis has observed that the jury might speculate to the detriment of the defendant, albeit the instructions which the expert received from the defence remain privileged. Dennis argues that in most cases, the prosecution will not be able to gain anything useful from knowledge of unused experts; thus, the duty of notification has been termed 'largely a waste of time.'[14]

It is against this backdrop that we proceed to discuss how the law of evidence deals with witnesses who wish to express an opinion in court. The vast majority of witnesses who testify are not considered experts of any sort but instead are regarded as witnesses to the fact. Their primary purpose will be to relate to the trier of fact what they did, saw, or heard at a particular point in time. We begin by examining the rules concerning the opinions of non-expert witnesses, before proceeding to consider the rules regulating the opinions of experts.

13.1 Non-expert witnesses

As a general rule, the role of a non-expert witness will be to provide evidence of what they perceived, which will be used by the prosecution or defence to either prove or disprove a particular fact in issue. This position is a natural corollary of the rule against hearsay, and it follows that witnesses are not permitted to express opinions about subjects that fall outside what they did, saw, or heard. Opinion evidence includes drawing inferences from facts and forming value judgments.[15] It would therefore be wrong for a witness to say 'I saw Tina there that evening, she's definitely guilty,' or 'It couldn't have been Adam, he would never have done something like this.' Such statements are regarded as extraneous, and may act to confuse or prejudice the jury. This is known as the 'ultimate issue' rule, and is discussed in greater depth below in the context of expert witnesses.

However, if the opinion of the witness is so closely interlinked with other aspects of their testimony, the courts have recognised an exception to the rule and will usually permit opinion evidence where it cannot be neatly severed from events about which the witness is testifying.

Example 13.1

Mary alleges she was the victim of a street robbery while walking home from the cinema. The attacker threatened her with a knife and stole her handbag. The defendant, James, claims he is the victim of mistaken identification and was at home alone on the evening in question. Mary will give evidence to the court as to where she was on the night in

---

13 Zander, M., 'Consultation on Proposals for Advance Disclosure of Defense Witness Lists and Unused Defense Expert Witness Reports' (2002), 12.

14 Dennis, I., *The Law of Evidence*, 5th edn (Sweet & Maxwell, 2013), p. 364.

15 Dennis, I., *The Law of Evidence* (Sweet & Maxwell, 2007), p. 846.

question, at what time she left the cinema, where she was going, etc. These are all potentially facts that Mary should be able to recollect from her memory. In addition, she will typically be asked by prosecuting counsel to describe her attacker. She may reply that he was male, tall, lean, fair-haired, and around 20 years old. James is, in fact, 23 years old, of medium height and build, and has blond hair. Mary's opinion thus differs slightly from James's actual physical appearance. However, this does not necessarily mean that she is lying or, indeed, that James was not her attacker. Her opinion simply represents what she perceived on the night in question. In particular, her perception of James as tall may be explained by the fact that she herself is small, and was comparing his height with her own. Similarly, the different hair tone could be explained by lighting conditions. Ultimately, it is for the jury to infer from her testimony whether James was, in fact, the assailant.

In this sense, the line between fact and opinion is not as clear-cut as it may *prima facie* appear. Ultimately, the accuracy of everything that a witness experiences first-hand, and later relays to the court, is dependent upon three key variables: perception, memory, and recall. Even where a witness states something as simple as 'I saw Joe at the restaurant,' they are relying upon their ability to correctly identify Joe as the person they believed that they saw.[16] They are also depending upon their memory of what they perceived at the time, and upon their ability to retrieve the necessary details from their memory in order to articulate them to the court. It would be nonsensical to exclude identification evidence on the basis that it was only an opinion, as it may be particularly cogent and may carry a lot of weight in the eyes of the jury. At the end of the day, there may be no other form in which such evidence could be put before the court. As the Law Reform Committee noted:

> Unless opinions, estimates and inferences, which men make in their daily lives and reach without conscious ratiocination as a result of their physical senses, were treated in the law of evidence as if they were statements of fact, the witnesses could find themselves unable to communicate to the judge an accurate impression of the events they were seeking to describe.[17]

Another example of this blurred boundary between fact and opinion frequently arises in relation to the complainant's evidence in rape and sexual assault trials. As noted in Chapter 6, such trials frequently boil down to a battle of credibility between the defendant and the complainant as to whether the latter was consenting. Thus, the defendant is entitled to express to the court an opinion that the victim was consenting. Indeed, without this information, he or she would be unable to establish their defence. In the same way, a complainant would be entitled to tell the court that it was clear to her that the accused knew that she was not consenting at the time of the intercourse. For that reason, the courts readily accept that witnesses may give evidence relatively freely about what they perceived and in what circumstances, even though some aspect of subjective interpretation in relation to perception or memory will naturally arise. It is therefore commonplace for witnesses to express opinions about appearance (such as age, hair/skin colour), the position or speed of vehicles, visibility, weather, and related matters. This rule has been devised in statutory form with regard to civil proceedings. Section 3(2) of the Civil Evidence Act 1972 provides:

---

16 On identification evidence, see discussion in Chapter 10.

17 Law Reform Committee, *Evidence of Opinion and Expert Evidence*, Cmnd 4489 (HMSO, 1970), at [3].

> It is hereby declared that where a person is called as a witness in any civil proceedings, a statement of opinion by him on any relevant matter on which he is not qualified to give expert evidence, if made as a way of conveying relevant facts personally perceived by him, is admissible as evidence of what he perceived.

On occasions, witnesses may also give opinions *about* those matters that they have directly perceived. In *R v Davies*,[18] the accused was tried for driving while unfit. Here, the witness's opinion that the defendant was drunk was held to be admissible since the witness had spoken to the accused moments after he had collided with a stationary vehicle. However, it would have been wrong for him to proceed to give evidence that the accused was unfit to drive simply because he was a driver himself. Similarly, in *R v Tagg*,[19] a passenger on board an aircraft was permitted to give evidence that the defendant appeared to have consumed excess alcohol. However, it should be underlined that witnesses in both of these cases would have been expected to substantiate *why* they believed the defendants to be drunk. They may, for example, have referred to the defendants' unstable stance, slurred speech, smelly breath, etc. There are clear policy reasons as to why this is so. Drunkenness in charge of a vehicle or on board an aircraft poses a significant risk to public safety, but, in the absence of a formal breath analysis, the chances of a successful prosecution are slim. Thus, the opinion of the witness may provide the prosecution with a crucial additional string in their bow to corroborate any other evidence. For the same reason, section 89(2) of the Road Traffic Regulation Act 1984 allows witnesses to estimate the speed of a vehicle.[20] Evidently, speed cameras cannot be everywhere all of the time, and if a victim happens to be injured or killed on the road due to excess speed, it may be difficult to establish this in the absence of concrete information from a speed camera. Thus, a witness's views about how fast a vehicle was travelling could serve to corroborate forensic evidence, such as tyre marks, and thus contribute towards the prosecution case against the suspect.

In certain circumstances, the courts have also permitted lay witnesses to give evidence of the mental state of another person. For example, in *Wright v Tatham*,[21] a testator had left a substantial estate to his steward. The will was contested by Tatham, who would have stood to inherit the property upon intestacy. He alleged that the will should be regarded as invalid, given that the testator was insane. Counsel for Wright introduced letters to show that, in the opinion of the letter writer, their intended recipient (the testator) was sane. Applying this to the context of a criminal hearing, it follows that witnesses may express an opinion about the mental state of another person, provided that they do not stray into territory that would require medical expertise.

Example 13.2

Billy is charged with murder, but his defence counsel alleges he was suffering from diminished responsibility at the material time. Billy's father, Geoff, testifies that his son seemed to be 'miserable, withdrawn, and depressed' for a period of weeks before the alleged murder. This is merely an observation of a father about the mental state of his son, and may or may not constitute a correct assessment of Billy's state of mind. The jury may well choose to place a considerable degree of weight on this evidence if the father and son had a reasonably close relationship, but they could not infer from Geoff's testimony that

18 [1962] 1 WLR 1111.

19 [2002] 1 Cr App R 22.

20 However, the same provision also stipulates that a defendant cannot be convicted for speeding solely on the testimony of one particular witness.

21 (1838) 4 Bing NC 489.

Billy suffered from an 'abnormality of mental functioning' as required for the defence of diminished responsibility to succeed.[22] Instead, if the defence wish to establish that Billy was suffering from a recognised medical condition, they will need to call an expert, most probably a psychiatrist. While the opinions of a lay witness may give the factfinder a useful insight into the mental state of an individual, they must not stray into an area of expertise that is outside their knowledge or experience.[23]

13.2 Expert evidence: context

In every criminal trial on indictment, the jury will always be the ultimate adjudicator of questions of fact, and it is self-evident that they will not be expected to be experts in all matters that they may be asked to decide upon. Moreover, neither the judge nor the advocates may be competent to explain complex or technical issues to them. In the above scenario, for example, presumably none could provide a diagnosis that Billy was suffering from an abnormality of mental functioning. For that reason, the law of evidence has created an exception to the general principle that opinion evidence should not be admissible in criminal proceedings. Where real evidence is adduced that falls outside the ordinary knowledge or understanding of the court, experts may give their professional opinion, and explain it where it would otherwise be difficult for the jury to comprehend. Section 30(1) of the Criminal Justice Act 1988 states that an expert report shall be admissible as evidence in criminal proceedings, whether or not the person making it attends to give oral evidence in those proceedings. Further to this, section 30(2) states that if it is proposed that the person making the report shall not give oral evidence, the report shall only be admissible with the leave of the court. In essence, the statute provides that where the expert attends as a witness, the report is admissible without leave; however, where the expert does not attend as a witness, the court's leave to use the report is required. Similarly, in civil proceedings, Rule 35.4(1) of the Civil Procedure Rules (CPR) 1998 provides that no party may call an expert or put in evidence an expert's report without the court's permission. Of course, this does not prevent a party from instructing an expert; it simply restricts the use of the expert at trial.

Traditionally, expert opinion evidence has predominantly fallen within well-established academic sciences, most commonly medicine and its allied forensic branches. There was traditionally widespread acceptance that members of professional bodies who held relevant qualifications would be qualified to act as expert witnesses where their opinion was needed. Throughout the twentieth century, science and technology both rapidly advanced, and so too did the tendency of lawyers to rely on the testimony of experts to establish their cases. In particular, our understanding of forensics and DNA is constantly evolving, and what may be considered a standard methodology or finding today may become debunked or superseded tomorrow. Thus, where either party in the trial wishes to rely on some form of real evidence that falls within such fields, it would be prudent for them to ensure that their expert's knowledge is up to date and that the expert is well respected within their field. Aronson has observed that the vast majority of issues with forensic

22 Homicide Act 1957, s 2(1B), provides that an abnormality of mental functioning provides an explanation for the defendant's acts or omissions in relation to the killing, thereby potentially reducing liability for murder to manslaughter.

23 However, as we note below, had Billy sought to rely on the defence of loss of self-control instead of diminished responsibility, expert evidence would not have been deemed necessary.

science and medicine in recent decades (including refining DNA processing, interpreting, and reporting) were identified by those who were not practising forensic analytics.[24]

The evidence of pathologists, fingerprint experts, psychiatrists, ballistic experts, and forensic handwriting analysts now plays a key role in case construction for both the defence and prosecution. It has also become increasingly commonplace to call experts from outside the traditional 'academic' sciences. It is no longer unusual for experts in engineering, computing, and communications systems to give evidence. Similarly, in cases involving fraud, experts in business transactions, banking, or accounting may testify. Dennis cites several examples where experts with more bizarre interests were called, including in *Browning*[25] (involving a specialist in identifying different models of the Renault 25) and in *R v Cooper*[26] (involving a zoologist specialising in the social behaviour of bottle-nosed dolphins). Certainly, so broad is the range of issues on which experts might potentially testify that it would be impossible to devise any sort of exhaustive list that would cover them all.[27]

However, as the range of fields of research continues to expand, and as the use of expert witnesses becomes ever more commonplace, questions are rightly being asked about when it is necessary to have an 'expert' give a view to the court. Where a party intends to rely on expert evidence, the trial judge will need to decide two matters: first, he or she must determine whether expert opinion is necessary and/or permissible; and second, he or she will need to evaluate the quality of the evidence in question in order to determine whether it ought to be admitted by the court.[28]

13.2.1 When is expert opinion necessary?

Not everything will be regarded as suitable for expert comment, and the general rule states that expert opinion will not be regarded as necessary where the matter in question does not call for specific expertise. As regards civil cases, Rule 35.1 of the Civil Procedure Rules 1998 states:

> Expert evidence shall be restricted to that which is reasonably required to resolve the proceedings.

A similar position is provided for in respect of criminal proceedings by paragraph 7.1.1 of the Criminal Practice Directions 2023:

> Expert opinion evidence is admissible in criminal proceedings at common law if, in summary, (i) it is relevant to a matter in issue in the proceedings; (ii) it is needed to provide the court with information likely to be outside the court's own knowledge and experience; and (iii) the witness is competent to give that opinion; and the expert opinion is sufficiently reliable to be admitted.

The Practice Direction largely reflects the traditional approach of the courts. Thus in *R v Anderson*,[29] the court refused to admit expert evidence on the question of whether certain articles in a satirical magazine were 'obscene' for the purposes of the Obscene Publications Act 1959; that was regarded

---

24 See Aronson, J., *Genetic Witness: Science, Law and Controversy in the Making of DNA Profiling* (Rutgers University Press, 2007); see also Kaye, D.H., *The Double Helix and the Law of Evidence* (Harvard University Press, 2010).

25 (1991) 94 Cr App R 109.

26 *The Times* (13 December 1991).

27 The UK Register of Expert Witnesses currently has over 17,000 entries in its subject list.

28 The procedures which govern the use of experts in both criminal and civil litigation can be found in the Criminal Procedure Rules 2020, Part 19, and the Civil Procedure Rules 1998, Part 35, respectively.

29 [1972] 1 QB 304.

as a question of fact for the jury to determine and it was not considered necessary for an expert to assist them in this task.[30] By contrast, a different approach to an obscenity charge was taken in *DPP v A and BC Chewing Gum*.[31] Here, the defendants had been charged with placing obscene cards with their product for sale contrary to section 2(1) of the 1959 Act. The Divisional Court held that the magistrate had improperly refused the prosecution the opportunity to call an expert to testify about the likely impact of the cards upon the minds of children. Since the jury was composed of adults, it was felt that an expert was needed to help them to determine how such cards might affect a child as young as 5 years old. These two decisions reflect the general rule as laid down in *Turner*:[32] if a particular issue does not require specialist knowledge, an expert should not be called and the matter should be left entirely to the jury. It should be noted, however, that the decision as to whether or not a matter requires expert comment will ultimately lie with the trial judge. There is, therefore, no guarantee that what the judge determines to be a matter of common sense will not need clarification in the eyes of the jury.

The particular facts of *Turner* provide a useful example. Here, D was charged with the murder of his girlfriend, and had admitted hitting her over the head with a hammer. However, the defendant raised the defence of provocation, and claimed that he lost his self-control after his girlfriend had admitted a string of affairs. The trial judge refused to grant leave for the defence to call a psychiatrist, who was prepared to testify that D suffered an immediate and explosive outburst of rage at the time of the attack. In the judge's view, the question of whether or not D had lost his self-control was a question of fact for the jury, and should not be the subject of expert comment. Dismissing the appeal, the Court of Appeal found that the expert evidence need not have been admitted as, through their own experience of human nature and behaviour, the jurors were in a position to determine for themselves whether or not D had been so affected by the events in question as to lose his self-control. In summary, then, the fundamental principle is that the purpose of expert evidence is to provide the court with information that is outside the experience and knowledge of a judge and jury. Where a particular matter falls within the knowledge and experience of the jury, or where it concerns an issue of human nature and behaviour within the limits of normality, expert evidence will not be admissible.

13.2.2 Restrictions on the scope of expert opinion

Interestingly, had the accused in *Turner* pleaded insanity or diminished responsibility, expert evidence would have been invariably permitted.[33] This underlines the fine line that courts will have to draw in relation to mental states. Unless the accused is suffering from a recognised medical condition that impacts upon the state of mind, expert evidence will not usually be allowed. Thus, in *Hegarty*,[34] the Court of Appeal stated that questions of emotional instability were not suitable for expert comment. Such a scenario also arose in *R v Toner*,[35] in which the Court of Appeal held that the defence had been wrongly prevented from asking a medical witness about the extent to which hypoglycaemia could impact upon the accused's ability to form specific intent. Similarly, in *R v Huckerby*,[36] it was held that the jury were entitled to hear expert evidence concerning the impact of post-traumatic stress disorder.

---

30 See also *Stamford* [1972] 2 QB 391.

31 [1968] 1 QB 159.

32 [1975] 1 All ER 70.

33 See *R v Holmes* [1953] 1 WLR 686 and *R v Bailey* (1977) 66 Cr App R 31, respectively. Similarly, a defence of automatism will usually be deemed to fall outside the jury's normal experience, and experts may also testify in this regard: *Smith* [1979] 1 WLR 1445.

34 [1994] Crim LR 353.

35 (1991) 93 Cr App R 382.

36 [2004] EWCA Crim 3251.

Occasionally, expert evidence may also be used as part of the defence's case to have a confession excluded on grounds of unreliability.[37] In *Ward*,[38] it was held that expert testimony was admissible to show that the confession was unreliable as a result of a severe personality disorder. However, such evidence will not be admissible in cases in which the accused was merely unstable or emotionally disturbed at the time of the confession, unless they suffer from a mental illness or are below the 'normal' intelligence threshold.[39]

The courts are equally unwilling to admit expert evidence concerning the formation of intention or *mens rea* generally. In *Chard*,[40] the court determined that the expert opinion on such matters fell outside the scope of the *Turner* criteria. Here, the appellant had been convicted of murder, but appealed on the grounds that the trial judge had refused to allow a prison doctor to give evidence that, in light of his personality, the accused could not have formed the requisite *mens rea* for murder. However, the Court of Appeal held that the trial judge was correct in refusing to allow expert opinion on this matter. Such evidence should be admissible only where D had an underlying medical condition that could interfere with his cognitive ability to form intention to kill or cause grievous bodily harm. In a similar vein, in *R v Weightman*,[41] a psychiatrist's evidence concerning the impact of stress upon the defendant was deemed inadmissible, and in *R v Browning*, a psychologist was not permitted to testify as to the likely extent of memory loss in a normal witness.[42] Even where the accused may have an abnormal personality trait, this will not justify admission where they are within the normal IQ range and are not suffering from a recognised medical condition.[43]

Yet this stipulation can prove contentious, as the case of *Masih*[44] illustrates. Here, D was charged with rape, and one of the defendants alleged that he was forced to commit the crime by his co-accused. D had an IQ of 72, and wished to call a psychiatrist to testify that he was immature and easily led. In these circumstances, the Court of Appeal again rejected the need for expert testimony. Although D had a low IQ, it was still within the 'normal' range and thus medical evidence was unnecessary. Had the defendant scored below 70, he would have been classed as 'mentally defective' and expert evidence to this effect would have been admissible. Although the logic for this position is that the jury will be less able to comprehend the actions of someone whose mental state is not 'normal,' such an artificial cut-off point raises the question as to whether justice can really be administered where the hands of the court are tied in such a rigid fashion.

Just as experts cannot usually comment on the state of mind of an accused, neither should they comment on the state of mind of a victim. In *Gilfoyle*,[45] a woman's body was found hanging in a garage. The prosecution alleged that she had been murdered by her husband, whereas the defence contended that the victim had committed suicide. They wished to call a forensic psychologist, who would review the life of the deceased and her medical records, and ultimately corroborate the defence's case that she was likely to have taken her own life. The evidence was excluded on the basis of *Turner* by the trial judge. This decision was subsequently upheld by the Court of Appeal on the grounds that an expert was no better placed to determine 'levels of happiness or unhappiness' than a layperson. The court cited two main reasons why his evidence should not be put before the court:

---

37 See Ch 8.
38 [1993] 2 All ER 577. See further below.
39 *R v Smith* [2003] EWCA Crim 927.
40 (1971) 56 Cr App R 268.
41 (1991) 92 Cr App R 291.
42 [1995] Crim LR 227.
43 *R v Wood* [1990] Crim LR 264.
44 [1986] Crim LR 395.
45 [2001] Cr App R 5.

> First ... he had never previously embarked on the task which he set himself in this case. Secondly, his reports identify no criteria by reference to which the court could test the quality of his opinion, there is no database comparing real and questionable studies and there is no substantial body of academic writing approving his methodology.[46]

Although the courts have generally remained loyal to the rule on *Turner*, there are a few cases that sit somewhat uncomfortably alongside it. In *Lowery v R*,[47] two co-defendants ran a cut-throat defence, each alleging that the other was to blame for the murder of an adolescent girl. One of the accused, K, successfully applied to the court to have a forensic psychologist testify to the fact that he was immature, vulnerable, easily led, and that he tended to be dominated by his co-accused, L, who had a much more dominant and aggressive character. In addition, the psychologist stated that L had a much more callous and impulsive personality and was not capable of relating well to others. In the view of the Privy Council, this evidence was admissible since it would have been unfair to K to have excluded it, as it tended to show his innocence. Where a party seeks to establish that a defendant is prone to certain forms of behaviour, but is not necessarily mentally defective, *Lowery* seems to indicate that expert evidence may be admissible depending on the particular circumstances of the case.

Although *Lowery* remains good law, there can be no doubting that it is something of an anathema to the line taken in the other decisions discussed above. In *Turner* itself, the Court of Appeal suggested that the decision in *Lowery* was based on its own particular facts and did not have any wider application. This line was followed in *Rimmer*,[48] in which an accused attempted to show it was more likely to be his co-accused who killed the victim as he had a history of mental illness. Here, the Court of Appeal upheld the decision of the trial judge. However, the House of Lords' decision in *R v Randall*[49] suggests that *Lowery* should be viewed as constituting a categorical exception to *Turner*. Two co-defendants, R and G, had been jointly charged with murder. As in *Lowery*, each defendant ran a cut-throat defence, and alleged that the other inflicted the fatal blows. While both co-accused had previous convictions, G had a considerably more serious record, which included convictions for violent burglary and robbery. The judge had directed the jury that the evidence undermining G's character was relevant only to the issue of credibility and did not have any bearing on whether G actually committed the offence. Subsequently, R was convicted of manslaughter and G was acquitted. R appealed, arguing that the evidence concerning G's propensity to use and threaten violence was not relevant to the issue of whether R had inflicted the fatal blows. The House of Lords proceeded to state that the propensity to violence of a co-accused may be relevant to the issues between the Crown and the accused tendering such evidence. As such, this would appear to imply that expert evidence to this effect would be admissible.

On the basis of *Randall*, it would thus seem that where D1 wishes to call an expert to testify against D2, even where both defendants are within the 'normal' psychological range, this will be regarded as relevant and admissible evidence insofar as it relates to character or psychological profiles. Admittedly, however, the House of Lords did not go so far as to state this and, as a result, some degree of legal uncertainty continues. Certainly, there seems to be little logical basis for one co-defendant to be able to call an expert against another, but the prosecution cannot call one in a trial against a single defendant. This anomaly, we assume, will have to be dealt with by the higher courts in due course.

---

46 Ibid., at [25]. See further *The Times* (25 February 2008). One of the experts who prepared an initial report for the CPS (but was refused permission to testify for the prosecution at trial) has since changed his mind in light of new research and is now convinced that the suicide note was genuine.

47 [1974] AC 85.

48 [1983] Crim LR 250.

49 [2004] 1 WLR 56.

All of these decisions illustrate the relatively high level of faith that is placed, first, in juries to arrive at factual judgments, and, second, in the ability of judges to make a determination whether something is or is not viable for expert comment. While the overall trend seems to indicate a marked reluctance to call experts too readily, there is a danger that the lack of clear guidance as to when experts should be called could result in inconsistent decisions. In questionable contrast to the line of authorities discussed above, in *Emery*,[50] the Court of Appeal seemed quite happy to allow an expert to opine on degrees of happiness or unhappiness in admitting the testimony of a counsellor that the appellant had been helpless and unable to protect her child from paternal abuse. In *Humphreys*,[51] the accused ran the defence of provocation, and was able to call upon a psychiatrist to testify to the fact that she was a compulsive attention-seeker and was prone to sudden and irrational behaviour. Indeed, there are some cases in which the appellate courts have criticised one of the parties for failing to produce expert witnesses. One such example was *Toohey v MPC*,[52] in which the Court of Appeal underlined that an expert should have been allowed to explain to the jury that alcohol may exacerbate hysteria, since the victim in question was more prone to hysteria than other people.

The freedom of the expert to testify is thus not unfettered. Experts must confine their comments to matters that fall within their area of competence. They may outline the results of research conducted by themselves or their peers or present an overview of the current state of knowledge. They should, however, be prepared to corroborate their evidence, if challenged, by citing other admissible evidence. It is therefore not unusual for experts to refer to their own works, experiments, scientific data, and publications, but they may also cite other authorities and works within their field. Under cross-examination, the expert should also be prepared to be asked about the significance of any contradictory studies.[53] Cole[54] argues that where techniques and opinions adduced by the state and admitted are unreliable, speculative, or 'shaky,' the obligations upon defence lawyers become onerous.

Experts may also wish to explain the basis of their opinion through citing findings or studies by others in their field. They may legitimately refer to such works as the basis for a particular opinion, and there is no requirement that any direct evidence be submitted to the court. Ultimately, it would be impractical for every witness to be able to account for and defend the findings of every piece of information that they have ever absorbed, and it would be equally unrealistic to call other experts to verify that studies of theirs that may have been referred to were accurate and relied upon in the correct context. In *R v Abadom*,[55] the expert testified concerning the refractive index of a piece of glass found in the shoe of the defendant, who was charged with robbery. The expert proceeded to state that, as the refractive index in question would be found in only 4 per cent of all glass, the piece found in the shoe was highly likely to have come from the window of the premises, since it had the same refractive index. The appellant argued that the expert had no personal knowledge of the analysis on which these statistics were based since, by his own admission, he had relied on unpublished statistics provided to him by the Home Office. The Court of Appeal rejected this contention, and stated that part of the reason for calling experts in the first place was their knowledge of, and ability to interpret, unpublished data. Provided that the expert had acknowledged the source as the basis for his findings, such evidence was admissible. Ultimately,

50 (1993) 14 Cr App R (S) 394.

51 [1995] 4 All ER 1008.

52 [1965] AC 595.

53 Cf *R v Weller* [2010] EWCA Crim 1085, and *R v Otway* [2011] EWCA Crim 3. As the case of Weller illustrates, although limitations might be successfully explained to the tribunal of fact during adversarial proceedings – through cross-examination, rebuttal expertise, or in closing address – there is no excuse for making defence lawyers the 'bulwark' against unreliable, speculative incriminating expert evidence.

54 See also Cole, S.A., 'A Cautionary Tale About Cautionary Tales About Intervention' (2009) 16 *Organization* 121.

55 [1983] 1 All ER 364.

if the source on which the expert is relying appears to the court to be especially weak or overly speculative, there is nothing to prevent the judge from excluding it under section 78 of the Police and Criminal Evidence Act (PACE) or at common law.[56]

13.2.3 The 'ultimate issue' rule

A further limitation on the expert's role was the operation of the 'ultimate issue' rule at common law. This prevented experts (and indeed all witnesses) from commenting on anything that was properly to be determined by the jury. For example, if an expert were explaining to the court that the fingerprints on a murder weapon matched a sample that the accused had provided to the police, the common law originally stated that they should not proceed to comment that D fired the weapon to kill V. The rationale behind this position was to prevent the lay jury from being swayed by the reasoning process of someone who was likely to be highly educated and renowned within a specialism. Over the years, however, the ultimate issue rule has largely fallen into disuse, and experts may now express an opinion on those issues that do ultimately fall to the jury for determination. As Parker CJ remarked in *DPP v A & BC Chewing Gum*:[57]

> Those who practise in the criminal courts see every day cases of experts being called on the question of diminished responsibility, and although technically the final question 'Do you think he was suffering from diminished responsibility?' is strictly inadmissible, it is allowed time and again without objection.[58]

The rule was expressly abolished in respect of civil cases by section 3 of the Civil Evidence Act 1972, while (as suggested above) in criminal cases it is now commonplace for experts to express opinions on what might properly be regarded as matters for the trier of fact. Arguably, however, this may be no bad thing, given that their specialist qualifications may mean that they are better placed to express such an opinion than lay witnesses. However, it remains the case that judges should intervene where the expert comments on an ultimate issue that is unrelated to their field of expertise. In *R v Doheny and Adams*,[59] the Court of Appeal reprimanded a scientist giving an opinion as to the probability of a random match between DNA found at the crime scene and that gathered from a sample provided by the defendant. While it was legitimate for the expert to explain the match between the DNA samples, he should not go so far as to give an opinion on the chances of the defendant having left a stain at the crime scene, as he was not qualified to do so. Furthermore, even where the expert does confine their comments to the scope of their field, the judge should issue a warning to the jury that they are not bound to adopt the opinion presented by the expert.[60] The jury are thus free to reject expert evidence as they see fit, and where they choose to do so this will not generally give rise to a ground for appeal. In *Lanfear*,[61] the Court of Appeal declined to quash the applicant's conviction for murder despite strong medical evidence at the trial that he was insane at the time of the killing. It was also stated that although an expert may be regarded as giving independent evidence to assist the court, it is wrong for the jury to be directed that his evidence should be accepted in the absence of reasons for rejecting it.

---

56 *R v Robb*, (1991) 93 Cr App R 161.
57 [1968] 1 QB 159.
58 Ibid., at 164.
59 [1997] 1 Crim App R 369.
60 *R v Stockwell* (1993) 97 Cr App R 260. See further Jackson, J., 'The Ultimate Issue Rule: One Rule Too Many' [1984] Crim LR 75.
61 [1968] 2 QB 77.

In *R v Hamilton*,[62] the Court of Appeal warned of the dangers of the trial whittling down to a battle between experts with opposing views. The accused had been charged with various cruelty and sexual offences against his daughter. The defence alleged that the allegations were false, and came about as the result of his daughter's mental illness. In particular, the defence wished to call an expert to support their contention that the allegations may have been prompted by memory recovery techniques that were used as part of her counselling treatment. The trial judge refused to allow the expert to testify, and the subsequent appeal against this decision was dismissed. The Court of Appeal held that the key issue here was both the reliability and credibility of the complainant, but these were factual assessments that ought to be carried out by the jury and it was not the proper role of expert witnesses to undertake such a task.

This matter has come before the courts on a number of occasions. First, in *R v Allad*,[63] an expert witness was called to explain, in factual terms, the meaning of so-called 'carousel-type VAT fraud.' In providing his explanation, however, the expert witness then began to offer an opinion as to whether it was possible for the defendant to have known, or at least been aware, of what was happening. This was a matter for which they were not called to give evidence on and, as Treacy LJ explained:

> It seems to us that the judge, and then prosecuting counsel, invited Mr Stone to enter forbidden territory. He had not been put forward as an expert; nor was he ever treated as such, for example by way of any direction in the summing-up. He was invited to and did opine on the single issue presented to the jury in the case of these appellants, namely whether they had knowingly participated in the fraud. He gave clear answers positively adverse to the defence, and the effect of what he said was repeated in the summing-up without qualification or warning. The questions posed and the impermissible answers given went to the very heart of the case. In our judgment, Mr Stone had moved from the primary facts of the case, into prohibited, secondary inference.

The Privy Council has explained the limitation on expert witnesses giving evidence on the ultimate issues in *Pora v The Queen*.[64] *Pora* involved the giving of evidence by an expert as to the reliability of the confession made by the defendant. In restricting the scope of the expert's comments, Lord Kerr stated that:

> It is the duty of an expert witness to provide material on which a court can form its own conclusions on relevant issues. On occasions that may involve the witness expressing an opinion about whether, for instance, an individual suffered from a particular condition or vulnerability. The expert witness should be careful to recognise, however, the need to avoid supplanting the court's role as the ultimate decision-maker on matters that are central to the outcome of the case. G trenchantly asserts that Pora's confessions are unreliable and he advances a theory as to why the appellant confessed ... This goes beyond his role. It is for the court to decide if the confessions are reliable and to reach conclusions on any reasons for their possible falsity. It would be open to G to give evidence of his opinion as to why, by reason of his psychological assessment of the appellant, Pora might be disposed to make an unreliable confession, but it is not open to him to assert that the confession is in fact unreliable.[65]

62 [2014] EWCA Crim 1555.
63 [2014] EWCA Crim 421.
64 [2015] UKPC 9.
65 Emphasis added.

Notwithstanding this approach, it is worth noting that the appellate courts may nonetheless quash a conviction where they feel that the jury has gone as far as to act contrary to the weight of the evidence. The murder conviction in *R v Bailey* was quashed in these circumstances,[66] since the prosecution had failed to rebut evidence adduced by a defence expert suggesting the accused suffered from diminished responsibility.[67]

13.3 Safeguarding the quality of expert evidence

The increasingly diverse range of matters that may lend themselves to expert testimony highlights the fact that the courts must take steps to ensure that all who purport to be experts have a sufficient level of competency in their fields. In the traditional sciences, such as medicine, membership of a professional body, such as the Royal College of Physicians, would generally suffice. However, as fields of research become both narrower and deeper, it becomes apparent that given individuals have a limited degree of expertise, even within their own particular field. The degree of knowledge and understanding any given person has will vary tremendously. For example, a recent medical graduate may well know more about coronary heart disease than the average layperson, but will know less than a junior doctor with two years' experience, and presumably will be much less well informed than a clinical professor of coronary medicine. Yet that same professor of medicine, owing to the specialist nature of their work, may know no more than the medical graduate about the most effective drugs that may be used to treat kidney disease, or the latest innovations in chemotherapy treatment. By contrast, only a century ago, medicine, engineering, and other scientific disciplines were considerably less specialised. Experts called to court may have had a broader knowledge base than their contemporary peers, although obviously the depth of that knowledge was considerably less given the rapid advances made in science and technology in the past few decades.

Unlike most other witnesses who testify, experts will not have perceived any of the contested events first-hand. Many of their opinions about the case will be based primarily on speculation about certain hypotheses that will be put to them by counsel. In criminal cases in particular, given the weight that may be attached by the jury to the evidence of someone who is a highly educated and respected professional, it is vital for the integrity of the criminal trial that those who are called to give evidence as experts are qualified to do so. As Bingham LJ stated in *R v Robb*:[68]

> We are alive to the risk that if, in a criminal case, the Crown are permitted to call an expert witness of some, but tenuous, qualifications the burden of proof may imperceptibly shift and a burden be placed on the defendant to rebut a case which should never have been before a jury at all. A defendant cannot be fairly asked to meet evidence of opinion given by a quack, a charlatan or an enthusiastic amateur.[69]

The competency of the expert was one of the key points of contention to arise from the *Sally Clark* case (see above). While Professor Meadow was a highly renowned paediatrician, he was neither trained in nor had he any expertise in statistics. The odds that he presented to the court of 1:73 million of two cot deaths within the same family were found by the Court of Appeal to be extremely dubious, as the expert had not taken into account other relevant variables such as sleep patterns, genetic determinations, type of bedding, and general living conditions. In the view of

66 (1961) 66 Cr App R 31.

67 Note that further limitations on an expert in civil proceedings can be found in the CPR 1998, r 35.4.

68 Op. cit., n. 56.

69 Ibid., 166.

the court, the prosecution's reliance on this evidence had contravened the core rule that experts should not give evidence on any matter outside their own field of expertise.

Arguably, the fault for this miscarriage of justice lay not with Professor Meadow, or even the prosecution, but with the trial judge. It is, after all, the responsibility of the trial judge to ensure that an expert witness is adequately qualified and to determine what information the factfinder should take into account. However, case law suggests that the judicial intervention on this point is relatively inconsistent, and there is certainly no blanket test of expert competence that can be applied as to what precisely an expert is or is not qualified to say. Certainly, professional qualifications may be a good indicator of expertise, but, as the *Clark* case illustrates, even well-established experts with numerous qualifications can still make mistakes. Thus, while judges should rightly attach a considerable degree of weight to the qualifications of a witness, they should not be the ultimate determinant. Indeed, in many cases, they have not even been a prerequisite. In *Silverlock*,[70] the court accepted the expert evidence of a solicitor who undertook the study of handwriting as a hobby in his spare time; in *Ajami v Controller of Customs*,[71] an experienced Nigerian bank official was permitted to give evidence of banking law in Nigeria, even though he had no legal qualifications. It should be noted that on average, prosecutors are better resourced than defence lawyers and those accused of criminal offences. They are also in a much better position than judges to undertake inquiries and review specialist literatures.[72]

In view of the above debates, recent years have witnessed increased discussion around the question as to who might legitimately be regarded as an expert witness. On occasion, legislation will lay down specific stipulations as to qualifications that a particular expert should hold. For example, legislation provides that a jury should not acquit on grounds of insanity or arrive at a finding of unfitness to plead unless evidence to this effect is provided by two or more medical experts who have been approved by the Secretary of State.[73] For the most part, however, competency in a particular field will be a question for the judge to determine within a *voir dire*.[74] It will be for the party calling the witness to establish, on the balance of probabilities, that the witness is competent to give an expert opinion to the court. The Court of Appeal has been unequivocal that all expert evidence must have a reliable scientific basis. In *R v Dlugosz and Others*,[75] it stated that it was

> essential to recall the principle which is applicable, namely in determining the issue of admissibility, the court must be satisfied that there is a sufficiently reliable scientific basis for the evidence to be admitted. If there is then the court leaves the opposing views to be tested before the jury.[76]

To this end, in *Luttrell*,[77] the Court of Appeal cited with approval the test laid down by the Supreme Court of South Australia in the case of the Australian case of *R v Bonython*.[78] Here it was established that there were two questions that needed to be asked by a trial judge in determining whether an expert is to be heard:

70 [1894] 2 QB 766.

71 [1954] 1 WLR 1405.

72 Edmond, G., Hamer, D., and Eunliffe, E., 'A Little Ignorance Is a Dangerous Thing: Engaging with Exogenous Knowledge Not Adduced by the Parties' (2016) 28 *Griffith Law Review*.

73 One of whom should be approved by the Secretary of State as having special experience in the diagnosis or treatment of mental disorders. Regarding unfitness to plead, see Criminal Procedure (Insanity and Fitness to Plead) Act 1991, s 1(1). Regarding fitness to stand trial, see Criminal Procedure (Insanity) Act 1964, s 4.

74 *R v Silverlock* [1894] 2 QB 766.

75 [2013] EWCA Crim 2.

76 Ibid., at para 11.

77 [2004] 2 Cr App R 31.

78 (1984) 38 SASR 45.

(i) The first is whether the subject matter of the opinion falls within the class of subjects upon which expert testimony is permissible. This may be divided into two parts:
  (a) whether the subject matter of the opinion is such that a person without instruction or experience in the area of knowledge or human experience would be able to form a sound judgment on the matter without the assistance of witnesses possessing special knowledge or experience in the area, and
  (b) whether the subject matter of the opinion forms part of a body of knowledge or experience which is sufficiently organised or recognised to be accepted as a reliable body of knowledge or experience, a special acquaintance with which by the witness would render his opinion of assistance to the court.

(ii) The second question is whether the witness has acquired by study or experience sufficient knowledge of the subject to render his opinion of value in resolving the issues before the court.

Although the courts have been relatively consistent in the need for quality control, abstract references to concepts such as 'sound judgment' and 'reliability' are very much subjective and likely to vary according to the experience and understanding of the individual judge. In its 2011 *Report on Expert Evidence in Criminal Proceedings*, the Law Commission advocated that trial judges ought to assume a much more robust 'gate-keeping' role, whereby they would make a decision as to whether the evidence concerned was deemed to be sufficiently reliable to be put before the jury. The draft Criminal Evidence (Experts) Bill was appended to the Law Commission's report. Clause 4 sets out how the court should determine the question of reliability:

4 Reliability: Meaning

(1) Expert opinion evidence is sufficiently reliable to be admitted if –
  (a) the opinion is soundly based, and
  (b) the strength of the opinion is warranted having regard to the grounds on which it is based.

(2) Any of the following, in particular, could provide a reason for determining that expert opinion evidence is not sufficiently reliable –
  (a) the opinion is based on a hypothesis which has not been subjected to sufficient scrutiny (including, where appropriate, experimental or other testing), or which has failed to stand up to scrutiny;
  (b) the opinion is based on an unjustifiable assumption;
  (c) the opinion is based on flawed data;
  (d) the opinion relies on an examination, technique, method or process which was not properly carried out or applied, or was not appropriate for use in the particular case;
  (e) the opinion relies on an inference or conclusion which has not been properly reached.

(3) When assessing the reliability of expert opinion evidence, the court must have regard to –
  (a) such of the generic factors set out in Part 1 of the Schedule as appear to the court to be relevant;
  (b) if any factors have been specified in an order made under Part 2 of the Schedule in relation to a particular field, such of those factors as appear to the court to be relevant;
  (c) anything else which appears to the court to be relevant.

While major statutory reform has not been forthcoming, there is some evidence that the recommendations of the Law Commission had been taken on board in the drafting of the Criminal Procedure Rules 2014. Part 33 of the 2014 Rules had been revised and a new Practice Direction included which drew heavily on the proposed reliability test recommended by the Law Commission for the admission of expert evidence. The 2014 Rules were replaced by the Criminal Procedure

Rules (Crim PR) 2015, which renumbered Part 33 to Part 19 and introduced new Criminal Practice Directions,[79] and now the Criminal Procedure Rules 2020 and Criminal Practice Directions 2023.

In determining whether expert evidence ought to be admitted, paragraph 7.1.2 of the Criminal Practice Directions 2023 stipulates that the court ought to have regard to the following factors:

(a) the extent and quality of the data on which the expert opinion is based;
(b) the validity of the methodology employed by the expert;
(c) if the expert's opinion relies on an inference from any findings, whether the opinion properly explains how safe or unsafe the inference is (whether by reference to statistical significance or in other appropriate terms);
(d) if the expert's opinion relies on the results of the use of any method (for instance, a test, measurement or survey), whether the opinion takes proper account of matters, such as the degree of precision or margin of uncertainty, affecting the accuracy or reliability of those results;
(e) the extent to which any material upon which the expert's opinion is based has been reviewed by others with relevant expertise (for instance, in peer-reviewed publications), and the views of those others on that material;
(f) the extent to which the expert's opinion is based on material falling outside the expert's own field of expertise;
(g) the completeness of the information which was available to the expert, and whether the expert took account of all relevant information in arriving at the opinion (including information as to the context of any facts to which the opinion relates);
(h) if there is a range of expert opinion on the matter in question, where in the range the expert's own opinion lies and whether the expert's preference has been properly explained; and
(i) whether the expert's methods followed established practice in the field and, if they did not, whether the reason for the divergence has been properly explained.

The Practice Direction then proceeds to set out a number of factors that may be used by the trial judge in assessing the potential reliability of the evidence in question:[80]

(a) being based on a hypothesis which has not been subjected to sufficient scrutiny (including, where appropriate, experimental or other testing), or which has failed to stand up to scrutiny;
(b) being based on an unjustifiable assumption;
(c) being based on flawed data;
(d) relying on an examination, technique, method or process which was not properly carried out or applied, or was not appropriate for use in the particular case; or
(e) relying on an inference or conclusion which has not been properly reached.

It remains to be seen whether they will be successful in encouraging higher standards among experts,[81] who may now need to take steps to provide assurance to the parties that seek to call them that their own evidence is of sufficiently high quality to be considered within a court of law.[82] While judges in the civil process are expected to exercise a similar level of vigilance in ensuring that the evidence is of sufficient quality, Part 35 of the Civil Procedure Rules 1998 and its associated Practice Direction offer relatively little by way of assistance to the judge in terms of

79 The relevant Practice Direction for this section is *Criminal Practice Direction V: Evidence*.

80 Para 7.1.3.

81 See Dennis, I., 'Tightening the Law on Expert Evidence' [2015] Crim LR 1–2.

82 The Court of Appeal in *R v Rogers* [2016] EWCA Crim 801 emphasised that as a matter of some importance 'the court should be able to have confidence that a person put forward as having the requisite expertise to give an opinion about matters … is appropriately qualified to express that opinion, and has sufficient data to support it' (per Lord Thomas CJ at [46]).

quality assessment. However, it is nevertheless expected that the judge will exercise a similar role as their criminal counterpart in ensuring that all evidence presented to the court is sufficiently relevant and cogent, and to this end similar factors are likely to operate in the civil courts.

13.3.1 New and emerging fields of expertise

Sometimes, resorting to experts who hold no formal qualifications reflects the fact that experts in these fields are difficult to find. For example, in *Hodges*,[83] a police officer gave expert testimony as to the market for heroin dealing in a particular vicinity, and in *Dallagher*,[84] expert evidence was given by a Dutch police officer who had worked with ear prints for over 10 years, even though he had no forensic qualifications. His evidence was accepted alongside that of a leading professor of forensic medicine, and it was agreed that ear prints were a new and emerging field of forensics with little consensus in the scientific community. However, the Court of Appeal seemed to analyse 'expertise' as something of a spectrum in stating that both scientific and non-scientific testimony should be subject to the 'ordinary tests of relevance and reliability.' In doing so, the court seemed to overlook the fact that forensic science, by its very nature, demands to be subjected to a specialist and scientific standard, rather than that used by the courts to receive non-specialist evidence.[85]

The courts have now accepted that the difficulty in finding suitably qualified experts in new or emerging fields means that, on occasions, the court may have to forgo the desirability of formal qualifications and rely on experience or personal knowledge instead. In *R v Clare and Peach*,[86] a police officer had undertaken a prolonged study of a poor-quality video-recording in order to gauge what precisely was happening in the footage. Although he had no personal qualifications in reading such footage or facial mapping (see below), the court held that his experience in watching the video some 40 times in slow motion had qualified him to make expert comment.

Of course, acquisition of a skill through experience will depend very much on the nature of the particular field. We can safely assume that the police officer in *Clare and Peach* could not have acquired through experience a skill such as forensic pathology, consulting engineering, or psychiatry. Since these established fields of expertise are all subject to regulation by professional bodies, there is usually little problem in finding someone who is well qualified to comment on a particular matter. Indeed, the Council for the Registration of Forensic Practitioners has maintained a database of competent practitioners in 13 specified fields, and plans are currently under consideration for a similar registration scheme for forensic psychologists.[87] However, this is not the case with all disciplines, and indeed there is some controversy as to whether the skills of some of the experts who testify have any scientific basis at all.[88]

In *R v Luttrell*,[89] the prosecution was attempting to show that the defendant was involved in a criminal conspiracy with several others. As part of the case against him, they sought to call a lip-reading expert, H, who had analysed CCTV footage of a conversation between the men. The ability to lip-read from televised evidence was such a specialised area that, at the time of the trial, there were apparently only four other people in the United Kingdom who would have been considered to have had the necessary expertise to testify in court. Before the Court of Appeal,

---

83 [2003] 2 Cr App R 15.

84 [2003] 1 Cr App R 195.

85 See further O'Brian, W., 'Scrutiny of Expert Evidence: Recent Decisions Highlight the Tensions' (2003) 7 *International Journal of Evidence and Proof* 172.

86 [1995] 2 Cr App R 333.

87 See Department of Health, *Applied Psychology: Enhancing Public Protection* (HMSO, 2005).

88 For an overview of the criticisms by attentive scholars and independent bodies, see Rinsinger, D.M., Denbauax, M., and Saks, M.J., 'Exercise of Ignorance as a Proxy for Rational Knowledge: The Lesson of Handwriting "Expertise"' (1989) 137 *University of Pennsylvania Law Review* 731; and Feigman, D.L., *Legal Alchemy: The Use and Misuse of Science in the Law* (WH Freeman, 1999).

89 [2004] 2 Cr App R 31.

the appellant argued that lip-reading evidence from video footage had never been shown to be reliable, and should therefore have been inadmissible. This argument was, however, rejected by the court. Lip-reading itself was a well-recognised skill and lip-reading from video footage was merely a further application of that skill, notwithstanding that it may increase the difficulty of the task. Noting that it was 'entirely appropriate' for the level of expertise to be challenged in court in order to establish the credibility of the expert, the court stated that trawling through the track record of the witness should not be repeated at subsequent trials. In an ironic twist, at another trial shortly afterwards, the defence was able to illustrate significant cracks in H's CV. Shortly afterwards, the CPS announced that it was reviewing all files in which H had been involved and would not be calling her again.[90]

Lip-reading is just one field of expertise that has been regarded with some degree of suspicion; other relatively novel and narrow fields within the realm of science and medicine have been similarly questioned. These have included the existence of Gulf War syndrome and battered woman syndrome. Particular concern seems to focus on the use of voice-identification techniques, facial mapping, and so-called low copy DNA evidence, all of which are becoming increasingly commonplace in criminal trials.[91]

13.3.1.1 Voice identification

The leading case regarding voice identification is that of *R v Robb*.[92] Here, a highly trained and experienced voice-identification expert gave evidence, even though he relied on a particular methodology that was accepted by many of his peers to be unreliable since it did not adopt acoustic analysis. Moreover, the expert had produced no empirical findings that were capable of lending weight to the reliability of his method. Despite the appellant arguing that his evidence should be regarded as unreliable, the Court of Appeal found that just because he held a minority viewpoint in his field, it would be wrong of the courts to exclude his evidence on that basis. Ultimately, it was for the judge to determine whether the expert had sufficient expertise, and it was sufficient that he had directed the jury that the opinion of the expert was not binding upon them. In the opinion of the judge, the expert was an experienced academic who had completed a doctorate and published widely in the area. On that basis, the expert was qualified to testify. This decision, however, remains the source of some consternation, particularly since the judge had not explained to the jury that they ought to pay attention to the fact that the expert held a minority academic opinion.[93] Currently, there are questions being asked over the use of ballistics and tool marks; foot and tyre prints; bite marks; voice recordings; gait, hair, fibre and document comparison; and soil analysis. These techniques are routinely adduced by prosecutors and admitted and relied upon in courts in Australia, England, Canada, New Zealand, Hong Kong, and the United States,[94] but, as Edmond and Thompson have argued, they lack formal validation and research-based standards.

---

90 See further Jackson, S., 'Read My Lips' (2004) 154 *New Law Journal* 1146.

91 More generally, see Saks, M.H. and Kochler, J., 'The Coming Paradigm Shift in Forensic Identification Science' (2005) 95 *American Journal of Public Health* 59.

92 Op. cit., n. 56.

93 Compare *R v O'Doherty* [2003] 1 Cr App R 77, in which the Northern Ireland Court of Appeal rejected voice-identification evidence where acoustic analysis had not been adopted. However, in *R v Flynn* [2008] 2 Cr App R 266, the Court of Appeal indicated that such a position would not be adopted in respect of voice-identification evidence in England and Wales.

94 Edmond, G., Thompson, M.B., and Tangen, J.M., 'A Guide to Interpreting Forensic Testimony: Scientific Approaches to Fingerprints Evidence' (2014) 13 *Law, Probability and Risk*.

13.3.1.2 Facial mapping

So-called facial mapping has also attracted considerable debate in recent years.[95] Facial mapping basically involves comparing two images of the accused. Generally, one of these images will have been retrieved from the crime scene, most commonly using CCTV or video stills. Where the footage obtained is of poor quality, experts may be appointed to analyse the CCTV image using image enhancement and various other technological tools with a view to identifying a suspect. Such evidence was first declared admissible in *R v Stockwell*,[96] in which the appellant had been convicted of a bank robbery. Since the robber was disguised, the prosecution sought to identify him through the testimony of an expert in facial mapping. The Court of Appeal rejected the appellant's contention that there was no need for expert evidence on such a matter and stated that the expert's evidence could provide the jury with a useful basis on which to conduct their fact-finding exercise.

In another case involving a bank robbery, *R v Clarke*,[97] the appellant argued that the technique of facial mapping was so novel that it was fundamentally unfair to allow an expert to testify at trial against the accused. It was suggested that evidence obtained in such a way should have been excluded under section 78 of PACE 1984. Rejecting this argument, the court held that the technique of facial mapping was a form of real evidence to which no different rules applied. However, if such evidence was not sufficiently intelligible to a jury, then an expert's opinion could be called upon in order to assist the jury in their interpretation of the real evidence. The probative value of such evidence depended on the reliability of the scientific technique, which was a matter of fact and had been fully explored in the *voir dire*. The trial judge had been fully justified in admitting the evidence. The court added that it would be slow to prevent experts from testifying in novel fields, since new techniques were constantly developing in relation to criminal investigations:

> There are no closed categories where such evidence may be placed before a jury. It would be entirely wrong to deny to the law of evidence the advantages to be gained from new techniques and new advances in science.[98]

The case of *R v Hookway* required more careful consideration.[99] Unlike *Stockwell* and *Clarke*, the case against the accused was based on facial mapping alone. Since there was no corroborating evidence linking the defendant to the crime scene, the appellant argued that his conviction should not have been based solely on the opinion of the expert. This contention was rejected by the court, which noted that the images were of exceptionally high quality and that, as such, the evidence was highly probative. However, this decision underlines the fact that the cogency of the evidence will always be a matter of degree. Had the video stills in this case been taken from a greater distance, or under poorer light, it may well have been determined that the evidence of the expert in itself would not have been a sound basis for the conviction.[100]

In *R v Atkins*,[101] the Court of Appeal held that it was permissible for an expert in facial mapping to identify the accused using expressions ranging from 'lends no support' to 'lends powerful support' despite the lack of any statistical database on which he could have based these statements. It was, however, stressed that this should be made 'crystal clear' to the jury and the court was not oblivious to the risks that such testimony posed:

---

95 See generally Costigan, R., 'Identification from CCTV: The Risk of Injustice,' [2007] Crim LR 591.
96 (1993) 97 Cr App R 260.
97 (1995) 99 2 Cr App R 425.
98 Ibid., 430.
99 [1999] Crim LR 750.
100 *Hookway* was doubted by Lord Thomas CJ (*obiter*) in *R v FNC* [2015] EWCA Crim 1732, at [31]–[33].
101 [2010] 1 Cr App R 8.

> We accept that there can be proper anxiety about new areas of expertise. Courts need to be scrupulous to ensure that evidence proffered as expert, for any party, is indeed based upon specialised experience, knowledge or study. Mere self-certification, without demonstration of study, method and expertise, is by itself not sufficient ... But the remedy is not to prevent all experts, good and bad, from expressing any informed opinion at all as to the import of their findings. The three principal remedies are: (i) to have such evidence examined and, if appropriate, criticised by an expert of equal experience and skill; (ii) to subject the evidence to rigorous testing in the witness box; and (iii) to ensure careful judicial exposition to the jury of the difference between factual examination/comparison or arithmetical measure on the one hand and, on the other, a subjective, but informed, judgment of the significance of the findings.

13.3.1.3 Low copy DNA evidence

Recent decades have seen DNA evidence become widely revered as sacrosanct in the courtroom, but its elevated status received something of a blow following the Northern Ireland decision of *R v Hoey*.[102] Sean Hoey, a renowned Irish Republican, faced a plethora of serious criminal charges in relation to terrorist activity in Northern Ireland between 1988 and 1998. These included 58 charges of murder, 29 of which related to the Omagh bomb atrocity in August 1998.

Giving the judgment of the court, Mr Justice Weir stated that the DNA evidence introduced by the prosecution could not be regarded as reliable because of the risk of interference or contamination. The risks were particularly acute given the type of DNA profiling used in this case. The profile created was based on 'low copy' DNA. Such evidence is usually resorted to where the sample found at the crime scene is too small to be analysed by more established scientific techniques. Instead, copies are made of the original sample until it can be usefully analysed. The perceived problem with this technique is that if the original sample was in any way damaged or contaminated, the copies produced from it will also be damaged in a similar fashion. In the view of the court, this meant that the risk of contamination was so great as to give rise to reasonable doubt. Hoey was subsequently acquitted.

The court noted that low copy DNA techniques had not been validated by the scientific community and that, at the time of the trial, only two other jurisdictions – New Zealand and the Netherlands – permitted its use in court. That pronouncement proved to be somewhat premature. Shortly afterwards, in *R v Reed and Reed; Garmson*,[103] the English Court of Appeal accepted that not only should low copy DNA be admissible, but also that challenges to the validity of the scientific method should no longer be permitted where the amount of genetic material was above the stochastic threshold (which the court determined to be 200 picograms). However, it was added that juries should also evaluate the DNA evidence and it should not form the sole basis of a conviction but should rather be considered in the context of the evidence as a whole.

13.4 Contesting expert evidence

One of the most frequent criticisms of the adversarial system is that, since parties are in charge of the evidence they present, they will actively seek out an expert whose evidence is likely to favour their case. There have certainly been a number of notorious cases in which the expert's evidence has fallen well short of being objective, and in North America it is not uncommon for parties to vet dozens of potential experts in order to find the one that will paint their case in the most

102 [2007] NICC 49.
103 [2010] 1 Cr App R 23.

favourable light. However, the idea that experts can simply be paid a fee to say what the advocate desires is probably still some way off the mark in England. Although the principle of free proof dictates that experts will generally support the case of the party that calls them, it should be underlined that an expert's primary duty is towards the court.[104] This principle is affirmed in Rule 35.1(3) of the Civil Procedure Rules 1998 and Rule 19.2 of the Criminal Procedure Rules 2020.

In addition to giving an objective and unbiased account of the evidence, the expert is under an obligation to state the facts or assumptions upon which their opinion is based,[105] and should inform the court if they do not have the necessary level of expertise within a particular area or if there is insufficient evidence on which to express an opinion.[106] If an expert fails to understand this duty to the court, then they should be debarred from giving evidence.[107] If, during the course of investigations, an expert should come across evidence that would tend to contradict or cast doubt upon their original opinion, they are under an obligation to inform the solicitor who has instructed them. This was another problem that arose in the *Sally Clark* case: a pathologist had failed to disclose that, in one of the two deceased children, a form of potentially lethal bacteria had been isolated during a post-mortem examination. Indeed, on occasions, the desire of experts to assist the prosecutor instructing them has caused them to depart from objectivity and be selective in their investigations, the results that are disclosed, or what they may say in court. As Medwed observed, appraised of the deep-seated problems, prosecutors should begin to re-evaluate their practices in ways that improve the quality of incriminating expert evidence relied upon in and out of court. Prosecutors have formal obligations to systematically address notorious problems with forensic science and medicine in the exercise of their discretions and in their trials and appellate practices, being 'repeat players ... with access to vast surges of information.'[108]

The most notorious case in which this occurred was that of Judith Ward,[109] who had been convicted of the murder of 12 people aboard a military coach in 1974. Having spent 18 years in prison, her conviction was quashed by the Court of Appeal in 1992, which felt that three government scientists had put objectivity to one side in an effort to help the police to secure a conviction. In the view of the court:

> [We] have identified the cause of the injustice done to the appellant on the scientific side of the case as stemming from the fact that three senior forensic scientists at RARDE regarded their task as being to help the police. They became partisan. It is the clear duty of government forensic scientists to assist in a neutral and impartial way in criminal investigations. They must act in the cause of justice. That duty should be spelt out to all engaged or to be engaged in forensic services in the clearest terms.[110]

Such cases underline the fact that just because an expert is highly trained and well renowned in a particular field does not necessarily mean that the evidence that eventually comes before the trier of fact will be accurate. Furthermore, even if experts do testify faithfully to the best of their ability, their opinion may not be shared by others within the scientific community.

In such cases, there is a clear risk that unless the defence are able to counter prosecution evidence with expertise of their own, the weight placed on expert evidence by the jury may result in

---

104 *National Justice Compania Naviera v Prudential Assurance Co Ltd* [1995] I Lloyd's Rep 455.
105 *The Ikarian Reefer* [1993] FSR 563.
106 Ibid. See also Civil Procedure Rules 1998, Practice Direction 35, [2.4].
107 *Stevens v Gullis* [2000] 1 All ER 527.
108 Medwed, D., *Prosecution Complex: America's Race to Convict and Its Impact on the Innocent* (New York University Press, 2012) 98, 20. See also Neuffield, P.J., 'The (Near) Irrelevance of Daubert to Criminal Justice' (2005) 95 *American Journal of Public Health* 107.
109 *R v Ward* [1993] 2 All ER 577.
110 Ibid., at 628.

a *de facto* reversal of the burden of proof. After all, it is ultimately for them to determine whether or not to accept the opinion presented by the expert. They are not under any obligation to do so,[111] but, by the same token, they should not be instructed that they may ignore such evidence if they so choose.[112] From the point of view of a lay juror, the fact-finding task may be complicated by the fact that there may exist a grey area between what constitutes an ascertainable forensic 'fact' and what amounts to a well-informed, although entirely subjective, opinion. Certainly, the trial judge will bear a considerable burden in effectively managing the evidence and in formulating a correct direction that instructs the jury in an appropriate and objective fashion.

The need for robust judicial management is greater still where expert evidence not only forms part of the prosecution case, but is also fundamental to it.[113] In *R v Henderson*,[114] the Court of Appeal noted that the receipt of expert evidence should lead to a 'logically justifiable outcome,' which will ultimately depend upon careful case management and the structure and quality of the directions in summing-up given by the judge:

> The essential medical issues which the jury have to resolve should be clear by the time the trial starts. Those issues should have been defined and the expert evidence, identifying the sources on which the evidence is based, should also be clear before the trial starts.

By the time the judge comes to sum up the case to the jury, the issues and the evidence relevant to the issues should be understood by everyone, including the jury. While it is conventional to discuss the law with counsel, the judge should, generally, take the opportunity to discuss the issues of medical evidence before the time comes for counsel to address the jury. The judge will thus be in a position carefully to structure his summing-up to those issues. He will be able to identify which evidence goes to the resolution of those issues. He should generally sum the case up to the jury issue by issue, dealing with the opinions and any written sources for those opinions issue by issue, unless there is good reason not to do so. Merely repeating the expert evidence in the order in which that evidence was given serves only to confuse. It is pointless, literally. It deflects the jury from their task. It does not save them, as they must be saved, from avoidable details. It blurs their focus on evidence going to the real issues. The summing-up should enable anyone concerned with an adverse verdict to understand how it has been reached.[115]

The court also approved guidance issued on the nature of the judicial direction by Cresswell J in *R v Harris*:[116]

> If the issue arises, a jury should be asked to judge whether the expert has, in the course of his evidence, assumed the role of an advocate, influenced by the side whose cause he seeks to advance. If it arises, the jury should be asked to judge whether the witness has gone outside his area of expertise. The jury should examine the basis of the opinion. Can the witness point to a recognised, peer-reviewed, source for the opinion? Is the clinical experience of the witness up-to-date and equal to the experience of others whose evidence he seeks to contradict?[117]

---

111 *R v Stockwell* (1993) 97 Cr App R 260.
112 *Anderson v R* [1972] AC 100.
113 *R v Holdsworth* [2008] EWCA Crim 971.
114 [2010] 2 Cr App R 24.
115 Ibid., at [214]–[215] *per* Moses LJ. Note that r 19.6(2) Criminal Procedure Rules 2020 provides for a pre-trial meeting of experts with a view to drawing up a statement outlining the areas of agreement and disagreement.
116 [2006] 1 Cr App R 55.
117 *Henderson*, op. cit., n. 114, at [219].

Harris has been considered by the Privy Council in *Myers v The Queen*[118] in relation to evidence of police officers who are also expert witnesses. The Board noted that:

> Compliance with these exacting standards can be difficult for a police officer who is effectively combining the duties of active investigator (if not of the current case) with those of independent expert. It is particularly important that such a witness should fully understand that once he is tendered as an expert he is not simply a part of the prosecution team, but has a separate duty to the court to give independent evidence, whichever side it may favour. In particular a police expert needs to be especially conscious of the duty to state fully any material which weighs against any proposition which he is advancing, as well as all the evidence on which he has based that proposition. When considering an application by the Crown to adduce the evidence of a police expert, it is incumbent on the judge to satisfy himself that these duties are recognised, and discharged.

13.4.1 Single joint experts

One means of avoiding the adversarial conflict that emerges from the conflicting opinion of experts would be to provide further incentives for both parties to agree on a single court-appointed expert. Rule 35.7 of the Civil Procedure Rules 1998 permits the court to issue such a direction in civil cases. Wherever possible, a joint expert report should be obtained, and this is now common practice for all cases allocated to the small claims track and the fast track. More complex cases may allow for each side to appoint one or more experts.[119]

Where the parties are unable to agree on who the expert should be, the court itself may select an expert from a list prepared by either party or direct that the expert should be selected in any other such manner as the court sees fit.[120] Although there is no presumption in favour of a joint expert agreed in this manner, it is increasingly the expectation that this is done in order to save costs.

In criminal matters, the court may appoint a single expert where multiple defendants wish to rely on expert evidence,[121] but it does not have the power to appoint a single joint expert to conduct investigations on behalf of both the prosecution and defence. This is likely to be attributable to the fact that adversarial argument remains more deeply entrenched in the criminal than the civil arena. There is at least an arguable case for stating that removing the defence's ability to appoint its own expert could conceivably interfere with their fair trial rights under Article 6(3)(d) of the European Convention on Human Rights (namely, the defendant's right to be able to effectively challenge all evidence adduced against him).

13.5 Expert evidence and hearsay

Section 30(1) of the Criminal Justice Act 1988 states that an expert report shall be admissible as evidence in criminal proceedings, whether or not the person making it attends to give oral evidence in those proceedings. Subsection (2) provides that if it is proposed that the person making the report shall not give oral evidence, the report shall only be admissible with the leave of the court. Therefore, where an expert is called as a witness at trial, their report is admissible without

118 [2015] UKPC 40.
119 See e.g. *ES v Chesterfield & North Derbyshire Royal Hospital NHS Trust* (2003) EWCA Civ 1284.
120 Civil Procedure Rules 1998, r 35.7(3).
121 Criminal Procedure Rules 2020, r 19.7.

leave as an exception to the hearsay rule. Where the expert does not attend, then the court's leave to use the report is required. In civil cases, the effective abolition of the hearsay rule pursuant to the Civil Evidence Act 1995 means that it is generally unproblematic for expert reports to be admitted in evidence, irrespective of whether the expert is called as a witness. However, Rule 35.4 of the Civil Procedure Rules 1998 does stipulate that no party may call an expert or put in evidence an expert's report without the court's permission.

In defending their opinion, experts are not curtailed by the hearsay rule to the same extent as non-expert witnesses. For example, a pathologist may wish to rely on primary facts discovered by a member of their staff during an investigation. Strictly speaking, if the individual pathologist did not uncover those facts, they should not testify about them, since to do so would infringe the hearsay rule. However, under section 127 of the Criminal Justice Act 2003, it is permissible for experts to give an opinion based on any primary facts where the investigation was carried out by an assistant.[122] In civil proceedings, the parties are free to adduce out-of-court statements by experts not present at trial, which may then be subject to comment by any experts who do testify.

13.6 Law reform and alternative approaches

There are no straightforward answers to the difficulties posed by expert evidence. Certainly, the courts seem reluctant to move on the issue, bar offering some generic guidance on the contents of experts' reports.[123] While some of the Law Commission's recommendations concerning the quality of evidence were incorporated into the original Criminal Procedure Rules 2014, any more far-reaching reform is likely to fall to Parliament. In the *Review of the Criminal Courts of England and Wales*, Lord Justice Auld recommended the establishment of a new governing body to oversee standards and maintain a register of experts from all disciplines.[124] Inclusion of an individual's name on the register would serve as an indicator of competence, thereby sidestepping the need for lengthy adversarial argument as to whether a particular expert was credible or not.[125] As of December 2014, several organisations maintain databases or registers of experts who have been vetted with varying degrees of rigour. These include the Society of Expert Witnesses, the Academy of Experts, the Expert Witness Institute, the Law Society, the UK Register of Expert Witnesses, and the Council for the Regulation of Forensic Practitioners.[126] In spite of the growing number of such bodies, inclusion of a name on their lists cannot be taken to be an absolute assurance of reliability. In the same way, there may be many other competent professionals who, for one reason or another, are not included on any such registers.

It is worth noting that other jurisdictions have attempted to overcome some of the problems discussed above in a range of ways, including the following:

- The introduction of a code of practice, with disciplinary sanctions attached for non-compliance. While such a move may further boost the overall quality of expert evidence, it may also be seen as a sticking plaster that fudges the question of much fundamental reform.
- The introduction of legislation that would regulate more closely expert accreditation in some of the more contentious fields of science to have emerged in recent years. However, this may be seen as tying the hands of trial judges, and could prove overly limiting.

---

122 Provided that the information supplied by the assistant related to matters of which the assistant had, or might reasonably be supposed to have had, personal knowledge. The court may decline, however, to admit such information where it would be contrary to the interests of justice under subs (4).

123 See comments of Gage LJ in *R v Lorraine Harris & others* [2006] 1 Cr App R 5.

124 Auld, Sir R., *Review of the Criminal Courts of England and Wales*, Cmnd 9376 (HMSO, 2002), [129]–[151].

125 Law Commission, *Expert Evidence in Criminal Proceedings in England and Wales*, Report No. 325 (HMSO, 2011).

126 The last of which receives a subsidy from the Home Office.

- The accreditation of a small pool of experts as 'court approved' would avoid lengthy courtroom battles about the credibility of witnesses, but the vetting procedure could prove costly and complex. Furthermore, there is a risk that experts who subscribe to minority views on unpopular theories would never be heard by juries. Issues would also arise as to how such experts should be selected and whether the prosecution or defence could object to their evidence.
- A single expert or a small conference of experts could be summoned to a pre-trial conference to devise a report on any contentious issues. This option could also prove costly, but the main problem would be that counsel would not have the opportunity to cross-examine the experts in court. This is the system followed in most inquisitorial jurisdictions, although the parties normally have the power to call their own expert evidence if so desired.
- A 'general acceptance' test could be adopted. This approach was followed by the US courts until the Federal Rules of Evidence were introduced in 1972. In order to be admitted, expert evidence had to have been 'sufficiently established to have gained general acceptance in the field where it belongs.'[127] Again, however, such an approach is open to the objection that it would exclude minority viewpoints, which may be perfectly valid.
- The current approach in the United States gives the courts greater discretion through following a 'check-list' of points in order to ensure the expert is competent in his field.[128]

Many of these options, however, would be likely to face stiff opposition by lawyers, policymakers, or experts themselves, who are handsomely remunerated for their time. As technology and forensic science continue to advance into new fields, expert evidence seems set to become an ever more familiar aspect of the adversarial trial.

13.7 Key learning points

- The general rule is that opinion evidence is inadmissible in court.
- For lay witnesses, opinion evidence may be admitted by eyewitnesses where it is difficult to separate it from the facts.
- A further exception applies to expert witnesses, who may give opinions provided that: (a) it is beyond the ordinary knowledge of the jury; and (b) they are adequately qualified to do so.
- Expert opinion regarding mental states is not usually admissible, unless the subject suffers from a medical condition that affects their mental state, or is classed as being mentally impaired.
- Expert evidence remains contentious following a number of high-profile miscarriages of justice. Particularly polemical is the role of experts in new or emerging fields of science and medicine.

13.8 Practice questions

1 'The general rule is that expert evidence of a psychologist or psychiatrist is inadmissible where the defendant is a normal person.' To what extent does this statement accurately reflect English law?

---

127 *Frye v United States* 293 F 1013 (1923). The test now applied is slightly different and can be found in r 702.

128 See *Daubert v Merrell Dow Pharmaceuticals* 113 S Ct 2786 (1993). These are: whether a theory or technique is scientific knowledge that will assist the trier of fact and whether it can be (and has been) tested; whether the theory or technique has been subjected to peer review and publication; the known or potential rate of error; and whether or not there is widespread acceptance of a particular technique.

2 Graeme is called to testify against Hugh, who is on trial for causing death by dangerous driving. Graeme was at the pub with Hugh on the evening in question. They had several pints of beer together, followed by some whisky. As they left the pub, Hugh appeared unstable on his feet and fell over twice. Graeme advised Hugh that he was very drunk and should not drive home, but Hugh ignored this advice and drove off. Will Graeme be able to tell the court that Hugh was unfit to drive?

3 Molly has recently been diagnosed with depression. She finds it difficult to concentrate and is easily agitated. She has recently been charged with the murder of her friend, Alisa, and wishes to run the defence of diminished responsibility. Will the defence be able to call an expert to testify in connection with these matters?

4 Andrew and Zack are charged with inflicting grievous bodily harm on George contrary to section 18 of the Offences Against the Person Act 1861. Andrew alleges that he kept watch while Zack beat George with a cricket bat in a nearby alleyway. Zack claims that he kept watch while Andrew attacked George. Andrew's counsel wishes to call a forensic psychologist to testify that Zack was more likely than Andrew to have carried out the attack since he had an aggressive personality and was prone to violent outbursts. Will he be allowed to do this?

13.9 Suggested further reading

Burns, S., 'Low Copy DNA on Trial' (2008) 158 NLJ 919.

Davies, G. and Piasecki, E., 'No More Laissez Faire? Expert Evidence, Rule Changes and Reliability: Can More Effective Training for the Bar and Judiciary Prevent Miscarriages of Justice?' (2016) 80(5) J Crim L 327.

Edmond, G., 'Legal versus Non-legal Approaches to Forensic Science Evidence' (2016) 20(1) E & P 3.

Law Commission, *Expert Evidence in Criminal Proceedings in England and Wales*, Report No. 325 (HMSO, 2011).

Morrison, S., 'The Likelihood-Ratio Framework and Forensic Evidence in Court: A Response to R v T' (2012) 16(1) E & P 1.

Naughton, M. and Tan, G., 'The Need for Caution in the Use of DNA Evidence to Avoid Convicting the Innocent' (2011) 15(3) E & P 245.

Redmayne, M., *Expert Evidence and Criminal Justice* (Oxford University Press, 2001).

Redmayne, M., 'Forensic Science Evidence in Question' (2011) Crim LR 347.

Shaw, K., 'Expert Evidence Reliability: Time to Grasp the Nettle' (2011) 75(5) Journal of Criminal Law 368.

Shelton, D.E., 'Juror Expectations for Scientific Evidence in Criminal Cases: Perceptions and Reality about the "CSI Effect" Myth' (2010) 27 Thomas M Cooley Law Review 1.

Ward, T., 'Expert Evidence and the Law Commission: Implementation Without Legislation?' (2013) Crim LR 561.

Ward, T., 'A New and More Rigorous Approach to Expert Evidence in England and Wales' (2015) 19(4) E & P 228.

Chapter 14

Public Interest Immunity

Chapter contents

DOI: 10.4324/9781003416098-14

As was stated in Chapter 1, the law of evidence concerns the use of material to prove the existence or non-existence of any elements of the substantive law. In order for a party to do so, however, the evidence in question needs to be disclosed. The meaning of disclosure in criminal and civil proceedings will be discussed later in this chapter. For the moment, however, it is important to note that the parties to the proceedings should observe 'the golden rule of full disclosure,'[1] which states that the parties should disclose to one another any and all relevant material to the proceedings. In criminal proceedings, the test for disclosure has been placed on a statutory footing by the Criminal Procedure and Investigations Act 1996, in particular section 3(1)(a) which states that the prosecutor must disclose to the accused any prosecution material which has not previously been disclosed to the accused and which 'might reasonably be considered capable of undermining the case for the prosecution against the accused or of assisting the case for the accused.' Similarly, in civil proceedings the test for 'standard disclosure' can be found in Rule 31.6 of the Civil Procedure Rules (CPR) 1998 which provides that a party is required to disclose the documents on which they rely and the documents which adversely affect their own case, adversely affect another party's case, or support another party's case.[2] However, as with many general rules in law, the criminal and civil 'golden rules' of disclosure are not absolute.

Full disclosure is not always possible with the operation of public interest immunity (PII). PII operates to prevent material held by a party from being disclosed, fully or even at all, where circumstances arise that could lead to the risk of serious prejudice to an important public interest. What amounts to an important public interest is part of a non-exhaustive list; however, the more settled interests include national security, the proper functioning of public service, and, more specifically to criminal proceedings, the identity of informants. Applications by the prosecution or the Government to the court to withhold material in these circumstances are known as PII applications. It is important to note at this stage that, although in certain circumstances some derogation from the golden rule of full disclosure may be justified, such derogation must always be 'the minimum derogation necessary to protect the public interest in question and must never imperil the overall fairness of the trial.'[3]

PII has long been subject to widespread criticisms and calls for review. By way of introduction to the topic, a good starting point is the infamous case of Matrix Churchill.[4] Matrix Churchill was a company specialising in the development of dual-use machine tools (civil engineering, with potential for use in military applications). In the case, three of the directors of the company were charged with supplying arms-making equipment to Iraq, in breach of the Government's published export guidelines. The defence argued that government ministers were complicit and authorised the exports, and sought the disclosure of documents from the Government to substantiate this accusation. These documents, however, had been made subject to PII certificates by government ministers. The judge ordered disclosure and allowed the documents to be used in cross-examination of the ministers in question, among others. During cross-examination, the then Minister of State at the Department of Trade and Industry, Alan Clark, admitted that the Government had been fully aware of the intended use of the equipment and was fully aware of the cover-up. Amid the allegations of a cover-up, the prosecution abandoned the case. As a result of the Matrix Churchill incident, Sir Richard Scott VC (a High Court judge) led an inquiry into the issue of PII and, on 15 February 1996,

---

1 *R v H and C* [2004] 2 AC 134 (Lord Bingham).
2 CPR 1998, r 31.6(a) and (b).
3 *R v H and C*, op. cit., n. 1.
4 Also referred to as the 'Arms to Iraq' incident.

Sir Richard published his report, which became known as the Scott Report.[5] The report contained a detailed analysis of the law relating to PII, the use of PII certificates, the circumstances in which they arose and how they came to be made, as well as serious observations and criticisms of ministers and law officers. The Scott Report led to widespread reforms in the law of PII, which will be discussed in greater depth below.[6]

14.1 Development of immunity

Prior to discussing the rules of PII in greater depth, it may be worth reflecting on the history and development of the concept of immunity. While largely of historical importance, the discussion below serves a useful purpose by way of providing the political context of the current PII regime. It also illustrates some of the reasons as to why the operation of immunity in criminal and civil cases has always been controversial, and, as noted below, a sense of general unease concerning the fairness of the current law remains intact to this day.

14.1.1 Crown privilege

Public interest immunity was previously referred to as 'Crown privilege.' Crown privilege reflected the position whereby the Crown could simply claim to retain information from disclosure as of right.[7] The law relating to Crown privilege developed largely in civil proceedings, with cases such as *Duncan v Cammell Laird & Co. Ltd*,[8] which concerned documents relating to the construction of a submarine. It was held that once a claim for Crown privilege was made by the Crown in a due and proper form, it was considered to be final and binding and could not and would not be overridden by the court. This principle applied irrespective of whether the claim related to the contents of a particular document or to a class of documents. It was added that this was the case despite the fact that the risk to the public interest may be minor when compared to the importance of the document to the litigant.

This final point in *Duncan* was widely criticised in subsequent cases,[9] and something of a judicial retreat began in 1964 with the Court of Appeal holding that the English courts had a residual power to inspect documents, in rare circumstances, and form their own opinion as to the PII.[10] However, it was only in 1968 that the so-called privilege came to a stark end with the landmark House of Lords decision in *Conway v Rimmer*,[11] where disclosure was sought for police files by a former police officer suing for wrongful prosecution. While not expressly overruling *Duncan*, their Lordships opted to distinguish it but held that it was for the court, not the Crown, to act as the final arbiter in relation to all PII claims.[12] Therefore, a ministerial certificate was no longer to be considered final, and the courts were then permitted to ask for clarification or amplification of the minister's objection and/or could inspect the documents themselves. At that stage, a balancing

5 Scott, Sir R., *Report of the Inquiry into the Export of Defence Equipment and Dual-Use Goods to Iraq and Related Prosecutions* (HMSO, 1996). See also Sir Richard Scott's article, 'The Acceptable and Unacceptable Use of PII' [1996] *Public Law* 427.

6 See discussion below.

7 As was expressly recognised in Crown Proceedings Act 1947, s 28.

8 [1942] AC 624.

9 See e.g. *Ellis v Home Office* [1953] 2 AB 135; and *Broome v Broome* [1955] P 190.

10 *Re Grosvenor Hotel, London (No. 2)* [1965] Ch 1210; see in particular Lord Denning's comments at 1244–46.

11 [1968] AC 910; see also *Rogers v Secretary of State for the Home Department* [1973] AC 388.

12 The House did, however, hold that the outcome in *Duncan* was correct on its particular facts, given the national security interests at stake.

test had to be performed by weighing up two public interests: that of the proper administration of justice in the actual disclosing of documents and that of interests of the state and the public in non-disclosure.

These developments in the civil courts can be contrasted with their relatively slow evolution in relation to criminal proceedings. Indeed, in *Duncan*, Viscount Simon LC had expressly stated that '[t]he judgment of the House in the present case is limited to civil actions,'[13] and *Conway v Rimmer* was also viewed by the court in a similar light. This remained true for a period as it was not until the mid-1990s when cases concerning PII first began to be reported in criminal cases. As with civil proceedings, this was because a decision of non-disclosure was left principally to the judgment of the prosecution, with the courts making a ruling only in exceptional circumstances. The first reported case concerning PII and its operation in criminal proceedings was *Osman*,[14] where it was held by Mann LJ that:

> The seminal cases in regard to public interest immunity do not refer to criminal proceedings but, the principles are expressed in general terms. Asking myself why those general expositions should not apply to criminal proceedings, I can see no answer but that they do. It seems correct in principle that they should apply. The reasons for the development of the doctrine seem equally applicable to criminal as to civil proceedings. I acknowledge that the application of the public immunity doctrine in criminal proceedings will involve a different balancing exercise to that in civil proceedings. Suffice it to say for the moment that a judge is balancing on the one hand the desirability of preserving the public interest in the absence of disclosure against, on the other hand, the interests of justice. Where the interests of justice arise in a criminal case touching and concerning liberty or conceivably on occasion life, the weight to be attached to the interests of justice is plainly very great indeed.[15]

The real change, however, came a few years later in the high-profile case of *Ward*,[16] where the Court of Appeal upheld the appeal of Judith Ward who had been convicted of multiple murder and explosives offences. The court ruled that it was, and is, for the court, rather than the prosecution, to be the final arbiter as to whether the prosecution was, and is, entitled to avoid disclosure on the basis of PII. Where a claim was made, the court could then, if necessary, rule on the legitimacy of the prosecution's claim of privilege. Where the prosecution refused or was not prepared to have the issue of PII determined by a court, they would be forced to drop the claim and possibly abandon the case as a whole. The decision of *Ward* is now reflected in the Criminal Procedure and Investigations Act 1996, section 21(2), which provides that the Act 'does not affect the rules of common law as to whether disclosure is in the public interest.' The criminal law has come a long way since the time before *Osman* and *Ward*. At present, the Criminal Procedure and Investigations Act (CPIA) 1996 is just one of a number of sources used in criminal litigation governing the operation of PII; other tools include the Criminal Procedure Rules (Crim PR) 2020, the Attorney General's Guidelines on Disclosure 2022, and the Crown Prosecution Service's (CPS) Disclosure Manual.

---

13 *Duncan v Cammell Laird*, op. cit., n. 8, at 628.

14 *R v Governor of Brixton Prison, ex parte Osman* [1992] 1 All ER 579.

15 Ibid., at 633–34.

16 [1993] 2 All ER 577.

These developments essentially mean that Crown privilege is no more and the preferred phrase now is 'public interest immunity,' which refers to matters excluded on grounds of public policy.[17]

In any event, 'Crown privilege' was an inaccurate phrase, which differed from the contemporary operation of PII in a number of ways:

(i) Under Crown privilege it was often not the Crown that initiated the proceedings but, rather, the Crown simply intervened to claim the 'privilege.'

(ii) An objection on the grounds of privilege could only have been made in relation to the production or inspection of the relevant document, whereas an objection on the grounds of public interest immunity is not restricted to the inspection of a document, but may also be made in relation to the disclosure of that document.[18]

(iii) Crown privilege implied that the matters at stake were of high national concern or great issues of state. In fact, Crown privilege often applied to neither of these. Durston affirms this, arguing that the reality was that it would normally concern 'much more mundane matters, such as the identity of a police informer or the efficient operation of a public service.'[19] Case law further demonstrates this misnomer with such authorities as *D v NSPCC*,[20] which concerned matters relating to the proper functioning of a public service, in that case the National Society for the Prevention of Cruelty to Children (NSPCC).

(iv) The word 'privilege' itself was an inappropriate description of the right held by the Crown. In *Rogers*, Lord Simon expressed his opinion that the term 'privilege,' in relation to disclosure, was applicable only to a claim that could be waived. Such privilege covered, and continues to cover, matters that directly affect and are personal to a particular party or witness, and it is their right alone to waive it. Examples of the most common privileges include litigation privilege, legal advice privilege, and the privilege against self-incrimination. Each of these can be waived, although PII cannot.[21]

It appears, however, in civil proceedings, that the law may not be so clear; in *R v Chief Constable of the West Midlands Police, ex parte Wiley*,[22] Lord Woolf commented that Lord Simon was referring to the

> situation *after* it had been determined that the public interest against disclosure outweighed that of disclosure in the interests of the administration of justice. When that is the determination that has been made, it is inevitable that the preservation of the document should follow so as to protect what has been held to be the dominant public interest. It was, however, unhelpful to talk of 'waiver' in the different situations where the balancing of the conflicting public interests *has not yet been carried out* or where it has been carried out and the result requires disclosure.

This appears to be an indication that waiving may be possible where a decision on PII has yet to be made. It thus seems that in civil proceedings there remains no definite answer as to whether PII can be waived, although the editor of *Phipson on Evidence* concludes that 'whether or not there can technically be a waiver, the distinction is unimportant in practice.'[23] By contrast, in criminal proceedings, the law is very clear that the CPS may voluntarily disclose to the defence documents

---

17 Ibid.

18 As provided in civil proceedings under CPR 1998, r 31.19(1).

19 Durston, G., *Evidence: Text & Materials*, 2nd edn (Oxford University Press, 2011), at 546.

20 [1978] AC 171.

21 *Rogers*, op. cit., n. 11, at 407 (Lord Simon). See also Lord Fraser's comments in *Air Canada v Secretary of State for Trade (No. 2)* [1983] 2 AC 394.

22 [1995] 1 AC 274.

23 Malek, H. (ed.), *Phipson on Evidence*, 18th edn (Sweet & Maxwell, 2016), at [25–16].

that would otherwise be in a class covered by PII, without referring the matter to the court for a ruling.[24]

(v) Where evidence is excluded by the operation of PII, not only are the documents that have been expressly withheld immune from use, the use of secondary evidence, such as copies of the documents and oral evidence as to the contents of the documents to prove a fact, is also forbidden. A good example is the case of *R v Lewes Justices, ex parte Home Secretary,*[25] where a copy of a letter, alleged to be libellous, had been obtained by the person to whom it referred; however, due to the operation of PII, he was not entitled to use that copy to prove his case. This is in direct contrast with a case of private privilege as that privilege only applies to the original document, and secondary evidence of the contents of that document is admissible.[26]

(vi) Similar to point (iv) above, the word 'privilege' implies a private right held by an individual. As noted above, Crown privilege was used for the protection of the public on either a national or local level, not protection of an individual. Indeed, this has been made clear in a number of judgments; in particular, Lord Scarman stated that 'we are in the realm of public law, not private right.'[27] A further distinction between the idea of a right and a duty was made by Bingham LJ, as he then was, in *Makanjuola v Commissioner of Police of the Metropolis.*[28] His Lordship stated that 'where a litigant asserts that documents are immune from production or disclosure on public interest grounds he is not (if the claim is well founded) claiming a right but observing a duty.'[29]

For the reasons stated above, Cross and Tapper describe Crown privilege as 'not a happy expression,'[30] and the issues stated above were effectively summarised by Brightman LJ in *Buttes Gas & Oil Co. v Hammer (No. 3)*[31] in the following terms: 'it is not a matter of privilege and it is not confined to the Crown.'[32]

14.1.2 Class claims and content claims

A claim for public interest immunity can take one of two forms: a class-based or content-based claim. In *Conway v Rimmer,*[33] their Lordships drew the distinction between class- and content-based claims: a class claim being one where a document, by virtue of the class to which it belonged, regardless of its contents, ought to be withheld; a contents claim, on the other hand, is about documents that ought to be withheld due to the contents in the document.[34] At one time, 'class immunity' might have been claimed by the Government or others for a document by virtue of the class to which it belonged and without reference to any harm which disclosure of the particular document might cause. As discussed above, where a claim was made by the Crown in proper form, it was conclusive on the matter and the court would not intervene. Indeed, this can be observed from Lord Reid's and Lord Upjohn's judgments in *Conway v Rimmer,* where their Lordships

---

24 This, however, is subject to the safeguard of first seeking the express written approval of the Treasury Solicitor, who should consult any other relevant government department and satisfy himself that the balance falls clearly in favour of disclosure: *R v Horseferry Road Magistrates, ex parte Bennett (No. 2)* [1994] 1 All ER 289.

25 [1973] AC 388.

26 See *Calcraft v Guest* [1889] 1 QB 759. The law was complicated by *Lord Ashburton v Pape* [1913] 2 Ch 469; however, that is outside the scope of this chapter.

27 *Science Research Council v Nassé* [1980] 1 AC 1028 at 1087.

28 [1992] 3 All ER 617.

29 Ibid. (Bingham LJ).

30 Tapper, C., *Cross & Tapper on Evidence*, 12th edn (Oxford University Press, 2010), at 477.

31 [1981] QB 223.

32 Ibid., at 262. See also *Lewes Justices, ex parte Secretary of State for the Home Department* [1973] AC 388 at 400 (Lord Reid).

33 *Conway v Rimmer*, op. cit., n. 11.

34 See also *Burmah Oil Co. Ltd v Bank of England* [1980] AC 1090, at 1111.

held that certain classes of documents, such as Cabinet papers and Foreign Office dispatches, should never be disclosed, regardless of their contents.[35]

Two rationales were given for this decision. In Lord Reid's eyes, 'the most important reason is that such disclosure would create or fan ill-informed or captious public or political criticism,'[36] while for Lord Upjohn, '[t]he reason for this privilege is that it would be quite wrong and entirely inimical to the proper functioning of the public service if the public were to learn of these high level communications.'[37] Irrespective of the rationale, the House of Lords has since made it clear that the courts should be prepared to evaluate and decide 'class' claims on their merits, just like any other type of document.[38] This is so even in cases concerning high-level government papers.[39] As a result, immunity from disclosure will no longer automatically be granted merely because of the nature of a document as a diplomatic correspondence or government report.

It is inaccurate to argue that a class claim can no longer be made or that class claims have now been eradicated. Rather, a class claim may still be made but there is no longer an automatic exclusion of the evidence simply because the document in question is in a certain class. The editors of *Archbold: Criminal Pleading, Evidence and Practice* submit that 'this approach has no place within modern criminal proceedings'[40] as disclosure is now governed by the CPIA 1996, the Criminal Procedure Rules, and the balancing exercise emphasised in *R v H and C* (discussed below).[41] The notion that class claims have no place in criminal cases was first mooted by Sir Richard Scott VC:

> Where class claims are concerned, the 'balance' between, on the one hand, the public interest in withholding the documents, and, on the other hand, the interests of justice would, in a criminal trial, unlike in civil litigation, be bound always to come down on the side of the interests of justice.[42]

Similarly, a class claim no longer has any place in civil proceedings that concern the Government, as confirmed in an official statement by the Lord Chancellor in December 1996, which stated that the division into class and contents claims would no longer be applied and, in particular, the Government would not seek to withhold a document simply on the grounds that the document fell within a particular class. Rather, ministers would:[43]

> focus directly on the damage that disclosure of sensitive documents would cause ... Ministers will only claim immunity when they believe that disclosure of a document will cause real damage or harm to the public interest. Damage will normally have to be in the form of a direct and immediate threat to the safety of an individual or to the nation's economic interests or relations with a foreign state, although in some cases the anticipated damage might be indirect or longer term, such as damage to a regulatory process.[44]

35 Op. cit., n. 11, at 952 and 993, respectively.

36 Ibid., at 943.

37 Ibid., at 993.

38 *Burmah Oil*, op. cit., n. 34, at 1134 (Lord Keith).

39 *Air Canada*, op. cit., n. 21, at 432. However, Lord Fraser also commented that 'while cabinet documents do not have complete immunity, they are entitled to a high degree of protection against disclosure.'

40 Richardson, J., *Archbold: Criminal Pleading, Evidence and Practice*, 65th edn (Sweet & Maxwell, 2017).

41 *R v H and C*, op. cit., n. 1.

42 Scott, op. cit., n. 5, at [G.18.83].

43 (1997) 147 NLJ 62. For a critique, see Supperstone, M. and Coppel, J., 'A New Approach to Public Interest Immunity?' [1997] *Public Law* 211.

44 Ibid.

In any event, the nature of the harm will have to be clearly explained, and ministers will no longer be able to claim immunity for internal advice or national security material merely by pointing to the general nature of the document. Roberts and Zuckerman note that this 'effectively established a new constitutional convention, though it is not a rule of law.'[45] Despite the lack of a strict law on the point, Choo argues that this approach is 'very much to be welcomed, but the situation is now somewhat anomalous'[46] in that, while the Government and particular ministers are no longer permitted to make class claims, non-government bodies such as the police may continue to do so. Indeed, there are numerous decisions of vital importance to the topic of the police and class claims.

To begin with, the House of Lords, in *R v Chief Constable of the West Midlands Police, ex parte Wiley*,[47] held that documents created for the purposes of an investigation into a complaint against the police for misconduct under Part IV of the Police Act 1996 no longer attracted immunity as a class of documents. Naturally, the court appreciated that documents of this kind may still obtain immunity from disclosure due to their specific contents; however, the court emphasised that the previous authorities on the matter, specifically *Neilson*,[48] had been wrongly decided on this point. Their Lordships did, however, leave open the question of whether class immunity applied to the actual reports of the investigating officers created for the purposes of an investigation into a complaint against the police for misconduct. Indeed, Lord Woolf stated in clear terms that 'it would not be right to close the door to a future attempt to establish that the reports are subject to class immunity.'[49] However, the Court of Appeal effectively closed the door on the question in *Taylor v Anderton (Police Complaints Authority Intervening)*,[50] holding that the actual reports of investigating officers fell into a sub-group category entitled to immunity by reason of class. Sir Thomas Bingham MR, as he then was, offered the rationale for such class immunity as being 'the prospect of disclosure other than in unusual circumstances would have an undesirably inhibiting effect on investigating officers' reports.'[51]

Additional cases demonstrating class immunity for police documents include *Kelly v Commissioner of Police of the Metropolis*,[52] which concerned forms used by the police and sent to the CPS and their use against the police subsequent to the proceedings for which they were created, and *Goodridge v Chief Constable*,[53] which related to correspondence and reports passing between the police and the Director of Public Prosecutions and reports to the Police Complaints Authority. In both cases, their Lordships held that the documents were entitled to immunity because of the class they belonged to. Again, it must be stressed that this entitlement to class immunity by the police does not equal automatic exclusion from disclosure. The balancing exercise is still necessary. As a result, it can be argued that 'the distinction between class and contents claims is not wholly dead,'[54] as their Lordships in *ex parte Wiley* might have assumed. However, even though class claims may still be made, in both criminal and civil proceedings, the use of such claims remains controversial and, therefore, 'there is a heavy burden of proof on any authority which makes such a claim.'[55] On the issue of government reports and the fact that it applies only to a government department and not

45 Roberts, P. and Zuckerman, A., *Criminal Evidence*, 2nd edn (Oxford University Press, 2010), at 332.
46 Choo, A.-L.T., *Evidence*, 4th edn (Oxford University Press, 2015), at 205.
47 *Ex parte Wiley*, op. cit., n. 22.
48 *Neilson v Laugharne* [1981] QB 736.
49 *Ex parte Wiley*, op. cit., n. 22, at 287 (Lord Woolf MR).
50 [1995] 1 WLR 447.
51 Ibid., at 465.
52 *The Times* (20 August 1997).
53 [1999] 1 WLR 1558.
54 Matthews, P. and Malek, H., *Disclosure*, 5th edn (Sweet & Maxwell, 2016), at 173.
55 *Ex parte Wiley*, op. cit., n. 22, at 247 (Lord Woolf MR).

to other statutory bodies, Choo concludes that 'what is required now is legislation which makes the approach of the Government of general application.'[56]

It makes sense to conclude this section by asking whether there is anything truly left of the class system. In light of the comments of Sir Richard Scott, in criminal proceedings class claims have 'all but disappeared,'[57] and in civil cases, because the Government will no longer make a class claim, they are now of 'limited importance.'[58] Despite these comments, it is inappropriate and wholly inaccurate to describe the class system as dead or removed. What has been removed is the old principle of Crown privilege, that is, once a claim was made in proper form, immunity was automatic. Class claims remain, although a heavy onus will be placed on the party claiming class immunity, and the claim will be determined by reference to the same balancing exercise as content claims.

14.2 Rules of disclosure

Before proceeding to a discussion of the current rules and procedures relating to the claiming of public interest immunity, it is important first to clarify some points surrounding the general law on disclosure in English litigation. Before the issue of PII even arises, the party seeking disclosure must establish that they have a 'legitimate interest' in the disclosure of the material. This simply means that the material must satisfy the disclosure test, whether in criminal or civil proceedings. If the material does not satisfy the disclosure test, no question of PII even arises.

14.2.1 Civil disclosure

In the context of civil proceedings, disclosure is defined in the CPR 1998 as 'stating that the document[59] exists or has existed.'[60] This is an unusual concept, especially when one considers it in contrast to the meaning of criminal disclosure (see below). In civil litigation, the physical delivery of materials or copies of materials (the type of disclosure understood by most) is referred to as inspection. Naturally, before a question of PII can even arise, the evidence in question is subject to the rules of disclosure. In civil proceedings, there are two forms of disclosure: standard disclosure[61] and specific disclosure.[62] This chapter will only deal with standard disclosure and that discussion will be brief. Rule 31.6 of the CPR 1998 provides the test for standard disclosure as follows:

Standard disclosure requires a party to disclose only –

(a) the documents on which he relies; and
(b) the documents which –
  (i) adversely affect his own case;
  (ii) adversely affect another party's case; or
  (iii) support another party's case; and
(c) the documents which he is required to disclose by a relevant practice direction.

---

56 Choo, A.-L.T., op. cit., n. 46, p. 210; see also Ormerod, D. (ed.), *Blackstone's Criminal Practice*, 27th edn (Oxford University Press, 2017), at [F9.4]: 'non-governmental bodies, although not bound by the report, should "adopt the same approach."'

57 Scott, op. cit., n. 5, at [25–15].

58 Ibid.

59 CPR 1998, r 31.4: A document is defined as: 'anything in which information of any description is recorded.'

60 CPR 1998, r 31.2.

61 Detailed rules on standard disclosure are found at CPR, r 31.10.

62 Detailed rules on specific disclosure are found at CPR, r 31.12 and Practice Direction 31A at [5.1].

The parties will disclose their documents by serving a disclosure list on the other party,[63] and then the party to whom a document has been disclosed has the right to inspect it, subject to a number of exceptions.[64] This duty of disclosure continues until the proceedings are concluded, and if documents to which that duty extends come to a party's notice at any time during the proceedings, they must immediately notify every other party.[65] When giving standard disclosure, a party is required to make a reasonable search for documents falling within Rule 31.6(b) or (c).[66] Should the party seeking disclosure fall at this hurdle, the question of PII will never arise.[67]

14.2.2 Criminal disclosure

Disclosure (other than by the accused) in criminal proceedings can be defined as 'providing the defence with copies of, or access to, any prosecution material'[68] that satisfies the disclosure test. There is no separate law relating to inspection of documents, as that is part and parcel of disclosure in criminal proceedings. The duties and responsibilities of the parties with regard to disclosure are governed by Parts I and II of the CPIA 1996, as amended by the Criminal Justice Act 2003. In addition to this, guidelines on disclosure of information in criminal proceedings were issued by the Attorney General in April 2005;[69] however, these guidelines have since been revised by the Attorney General, most recently in May 2022.

Section 3(1) of the CPIA 1996 sets out the 'disclosure test' for prosecution material. It provides that the prosecutor must:

> (a) disclose to the accused any prosecution material[70] which has not previously been disclosed to the accused and which might reasonably be considered capable of undermining the case for the prosecution against the accused or of assisting the case for the accused, or
> (b) give to the accused a written statement that there is no material of a description mentioned in paragraph (a).

It is thus evident that a prosecutor is under no duty or obligation to disclose to the accused any neutral material or material damaging to the defendant.[71] The former is in concord with the civil rule that neutral information need not be disclosed (unless required by a practice direction in civil proceedings), whereas the latter is in direct contrast with the civil rules whereby a party must disclose documents that adversely affect another party's case.

As a result, where a prosecutor wishes to withhold this type of information from the accused in a criminal case on the ground of a risk to a public interest, they need not apply to the court for a ruling, nor need they bring the material to the attention of the court.[72] This point shall be returned to later in the chapter. Further, under section 7A of the 1996 Act, the prosecutor is under

---

63 CPR 1998, r 31.10(2).

64 CPR 1998, r 31.3; the most important for this chapter being r 31.3(1)(b), which states that a document need not be delivered for inspection where the party disclosing the document has a right or a duty to withhold inspection of it.

65 CPR 1998, r 31.11(1) and (2), respectively.

66 CPR 1998, r 31.7(1). See also r 31.7(2), which provides the following factors as being relevant in deciding the reasonableness of a search: (a) the number of documents involved; (b) the nature and complexity of the proceedings; (c) the ease and expense of retrieval of any particular document; and (d) the significance of any document which is likely to be located during the search.

67 See *Evans v Chief Constable of Surrey* [1989] 2 All ER 594.

68 Attorney General's Guidelines on Disclosure for Investigators, Prosecutors and Defence Practitioners (Attorney General's Office, 2013), at [4].

69 These were supplemented by further guidelines in respect of digitally stored material on 14 July 2011.

70 Material is defined in s 3(2) as material which (a) is in the prosecutor's possession, and came into his possession in connection with the case for the prosecution against the accused, or (b) in pursuance of a code operative under Part II, he has inspected in connection with the case for the prosecution against the accused.

71 AG's Guidelines on Disclosure, op. cit., n. 68, at [65], and the Disclosure Manual (CPS, 2004), at [8.23].

72 Ibid.

a continuing duty to keep under review the question of whether at any given time (and, in particular, following the giving of a defence statement) there is prosecution material that satisfies the disclosure test and has not yet been disclosed to the accused. The Court of Appeal in *R v Austin (Herbert)*[73] has warned judges, however, to avoid interfering with the prosecution's duty under section 7. Irwin J specifically warned that:

> It was the Crown's responsibility to carry out the duties of disclosure. Judicial involvement could only properly be triggered by an application under the Criminal Procedure and Investigations Act 1996 by the prosecutor or by the defence. There was no provision for a trial judge to superintend the decisions of disclosure made by the prosecution on his own motion by inspecting unused material himself.

Of course, the rules of disclosures under the 1996 Act do not apply solely to the prosecution and to prosecution material. Rather, the Act also provides for a systematic process for defence disclosure for which the main rules can be found in sections 5, 6, and 6A.[74] Given that a claim for withholding material on the ground of PII is an application made by the prosecution, the law relating to defence disclosure is outside the scope of this chapter.

It is hoped that an understanding, albeit a limited one, of the rules relating to the disclosure and the test to be satisfied in both civil and criminal law before material is passed to the other side, will assist the reader's understanding of the operation of PII and the circumstances in which it arises. We shall now look at the so-called doctrine of public interest immunity and the range of categories traditionally recognised by the courts therein.

14.3 The doctrine of PII

The doctrine of PII, as it now operates in criminal proceedings, was summarised in *R v H and C* in the following terms:

> Circumstances may arise in which material held by the prosecution and tending to undermine the prosecution or assist the defence cannot be disclosed to the defence, fully or even at all, without the risk of serious prejudice to an important public interest. The public interest most regularly engaged is that in the effective investigation and prosecution of serious crime, which may involve resort to informers and undercover agents, or the use of scientific or operational techniques (such as surveillance) which cannot be disclosed without exposing individuals to the risk of personal injury or jeopardising the success of future operations. In such circumstances some derogation from the golden rule of full disclosure may be justified but such derogation must always be the minimum derogation necessary to protect the public interest in question and must never imperil the overall fairness of the trial. However, as Pitcher contends, 'to what extent that serves the common good ... includes paying proper regard to the interests and rights of all those who are affected by crime and the criminal justice system and maintaining a seat of legitimate institutions that can justly pursue those aims.'[75]

---

73 [2013] EWCA Crim 1028.

74 In the Crown Court, the defence is obligated to serve the prosecution with a defence statement under s 5 CPIA 1996. In the magistrates' court, however, the defence has the option of serving a defence statement under s 6 CPIA 1996.

75 Pitcher, K.M., 'Rights-Analysis in Addressing Pre-trial Impropriety: An Obstacle to Fairness?,' in J.D. Jackson and S.J. Summers (eds), *Obstacles to Fairness in Criminal Proceedings, Individual Rights and Institutional Forms* (Hart Publishing, 2018).

The need for there to be a real 'risk of serious prejudice to an important public interest' must be emphasised. Paragraph 8.17 of the Disclosure Manual[76] expressly states that the prosecutor must be satisfied that the risk is 'real, not fanciful.' Similarly, paragraph 8.19 provides that the prosecutor must be satisfied that the prejudice that is anticipated from disclosure of a document is a 'serious, not a trivial, risk.' It is also important to recall that the doctrine only operates in criminal proceedings where the material held by the prosecutor satisfies the disclosure test in section 3 of the 1996 Act. Material that falls outside this test (neutral material or material damaging to the accused) need not be disclosed, nor need it be brought to the attention of the court.

The doctrine and operation of PII in civil proceedings are not dissimilar to those in criminal proceedings. The law and its conditions in relation to civil PII are mainly to be found in the decisions of the House of Lords in *Burmah Oil Co Ltd v Governor and Co of the Bank of* England[77] and *Conway v Rimmer.*[78]

The law as it stands provides that certain documents must be withheld from production to the other side on the grounds that disclosure would be 'injurious to the public interest.' As with criminal proceedings, a document need not be disclosed to the other side and may be withheld where the disclosure test in Rule 31.6 of the CPR is not satisfied (neutral documents).

Naturally, for the purposes of this chapter, we shall focus on material that does satisfy the disclosure test, and will turn below to look at examples of cases (both in criminal and civil proceedings) where there may be a risk to a public interest. First, however, let us explore the nature of the test to be applied when the court is confronted by a PII application.

14.3.1 The test to be applied (a balancing act)

Prior to the case of *Conway v Rimmer*, the decision as to non-disclosure was one for the responsible minister. Upon taking control of the decision as to whether information is within the public interest to disclose, the court was required to formulate a test to be applied. In *Conway v Rimmer*, their Lordships established a *prima facie* simple balancing act whereby the judge would balance the interests of justice in disclosing the evidence in question on the one hand, against the public policy for excluding it on the other hand:

> It is universally recognised that here there are two kinds of public interest which may clash. There is the public interest that harm shall not be done to the nation or the public service by disclosure of certain documents, and there is the public interest that the administration of justice shall not be frustrated by the withholding of documents which must be produced if justice is to be done.[79]

In the latter part of his speech, Lord Reid proceeded to state:

> Courts have and are entitled to exercise a power and duty to hold a balance between the public interest, as expressed by a Minister, to withhold certain documents or other evidence, and the public interest in ensuring the proper administration of justice.[80]

---

76 The CPS Disclosure Manual is designed to provide a practical guide to disclosure principles and procedures, building on the framework of the CPIA 1996, the Code of Practice, and the Attorney General's Guidelines. When properly applied, it will assist investigators and prosecutors to perform their disclosure duties effectively, fairly, and justly, which is vitally important to the integrity of the criminal justice system and the way in which it is perceived by the public.

77 *Burmah Oil*, op. cit., n. 34.

78 Op. cit., n. 11.

79 Ibid., at 940.

80 Ibid., at 952.

Durston argues that this original formulation of a balancing act is 'the essence of any modern exercise of PII';[81] however, he also argues that the operation of the balancing exercise is 'nearly always a matter of choosing the lesser evil.'[82] The balancing exercise was possibly taken one step further by Lord Simon's comments in *D v NSPCC*, where his Lordship remarked that excluding relevant evidence is a serious step to take and, as such, 'any hindrance to its seeker needs to be justified by a convincing demonstration that an even higher public interest requires that only part of the truth should be told.'[83]

The balancing exercise, however, only applies to civil proceedings. Following *Osman*, a different balancing exercise applies to criminal proceedings. The key difference is that the weight to be attached to the 'interests of justice' in a criminal case will be much higher than in its civil counterpart, especially when there is a risk to the defendant's liberty. As will be discussed below, if there is the possibility that disputed material 'may prove the defendant's innocence or avoid a miscarriage of justice, then the balance comes down resoundingly in favour of disclosing it.'[84] It may appear from this that there is no balancing act to be applied as once it has been established that the material may assist the defendant, it must be disclosed. However, their Lordships, in *Keane*, made it clear that the court was in favour of 'performing the balancing exercise, not ... dispensing with it.'[85]

In conducting the balancing exercise, it is unquestionable that the trial judge has the power to inspect the documents in question to assist in their decision. However, the discretion as to the basis on which the power is exercised has been subject to a difference of opinion among the judiciary. The arguments that have been put forward include the fact that in cases where public interest is high, such as national security cases, the court is not equipped to assess the possible harm to the public interest as competently as the minister seeking that the information be withheld. Indeed, this was the view taken by the Court of Appeal in *Balfour v Foreign and Commonwealth Office*,[86] where it was held that once a certificate demonstrates that there is an actual or potential risk to national security, the court should not exercise its right to inspect. In *Burmah Oil*, the House of Lords argued that the court should inspect the documents where it would be necessary in disposing fairly of the matter before it, and which will invariably be the case in respect of criminal proceedings.[87]

Having made such a decision, the trial judge must keep the situation under review, during the course of the trial, in case the balance changes. This was the decision in *R v Davis (No. 1)*,[88] where Lord Taylor CJ commented that a 'ruling is not necessarily final. In the course of the hearing the situation may change.' The decision in *Davis* was put on a statutory footing by section 14 of the CPIA 1996, and will discussed in greater detail below.[89]

A point on which the authorities seem to conflict is on which party the burden of proof lies in seeking to show that the balancing exercise should be resolved in their favour. First, in *Campbell v Tameside MBC*,[90] Ackner LJ commented that 'there is a heavy burden upon the appellants [the party claiming the documents be withheld] to justify withholding them from disclosure.'[91] In contrast, in *Burmah Oil*, Lord Edmund-Davies commented that it is for the person seeking disclosure

81 Durston, op. cit., n. 19, at 554.
82 Ibid., at 545.
83 *D v NSPCC*, op. cit., n. 20, at 1127.
84 Ibid., at 1127.
85 *R v Keane* [1994] 1 WLR 746.
86 [1994] 1 WLR 681.
87 *Burmah Oil*, op. cit., n. 34.
88 [1993] 1 WLR 613.
89 See below.
90 [1982] QB 1065.
91 Ibid., at 1075.

to establish that the public interest in disclosing the documents 'tips the scales decisively in his favour.'[92] Further to this, in *Air Canada v Secretary of State for Trade* (No. 2),[93] Lord Wilberforce observed that it was for the party seeking disclosure and inspection to

establish clearly that the scale falls decisively in favour of [the public interest in the administration of justice] if he is to succeed in his quest. If he fails, even material clearly necessary ... for disposing fairly of the case or matter must be withheld. Murphy welcomes the emphasis placed on the burden resting with the party seeking non-disclosure;[94] however, the authorities seem clear that the burden lies with the party seeking disclosure.

The court in *Conway v Rimmer*, and the courts in numerous authorities that have applied that case, seemed to suggest that the judge must balance two different public interests. Indeed, this would make sense given that one is in favour of disclosure and the other not. However, the more appropriate view of the conflicting interests, we submit, is in line with the comment by Lord Woolf in *ex parte Wiley*, that it is strictly inappropriate to refer to them as two different public interests; rather, 'the conflict is more accurately described as being between two different aspects of the [same] public interest.'[95]

14.3.2 Sensitive material

Sensitive material has been defined as material which if disclosed would give rise to a real risk of serious prejudice to an important public interest.[96] That definition was given solely for criminal proceedings, although it is submitted that it is as equally applicable to civil litigation. Before we examine certain examples of sensitive material, it is worth recalling the words of Lord Hailsham in *D v NSPCC*, that the 'categories of public interest are not closed, and must alter from time to time whether by restriction or extension as social conditions and social legislation develop.'[97]

A helpful starting point, however, is found in the Code of Practice, as created by section 23(1) of Part II of the CPIA 1996, para 6.12, which provides a non-exhaustive list[98] of examples of sensitive material:[99]

(i) material relating to national security;
(ii) material received from the intelligence and security agencies;
(iii) material relating to intelligence from foreign sources which reveals sensitive intelligence gathering methods;
(iv) material given in confidence;
(v) material relating to the identity or activities of informants, or undercover police officers, or witnesses, or other persons supplying information to the police who may be in danger if their identities are revealed;
(vi) material revealing the location of any premises or other place used for police surveillance, or the identity of any person allowing a police officer to use them for surveillance;
(vii) material revealing, either directly or indirectly, techniques and methods relied upon by a police officer in the course of a criminal investigation, for example covert surveillance techniques, or other methods of detecting crime;
(viii) material whose disclosure might facilitate the commission of other offences or hinder the prevention and detection of crime;

---

92 *Burmah Oil*, op. cit., n. 34, at 1075.
93 *Air Canada*, op. cit., n. 21.
94 Glover, R. *Murphy on Evidence*, 15th edn (Oxford University Press, 2017), at 484.
95 *Ex parte Wiley*, op. cit., n. 22, at 298.
96 CPIA Code of Practice, at [2.1].
97 *D v NSPCC*, op. cit., n. 20, at 230.
98 This list has been supplemented by a further list in [8.4] of the Disclosure Manual.
99 These examples are equally relevant to civil law.

(ix) material upon the strength of which search warrants were obtained;
(x) material containing details of persons taking part in identification parades;
(xi) material supplied to an investigator during a criminal investigation which has been generated by an official of a body concerned with the regulation or supervision of bodies corporate or of persons engaged in financial activities, or which has been generated by a person retained by such a body;
(xii) material supplied to an investigator during a criminal investigation which relates to a child or young person and which has been generated by a local authority social services department, an area child protection committee or other party contacted by an investigator during the investigation;
(xiii) material relating to the private life of a witness.

Paragraph 8.18 of the CPS Disclosure Manual provides guidance on the use of this list. It states:

> The examples of material that might attract public interest immunity (PII) in paragraph 6.12 of the Code of Practice do not define classes of material; they are examples only and whether the disclosure of an individual document would be likely to give rise to a real risk of serious prejudice to an important public interest must be assessed in each case. Whilst some of the examples are always likely to carry that real risk, not all will and the prosecutor must assess the risk to the public interest of the disclosure of that document in the individual case, whilst also having regard to the risk of incremental or cumulative damage to the public interest.

This list was created for application to criminal proceedings; however, it is submitted that numerous items on that list, mainly numbers (i)–(iv) and (xiii), are of general application across both the criminal and civil litigation processes. In addition, there are several areas often affected by the immunity that do not appear on that list, but which must be discussed due to their significance in proceedings.[100]

We shall now consider in detail some of the more notable categories of sensitive material. However, it is worth noting at this stage that different principles will apply to the different categories; for example, documents relating to national security will have a higher level of importance than documents affecting local government or the police. Similarly, documents used in civil proceedings are unlikely to have as high a level of importance when compared to documents used in criminal proceedings against an accused and his or her liberty.[101]

14.3.2.1 National security

In the case of national security, documents falling within this category are those most readily protected against disclosure. In fact, it was this type of category that previously led to automatic exclusion by the courts.[102] It is submitted that the position has not changed much, given that in many cases it appears that a ministerial certificate will be conclusive on the matter anyway. According to the Court of Appeal in *Balfour*, a case that concerned material relating to the security and intelligence services, 'once there is an actual or potential risk to national security demonstrated by an appropriate ministerial certificate, the court should not exercise its right to inspect.'[103] This does not mean that a ministerial certificate without evidence or grounds should

---

100 See also *Duncan v Cammell Laird*, op. cit., n. 8, where Viscount Simon suggested that PII would normally be raised in the following three situations: those where disclosure would be 'injurious to national defence, or to good diplomatic relations, or where the practice of keeping a class of documents secret is necessary for the proper functioning of a public service.'

101 Durston, op. cit., n. 19, at 688.

102 *Duncan v Cammell Laird*, op. cit., n. 8.

103 *Balfour v Foreign and Commonwealth Office*, op. cit., n. 86, 688 (Lord Justice Russell).

be accepted automatically, for to do so would revert back to the old principle of Crown privilege. Rather, what appears from subsequent judgments handed down is that the courts are unlikely to question the view of the responsible minister that it would be contrary to the public interest to make public the contents of a particular document, especially when it comes to issues such as national security where the minister's conclusions are properly evidenced and supported.[104]

The examples of claims for immunity from disclosure on the grounds of national security are numerous and have included information such as documents relating to the construction of a submarine,[105] government plans relating to the conduct of a military campaign in the First World War,[106] and confidential documents to or from a foreign secretary concerning the interests of a foreign state in connection with a territorial dispute.[107]

Numerous publications on the law of evidence have argued that *Balfour* is authority for the principle that a ministerial certificate is conclusive on the topic of national security.[108] We submit that this is not the case. A number of relatively recent decisions have brought into question the real weight to be attached to a ministerial certificate and the procedure to be followed in national security cases. First, the case of *R (Al-Sweady) v Secretary of State for Defence*[109] concerned the question of whether or not members of the British army had killed or ill-treated Iraqis, whom they had taken prisoners. The claimants sought an adequate and independent investigation into the alleged violations of their human rights under Articles 1, 2, 3, and 5 of the European Convention on Human Rights (ECHR). In that case, the Minister of State for the Armed Forces had signed a PII certificate, stating that it was not in the public interest, on national security grounds, to disclose certain redacted aspects of documents otherwise disclosed to the claimants. Subsequently, during the trial, the court was provided with a supplemental certificate, pointing out that the previous certificate was signed on a partly false basis because a great deal of the information referred to in the PII certificate was already in the public domain. As a result of the 'potentially very serious damage caused by the failure of the Ministry of Defence in this case to the integrity of the PII process,' the court handed down a separate judgment dealing solely with the issues of PII.[110] In that judgment, Baker LJ (who handed down the judgment) stated unequivocally that:

> [u]ntil such time as the MOD has demonstrated this to be the case [that being that false assertions are never again made in a Ministerial Certificate and Schedule and in future the whole content of such documents are scrupulously accurate] it will, in our view, be incumbent on the courts to approach the content of any Ministerial Certificate and Schedule from the MOD with very considerable caution.[111]

This appears to be a departure from the traditional conclusive nature of a ministerial certificate on national security grounds and could be a sign of the courts taking an even greater interest in the claims made by the Government.

---

104 *R (Binyam Mohammed) v Secretary of State for Foreign and Commonwealth Affairs* [2010] 3 WLR 554.

105 *Duncan v Cammell, Laird*, op. cit., n. 8. See further Durston, op. cit., n. 19, at 547, who argues that the decision in *Duncan* is 'unsurprising' as the country at that time could not afford to risk any information regarding construction of a naval vessel falling into the hands of the enemy.

106 *Asiatic-Petroleum Oil Co. Ltd v Anglo-Persian Oil Co. Ltd* [1961] 1 KB 822.

107 *Buttes Gas & Oil Co. v Hammer (No. 3)*, op. cit., n. 31.

108 Keane, A. and McKeown, P., *The Modern Law of Evidence*, 11th edn (Oxford University Press, 2016), at 570; Choo, op. cit., n. 46, at 206; Glover, op. cit., n. 94, at 477 and 480.

109 [2009] EWHC 2387 (Admin).

110 Ibid.

111 Ibid., at [25].

R (Binyam Mohammed) v Secretary of State for Foreign and Commonwealth Affairs[112] was the next major case to emerge. In simple terms, the issue at the heart of the case concerned the disclosure of intelligence material provided by the United States to the British security services, which, as it was certified by the Secretary of State, should remain under the control of the United States and not be disclosed in an open judgment of the court. This is known as the 'control principle,' and it was argued that a breach of the control principle would prejudice national security. Lord Judge CJ concluded his judgment with the following principles (emphasis added):

> 44. As the executive, not the judiciary, is responsible for national security and public protection and safety from terrorist activity, the judiciary defers to it on these issues, unless it is acting unlawfully, or, in the context of litigation, the court concludes that the claim by the executive for public interest immunity is not justified. Self-evidently, that is not a decision to be taken lightly …
>
> 46. Although the Foreign Secretary accepts that the [control] principle is not absolute, he contends that, having made his own examination of the overall interests of justice, the control principle should be upheld. On the basis of all the evidence including sensitive schedules, I have been unable to eradicate the impression that we are being invited to accept that once the Foreign Secretary has made his judgement of all the relevant considerations, including the interests of justice, and notwithstanding that in law the control principle is not absolute, so far as this court is concerned, as a matter of practical reality, that should be that. *However, although in the context of public safety it is axiomatic that his views are entitled to the utmost respect, they cannot command the unquestioning acquiescence of the court.*

The ruling in *Binyam Mohammed* was subsequently applied in *Secretary of State for Foreign and Commonwealth Affairs v Assistant Deputy Coroner for Inner North London.*[113] The case is more commonly referred to as the Litvinenko Inquiry. The facts in brief are as follows: Alexander Litvinenko died on 23 November 2006, having ingested Polonium-210, a radioactive isotope. On 11 January 2012, the coroner for Inner North London (Sir Robert Owen), in a detailed letter, requested disclosure from all government departments and agencies of documents held by them relating to the circumstances of Mr Litvinenko's death. The Secretary of State claimed a right to withhold the documents on the ground of PII and the risk to national security; however, in May 2013 the Coroner for the Inquest partially rejected the ministerial certificate and ordered disclosure. A panel of three judges of the High Court, led by Goldring LJ, unanimously quashed that ruling. Lord Justice Goldring quashed the coroner's decision to order disclosure, deciding that there was a real and significant risk to national security from disclosure; that the weight given to the views of the Foreign Secretary was insufficient and amounted to an error in law; and that no coroner could reasonably have found that the balance was in favour of disclosure. Although his Lordship found in favour of the Government, he provided the following conclusions and guidance on the weight of ministerial certificates in general:

> First, it is axiomatic … that public justice is of fundamental importance. *Even in cases in which national security is said to be at stake, it is for courts, not the Government,* to decide whether or not PII should prevent disclosure of a document or part of a document.
>
> Second, as I have said, the issues which we have had to resolve only concerned national security. The context of the balancing exercise was that of national security as against the proper administration of justice.

112 [2010] EWCA Civ 65.
113 [2013] EWHC 3724 (Admin).

Third, when the Secretary of State claims that disclosure would have the real risk of damaging national security, the authorities make it clear that *there must be evidence to support his assertion*. If there is not, the claim fails at the first hurdle.

Fourth, if there is such evidence and its disclosure would have a sufficiently grave effect on national security, *that would normally be an end to the matter*. There could be no disclosure. If the claimed damage to national security is not 'plain and substantial enough to render it inappropriate to carry out the balancing exercise,' then it must be carried out.

Fifth, when carrying out the balancing exercise, the Secretary of State's view regarding the nature and extent of damage to national security which will flow from disclosure should be accepted unless there are cogent or solid reasons to reject it. If there are, those reasons must be set out.

Sixth, *the Secretary of State knew more about national security than the Coroner. The Coroner knew more about the proper administration of justice than the Secretary of State.*

Seventh, a real and significant risk of damage to national security will generally, but not invariably, preclude disclosure. *As I have emphasised, the decision was for the Coroner, not the Secretary of State.*

Eighth, in rejecting the Certificate the Coroner must be taken to have concluded that the damage to national security as assessed by the Secretary of State was outweighed by the damage to the administration of justice by upholding the Certificate.

Ninth, it was incumbent on the Coroner to explain how he arrived at his decision, particularly given that he ordered disclosure in the knowledge that by doing so there was a real and significant risk to national security.[114]

From above, therefore, the principles appear clear. The court remains the final arbiter on PII claims, even in cases of national security. This may not sit well with the decision in *Balfour*; however, it has been emphasised that the court will give the utmost respect to the views of the minister to the extent that if justified, their views may be accepted at face value.

14.3.2.2 Proper functioning of a public service

Case law provides without a doubt that the proper functioning of a public service, whether it be central government, local government, the police, or other public organisations, may found a claim of PII in certain circumstances.[115] In this context, PII attaches to a broad spectrum of issues ranging from high-level security documents and Cabinet minutes[116] to the functioning of local authorities.[117] Additional examples include the proper functioning of the Gaming Board,[118] the Law Society,[119] and, most famously in the study of PII, the NSPCC.[120] In *D v NSPCC*, it was the NSPCC that was alleged to have been negligent. The claimant sought disclosure of documentation in the possession of the defendant that concerned a complaint by a third-party informer that the claimant had maltreated her child. The NSPCC claimed immunity from disclosing the documents containing the identity of the informant, which was agreed by the House of Lords. The rationale given for this decision is one analogous to that of the police in that disclosure would cause those sources of information to dry up so that NSPCC protection of that part of the community which consists of children who may be in peril would be impaired. Lord Woolf, in *ex parte Wiley*, described the significance of *D v NSPCC*, explaining that

114 Ibid. [53]–[61] (emphasis added).

115 *Ex parte Wiley*, op. cit., n. 22; *Conway v Rimmer*, op. cit., n. 11; *Burmah Oil*, op. cit., n. 34.

116 *Conway v Rimmer*, op. cit., n. 11.

117 *Re D (Infants)* [1970] 1 All ER 1086.

118 *R v Lewes Justices, ex parte Secretary of State for the Home Department* [1973] AC 388.

119 *Buckley v Law Society (No. 2)* [1984] 3 All ER 313.

120 *D v NSPCC*, op. cit., n. 20.

> it made clear that immunity does not only exist to protect the effective functioning of departments or organs of central government or the police, but also could protect the effective functioning of an organisation such as the NSPCC which was authorised under an Act of Parliament to bring legal proceedings for the welfare of children.[121]

The Court of Appeal considered the extent of disclosure in relation to an appeal from the Employment Appeal Tribunal (EAT). In *Kiani v The Secretary of State for the Home Department*,[122] the appellant, dismissed from his employment without reason, appealed against the ruling of the EAT that the respondent did not have to disclose evidence or the gist of the evidence against the claimant, in turn preventing the claimant from giving full instructions to his advocate. His appeal was on the basis that such refusal to disclose was a breach of his Article 6 right to a fair trial. The Court of Appeal dismissed the appeal, finding that evidence can be withheld on the grounds of national security or where the information would be contrary to the effective running of a service. Specifically, Lord Dyson MR concluded that:

> [T]he requirements of article 6 depend on context and all the circumstances of the case. The particular circumstances in [this case] included the fact that (i) it did not involve the liberty of the subject; (ii) the claimant had been provided with a degree of information as to the basis for the decision to withdraw his security vetting: he was not completely in the dark; (iii) there was real scope for the special advocate to test the issue of discrimination without obtaining instructions on the facts from the claimant; and (iv) this was a security vetting case and it was clearly established in the Strasbourg jurisprudence that an individual was not entitled to full article 6 rights if to accord him such rights would jeopardise the efficacy of the vetting regime itself. The Court of Appeal in *Kiani* has effectively reaffirmed the proposition that although reasons relied on against disclosure are well-founded, the court must strike an effective balance between the right to a fair trial through full and frank disclosure and the requirements of state security.

Bridges[123] has previously argued that an important institutional aspect to the fair trial standards is that public interest is taken into account, alongside the interests of the individual defendant caught up in the criminal process. Jackson and Summers[124] have also highlighted that there is public interest and not merely individual interest in promoting fair trial standards, and public interest comprises the need to ensure that the rule of law prevails through the institutional safeguards of judicial impartiality and adversarial testing.

14.3.2.3 Diplomatic relations and foreign interests

The public interest spoken of throughout this chapter relates to those interests of the United Kingdom. There is no equivalent immunity for documents that are likely to hinder the interests of a foreign state.[125] However, there is an established public interest in protecting the diplomatic relations and international comity of the United Kingdom and other states. This was decided in the *Buttes Gas* case, which concerned a drilling dispute between two oil companies and the extent of their respective territorial waters. The Court of Appeal held that:

---

121 *Ex parte Wiley*, op. cit., n. 22, at 291.

122 [2015] EWCA Civ 776.

123 See Bridges, L., 'The Ethics of Representation on Guilty Pleas' (2006) 9 *Legal Ethics* 80.

124 Jackson, J.D., and Summers, S.J., 'Seeking Core Fair Trial Standards Across National Boundaries: Judicial Impartiality, the Prosecutorial Role and the Right to Counsel,' in J.D. Jackson and S.J. Summers (eds), *Obstacles to Fairness in Criminal Proceedings, Individual Rights and Institutional Forms* (Hart Publishing, 2018).

125 *Buttes Gas v Hammer (No.3)*, op. cit., n. 31.

> it is in the public interest of the United Kingdom that the contents of confidential documents addressed to, or emanating from sovereign states, or concerning the interests of sovereign states, arising in connection with an international territorial dispute between sovereign states, shall not be ordered by the courts of this country to be disclosed ... without the consent of the sovereign states concerned.[126]

This category is thus given similar respect to that of national security.[127]

14.3.2.4 Informants

The public interest in preserving the anonymity of informants has long been recognised.[128] This applies not only to police informants, as is mainly the case, but also to informants for other bodies (as illustrated by *D v NSPCC*). The rationale of the rule was explained by Lawton LJ, in *R v Hennessey*,[129] as follows: '[t]he courts appreciate the need to protect the identity of informers, not only for their own safety but to ensure that the supply of information about criminal activities does not dry up.'[130]

This rationale has been developed and manipulated to provide a basis for informants other than the police.[131] The historical cases have mainly dealt with withholding the identity of the informant, the information itself held by the informant, and information that will enable the informant to be identified; however, as *R v Roussow*[132] demonstrates, the law also allows for the prosecution to claim the right to neither confirm nor deny the actual existence of an informant. In that case, the Court of Appeal concluded that simply revealing the fact of there being an informant, if it be the case, could itself be dangerous.

The judge is obliged to apply this rule even if it is not invoked by the party entitled to object to disclosure.[133] In practice, this essentially means that where a witness is asked about information relating to an informant, whether it be their identity or material which may lead to uncovering their identity, and the prosecution does not rise and object, the judge is under an obligation to make the objection personally. This should be the clearest indication of how seriously the law seeks to protect informants, although the presumption of innocence means that the need for disclosure will prevail where the material in question could establish the innocence of the accused. In *Marks v Beyfus*, Lord Esher MR commented that:

> if upon the trial of a prisoner the judge should be of opinion that the disclosure of the name of the informant is necessary or right in order to show the prisoner's innocence, then one public policy is in conflict with another public policy, and that which says that an innocent man is not to be condemned when his innocence can be proved is the policy that must prevail.[134]

Similarly, in *Keane*, Lord Taylor CJ remarked:

> If the disputed material may prove the defendant's innocence or avoid a miscarriage of justice, then the balance comes down resoundingly in favour of disclosing it.[135]

---

126 Ibid., at 265 (Brightman LJ).
127 *Asiatic Petroleum Co. v Anglo-Persian Oil Co.*, op. cit., n. 106.
128 *D v NSPCC*, op. cit., n. 20, 218.
129 (1978) 68 Cr App R 419.
130 Ibid., at 425. See also McLachlin J's comments in the Canadian case of *R v Leipert* (1997) 143 DLR (4th) 38, 43–44.
131 *D v NSPCC*, op. cit., n. 20, 218.
132 [2006] EWCA Crim 2980.
133 See *Marks v Beyfus* (1890) 25 QBD 494, at 500 (Lord Esher MR); *Rankine* [1986] QB 861 at 867 (Mann J).
134 *Marks v Beyfus*, op. cit., n. 133, at 498; see also Lord Eyre's comments in *R v Hardy* (1794) 24 St Tr 199.
135 Op. cit., n. 19, at 751–52.

It would appear at this stage that the balancing exercise used by the courts has no such application where the accused's liberty is at risk. As Durston argues, in such cases 'no "balancing" process is possible. Once the court concludes that disclosure is necessary to help the accused person establish his innocence, the issue is decided and disclosure must be ordered.'[136] This can clearly be demonstrated by the case of *Agar*,[137] where the defendant alleged that the police had arranged with an informer to ask the accused to go to the informer's house, where drugs allegedly found on the defendant had been planted by the police. The court held that disclosure of the identity of the informant was necessary to enable the accused to put forward the tenable defence that he had been set up by the police and the informer acting in concert.

A point of interest to be mentioned is on whom the burden of proof sits. It was made clear in *Hennessey*, by Lawton LJ, that it is for the accused to show that disclosure of information relating to the informer is necessary to prove his innocence.[138]

One might think that this is a simple matter, but the process is somewhat delicate given that the defendant's liberty may be at stake. Indeed, their Lordships were explicit in the case of *Keane* that, once an accused shows that disclosure will assist him in establishing his innocence, the judge:[139]

> has to perform the balancing exercise by having regard on the one hand to the weight of public interest in non-disclosure. On the other hand, he must consider the importance of the documents to the issues of defence, present and potential, so far as they have been disclosed to him or he can foresee them. Accordingly, the more full and specific the indication the defendant's lawyers give of the defence or issues they are likely to raise, the more accurately both prosecution and judge will be able to discuss the value to the defence of the material.

In that case, Lord Taylor CJ concluded that (i) there was undoubtedly a public interest in not disclosing the material withheld by the Crown and (ii) the material, had it been disclosed, would not have assisted the defence at all. The same decision was reached in the case of *Slowcombe*,[140] where disclosure of the identity of an informer would have contributed little or nothing to the issue that the jury had to consider. So, although the possibility of a miscarriage of justice may command disclosure, the judge is still expected to balance the competing interests and decide whether the information is truly useful to the accused, even if the balance may come resoundingly down in favour of disclosure.

A question that then arises is what is the degree of necessity, so to speak, that is required to be proven by the accused? In *R v Hallett*,[141] it was the Court of Appeal which suggested the threshold be to the level that the accused need merely prove that he may be 'deprived of the opportunity of casting doubt on the case against him.' Lord Taylor CJ gave more detailed guidance, in *R v Turner*,[142] as to how a judge should approach a defence application for disclosure. Here, the defendant was accused of robbery of a shop and numerous firearm offences. He put forward the defence of alibi and claimed that he was being set up. He sought disclosure of an informant who had tipped off the police as to the precise location where the gun and the defendant's clothing could be found; however, the trial judge approved the prosecution's application to withhold the identity of the

---

136 Durston, op. cit., n. 19, at 558.
137 [1990] 2 All ER 442. Applied in *R v Langford* [1990] Crim LR 653.
138 *Hennessey* (1978) 68 Cr App R 419 (Lawton LJ), and *Hallett* [1986] Crim LR 462.
139 Op. cit., n. 19, at 752.
140 [1991] Crim LR 198.
141 Op. cit., n. 19.
142 [1995] 1 WLR 264.

informant. The Court of Appeal concluded that disclosure was necessary and the identity of the informant ought to have been disclosed for two reasons: (i) the nature of the evidence, specifically a strong support that the informant was involved in the crime, and (ii) the defence run had always been alibi and the fact that the defendant was set up. Although their Lordships found in favour of the accused, Lord Taylor took it upon himself to give the following guidance:

> We wish to alert judges to the need to scrutinise applications for disclosure of details about informants with very great care. They will need to be astute to see that assertions of a need to know such details, because they are essential to the running of the defence, are justified. If they are not so justified, then the judge will need to adopt a robust approach in declining to order disclosure. Clearly, there is a distinction between cases in which the circumstances raise no reasonable possibility that information about the informant will bear upon the issues and cases where it will. Again, there will be cases where the informant is an informant and no more; other cases where he may have participated in the events constituting, surrounding, or following the crime. Even when the informant has participated, the judge will need to consider whether his role so impinges on an issue of interest to the defence, present or potential, as to make disclosure necessary.[143]

It was discussed towards the start of this chapter as to whether PII can be waived. The Court of Appeal, in *Savage v Chief Constable of Hampshire*,[144] held that a police informer has the right, if he wishes to do so, to voluntarily sacrifice his own anonymity.[145] This is in direct contrast to the principle set down in *Rogers*, namely, that PII cannot be waived. However, Judge LJ explained that this right to waive anonymity does not follow 'from waiver of privilege attaching personally to the informer, but from the disappearance of the primary justification for the claim for public interest immunity,'[146] specifically, the informant's safety. As such, this can be seen as not an exception to the 'PII cannot be waived' rule, but rather as an understanding of the reach that PII has on the law. Importantly, where the informant does not consent to their identity being revealed, and the prosecutor believes that it is in the interests of justice to do so, the CPS should apply to the court for a ruling; it should not break the anonymity itself. Further, the court should reach its own decision and not simply defer to the view of the prosecutor.[147]

14.3.2.5 Premises used for surveillance

The above rule in relation to informants has been extended to protect the identity of persons who have allowed their premises to be used for surveillance, as well as the identity of their premises. The type of surveillance protected includes that of the police and other law enforcement officers, such as HM Revenue and Customs. The rationale for this category has been deemed the same as for that of informers.[148]

To put it plainly in this context, the identity of an individual's premises is likely to cause them to be extremely frightened at the thought of harm to themselves or damage to their property. Further, to reveal a person's property may well lead to other persons refusing to allow their property to be used for a similar purpose. The two categories are indistinguishable: both concern the safety of the individual but also the safety of future information that may assist in the detection

143 Ibid., at 267.

144 [1997] 2 All ER 631.

145 In that case, the informant had sacrificed his own anonymity by the bringing of civil proceedings.

146 *Savage v Chief Constable of Hampshire*, op. cit., n. 141, at 636.

147 *R (WV) v CPS* [2011] EWHC 2480 (Admin).

148 *R v Rankine*, op. cit., n. 130.

of crime. Under this category, should a defendant prove that the location of the observation point is necessary for their defence or liberty, the judge must resort to the balancing act and weigh up where, in those interests, the balance lies. In such a case, the judge may nonetheless exclude the evidence, so long as the prosecution has provided a proper evidential basis for such exclusion.

A detailed evaluation of the law relating to premises used for observation was given by the Court of Appeal in the case of *Johnson*,[149] where the defendant was charged on numerous counts for the unlawful supply of controlled drugs. The main evidence against the defendant at trial came from police officers who were stationed at several points inside buildings and who observed the defendant selling cannabis and cocaine in the street on six occasions. The defendant alleged that due to the layout of the street, the observation must have been impeded and thus, in order to properly test the prosecution's case, the exact location of the officers should have been disclosed. The trial judge refused disclosure on the ground that a miscarriage of justice was unlikely and the balance fell in favour of non-disclosure. Further, the jury were well aware of the restraints on the part of the defendant, and were carefully directed about the special care they had to give to any disadvantage the restraints may have brought to the defence. The Court of Appeal agreed and made a point to give the following guidance as to the minimum evidential requirements in this regard:[150]

(a) The police officer in charge of the observations to be conducted, no one of lower rank than a sergeant should usually be acceptable for this purpose, must be able to testify that beforehand he visited all observation places to be used and ascertained the attitude of occupiers of premises, not only to the use to be made of them, but to the possible disclosure thereafter of the use made and facts which could lead to the identification of the premises thereafter and of the occupiers. He may of course in addition inform the court of difficulties, if any, usually encountered in the particular locality of obtaining assistance from the public.

(b) A police officer of no lower rank than a chief inspector must be able to testify that immediately prior to the trial he visited the places used for observations, the results of which it is proposed to give in evidence, and ascertained whether the occupiers are the same as when the observations took place and whether they are or are not, what the attitude of those occupiers is to the possible disclosure of the use previously made of the premises and of facts which could lead at the trial to identification of premises and occupiers.

Such evidence will, of course, be given in the absence of the jury when the application to exclude the material evidence is made. The judge should explain to the jury, as this judge did, when summing up or at some appropriate time before that, the effect of his ruling to exclude, if he so rules.

Johnson was applied and approved in the cases of *R v Hewitt*[151] and *R v Grimes*.[152] A number of points that have arisen as a result of *Johnson* should be discussed:

(i) The guidelines in *Johnson* do not require a threat of violence to the occupier before protection can be afforded. Rather, it will suffice if the occupier is in fear of harassment from those being observed.[153]

149 [1988] Cr App R 131.
150 Ibid., at 139 (Watkins LJ).
151 (1992) 95 Cr App R 81.
152 [1994] Crim LR 213.
153 *Blake and Austin v DPP* (1993) 97 Cr App R 169.

(ii) Information that can be revealed without identifying the occupier should be revealed,[154] unless PII can be justified on another ground.

The protection of informants and police observation points remains the most frequent area of PII that tends to arise in contemporary criminal practice.

14.4 The procedure for claiming PII

Having outlined the test to be applied by the courts and the sort of circumstances in which the law of PII operates, we will now turn to discuss the procedure involved.

14.4.1 Ministerial certificates and the sensitive schedule

First, in proceedings where the Government is a party to proceedings or has intervened to claim the immunity,[155] the procedure to be adopted by the Government, through its appropriate minister, is set down in the Scott Report of 1996. The report sets out a three-stage approach that must be considered by the Government in both criminal and civil cases:

First: A decision must be taken on whether there is a duty to disclose the document at all. Broadly speaking, the question in civil and criminal cases will be whether the document is relevant or potentially relevant to an issue in the case. If there is no duty to disclose the document, questions of PII do not arise.

Second: If there is a duty to disclose, a decision must be taken on whether the document attracts PII. Existing practice has been to determine this question by asking whether the document attracts PII because of its 'contents' or because it falls into a 'class' of documents that attracts PII. The Government regards this distinction as no longer helpful. It proposes to abandon it and adopt a new approach that applies the fundamental test of whether the maker of the certificate believes that disclosure would cause real damage.

Third: This step applies to some claims, including those made by ministers. If the document attracts PII, the decision-maker will consider (so far as he can judge it) the strength of the public interest in disclosing the document. This will require an assessment of the issues in the case. The decision-maker performs what is described in this report as the Wiley balancing exercise, usually after taking advice from counsel in the case or Treasury Counsel. If the balance appears to him to favour disclosure, he is entitled to disclose the document. If the balance appears to go the other way, or if the decision-maker is uncertain, he will put a certificate to the court explaining clearly his reasons for asserting PII; and the court will then be invited to determine whether disclosure should be made.[156]

In such cases where the Government is involved, it is the usual practice for the responsible minister (normally the head of the department) to object to disclosure on the grounds of PII. The minister should have seen and considered the contents and have formed the view that it would be contrary to the public interest to produce them – either because of their actual contents or because of the class of documents to which they belong. In *Bennett v Commissioner of Police for the Metropolis*,[157]

154 *Johnson*, op. cit., n. 149, at 134.

155 As they are empowered to do so in criminal proceedings by the Criminal Procedure and Investigations Act 1996, s 16; and in civil proceedings by CPR, r 19.4. Alternatively, a party may seek disclosure where the Government is not a party to the proceedings by satisfying the test in r 31.17.

156 Scott, op. cit., n. 5, at [2.3].

157 [1995] 2 All ER 1.

it was held that it is 'at least arguable'[158] that the Secretary of State concerned is under a duty to consider, before objecting to disclosure, the balancing exercise. However, as was observed above in the Scott Report, it is not merely 'arguable' that they must do so; rather, it seems mandatory for the minister to consider the balancing exercise. The latter opinion is to be preferred. The minister must consider whether the public interest in non-disclosure is outweighed by the public interest in the documents being available in the interests of the administration of justice. The minister is required to support their claim by an affidavit or by providing a PII certificate stating the grounds for the objection[159] to the individual documents in question;[160] however, this ministerial certificate is not conclusive, final, or binding on the court. As made clear in *Conway v Rimmer*, the final arbiter as to whether material should be disclosed is the court, not the minister. As discussed above, it is questionable whether in cases where there is high-level information, such as national security cases, the certificate is conclusive. Since the case of *Balfour*,[161] it has been the opinion that the ministerial certificate is conclusive in cases of national security as the minister is in a better position to assess what is in the public interest than a trial judge. However, cases such as *Al-Sweady* and *Litvinenko* demonstrate that *Balfour* may no longer be the authority in this area and the courts remain the final arbiter on PII decisions. Further, although in general an objection by the Crown to the disclosure of material is entitled to the greatest weight, the court is entitled to ask for clarification or amplification of the objection,[162] and has the power to inspect documentary evidence privately and to order its production to the other side notwithstanding the minister's objection.[163] In contrast, where the Government is not a party or has not intervened, a claim for immunity may still be made. This may be done in one of three ways: on the party's[164] own initiative; at the request of the relevant government department; or, if necessary, the judge herself should raise the issue.[165]

In criminal cases, the responsibilities on the part of the police in retaining evidence are detailed in numerous sources. In particular, the retention of material that may in due course be the subject of a PII claim is detailed in the Code of Practice under the CPIA 1996 and the CPS Disclosure Manual. Paragraph 6.12 of the Code of Practice provides that the disclosure officer[166] 'must list on a sensitive schedule[167] any material, the disclosure of which he believes would give rise to a real risk of serious prejudice to an important public interest, and the reason for that belief.' The schedule must include a statement that the disclosure officer believes the material is sensitive. Detailed guidance as to the assessment of sensitivity and the preparation of the schedule is contained in Chapter 8 of the Disclosure Manual. To assist the prosecutor to decide how to deal with disclosable sensitive material, the investigator and disclosure officer should provide detailed information dealing with the following issues:

- the reasons why the material is said to be sensitive;
- the degree of sensitivity said to attach to the material; in other words, why it is considered that disclosure will create a real risk of serious prejudice to an important public interest;

158 Ibid., at 13 (Rattee J).

159 A defective ministerial certificate may be amended: *R (Binyam Mohammed) v Secretary of State for Foreign and Commonwealth Affairs* [2008] EWHC 2100 (Admin).

160 *Duncan v Cammell Laird*, op. cit., n. 8, at 638.

161 *Balfour v Foreign and Commonwealth Office*, op. cit., n. 86.

162 CPR, r 31.19(6).

163 *Conway v Rimmer*, op. cit., n. 11.

164 See *Burmah Oil*, op. cit., n. 34.

165 *Duncan v Cammell Laird*, op. cit., n. 8, at 642 (Viscount Simon LC).

166 Defined in the CPIA Code of Practice at [2.1] as 'the person responsible for examining material retained by the police during the investigation; revealing material to the prosecutor during the investigation and any criminal proceedings resulting from it, and certifying that he has done this; and disclosing material to the accused at the request of the prosecutor.'

167 Also known as the MG6D form.

- the consequences of revealing to the defence;
- the material itself;
- the category of the material;
- the fact that an application may be made;
- the apparent significance of the material to the issues in the trial;
- the involvement of any third parties in bringing the material to the attention of the police;
- where the material is likely to be the subject of an order for disclosure, what the police view is regarding continuance of the prosecution;
- whether it is possible to disclose the material without compromising its sensitivity.[168]

To assist in determining the degree of sensitivity, consideration should be given to the fact that the public interest may be prejudiced either directly or indirectly through incremental or cumulative harm.[169] As with ministerial certificates, inclusion of material in the MG6D form is not conclusive as to whether disclosure is in the public interest. The question is one for the courts. This was the ruling in *R v Ward*,[170] as discussed above. The common law has been reinforced by the provisions of the CPIA 1996, which make it clear that it is for the court, not the prosecutor, not the CPS, and certainly not the investigator or disclosure officer, to be the final arbiter as to whether material should be disclosed.

14.4.2 Making the application

14.4.2.1 Civil proceedings

Under the CPR 1998, Rule 31.19 sets out the procedure to be adopted by the party seeking the withholding of the material in question. The Rule is set out exactly as it appears in the CPR 1998, so that the reader is aware of the exact wording.
Rule 31.19 provides that:

> (1) A person [who need not be a party] may apply, without notice, for an order permitting him to withhold disclosure of a document on the ground that disclosure would damage the public interest.
> (2) Unless the court orders otherwise, an order of the court under paragraph (1) –
> (a) must not be served on any other person; and
> (b) must not be open to inspection by any person.
> (3) A person who wishes to claim that he has a right or a duty to withhold inspection of a document, or part of a document, must state in writing –
> (a) that he has such a right or duty; and
> (b) the grounds on which he claims that right or duty.
> (4) The statement referred to in paragraph (3) must be made –
> (a) in the list in which the document is disclosed; or
> (b) if there is no list, to the person wishing to inspect the document.
> (5) A party may apply to the court to decide whether a claim made under paragraph (3) should be upheld.
> (6) For the purpose of deciding an application under paragraph (1) (application to withhold disclosure) or paragraph (3) (claim to withhold inspection) the court may –
> (a) require the person seeking to withhold disclosure or inspection of a document to produce that document to the court; and
> (b) invite any person, whether or not a party, to make representations.

168 Disclosure Manual, op. cit., n. 71, at [8.13].
169 Ibid. [8.14]. Examples of direct harm and incremental or cumulative harm are given in [8.15] and [8.16], respectively.
170 *R v Ward*, op. cit., n. 16.

(7) An application under paragraph (1) or paragraph (5) must be supported by evidence.
(8) This Part does not affect any rule of law which permits or requires a document to be withheld from disclosure or inspection on the ground that its disclosure or inspection would damage the public interest.

14.4.2.2 Criminal proceedings

Under the Crim PR 2020, Rule 15.3 sets out the procedure that the prosecutor must follow in making an application for a public interest ruling. Detailed guidance is also contained in Chapter 13 of the Disclosure Manual. Before making such an application, however, the Attorney General's Guidelines on Disclosure provide that prosecutors should aim to disclose as much of the material as they properly can (for example, by giving the defence redacted or edited copies or summaries). This is in accord with the guidance given in *R v H and C* (below) that the court should consider disclosure of documents in an edited or anonymised form.

Further to this, para 13.1 of the CPS Disclosure Manual states that where sensitive material is identified as meeting the disclosure test and the prosecutor is satisfied that disclosure would create a real risk of serious prejudice to an important public interest, the options are to: (i) disclose the material in a way that does not compromise the public interest in issue; (ii) obtain a court order to withhold the material; (iii) abandon the case; or (iv) disclose the material because the overall public interest in pursuing the prosecution is greater than in abandoning it. The guidance makes it clear that option (ii) should be considered only if the other options of disclosing the material have been discounted or there is no agreement between the prosecutor, investigators, or agencies, or the court's assistance is required to assess whether material should be disclosed. As you will see, Rule 15.3(3)(a)(iii) below supports this statement.

Rule 15.3 of the Crim PR 2020 provides the following:

(1) This rule applies where –
  (a) without a court order, the prosecutor would have to disclose material; and
  (b) the prosecutor wants the court to decide whether it would be in the public interest to disclose it.
(2) The prosecutor must –
  (a) apply in writing for such a decision; and
  (b) serve the application on –
    (i) the court officer,
    (ii) any person who the prosecutor thinks would be directly affected by disclosure of the material, and
    (iii) the defendant, but only to the extent that serving it on the defendant would not disclose what the prosecutor thinks ought not be disclosed.

1. (3) The application must –
  (a) describe the material, and explain why the prosecutor thinks that –
    (i) it is material that the prosecutor would have to disclose,
    (ii) it would not be in the public interest to disclose that material, and
    (iii) no measure such as the prosecutor's admission of any fact, or disclosure by summary, extract or edited copy, adequately would protect both the public interest and the defendant's right to a fair trial;
  (b) omit from any part of the application that is served on the defendant anything that would disclose what the prosecutor thinks ought not be disclosed (in which case, paragraph (4) of this rule applies); and
  (c) explain why, if no part of the application is served on the defendant.
(4) Where the prosecutor serves only part of the application on the defendant, the prosecutor must –
  (a) mark the other part, to show that it is only for the court; and
  (b) in that other part, explain why the prosecutor has withheld it from the defendant.

2. (5) Unless already done, the court may direct the prosecutor to serve an application on –

(a) the defendant;
(b) any other person who the court considers would be directly affected by the disclosure of the material.

(6) The court must determine the application at a hearing which –
(a) must be in private, unless the court otherwise directs; and
(b) if the court so directs, may take place, wholly or in part, in the defendant's absence.

3. (7) At a hearing at which the defendant is present –
(a) the general rule is that the court must consider, in the following sequence –
(i) representations first by the prosecutor and any other person served with the application, and then by the defendant, in the presence of them all, and the
(ii) further representations by the prosecutor and any such other person in the defendant's absence; but
(b) the court may direct other arrangements for the hearing.

(8) The court may only determine the application if satisfied that it has been able to take adequate account of –
(a) such rights of confidentiality as apply to the material; and
(b) the defendant's right to a fair trial.

(9) Unless the court otherwise directs, the court officer –
(a) must not give notice to anyone other than the prosecutor –
(i) of the hearing of an application under this rule, unless the prosecutor served the application on that person, or
(ii) of the court's decision on the application;
(b) may –
(i) keep a written application or representations, or
(ii) arrange for the whole or any part to be kept by some other appropriate person, subject to any conditions that the court may impose.

14.4.3 Categories of hearings

In *R v Ward*, the court ruled that it is to be the final arbiter in a decision as to whether material ought to be disclosed. However, the court also ruled that 'it would be wrong to allow the prosecution to withhold material documents without giving any notice of that fact to the defence.'[171] In essence, the court in *Ward* established a rule that in all criminal cases, regardless of the nature of the material, the prosecution is required to give notice to the defence. This appears flawed, given that highly relevant material could be compromised by the mere fact of alerting the defence that material will be withheld. A few months after *Ward* was decided, the Court of Appeal, in *Davis*, had a second chance to set the guidance needed in PII cases. Lord Taylor CJ felt the need to set principles for three different categories of hearing, depending on the level of public interest at stake:

> Type one (Least sensitive)
>
> If the prosecution wish to rely on public interest immunity to justify non-disclosure then, in most cases, they must notify the defence that they are applying for a ruling by the court, and indicate to the defence at least the category of the material which they hold. The defence must then have the opportunity of making representations to the court.
>
> Type two (Moderately sensitive)
>
> This procedure is followed where the prosecution contend that the public interest would be injured even if disclosure was made of the category of material in question. The prosecution should still notify the defence that an application to the court is made, but need not specify the category of material. The defence would be able to address the court on the procedure to be adopted but the application itself would be *ex parte*. If the court on that

171 Ibid. (Glidewell J).

application found that there should be an *inter partes* application it would so order. If not, it would rule on the *ex parte* application.

Type three (Most sensitive)

In a highly exceptional case, where even to reveal that an *ex parte* application was to be made would injure the public interest, the prosecution could apply to the court *ex parte* without notifying the defence of the actual application to the court at all. Again, if the court on hearing the application considered that notice should have been given to the defence (Type 2), or even that the normal *inter partes* hearing should have been adopted (Type 1), it would so order. Special counsel may need to be appointed to represent the defendant's interests.[172]

Rule 15.3 of the Crim PR 2020 in effect reproduces the procedure laid down by Lord Taylor CJ in *Davis*. In particular, Rule 15.3(2) provides that the prosecutor must (a) apply in writing for a decision as to whether it is in the public interest to disclose the material; and (b) serve the application on (i) the court officer, (ii) any person who the prosecutor thinks would be directly affected by disclosure of the material, and (iii) the defendant, but only to the extent that serving it on the defendant would not disclose what the prosecutor thinks ought not be disclosed.[173] The importance of proper notice in Type 1 and 2 applications, or lack thereof in Type 3 applications, is made clear in the Judicial Protocol on the Disclosure of Unused Material in Criminal Cases, paragraph 55b, which states:

> When the PII application is a Type 1 or Type 2 application, proper notice to the defence is necessary to enable the accused to make focused submissions to the court and the notice should be as specific as the nature of the material allows. It is appreciated that in some cases only the generic nature of the material can be identified. In some wholly exceptional cases (Type 3 cases) it may be justified to give no notice at all. The judge should always ask the prosecution to justify the form of notice (or the decision to give no notice at all).

As discussed below at 14.4.5, the judge is required to keep the situation and the category of material under continuous review.[174]

14.4.4 Approach of the courts

14.4.4.1 Civil proceedings

In the leading case of *Al-Rawi v The Security Service*,[175] Lord Clarke accepted that the following principles correctly state the current approach to a PII application in civil proceedings:

(i) A claim for PII must ordinarily be supported by a certificate signed by the appropriate minister relating to the individual documents in question.

(ii) Disclosure of documents which ought otherwise to be disclosed under CPR Part 31 may only be refused if the court concludes that the public interest which demands that the evidence be withheld outweighs the public interest in the administration of justice.

(iii) In making that decision, the court may inspect the documents. This must necessarily be done in an *ex parte* process from which the party seeking disclosure may properly be excluded. Otherwise the very purpose of the application for PII would be defeated.

172 *R v Davis*, op. cit., n. 88, at 617.

173 More of the rules in Part 15.3 are discussed above in Section 14.4.2.

174 *R v Davis*, op. cit., n. 88.

175 [2011] UKSC 34 at [145].

(iv) In making its decision, the court should consider what safeguards may be imposed to permit the disclosure of the material. These might include, for example, holding all or part of the hearing in camera; requiring express undertakings of confidentiality from those to whom documents are disclosed; restricting the number of copies of a document that could be taken, or the circumstances in which documents could be inspected (e.g. requiring the claimant and his legal team to attend at a particular location to read sensitive material); or requiring the unique numbering of any copy of a sensitive document.

(v) Even where a complete document cannot be disclosed it may be possible to produce relevant extracts, or to summarise the relevant effect of the material.

(vi) If the public interest in withholding the evidence does not outweigh the public interest in the administration of justice, the document must be disclosed unless the party who has possession of the document concedes the issue to which it relates.[176]

14.4.4.2 Criminal proceedings

In the landmark criminal decision of *R v H and C*,[177] the House of Lords held that where any issue of derogation from the golden rule of full disclosure comes before a court, it must address a series of questions[178] (questions 3 and 4 being the most prominent):

(1) What is the material which the prosecution seeks to withhold? This must be considered by the court in detail.

(2) Is the material such as may weaken the prosecution case or strengthen that of the defence?
If No, disclosure should not be ordered.
If Yes, full disclosure should (subject to (3), (4) and (5) below) be ordered.

(3) Is there a real risk of serious prejudice to an important public interest (and, if so, what) if full disclosure of the material is ordered?
If No, full disclosure should be ordered.

(4) If the answer to (2) and (3) is Yes, can the defendant's interest be protected without disclosure or disclosure be ordered to an extent or in a way which will give adequate protection to the public interest in question and also afford adequate protection to the interests of the defence?

This question requires the court to consider, with specific reference to the material which the prosecution seek to withhold and the facts of the case and the defence as disclosed, whether the prosecution should formally admit what the defence seek to establish or whether disclosure short of full disclosure may be ordered.

This may be done in appropriate cases by the preparation of summaries or extracts of evidence, or the provision of documents in an edited or anonymised form, provided the documents supplied are in each instance approved by the judge. In appropriate cases, the appointment of special counsel may be a necessary step to ensure that the contentions of the prosecution are tested and the interests of the defendant protected.

(5) Do the measures proposed in answer to (4) represent the minimum derogation necessary to protect the public interest in question?
If No, the court should order such greater disclosure as will represent the minimum derogation from the golden rule of full disclosure.

(6) If limited disclosure is ordered pursuant to (4) or (5), may the effect be to render the trial process, viewed as a whole, unfair to the defendant?
If Yes, then fuller disclosure should be ordered even if this leads or may lead the prosecution to discontinue the proceedings so as to avoid having to make disclosure.

(7) If the answer to (6) when first given is No, does that remain the correct answer as the trial unfolds, evidence is adduced and the defence advanced?

---

176 See *Secretary of State for the Home Department v MB* [2007] UKHL 46, at [51] (Lord Hoffmann).

177 *R v H and C*, op. cit., n. 1.

178 Ibid., pp. 155–56, at [36].

> It is important that the answer to (6) should not be treated as a final, once-and-for-all, answer but as a provisional answer which the court must keep under review.

The Attorney General's Guidelines on Disclosure emphasise that the principles set out in *R v H and C* should be:

> applied rigorously, firstly by the prosecutor and then by the court considering the material. It is essential that these principles are scrupulously adhered to, to ensure that the procedure for examination of material in the absence of the accused is compliant with Article 6.[179]

The decision of the House of Lords, in *R v H*, has been the subject of great commendation by subsequent authorities. In particular, in *R v Twomey*,[180] Lord Judge CJ, as he then was, remarked that the guidance given in *R v H* is now 'well understood and form[s] part of the day-to-day administration of criminal justice.'[181] Where the judge rules in favour of disclosure, the prosecution must decide whether to refuse disclosure and abandon the case or give disclosure and continue the case. Where, however, the court has ruled in favour of the party seeking the documents to be withheld, the decision must be kept under continuous review.

14.4.5 Review of PII decisions

It has been made clear throughout this chapter that once the court has made its decision to withhold information from disclosure on the grounds of PII, that is not the end of the matter. The review of PII decisions is of great importance to the party seeking disclosure in both criminal and civil proceedings, especially when the material may be of significant assistance to their case.

In civil proceedings, under the CPR 1998, Rule 31.19(5), a party may apply to the court to decide whether a claim for PII should be upheld. There is no duty, as such, on the court to review its own decision throughout the trial. Rather, the burden of seeking a review seems to rest on the shoulders of the party seeking disclosure. In criminal proceedings, however, the reviewing of a PII decision varies, depending on whether the case is tried summarily or tried on indictment. Under section 14(2) of the CPIA 1996, in summary trials, it is the accused's responsibility to apply for the magistrates' decision to be reviewed. This appears to follow the procedure in civil litigation. This is in contrast with section 15 of the Act, which concerns trials on indictment and provides that the court is under a continuous duty to keep under review the question as to whether it is still not in the public interest to disclose the material in question. Rule 15.6 of the Crim PR 2015 provides for the procedure to be followed by the accused or court, depending on whether the trial is summary or on indictment.

14.5 PII and human rights

As discussed towards the beginning of this chapter, the operation of PII naturally leads to controversial results.[182] Should information and relevant evidence be withheld from the defence,

---

179 AG's Guidelines on Disclosure, op. cit., n. 68, at [68].

180 [2011] EWCA Crim 8.

181 Ibid., at 42.

182 Including many cases of potential miscarriages of justice. In particular, see *R v Jones (Conrad) (No. 2)* [2014] EWCA Crim 1337 where the defendant served six years in prison after being wrongly convicted based on evidence which remained withheld for PII reasons. See further 'CPS to pay six-figure sum to man over wrongful conviction,' *The Guardian* (6 October 2016) https://www.theguardian.com/uk-news/2016/oct/06/cps-to-pay-six-figure-sum-to-man-over-wrongful-conviction (last accessed 20 July 2017).

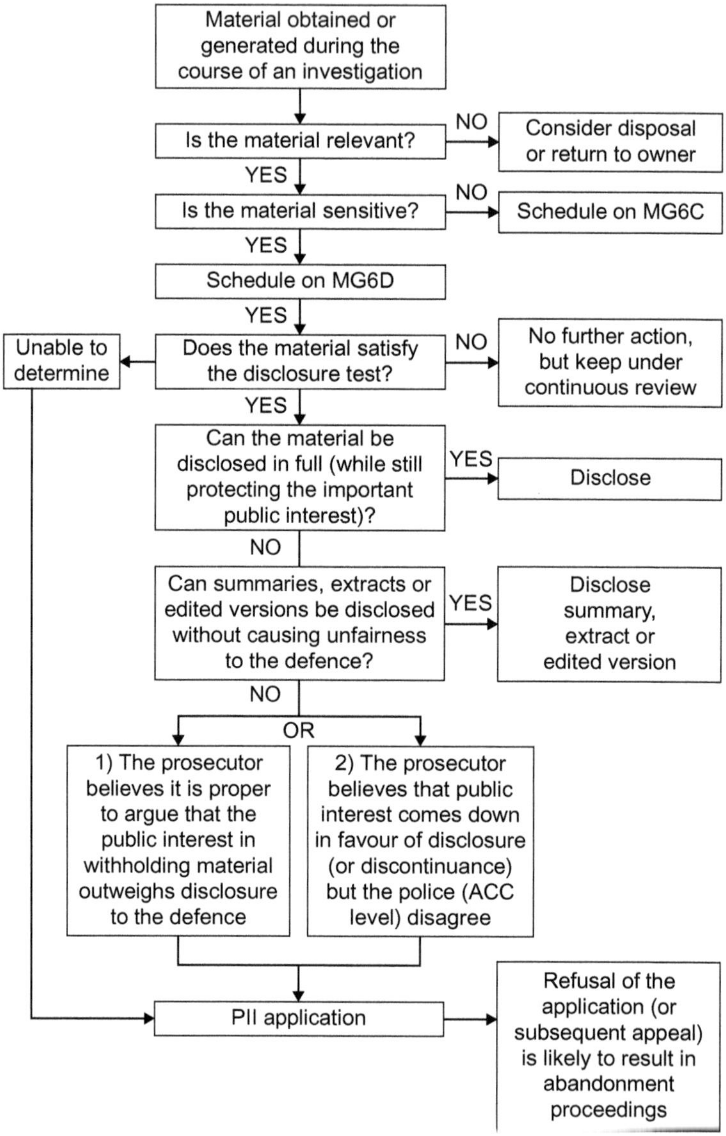

Figure 14.1 The PII procedure

questions arise as to whether the defendant's right to a fair trial under Article 6(1) of the ECHR has been impugned.[183] As the Attorney General's Guidelines on Disclosure state, '[f]air disclosure to the accused is an inseparable part of a fair trial.'[184] In light of that, the procedural fairness of PII will now be explored. As the case of *Al-Khawaja and Tahery v UK* has explored, other interests must also be taken into consideration in guaranteeing fairness; those of the European Court of Human

183 Note, however, that the Court of Appeal in *R v Gray and Others* [2014] EWCA Crim 2372 was very clear that simply because a PII hearing has taken place does not mean that the defendant has been deprived of any relevant material.

184 AG's Guidelines on Disclosure, op. cit., n. 68, at [2].

Rights (ECtHR) recognise that the right to a fair trial is not an absolute guarantee but is open to balancing the competing interests of the defence, the victim, witnesses, and the public interests in the administration of justice.[185]

The leading case from Strasbourg on the issue is *Rowe and Davis v UK*,[186] which concerned three defendants charged with murder and numerous robberies. As a result of an unidentified informant, the police searched the accuseds' homes and found items that had been taken during the robbery. During the defendants' original trial, the prosecution decided, without notifying the judge, to withhold certain relevant evidence on grounds of public interest. Of course, since the decision in *Ward*, it is the court who acts as the final arbiter on whether information can be withheld, not the prosecution. Therefore, the procedure adopted at that stage was naturally unfair. However, the Court of Appeal nevertheless upheld the convictions, ruling that the evidence was sufficient and the convictions were safe.[187] The matter was then brought before the ECtHR where it was held that the convictions were in fact unsafe as the appellants' rights under Article 6(1) had been violated. The following extract of the judgment, from the Strasbourg Court's unanimous decision, concerns the approach to be adopted by a court when a determination on PII is required:

> Article 6(1) requires ... that the prosecution authorities disclose to the defence all material evidence in their possession for or against the accused.
>
> ... entitlement to disclosure of relevant evidence is not an absolute right. In any criminal proceedings there may be competing interests, such as national security or the need to protect witnesses at risk of reprisals or keep secret police methods of investigation of crime, which must be weighed against the rights of the accused ... In some cases it may be necessary to withhold certain evidence from the defence so as to preserve the fundamental rights of another individual or to safeguard an important public interest. However, only such measures restricting the rights of the defence which are strictly necessary are permissible under Article 6(1) ...
>
> In order to ensure that the accused receives a fair trial, any difficulties caused to the defence by a limitation on its rights must be sufficiently counterbalanced by the procedures followed by the judicial authorities ...
>
> In cases where evidence has been withheld from the defence on public interest grounds, it is not the role of this Court to decide whether or not such non-disclosure was strictly necessary since, as a general rule, it is for the national courts to assess the evidence before them. Instead, the European Court's task is to ascertain whether the decision-making procedure applied in each case complied, as far as possible, with the requirements of adversarial proceedings and equality of arms and incorporated adequate safeguards to protect the interests of the accused.[188]

The convictions in *Rowe and Davis* were subsequently referred back to the Court of Appeal, and the convictions were quashed.[189]

Ex parte hearings, where the judge considers whether to admit evidence without the presence of the opposing party, are relatively common devices that are used to consider non-disclosure requests. *Prima facie*, such hearings appear to run contrary to the principle of natural justice since the absent party will be unaware of the nature of the evidence and the nature of the arguments

---

185 *Al-Khawaja and Tahery v UK* [GC] (2012) 54 EHRR, 23.

186 (2000) 30 EHRR 1.

187 *R v Davis*, op. cit., n. 88.

188 Ibid. at [60]–[65] (emphasis added). See also *Atlan v UK* (2002) 34 EHRR 833 and *Dowsett v UK* [2003] Crim LR 890, where the court reached the same conclusion as in *Rowe*.

189 *R v Davis, Johnson, and Rowe* [2001] 1 Cr App R 115.

being considered by the court. The fairness of the procedure was considered by the ECtHR in *Jasper v UK*,[190] where it was held by a majority of nine to eight that such a hearing would not breach Article 6(1). The key reasons given were that (i) the defence were notified that the application had been made; (ii) the trial judge gave them as much information regarding the nature of the withheld evidence as possible without revealing what it was; (iii) the defence were permitted to outline their case to the judge; (iv) the defence were permitted to make submissions and participate in the decision-making process as far as possible without revealing the information sought after; and (v) the judge kept under review the need for disclosure at all times throughout the trial.[191]

The potential unfairness of an *ex parte* hearing arose yet again in the case of *Botmeh*,[192] where the defence argued that the *ex parte* procedure could not be used in the Court of Appeal as it was limited (as per the decision in *Jasper*) to use in proceedings at first instance. The Court of Appeal rejected this argument, ruling that the decisions in *Rowe*, *Jasper*, and *Atlan* provided no basis to suggest that use of an *ex parte* procedure by the Court of Appeal was unfair in itself. By contrast, in *Edwards v UK*,[193] the Strasbourg Court found a breach of Article 6 due to the limitations the *ex parte* procedure placed on the defence to argue their case. Edwards was charged with numerous drug offences after an undercover operation revealed his actions as a drug dealer. In an *ex parte* hearing, the prosecution applied to withhold evidence, which the judge approved. The defendant subsequently applied for the evidence of the undercover officer to be excluded by section 78 of PACE 1984 on the grounds of entrapment. The trial judge had ruled that there was nothing present in the evidence given in the *ex parte* hearing that would have assisted the defendant in arguing that the evidence ought to be excluded. The European Court held that the defendant's rights under Article 6 had been breached as the defence was not able to fully argue their case of entrapment. Despite the judge's confidence that the evidence would not have assisted the defendant, his ruling ignored the fact that the defendant could have made use of the evidence and countered it or proved it to be wrong or mistaken.

As Dennis argues, the principle of fair treatment forms part of the justification of the defendant's right to a fair trial but this principle does not apply uniquely to the defendant. As he has explored, reliance on terms like dignity and autonomy does little in itself to justify why the accused should be accorded certain process rights, such as a right to disclose information or the right to examine witnesses when such rights risk impacting unfairly on other participants.[194]

All of the above cases were criminal in nature. In terms of civil actions, the authors of *Blackstones' Civil Practice* argue that it is in fact 'questionable'[195] whether the civil procedures, specifically Rule 31.19 which allows an order to be made 'without giving any information to the parties,' as well as that decisions can be made by judges other than the trial judge, 'would seem to fall short of the safeguards contemplated by the European Court' in *Rowe*.[196] Given that (i) class claims are rarely made in civil proceedings, and no longer relied upon at all by the Government, (ii) a *Wiley* balancing exercise must be undertaken by the judge, and (iii) the court must be the final arbiter on the decision as to whether to disclose, it would only make sense to submit that civil proceedings and the procedures therein are in line with Article 6(1). However, this assertion has yet to be tested before the European Court. The most salient points from the Strasbourg case law to date are summarised as follows:

---

190 (2000) 30 EHRR 441.

191 The court reached the same conclusion in *Fitt v UK* (2000) 30 EHRR 480, which interestingly was decided on the same day on similar grounds.

192 [2002] 1 WLR 531.

193 (2003) 15 BHRC 189.

194 Dennis, I., 'The Right to Confront Witnesses: Meanings, Myths and Human Rights' [2010], Crim LR 226, 268.

195 Sime, S. (ed.), *Blackstones' Civil Practice*, 17th edn (Oxford University Press, 2017), at [48.71].

196 Ibid.

(i) An adversarial trial and the equality of arms are fundamental prerequisites to ensuring the defendant receives a fair trial.
(ii) The entitlement to disclosure is not an absolute right.
(iii) Only such measures that restrict the defendants' rights that are 'strictly necessary' are legal under Article 6.
(iv) Any difficulties caused to the defence by PII must be sufficiently counterbalanced by the procedures in place.

The fairness of a defendant's trial when faced with non-disclosure for reasons of PII was clearly evident in the case of *Barkauskas and Ors v R*,[197] in which the Court of Appeal noted that the trial judge 'had the fairness of the trial well in mind and thereafter kept the position under constant review.'[198] The defendants in this case were charged and convicted with (*inter alia*) conspiracy to steal motor vehicles and handling stolen goods. One of the grounds of appeal against conviction was based on the prosecution's failure to disclose evidence relating to 'covert markings' that were used by the police and Mr King, an expert in this field, to identify stolen cars and parts. The prosecution alleged, with which the trial judge agreed, that such evidence of covert markings might 'facilitate other offences, hinder the prevention and detection of crime and deter manufacturers from sharing information in the future.'[199] Defence counsel accepted that the material was covered by PII, but questioned whether the defendants could be afforded a fair trial in absence of its disclosure. The Court of Appeal commended the trial judge for her conduct in:

> [M]eticulously checking that prosecution counsel had seen and verified the marks relied upon by the expert, that both the experts and counsel agreed that 'nothing undermined the prosecution or assisted the defence' and that the schedule accurately recorded the data.[200]

On the basis of the trial judge's review of the evidence, the relatively small part the covert markings played in the prosecution case and the sufficiency of all other material served on the defence meant that the convictions were safe and the defendants had secured a fair trial.

In our view, it appears from the aforementioned authorities that the procedures adopted by the English courts for determining PII applications are, at this moment in time, compliant with Article 6(1). The specific use of the phrase 'at this moment in time' was intentional on our part, and the reasons for its use will become transparent in the next section.

14.6 New trends and the future of PII

The last part of this chapter will look at some recent trends in relation to PII and will consider the future direction of the law. Recent years have seen unease being expressed at the increasingly widespread use of PII applications, and, as noted below, a number of safeguards that have been hitherto present for the accused in criminal trials may now be under threat.

14.6.1 Special counsel/advocates

The use of special counsel in England and Wales began with the Special Immigration Appeals Commission Act 1997.[201] Under this legislation, where it is necessary on national security grounds

197 [2017] EWCA Crim 1210.
198 Ibid., at [44] (Hallett LJ).
199 Ibid., at [24] (Hallett LJ).
200 Ibid., at [44] (Hallett LJ).
201 As introduced in response to the ECtHR's ruling in *Chahal v UK* (1997) 23 EHRR 413.

for the relevant tribunal to sit *in camera* (i.e. in the absence of the defendant and their legal representatives), the Attorney General may appoint a special counsel to represent the interests of the individual in the proceedings.[202] The legislation provides that the special counsel is not, however, 'responsible to the person whose interest he is appointed to represent,'[203] thus ensuring that the special counsel is both entitled to and obliged to keep confidential any information that cannot be disclosed.

The appointment of special counsel in cases where a decision has been made to refuse disclosure of documents has been discussed by numerous authorities. First, in *Rowe and Davis*, it was argued on behalf of the defendant that exclusion of the defence from this, and any *ex parte* procedure for that matter, should be counterbalanced by the introduction of a special independent counsel. Their role would be to argue the 'relevance of the undisclosed evidence, test the strength of the prosecution claim to public interest immunity, and safeguard against the risk of judicial error or bias.'[204] The Court found a violation of Article 6 without the need to address the question of special counsel. The issue arose again in *Edwards v UK*, where the Court referred to Sir Robin Auld's *Review of the Criminal Courts of England and Wales*[205] and his recommendations that special counsel should be introduced in trials at first instance and on appeal to represent the interests of the accused where the defence have been excluded from the hearing of PII applications.

Most prominently in *H and C*, the House of Lords was invited by the defence to state that special counsel should be appointed in every case where material that the prosecution seeks to withhold is, or may be, relevant to a disputed issue of fact. Their Lordships, however, declined to do so and held that there is 'no absolute rule which requires the appointment of special counsel in any particular kind of case.'[206] To routinely appoint a special advocate in all *ex parte* PII hearings would 'seek to place the trial judge in a straitjacket.'[207] Although Lord Bingham made it clear that there was no such absolute rule of law, he proceeded to state that there will be cases that arise in which the appointment of an approved advocate as special counsel is necessary, in the interests of justice, to secure protection of a criminal defendant's right to a fair trial.[208]

His Lordship went on to discuss both the ethical and practical problems involved in appointing special counsel:

> Such an appointment does however raise ethical problems, since a lawyer who cannot take full instructions from his client, nor report to his client, who is not responsible to his client and whose relationship with the client lacks the quality of confidence inherent in any ordinary lawyer-client relationship, is acting in a way hitherto unknown to the legal profession.
>
> The appointment is also likely to cause practical problems: of delay, while the special counsel familiarises himself with the detail of what is likely to be a complex case; of expense, since the introduction of an additional, high-quality advocate must add significantly to the cost of the case; and of continuing review, since it will not be easy for a special counsel to assist the court in its continuing duty to review disclosure, unless the special counsel is present throughout or is instructed from time to time when need arises.[209]

---

202 Special Immigration Appeals Commission Act 1997, s 6(1).
203 Ibid., s 6(4).
204 Op. cit., n. 189, at [55].
205 *Edwards*, op. cit., n. 193, at paras [193]–[197].
206 *R v H and C*, op. cit., n. 1, at [32].
207 Ibid., at [33].
208 Ibid., at [22].
209 Ibid., at [22]. See also Chamberlain, M., 'Special Advocates and Procedural Fairness in Closed Proceedings' (2009) 28 *Civil Justice Quarterly* 314, for detailed statements by barristers appearing as special advocates.

Having referred to the numerous drawbacks, however, his speech concluded in the following terms:

> None of these problems should deter the court from appointing special counsel where the interests of justice are shown to require it. But the need must be shown. Such an appointment will always be exceptional, never automatic; a course of last and never first resort. It should not be ordered unless and until the trial judge is satisfied that no other course will adequately meet the overriding requirement of fairness to the defendant.[210]

As has been noted above, the possible use of special counsel was included by their Lordships in the questions that need to be asked by a trial judge in determining a PII application. This issue further arose in the case of *Austin*,[211] where the Court of Appeal held that it was open for the trial judge to appoint counsel in the case given the unusual history of the case; however, that was a matter for him and at no stage was he obliged to do so.

From the above discussion, it can be seen that the role of special counsel, although continuing to develop, has not yet had a substantial impact upon the PII process. Indeed, the role provides a form of counterbalancing measures as required by the Strasbourg authorities; however, it is explicit from R v H *and* C that other forms of methods, such as disclosure of redacted or edited statements, remain the preference of the courts and must first be exhausted before special counsel may even be considered. As Waldron has pointed out, when enquiring into the fairness of criminal proceedings, we must enquire more deeply into why public interest immunity functions in the way that it does.[212]

14.6.2 Closed material procedures

The law on closed material procedures has expanded rapidly, especially since the introduction of the Justice and Security Act 2013.[213] The definition of a closed material procedure (CMP) was helpfully given by Lord Dyson in the opening of his judgment in the high-profile case of R v *Al-Rawi*:[214]

> A 'closed material procedure' means a procedure in which:
>
> (a) a party is permitted to
>   (i) comply with his obligations for disclosure of documents, and
>   (ii) rely on pleadings and/or written evidence and/or oral evidence without disclosing such material to other parties if and to the extent that disclosure to them would be contrary to the public interest (such withheld material being known as 'closed material'); and
>
> (b) disclosure of such closed material is made to special advocates and, where appropriate, the court; and
>
> (c) the court must ensure that such closed material is not disclosed to any other parties or to any other person, save where it is satisfied that such disclosure would not be contrary to the public interest.

For the purposes of this definition, disclosure is contrary to the public interest if it is made contrary to the interests of national security, the international relations of the United Kingdom, the

210 Ibid., at [22].
211 [2013] EWCA Crim 1028.
212 Waldron, J., *Political Theory: Essays on Institutions* (Harvard University Press, 2016).
213 See Forsyth, C., 'Principle or Pragmatism: Closed Material Procedure in the Supreme Court,' UK Const. L. Blog (29 July 2013) http://ukconstitutionallaw.org (last accessed 20 July 2017).
214 R v *Al-Rawi*, op. cit., n. 175, at [34].

detection and prevention of crime, or in any other circumstances where disclosure is likely to harm the public interest.

CMP has been expressly sanctioned[215] in statute and deemed lawful in accordance with Article 6 for cases of alleged terrorism,[216] immigration proceedings,[217] and Employment Tribunal cases.[218]

In each of the cases the justification for holding such a procedure has been that it is in the interests of national security to do so. However, prior to the Justice and Security Act 2013, there was no specific statutory provision applicable to general civil claims for damages. In fact, both the Court of Appeal and the Supreme Court in *Al-Rawi* confirmed that the court had no power at common law to conduct a CMP in ordinary civil claims. Lord Dyson, giving the lead judgment, with which Lords Hope, Brown, and Kerr agreed, was clear that:

> Closed material procedures and the use of special advocates continue to be controversial. In my view, it is not for the courts to extend such a controversial procedure beyond the boundaries which Parliament has chosen to draw for its use thus far.[219]

The rationale for such a ruling was that their Lordships believed the procedure to be contrary to the principles of open and natural justice. The feature of open justice is that trials should be conducted and judgments given in public. In a similar vein, natural justice requires that: (i) a party has a right to know the case against them and the evidence on which it is based; (ii) a party is entitled to have the opportunity to respond to any such evidence and to any submissions made by the other side; (iii) the other side may not advance contentions or adduce evidence of which they are kept in ignorance; and (iv) the parties should be given an opportunity to call their own witnesses and to cross-examine the opposing witnesses. Lord Dyson concluded his criticism of the CMP stating that:

> unlike the law relating to PII, a closed material procedure involves a departure from both the open justice and the natural justice principles.[220]

At this stage it may be useful to set out some of the major and most controversial differences between a PII procedure and a CMP. To begin with, Lord Dyson described the CMP as 'the very antithesis of a PII procedure.'[221] It is suggested that this description was apt for three main reasons:

(i) In PII, the court must conduct the balancing exercise (the *Wiley* Balance) between the public interest in non-disclosure and the public interest in the administration of justice; in CMP, there is no equivalent balancing exercise by the court: the court's task is to ensure that material is not disclosed if its disclosure would cause harm to the public interest.

(ii) In PII, where the judicial balance comes out against disclosure, the material is excluded altogether from the case and cannot be used by either party or the court; in CMP, material which the court agrees should be 'closed' is admissible: it can be seen by the court and can be relied on by one party (the party who wishes it to be withheld from the other side).

---

215 Although that wording is not expressly used.

216 Terrorism Prevention and Investigation Measures Act 2011, Sch 4, or the Counter-Terrorism Act 2008, Pt 6. Formerly, the Prevention of Terrorism Act 2005 was also applicable; however, this was repealed by the Terrorism Prevention and Investigation Measures Act 2011, s 1.

217 The Special Immigration Appeals Commission Act 1997.

218 Employment Tribunals Act 1996; Employment Tribunals (Constitution and Rules of Procedure) Regulations; and *Tariq v Home Office* [2011] UKSC 34, where the Supreme Court held that closed material procedures in employment tribunal cases were lawful.

219 *R v Al-Rawi*, op. cit., n. 175, at [47].

220 Ibid., at [14]. An opinion reiterated in the subsequent Supreme Court case of *Re A (A Child)* [2012] UKSC 60, at [34].

221 Ibid., at [41].

(iii) An argument often raised is that the PII exercise is much longer and more time-consuming than a CMP, and that this is, therefore, a reason for preferring CMP over PII. In fact, there are no reasons nor grounds to substantiate why a CMP should take any less time than a PII exercise.

The Government was quick to respond to the Supreme Court's ruling in *Al-Rawi* with the enactment of the Justice and Security Act 2013.[222] Part 2 of this Act allows the civil courts to order a CMP in ordinary civil actions where the disclosure of material would be 'damaging to the interests of national security.'[223] Section 6 of the 2013 Act provides the power to direct a CMP:

(1) The court seised of relevant civil proceedings[224] may make a declaration that the proceedings are proceedings in which a closed material application may be made to the court.
(2) The court may make such a declaration –
 (a) on the application of –
  (i) the Secretary of State (whether or not the Secretary of State is a party to the proceedings), or
  (ii) any party to the proceedings, or
 (b) of its own motion.

The conditions to be satisfied in order for a declaration under section 6 to be made can be found in sub-sections (3)–(6).

(3) The court may make such a declaration if it considers that the following two conditions are met.
(4) The first condition is that –
 (a) a party to the proceedings would be required to disclose sensitive material in the course of the proceedings to another person (whether or not another party to the proceedings), or
 (b) a party to the proceedings would be required to make such a disclosure were it not for one or more of the following –
  (i) the possibility of a claim for public interest immunity in relation to the material,
  (ii) the fact that there would be no requirement to disclose if the party chose not to rely on the material,
  (iii) section 17(1) of the Regulation of Investigatory Powers Act 2000 (exclusion for intercept material),
  (iv) any other enactment that would prevent the party from disclosing the material but would not do so if the proceedings were proceedings in relation to which there was a declaration under this section.
(5) The second condition is that it is in the interests of the fair and effective administration of justice in the proceedings to make a declaration.[225]
(6) The two conditions are met if the court considers that they are met in relation to any material that would be required to be disclosed in the course of the proceedings (and an application under subsection (2)(a) need not be based on all of the material that might meet the conditions or on material that the applicant would be required to disclose).

222 Received royal assent on 25 April 2013.

223 Section 6(11).

224 'Relevant civil proceedings' means any proceedings (other than proceedings in a criminal cause or matter) before (a) the High Court, (b) the Court of Appeal, (c) the Court of Session, or (d) the Supreme Court (s 6(11)).

225 In *CF v The Security Service & Ors* [2013] EWHC 3402, Irwin J commented (at [36]) that 'whether it is in the interests of the fair and effective administration of justice in the proceedings to make a declaration, must turn on the specific circumstances of the case in hand, and cannot properly turn on objections which would arise in every case, and which would therefore, if successful, subvert the intention of Parliament.' Further, Irwin J stated (at [41]) that: 'The question becomes whether there are considerations special to this case, taking the matter as a whole, bearing in mind all the circumstances, which mean that it would not be in the interests of "the fair and effective administration of justice" to make a declaration here.' Whether this is the interpretation that the courts will follow is yet to be seen.

The legislation has placed an additional hurdle where an application is made by the Secretary of State. Section 6(7) provides that:

> The court must not consider an application by the Secretary of State under subsection (2)(a) unless it is satisfied that the Secretary of State has, before making the application, considered whether to make, or advise another person to make, a claim for PII in relation to the material on which the application is based.

It may appear *prima facie* that section 6(7) requires the Secretary of State to take part in the PII process before seeking a declaration. Indeed, this was the argument of the claimants in the High Court case of *CF v The Security Service & Others*.[226] It was their contention that section 6(7) imposes an obligation on the court to conclude the PII process in *every case* before it considers making a declaration.[227] Irwin J, who presided over this case, declined to agree with the claimants and instead found in favour of the defendants, and held that the wording of section 6(7) is quite clear. Parliament has declined to make it a pre-condition of a declaration that PII proceedings should be conducted in every case. Rather, the actual pre-condition is that the Secretary of State should have *considered making* such an application. Irwin J concluded that:

> In my view ... the court may make a declaration, and adopt a closed material procedure, before disclosure has been given and without a PII claim having been made or determined.[228]

Part 2 of the Justice and Security Act 2013 has been heavily criticised by human rights groups and civil society organisations. It has been argued that the core provisions are unfair, unjust, and have even been likened to the Star Chamber.[229] It remains to be seen how the Act will continue to interact with the long-standing principles of PII, and whether PII in civil cases, when the interests of national security are concerned, is to be replaced.

Briefly, there are additional rules found within the 2013 Act that are relevant here. They are as follows:

- Section 7: the court must keep the declaration under review, and may at any time revoke it if it considers that the declaration is no longer in the interests of the fair and effective administration of justice in the proceedings;
- Section 8: the court is required to give permission for material not to be disclosed if it considers that the disclosure of the material would be damaging to the interests of national security;
- Section 9: the appropriate law officer (e.g. the Attorney General) may appoint a special advocate to represent the interests of a party in any section 6 proceedings from which the party (and any legal representative of the party) is excluded. However, this course of action is not mandatory;
- Section 12: the Secretary of State must prepare a report for the period of 12 months beginning with the day on which section 6 comes into force, and every subsequent 12-month period, and lay a copy of each such report before Parliament.[230]

---

226 [2013] EWHC 3402. This was the first case decided under the Justice and Security Act 2013.

227 Ibid., at [25].

228 Ibid., at [36].

229 See e.g. Peto, A. and Tyrie, A., *Neither Justice nor Fair: The Justice and Security Bill* (Centre for Policy Studies, 2013).

230 The report published on 22 July 2014 stated that in the six-month period preceding, five applications under s 6 had been made, two of which were granted (one, of course, being in *CF v The Security Service*).

The detailed procedural rules in relation to CMPs and the Justice and Security Act are provided in Part 82 of the CPR 1998.[231] These rules, however, are outside the scope of this work and any interested reader is advised to refer to the most recent edition of the White Book[232] or the website of the Ministry of Justice.[233]

14.7 Key learning points

- The general rule is the prosecution must give 'full disclosure.'
- Any derogation from this rule must be kept to an absolute minimum.
- Formerly, the Crown could simply claim a privilege over information. This is no longer the case.
- The judge must balance two competing interests: the administration of justice and the protection of national interests.
- Strasbourg Court authorities are clear that it must be 'strictly necessary' to withhold disclosure.
- Civil courts may now order a CMP where disclosure of information would be likely to damage interests in the national security.

14.8 Practice questions

1. 'The old class system was justified. There are certain types of documents that should never be exposed as a matter of principle.' Discuss with regard to the old principle of Crown privilege and the current law as it stands regarding class claims.
2. It has been said that the operation of PII can lead to unfairness with potentially relevant material being withheld. Where should the balance lie?
3. Robin is a shop owner on a street that is prone to drug-related offences by a notorious gang. The police are sure that the gang are the perpetrators, although they have little evidence to bring a case against them. The police request permission from Robin to use his shop as an observation point where they can watch the street and any activities that go on there. Robin is reluctant; however, upon being informed by the police that his premises will not be revealed in court, he gives the police permission. The police stake out the street for a total of two weeks and in that time witness several drug dealings and numerous takings of illegal drugs. The police charge members of the gang with these offences and seek to withhold the location of their observation point from the defence. The defence apply for the information to be revealed.
   (a) What is the court's likely approach to this issue?
   (b) What if Robin was not allowing his premises to be used, but rather was an informant who saw all offences take place?
   (c) Should the defendants bring civil actions against the police, what information or communication may be revealed?

14.9 Suggested further reading

Allen, T.R.S., 'Public Interest Immunity and Ministers' Responsibilities' (1993) Crim LR 660.
Bisgrove, M., 'Judges as Tribunals of Fact . . . Where Issues of PII are Present?' (2010) Crim LR 702.

---

231 As inserted by the Civil Procedure (Amendment No. 5) Rules 2013 (SI 2013/1571).
232 Jackson L.J. (ed.), *Civil Procedure: The White Book Service* 2023 (Sweet & Maxwell, 2023).
233 https://www.justice.gov.uk/courts/procedure-rules/civil/rules.

Chamberlain, M., 'Special Advocates and Procedural Fairness in Closed Proceedings' (2009) 28 Civil Justice Quarterly 314.
Gray, A., 'A Comparison and Critique of Closed Court Hearings' (2014) 18(3) E & P 230.
Taylor, C., 'The Courts and Applications for Public Interest Immunity: R v H and C' (2004) E & P 179.
Taylor, C., 'What Next for Public Interest Immunity' (2005) 69 Journal of Criminal Law 75.
Tomkins, A., 'Justice and Security in the United Kingdom' (2014) 47(3) Israel Law Review 305.
Yip, J., 'Al-Rawi, Tariq and the Future of Closed Material Procedures and Special Advocates' (2012) 75(4) Modern Law Review 606.

Index

For Product Safety Concerns and Information please contact our EU
representative GPSR@taylorandfrancis.com
Taylor & Francis Verlag GmbH, Kaufingerstraße 24, 80331 München, Germany

www.ingramcontent.com/pod-product-compliance
Ingram Content Group UK Ltd.
Pitfield, Milton Keynes, MK11 3LW, UK
UKHW051010280325
456830UK00011B/192
* 9 7 8 1 0 3 2 5 4 2 7 7 5 *